Rorschach Assessment
of the Personality Disorders

The LEA Series in Personality and Clinical Psychology
Irving B. Weiner, Editor

Rorschach Assessment
of the Personality Disorders

Edited by

Steven K. Huprich
Eastern Michigan University

LAWRENCE ERLBAUM ASSOCIATES, PUBLISHERS
2006   Mahwah, New Jersey   London

Lawrence Erlbaum Associates, Inc., Publishers
10 Industrial Avenue
Mahwah, New Jersey 07430
www.erlbaum.com

Cover design by Tomai Maridou

Library of Congress Cataloging-in-Publication Data

Rorschach assessment of the personality disorders / edited by Steven
 K. Huprich.

        p. cm.
Includes bibliographical references and index.
ISBN 0-8058-4786-3 (h.: alk. paper)
 1. Rorschach Test. 2. Personality disorders. I. Huprich, Steven Ken,
 1966–

RC474.R6R67 2005
155.2'842—dc22   2204056255
                                                             CIP

Books published by Lawrence Erlbaum Associates are printed on acid- free
paper, and their bindings are chosen for strength and durability.

Printed in the United States of America
10 9 8 7 6 5 4 3 2 1

Contents

III: CLUSTER B PERSONALITY DISORDERS

IV: CLUSTER C PERSONALITY DISORDERS

V: OTHER PERSONALITY DISORDERS

VI: PERSONALITY DISORDERS, PSYCHOANALYTIC SCIENCE, AND THE RORSCHACH

List of Contributors

Marvin W. Acklin, PhD, ABPP

Matthew R. Baity, PhD

Mark A. Blais, PsyD

Robert F. Bornstein, PhD

Dana Deardeuff Foley, PhD

Ronald J. Ganellen, PhD

Galit Gerevitz-Stern, MS

Leonard Handler, PhD

Mark J. Hilsenroth, PhD

Steven K. Huprich, PhD

Nancy Kaser-Boyd, PhD

James H. Kleiger, PsyD, ABPP

Alan J. Lee, PsyD

Paul M. Lerner, EdD

Susan H. S. Li, MS

James L. Loving, PsyD

Joni L. Mihura, PhD

Barry Ritzler, PhD

Robert B. Schneider, PsyD

James Tyson, MS

Thomas A. Widiger, PhD

Preface

When I began graduate training in personality assessment, my initial reaction to the Rorschach was, "How can you understand personality with inkblots?" My earliest skepticism disappeared, yet I remained wary of an instrument that seemed so difficult to learn and master. As my training continued, I encountered clinical supervisors who were masters of Rorschach scoring and interpretation. It was during my clinical internship at the State University of New York Health Science Center (now Upstate Medical University) in Syracuse, New York that I began to appreciate the brilliance of the Rorschach and what it offered in understanding human personality and its problems. Little did I think as a young student that I would teach, research, and write about the Rorschach.

Contrary to my early ambivalence with the Rorschach, I entered graduate school very interested in studying personality disorders. Perhaps this reflected my ongoing interest in how an individual's biological and experiential bases contributed to his current state of being, as well as my interest in how, by understanding these factors, a clinical psychologist could lead the individual toward new ways of being that yielded greater satisfaction in one's relationships and work. My earliest research on the personality disorders was conducted under the supervision of Dr. Mark Fine at the University of Dayton. I found certain similarities in the DSM-III-R category of self-defeating personality disorder and dependent personality disorder. That is, both disorders involved high external loci of control, along with putting oneself in a position to be influenced by another person, apparently with little concern about the high degree of influence that other person wields. While my thesis evaluated clinicians' ability to differentially diagnose these two disorders, I wondered what types of dynamics and motives would shape an individual's personality in such a way: Low self-esteem and self-regard? Fear of others that could only be expressed through excessive submission? Might such personality types be motivated and gratified by such submission, ergo suffering?

As I continued my doctoral work at the University of North Carolina at Greensboro, under the direction of Dr. Rosemery Nelson-Gray, I learned much about various self-report instruments used to assess personality disorders. In my research, however, I quickly became dismayed by several observations: First, many people meet criteria for more than one personality disorder. (Can a person really have two or more personality disorders? There is only one personality.) Second, some people have features of one or more personality disorders, but do not meet DSM criteria. Yet, in reflecting upon their answers and my reactions to what they said, I wondered if such individuals actually had a maladaptive personality that was not being detected. And finally, I observed that a research participant might say or do something that made me question the diagnostic assessment I had just conducted with a semistructured interview. For instance, a young man with a below threshold score on a semistructured interview for narcissistic personality disorder made a point of commenting upon the questions in a manner that many would describe as smug and devaluing. I thought that those who interacted with this person may believe he was somewhat insolent. Despite my novice interviewing skills, this individual seemed to have many narcissistic qualities.

My clinical work, too, provided me with insights into personality disorders that I did not learn in the traditional DSM description of the disorders. For instance, many individuals with a cluster B personality disorder seem to have features of other cluster B disorders. A borderline patient failed to recognize or acknowledge our last session together, which involved a year's worth of intense work. "How self-absorbed is this guy to not discuss our final session until the very end?" I thought. In addition, it seemed that the distinction between Axis I and Axis II, as well as the distinction between state and trait phenomena are blurry. One supervisor and I contemplated whether a socially anxious, interpersonally secluded young man should be diagnosed as socially phobic or avoidant personality disorder.

All of these observations, along with many others, led me to recognize that personality disorders are not easily assessable (a point that I will elaborate upon in chapter 2). How, then, does one begin to phenomenologically understand the individual when many factors work against an accurate degree of measurement? For me, it appears that the Rorschach is an instrument poised to address these issues nicely. In short, providing an ambiguous stimulus to an individual and allowing him or her to tell the examiner what the stimulus might be and why it might be that is perhaps one of the most ingenious ways to access the person's inner world of thoughts, feelings, wishes, impulses, and ideas. While an examinee may rightly note that the examiner is showing him or her an inkblot, it is the speculative process of what the blot "might be" that is of interest to the personality assessor. Here, Rappaport, Gill, and Schafer (1968) so eloquently make the point: "It is clear now that no sensory stimulation falls on an empty, passive-receptive organ but that all stimuli are taken in by a complicated receiving system, and that this receiving system is structured and directed by basic needs and interests of the organism, modified by experiences long past and 'set' by experiences of recent past" (p. 272). More recent cognitive models have described a similar process, whereby the individual develops schemas that are organized around affectively charged material that involves the way in which one relates to him or herself and others (Beck, Freeman, Davis, & Associates, 2004). As the individual engages in this speculative process, he or she cannot help but be influenced by his "receiving system." The result of this process is a perceptual, verbal, and behavioral product that may be considered a sampling of the predominant thoughts, feelings, needs, wishes, and ideas of the individual. For the person with a personality disorder, such a product is likely to contain elements representative of the personality disorder. This being the case, I believe that the Rorschach has much to offer the clinician or researcher who wants to assess for a personality disorder.

The current text seeks to fill a gap in the Rorschach and personality disorder literatures. While some researchers have extensively studied certain personality disorders with the Rorschach (i.e., antisocial personality disorder and the work of Carl Gacono and Reid Meloy) or personality traits and patterns (i.e., interpersonal dependency and the work of Robert F. Bornstein), there has not been published a text on the assessment of personality disorders with the Rorschach. As such, the present text will serve as an introductory work to a field where additional research and clinical description is needed.

In preparing to write and edit this book, contributors were instructed to: (a) Describe the personality disorder of interest, especially in light of the Comprehensive System (Exner, 2003) clusters; (b) Review relevant research on the disorder of interest that would inform the clinician of patterns and findings that would be expected on the Rorschach; and (c) Provide a clinical example of a Rorschach protocol of a patient with the personality disorder of interest. Although this task was quite demanding and challenging, I believe that the contributors to this book have done an excellent job of presenting the material in a way that is easy to follow and readily stimulates critical evaluation and research.

This text begins with an overview by Dr. Thomas Widiger on the theoretical models commonly utilized for understanding personality disorders, along with a discussion of the categorical and dimensional models of classification. It is followed by a key chapter, in which Dr. Ron Ganellen and I provide a discussion of the advantages the Rorschach offers when assessing personality disorders. The next three sections of the book are organized by DSM-IV (American Psychological Association, 2001) personality disorder clusters, and a chapter is devoted to each personality disorder in that cluster to discuss the Rorschach findings that would be anticipated for that disorder. The subsequent section includes chapters on two proposed personality disorders—passive–aggressive and depressive. Although these disorders remain controversial as to their validity and utility, it appears that the Rorschach may provide important information about the internal dynamics of individuals who meet the diagnostic criteria for the disorders. The final section of the text provides a discussion of two important domains in which the Rorschach can be of utility to the psychoanalytic/psychodynamic clinician researcher. Dr. Paul Lerner discusses how object relations may be assessed on the Rorschach and reviews evidence supporting the use of the Rorschach in this way. Next, Dr. Marvin Acklin and his students, Susan Li and James Tyson, discuss the science of psychological assessment and the way in which the Rorschach provides important information into the inner world of examinee.

It is my hope that, after reading part or all of this text, students, researchers, and clinicians will be inspired to critically evaluate the use of the Rorschach to assess personality disorders. Theses, dissertations, research reports, and case studies on this topic would be the richest fruits of the authors' labor. Moreover, I believe the field of clinical psychology and assessment psychology will be all the better, as will our ability to assess those individuals who come to us for relief of their suffering and pain.

In closing, I must express my sincerest appreciation to all individuals who contributed to the chapters in this text. I could not be more pleased with their willingness and eagerness to write about this important topic. Special thanks are extended to Dr. Susan Milmoe, Ms. Kristen Depken, Steven Rutter, Sarah Wahlert and Mr. Lawrence Erlbaum. Your support, aid, advice, and assistance in the preparation of this book were invaluable. Clearly, you made this enormous project much more manageable. Similarly, I am very appreciative of the support provided by Dr. Wallace Daniel, Dean of the College of Arts and Science at Baylor University, who provided me with a reduced teaching load in the Fall of 2003 to work on this book. Countless contributors and consultants have also facilitated the development of this text. Some of these include Drs. Irving Weiner, Ronald Ganellen, Mark Hilsenroth, Robert Bornstein, Marshall Silverstein, John Porcerelli, Barry Ritzler, and Philip Erdberg.

My last expressions of gratitude deserve separate paragraphs. First, I am indebted to Dr. Carl Gacono's words of counsel, encouragement, and direction in the early planning of this book. While I was initially skeptical in pursuing the ideas in this book, Carl provided the encouragement to make this happen. For this, I am deeply appreciative and thankful.

Second, I want to express my appreciation to dear friends who forever have changed my life: Robert and Betty Young, Robert and Susan Gibson, and Robert Sanders. Your friendship over the past five years has made my life richer and better. Although we have never really spoken much about this book, your kindness, intellectual curiosity, direction, and support have made me a better person and helped me through very good and very difficult times. Thank you for such a gift.

Finally, and most importantly, I want to acknowledge my wife, Donna. We were married shortly after this project began, and I have found myself to be energized and invigorated by her love and encouragement throughout the writing of this book. This process has had its highs and lows, and I have found her support to be unwavering and deeply loving. In charting the ambiguous stimuli in the world of writing and editing this book, Donna has been a secure base to which I have returned time and time again for comfort and support. I am a better person because of her. I hope we spend many more wonderful years together in our life journeys.

REFERENCES

American Psychiatric Association. (2001). *Diagnostic and statistical manual of mental disorders* (4th ed., text revision). Washington, DC: Author.

Beck, A. T., Freeman, A. T., Davis, D. D., & Associates. (2004). *Cognitive therapy of personality disorders* (2nd ed.). New York: Guilford.

Exner, J. E. (2003). *The Rorschach: A comprehensive system* (Vol. 1). Hoboken, NJ: John Wiley.

Rapaport, D., Gill, M. M., & Schafer, R. (1968). *Diagnostic psychological testing*. New York, NY: International Universities Press.

I

INTRODUCTORY ISSUES

Understanding Personality Disorders

Thomas A. Widiger
University of Kentucky

The American Psychiatric Association's (APA) *Diagnostic and Statistical Manual of Mental Disorders,* 4th edition, Text Revision (DSM-IV-TR; APA, 2000) includes 10 personality disorders: antisocial, avoidant, borderline, dependent, histrionic, narcissistic, obsessive–compulsive, paranoid, schizoid, and schizotypal. Two additional disorders are placed in an appendix to the DSM-IV for diagnoses provided for further study: passive–aggressive and depressive.

Personality disorders currently have a singular importance in the diagnostic manual. This was noted especially in the third edition of the APA diagnostic manual (APA, 1980), in which personality disorders were placed on a separate axis: Axis II (Spitzer, Williams, & Skodol, 1980). As stated in the DSM-III, "this separation ensures that consideration is given to the possible presence of disorders that are frequently overlooked when attention is directed to the usually more florid Axis I disorder" (APA, 1980, p. 23).

One reason that the authors of the multiaxial system of the DSM-III wanted to draw attention to the personality disorders was because of the "accumulating evidence that the quality and quantity of preexisting personality disturbance may … influence the predisposition, manifestation, course, and response to treatment of various Axis I conditions" (Frances, 1980, p. 1050). In fact, the presence of a personality disorder does increase the likelihood that particular Axis I disorders will develop, and often affects significantly their course and treatment (Gunderson, Triebwasser, Phillips, & Sullivan, 1999; Klein, Wonderlich, & Shea, 1993). Before DSM-III, clinicians often failed to recognize or appreciate the existence of patients' maladaptive personality traits (Frances, 1980), and research has since suggested that the separate Axis II placement has indeed increased the recognition of personality disorders in clinical practice (Loranger, 1990).

The purpose of this chapter is to provide a general introduction to the personality disorders for this volume on their assessment with the Rorschach Inkblot Method (RIM). The discussion first focuses on their conceptualization, emphasizing some of the core, fundamental features of a personality disorder (age of onset, stability in course, distortions in self-image, and categorical distinctions) that are particularly important in their assessment. It then presents predominant theories of etiology or pathology that might be especially pertinent to their assessment with RIM.

CONCEPTUALIZATION

Personality disorders concern the characteristic manner of thinking, feeling, behaving, and relating to others that is generally evident in everyday functioning. In this respect, personality disorders are sometimes described as being "ego syntonic" rather than "ego dystonic" (Frances, First, & Pincus, 1995, p. 361). Most Axis I disorders, like most medical disorders, are experienced by persons as conditions or syndromes that happen to or come upon them. Personality disorders, in contrast, often are related to the way persons consider themselves to be—their sense of self and identity.

A personality disorder is defined in the DSM-IV-TR as "an enduring pattern of inner experience and behavior that deviates markedly from the expectations of the individual's culture, is pervasive and inflexible, has an onset in adolescence or early adulthood, is stable over time, and leads to distress or impairment" (APA, 2000, p. 686). A number of points in this definition are worth extended consideration. Discussed in particular are age of onset, temporal stability, and distortions in self-image, as well as the categorical distinctiveness of a personality disorder.

Onset of Personality Disorder in Late Adolescence or Young Adulthood

Personality disorders have "an onset in late adolescence or early adulthood" (APA, 2000, p. 686). They can be diagnosed before the age of 18 years, but this is generally discouraged. "Personality disorder categories may be applied to children or adolescents in those relatively unusual instances in which the individual's particular maladaptive personality traits appear to be pervasive, persistent, and unlikely to be limited to a particular developmental stage or an episode of an axis disorder" (APA, 2000, p. 687). An additional, important implication of the age of onset requirement is that the DSM-IV does not recognize the existence of adult onset personality disorders, unless their etiology can be attributed to the neurophysiologic effects of a known medical condition (i.e., personality change attributable to a medical condition). The World Health Organization (WHO), in contrast, includes within its diagnostic manual, the *International Classification of Diseases* (ICD-10; WHO, 1992), two additional adult onset personality disorders: personality change secondary to catastrophic experiences (Shea, 1996) and personality change secondary to the experience of a severe mental disorder (Triebwasser & Shea, 1996).

A reason for the DSM-IV restriction to an onset no later than young adulthood is to avoid confusing the assessment of a mood, anxiety, substance dependence, or other Axis I mental disorders with a personality disorder (Triebwasser & Shea, 1996), because such Axis I disorders often are comorbid, impacting the assessment of the individual's personality. More specifically, persons who are significantly anxious, depressed, angry, or distraught often fail to provide an accurate description of their usual way of thinking, feeling, behaving, and relating to others (Farmer, 2000; Kaye & Shea, 2000; Widiger & Coker, 2002). Requiring that the assessment of a personality disorder document its presence as far back as late childhood is one way to ensure that the personality disorder was, in fact, present before the onset of a current Axis I disorder (Triebwasser & Shea, 1996).

The task of considering age of onset can become especially difficult as the person ages. A 75-year-old man can be diagnosed with a dependent personality disorder, or a 45-year-old woman with a borderline personality disorder, but the disorder must have been present throughout the entire duration of adulthood (e.g., since the age of 18 years). It is unclear whether judgments concerning the consistencies of particular diagnostic criteria over the course of 50 to 70 years can be asserted confidently. Studies investigating personality disorders in the aging population suggest that it can be unclear whether the instruments being used are in fact documenting the existence of the personality traits across the individual's adult life (Abrams & Horowitz, 1999; Agronin, 1998; Widiger & Seidlitz, 2002).

Stable and Enduring Personality Traits

A personality disorder also is "stable over time" (APA, 2000, p. 686) and there is considerable empirical support for the temporal stability of personality functioning (Costa & McCrae, 1994). As such, personality disorders are among the more difficult of disorders to treat, in part because they involve pervasive and entrenched behavior patterns that have been present throughout much of a person's life, and persons consider many aspects of their personality to be integral to their sense of self (Millon et al., 1996; Stone, 1993). However, maladaptive personality traits often are the focus of clinical treatment (Beck, Freeman, Davis, & Associates, 2004; Benjamin,

1996a; Gunderson & Gabbard, 2000; Millon et al., 1996; Paris, 1998; Stone, 1993), and "psychotherapy studies indicate that, as a group, personality disorders improve with treatment" (Perry & Bond, 2000, p. 25). In fact, there is compelling empirical support to indicate that meaningful effects of treatment do in fact occur (Leichsenring & Leibing, 2003; Perry, Banon, & Ianni, 1999; Salekin, 2002; Sanislow & McGlashan, 1998).

However, recognizing that personality traits can change does not necessarily imply that sudden, dramatic changes are likely to occur. "The personality traits that define these disorders must ... be distinguished from characteristics that emerge in response to specific situational stressors or more transient mental states (e.g., mood or anxiety disorders, substance intoxication)" (APA, 2000, p. 686). In fact, it would be necessary to question the validity of the concept of a personality trait, or at least its assessment, if the assessment proved to be markedly unstable over time. Such was the case with DSM-III-R's (APA, 1987) self-defeating personality disorder. It was not included in the DSM-IV, in part because the self-defeating behavior seen in persons with this diagnosis too often was attributable to their existence in an abusive relationship (Widiger, 1995).

The extent of stability and instability present, however, is controversial. One of the more intriguing findings of the Collaborative Longitudinal Study of Personality Disorders (Gunderson et al., 2000) has been the extent to which persons fail to maintain personality disorder symptoms over time. For example, 23 of 160 persons (14%) with a diagnosis of borderline personality disorder at the study's baseline assessment met criteria for two or fewer of the nine diagnostic criteria 6 months later. Whereas 18 of these persons sustained this reduction 6 months to 1 year, 14 continued to have two or fewer diagnostic criteria in the subsequent blind assessments of outcome 2 years later. Gunderson et al. (2003) concluded that only 1 of these 18 persons had been inaccurately diagnosed at baseline. The rest were considered to be valid instances of borderline personality disorder who did, in fact, experience sudden and dramatic remissions. However, in one instance, the person's original symptoms were determined to result from the use of a stimulant for weight reduction. For others, the dramatic changes occurred when they left highly volatile, provocative, and unstable life situations. It is possible that some of these sudden dramatic remissions may have been attributable to inadequacies in the assessments by the self-report inventories and semistructured interviews that provided the baseline diagnoses (Westen, 1997).

Distortions in Self-Image and Presentation

A personality disorder involves a characteristic "way of perceiving and interpreting self, other people, and events" (APA, 2000, p. 689). In fact, many personality disorders can be distinguished, in part, by a characteristically distorted view of the self, others, or the future. Therefore, the self-description of persons with personality disorders should not be taken at face value because there is a good possibility that these descriptions will be comparably distorted, inaccurate, or misleading (Bornstein, 1995; Westen, 1997). For example, the paranoid person often will demonstrate great reluctance to be forthrightly honest; the antisocial person will be characteristically dishonest and evasive; and narcissistic persons may deny their faults, foibles, and inadequacies.

It is not yet clear whether these characteristic distortions in self-image and self-presentation prevent self-report inventories or semistructured interviews from providing valid personality disorder assessments. For example, some have suggested that self-report inventories should not be used for assessment of psychopathy (Hare, 1991). Self-report inventories and semistructured interviews do not rely entirely on the ability or motivation of respondents to provide valid self-descriptions because they do include quite a few indirect items and probes, and, in the case of semistructured interviews, observations and clinical judgments of the interviewee's behavior and responses (Widiger & Coker, 2002). Nevertheless, it is possible that projective tests, such as the RIM, may be particularly useful in addressing this concern (Bornstein, 1996, 1999; Gacono & Meloy, 2002; Hilsenroth, Handler, & Blais, 1996; Wiggins, 2003). This issue is given detailed discussion in the next chapter by Drs. Ganellen and Huprich.

Categorically Distinct

"DSM-IV is a categorical classification that divides mental disorders into types based on criterion sets with defining features" (APA, 2000, p. xxxi). "The diagnostic approach [used in the DSM-IV] represents the categorical perspective that personality disorders are qualitatively distinct clinical syndromes" (APA, 2000, p. 689). This categorical model of classification is consistent with traditional medical diagnosis, but compelling concerns have been raised regarding its validity and utility for understanding personality disorders (Livesley & Jang, 2000; Widiger, 1993).

Studies have indicated that prototypic cases of each personality disorder are infrequent exceptions rather than the rule (Bornstein, 1998; Westen & Arkowitz-Westen, 1998; Widiger, 1993). It is a rare patient who meets all the diagnostic criteria for one personality disorder and lacks any of the diagnostic criteria for any other personality disorder. Heterogeneity among persons sharing the same diagnosis and excessive diagnostic co-occurrence are the norm (Bornstein, 1998). Research also has failed to identify a nonarbitrary point of demarcation between normal and abnormal personality functioning. Most of the diagnostic thresholds provided in the

DSM-IV are not based on empirical data, and none are guided by an explicit rationale (e.g., that point at which avoidant behavior results in a clinically significant level of impairment, or that point at which an underlying pathology is most likely to be present). In fact, the most popular diagnosis in clinical practice often is personality disorder not otherwise specified, suggesting that the existing diagnostic categories are failing to identify all the clinically relevant maladaptive personality functioning (Westen & Arkowitz-Westen, 1998).

A variety of alternative dimensional models of personality disorder classification have been developed, and most, if not all, complement well the existing diagnostic categories. The alternative dimensional models do not imply that the diagnostic categories are failing to identify clinically meaningful maladaptive personality traits, but suggest that a more accurate description of any particular person will be provided by a more quantitative classification. Some of the dimensional models, in fact, retain the existing diagnostic categories. For example, Oldham and Skodol (2000) proposed implementing a system whereby each personality disorder (e.g., borderline) could be described more quantitatively as absent (no diagnostic criteria present), traits (only 1 or 2 diagnostic criteria present), subthreshold (one criterion short of categorical diagnosis), threshold (just barely meeting criteria for categorical diagnosis), moderate (2 or more criteria present than necessary), or prototypic (all diagnostic criteria present). For the patient above the threshold for three or more personality disorders, the diagnosis could be "extensive personality disorder" characterized (for example) by borderline (prototypic), histrionic (moderate), and dependent (threshold) features.

An advantage of this proposal is that it would provide a significant step toward a dimensional model of classification without requiring that clinicians learn new diagnostic constructs (Widiger & Sanderson, 1995). Similarly, the proposals of Livesley and Jang (2000) and Clark (1993) also would retain much of the existing personality disorder symptomatology, but would reorganize them into more clinically distinct dimensions, such as anxiousness, compulsivity, self-harm, intimacy problems, entitlement, detachment, and affective lability rather than diagnostic categories comprising constellations of these problems.

Westen and Shedler's (2000) prototypal matching proposal is similar to the proposal of Oldham and Skodol (2000) in that the diagnostic manual would retain much of the existing diagnoses, each of which would be rated on a 5-point scale. However, an important difference is that the 5-point rating would not be based on the number of diagnostic criteria, but rather the clinician's judgment of the extent to which the patient's personality matched a brief, narrative description of a prototypic case: 1 (description does not apply), 2 (only minor features), 3 (significant features), 4 (strong match, patient has the disorder), and 5 (exemplifies the disorder, prototypic case). Westen and Shedler (2000) suggested that the diagnostic criterion sets are not really necessary for reliable and valid diagnoses, and that the assessment should be based instead on the assessment procedures that each clinician finds most informative, which certainly could include the RIM. An additional distinction is that Westen and Shedler (1999) also suggested that the narrative descriptions would be based optimally on descriptions they have generated with the Shedler–Westen Assessment Procedure-200 (SWAP-200). The SWAP-200 is a clinician rating form of 200 items (only half of which are the DSM-IV diagnostic criterion sets) drawn from the psychoanalytic and personality disorder literature (Shedler, 2002; Westen & Shedler, 1999).

More radical proposals are offered by Cloninger (2000) and Widiger, Costa, and McCrae (2002). Cloninger's model is informed largely from the neurobiologic and humanistic literature. He proposes that four fundamental temperaments (i.e., reward dependence, persistence, harm avoidance, and novelty seeking) are associated with relatively distinct neurotransmitter systems, and that three character dimensions (self-directedness, cooperativeness, and self-transcendence) are associated with early experiences in one's development. The presence of a personality disorder would be indicated by low levels of cooperativeness, self-transcendence, and, most importantly, self-directedness (the ability to control, regulate, and adapt behavior). The specific variants of personality disorder would be governed by the temperaments of novelty seeking, harm avoidance, reward dependence, and persistence (Cloninger, 2000).

Widiger and Costa (1994) proposed integrating the DSM-IV personality disorder nomenclature with a predominant dimensional model of general personality functioning, the five-factor model, consisting of the following dimensions: neuroticism versus emotional stability, extraversion versus introversion, openness versus closedness to experience, agreeableness versus antagonism, and conscientiousness versus undependability. The five-factor model has established a firm empirical foundation in general personality theory (McCrae & Costa, 1999), and it does appear to include the maladaptive personality traits described by the DSM-IV personality disorders (Widiger & Costa, 2002).

Widiger, Costa, and McCrae (2002) proposed a four-step procedure for the diagnosis of a personality disorder. The first step is to describe an individual's personality structure in terms of the five-factor model. The second step involves identifying problems and impairments associated with these personality traits (a comprehensive list of problems and impairments associated with each of the 30 facets of the five-factor model is provided). The third step is to determine whether these impairments reach a specified level of clinical significance (e.g., whether the traits significantly interfere with work or social functioning, according to Axis V of the DSM-IV). In the fourth step, the personality profile is matched with prototypic cases to determine whether a single, parsimonious diagnostic label can be meaningfully applied.

There is, as yet, relatively little research on the use of the RIM to assess the dimensional models of personality disorder. However, generalization of the RIM findings obtained with the DSM-IV personality disorders to the proposals of Oldham and Skodol (2000) or Westen and Shedler (1999) would be relatively straightforward because both include the same or only slightly modified DSM-IV constructs. In addition, many of the constructs included in the dimensional models of Livesley and Jang (2000) and Clark (1993) that concern components of the existing personality disorders (e.g., self-harm, identity problems, narcissism, insecure attachment, detachment, and dependency) might be more readily assessed by the RIM than the existing diagnostic categories (Blais, Hilsenroth, Fowler, & Conboy, 1999; Bornstein, Hilsenroth, Padawer, & Fowler, 2000; Fowler, Hilsenroth, & Nolan, 2000). On the other hand, it might be more difficult to make inferences regarding the models proposed by Cloninger (2000) and Widiger (2000) with the RIM, although initial efforts toward this goal are being published (Meyer, Bates, & Gacono, 1999; Mihura, Meyer, Bel-Bahar, & Gunderson, 2003).

THEORETICAL MODELS
OF ETIOLOGY AND PATHOLOGY

The DSM-IV personality disorders have a rich clinical history, detailed well in the seminal text by Millon et al. (1996). In addition, a substantial amount of systematic research has accumulated regarding many of these personality disorders, particularly the antisocial (Stoff, Breiling, & Maser, 1997; Sutker & Allain, 2001), the borderline (Gunderson, 2001), and the schizotypal (Raine, Lencz, & Mednick, 1995). Currently, also, a considerable amount of research is available concerning maladaptive dependency (Bornstein, 1992, 1993) and narcissism (Baumeister, Smart, & Boden, 1996; Widiger & Bornstein, 2001). The diagnoses in the appendix to the DSM-IV, the passive–aggressive and the depressive, also are developing a strong empirical base (Huprich, 1998, 2003a, 2003b; Joiner & Rudd, 2003; McDermut, Zimmerman, & Chelminski, 2003; Wetzler & Morey, 1999).

There is no single, authoritative model for understanding the etiology and pathology of any mental disorder. There are, instead, alternative models of psychopathology that in some respects provide competing perspectives, but that in many other respects actually are quite complementary. Some clinicians affiliate themselves primarily with one particular theoretical perspective, whereas others are more eclectic, drawing on a variety of theoretical models to inform and guide their clinical practice. At least eight alternative theoretical models are actively involved in accounting for psychopathology: the neurobiologic (Hyman, 2002; Kandel, 1998), sociobiologic (Buss, Haselton, Shackelford, Bleske, & Wakefield, 1998), psychodynamic (Gabbard, 2000; Westen, 1998), behavioristic (Folette & Houts, 1996; Plaud, 2001), cognitive (Pretzer & Beck, 1996), interpersonal and systems (Kaslow, 1996; Reiss & Emde, 2003), humanistic (Greenberg, Elliott,, & Lietar, 2003; Rychlak, 1993) and anthropologic or social–cultural (Alarcon, 1996; Lopez & Guarnaccia, 2000). Each of these perspectives can provide a clinically meaningful understanding of each of the DSM-IV personality disorders. Space limitations prevent an adequate summary or illustration for each of them. This presentation is confined to the three models that might be particularly compatible with the RIM, specifically the psychodynamic, cognitive, and interpersonal models.

Psychodynamic

Many of the personality disorders, perhaps the narcissistic, borderline, histrionic, dependent, and obsessive–compulsive, in particular, trace their primary historical foundation to the observations of psychodynamic clinicians and theorists, although precedents and variants of these personality disorders also were proposed by more biologically oriented clinicians (Kraepelin, 1904; Millon et al., 1996; Schneider, 1923). Early precursors for obsessive–compulsive personality disorder include Freud's (1908) speculations on character and anal eroticism, Abraham's (1921) observations of obsessional character traits, and Reich's (1933) formulation of the compulsive character. The histrionic personality disorder was described by Reich, as well as by Fenichel (1945), Chodoff and Lyons (1958), and Easser and Lesser (1965). The dependent personality disorder can trace its history to discussions of oral character traits by Freud (1908), Abraham (1921, 1927), and Fenichel (1945). Narcissistic personality disorder was a new addition to the DSM-III (APA, 1980; Frances, 1980). "The stimulus for the inclusion of a narcissistic personality disorder category in the DSM-III derived from the widespread usage of the term by psychodynamically informed clinicians" (Gunderson, Ronningstam, & Smith, 1991, p. 167), particularly Akhtar and Thomson (1982), Bursten (1973, 1982), Cooper (1981), Kernberg (1970, 1975), and Kohut (1966, 1971). Narcissistic personality disorder, however, still is not included in the international diagnostic nomenclature of WHO (1992). Borderline personality disorder was another new addition to the DSM-III (APA, 1980), and its inclusion again was largely attributed to psychodynamic research, particularly the work of Stern (1938), Grinker, Werble, and Drye (1968), Gunderson and colleagues (Gunderson & Kolb, 1978; Gunderson & Singer, 1975), Kernberg (1967, 1975), Knight (1953), and Stone

(1980). Gunderson and Singer (1975) actually emphasized the use of the RIM for its diagnosis, suggesting that the "propensity to regress when structure is low becomes an important and perhaps pathognomonic criterion for defining any sample of borderline persons" (p. 2). These authors suggested in particular that "borderline persons are believed to connect unrelated percepts illogically, overelaborate on the affective meaning of percepts, and give circumstantial and unpleasant associations to the Rorschach inkblots" (Gunderson & Singer, 1975, p. 6).

Psychodynamic theory was the predominant perspective in psychiatry for much of the first half of the 20th century (Stone, 1997). Credit for the substantial impact and importance of this perspective can be traced to the innovative brilliance of one particular person: Sigmund Freud. Some of Freud's original hypotheses have been discredited (Crews, 1996), but this reflects in large part the natural growth of any body of knowledge. "To reject psychodynamic thinking because Freud's instinct theory or his view of women is dated is like rejecting modern physics because Newton did not understand relativity" (Westen, 1998, p. 334). Freud was innovative in his rich development of a perspective that psychopathology reflects, at least in part, unconscious psychological conflicts (Gabbard, 2000; Westen, 1998). Freud had placed particular emphasis on conflicts involving primitive sexual and aggressive impulses, whereas contemporary clinicians emphasize instead conflicts regarding self-esteem, intimacy, control, and interpersonal relatedness (Gabbard, 2000; Westen, 1998; Westen & Gabbard, 1999; Wiggins, 2003).

Attachment theory illustrates well the changing nature of psychodynamic theory from concerns regarding the control of instinctual impulses to matters of interpersonal relatedness. Attachment theory is "a way of conceptualizing the propensity of human beings to make strong affectional bonds to particular others" (Bowlby, 1977, p. 201). The theory proposes the existence of an innate motivational system to maintain proximity with a caregiver. A caregiver's sensitivity and responsivity to an infant's signals (e.g., crying or clinging) is of fundamental importance in developing within the infant a sense of security and support. Bowlby (1982) proposed that children internalize over time their experiences with their caregiver in the form of a working model, or cognitive schema, about the self, close others, and the self in relationship with others. These schemas were classified as indicating the state of being largely secure, ambivalent, or avoidant by Ainsworth, Blehar, Waters, and Wall (1978), and as indicating the state of being secure, preoccupied, fearful, or dismissing by Bartholomew and Horowitz (1991). Bartholomew, Kwong, and Hart (2001) described well how these different forms of attachment might relate to some of the DSM-IV personality disorders. For example, histrionic personality disorder may be closely related to a preoccupied attachment orientation. Experiences of inconsistent and insensitive caretaking are thought to contribute to a preoccupation with attachment needs. "Because past attachment figures are likely to have responded inconsistently to their distress, the preoccupied have learned to express their needs actively and unrelentingly in order to maximize their chances of gaining support" (Bartholomew et al., 2001, p. 203). Illustrative personality disorder attachment studies are provided by Allen, Coyne, and Huntoon (1998), Besser and Priel (2003), Brennan and Shaver (1998), Fonagy et al. (1996), Nickell, Waudby, and Trull (2002) and Wilson and Constanzo (1996).

Cognitive

A fundamental component of cognitive models of personality psychopathology is the concept that underlying mental disorders are irrational, illogical cognitive schemas that dominate a person's reasoning or processing of information. These schemas contribute to maladaptive negative affect (anxiety, depression, or anger) by imparting a meaning that is both exaggerated and disturbing. Persons acting on these perceptions also further exacerbate their difficulties and escalate their conflicts through their ineffective, inaccurate, and distorted understanding of what is in fact problematic.

> Once such a pattern is established, the individual's schemas tend to bias his or her perception of events in such a way that experiences that otherwise would contradict his/her assumptions are overlooked, discounted, or misinterpreted while, at the same time, his/her interpretation of events and his/her interpersonal behavior result in experiences which seem to confirm his/her dysfunctional schemas. (Pretzer & Beck, 1996, p. 55)

Beck et al. (1990) developed a cognitive model for the conceptualization and treatment of each personality disorder. For example, they described the core pathologic beliefs of the dependent as "I am completely helpless," "If I am not loved, I will always be unhappy," and "Be subservient in order to bind him or her" (p. 45). These core beliefs are distinguished from those observed in persons with simple Axis I disorders because they are considered to be more fundamental, generalized, and pervasive. For example, the depressed person may say "I am a failure," whereas, the borderline person may believe he or she is fundamentally worthless. Irrational cognitive schemas associated with Axis I disorders generally remit with effective treatment of those disorders, whereas they are more chronic and characteristic in persons with a personality disorder (Cottraux & Blackburn, 2001). Illustrative studies on cognitive models of the personality disorders are provided by Nelson-Gray, Huprich, Kissling, and Ketchum (2004), Young (1994), and Young and Lindemann (1992).

One of the classic texts in the history of psychiatry was provided by Shapiro (1965). Shapiro sought to bridge psychodynamic and cognitive psychology, providing rich and detailed descriptions of the cognitive styles (irrational cognitive schemas) that characterize personality disorders, notably the hysterical, the obsessive–compulsive, the impulsive, and the paranoid. For example, he contrasted the hysterical and the obsessive–compulsive:

> Hysterical cognition in general is global, relatively diffuse, and lacking in sharpness, particularly in sharp detail. In a word, it is impressionistic. In contrast to the active, intense, and sharply focused attention of the obsessive–compulsive, hysterical cognition seems relatively lacking in sharp focus of attention; in contrast to the compulsive's active and prolonged searching for detail, the hysterical person tends cognitively to respond quickly and is highly susceptible to what is immediately impressive, striking, or merely obvious. (Shapiro, 1965, pp. 111–112)

The irrational cognitive schemas identified by cognitive therapists complement well the defense mechanisms identified by psychodynamic clinicians (Westen, 1991). Both involve habitual distortions in the perceptions of oneself and other persons. For example, Beck et al. (1990) described the borderline person as characterized by a "dichotomous thinking." "The effect of this black-or-white thinking is to force extreme interpretations on events that would normally fall in the intermediate range of a continuum, since there are no intermediate categories … [and] according to the cognitive view, extreme evaluations of situations lead to extreme emotional responses and extreme actions" (Beck et al., 1990, p. 187). This is similar to the description of splitting by Kernberg (1967) and Klein (1946). "Within the larger mental health community, this defense became identifiable by the borderline patient's tendency to perceive others in dichotomous, 'all-good' or 'all-bad' terms and then to treat others very differently (idealized or devalued, respectively), depending on which side of the internal split they occupied" (Gunderson, 2001, p. 103). Both of these are cognitive pathologies in which the person fails to perceive himself, other persons, and events in an accurate manner. A fundamental difference, however, is that psychodynamically oriented clinicians suggest that a person has an unconscious motivation for developing and maintaining these irrational cognitive schemas. Splitting is used by a person to avoid the anxiety and despair that would accompany an accurate perception of others (e.g., accurately perceiving that a parent was both abusive or denigrating and protective or loving). For the cognitive theorist, the schemas may simply be the result of instruction, reinforcement, and modeling.

Interpersonal

Fundamental to an understanding and description of personality is the characteristic manner of relating to others (Millon et al., 1996; Wiggins, 1982). No model of personality can fail to include interpersonal relatedness. It even has been suggested that personality disorders are essentially, if not entirely, disorders of interpersonal relatedness (Benjamin, 1996a; Kiesler, 1986, 1996).

A fundamental principle of some interpersonal models of psychopathology is that human behavior should be understood in a wider context of social, interpersonal relationships. As expressed by one of the earliest proponents of interpersonal models of psychopathology, "scientific psychiatry has to be defined as the study of interpersonal relations, and this end calls for the use of the kind of conceptual framework that we now call field theory" (Sullivan, 1953, p. 368). "The theory holds that we come into being as persons as a consequence of unnumbered interpersonal fields of force and that we manifest intelligible human processes only in such interpersonal fields" (Sullivan, 1948, p. 3). Carson (1969) has suggested that personality may itself be an arbitrary and illusory demarcation of the individual outside the context of this interpersonal field, "nothing more (or less) than the patterned regularities that may be observed in an individual's relations with other persons" (p. 26). The pathology that has resulted in a maladaptive behavior pattern may not reside within the person as an organismic mental disorder, but may instead lie in the social system in which the person is functioning. A diagnosis of psychopathology of an individual acting within this social system may in fact be counterproductive because it could identify incorrectly the individual as the sole or primary source for the dysfunctional behaviors, feelings, and ideas, distracting attention away from the wider social network controlling the actions of the individual (Reiss & Emde, 2003).

One of the diagnoses proposed for the DSM-III-R (APA, 1987) was a self-defeating or masochistic personality disorder. The intention of the diagnosis was to identify persons who are characteristically pessimistic, self-blaming, and self-defeating. However, it was apparent that a proportion of these persons would be within physically abusive relationships, and that their self-defeating behaviors may say more about the constant threat of physical harm than any organismic cognitive, neurobiologic, or psychodynamic pathologies that may be present (Widiger, 1995). A diagnosis of masochistic or self-defeating personality disorder could even be used to blame the victim rather than the perpetrator. An historical example is provided by Snell, Rosenwald, and Robey (1964), who reported 12 husbands charged with assault as "filling masochistic needs of the wife" (p. 110). On the other hand, women who have been repeatedly physically, sexually, or psychologically abused during childhood do have an increased risk of developing cognitive, neurobiologic, and psychodynamic pathologies that may increase the likelihood of their victimization again as adults. Yet, many current victims of abuse who seem unwilling or unable to extricate themselves from a relationship could be acting realistically in response to threats of physical harm and to the absence of a safe or meaningful alternative (Walker, 1989). Feelings of insecurity in women regarding their romantic and intimate relationships may say less about the women than the persons with whom the women are involved. "Men and women may differ in what they seek from relationships, but they may also differ in what they provide to each other" (Coyne & Whiffen, 1995, p. 368). In other words, "women might appear (and be) less dependent if they weren't involved with such undependable men" (Widiger & Anderson, 2003, p. 63).

Interpersonal models of personality, however, also support assessment and classification of personality disorders with respect to an individual's typical manner or style of interpersonal relatedness. "In 1947, a University of California faculty member (Hubert Coffey) and three graduate students (Mervin Freedman, Timothy Leary, and Abel Ossorio) initiated a psychodiagnostic investigation of patients who were undergoing group psychotherapy at a Unitarian church in Berkeley" (Wiggins, 2003, p. 68), an effort that eventually led to the widely influential interpersonal circumplex text of Leary (1957). Leary suggested, and many studies since have confirmed, that most (if not all) forms of interpersonal relatedness can well be described as some combination of two fundamental dimensions, identified by Wiggins (2003) as agency (dominance vs. submission) and communion (affiliation, or love vs. hate). Freedman, Leary, Ossorio, and Coffey (1951) suggested that each of the interpersonal traits would have both normal and maladaptive variants, and Leary and Coffey (1955) subsequently described six personality disorders (psychopathic, schizoid, obsessive, phobic, hysteric, and psychosomatic) with respect to this circumplex. Subsequent efforts at classification were provided by Lorr, Bishop, and McNair (1965) and Plutchik and Platman (1977), as well as by Leary (1957), and more recent interpersonal circumplex models of personality disorder have been provided by Benjamin (1996a), Kiesler (1996), Pincus (1994; Pincus & Wiggins, 1990; Pincus & Wilson, 2001; Wiggins & Pincus, 1989), and Trobst, Ayearst, and Salekin (2004).

The interpersonal models of personality disorder complement well the object-relational psychodynamic and cognitive models. Cognitive models of personality disorder overlap substantially with interpersonal, interactive models because "differences in basic [cognitive] assumptions lead to very different patterns of interpersonal interaction, elicit different responses from others, and establish a cognitive–interpersonal cycle that is strongly self-perpetuating" (Pretzer & Beck, 1996, pp. 55–56). Attachment theory is as much an interpersonal model of personality disorder as it is a psychodynamic model (Benjamin, 1996b; Pincus & Wilson, 2001).

An explicit integration of the interpersonal circumplex and psychodynamic models is provided by Benjamin's (1996a, 1996b, 1997) structural analysis of social behavior (SASB). The SASB contains three interpersonal circumplex surfaces: a focus on self, a focus on others, and the introjection of others' treatment of self. The model is creative in its integration of the two interpersonal circumplex dimensions of agency (power) and communion (affiliation) with the psychodynamic hypothesis that self-image is a function of one's relationships with one's caregivers. The fundamental psychodynamic perspective that personality is a reflection of identification (to be like him or her) and introjection (to treat yourself as one was treated), and that intense, significant interpersonal relationships are largely transferential (to act as if he or she is still there) is operationalized and studied in terms of the interpersonal dimensions of dominance and affiliation (e.g., dominating parental behavior is introjected by the self in the belief that one is helpless and should submit to others).

The assessment of personality disorders can be of substantial importance to a clinical intervention and treatment planning (Frances, 1980; Millon et al., 1996). There is considerable literature and research on their assessment with clinical interviews and self-report inventories, but, at least for some of the personality disorders, relatively less has been written on the use of the RIM (Widiger & Coker, 2002). The RIM can provide a uniquely informative and complementary contribution to our understanding of maladaptive personality functioning (Wiggins, 2003), and this volume should make a significant contribution to this effort.

REFERENCES

Abraham, K. (1921). *On character and libido development*. New York: Basic Books.

Abraham, K. (1927). The influence of oral eroticism on character formation. In *Selected papers on psychoanalysis*. London: Hogarth.

Abrams, R. C., & Horowitz, S. V. (1999). Personality disorders after age 50: A meta-analytic review of the literature. In E. Rosowsky, R. C. Abrams, & R. A. Zweig (Eds.), *Personality disorders in older adults: Emerging issues in diagnosis and treatment* (pp. 55–68). Mahwah, NJ: Lawrence Erlbaum Associates.

Agronin, M. E. (1998). Personality and psychopathology in late life. *Geriatrics, 53*, 35–40.

Ainsworth, M. D. S., Blehar, M. C., Waters, E., & Wall, S. (1978). *Patterns of attachment: Psychological study of the Strange Situation*. Hillsdale, NJ: Lawrence Erlbaum Associates.

Akhtar, S., & Thomson, J. (1982). Overview: Narcissistic personality disorder. *American Journal of Psychiatry, 139*, 12–20.

Alarcon, R. D. (1996). Personality disorders and culture in DSM-IV: a critique. *Journal of Personality Disorders, 10*, 260–270.

Allen, J. G., Coyne, L., & Huntoon, J. (1998). Complex posttraumatic stress disorder in women from a psychometric perspective. *Journal of Personality Assessment, 70*, 277–298.

American Psychiatric Association. (1980). *Diagnostic and statistical manual of mental disorders* (3rd ed.). Washington, DC: Author.

American Psychiatric Association. (1987). *Diagnostic and statistical manual of mental disorders* (3rd rev. ed.). Washington, DC: American Psychiatric Association.

American Psychiatric Association. (2000). *Diagnostic and statistical manual of mental disorders: Text revision* (4th rev. ed.). Washington, DC: American Psychiatric Association.

Bartholomew, K., & Horowitz, L. M. (1991). Attachment styles among young adults: A test of a model. *Journal of Personality and Social Psychology, 61*, 226–244.

Bartholomew, K., Kwong, M. J., & Hart, S. D. (2001). Attachment. In W. J. Livesley (Ed.), *Handbook of personality disorders. Theory, research, and treatment* (pp. 196–230). New York: Guilford.

Baumeister, R. F., Smart, L., & Boden, J. M. (1996). Relation of threatened egoism to violence and aggression: The dark side of high self-esteem. *Psychological Review, 103*, 5–33.

Beck, A. T., Freeman, A., & Associates. (1990). *Cognitive therapy of personality disorders.* New York: Guilford.

Beck, A. T., Freeman, A., Davis, D. D., & Associates. (2004). *Cognitive therapy of personality disorders* (2nd ed.). New York: Guilford.

Benjamin, L. S. (1996a). *Interpersonal diagnosis and treatment of personality disorders* (2nd ed.). New York: Guilford.

Benjamin, L. S. (1996b). An interpersonal theory of personality disorders. In J. F. Clarkin & M. F. Lenzenweger (Eds.), *Major theories of personality disorder* (pp. 141–220). New York: Guilford.

Benjamin, L. S. (1997). Personality disorders: Models for treatment and strategies for treatment development. *Journal of Personality Disorders, 11*, 307–324.

Besser, A., & Priel, B. (2003). A multisource approach to self-critical vulnerability to depression: The moderating role of attachment. *Journal of Personality, 71*, 515–556.

Blais, M. A., Hilsenronth, M. J., Fowler, J. C., & Conboy, C. A. (1999). A Rorschach exploration of the DSM-IV borderline personality disorder. *Journal of Clinical Psychology, 55*, 563–572.

Bornstein, R. F. (1992). The dependent personality: Developmental, social, and clinical perspectives. *Psychological Bulletin, 112*, 3–23.

Bornstein, R. F. (1993). *The dependent personality.* New York: Guilford.

Bornstein, R. F. (1995). Sex differences in objective and projective dependency tests: A meta-analytic review. *Assessment, 2*, 319–331.

Bornstein, R. F. (1996). Sex differences in dependent personality disorder prevalence rates. *Clinical Psychology: Science and Practice, 3*, 1–12.

Bornstein, R. F. (1998). Reconceptualizing personality disorder diagnosis in the DSM-V: The discriminant validity challenge. *Clinical Psychology: Science and Practice, 5*, 333–343.

Bornstein, R. F. (1999). Criterion validity of objective and projective dependency tests: A meta-analytic assessment of behavioral prediction. *Psychological Assessment, 11*, 48–57.

Bornstein, R. F., Hilsenroth, M. J., Padawer, J. R., & Fowler, J. C. (2000). Interpersonal dependency and personality pathology: Variations in Rorschach oral dependency scores across Axis II disorders. *Journal of Personality Assessment, 75*, 478–491.

Bowlby, J. (1977). The making and breaking of affectional bonds. *British Journal of Psychiatry, 130*, 201–210.

Bowlby, J. (1982). *Attachment and loss: Vol. 1. Attachment* (2nd ed.). New York: Basic Books.

Brennan, K. A., & Shaver, P. R. (1998). Attachment styles and personality disorders: Their connections to each other and to parental divorce, parental death, and perceptions of parental caregiving. *Journal of Personality, 66*, 835–878.

Bursten, B. (1973). Some narcissistic personality types. *International Journal of Psychoanalysis, 54*, 287–300.

Bursten, B. (1982). Narcissistic personality in DSM-III. *Comprehensive Psychiatry, 23*, 409–420.

Buss, D. M., Haselton, M. G., Shackelford, T. K., Bleske, A. L., & Wakefield, J. C. (1998). Adaptations, exaptations, and spandrels. *American Psychologist, 53*, 533–548.

Carson, R. C. (1969). *Interaction concepts of personality*. Chicago: Aldine.

Chodoff, P., & Lyons, H. (1958). Hysteria, the hysterical personality and "hysterical" conversion. *American Journal of Psychiatry, 114*, 734–740.

Clark, L. A. (1993). *Manual for the schedule for nonadaptive and adaptive personality*. Minneapolis, MN: University of Minnesota Press.

Cloninger, C. R. (2000). A practical way to diagnosis personality disorders: A proposal. *Journal of Personality Disorders, 14*, 99–108.

Cooper, A. M. (1981). Narcissism. In S. Arieti (Ed.), *American handbook of psychiatry* (Vol. 7, 2nd ed., pp. 297–316). New York: Basic Books.

Costa, P. T., & McCrae, R. R. (1994). Set like plaster? Evidence for the stability of adult personality. In T. Heatherton & J. L. Weinberger (Eds.), *Can personality change?* (pp. 21–40). Washington, DC: American Psychological Association.

Cottraux, J., & Blackburn, I. M. (2001). Cognitive therapy. In W. J. Livesley (Ed.), *Handbook of personality disorders: Theory, research, and treatment* (pp. 377–400). New York: Guilford.

Coyne, J. C., & Whiffen, V. E. (1995). Issues in personality as diathesis for depression: The case of sociotropy–dependency and autonomy–self-criticism. *Psychological Bulletin, 118*, 358–378.

Crews, F. (1996). The verdict on Freud. *Psychological Science, 7*, 63–67.

Easser, R., & Lesser, S. (1965). Hysterical personality: A reevaluation. *Psychoanalytic Quarterly, 34*, 390–402.

Farmer, R. F. (2000). Issues in the assessment and conceptualization of personality disorders. *Clinical Psychology Review, 20*, 823–851.

Fenichel, O. (1945). *The psychoanalytic theory of the neurosis*. New York: Norton.

Folette, W. C., & Houts, A. C. (1996). Models of scientific progress and the role of theory in taxonomy development: A case study of the DSM. *Journal of Consulting and Clinical Psychology, 64*, 1120–1132.

Fonagy, P. Leigh, T., Steele, M., Steele, H., Kennedy, R., Mattoon, G., et al. (1996). The relation of attachment status, psychiatric classification, and response to psychotherapy. *Journal of Consulting and Clinical Psychology, 64*, 22–31.

Fowler, J. C., Hilsenroth, M. J., & Nolan, E. (2000). Exploring the inner world of self-mutilating borderline patients: A Rorschach investigation. *Bulletin of the Menninger Clinic, 64*, 365–385.

Frances, A. J. (1980). The DSM-III personality disorders section: A commentary. *American Journal of Psychiatry, 137*, 1050–1054.

Frances, A. J., First, M. B., & Pincus, H. A. (1995). *DSM-IV guidebook*. Washington, DC: American Psychiatric Press.

Freedman, M. B., Leary, T. F., Ossorio, A. G., & Coffey, H. S. (1951). The interpersonal dimension of personality. *Journal of Personality, 20*, 143–161.

Freud, S. (1908/1959). Character and anal eroticism. In J. Strachey (Ed. and Trans.), *The standard edition of the complete psychological works of Sigmund Freud* (Vol. 9). London: Hogarth Press.

Gabbard, G. O. (2000). *Psychodynamic psychiatry in clinical practice* (3rd ed). Washington, DC: American Psychiatric Press.

Gacono, C. B., & Meloy, J. R. (2002). Assessing antisocial and psychopathic personalities. In J. N. Butcher (Ed.), *Clinical personality assessment: Practical approaches* (2nd ed., pp. 361–375). New York: Oxford University Press.

Greenberg, L. S., Elliott, R., & Lietar, G. (2003). Humanistic-experiential psychotherapy. In G. Stricker, T. A. Widiger, & I. B. Weiner (Eds.), *Handbook of psychology*. Vol. 8. *Clinical psychology* (pp. 301–325). New York: John Wiley.

Grinker, R., Werble, B., & Drye, R. (1968). *The borderline syndrome: A behavioral study of ego functions*. New York: Basic Books.

Gunderson, J. G. (2001). *Borderline personality disorder: A clinical guide*. Washington, DC: American Psychiatric Press.

Gunderson, J. G., Bender, D., Sanislow, C., Yen, S., Rettew, J. B., Dolan-Sewell, R. et al. (2003). Plausibility and possible determinants of sudden "remissions" in borderline patients. *Psychiatry, 66*, 111–119.

Gunderson, J. G., & Gabbard, G. O. (2000). *Psychotherapy for personality disorders*. Washington, DC: American Psychiatric Press.

Gunderson, J. G., & Kolb, J. E. (1978). Discriminating features of borderline patients. *American Journal of Psychiatry, 135*, 792–796.

Gunderson, J. G., Ronningstam, E., & Smith, L. E. (1991). Narcissistic personality disorder: A review of data on DSM-III-R descriptions. *Journal of Personality Disorders, 5*, 167–177.

Gunderson, J. G., Shea, M. T., Skodol, A. E., McGlashan, T. H., Morey, L. C., Stout, R. L., et al. (2000). The Collaborative Longitudinal Personality Disorders Study, I: Development, aims, design, and sample characteristics. *Journal of Personality Disorders, 14*, 300–315.

Gunderson, J. G., & Singer, M. (1975). Defining borderline patients: An overview. *American Journal of Psychiatry, 132*, 1–10.

Gunderson, J. G., Triebwasser, J., Phillips, K. A., & Sullivan, C. N. (1999). Personality and vulnerability to affective disorders. In C. R. Cloninger (Ed.), *Personality and psychopathology* (pp. 3–32). Washington, DC: American Psychiatric Press.

Hare, R. D. (1991). *The Hare Psychopathy Checklist–Revised manual.* North Tonawanda, NY: Multi-Health Systems.

Hilsenroth, M. J., Handler, L., & Blais, M. A. (1996). Assessment of narcissistic personality disorder: A multimethod review. *Clinical Psychology Review, 16,* 655–683.

Huprich, S. K. (1998). Depressive personality disorder: Theoretical issues, clinical findings, and future research questions. *Clinical Psychology Review, 18,* 477–500.

Huprich, S. K. (2003a). Depressive personality and its relationship to depressed mood, interpersonal loss, negative parental perception, and perfectionism. *Journal of Nervous and Mental Disease, 191,* 1–7.

Huprich, S. K. (2003b). Evaluating facet-level predictions and construct validity of depressive personality disorder. *Journal of Personality Disorders, 17,* 219–232.

Hyman, S. (2002). Neuroscience, genetics, and the future of psychiatric diagnosis. *Psychopathology, 35,* 139–144.

Joiner, T. E., & Rudd, M. D. (2003). The incremental validity of passive–aggressive personality symptoms rivals or exceeds that of other personality symptoms in suicidal outpatients. *Journal of Personality Assessment, 79,* 161–170.

Kandel, E. R. (1998). A new intellectual framework for psychiatry. *American Journal of Psychiatry, 155,* 457–469.

Kaslow, F. W. (Ed.). (1996). *Handbook of relational diagnosis and dysfunctional family patterns.* New York: John Wiley.

Kaye, A. L., & Shea, M. T. (2000). Personality disorders, personality traits, and defense mechanisms measures. In A. Rush, H. Pincus, M. First, D. Blacker, J. Endicott, S. Keith, et al. (Eds.), *Handbook of psychiatric measures* (pp. 713–749). Washington, DC: American Psychiatric Association.

Kernberg, O. (1967). Borderline personality organization. *Journal of the American Psychoanalytic Association, 15,* 641–685.

Kernberg, O. (1970). A psychoanalytic classification of character pathology. *Journal of the American Psychoanalytic Association, 18,* 800–822.

Kernberg, O. (1975). *Borderline conditions and pathological narcissism.* New York: Jason Aronson.

Kiesler, D. J. (1986). The 1982 interpersonal circle: An analysis of DSM-III personality disorders. In T. Millon & G. Klerman (Eds.), *Contemporary directions in psychopathology: Toward DSM-IV* (pp. 571–597). New York: Guilford.

Kiesler, D. J. (1996). *Contemporary interpersonal theory and research: Personality, psychopathology, and psychotherapy.* New York: John Wiley.

Klein, M. (1946). Notes on some schizoid mechanisms. *International Journal of Psychoanalysis, 27,* 99–110.

Klein, M. H., Wonderlich, S., & Shea, M. T. (1993). Models of relationship between personality and depression: Toward a framework for theory and research. In M. H. Klein, D. J. Kupfer, & M. T. Shea (Eds.), *Personality and depression* (pp. 1–54). New York: Guilford.

Knight, R. (1953). Borderline states. *Bulletin of the Menninger Clinic, 17,* 1–12.

Kohut, H. (1966). Forms and transformations of narcissism. *Journal of the American Psychoanalytic Association, 145,* 243–272.

Kohut, H. (1971). *The analysis of the self.* New York: International Universities Press.

Kraepelin, E. (1904). *Lectures on clinical psychiatry* (Trans. and Ed. by Thomas Johnstone). New York: William Wood.

Leary, T. (1957). *Interpersonal diagnosis of personality*. New York: Ronald Press.

Leary, T., & Coffey, H. S. (1955). Interpersonal diagnosis: Some problems of methodology and validation. *Journal of Abnormal and Social Psychology, 50,* 110–124.

Leichsenring, F., & Leibing, E. (2003). The effectiveness of psychodynamic therapy and cognitive behavior therapy in the treatment of personality disorders: A meta-analysis. *American Journal of Psychiatry, 160,* 1223–1232.

Livesley, W. J., & Jang, K. L. (2000). Toward an empirically based classification of personality disorder. *Journal of Personality Disorders, 14,* 137–151.

Lopez, S. R., & Guarnaccia, P. J. (2000). Cultural psychopathology: Uncovering the social world of mental illness. *Annual Review of Psychology, 51,* 571–598.

Loranger, A. W. (1990). The impact of DSM-III on diagnostic practice in a university hospital. *Archives of General Psychiatry, 47,* 672–675.

Lorr, M., Bishop, P. F., & McNair, D. M. (1965). Interpersonal types among psychiatric patients. *Journal of Abnormal Psychology, 70,* 468–472.

McCrae, R. R., & Costa, P. T. (1999). A five-factor theory of personality. In L. A. Pervin & O. P. John (Eds.), *Handbook of personality: Theory and research* (2nd ed., pp. 139–153). New York: Guilford.

McDermut, W., Zimmerman, M., & Chelminski, I. (2003). The construct validity of depressive personality disorder. *Journal of Abnormal Psychology, 112,* 49–60.

Meyer, G. J., Bates, M., & Gacono, C. (1999). The Rorschach Rating Scale: Item adequacy, scale development, and relations with the Big Five model of personality. *Journal of Personality Assessment, 73,* 199–244.

Mihura, J. L., Meyer, G. J., Bel-Bahar, T., & Gunderson, J. (2003). Correspondence among observer ratings of Rorschach, Big Five model, and DSM-IV personality disorder constructs. *Journal of Personality Assessment, 81,* 20–39.

Millon, T., Davis, R. D., Millon, C. M., Wenger, A. W., Van Zuilen, M. H., Fuchs, et al. (1996). *Disorders of personality. DSM-IV and beyond*. New York: John Wiley.

Nelson-Gray, R. O., Huprich, S. K., Kissling, G. E., & Ketchum, K. (2004). A preliminary examination of Beck's cognitive theory of personality disorders in undergraduate analogues. *Personality and Individual Differences, 36,* 219–233.

Nickell, A. D., Waudby, C. J., & Trull, T. (2002). Attachment, parental bonding, and borderline personality disorder features in young adults. *Journal of Personality Disorders, 16,* 148–159.

Oldham, J. M., & Skodol, A. E. (2000). Charting the future of Axis II. *Journal of Personality Disorders, 14,* 17–29.

Paris, J. (1998). Psychotherapy for the personality disorders: Working with traits. *Bulletin of the Menninger Clinic, 62,* 287–297.

Perry, J. C., Banon, E., & Ianni, F. (1999). Effectiveness of psychotherapy for personality disorders. *American Journal of Psychiatry, 156,* 1312–1321.

Perry, J. C., & Bond, M. B. (2000). Empirical studies of psychotherapy for personality disorders. In J. M. Oldham & M. B. Riba (Eds.), *Psychotherapy for personality disorders* (pp. 1–31). Washington, DC: American Psychiatric Press.

Pincus, A. L. (1994). The interpersonal circumplex and interpersonal theory: Perspectives on personality and its pathology. In S. Strack & M. Lorr (Eds.), *Differentiating normal and abnormal personality* (pp. 114–136). New York: Springer.

Pincus, A. L., & Wiggins, J. S. (1990). Interpersonal problems and conceptions of personality disorders. *Journal of Personality Disorders, 4,* 342–352.

Pincus, A. L., & Wilson, K. R. (2001). Interpersonal variability in dependent personality. *Journal of Personality, 69,* 223–252.

Plaud, J. J. (2001). Clinical science and human behavior. *Journal of Clinical Psychology, 57,* 1089–1102.

Plutchik, R., & Platman, S. (1977). Personality connotations of psychiatric diagnoses. *Journal of Nervous and Mental Disease, 165,* 418–422.

Pretzer, J. L., & Beck, A. T. (1996). A cognitive theory of personality disorders. In J. F. Clarkin & M. F. Lenzenweger (Eds.), *Major theories of personality disorder* (pp. 36–105). New York: Guilford.

Raine, A., Lencz, T., & Mednick, S. A. (Eds.). (1995). *Schizotypal personality.* New York: Cambridge University Press.

Reich, W. (1933). *Character analysis.* NY: Farrar, Strauss, and Giroux.

Reiss, D., & Emde, R. N. (2003). Relationship disorders are psychiatric disorders: Five reasons they were not included in DSM-IV. In K. A. Phillips, M. B. First, & H. A. Pincus (Eds.), *Advancing DSM. Dilemmas in psychiatric diagnosis* (pp. 191–223). Washington, DC: American Psychiatric Association.

Rychlak, J. F. (1993). *Discovering free will and personal responsibility.* New York: Oxford University Press.

Salekin, R. T. (2002). Psychopathy and therapeutic pessimism: Clinical lore or clinical reality? *Clinical Psychology Review, 22,* 79–112.

Sanislow, C. A., & McGlashan, T. H. (1998). Treatment outcome of personality disorders. *Canadian Journal of Psychiatry, 43,* 237–250.

Schneider, K. (1923). *Psychopathic personalities.* London: Cassell.

Shapiro, D. (1965). *Neurotic styles.* New York: Basic.

Shea, M. T. (1996). Enduring personality change after catastrophic experience. In T. A. Widiger, A. J. Frances, H. A. Pincus, R. Ross, M. B., First, & W. W. Davis (Eds.), *DSM-IV sourcebook* (Vol. 2, pp. 849–860). Washington, DC: American Psychiatric Association.

Shedler, J. (2002). A new language for psychoanalytic diagnosis. *Journal of the American Psychoanalytic Association, 50,* 429–456.

Snell, J., Rosenwald, R., & Robey, A. (1964). The wife-beater's wife: A study of family interaction. *Archives of General Psychiatry, 11,* 107–112.

Spitzer, R. L., Williams, J. B. W., & Skodol, A. E. (1980). DSM-III: The major achievements and an overview. *American Journal of Psychiatry, 137,* 151–164.

Stern, A. (1938). Psychoanalytic investigation and therapy in the borderline group of neuroses. *Psychoanalytic Quarterly, 7,* 467–489.

Stoff, D. M., Breiling, J., & Maser, J. D. (Eds.). (1997). *Handbook of antisocial behavior.* New York: John Wiley.

Stone, M. H. (1980). *The borderline syndromes.* New York: McGraw-Hill.

Stone, M. H. (1993). *Abnormalities of personality. Within and beyond the realm of treatment.* New York: W. W. Norton and Company.

Stone, M. (1997). A brief history of psychiatry. In A. Tasman, J. Kay, & J. A. Lieberman (Eds.), *Psychiatry* (Vol. 2, pp. 1853–1875). Philadelphia, PA: W. B. Saunders.

Sullivan, H. S. (1948). The meaning of anxiety in psychiatry and in life. *Psychiatry, 11,* 1–13.

Sullivan, H. S. (1953). *The interpersonal theory of psychiatry.* New York: Norton.

Sutker, P. B., & Allain, A. N. (2001). Antisocial personality disorder. In P. B. Sutker & H. E. Adams (Eds.), *Comprehensive textbook of psychopathology* (3rd ed., pp. 445–490). New York: Plenum Publishers.

Triebwasser, J., & Shea, M. T. (1996). Personality change resulting from another mental disorder. In T. A. Widiger, A. J. Frances, H. A. Pincus, R. Ross, M. B. First, & W. W. Davis (Eds.), *DSM-IV sourcebook* (Vol. 2, pp. 861–868). Washington, DC: American Psychiatric Association.

Trobst, K., Ayearst, L. E., & Salekin, R. T. (2004). Where is the personality in personality disorder assessment? A comparison across four sets of personality disorder scales. *Multivariate Behavioral Research, 39,* 231–271.

Walker, L. E. A. (1989). Psychology and violence against women. *American Psychologist, 44,* 695–702.

Westen, D. (1991). Social cognition and object relations. *Psychological Bulletin, 109,* 429–455.

Westen, D. (1997). Divergences between clinical and research methods for assessing personality disorders: Implications for research and the evolution of Axis II. *American Journal of Psychiatry, 154,* 895–903.

Westen, D. (1998). The scientific legacy of Sigmund Freud: Toward a psychodynamically informed psychological science. *Psychological Bulletin, 124,* 333–371.

Westen, D., & Arkowitz-Westen, L. (1998). Limitations of Axis II in diagnosing personality pathology in clinical practice. *American Journal of Psychiatry, 155,* 1767–1771.

Westen, D., & Gabbard, G. O. (1999). Psychoanalytic approaches to personality. In L. Pervin & O. P. John (Eds.), *Handbook of personality: Theory and research* (2nd ed., pp. 57–101). New York: Guilford.

Westen, D., & Shedler, J. (1999). Revising and assessing Axis II: Part II. Toward an empirically based and clinically useful classification of personality disorders. *American Journal of Psychiatry, 156,* 273–285.

Westen, D., & Shedler, J. (2000). A prototype matching approach to diagnosing personality disorders: toward DSM-V. *Journal of Personality Disorders, 14,* 109–126.

Wetzler, S., & Morey, L. C. (1999). Passive-aggressive personality disorder: The demise of a syndrome. *Psychiatry, 62,* 49–59.

Widiger, T. A. (1993). The DSM-III-R categorical personality disorder diagnoses: A critique and an alternative. *Psychological Inquiry, 4,* 75–90.

Widiger, T. A. (1995). Deletion of the self-defeating and sadistic personality disorder diagnoses. In W. J. Livesley (Ed.), *The DSM-IV personality disorders* (pp. 359–373). New York: Guilford.

Widiger, T. A. (2000). Personality disorders in the 21st century. *Journal of Personality Disorders, 14,* 3–16.

Widiger, T. A., & Anderson, K. (2003). Personality and depression in women. *Journal of Affective Disorders, 74,* 59–66.

Widiger, T. A., & Bornstein, R. F. (2001). Histrionic, narcissistic, and dependent personality disorders. In H. E. Adams & P. Sutker (Eds.), *Comprehensive handbook of psychopathology* (3rd ed., pp. 507–529). New York: Plenum.

Widiger, T. A., & Coker, L. A. (2002). Assessing personality disorders. In J. N. Butcher (Ed.), *Clinical personality assessment. Practical approaches* (2nd ed., pp. 407–434). New York: Oxford University Press.

Widiger, T. A., & Costa, P. T. (1994). Personality and personality disorders. *Journal of Abnormal Psychology, 103,* 78–91.

Widiger, T. A., & Costa, P. T. (2002). Five factor model personality disorder research. In P. T. Costa & T. A. Widiger (Eds.), *Personality disorders and the five factor model of personality* (2nd ed., pp. 59–87). Washington, DC: American Psychological Association.

Widiger, T. A., Costa, P. T., & McCrae, R. R. (2002). A proposal for Axis II: Diagnosing personality disorders using the five factor model. In P. T. Costa & T. A. Widiger (Eds.), *Personality disorders and the five-factor model of personality* (2nd ed., pp. 431–456). Washington, DC: American Psychological Association.

Widiger, T. A., & Sanderson, C. J. (1995). Towards a dimensional model of personality disorders in DSM-IV and DSM-V. In W. J. Livesley (Ed.), *The DSM-IV personality disorders* (pp. 433–458). New York: Guilford.

Widiger, T. A., & Seidlitz, L. (2002). Personality, psychopathology, and aging. *Journal of Research in Personality, 36,* 335–362.

Wiggins, J. S. (1982). Circumplex models of interpersonal behavior in clinical psychology. In P. Kendall & J. Butcher (Eds.), *Handbook of research methods in clinical psychology* (pp. 183–221). New York: John Wiley.

Wiggins, J. S. (2003). *Paradigms of personality assessment.* New York: Guilford.

Wiggins, J. S., & Pincus, A. L. (1989). Conceptions of personality disorders and dimensions of personality. *Psychological Assessment, 1,* 305–316.

Wilson, J. S., & Constanzo, P. R. (1996). A preliminary study of attachment, attention, and schizotypy in early adulthood. *Journal of Social and Clinical Psychology, 15,* 231–260.

World Health Organization. (1992). *The ICD-10 classification of mental and behavioural disorders: Clinical descriptions and diagnostic guidelines.* Geneva, Switzerland: Author.

Young, J. E. (1994). *Cognitive therapy for personality disorders: A schema focused approach.* Sarasota, FL: Professional Resource Exchange.

Young, J. E., & Lindemann, M. D. (1992). An integrative schema-focused model for personality disorders. *Journal of Cognitive Psychotherapy: An International Quarterly, 6,* 11–23.

2

The Advantages of Assessing Personality Disorders With the Rorschach

Steven K. Huprich
Eastern Michigan University

Ronald J. Ganellen
Northwestern University

The obstacles to assessing personality disorders and their solutions remain a conundrum in clinical practice. In part, some of the obstacles are related to the elusive construct of "personality" and what makes it "disordered." Likewise, measurement of any construct is dependent on the stability and accuracy of the measurement, as well as the nature of the tool used to perform the measurement. Physicians, for instance, suspected that microorganisms were responsible for certain disease processes, but only with the advent of a microscope and microbiologic techniques were they able to understand the nature of the pathologic agent and how to change the action of that agent. So it is with personality disorders. Identifying the quintessential elements of personality has been challenging, as has been finding the right tool to measure it.

However, it is suggested in this chapter that the Rorschach Inkblot Method (RIM) has many advantages as a technique for assessment of personality disorders. Although this approach to measurement is not without its drawbacks, it appears that the RIM provides alternatives to assessment that many other traditional assessment devices do not offer, such as self-report, informant report, or interview measures. Of course, this approach to assessment has received mixed attention in the research and clinical literature. Because some of this may be attributable to a disdain for projective techniques and the belief that the Rorschach is not empirically justified

(Hunsley & Bailey, 1999; Wood, Nezworski, Garb, & Lilienfeld, 2001), this chapter aims to provide a foundation upon which personality disorders can be researched and assessed with the RIM. With such a framework in place, interested parties can engage in empirically justified and clinically informed assessment of personality disorders, and the merits of such an approach can be further evaluated for their contributions to scientifically informed clinical practice. The following discussion presents the problems encountered when traditional self-report, informant report, and interview measures are used for personality disorder assessment and provides several advantages offered by the RIM.

LIMITATIONS OF SELF-REPORTS AND INFORMANT REPORTS AS MEASURES OF PERSONALITY DISORDERS

Assessment of personality disorders in clinical and research settings usually is based on information provided by the patient, supplemented by observations of the patient's behavior. In some cases, additional information is provided by a person familiar with the patient's behavior such as a partner or family member. Methods used to identify personality disorders include scales designed to identify personality disorders contained in an omnibus self-report inventory, such as the Minnesota Multiphasic Personality Inventory-2 (MMPI-2) or Millon Clinical Multiaxial Inventory-III (MCMI-III), self-report inventories focused specifically on characteristics of personality disorders, informant reports, clinical interviews, semistructured interviews such as the Personality Disorder Examination (Loranger, 1988) or Structural Clinical Interview for the DSM-III-R (SCID-II) (First, Spitzer, Gibbon, & Williams, 1995), and attempts to combine multiple sources of information obtained over time, such as the Longitudinal Expert and All Data (LEADS) method (Spitzer, 1983).

It is well established that the level of agreement among different approaches to the diagnosis of personality disorders is low (Zimmerman, 1994; Zimmerman & Coryell, 1990). Low concordance rates are the norm rather than the exception both within and between different methods of assessing personality disorders. For instance, not only are correlations between parallel MMPI and MCMI personality disorder scales weak, as are relationships between self-report measures and structured clinical interviews (Renneberg, Chambless, Dowdall, & Fauerbach, 1992), but findings have shown that the rates of agreement between patient and informant reports also are low (Bernstein et al., 1997; Ferro & Klein, 1997; Klonsky, Oltmanns, & Turkheimer, 2002; Reich, 1988; Riso, Klein, Anderson, Ouimette, & Lizardi, 1994; Zimmerman, 1994; Zimmerman, Pfohl, Coryell, Stangl, & Corenthal, 1988). Low levels of agreement exist not only among attempts to identify specific personality disorders, but also at the most basic level of whether a personality disorder exists. For example, in three studies that examined agreement between information provided by patients and knowledgeable informants responding to semistructured interviews, the rate of agreement, as measured by kappa, ranged from .06 to .13, with a median value of .06 (Dreessen, Hildebrand, & Arntz, 1998; Riso et al., 1994; Zimmerman et al., 1988).

Different explanations have been offered to account for these disappointing findings. In addition to theoretical and methodologic critiques concerning the validity of current approaches to classifying personality disorders, such as those made by proponents of the Five-Factor Model (Costa & Widiger, 2002), important questions have been raised about the strengths and weaknesses of different approaches used to assess personality disorders. The following sections discuss the advantages and disadvantages inherent in self-report methods as well as methods that assess personality disorders by collecting information from informants who know well the person being evaluated.

SELF-REPORT METHODS

According to the *Diagnostic and Statistical Manual of Mental Disorders*, 4th Edition (DSM-IV) Text Revision (American Psychological Association, [APA], 2000), a personality disorder is diagnosed if an individual has "an enduring pattern of inner experience and behavior that deviates markedly from the expectations of the individual's culture" (p. 629). These problematic reactions can be manifested in terms of inappropriate or distorted ways of viewing oneself or others, difficulties in managing emotional responses, difficulties in establishing and maintaining mutually satisfying interpersonal relationships, or behavior demonstrating problems with impulse control (criterion A). Not only must the clinician identify patterns of cognition, affect, interpersonal functioning, and impulse control, but it also must be determined that the patterns are inflexible and pervasive across a broad range of personal and social situations (criterion B) and lead to "clinically significant distress in impairment in social, occupational, or other important areas of functioning" (criterion C; p. 629).

A reading of these criteria suggests some obvious reasons why individuals may have difficulty describing themselves accurately when responding to a clinical or semistructured interview that explores characteristics of personality disorders, or when completing a self-report inventory that has items relevant to personality disorders. For instance, the general guidelines provided in the DSM-IV to identify personality disorders, as well as some of the specific criteria required for the diagnosis of individual DSM-IV personality disorders, involve concepts and terminology to which some individuals may have difficulty responding because the terms are unfamiliar or because the abstraction level of the criteria is prohibitive.

For example, one aspect of borderline personality disorder involves perceptions of others that alternate between extremes of idealization and devaluation. It is unlikely that the average person on the street is sufficiently familiar with these terms and concepts to rate reliably whether their views of others shift between the extremes of idealization and devaluation. Similarly, it may be difficult for a person to rate whether his or her speech is overly impressionistic, a feature of histrionic personality disorder, unless the person has a conceptual grasp of what it means for speech to be impressionistic, vague, and lacking in detail.

The impact of the abstract nature of diagnostic criteria and the degree to which individuals are familiar with these concepts may be mitigated if interview or test items are clearly written in everyday language and anchored by easily understood examples. Assuming that an individual has a firm conceptual understanding of the characteristics under investigation, the DSM-IV criteria do not provide any clear guidelines an individual can use to determine whether his or her patterns of thinking, feeling, and acting deviate from or conform to the norms and expectations of his or her culture and, if so, whether the deviation is mild, moderate, or marked. For instance, an individual may report viewing other people with suspicious mistrust and being wary, vigilant, and cautious about contact with others. This description may be quite accurate. There clearly is considerable room for judgment, however, in determining whether these attitudes and expectations are deviant, as required for a diagnosis of a paranoid personality disorder, or whether they reflect a realistic awareness of human nature and the way the world operates. Similarly, the demarcation between a robust sense of self-confidence and an inflated view of one's importance, a feature of a narcissistic personality disorder, is not well-defined in the DSM-IV.

Individuals also may have difficulty determining whether their patterns of cognition, affect, and behavior contribute to clinically significant distress or impairment in functioning, as required by the DSM-IV. For instance, a man may acknowledge a pattern of becoming easily irritated when his domestic partner requests that he do particular chores or questions his absences from home, reacting with a hostile counterattack, and engaging in repeated instances of physical abuse. However, if these reactions occur in the context of an antisocial personality disorder, the man may accurately state that he is not distressed, is not likely to define his reactions as problematic in the least, and instead, is more likely to insist adamantly that his partner is the problem.

It should be noted that the brief examples provided concerning suspicious mistrust, self-confidence, and physical abuse do not involve the issue of insight, an issue discussed later. Instead, these examples illustrate that there is considerable room for interpretation when an individual is asked to describe him- or herself in terms of whether he or she exhibits a pattern that is abnormal, and whether that pattern causes either significant distress or difficulties in functioning. These factors each may contribute to the low levels of agreement found when methods of diagnosing personality disorders relying on self-report are compare with other methods.

Assuming that individuals understand the terms and concepts addressed in interview questions or test items, as well as the guidelines for distinguishing when a pattern of thinking, emotional reactions, and behavior is persistent and maladaptive, accurate self-reports depend on truthful and realistic responding. Patients' accounts of their functioning may be skewed consciously or unconsciously in ways that render self-report untrustworthy or unreliable. Some individuals may consciously and deliberately misrepresent their history for a variety of reasons. For instance, in some circumstances an individual with an antisocial personality disorder may deny a history of repeated infractions involving authority figures or other irresponsible, amoral behavior that is well documented in other sources of information. Of course, finding such an obvious discrepancy may confirm that the individual has a tendency to be deceitful, manipulative, and dishonest. This is useful information when a diagnosis of antisocial personality disorder is being considered. On the basis of their clinical experiences, Widiger, Mangine, Corbitt, Ellis, and Thomas (1995) also have found that some individuals with an antisocial personality disorder intentionally mislead and deceive clinicians "simply for their own amusement and pleasure" (p. 21).

It also is possible that some individuals deny having certain characteristics of a personality disorder not because they do not have them, but because agreeing that they do would make an unflattering statement about themselves. For instance, how many people are likely to agree that they express emotions in a shallow manner, one of the criteria used to diagnose a histrionic personality disorder? Similarly, many people are reluctant to say they lack empathy with others, even if they know this is true of them, because this description is uncomplimentary.

Individuals may portray their functioning in a biased manner that is not as blatant or deliberate as described earlier. For a variety of reasons, individuals may engage in impression management strategies that are not consciously selected or acted on. This can occur for different reasons. In some instances, an individual simply may not recognize how his or her behavior is seen by and affects others. For instance, an individual who frequently spends most or all of his or her leisure time engaged in work-related tasks may perceive him- or herself as a conscientious, responsible, productive employee without recognizing that his or her behavior pushes others away and interferes with the development of close bonds with them. Individuals with these characteristics who carry a diagnosis of an obsessive–compulsive personality disorder may not rate themselves as excessively devoted to work. In their view, they may consider their dedication to work as necessary, if not praiseworthy. In this example, the individual does not recognize or acknowledge the impact of his behavior. Stated differently, he does not understand the toll that his choices, priorities, and actions take on interpersonal relationships. This reflects a lack of insight.

A similar lack of insight may influence how an individual with a paranoid personality disorder responds when asked whether he tends to read too much into benign remarks or events. This individual may not endorse criterion 4 of the DSM-IV, even in response to a thoughtful, sensitive inquiry about it, not because the described characteristics do not apply to him, but because he is convinced interactions and circumstances are anything but benign. This individual is not likely to recognize that he misinterprets casual remarks or to be aware that he attributes unintended meanings to others' actions. Thus, persistent, maladaptive patterns of thinking, feeling, and behaving characteristic of a personality disorder may result in a lack of self-awareness that leads an individual to deny truthfully a manifestation of personality disorder features that others might readily identify as applying to him or her.

The preceding outlined issues present a number of reasons why self-report methods may not be accurate or reliable. In addition to a deliberate reporting of inaccurate information, some individuals may lack awareness that they exhibit certain characteristics, may not realize the impact of the way they customarily structure their lives, or may not want to acknowledge characteristics they consider unflattering or socially undesirable. Moreover, self-reports may be unreliable if individuals are not familiar with the concepts and terms being investigated or do not understand them. This highlights the importance of obtaining information from other sources given the possibility that a self-report may be limited, incomplete, self-serving, or inaccurate.

INFORMANT REPORTS

As noted, ratings of personality characteristics made by patients about themselves and ratings of them made by others who know them intimately often do not match well (Klonsky et al., 2002; Zimmerman, 1994). This should not be surprising because similar findings are reported frequently when ratings of other psychological characteristics obtained from different sources are compared. It might be concluded that this discrepancy occurs as a function of the biases and inaccuracies in self-report discussed earlier. Individuals may provide unreliable, inaccurate ratings of themselves for a variety of reasons, including limited self-awareness or differences in definitions of whether behaviors are problematic. Discrepancies between self-report and informant reporting can have a marked impact on the conclusions reached about a personality disorder diagnosis. For instance, Zimmerman, Pfohl, Stangl, and Corenthal (1986) reported that they changed an initial diagnosis of a personality disorder reached on the basis of self-report material alone in 20% of their cases after additional information was obtained from an informant. The change in diagnosis usually occurred after the informant provided information indicating pathology not disclosed or acknowledged by the individual.

Whereas these factors may account for some of the reasons why discrepancies between self-ratings and observer ratings occur, they do not explain another well-documented finding—namely, that substantial disagreement is found frequently among ratings of an individual provided by different informants. For instance, ratings of a child made by different adults more often disagree than agree. This occurs when ratings of behavior made by a child's mother are compared with ratings made by the child's father, as well as when parental ratings are compared with teacher ratings. Studies have replicated the finding that different informants often provide contradictory information in a variety of behavior domains using different rating instruments including the Child Behavior Checklist (Achenbach, 1991; Achenbach, McConaughy, & Howell, 1987) and ratings of symptoms associated with attention deficit hyperactivity disorder (Zucker, Morris, Ingram, Morris, & Bakeman, 2002).

One might question whether finding that two raters provide different descriptions of an individual indicates that one rater knows the person better than the other. Along this vein, in the Child Behavior Checklist literature, some authors have suggested that mothers' ratings of their children may be more valid than ratings made by fathers because, in general, mothers spend more time with their children than fathers (Fitzgerald, Zucker, Maguin, & Reider, 1994). This is an important consideration in assessments to determine whether an individual's condition should be diagnosed as a personality disorder. One might naturally put more stock in ratings made by the person most familiar with that individual, particularly when discrepant reports are obtained from different informants.

Another explanation has been offered to explain the discrepancies frequently found between ratings of children made by their mothers and fathers. Some writers have suggested that fathers may be more tolerant of certain behaviors, such as roughhousing or play fighting, than mothers, whereas mothers may be more tolerant than their husbands of other behaviors, such as a daughter's moodiness. These writers have suggested that parents are more likely to accept and view as normal behaviors they engaged in as youngsters, even when their partner disapproves of their child's actions and believes a problem exists that requires attention. Stated in more general terms, disagreements in ratings made by different informants may reflect differences in the raters' tolerance for a particular characteristic.

The differences in levels of tolerance for particular behaviors and personality characteristics may be one factor explaining low concordance when different informants rate an individual for features of a personality disorder. For instance, in marital therapy, it is quite common for a couple to consist of an individual with obsessive personality features and an individual with histrionic characteristics. An obsessive male may not view his partner' emotional intensity as a liability that deserves a rating for pathology, but instead may describe his partner as having a warm heart and admire and enjoy her uninhibited spontaneity. Other people, however, may be impatient or irritated with the constant drama this woman creates in her life, readily rating her as egocentric, attention seeking, and subject to rapidly shifting moods and shallow emotions. This example illustrates the point that in some cases, differences in ratings relevant to a personality disorder diagnosis may occur not because observers disagree as to whether the person they are rating exhibits a pattern of behavior, but because they disagree as to whether they approve or disapprove of certain personality characteristics and view a pattern of behavior as deviant or maladaptive.

Other more complex explanations for disagreements between raters exists. To some writers, findings showing that different people have divergent views of an individual are not at all troubling. These writers believe such divergence should be expected to occur naturally and frequently. These low levels of agreement between different observers are thought to reflect the fact that an individual does not have the same type of relationship with everyone in his or her life, but instead develops unique relationships with others that are shaped by the give and take that occurs between people over time.

Thus, for instance, just as it is common for a man to act differently with his drinking buddies than he does with his in-laws, it is equally understandable that a patient with a personality disorder can have different kinds of relationships with different people. Problematic patterns of thinking, reacting, and social behavior may be more readily rated by some people than others. For instance, an individual with an avoidant personality disorder may feel relaxed and appear self-confident with a person he or she knows well, feels accepted by, and is comfortable with, whereas the same person may become apprehensive, inhibited, and uptight when spending time with a new acquaintance who has a critical, judgmental edge. One would naturally expect ratings of the patient made by these two people to differ considerably, not because one is right and the other wrong, nor because one knows the patient better than the other, but as a function of the type of dyadic relationship that exists with each person. This perspective assumes that relationships are dynamic in nature, and that they are shaped and colored by the needs, expectations, and behaviors each person brings to the relationship.

It also is possible that the type of unique relationship a patient develops with a friend or partner may be colored by his associate's own psychological issues and problems. This possibility is suggested by research investigating the reasons why low levels of agreement between parents in their ratings of their child are the norm rather than the exception. Some studies have suggested that disagreement between parents can occur if one parent has current psychological problems, such as depression (Achenbach et al., 1987). The presence of psychopathology may influence how parents view their children's behavior or how tolerant they are of their children's problems.

Recognizing the possibility that informants' psychological characteristics have a considerable influence on what they say about another person has an important implication for the assessment of personality disorders. One must be aware that descriptions of an individual's behavior and personality characteristics may be biased by the informant's psychological dynamics, and in some cases may reveal as much about the informant as about the person the informant is rating. For instance, a romantic partner may minimize or gloss over her partner's irresponsible behavior, multiple sexual infidelities, and absence of remorse if her loyalty is motivated by fears of abandonment, a dynamic that is not uncommon among individuals who meet diagnostic criteria for a dependent personality disorder. A very different description of the same person may be provided by a relative who is angry, bitter, and resentful about the impact the patient's behavior has had on the family over the course of years.

Furthermore, some researchers have remarked that ratings of personality disorder characteristics by an observer often are correlated with characteristics of a personality disorder exhibited by that observer. Widiger et al. (1995), for instance, commented that whereas "narcissistic persons may devalue the subject, a borderline informant may idealize the subject" (p. 32). These writers remind us that not all informants are able to be objective and to provide a balanced, unbiased account of another person' strengths and weaknesses. The data any informant gives about another person should therefore be viewed as involving some mixture of objective facts, subjective interpretations of these facts, and the dynamics of the informant's relationship with that person. These factors bias what the informant knows about the person and, what he or she is willing to say about that person.

IMPLICATIONS FOR ASSESSMENT
OF PERSONALITY DISORDERS

These findings have a number of important implications for the assessment of personality disorders. Obviously, a reliable, valid diagnosis of a personality disorder is contingent on acquisition of accurate information about an individual's patterns of behavior, thought, emotions, and interpersonal relationships. The aforementioned findings suggest that we should expect to find discrepancies between information provided by an individual about him- or herself and information provided by an observer, such as a family member or close friend, as well as discrepancies among different observers.

It is reasonable to question whether one source of information (self-report vs. observer ratings) consistently provides more accurate data than other sources of information (Zimmerman, 1994). It is not clear from the literature whether to weight data provided by an individual about himself or herself when responding to an interview or to weight a self-report instrument more heavily than material provided by knowledgeable informants. One reason it may not be possible to identify which source consistently provides the most valuable information on which to rely in evaluating whether an individual meets diagnostic criteria for a personality disorder is that no accepted, recognized gold standard for diagnosing a personality disorder exists against which relevant self-report and observer ratings can be compared. For instance, given the questions that have been raised about the conceptual and psychometric foundations of the system used to identify personality disorders in the DSM-IV (Clark, Lively, & Morey, 1997), it is not clear whether self-report or observer ratings of personality disorders should be expected to predict clinician-generated diagnoses.

Although the possibility must be taken seriously that patient ratings may be more accurate than informant ratings or vice versa, one also might argue that it is essential to obtain information from multiple sources given the complexities of diagnosing personality disorders. For example, the discrepancies found among different informants in the child assessment literature discussed earlier have led some researchers to recommend that a more complete picture of an individual's problems and behavior may be obtained if it is based on information gathered from multiple sources rather than material provided by one informant.

A similar suggestion was made recently by Klein (2003), who used longitudinal data to compare depressed patients' and informants' reports of personality disorders in predicting depressive symptoms, social adjustment, and global functioning over 7½ years. Klein found that information from both patients and informants made significant, independent contributions to the prediction of depressive symptoms and global functioning at follow-up assessments. In some analyses, however, patient reports were more strongly related to outcome measures than informants' ratings, whereas in other analyses, observer ratings were stronger predictors of outcome than patients' ratings. These findings reinforce the perspective that patient self-report and informant reports make independent contributions, and that information may be lost if there is reliance on only one source of information.

Klein (2003) noted one interesting exception to this finding for patients with passive–aggressive personality disorder. Patient self-reports of passive–aggressive personality disorder features were not associated with any outcome measures, whereas informant ratings of passive–aggressive features were significantly associated with outcome. Klein speculated that, whereas passive–aggressive behaviors may be recognized by others, patients may not be aware they are expressing anger in passive–aggressive ways, or may not recognize the impact such behavior has on others.

Although Klein's (2003) study did not directly address whether individuals or observers provide more accurate information about the presence or absence of a personality disorder, it did suggest that both patients and informants can provide useful information, even when they do not agree. These findings also underscore the point discussed earlier that the accuracy of self-reported personality disorders may be limited when the criteria being assessed are not consciously recognized and acknowledged. For example, informants may provide more reliable, valid information about certain behaviors, such as a tendency to express anger in indirect, passive–aggressive ways, than individuals with passive–aggressive characteristics are able to provide about themselves.

In contrast, patients may be better sources of information about certain personality disorder criteria than informants if the criteria involve subjective, inner experiences. For instance, individuals with an avoidant personality disorder are troubled by feelings of inadequacy and fears of being shamed or ridiculed. An observer may accurately rate such an individual as avoiding contact with others, appearing uncomfortable and uneasy in social situations, or expressing him- or herself in a restrained, if not inhibited, manner. However, unless the individual confides that he or she is bothered by a sense of inadequacy and apprehensive about being humiliated, observers often have no way of knowing the person's inner experience with any certainty. Similarly, although an observer may see that a friend becomes agitated and frantic each time an end to a romantic relationship seems imminent, and may accurately recognize that the friend is upset, the observer may not understand that the distress reflects a fear of abandonment unless the friend says so. It is understandable that a person can be totally ignorant about some of the feelings, cognitions, or perceptions another person has if that person has not discussed these reactions. Thus, an individual may be a better source of information about his or her own feelings, thoughts, and expectations than others, assuming, of course, that the individual is aware of these inner experiences.

Given the aforementioned factors that limit self-report and observer ratings in clinical evaluations of personality disorders, it seems reasonable to search for a method that contributes to an assessment of personality disorders that does not share these limitations, and that has the potential to provide reliable, valid information independent of the information an individual can provide about him- or herself or that could be provided by a knowledgeable informant.

THE RORSCHACH PROVIDES A VIABLE ALTERNATIVE METHOD OF ASSESSMENT

The RIM is a measure that assesses the individual's perceptual organizational (Exner, 2003) processes and associational/projective processes (Weiner, 2003). One way to conceptualize this is to put the Rorschach into operant learning terms. The RIM provides a means by which an observer can determine how a given stimulus is associated with a given response for a specific individual. In this process, the examinee must evaluate his or her perceptual field and draw upon contents within his or her psyche to produce the response. When the stimulus field readily matches an object of common experience, a response is likely to be produced that is consensually validated in form, content, or both (card V often is described as "a bat"). But, as the stimulus becomes less and less representative of an object of common experience, the individual must draw upon greater avenues and arenas of experience to produce a response. Thus, the resulting behavior (i.e., response) becomes more the product of multifaceted experiences that are distinctively the product of the individual's learning history. For this reason, the RIM also is often considered a test of association or projection, because responses come from experience that reflects the uniqueness of the person producing the response. In other words, the verbal behavior is the product of multidetermined, idiographic mental processes.

In one sense, self-reports and interviews involve similar cognitive processes. An individual responds to a stimulus set, (e.g., a statement about his or her personality) and produces a response based upon his or her experience. Although the statements on self-report inventories may seem to be clear-cut and objective, many (Ganellen, 1996; Greene, 1991; Weiner, 2003) have observed that several items on self-report inventories can have different meanings for different individuals (e.g., "I am generous with my time" or "I often lose my temper"). In other words, even a stimulus set that is semantically perceived in commonly understood ways can be evaluated ideographically.

In contrast to self-reported information requested from an examiner, a response to a Rorschach inkblot is an observed verbal behavior recorded verbatim by an observer (i.e., examiner). The observer codes the response according to objectively defined criteria. The coding for all the responses generated by an individual are then combined to form the variables contained in the Structural Summary. The examiner is then able to interpret Rorschach data at the structural (objective and observable) level while also examining the themes, issues, and conflicts expressed by the person (projective and associational level). In this sense, the RIM provides an empirically quantifiable way to assess the distinctive perceptual, organizational, and associational processes that are not subject to the inherent limitations of self-report and informant report measures, as discussed earlier. As discussed in the following sections and throughout this book, the authors believe that the RIM provides a viable alternative for assessing personality disorders because it is not biased in the ways other assessment methods may be.

It should noted that information derived from the RIM does not link directly to each criterion required to diagnose personality disorders described in the DSM-IV. For instance, no RIM variable directly assesses the tendency to prefer solitary activities most of the time, a criterion for schizoid personality disorder. Similarly, no RIM variable directly assesses a history of self-destructive behaviors such as impulsive spending, sex, substance abuse, reckless driving, or self-mutilating behavior, which are features of borderline personality disorder. As discussed later and throughout this book, however, Rorschach variables do identify and describe many enduring patterns of maladaptive inner experience and behavior characteristic of many of the DSM-IV personality disorder diagnostic criteria. These include characteristic ways of perceiving oneself and others, the manner by which one interprets events, the capacity to manage emotional responses and affective intensity, interpersonal functioning, and impulse control.

The position taken in this chapter is that the Rorschach can make a meaningful contribution to the complex process of determining whether an individual has a personality disorder despite the fact that each DSM-IV personality disorder criterion is not directly represented on the RIM. According to the DSM-IV, an individual has a personality disorder if that individual exhibits a certain number of problems in his or her characteristic ways of thinking, feeling, behaving, and relating interpersonally that are typical of that disorder. Rorschach findings relevant to these characteristics can provide evidence indicating whether the individual does or does not manifest the difficulties outlined in the DSM-IV. Data from the Rorschach can be compared with interview, self-report, other report, and clinician–therapist interaction to facilitate the clinician's diagnosis, evaluation, and treatment of the patient/examinee (Ganellen, 1996; Meyer et al., 1998). Thus, although there may not be a direct one-to-one correspondence between DSM-IV criteria and Rorschach variables, information provided by the RIM complements the information obtained from other sources when a diagnosis of a personality disorder is being investigated, and can in some instances supply data other sources do not provide, as discussed in the sections that follow.

AS AN IMPLICIT MEASURE OF PERSONALITY, THE RORSCHACH CAN BE LINKED WITH REAL-WORLD BEHAVIORS

As discussed earlier, information provided by individuals about themselves in a self-report format, either when completing a questionnaire or when responding to a clinical interview, may be limited or inaccurate, either because the individuals are reluctant to describe themselves in unfavorable terms or because they have limited insight into their emotional world, patterns of thinking, interpersonal style, or behavior. However, the RIM has the capacity to provide knowledge about the person that may be unknown to him or her, and that he or she may not wish to acknowledge. As the Comprehensive System has evolved, data has accumulated on associations between Rorschach variables and meaningful behavioral criteria, traits, or personality characteristics, associations that in many instances are distinct from associations among self-report and behavioral criteria (Exner, 2003; Meyer & Archer, 2001; Viglione & Hilsenroth, 2001). This advantage is nested in RIM's nature as an implicit measure of personality.

McClelland, Koestner, and Weinberger (1989) initially formulated the implicit–explicit distinction in personality assessment. They stated that implicit measures are those that assess an individual's automatic, unconscious patterns of behavior, whereas explicit measures are those that assess an individual's self-attributed motives. They added that implicit measures provide a more direct measure of one's motivational and emotional experiences than do explicit measures because they are less subject to being filtered and are more a product of early "prelinguistic affective experiences." Stated differently, information derived from implicit methods of assessment provide information about patterns of thinking, reacting, and behaving that individuals may not recognize as characteristic of them. This information may be relevant in assessing features of personality disorders that may not be accessible to a patient responding to questions during an interview or completing a self-report measure. For instance, a man with symptoms of depression who seeks treatment may not describe himself as having excessive needs for affirmation, admiration, and recognition, characteristics strongly associated with an elevated number of reflection responses and possibly a narcissistic personality disorder (Exner, 2003).

McClelland et al. (1989) suggested that implicit measures are less susceptible to a self-presentation bias than explicit measures. This issue has been given detailed discussion in two recent works (Ganellen, 1996; Weiner, 2003). For the purpose of discussion here, one well-documented example of the implicit–explicit relationship will be reviewed. It is a good exemplar of how the Rorschach can provide meaningful information about real-world behavior that may not otherwise be acknowledged (i.e., that may be susceptible to self-report bias).

The Rorschach Oral Dependency Scale (ROD; Masling, Rabie, & Blondheim, 1967) is a measure that evaluates RIM content for instances of oral dependency. These instances of oral dependency fall into 16 categories including food and drinks, food objects, food providers, passive food receivers, or themes of passivity and helplessness. One point is assigned for each response that has content falling into one of these categories. The ROD score is computed by dividing this score by the total number of responses provided by the examinee. In summarizing the results from several years' of studies, Bornstein (1996) concluded that the ROD is a valid, implicit measure of interpersonal dependency.

In contrast, the Interpersonal Dependency Inventory (IDI; Hirschfeld, Klerman, Gough et al., 1977) is a 48-item Likert measure that assesses self-reported (i.e., explicit) levels of interpersonal dependency. Three subscales can be computed on the IDI: Emotional Reliance on Others, Lack of Social Self-Confidence, and Assertion of Autonomy. Bornstein (1994) reviewed several years of studies on the IDI and concluded that it is a reliable and valid measure of interpersonal dependency. Furthermore, Bornstein (2002) reviewed studies on the relation between the ROD and the IDI. He concluded that these two measures are modestly correlated (mean $r = .29$), and that each measure is associated with different aspects of interpersonal dependency (consistent with the explicit and implicit distinction). Some examples of these distinctions follow.

Bornstein (1998) evaluated the implicit–explicit distinction in the assessment of interpersonal dependency in undergraduate students. Using the ROD and IDI, he first identified four groups of individuals: those with high dependency (HD; high scores on both the IDI and ROD), those with unacknowledged dependency (UD; high score on the ROD and low score on the IDI), those with dependent self-presentation (DSP; high score on the IDI and low score on the ROD), and those with low dependency (LD; low scores on both the IDI and ROD). After classifying individuals into one of four categories, Bornstein (1998) assigned individuals to one of two experimental groups. The individuals in one group were told that they were going to engage in a study of problem solving, whereas the other group was told that they were in a study of dependency and help seeking. Thus, a four (group) by two (instructions) between-subjects design was used. Bornstein predicted that dependency classification status would interact with instructions to produce differential help-seeking behaviors, which were defined as the number of times a participant asked for help or guidance in the experimental task (which consisted of solving anagrams).

Consistent with these predictions, Bornstein (1998) found that study instructions did interact with dependency group status. Specifically, the UD group engaged in help seeking at rates similar to those for the HD group when they believed they were involved in a problem-solving task. Yet, the UD group did not engage in low rates of help-seeking behavior when they believed they were in a study of dependency. In fact, their rate of help seeking did not significantly differ from that for the LD group. In contrast, the DSP group engaged in moderate amounts of help seeking when they believed they were involved in a problem-solving task. However, when told they were in a study of dependency, the DSP group engaged in help-seeking behavior at a rate similar to that for the HD group. Thus, as predicted, individuals who consciously described themselves as having high or low dependency acted differently when they were led to believe that their level of interpersonal dependency was being assessed.

In another set of studies, Bornstein, Bowers, and Bonner (1996) induced a positive, negative, or neutral mood in participants with the Velten (1968) and Baker and Gutterfreund (1993) mood induction procedures. They hypothesized that implicit levels of dependency should increase when a negative mood was induced, whereas self-reported dependency should remain relatively unchanged. These hypotheses were based on past findings demonstrating that depressed mood increases individuals' dependent feelings (Hirschfeld, Klerman, Andreason, Clayton, & Keller, 1986; Zuroff & Mongrain, 1987). In both studies, ROD scores significantly increased when induced with a negative mood, whereas ROD scores remained the same for positive and neutral mood induction. In contrast, IDI scores remained relatively unchanged for both males and females. Bornstein et al. (1996) concluded that implicit levels of dependency may be manipulated. In other words, there are elements of dependency capable of modification that are not subject to conscious control.

Bornstein, Rossner, Hill, and Stepanian (1994) evaluated the impact of test instructions on levels of self-reported and implicit measures of dependency in three studies. In short, the findings for all three studies showed that when either positive or negative information about dependency was provided before measures of dependency were administered, explicit (IDI), but not implicit (ROD), scores were affected. As predicted, when dependency was presented as a positive characteristic, IDI ratings of dependency increased. In contrast, when dependency was presented as a negative characteristic, IDI ratings of dependency decreased. Bornstein et al. (1994) concluded that implicit measures of dependency are not affected by self-monitoring of reported dependency, whereas self-reported dependency scores are. Thus, when the evidence about the implicit–explicit assessment of interpersonal dependency with the Rorschach is reviewed, it appears that the ROD offers a clear advantage in assessment, as compared with self-report measures. Whereas self-report measures of dependency can be skewed deliberately by self-presentational pressures, implicit measures of dependency, such as the ROD, are less susceptible to impression management strategies. This suggests that more reliable, accurate information may be obtained when the personality characteristic of dependency is assessed with an implicit measure in a clinical situation wherein individuals are reluctant to report honestly their need to rely on others and their desire to obtain reassurance and support.

Although the aforementioned findings are focused on measurement of dependency with the ROD, they also illustrate some of the reasons why implicit measures of personality characteristics, including the RIM, can provide information relevant to the evaluation of personality disorders that may not be obtained by other assessment approaches. As discussed earlier, some individuals may be reluctant to acknowledge information about themselves that could be considered negative, unflattering, or unfavorable, or they simply may not be aware of certain aspects of their behavior, interpersonal style, or emotional reactions. Whereas self-awareness and self-presentational concerns could bias responses on self-report inventories, this is less likely to be a concern when implicit measures of personality functioning are used. For example, some individuals may not describe themselves as having a tendency to react to situations with considerable emotional intensity, a characteristic associated with a histrionic personality style. This aspect of psychological functioning is reflected on the RIM by the FC:CF+C ratio. Skewed scores on this ratio are associated with ratings of histrionic personality features (Blais, Hilsenroth, Castlebury, Fowler, & Baity, 2001). A clinician might be alerted to an individual's tendency to have very strong, unrestrained emotional reactions if he or she has a skewed score on the FC:CF+C ratio, even if that individual is reluctant to describe him- or herself as having this characteristic. As discussed in more detail throughout this book, many RIM variables are considered implicit measures of psychological functioning that provide clinically relevant information that may agree with or augment data obtained using explicit measures provided by an individual about him- or herself as well as information provided by informants.

THE RORSCHACH PROVIDES A WEALTH OF INFORMATION THAT MAY BE USED IN TREATMENT PLANNING

Unlike many self-report inventories and semistructured interviews developed specifically to determine whether an individual meets diagnostic criteria for a personality disorder (e.g., structured clinical interview for DSM-IV Axis II disorder or the Personality Disorder Examination), the RIM assesses multiple aspects of personality including affective regulation, self-perception, and interpersonal relationships. Such aspects are characteristic of personality disorders and other arenas of psychological functioning. Although personality disorders and other aspects of psychological functioning can be evaluated using other assessment methods (e.g., MMPI-2, Personality Assessment Inventory, NEO Personality Inventory–Revised), the RIM is not limited in the ways that self-report measures are (discussed earlier). As such, the RIM may provide valuable information about a person's personality, overall level of functioning, and psychological strengths and liabilities that can help clinicians anticipate their patients' immediate therapeutic needs and select among various treatment approaches.

For instance, recent approaches to the treatment of patients with borderline personality disorder suggest that whereas psychotherapy usually is the primary method for treatment, a combination of psychotherapy and medication may be most effective for certain patients (Oldham et al., 2002). More specifically, these writers have recommended that treatment interventions for patients with a borderline personality disorder (BPD), including the selection of specific medications and goals for psychotherapy, be based on a patient's clinical presentation and the specific problems he or she exhibits.

To elaborate this point, research has found a high rate of comorbid mood and anxiety disorders among patients with BPD. Some estimates suggest that as many as 90% of patients with BPD will meet diagnostic criteria for an episode of depression at some point during their life, whereas up to 70% will meet diagnostic criteria for an Axis I anxiety disorder throughout their lifetime. Thus, Oldham et al. (2002) recommended that a patient with BPD whose clinical presentation involves affective dysregulation, manifested by significant symptoms of depression, anxiety, irritability, or rejection sensitivity, should be treated with an antidepressant, anxiolytic, or mood stabilizing medication in addition to psychotherapy.

Furthermore, different treatment interventions may be required for BPD patients whose clinical picture involves primary difficulties other than affective dysregulation. Soloff (1998, 2000) suggested that borderline patients who exhibit impulsive, aggressive, or self-destructive behavior may respond best to certain medications. He considered that severe behavioral impulsivity, mood lability, or extreme anger is most effectively controlled by a mood stabilizing agent or a selective serotonin reuptake inhibitor. In contrast, he suggested that patients with significant cognitive–perceptual distortions, such as paranoia or ideas of reference, be treated with a neuroleptic medication, such as Risperdal or Seroquel. Not only can medication decrease impulsivity or cognitive–perceptual distortions, but these interventions also can facilitate progress in psychotherapy. For instance, appropriate pharmacotherapy of a patient with BPD can decrease impulsive acting out or reduce misperceptions of what occurs between therapist and patient, which otherwise may lead to negative, hostile transference–countertransference dynamics or damage a fragile sense of collaboration and trust in the therapeutic alliance. Thus, these authors suggested that treatment is most effective if decisions about the goals of treatment and selection of medications target specific problem areas.

Whereas the preceding examples draw from recent literature providing guidelines for the treatment of patients with BPD, similar recommendations are likely applicable to treatment decisions concerning other personality disorders (Gabbard, 2000). For instance, one review of the literature found prevalence rates of depression ranging between 30% and 70% in Axis II populations (Farmer & Nelson-Gray, 1990). Although difficulties in the specific aforementioned symptom domains may be reported or exhibited by some patients with a personality disorder during a clinical interview, such problems are not always obvious or acknowledged. Rorschach data, on the other hand, can assist clinicians in setting priorities for treatment by providing objective information to help them identify which specific issues and problems exist, which require immediate attention, and which intervention approaches are the most appropriate. For instance, Rorschach variables relevant to identifying a potential for impulsive behavior (e.g., D Score, pure C), affective dysregulation (e.g., FC:CF+C ratio), and cognitive distortions (Wsum6, XA%, WDA% and X–%) all may provide meaningful information for treatment planning with both psychotherapy and pharmacotherapy.

Specific examples of how the Rorschach may be useful in treatment planning are found in the empirical literature. Gacono and Meloy (1994) observed that although the DSM may provide behavioral criteria for detecting antisocial behavior, "this model has failed to satisfy ... [the] clinical understanding of the disorder." They note that, "a search for clinical knowledge leads to questions of motivation and meaning, prompting further inquiry into the thought organization, affective life, defensive operations, impulses, and object relations of psychopaths and other aggressive individuals" (pp. 2–3). Thus, they suggested that the DSM's description of antisocial personality disorder fails to capture many aspects of the persona related to assessment treatment of psychopathic individuals. For example, although antisocial personalities often are considered to be free of psychic turmoil, Gacono and Meloy (1994) noted that

45% of both male and female patients with a diagnosis of antisocial personality disorder experienced some level of stress at the time the Rorschach was administered (D ≤ −1), and 20% manifested signs of chronic distress (adjusted D ≤ −1). These findings suggest that an evaluation of Rorschach findings could identify those individuals with antisocial personality disorder who are experiencing more psychological distress than is stereotypically judged to be possible and could benefit from psychological treatment that helps them better manage the stressors in their lives. Likewise, additional scrutiny of the individual's protocol may yield information about current affective distress (sum shading), poor self-image (MOR), and other problematic areas that could be the focus of treatment.

One domain of critical importance in treatment planning in general is the assessment of suicidality. Whereas it generally is recognized that in comparison with the general population, BPD patients have a relatively high rate of suicide (Overholser, Stockmeir, Dilley, & Freiheit, 2002; Soloff, Lynch, Kelly, Malone, & Mann, 2000), recent research has shown that suicide attempts occur more frequently in all three clusters of personality disorders than in the general population (Heikkinen et al., 1997; Isometsa et al., 1996; Overholser et al., 2002; Yen et al., 2003). Thus, clinicians should be prepared to identify and manage suicidal risk when they work with an Axis II population.

In a review of measures used to assess suicide potential, Shaffer (1996) noted that no self-report scale currently exists that imminently predicts suicide with useful accuracy. One of the most widely used self-report measures, the Beck Hopelessness Scale (Beck, Brown, & Steer, 1989), has been found to predict future suicide within a 10-year period with 90% accuracy, and the Linehan Reasons for Living Inventory (LRLF; Linehan, Goodstein, Nielsen, & Chiles, 1983) has discriminated patients who made a previous suicide attempt from a matched clinical sample (Osman et al., 1999). Thus, some self-report measures may be useful in identifying an increased risk of suicide. However, the Rorschach Suicide Constellation (S-CON) appears to assess accurately the likelihood of a completed suicide within a 60-day period (Exner, 1993), possibly making it a more preferred measure to use when the likelihood of suicide within a 2-month period is needed.

Results of a recent study by Fowler, Piers, Hilsenroth, Holdwick, and Padawer (2001) suggest that the Rorschach S-CON may provide a useful alternative to self-report measures of suicidality for those working with Axis II patients. As noted earlier, the S-CON successfully identified 80% of the patients who completed suicide within 60 days after administration of the Rorschach, using a criterion cutoff score of 8. In a recent study with Axis II patients, Fowler et al. (2001) found that the S-CON also did a good job of accurately discriminating near-lethal, parasuicidal, and nonsuicidal individuals from each other. More specifically, scores of 7 on the S-CON produced the following diagnostic efficiency statistics in a comparison of patients who had engaged in near-lethal and parasuicidal behavior: sensitivity (.70), specificity (.87), positive predictive power (.81), negative predictive power (.78), and overall correct classification rate (.79). These data were even stronger when near-lethal and nonsuicidal college students were compared: sensitivity (.70), specificity and positive predictive power (1.0), negative predictive power (.85), and overall correct classification rate (.89). These authors also reported that S-CON was positively correlated with the incidence of overdose ($r = .32; p < .001$) and emergency medical transfers because of instrumental suicidal behaviors ($r = .28; p < .004$), but not self-inflicted superficial lacerations ($r = .08$, not significant). These findings provide support for the convergent and discriminant validity of the S-CON because it is significantly associated with real-world suicidal behaviors, but not less serious forms of self-injury.

To evaluate further the relationship of the S-CON with self-report measures of suicide, Fowler et al. (2001) compared the LRLF and Beck Hopelessness Scale (BHS) with the S-CON. They found that, although the LRLF was able to discriminate individuals who had made a suicide attempt from matched nonclinical controls, it did not predict future suicide attempts. Thus, there was no evidence for the predictive validity of the LRLF. For the BHS, Fowler et al. (2001) computed diagnostic efficiency statistics based upon information reported by the test authors and compared it with their findings. Although the BHS had better sensitivity (.91) and negative predictive power (.99) than the S-CON, it did not demonstrate good positive predictive power (.12) or an overall correct classification rate (.51). Furthermore, when their base rates were adjusted to match Beck's base rates, the S-CON's positive predictive power was more than double that of the BHS, and the overall correct classification rate was substantially higher (.86).

Thus, as an implicit measure of suicidality, the S-CON offers advantages for assessment not found in many self-reports. Given that a diagnosis of a personality disorder carries an increased risk of suicide (as discussed earlier) and considering that self-reports of personality disordered individuals are not always reliable, the S-CON may, in fact, be a valuable assessment tool for some individuals who have a personality disorder.

THE RORSCHACH ASSESSES BOTH STATES AND TRAITS

Hirschfeld et al. (1983) found that among depressed individuals, depressed mood state tended to produce exaggerated elevations in personality traits that were not reported when the same individuals were not depressed. Such an issue is problematic because many individuals who have a personality disorder also have a mood disorder (Farmer & Nelson-Gray, 1990). Likewise, as noted earlier, personality disordered patients may lack insight when reporting their personality characteristics. Therefore, not only are patients' self-reports likely to be skewed as a result of their personality disorders, they also are likely to be influenced by their mood state. On the RIM, D and Adjusted D allow one to determine the current and chronic levels of distress an individual experiences. Such information can be clinically useful for reconciling an individual's self-report with his or her present distress. Furthermore, research on the RIM also has indicated that at least 30 variables have strong 3-year stability (Exner, 2003), ranging in value between .72 and .90. These results suggest that current mood state may not have a substantial impact on the observed scores for many RIM variables. This being the case, the RIM offers the advantage of assessing current levels of distress while also measuring personality traits not likely to be affected by psychological state and subsequently varying over time.

LIMITATIONS TO RORSCHACH ASSESSMENT

Although many advantages have been offered about the RIM assessment of personality disorders, there clearly are limitations and drawbacks to its use. Some of these are discussed.

First, the RIM is difficult to learn. Huprich (2002) identified at least five difficulties in teaching the Rorschach: (a) students often enter their RIM training with some degree of skepticism; (b) learning the RIM is costly in terms of time, mental resources, and money; (c) faculty members and supervisors tend to give mixed messages about the utility and validity of the RIM; (d) providing adequate supervision for trainees is very time expensive; and (e) with all the rhetoric about the RIM, students may come to premature conclusions about the utility of the measure.

Second, administration and scoring errors can have big implications for the interpretive process. For instance, one Texture response is expected and desired from examinees as a measure of healthy dependency in relationships (Exner, 2003; Weiner, 2003), yet 0 or 2+ responses are potentially problematic, indicating a lack of interest or ability in expressing dependency or an excessive degree of dependency seeking, respectively. An examiner who fails to score or inquire properly may inadvertently omit or prompt a Texture response. Similarly, poor administration may prompt certain responses (e.g., "What does this remind you of?" vs. "What might this be?") or fail to obtain a sufficient number of responses (thereby affecting many of the obtained scores and ratios in the Structural Summary).

Third, contrary to the belief that personality tests can provide a diagnosis, the RIM is not meant to be a diagnostic instrument in and of itself. This also is true of other widely used self-report personality measures not designed for diagnostic use (e.g., MMPI-2, MCMI-III, PAI, 16PF). Personality assessment is a process that integrates "the results of several carefully selected tests with relevant history, information, and observation [and] enables the sophisticated clinician to form an accurate, in-depth understanding of the patient; formulate the most appropriate and cost-effective treatment plan, and later, monitor the course of intervention" (p. 3; Meyer et al., 1998). In other words, diagnosis is an activity performed by the assessor after all relevant available data have been considered, including test results. Weiner (2003) expanded on this point. He noted that the RIM is not a test per se, but rather a multifaceted method for obtaining structural, thematic, and behavioral data that can be applied in both quantitative and qualitative terms. Weiner recommended that the RIM be used as one tool in the process of deriving a diagnosis. Thus, to assume that RIM results can provide a diagnosis is misleading and inaccurate. For these same reasons, a book about using the RIM to assess personality disorders can be written without assuming that there is a standard pattern of results that necessitates a diagnosis of a personality disorder.

To highlight this point further, it should be noted that past efforts to use RIM variables to identify individuals who have a given disorder have yielded mixed empirical results. This is evident when the histories of the Depression Index (DEPI) and the Schizophrenia Index (SCZI) are examined. Most recently, Exner (2003) concluded that, "positive DEPI values probably are best interpreted as representing an affective problem rather than specifically equating positive values with diagnostic categories" (p. 312). As for SCZI, Exner (2003) modified the Comprehensive System so that SCZI is no longer computed, and replaced it with the Perceptual Thinking Index (PTI). This change occurred, in part, because of the substantial false positive rate found in clinical samples. Exner (2003) stated that the, "main purpose [of the PTI] is to alert interpreters about the likelihood of mediational and ideational difficulties" (p. 393). Thus, the primary aim of the PTI is not diagnostic.

This chapter identifies several problems inherent in the use of self-report, informant report, and interviews in assessment for a personality disorder. It has been suggested that the RIM provides some solutions to these problems, thus offering some advantages over these measures. Although the RIM is not without its limitations, it is the authors' premise that the RIM has utility for the assessment of personality disorders. With these issues in mind, attention can now be drawn to assessing individual personality disorders with the RIM.

REFERENCES

Achenbach, T. M. (1991). *Manual for the Child Behavior Checklist and 1991 Child Behav-ior Profile*. Burlington: University of Vermont, Department of Psychiatry.
Achenbach, T. M., McConaughy, S. H., & Howell, C. T. (1987). Child/adolescent be-havioral and emotional problems: Implications of cross-informant correlation for situational specificity. *Psychological Bulletin, 101,* 213–232.
American Psychiatric Association. (2000). *Diagnostic and statistical manual of mental disorders* (4th ed., text revision), Washington, DC: Author.
American Psychiatric Association. (1994). *Diagnostic and statistical manual of mental disorders* (4th ed.), Washington, DC: Author.
Baker, R. C., & Gutterfreund, D. G. (1993). The effects of written autobiographical recollection induction procedures on mood. *Journal of Clinical Psychology, 49,* 563–568.
Beck, A. T., Brown, G., & Steer, R. A. (1989). Prediction of eventual suicide in psychi-atric inpatients by clinical ratings of hopelessness. *Journal of Consulting and Clini-cal Psychology, 57,* 309–310.
Bernstein, D. P., Kasapis, Ch., Bergman, A., Weld, E., Mitropoulou, V., Horvath, T., et al. 1997). Assessing Axis II disorders by informant interview. *Journal of Personal-ity Disorders, 11,* 158–167.
Blais, M., Hilsenroth, M., Castlebury, F., Fowler, J., & Baity, M. (2001). Predicting DSM-IV Cluster B personality disorder criteria from MMPI-2 and Rorschach data: A test of incremental validity. *Journal of Personality Assessment, 76,* 150–168.
Bornstein, R. F. (1994). Construct validity of the interpersonal dependency inven-tory: 1977–1992. *Journal of Personality Disorders, 8,* 64–76.
Bornstein, R. F. (1996). Construct validity of the Rorschach Oral Dependency Scale: 1967–1995. *Psychological Assessment, 8,* 200–205.
Bornstein, R. F. (1998). Implicit and self-attributed dependency strivings: Differen-tial relationships to laboratory and field measures of help-seeking. *Journal of Per-sonality and Social Psychology, 75,* 779–787.
Bornstein, R. F. (2002). A process dissociation approach to objective-projective test score interrelationships. *Journal of Personality Assessment, 78,* 47–68.
Bornstein, R. F., Bowers, K. S., & Bonner, S. (1996). Relationships of objective and projective dependency scores to sex role orientation in college student partici-pants. *Journal of Personality Assessment, 66,* 555–568.
Bornstein, R. F., Rossner, S. C., Hill, E. L., & Stepanian, M. L. (1994). Face validity and fakability of objective and projective measures of dependency. *Journal of Person-ality Assessment, 63,* 363–386.
Clark, L. A., Livesley, W. J., & Morey, L. (1997). Personality disorder assessment: The challenge of construct validity. *Journal of Personality Disorders, 11,* 205–231.
Costa, P. T., Jr., & Widiger, T. A. (2002). *Personality disorders and the five-factor model of personality* (2nd ed.). Washington, DC: American Psychological Association.
Dreesen, L., Hildebrand, M., & Arntz, A. (1998). Patient–informant concordance on the Structured Clinical Interview for DSM-III-R personality disorders (SCID-II). *Journal of Personality Disorders, 12,* 149–161.
Exner, J. E. (1993). *The Rorschach: A comprehensive system* (Vol. 1). *Basic foundations* (3rd ed.). New York: John Wiley.
Exner, J. E. (2003). *The Rorschach: A comprehensive system* (Vol. 1). *Basic foundations* (4th ed.). New York: John Wiley.

Farmer R. A., & Nelson-Gray, R. O. (1990). Personality disorders and depression: Hypothetical relations, empirical findings, and methodological considerations. *Clinical Psychology Review, 10*, 453–476.

Ferro, T., & Klein, D. N. (1997). Family history assessment of personality disorders: I. Concordance with direct interview and between pairs of informants. *Journal of Personality Disorders, 11*, 123–136.

First, M. B., Spitzer, R. L., Gibbon, M., & Williams, J. B. W. (1995). The Structured Clinical Interview for DSM-III-R Personality Disorders (SCID-II). *Journal of Personality Disorders, 9*, 83–91.

First, M. B., Spitzer, R. L., Gibbon, M., Williams, J. B. W., Davies, M., Borus, J., et al. (1995). The Structured Clinical Interview for DSM-III-R Personality Disorders (SCID-II): Part II. Multisite test–retest reliability study. *Journal of Personality Disorders, 9*, 92–104.

Fitzgerald, H. E., Zucker, R. A., Maguin, E. T., & Reider, E. E. (1994). Time spent with child and parental agreement about preschool children's behavior. *Perceptual and Motor Skills, 79*, 336–338.

Fowler, J. C., Piers, C., Hilsenroth, M. J., Holdwick, D. J., & Padawer, J. R. (2001). The Rorschach Suicide Constellation: Assessing various degrees of lethality. *Journal of Personality Assessment, 76*, 333–351.

Gabhard, G. O. (2000). *Psychodynamic psychiatry in clinical practice* (3rd ed.). Washington, DC: American Psychiatric Press.

Gacono, C. B., & Meloy, J. R. (1994). *Rorschach assessment of aggressive and psychopathic personalities*. Mahwah, NJ: Lawrence Erlbaum Associates.

Ganellen, R. J. (1996). *Integrating the Rorschach and the MMPI-2 in personality assessment*. Mahwah, NJ: Lawrence Erlbaum Associates.

Greene, R. (1991). *The MMPI/MMPI-2: An interpretive manual*. Boston, MA: Allyn & Bacon.

Heikkinen, M. E., Isometsae, E. T., Henriksson, M. M., & Marttunen, M. J. (1997). Psychosocial factors and completed suicide in personality disorders. *Acta Psychiatrica Scandinavia, 95*, 49–57.

Hilsenroth, M. J., Fowler, J. C., & Padawer, J. R. (1998). The Rorschach Schizophrenia Index (SCZI): An examination of reliability, validity, and diagnostic efficiency. *Journal of Personality Assessment, 70*, 514–534.

Hilsenroth, M. J., Fowler, J. C., Padawar, J. R., & Handler, L. (1997). Narcissism in the Rorschach revisited: Some reflections on empirical data. *Psychological Assessment, 9*, 113–121.

Hilsenroth, M, J., Handler, L., & Blais, M. A. (1996). Assessment of narcissistic personality disorder: A multimethod review. *Clinical Psychology Review, 16*, 655–683.

Hirschfeld, R. M. A., Klerman, G. L., Andreason, N. C., Clayton, P. J., & Keller, M. B. (1986). Psychosocial predictors of chronicity in depressed patients. *British Journal of Psychiatry, 148*, 648–654.

Hirschfeld, R. M. A., Klerman, G. L., Clayton, P. J., Keller, M. B., MacDonald-Scott, P., & Larkin, B. (1983). Assessing personality effects of the depressive state on trait measurement. *American Journal of Psychiatry, 140*, 695–699.

Horowitz, M. J. (1988). *Introduction to psychodynamics: A new synthesis*. New York: Basic Books.

Hunsley, J., & Bailey, J. M. (1999). The clinical utility of the Rorschach: unfulfilled promises and an uncertain future. *Psychological Assessment, 11*, 266–277.

Huprich, S. K. (2002). Why instructors and supervisors must advocate for the Ror-
    schach. *SPA Exchange, 14*(1), 4–6.
Isometsa, E. T., Henriksson, M. H., Heikkinen, M. E., Aro, H. M., Marttuen, M. J.
    Kauppasalami, K. I., et al. (1996). Suicide among subjects with personality disor-
    ders. *American Journal of Psychiatry, 153,* 667–673.
Klein, D. N. (2003). Patients' versus informants' reports of personality disorders in
    predicting 7½-year outcome in outpatients with depressive disorder. *Psychologi-
    cal Assessment, 15,* 216–222.
Linehan, M. M., Goodstein, J. L., Nielsen, S. L., & Chiles, J. K. (1983). Reasons for
    staying alive when you are thinking of killing yourself: The Reasons for Living
    Inventory. *Journal of Consulting and Clinical Psychology, 51,* 276–286.
Lorganer, A. (1988). *Personality disorder examination.*
Maffei, C., Fossati, A., Agostoni, H., Barraco, A., Bagnato, M., Deobrah, D., et al.
    (1997). Interrater reliability and internal consistency of the Structured Clinical
    Interview for DSM-IV Axis II Personality Disorders (SCID-II), Version 2.0. *Jour-
    nal of Personality Disorders, 11,* 279–284.
McClelland, D. C., Koestner, R., & Weinberger, J. (1989). How do self-attributed and
    implicit motives differ? *Psychological Review, 96,* 690–702.
Meyer, G. J., Finn, S. E., Eyde, L. D., Kay, G. G., Kubiszyn, T. W., Moreland, K. L., et al.
    (1998). *Benefits and costs of psychological assessment in healthcare delivery: Report of
    the Board of Professional Affairs Work Group, Part I.* Washington, DC: American
    Psychological Association.
Oldham, J. M., Gabbard, G. O., Goin, M. K., Gunderson, J., Soloff, P., Spiegel, D.,
    Stone, M., & Phillips, K. A. (2002). Practice guideline for the treatment of patients
    with borderline personality disorder. *American Psychiatric Association practice
    guidelines for the treatment of psychiatric disorders: Compendium 2002* (pp. 767–855).
    Washington, DC: American Psychiatric Association.
Osman, A., Kopper, B. A., Linehan, M. M., Barrios, F. X., Guiterrez, P. M., & Bagge, C.
    L. (1999). Validation of the Adult Suicidal Ideation Questionnaire and the Rea-
    sons for Living Inventory in an adult psychiatric inpatient sample. *Psychological
    Assessment, 11,* 115–123.
Overholser, J. C., Stockmeier, C., Dilley, G., Freiheit, S. (2002). Personality disorders
    in suicide attempters and completers: Preliminary findings. *Archives of Suicide
    Research, 6,* 123–133.
Reich, J. H. (1988). A family history method for DSM-III anxiety and personality dis-
    orders. *Psychiatry Research, 26,* 131–139.
Riso, L. P., Klein, D. N., Anderson, R. L., Ouimette, P. C., & Lizardi, H. (1994). Con-
    cordance between patients and informants on the personality disorder examina-
    tion. *American Journal of Psychiatry, 151,* 568–573.
Shaffer, D. (1996). Predictive validity of the Suicide Probability Scale among adoles-
    cents in group home treatment: Discussion. *Journal of the American Academy of
    Child and Adolescent Psychiatry, 35,* 172–174.
Soloff, P. H. (1998). Symptom-oriented psychopharmacology for personality disor-
    ders. *Journal of Practical Psychiatry and Behavioral Health, 4,* 3–11.
Soloff, P. H. (2000). Psychopharmacology of borderline personality disorder. *Psychi-
    atric Clinics of North America, 23,* 169–192.

Soloff, P. H., Lynch, K. G., Kelly, T. M., Malone, K. M., Mann, J. J. (2000). Characteristics of suicide attempts of patients with major depressive episode and borderline personality disorder: A comparative study. *American Journal of Psychiatry, 157,* 601–608.

Spitzer, R. L. (1983). Psychiatric diagnosis: Are clinicians still necessary? *Comprehensive Psychiatry, 24,* 399–411.

Sullivan, H. S. (1953). *The interpersonal theory of psychiatry.* New York: Norton.

Velten, E. (1968). A laboratory task for induction of mood states. *Behavior Research and Therapy, 6,* 473–482.

Viglione, D. J., & Hilsenroth, M. J. (2001). The Rorschach: Facts, fictions, and future. *Psychological Assessment, 13,* 452–471.

Weiner, I. B. (1994). The Rorschach Inkblot Method (RIM) is not a test: Implications for theory and practice. *Journal of Personality Assessment, 62,* 498–504.

Weiner, I. B. (2003*). Principles of Rorschach interpretation* (2nd ed.). Mahwah, NJ: Lawrence Erlbaum Associates.

Widiger, A. T., Mangine, S., Corbitt, E. M., Ellis, C. G., & Thomas, G. V. (1995). *Personality Disorder Interview-IV: A semistructured interview for the assessment of personality disorders.* Odessa, FL: Psychological Assessment Resources.

Wood, J. M., Nezworski, M. T., Garb, H. N., & Lilienfeld, S. (2001). The misperception of psychopathology: Problems with the norms of the Comprehensive System for the Rorschach. *Clinical Psychology: Science and Practice, 8,* 350–373.

Yen, S., Shea, T., Pagano, M., Sanislow, C. A., Grilo, C. M., McGlashan, T. H., et al. (2003). Axis I and Axis II disorders as predictors of prospective suicide attempts: Findings from the Collaborative Longitudinal Personality Disorders Study. *Journal of Abnormal Psychology, 112,* 375–381.

Zimmerman, M. (1994). Diagnosing personality disorders: A review of issues and research methods. *Archives of General Psychiatry, 51,* 225–245.

Zimmerman, M., & Coryell, W. (1990). Diagnosing personality disorders in the community: A comparison of self-report and interview measures. *Archives of General Psychiatry, 47,* 733–737.

Zimmerman, M., Pfohl, B., Coryell, W., Stangl, D., & Corenthal, C. (1988). Diagnosing personality disorder in depressed patients: A comparison of patient and informant interviews. *Archives of General Psychiatry, 45,* 733–737.

Zimmerman, M., Pfohl, B., Stangl, D., & Corenthal, C. (1986). Assessment of DSM-III personality disorders: The importance of interviewing an informant. *Journal of Clinical Psychiatry, 47,* 261–263.

Zucker, M., Morris, M. K., Ingram, S. M., Morris, R. D., & Bakeman R. (2002). Concordance of self- and informant ratings of adults' current and childhood attention-deficit/hyperactivity disorder symptoms. *Psychological Assessment, 14,* 379–389.

Zuroff, D. C., & Mongrain, M. (1987). Dependency and self-criticism: Vulnerability factors for depressive affective states. *Journal of Abnormal Psychology, 96,* 14–22.

II

CLUSTER A
PERSONALITY DISORDERS

Rorschach Assessment
of Paranoid Personality Disorder

Nancy Kaser-Boyd
UCLA School of Medicine

Paranoid personality disorder (PPD) is one of the most difficult disorders to detect and treat. In part, this comes from the paranoid person's infrequent use of clinical services, as well as his or her inherent suspicion of the assessment and treatment process. Nevertheless, the assessment of individuals with PPD has yielded important information about this inner world, which allows clinicians to understand and interact better with such individuals. This chapter discusses what information the Rorschach can provide assessors about individuals with PPD and presents a real case of an individual with a diagnosis of PPD. This exemplar demonstrates how the Rorschach can elucidate the cognitive processing style of the person with PPD and provide meaningful information about the individual's interpersonal relatedness and other personality features.

A chapter on paranoid personality disorder should begin with a statement of the limitations inherent in studying paranoid personality. Not only is this personality disorder perhaps the least likely to be seen frequently in clinical settings, but it also is more likely to be analyzed postmortem (e.g., Siegel's [1994] analysis of Adolph Hitler), or after a crime related to paranoid ideation. In contrast, however, paranoid individuals may be in touch with legal professionals. For example, litigious individuals haunt lawyers' offices; grandiose patients join or form cults; and individuals with paranoid jealousy may run afoul of the law (Munro, 1992). In fact, a number of domestic murders and other crimes such as stalking are carried out by individuals with paranoid personality features.

There also have been many famous cases of PPD, often in the realm of politics and international affairs. Political terrorists such as Osama Bin Laden and Saddam Hussain illustrate the early origins of paranoia, with early wounds (Coughlin, 2002) and layers of psychological defense that include the projection of evil onto an external enemy (Kaser-Boyd, 2002).

When seen for evaluation, the paranoid person is more likely than many personality disordered clients to be court referred. On the Mental Status Examination, the paranoid individual typically is intact in the domains of thinking, orientation, attention, memory, and perception (Manschreck, 1992). In fact, individuals with PPD often are intelligent and very alert. In the evaluation itself, they may be minimally cooperative, suspicious, guarded and defensive, and working hard to guard their privacy and safety. It also is possible that they will be referred at a time when they have come "unwrapped" (when their rigid defense structure has been weakened) so that their interview behavior and test protocols may look more disorganized or frankly "paranoid."

Because the individual with PPD is likely to be guarded and suspicious in the clinical evaluation, self-report measures often yield inconclusive findings. For example, scales L and K of the Minnesota Multiphasic Personality Inventory (MMPI-2) are often elevated, and clinical scales fall with normal limits, and though scale 6 of the MMPI-2 has many obvious items, a truly paranoid personality may deny most of them. On the Millon Clinical Multiaxial Inventory (MCMI-III; Millon, 1994) the Social Desirability and Compulsive scales often are elevated, or the Disclosure scale may be very low. The Paranoid scale of the MCMI-III has a low sensitivity rate (27.7% for a base rate of 75 or higher), although specificity rates are better (90.4%), making it possible to rule out paranoid personality traits with this measure (Retzlaff, 1996). The MCMI-II Paranoid scale is believed to have better construct validity, allowing clinicians to offer more trustworthy hypotheses about the individual being assessed (Rogers, Salekin, & Sewell, 1999).

The Rorschach, with its often-discussed ability to elicit features of personality functioning of which the patient is less consciously aware (Exner, 2003; Lerner, 1991; Weiner, 2003), assesses patient defensiveness in a different way (discussed later). This does not mean that the individual with PPD will be unable to sabotage efforts for more complete evaluation. However, the Rorschach is the instrument most likely to capture the dynamics of PPD in the context of the subject's normal defensiveness.

DIAGNOSTIC ISSUES

DSM-IV Criteria

In descriptive terms, the paranoid individual is observed to be hypersensitive, fearful, angry, defensive, resentful, suspicious, irritable, critical and accusatory, preoccupied with details, humorlessness, litigious, secretive, obstinant, seclusive, self-righteous, and jealous (Manschreck, 1992). *The Diagnostic and Statistical Manual of Mental Disorders*, 4th Edition (DSM-IV; American Psychiatric Association, 1994) states, "The essential feature of Paranoid Personality Disorder is a pattern of pervasive distrust and suspiciousness of others such that their motives are interpreted as malevolent. This pattern begins by early adulthood and is present in a variety of contexts" (p. 634).

For a diagnosis of PPD, the individual must be characterized by at least four of the following:

1. Suspects, without sufficient basis, that others are exploiting, harming, or deceiving him or her
2. Is preoccupied with unjustified doubts about the loyalty or trustworthiness of friends of associates
3. Is reluctant to confide in others because of unwarranted fear that the information will be used maliciously against him or her
4. Reads hidden demeaning or threatening meanings into benign remarks or events
5. Persistently bears grudges, is unforgiving of insults, injuries, or slights
6. Perceives attacks on his or her character or reputation that are not apparent to others and is quick to react angrily or to counterattack
7. Has recurrent suspicions, without justification, regarding fidelity of spouse or sexual partner

These symptoms must not occur only during an Axis I disorder such as a mood disorder with psychotic features. Other rule-outs include paranoid schizophrenia, personality change attributable to a general medical condition or physical handicap, and other personality disorders, such as antisocial and narcissistic personalities, which have the highest comorbidity levels.

The prevalence of the disorder is set between .5 and 2% of the general population and between 2 and 10% of the outpatient population. These estimates of prevalence are somewhat unreliable, however, because this disorder, as compared with other diagnostic groups, often is masked by rigid defenses and social avoidance. In fact, individuals with rather serious paranoid traits can present as relatively well-organized and logical until the object of their paranoia is touched (Siegel, 1994).

Differential Diagnosis

Paranoid symptoms or features are evident in several other personality disorders (e.g., narcissistic, antisocial, passive–aggressive, and borderline personalities) as well as Axis I disorders (e.g., bipolar disorder, mania, paranoid schizophrenia, and delusional disorder). Millon (1981) provided descriptive pictures representing some of these mixed paranoid personality disorders. For instance, the paranoid–antisocial personality has more overt hostility and acting out; the paranoid–narcissistic personality has more of a sense of specialness and entitlement; and the paranoid–borderline personality has more mood instability.[1] Millon (1981) also noted that the paranoid individual is extremely vulnerable to the strains of life and can decompensate dramatically despite a rather formidable defensive structure. Millon added that, when they do decompensate, they change more dramatically than those with other personality disorders, often becoming totally absorbed in fantasy and preoccupied with their idiosyncratic beliefs. This means that there may be some shift between PPD and Axis I paranoid states, with delusions or hallucinations. Psychotic episodes, however, may be brief, particularly if the stressor or stressors are short-lived and the typical defensive moves of externalization ward off overwhelming anxiety.

Paranoid symptoms also are to be expected for those who have a history of abuse or trauma. This is made obvious by criterion D of DSM-IV's posttraumatic stress disorder, especially with regard to hypervigilence and irritability. Hypersensitivity to danger occurs when there has been only one incident of trauma, and for those who have experienced repeated harm, the development of a paranoid stance is possible and even likely. This is an even greater likelihood if the harm has resulted from interpersonal violence. Herman (1992) described the personality changes that occur in such cases. The self is experienced as vulnerable and fragmented, with fears of annihilation. Others are experienced as unpredictable and dangerous, and avoidance of attachments is perceived as the safest position. A careful life history interview can easily answer the question concerning the etiology of paranoid symptoms. Although individuals with trauma histories may be reluctant to discuss early traumas because recalling these memories is inherently provocative, a patient and empathic evaluator can get enough information to distinguish between paranoid personality disorder and what are now referred to as disorders of extreme stress.

Paranoid symptoms also are common in a number of medical conditions, making careful medical evaluation an important precursor to diag-

---

[1]In terms of Axis I disorders, Millon (1981) indicated that the progression from paranoid personality disorder to paranoia to "paranoid disorder" to "schizophrenia, paranoid type" reflects differences in degree of personality deterioration. In paranoia, the delusions are highly systemized and the personality largely intact. In the "paranoid disorder," the delusions lack the systemization seen in paranoid personality, but fall short of the fragmentation and deterioration of the paranoid schizophrenic. Numerous others make a similar distinction.

nosis. Manschreck and Petri (1978) identified 85 medical conditions in which paranoid symptoms could be present, including endocrine disorders, pharmacologic toxicity, human immunodeficiency virus infection, diseases of aging, and drug and alcohol abuse. The latter would include excessive use of over-the-counter drugs (such as diet pills), steroids, and illegal drugs such as methamphetamines and cocaine (Manschreck, 1992).

THEORETICAL PERSPECTIVES ON PARANOID PERSONALITY DISORDER

There is much to be learned from the clinical literature on paranoid personality. The origin of the term *paranoia* was Greek and meant "to think beside oneself." The term initially was used broadly to denote a variety of mental disorders. Its use did not approximate the current usage until Kraepelin (1909–1915) narrowed the meaning to describe the systemized and well-contained delusions in patients who otherwise lacked signs of personality deterioration (Millon, 1981, p. 375.) Millon (1981) credits Kretschmer and Sheldon with explaining and describing paranoid character (i.e., paranoid personality disorder). They characterized those with paranoid character as inclined to fight and to be antagonistic and resentful of others. These individuals were seen as sometimes openly aggressive, and at other times as less direct, limiting themselves to ruminations of hostility or persecution. In general, they were described as overly sensitive, suspicious, irritable, tenacious, and combative.

Ironically, the most famous psychoanalytic case of paranoid character—that of Freud's Schreber—ultimately seemed to have been a case of child abuse. Neiderland (1974) studied the writings of Schreber's father, who was a physician and an authority on child rearing. He was an advocate of extreme procedures to instill moral values and character, including the use of belts and straps to restrain children, and the withholding of food to encourage them to renounce their basic needs, methods he likely used with his children.

Shapiro (1981) described the paranoid character as "rigid," preoccupied with issues of "will and self-control." In his view, the paranoid character has rigid ideas of right and wrong and exceptionally high standards. When the paranoid individual fails to meet those standards, he or she feels shame, which Shapiro described as an internal threat. Through the process of defense, this threat is projected outward, as a belief that others are thinking bad things or harboring malevolence toward the paranoid individual. As such, the threat becomes externalized. Shapiro (1981) stated: "The projective identification of the enemy in the shadows can be seen as the product of a nervous, defensively searching and anticipating, suspicious attention.

Once the paranoid person has identified the threat, there is further mobili-zation—an intensification of guardedness, suspiciousness, defensive an-tagonism—against it" (p. 127). This description alludes to the clinical symptoms of hypervigilence.

Shapiro (1981) next identified the narcissistic features of PPD:

> The paranoid person—often grandiose and arrogant though underneath feeling ashamed and small, determined to be strong and to be "on top of things," though underneath feeling weak—is constantly, pridefully, con-cerned with those who, on account of their rank or superior authority, can make him feel small and powerless. He is extremely conscious of status and rank.... Acute feelings of inferiority, shame, and weakness ... are always at the edge of his consciousness. (p. 137)

When feeling threatened, the paranoid character goes into a state of hyperrigidity (i.e., mobilizing his defenses and becoming even more rigid). The projection may not be an exact duplicate of the internal threat, but it re-sults from the typical defensive concerns of rigid characters. These con-cerns often include being slighted, humiliated, controlled by others, trapped, or harmed. The rigid character of paranoid persons makes them admiring and respectful toward authority figures, but, at the same time, resistant, defensive, and resentful.

Millon (1981) touched briefly on the possible developmental roots of PPD, citing Cameron (1943, 1963), who stated:

> The paranoid personality is one that has its origin in a lack of basic trust. There is evidence that in many cases the paranoid person has received sadis-tic treatment during early infancy and that he has, in consequence, internal-ized sadistic attitudes toward himself and others. Because of his basic lack of trust in others, the paranoid personality must be vigilant in order to safe-guard himself against sudden deception and attack. He is exquisitely sensi-tive to traces of hostility, contempt, criticism or accusation. (p. 378)

Millon (1981) and Munro (1992) both have commented on the cognitive style of the individual with PPD, and their discussions provide descrip-tive clinical material rich in significance for Rorschach performance. Millon (1981) stated:

> The paranoid's lack of trust seriously distorts perceptions, thoughts and memories.... They are notoriously oversensitive and disposed to detect signs everywhere of trickery and deception; they are preoccupied,... ac-tively picking up minute cues, then magnifying and distorting them so as to confirm their worst expectations.... Paranoids dismiss contradic-tions and confirm their expectations by seizing upon real, although triv-ial or irrelevant, data.... The unwillingness of paranoids to trust sharing

their doubts and insecurities leaves them isolated and bereft of the reality checks that might restrain their suspicions. Driven to maintain secrecy, they become increasingly unable to see things as others do.... Lacking closeness and sharing,... they concoct events ... and build an intricate logic to justify their distortions.... Little difference exists in their mind between what they have seen and what they have thought. Momentary impressions and hazy memories become fact. Chains of unconnected facts are fitted together.... Delusions are a natural outgrowth of the paranoid pattern. Two factors, dependence on self for both stimulation and reinforcement, are conducive to their development. Insistent on retaining their autonomy, paranoids isolate themselves and are unwilling to share the perspective and attitudes of others. Withdrawn from social communion, they have ample time to cogitate and form idiosyncratic suppositions and hypotheses.... Accustomed to independent thought and convinced of their superiority, they are skillful in formulating beliefs and confident in their correctness. (pp. 380–383)

Munro (1992) noted that paranoid patients "tend to react rapidly to stimuli, but often with rigid and inappropriate responses. There is a marked tendency to lead an isolated lifestyle, thereby reducing their contact with reality and exacerbating their beliefs. Although showing extreme sensitivity to their environment, they frequently misinterpret important elements in it" (p. 234).

There has been conjecture for some time about biologic or genetic causes of paranoid and other personality disorders. Nigg and Goldsmith (1994) reviewed data examining the hypothesis that paranoid personality disorder is part of the schizophrenia spectrum. The authors concluded that across family studies using varying methods, evidence consistently shows that schizotypal and paranoid personality disorders are more likely in relatives of schizophrenic probands, and that schizotypal and paranoid symptoms are familial. Yet, the studies also found that the increased risk for PPD is small. Winokur (1977, 1985) examined two groups of families: those in which at least one individual had a delusional disorder and those in which at least one individual had schizophrenia. He found PPD more common in families with delusional disorders, again suggesting a biogenetic association between the two disorders.

Neuropharmacologists hypothesize that paranoid symptoms are related to an excess of dopamine activity (Munro, 1992), and some neurophysiologists have implicated various brain structures. For instance, Siegel (1994) discussed the limbic system as "the neurophysiological hideaway" of paranoia because of the limbic system's role in the experience of fear and danger. He described chemically and electrically induced paranoid reactions that mimic paranoid disorders and suggested that clinical paranoia may be related to overactivity in this system.

PARANOID PERSONALITY AND DANGEROUSNESS

A discussion of paranoid personality would not be complete without attention to the issue of dangerousness. The percentage of individuals with PPD who become violent is unknown. Small studies investigating certain types of violence have been conducted. For example, features of PPD have been identified in a proportion of stalkers (Meloy, 1998). Batterers frequently demonstrate PPD (Kaser-Boyd, 2004). A number of individuals who have committed workplace violence have features of PPD (Resnick & Kausch, 1995; Douglas & Martinko, 2001).

Although the prediction of danger is an often-noted pitfall in psychological assessment with an inherent potential for false positives (Megarghee, 1976), and although the assessment of violence involves dynamic rather than a static processes (Maloney, 1985), the potential for dangerous or frightening behavior is nevertheless present in individuals with PPD. When hostility is disavowed and projected onto a "bad object," there is clearly the potential for harm. A first step for a violent act often involves devaluation of the "object"—the hated or feared person is "evil," "immoral," or the like. A next step is communication with the person. Here, there typically is an intent to cause fear or to control the other person. There may even be a need or intent to destroy the person. These represent increasing levels of severity of pathology and dangerousness.

The paranoid patient may communicate threat directly (e.g., by a verbal statement to the therapist or others, letters to the person) or indirectly (e.g., in journals, songs recorded for the person, art or religious prophecy). The most challenging question is how likely the violent behavior is to occur. As with other diagnostic groups, dangerousness is an interaction between a thought or impulse and psychological–behavioral controls (Megarghee, 1976). Individuals with PPD may have a chronically high degree of suspiciousness, with vaguely formulated threats, but at the time of a crisis (e.g., threatened loss of work), they may focus their anger and suspicion on one or two people, formulating specific thoughts about their badness. The stress may cause a chain reaction that lessens controls. For example, sleep may become impaired, or substance abuse may increase. Millon (1981) noted that individuals with PPD are extremely vulnerable to stressors and can decompensate dramatically.

An example showing the explosive nature of stress in individuals with PPD is that of a batterer whose partner has finally made the decision to leave him. In these cases, threat is dramatically increased by the following factors: presence of weapons (many of these individuals are gun collectors), previous threats to kill, previous attempts to kill, suicide attempts, and substance abuse (Kaser-Boyd, 2004). White and Cawood (1998) identified the following risk factors for stalkers: male, direct verbal threats, suicide threats, anger and grandiosity, a likely personality disorder, depressive symptoms, underemployment, long-term preoccupation with the victim, history of involvement with firearms, and current feelings of desperation.

PARANOID PERSONALITY DISORDER AND THE RORSCHACH

Because of the difficulty involved in studying PPD, the Rorschach as an assessment tool for PPD has been a relatively neglected area of clinical inquiry and writing (Lerner, 1991). The early Rorschach work on paranoia was flawed by the widely accepted belief at the time that paranoid features were a product of repressed homosexual urges, a theory first offered by Freud (see Shapiro's [1981] discussion of Freud's Schreber, and Goldfried, Stricker, & Weiner's, [1971] discussion of the Rorschach.[2]) Once the American Psychiatric Association depathologized homosexuality, this literature was abandoned.

Hertz (1942), Lindner (1947), and others (Phillips & Smith, 1953) have compared Rorschach findings in paranoid personalities with other diagnostic groups. For example, Phillips and Smith (1953) noted that form quality may have some tendency toward the violation of reality (minus form quality responses), but because thought processes remain integrated in paranoid people, the proportion of form quality minus responses may be within normal limits. Linder (1947) explored human and humanoid content and found a greater amount of the latter in the records of those with paranoid features. Linder suggested that (H) reflects the paranoid's social anxiety and hypersensitivity.

Paranoid personality style has received little research attention since Exner (1974) published his Comprehensive System, except for Exner's (2003) work with the Hypervigilance Index (HVI; Table 3.1). Exner's (1986) early work on paranoid characteristics was conceptual, because he hypothesized that a set of Rorschach variables are related to a paranoid style. The cluster of variables that came to make up the HVI emerged from a study of 150 paranoid schizophrenics. In that study, 150 paranoid schizophrenics were compared with 150 nonparanoid schizophrenics. In the paranoid schizophrenic sample, 70% were positive for five of the variables and 85% were positive for four variables, as compared to 13% and 17% respectively, in the sample of nonparanoid schizophrenics. When the HVI was exam-

---

[2]To quote from this classic Rorschach text: "Freud has maintained that a homosexual conflict lies at the root of all paranoid delusions.... The Rorschach homosexual signs have been used by Aronson (1952), Grauer (1954), and Meketon, et al. (1962) in testing the psychoanalytic hypothesis directly, and by Chapman and Reese (1953) in a less direct test of the theory."

TABLE 3.1
Exner's Hypervigilence Index (HVI)

---

1. FT + TF + T = 0
2. Zf > 12
3. Zd > +3.5
4. S > 3
5. H + (H) + Hd + (Hd) > 6
6. (H) + (A) + (Hd) + (Ad) > 3
7. H + A: Hd + Ad
8. Cg > 3

Note. Positive if condition 1 is true and at least four of the others are true.

ined in a sample of 20 subjects with a diagnosis of PPD, 12 of the 20 had all five variables in their records. This made the HVI appear to be a promising way to measure at least one aspect of a paranoid style. Dies (1995) noted that HVI has received very little attention in professional journals, and a recent literature search indicated that this is still true.

Many variables are evaluated within the HVI (Table 3.1). Texture (T) must be absent from the record. The sum of H, (H), Hd, and (Hd) must be greater than 6. When this variable is present, the examinee is paying considerable attention to people. At the same time, much of the content is parenthesized [(H)+(A)+(Hd)+(Ad) > 3], indicating that there is a need to distance oneself from others by seeing people or animals as imaginary rather than real. There also is a tendency to focus on parts of figures rather than wholes, perhaps related to carefulness in scanning, or perhaps to hypercriticism (H+A:Hd+Ad < 4:1). Overall, the HVI is believed to assess concerns about protecting oneself, concerns about not being able to perceive others' actions accurately, and difficulty discerning the motives of others [Cg > 3]. There also are markers of overincorporation, whereby the individual searches the environment carefully and thoroughly before coming to closure [Zf > 12, Zd > +3.5]. Finally, the HVI captures anger or resentment "channeled in some maladaptive way" [S > 3].

Weiner (2003) noted that a positive HVI rarely occurs in nonpatients and "is a pervasive frame of reference that colors many different facets of a person's behavior" (p. 176). When HVI is positive, the examinee is "inordinately alert to potential sources of danger or threat ... usually as a consequence of feeling unable to trust the motives of others and depend on the safety of their surroundings" (p. 176). Weiner noted that HVI incorporates three dimensions of personality functioning: (a) relating to others, (b) a hypervigilant style of processing incoming stimuli, and (c) anger. Regarding the latter, he commented that anger plays a role in hypervigilance via the mechanism of projection, or disavowing one's own anger and attributing it to others.

As noted previously, a central variable in the HVI is the finding that T equals 0. Exner (1993, p. 383) reported that 89% of the normative sample gave at least one T response. Klopfer postulated that texture is related to affection and dependency (Exner, 1993, p. 383), and empirical studies have found a relationship between T and emotional need. For example, Exner and Bryant (1974) found that recently divorced or separated subjects had significantly more T than matched controls (3.57 vs. 1.31). Leura and Exner (1976) compared 32 foster children who had no placement lasting longer than 14 months with a control group of 32 children who had lived with their own parents since birth. Of the 32 foster children, 20 had T-less records, with a mean of .045, as compared with 1.47 for the comparison group. Battered women on trial for killing their batterers also were found to have a T = 0 (Kaser-Boyd, 1993). Exner (Personal Communication, Rorschach Workshops, 1991) stated that in these samples, a lack of texture may be a result of painful human interaction and subsequent avoidance. Weiner (2003) suggested that the lack of T probably represents a character trait, likely resulting from a lack of early attachment or disturbed attachment. He noted that those who give T-less records rarely give subsequent records with T unless they become significantly attached, whereas those with a T > 0 may vary in the amount of T depending of situational events. For example, T may increase at a time of object loss. At a minimum, it appears that there is something different about the person with no T responses in the way he or she relates to others.

Findings show that HVI is not routinely positive in groups other than those with significant paranoia. As such, the HVI appears to have substantial discriminative power. In various Exner (1993) samples, HVI is positive in 10% of inpatient depressives, 18% of inpatient schizophrenics, 7 % of general character disorders, and 4% of general outpatients.

As with other Rorschach indices, HVI may be less accurate with brief, high lambda records (Meyer, 1993), and computer-generated narratives may not make this clear. This means that the examiner needs to take a close look at these records to detect whether they could be false negative presentations of PPD. There may be other individuals who have T in their record, but who otherwise carefully scan the stimulus field, are vigilant to danger, and have the clinical presentation of PPD.

The content of Rorschach responses often is a window into the examinee's experience of the world. The Exner (1986, 1993, 2003) system, following the lead of older Rorschach scoring systems, did not include a category for threatening percepts or for fear, although there is a special score for aggressive content (AG) and one for morbid content (MOR) that captures the fear of harm or sense of imminent disintegration. Ephraim and Kaser-Boyd (2003) proposed the Preoccupation with Danger Index, which includes four content categories: (a) fear, (b) threat, (c) harm, and (d) violent confrontation.[3] The scoring categories were derived from clinical work with survivors of severe domestic violence and survivors of torture/state violence. To date, the Danger Index (DI) has been formally studied with two groups of trauma survivors: refugee seekers who had been victims of torture–state violence and battered women referred for pretrial evaluation. Both groups were significantly higher on the DI than a group of normal volunteers. The mean number of danger contents was 5.55 for battered women and 6.33 for refugees. The mean number of danger contents for the comparison group was 1.25. Although more research investigating the DI is needed, it appears that nonpatients are likely to have no more than one danger content, whereas severely traumatized individuals have four or five times as many. Although no research has investigated the DI and paranoid personality, it is proposed as a potentially useful index for individuals with paranoid personality traits and will be applied to the case reported later.

Rorschach Hypotheses—Paranoid Personality Disorder

Whereas the protocol of an examinee with PPD may vary depending on the level of stress and decompensation (in which defended vs. undefended protocols may be captured by low R vs. high R, and by Lambda > 1.0 vs. Lambda < .99), there are some fundamental features of Rorschach performance that should remain relatively constant. The examinee's approach to the Rorschach task should resemble his or her approach to the world. Hypervigilant alertness should be manifested in an over-incorporative approach to the stimuli (Zd > +1). Because of the effort expended to scan the stimulus field, there should be more D and Dd responses than in the average protocol. At the same time, the examinee likely will struggle to keep feelings at bay, to the extent that this is possible, and guard against revealing his or her thoughts and feelings (Lambda > 1.0). Consistent with this, the number of shading responses likely will be low, if present at all. Populars can be expected to fall within normal range, but Form Quality for nonpopulars may be less than satisfactory (i.e., below .70) because of the tendency to misperceive and personalize percepts. While the examinee may strive to give a bland,

---

[3]*Fear:* A living or imaginary being is portrayed as endangered or fearful. *Threat:* A living or imaginary being, or force, is portrayed as endangering, scary, threatening, destructive, or malevolent. *Violent confrontation:* Portrayal of a fight, clash, combat, or war. *Harm:* Portrayal of destruction, violent disruption, or failure to protect body boundaries; includes also barrier responses that emphasize the need to protect/shelter the body-self against danger.

ordinary protocol response, with popular and unimaginative percepts, certain cards may assess the examinee's issues. That is, they may trigger associations about danger or other idiosyncratic content related to threat. When controls slip, color or shading scores may appear, as well as Special Scores. Danger content probably will be greater than in an average record, although in an individual with long-established paranoid tendencies, the elements of danger may be symbolic or disguised. Because the world is perceived as hostile, AG content may be higher than in the average record. The guarded, defensive stance also may result in more personalization responses. The HVI also may be elevated, or if its elevation is absent because texture is present, other variables of the HVI may be elevated, particularly those that surround interpersonal distance. Finally, because of the paranoid person's primitive defensiveness and intense self-focus, the protocol may have one or more reflection responses.

The following case was selected for inclusion in this chapter before the Rorschach was administered (i.e., after a clinical interview and diagnosis) and before it was clear whether the Rorschach would illustrate some of these hypotheses.

CASE EXAMPLE: MS. JENSEN

Ms. Jensen was referred for an independent medical examination by opposing legal counsel. She was suing her employer for discrimination resulting from his demands of improved performance. She cited special disabilities that required consideration in her employment supervision. Ms. Jensen had been badly injured in a car accident shortly after she finished college. After a period of recovery and rehabilitation, she began working and had worked for about 5 years in this and a related field.

Ms. Jensen presented as an attractive 34-year-old woman She was neatly and pleasantly groomed in professional attire. She was polite and very formal in her interactions. She brought a tape recorder to her sessions, although she struggled to use it. She seemed clearly above average in intelligence, with an excellent vocabulary. Her behavior caused alarm from the beginning of her first session, however, as she claimed that she "smelled gas" in the waiting room and could not complete testing there. In the inner office, she refused to sit in the first chair offered to her, stating that it "felt dirty." She moved to a similar chair, which was of the same age and condition.

At her second appointment, Ms. Jensen insisted that the examiner was late, had called her attorney, and said she was going to leave, but later indicated that she sets her watch "fast." In general, she seemed argumentative and rigid. At the end of the evaluation, she said she felt as though the evaluator had "kicked her in the chest" because the evaluation questions had stirred up painful emotions. She believed the evaluator probably would be calling opposing counsel and "laughing" about her, especially because opposing counsel had called her "obese." A review of the report provided by the plaintiff's psychologist at the end of the evaluation showed that Ms. Jensen had withheld certain important aspects of her history (e.g., that her mother and sister had both suffered from severe depression).

Traditional psychological testing proved difficult. On the MMPI-2, Ms. Jensen omitted more than 50 questions, characterizing these as "silly," "stupid," or "bizarre," and implying that she should not have to answer them. When these items were read aloud to her, she wanted to argue about the meaning of each question, making this a laborious process. Ms. Jensen frequently demeaned and devalued the test, which seemed like a coping mechanism activated by her considerable anxiety about being judged. She was somewhat less defensive with the MCMI-III, leaving virtually no items unmarked and making no devaluing comments. Interestingly, when the Rorschach was administered, she made a concerted effort to process the stimuli.

Ms. Jensen, by all accounts, had experienced a difficult childhood. Her parents had divorced before she entered first grade. Her father was a highly skilled professional, and her mother was a housewife who did not believe in divorce. Her mother never remarried, and she apparently was quite bitter toward Ms. Jensen's father. As such, all contact with the father was terminated for many years. Her father moved to another state and remarried, and Ms. Jensen had no contact with him until her accident (described later). It seemed that her mother had provided a model of emotional rigidity and interpersonal suspicion. In part, this may have resulted from severe levels of depression. Depression also was reported in Ms. Jensen's sister. As a result of economic hardship, Ms. Jensen, her mother, and older siblings moved frequently. Ms. Jensen, out of necessity, began to work part-time while still in high school.

Ms. Jensen told her own expert that she had been a premature baby, deprived of oxygen at birth. She also reported being enuretic until the age 8 years and receiving speech and language services in elementary school. By high school, however, she said she had "really enjoyed school" and had been a good student without studying. She described herself as a leader with "plenty of friends." She added that the best-looking boy on campus had been her boyfriend.

When Ms. Jensen was a senior in high school, a car she was driving was hit by a drunk driver. She stated that she almost died, and that she was not aware of her surroundings for about 2 weeks. She had many facial injuries, the result of her face hitting the windshield. She said that magnetic resonance images found brain damage in her left frontal lobe, although this was not substantiated by defense experts. Ms. Jensen also had trauma to her hips, and was in a wheel chair for almost a year after her accident. Nevertheless, she was determined to attend college. While there, she continued to support herself by working part-time at her college campus.

At the time of Ms. Jensen's injury, someone called her estranged father to inform him of the accident. Before he would visit her, however, he demanded that she and her siblings sign documents giving up their rights to past child support. This was a sensitive subject, and there was clear evidence of Ms. Jensen feeling hurt and rejected in this relationship.

Ms. Jensen believed that her cognitive abilities were affected by her accident. She reported having difficulty processing verbal information and putting things in order. Although she graduated from college with good grades, she stated that she had to work extra hard to achieve such grades. Throughout this period in her life, Ms. Jensen reported a number of other troubling reminders of her accident, including numbness and tingling in her face and extremities.

Ms. Jensen began working full-time after college graduation. There were no real problems with her first job, which lasted about 2 years. At her second job, her employer began to document her need for improvement in performance in several memos. When the examiner showed Ms. Jensen that she had copies of these complaints, Ms. Jensen became visibly angry. Instead of discussing the complaints about her performance, she began a long discussion about the deficiencies of the employer. During this discussion, she conveyed a sense that she was better at knowing "what's right" than others around her. She spoke disdainfully about those both above and below her in the corporate structure. Although the complaints about her performance began as relatively minor, (e.g., tardiness and poor interpersonal skills with colleagues), her reaction to them was poor, and subsequent evaluations of her performance became more globally negative. She then began to accuse her employer of discrimination against the handicapped. Ultimately, she filed suit for emotional distress.

Ms. Jensen's Rorschach

Ms. Jensen produced a Rorschach record of 27 responses, which is above average for an adult. Lambda was .93, indicating that the record was not as constricted and defended as might be expected. She made a concerted effort to process the blots, and although she worked to "pull" stimuli together, this was sometimes at the expense of accurate reality testing. Of her 27 responses, only 7 were scored D, and the remainder were Ws. Her W:M ratio suggested that she had a strong achievement orientation. She did not show the tendency to overincorporate (Zd > 1.0), but she was positive on HVI, indicating a heightened effort to notice and account for events in the environment. The HVI was positive mostly because of her focus on human percepts, which tended to be whole, but fictional, figures (H). These plus an absence of Texture (T) indicated she had limited capacity to form close attachments and preferred to keep people at "arm's length."

Despite Ms. Jensen's angry and confrontational demeanor in the interview, she had no Space (S) responses. She did have one reflection response, indicating a clear tendency to overvalue her worth or to be preoccupied with her needs at the expense of concern about others. Reflection responses also can indicate a sense of entitlement and a tendency to externalize blame to others, features that were very clear in her clinical interview. Ms. Jensen's record also was remarkable for its number of personalizations (PER = 5). As predicted, she was defensive and argumentative when asked to describe her percepts.

Ms. Jensen's record spoke clearly of her damaged sense of self (MOR = 2; An + Xy = 1), and her dysphoric affect was evident (C' = 3; Y = 2). Also evident was Ms. Jensen's pervasive sense of helplessness (m = 3). Her DEPI results were positive, and she had two Color-Shading Blends, clearly marking the sense of desperate vulnerability that characterized her behavior in and around the evaluation.

Although these variables were not hypothesized to characterize PPD, Ms. Jensen was pretty much at the "end of her rope." She had been working at an underpaid menial job for more than 1 year while waiting for her suit to be heard, and she found the whole series of evaluations and depositions humiliating and threatening. It also is quite likely that repeated interviewing about her automobile accident triggered memories from which she had worked to distance herself.

Ms. Jensen's thinking was more complex (Blends = 6) than what likely was functional for her, especially when the topic was emotionally laden. The low X+% and F+% documented the misperception and personalization described for paranoid personality. As expected, she had few special scores associated with thought disorder, with unusual beliefs only about how others regarded her.

Ms. Jensen had a number of percepts that would be considered for a score on the Danger Index for Harm. For example, on Card IV, she saw a tree "that's being uprooted and it's dying, falling over." On Card V, she saw a pelvis and commented: "It could look like the pelvis crushed on my body; it reminded me of x-rays I've looked at so many times." There was little other Danger content, although it could be argued that it was a disguised or minimized form of potential threat or harm. For instance, on Card I, she reported a mask, on Card IV, "a creepy, crawly bug," and on Card V, a bat, and "bats are pretty creepy to me." Alternatively, it may be that her many childlike and fantasy percepts represented a form of denial of threat.

For a person involved in a service delivery field, there was a paucity of human content (H = 4; A = 9). Although she had Cooperative Movement (COP) of 1, her whole human responses were children or distanced, odd, or lifeless forms.

What about the other test results? The MCMI-III was elevated on Anxiety Disorder and on Borderline Personality Disorder, but not on Paranoid Personality Disorder or Delusional Disorder. On the MMPI-2, Ms. Jensen was moderately defensive, but obtained a classic elevation on scale 6. The Caldwell Report (2000) provided the following descriptors about such a protocol:

> She would be seen as painfully sensitive to criticism, with projections and fixed misinterpretations of the motives of others.... She would be seen as rigidly self-controlling and generally lacking in insight. She would minimize shortcomings and limitations both in herself and others, righteously reacting as though everyone somehow were or ought to be more virtuous than they are. Despondency, worry, self-criticism, marked social discomfort, and underlying pessimism are indicated. At other times, she would fixedly blame others and seek to externalize the focus of her conflicts away from herself....
>
> Her moral inflexibility would conflict with allowing natural expressions of anger. Hostility toward members of her family appears poorly recognized and carefully rationalized.... Her expressions of anger are apt to be self-righteous, displaced, and at times inappropriate. Her tendency to provoke others would leave them frustrated and resentful of her.... Continuing self-control and careful avoidance of criticism are self-protective behaviors that would influence many aspects of her lifestyle.... Underneath, this would be overlearned but unverbalized fears lest she be attacked and be caused pain and humiliation by loved ones. Along with this may be a strong underlying fear of body failure and of dying.... The profile has often been associated with acute paranoid episodes and more chronic paranoid trends. (p. 3)

Ms. Jensen did not prevail in her suit. There was little doubt that Ms. Jensen's automobile accident and long struggle to recuperate played a significant role in her perception of threat in the world. She felt profoundly changed, and she assumed that everyone saw her as damaged. Whereas her stubborn resilience had propelled her through college despite enormous physical difficulties, this same personality feature drove her to seek a level of work achievement that probably was too demanding. Her fragile self-esteem would not let her give up or accept the possibility of personal weaknesses, and blame was therefore externalized to others. Her belief that this examiner would call the lawyer, and that they would laugh at her was a suspicion misplaced and particularly poignant. Whereas her accident greatly influenced her sense of threat, her childhood and family dynamics also seemed important in that bitterness and resentment were modeled by her mother, and the experience of abandonment, greed, and manipulation were quite real.

Although case studies such as the one provided allow researchers and clinicians to understand better the Rorschach presentation of PPD, there are obvious limitations to the single case study. Thus, there is a clear need for Rorschach research with PPD. In particular, large group data on a sample of individuals with PPD would allow further evaluation of the presented hypotheses. However, individuals with this personality disorder, more than others, are unlikely to volunteer for studies and rarely present in outpatient clinical settings, making it difficult to collect samples of sufficient size. As such, the prison population might be more fruitful when this endeavor is begun because there are sufficient numbers of individuals with PPD in this setting. Because several other personality disorders exhibit paranoid symptoms (e.g., narcissistic, antisocial personalities), research should continue to evaluate Rorschach data to determine whether these groups may be differentiated by the Rorschach. A positive finding in this regard would provide incremental validity of the Rorschach for these populations.

Another area of research involves the use of the HVI to assess paranoid features and traits. Because the HVI is seldom positive for nonpatients (Exner, 2003), it would be interesting to determine both the sensitivity and specificity of the HVI in detecting PPD. Although the Rorschach is not to be used for diagnostic purposes, strong findings in this line of research may provide evidence for the utility and validity of the Rorschach in detecting paranoia, especially in individuals who may be prone to deny such feelings. Furthermore, evaluation of differences on the HVI and other Rorschach variables between patients with PPD and those with posttraumatic stress disorder would be particularly helpful. Because patients with posttraumatic stress disorder often are hypervigilant to their environment, there may be other ways in which the two disorders are differentiated, such as the quality of human figure representation, Ephraim and Kaser-Boyd's Danger (2003) Index, and an evaluation of the defensive style presented by the groups. Individuals with PPD fluctuate in symptoms and defenses. Therefore, dividing records into high Lambda and low Lambda groups will be a prerequisite of careful research.

REFERENCES

American Psychiatric Association. (1994). *Diagnostic and statistical manual of mental disorders* (4th ed.). Washington, DC: Author.

Aronson, M. L. (1952). A study of the Freudian theory of paranoia by means of the Rorschach test. *Journal of Projective Techniques, 16,* 397–411.

Caldwell, A. (2000). *The Caldwell Report.* Los Angeles, CA: Clinical Psychological Services, Inc.

Cameron, N. (1943). The paranoid pseudo-community. *American Journal of Sociology, 49,* 32–38.

Cameron, N. (1963). *Personality Development and Psychopathology.* Boston: Houghton Mifflin.

Chapman, A. H., & Reese, D. G. (1953). Homosexual signs in Rorschachs of early schizophrenics. *Journal of Clinical Psychology, 9,* 30–32.

Coughlin, C. (2002). *Saddam: King of terror.* New York: Harper/Collins.

Dies, R. R. (1995). Conceptual issues in Rorschach research. In J. E. Exner (Ed.), *Issues and methods in Rorschach research.* Mahwah, NJ: Lawrence Erlbaum Associates.

Douglas, S. C., & Martinko, M. J. (2001). Exploring the role of individual differences in the prediction of workplace aggression. *Journal of Applied Psychology, 86*(4), 547–559.

Ephraim, D., & Kaser-Boyd, N. (2003, March). *A Rorschach index to assess preoccupation with danger.* Paper presented at the Annual Meeting of the Society for Personality Assessment, San Francisco, CA.

Exner, J. E. (1974). *The Rorschach: A comprehensive system: Volume 1.* New York: John Wiley.

Exner, J. E. (1986). *The Rorschach: A comprehensive system: Volume 1. Basic foundations* (2nd ed.). New York: John Wiley.

Exner, J. E. (1993). *The Rorschach: A comprehensive system: Volume 1. Basic foundations* (3rd ed.). New York: John Wiley.

Exner, J. E. (2003). *The Rorschach: A comprehensive system: Volume 1. Basic foundations* (4th ed.). New York: John Wiley.

Exner, J. E., & Bryant, E. L. (1974). *Rorschach responses of subjects recently divorced or separated.* Workshops Study No. 206 (unpublished). Asheville, NC: Rorschach Workshops.

Gacano, C. B., & Meloy, J. R. (1994). *The Rorschach assessment of aggressive and psychopathic personalities.* Hillsdale, NJ: Lawrence Erlbaum Associates.

Goldfried, M. R., Stricker, G., & Weiner, I. B. (1971). *Rorschach handbook of clinical and research applications* (pp. 210–212). Englewood Cliffs, NJ: Prentice-Hall.

Grauer, D. (1954). Homosexuality in paranoid schizophrenia as revealed by the Rorschach test. *Journal of Consulting Psychology, 18,* 459–462.

Herman, J. (1992) Complex PTSD: A syndrome in survivors of prolonged and repeated trauma. *Journal of Traumatic Stress, 5,* 377–389.

Hertz, M. R. (1942). *Frequency tables to be used in scoring the Rorschach inkblot test* (rev. ed.). Cleveland, OH: Western Reserve University Press.

Kaser-Boyd, N. (1993). Rorschachs of women who commit homicide. *Journal of Personality Assessment, 60,* 458–470.

Kaser-Boyd, N. (2002, March). *Hatred and fanaticism: Understanding the terrorist.* Paper presented at the Annual Meeting of the Society for Personality Assessment, San Antonio, TX.

Kaser-Boyd, N. (2004). Battered woman syndrome: Clinical features, evaluation, and expert testimony. In B. J. Cling (Ed.), *Sexualized violence against women and children.* New York: Guilford.

Kraepelin, E. (1909–1915). *Psychiatrie: Ein Lehrbuch* (Vol. 3, 8th ed.). Leipzig: Barth.

Leura, A. V., & Exner, J. E. (1976). Rorschach performances of children with a multiple foster home history. Workshops Study No. 220 (unpublished). Asheville, NC: Rorschach Workshops.

Lerner, P. M. (1991). *Psychoanalytic theory and the Rorschach*. Hillsdale, NJ: The Analytic Press.

Lindner, R. M. (1947). Analysis of Rorschach test by content. *Journal of Clinical Psychopathology, 8,* 707–719.

Maloney, M. P. (1985). *A clinician's guide to forensic psychological assessment*. New York: Free Press.

Manschreck, T. C. (1992). Delusional disorders: Clinical concepts and diagnostic strategies. *Psychiatric Annals, 22,* 241–251.

Manschreck, T. C., & Petri, M. (1978). The paranoid syndrome. *Lancet, 2,* 251–253.

Megarghee, E. (1976). The prediction of dangerous behavior. *Criminal Justice and Behavior, 3,* 3–21.

Meketon, B. W., Griffith, R. M., Taylor, V. H., & Wiedeman, J. S. (1962). Rorschach homosexual signs in paranoid schizophrenics. *Journal of Abnormal and Social Psychology, 65,* 280–284.

Meloy, J. R. (1998). *The psychology of stalking*. New York: Academic Press.

Meyer, G. J. (1993). The impact of response frequency on Rorschach Comprehensive System constellation indices and on their validity with diagnostic and MMPI-2 criteria.

Millon, T. (1981). *Disorders of personality*. New York: John Wiley.

Millon, T. (1996). *Disorders of personality* (3rd ed). New York: John Wiley.

Millon, T. (1994). *MCMI-III manual*. Minneapolis, MN: National Computer Systems.

Munro, A. (1992). Psychiatric disorders characterized by delusions: Treatment in relation to specific types. *Psychiatric Annals, 22,* 232–240.

Niederland, W. G. (1974). *The Schreber case: Psychoanalytic profile of a paranoid personality*. New York: Quadrangle.

Nigg, J. T., & Goldsmith, H. H. (1994). Genetics of personality disorders: Perspectives from personality and psychopathology research. *Psychological Bulletin, 115,* 346–380.

Phillips, L., & Smith, J. G. (1953). *Rorschach interpretation: Advanced technique*. New York: Grune & Stratton.

Resnick, P. J., & Kausch, O. (1995). Violence in the workplace: Role of the consultant. *Consulting Psychology Journal: Practice and Research, 47*(4), 213–222.

Retzlaff, P. (1996). MCMI-III validity: Bad test or bad validity. *Journal of Personality Assessment, 66,* 431–437.

Rogers, R., Salekin, R. T., & Sewell, K. W. (1999). Validation of the Millon Clinical Multiaxial Inventory for Axis II Disorders: Does it meet the Daubert standard? *Law and Human Behavior, 23,* 425–443.

Shapiro, D. (1981). *Autonomy and rigid character*. New York: Basic Books.

Siegel, R. K. (1994). *Whispers: The voices of paranoia*. New York: Crown Publishers.

Weiner, I. B. (2003). *Principles of Rorschach interpretation* (2nd ed.). Mahwah, NJ: Lawrence Erlbaum Associates.

White, S. G. & Cawood, J. S. (1998). Threat management of stalking cases. In J. R. Meloy (Ed.), *The psychology of stalking.* New York: Academic Press.
Winokur, G. (1977). Delusional disorder (paranoia). *Comprehensive Psychiatry, 18,* 518–521.
Winokur, G. (1985). Familial psychopathology in delusional disorder. *Comprehensive Psychiatry, 26,* 241–248.

Free Association	Inquiry
Card I	
1. Could be a bug.	1. The segmented body parts there, and these could be little antler things, and it's pretty symmetrical, an anthropod.
2. (v) Could be a lamp…It could be anything really.	2. When I turned it around like this, these kinds of things are those long lamps, the foot of a lamp and the light would just come out here.
3. (v) Could be some kind of design for a gate.	3. Sometimes you see something like that on a gate, not exactly, but it kind of arches. Sometimes even with a gate, it opens up automatically and they make them ornate, decorative.
4. (v) Could be a mask.	4. If you have it like this, it could be a mask. People could see out of there and breathe.
5. Could be a funny little animal.	5. I forgot where I found that one. I don't know, could be a crown, too. Oh, now I see, like one of those really long, ferret kind of animals, like a long nose and a long tail, the bottom part…like an animal a kid would draw.
Card II	
6. Two elephants playing at a circus.	6. Their trunks up in the air, and their feet are up on something like a little stool, and they are twirling, doing some kind of trick.
7. Looks like a student's art work.	7. (Smiles). Well, because children like to use black a lot, and they smear them together, and they like to try to draw hearts, and this red part looks like a heart, and there is other red. And it looks like some of their fingerprints.
8. Or it could be a hole in the wall.	8. When I turned it, mostly like diagonal, not straight up and down. (I'm not sure I see it like you do). Just the center part, and the outside of it looks like it was blasted through the center, because of the red part on the outer side there.
Card III	
9. Maybe two people facing each other, like a teeter totter but not because they don't have anywhere to sit.	9. It's a game we used to play where you would put your feet together and rock back and forth. Kind of looks like two people facing each other, kind of bent over you know.

10. (v) But if you turn it upside down, it looks like a bug.

10. Yes, but mostly, if you think of these as the eyes of a robin and the red as a red breasted bird, it looks like a robin, and I like it better that way. If you wanted to make it ugly, it looks like a bug. And if you just look at the outside, the bigger circles make it look like a bird with a beak in the center.

11. Or it could be a bird with big eyes, and a red chest, like a robin.

11. Shape of a bird, and with a red chest.

Card IV
12. Big clown feet.

12. These look like big clown feet on the outer side. And the way this is drawn, reminds me of those clown collars and the shading makes it look like a checkered kind of suit.

13. Or like a mountain, far away, to climb up to the top would be far away (turns).

13. If you just look at the very very tip, over here, could be a very high distance, because it's so small compared to down here at the bottom, which is very large.

14. (>) Or could just be a tree that's being uprooted, if you look at it sideways and it's dying, because the leaves are dying, a dying tree falling over.

14. These could be like dead branches. And these look like roots coming out of the ground.

15. (v) But if you look at it this way, it could be a bug.

15. This way it looks like an ugly bug...mostly because if you just look at it this direction, the thing that catches my eye are tentacles. I don't like bugs and spiders. It's like a little creepy crawly bug.

16. (v) When I look at it this way, it looks like a mosaic, and little figurines, maybe a wolf and a person within it, with lots of little figurines. Not a mosque, but some of those older churches have those things engraved.

16. Well if this is really a figurine, it has to be attached to something larger to be part of a mosaic...has to be some permanent thing it's attached to, something bigger. The wolf is howling. I've seen pictures.

Card V

17. (v) The blue spot throws off the symmetry, but it looks like a bat.

17. I don't particularly like bats. I've been caving before when I was younger. Bats are pretty creepy to me. The two parts here look like ears, and the feet and the large wings.

18. Could be one of those horns, moose horns where they have the big things.

18. Oh, when I turned it over, antlers people save when they go hunting. I don't know if they are moose or some kind of animal horns. I have to think of it kind of skinnier.

19. (v) Or if you turn it this way, it could look like the pelvis crushed on my body. This one isn't crushed, but it's not the right shape. And your blue spot happens to be the spot that is messed up on mine.

19. Because the ink that is not supposed to be there drew my attention to that it's the left side of my pelvis that is injured. Maybe if the ink spot wasn't there, I wouldn't have even noticed it. It just reminded me of X-rays I've looked at so many times, the blacks and the grays, and I've seen this particular shape many times.

Card VI

20. Could be an Indian rug or something.

20. Just how it has fringes on the outer sides. And this reminds me of my elderly friend who has lots of Indian rugs in her house, or she used to before she passed away. And all the fringes, and they are perfectly symmetrical. They always have some kind of ornate thing hung off the side.

Card VII

21. Two little kids looking at each other with pony tails, flying in the air, could be on a teeter totter.

21. Because they are small and look so goofy, but they are having fun. Just with pony tails, little people, and they are short. They look like they are having fun. Place where their mouths could be looks like smiles. Most little kids have their hair up in pony tails with little bangs.

22. When you turn it upside down, it looks like two people with big hair, back to back, with those big beehives. And their head is touching.

22. This is their big beehives and their faces are very small because their hair is so big, and kind of standing there in a pose, like they are going to do a dance or something.

Card VIII

23. Looks like a dissected fish.

23. Oh, because it looks like a school science project I've seen. You cut them in half, and everything is symmetrical and in the center it looks like bones.

24. (>) When you turn it vertical, it looks like it could be a bear climbing and like water reflecting. Reflection over there. It reminds me of when you do kids names and you make a mirror image, so it could be like water, and maybe rocks.

24. Could be a bear or lion. I didn't think of another animal until I saw this part. Probably a regular bear, because a lion would have a mane. I thought maybe this was a rock because it looks like a little mountain. I was thinking of the scene itself, what would make it look nice. The bear wouldn't just be standing in the air. Plus, it looks kind of nice as a rock. It could be like two different animals, one coming over the top and one over the bottom, looking into the water or something. It looks like a peaceful place if you're looking at it as a lake, with a reflection. A nice lake, the blue color of the water, with the reflection, and this part suggests a forest, peaceful.

Card IX
25. Maybe two canaries at the bottom.

25. Like these could be birds' feet, hanging onto something, a rope or wire. And these look like little canaries, like their face or something could be an animal. Could be clouds on the top, little rain clouds. Well, if the birds are sitting on a wire, they would have that above them, not so much dark clouds, but maybe blue skies with puffy clouds. There is a lighter one, lighter bluish color and could be a cave in the middle, farther back, through these two little holes. There is nothing there, so could be a cave in the background, but if this is the sky, I don't know what the red part is supposed to be.

Card X
26. If I look at it this way, it could be a silhouette of a person standing in the very center, down the middle line, very faint.

27. And the outside could be just like fireworks. I don't know, bright lights.

26 & 27. Fourth of July, that's what it looks like. (Long silence). Well, I'm trying to make sense of it. If you try to tear the parts apart, the colors and the shapes look like fireworks.

RORSCHACH SEQUENCE OF SCORES FOR MS. JENSEN

Card	Resp	Loc (DQ)	Loc N	Determinants (FQ)	(2)	Content(s)	P	Z	Special Scores
I	1.	Wo	1	Fo		A		1.0	DV
	2.	Wo	1	F-		Hh		1.0	
	3.	Wo	1	Fu		Hh		1.0	
	4.	WSo	1	Fo		Hd		3.5	GHR
	5.	Do		Fo		A, Art			
II	6.	D+		FMao	(2)	A	P	5.5	
	7.	Wo	1	C'F.FC.YFo		Art		4.5	PER
	8.	DSo		FC'.FCo		Id			
III	9.	D+		Mao	(2)	H	P	4.0	COP, GHR
	10.	Wo	1	Fu		A		5.5	
	11.	Wo	1	FCu		A		5.5	
IV	12.	W+	1	FYo		(H)		4.0	GHR
	13.	Wo	1	FDo		Ls		2.0	
	14.	Wo	1	mpu		Bt		2.0	MOR
	15.	Do		Fu		A			
V	16.	W+	1	Fu		Art, Ad, (H)		4.0	PER, GHR
	17.	Wo	1	Fo		A	P	1.0	PER
	18.	Do		Fo		(Ad)			
VI	19.	Wo	1	FC'u		Xy		1.0	PER
	20.	Wo	1	Fo		Ay		2.5	
VII	21.	W+	1	Ma.mp+	(2)	H	P	2.5	GHR
	22.	W+	1	Mpo	(2)	H		4.5	GHR
VIII	23.	Wo	1	Fu		(Ad)		4.5	MOR, PER
	24.	W+	1	Fr.CFo		A, Ls	P	4.5	
IX	25.	WS+	1	FMp.CF.FD-	(2)	A, Na		5.5	
	26.	Do		Fo		H			
X	27.	Wv/+	1	mp.CFu		Ex		5.5	GHR

Location Features	Determinants	Contents	Approach

Location Features

Zf = 22
ZSum = 73.0
Zest = 73.5

W = 20
D = 7
W+D = 27
Dd = 0
S = 3

Developmental Quality
+ = 8
o = 18
v = 1
v/+ = 0

Determinants

Blends
C'F.FC.YF
FC'.FC
M.m
Fr.CF
FM.CF.FD
m.CF

Single
M = 2
FM = 1
m = 1
FC = 1
CF = 0
C = 0
Cn = 0
FC' = 1
C'F = 0
C' = 0
FT = 0
TF = 0
T = 0
FV = 0
VF = 0
V = 0
FY = 1
YF = 0
Y= 0
Fr = 0
rF = 0
FD = 1
F = 13
(2) = 5

Form Quality

	FQx	MQual	W+D
+	= 1	= 1	= 1
o	= 15	= 2	= 15
u	= 9	= 0	= 9
-	= 2	= 0	= 2
none	= 0	= 0	= 0

Contents

H = 4
(H) = 2
Hd = 1
(Hd) = 0
Hx = 0
A = 9
(A) = 0
Ad = 1
(Ad) = 2
An = 0
Art = 3
Ay = 1
Bl = 0
Bt = 1
Cg = 0
Cl = 0
Ex = 1
Fd = 0
Fi = 0
Ge = 0
Hh = 2
Ls = 2
Na = 1
Sc = 0
Sx = 0
Xy = 1
Id = 0

Approach

I: W.W.W.WS.D
II: D.W.DS
III: D.W.W
IV: W.W.W.D.W
V: W.D.W
VI: W
VII: W.W
VIII: W.W
IX: WS
X: D.W

Special Scores

	Lv 1	Lv 2
DV =	1x1	= 0x2
INC =	0x2	= 0x4
DR =	0x3	= 0x6
FAB =	0x4	= 0x7
ALOG =	0x5	
CON =	0x7	

Raw Sum 6 = 1
Wgtd Sum 6 = 1

AB = 0	GHR = 7
AG = 0	PHR = 0
COP = 1	MOR = 2
CP = 0	PER = 5
	PSV = 0

Ratios, Percentages, and Derivations

Core

R = 27	L = .93	
EB = 3:4.5	EA = 7.5	EBPer = N/A
eb = 5:5	es = 10	D = 0
	Adj es = 7	Adj D = 0
FM = 2	SumC' = 3	SumT = 0
m = 3	Sum V = 0	Sum Y = 2

Affect

FC: CF+C = 3:3
Pure C = 0
SumC':WSumC = 3:4.5
Afr =.23
S =3
Blends:R = 6:27
CP = 0

Interpersonal

COP = 1	AG = 0
GHR: PHR = 7:0	
a:p = 3:5	
Food = 0	
Sum T = 0	
Human Cont = 7	
Pure H = 4	
PER = 5	
Isol Indx = .19	

Ideation

a:p = 3:5	Sum6 = 1
Ma:Mp = 2:1	Lv2 = 0
2AB+Art+Ay = 4	WSum6 = 1
MOR = 2	M- = 0
	M none = 0

Mediation

XA% = .92
WDA% = .92
X-% = .07
S- = 1
P = 5
X+% = .59
Xu% = .33

Processing

Zf = 22
W:D:Dd = 20:7:0
W:M = 20:3
Zd = -0.5
PSV = 0
DQ+ = 8
DQv = 0

Self-Perception

3r+(2)/R = .30
Fr+rF = 1
SumV = 0
FD = 2
An+Xy = 1
MOR = 2
H:(H)+Hd+(Hd) = 4:3

PTI = 0   *DEPI = 6   CDI = 3   S-CON = 4   *HVI = 5   OBS = 1

Rorschach Assessment
of Schizoid Personality Disorder

James H. Kleiger
Private Practice, Maryland

Steven K. Huprich
Eastern Michigan University

Divergent views of schizoid personality disorder in terms of phenomenology, diagnostic criteria, and conceptual understanding are found in the psychoanalytic literature (Akhtar, 1987; Gabbard, 2000) as well as the *Diagnostic and Statistical Manual of Mental Disorders,* 4th Edition (DSM-IV) and DSM-IV—Text Revison (DSM-IV-TR) (American Psychiatric Association, 1994, 2000). Whether one views schizoid personality as a unitary phenomenon or as a more complex and inherently contradictory one depends on one's theoretical orientation, interest in descriptive versus dynamic diagnosis, and basic preference for diagnostic "lumping" versus "splitting." Official psychiatric classification is based on a contemporary descriptive–consensual approach, which according to the DSM-IV (American Psychiatric Association, 1994), seeks to reduce diagnostic uncertainty and increase the reliability and discriminatory power of psychiatric diagnosis to "enable clinicians and investigators to diagnose, communicate about, and study people with various mental disorders" (p. xi). Psychodynamic perspectives, on the other hand, have traditionally opted for a more textured or layered view of mental and personality disorders, which strives to explain the relation between surface behavioral manifestations and underlying personality structure and dynamics. For the most part, the DSM-IV tries to minimize or eliminate apparent contradictions and paradox, whereas psychodynamic diagnosis tends to embrace these as part of mental phenomena.

DSM AND THE DESCRIPTIVE APPROACH

The evolution of the modern DSM system has led to narrower and more homogeneous diagnostic criteria for schizoid personality disorder, with concurrent attempts to capture diagnostic discontinuities by formulating a separate category of avoidant personality (American Psychiatric Association, 1980, 1987, 1994, 2000). The committee that formulated the DSM-III believed that the DSM-II (American Psychiatric Association, 1968) had been overly broad in describing the schizoid personality disorder. The result was a subdivision of the disorder into three different categories: schizoid, avoidant, and schizotypal personalities.

Schizoid personality, in DSM-II, was originally defined as a behavior pattern manifesting

> shyness, oversensitivity, seclusiveness, avoidance of close or competitive relationships, and often eccentricity. Autistic thinking without loss of capacity to recognize reality is common, as are daydreaming and the inability to express hostility and ordinary aggressive feelings. These patients react to disturbing experiences and conflicts with apparent detachment. (p. 42)

The juxtaposition of the concepts of "avoidance of close and competitive relationships" and "apparent detachment," on the one hand, with that of "oversensitivity" on the other provided the background for the eventual splitting of the category into two distinct personality diagnoses. The concept of "autistic thinking" served as the basis for creating a third type, and also, in this case, schizotypal personality disorder.

Millon (1969, 1974, 1981, 1996) was a major influence in the creation of the personality disorders section of the DSM-III. He proposed a schema for conceptualizing the differences between different personality disorders in terms of the types of reinforcements (positive/pleasure versus negative/pain) an individual has sought the sources the individual has learned as providers of these reinforcements' (self vs. others), and the instrumental behaviors used to achieve them (passive vs. active). A person seeks gratification either by turning to him- or herself, by turning to others, or by detaching and looking to neither as a source of reinforcement. The schizoid personality, according to Millon (1981) employs a "passive-detached" strategy whereas, the avoidant personality uses an "active-detached" strategy to manage anxiety and achieve security.

Millon (1981) reviewed the historical and theoretical antecedents of the schizoid diagnosis, pointing to the work of Kretschmer (1925) in particular, who introduced subtle refinements in the nature of the schizoid character, which foreshadowed the DSM-III differentiation of schizoid from avoidant personality types. According to Kretschmer, there are two distinct subtypes of schizoid character. The one group, he termed "hyperaesthetic" and the other "anaesthetic." Hyperaesthetics are timid and shy individuals, who are anxious, excitable, extremely sensitive, and easily wounded. They feel things too intensely and seek to avoid painful stimulation from the outside world. They compare themselves negatively with others, feeling that they do not measure up. In contrast, the schizoid–anaesthetic type is an emotionally vacuous individual, whose external blandness and constriction mirrors his or her internal emptiness. These schizoid persons suffer what Kretschmer termed "affective lameness," or the lack of connection between emotional stimulus and motor–behavioral response. Humorless and dull, these individuals keep their distance, not so much for protection, but more because they lack any interest in connecting with the outside world, especially the world of relationships.

Millon (1981) drew a strong parallel between Kretschmer's (1925) schizoid subtypes and the subsequent parsing of the schizoid concept into two distinct personality disorders: the schizoid and the avoidant personalities. One can see the natural convergence between the hyperaesthetic subtype and the avoidant personality, who appreciates, but fears, social contact, and similarly, between aesthetic and schizoid personality, who eschews it entirely. Although Kretschmer (1925) apparently considered both the hyperaesthetic and anaesthetic subtypes both variants of a schizoid character, the DSM-III created two separate personality diagnoses as follows (Table 4.1).

According to the DSM III and IV, both personality types may appear isolated, detached, and lonely. However, if the patient is unambivalent about this detachment, then a diagnosis of schizoid personality is more appropriate. On the other hand, if the individual expresses any ambivalent wishes and fears regarding intimacy, then a diagnosis of avoidant personality disorder is indicated. Interestingly, in the modern DSM, schizoid personality is placed among the most severe "prepsychotic" personality disorders (cluster A), whereas avoidant personality is grouped among those higher level personality disorders for which anxiety management plays a more prominent role (cluster C). The result is two distinctly different diagnostic categories: one characterized by deficient interest in and ability to form intimate connections, and the other characterized by conflicts between intimacy wishes and fears of rejection.

The DSM schizoid personalities are remote because of preference (perhaps constitutionally based). Their affective and fantasy life are constricted and bland. They have little interest in sex and are indifferent to positive and negative feedback from others. Their remoteness and emotional coldness are quite egosyntonic. Nonetheless, in the text revision of the DSM-IV (American Psychiatric Association, 2000), it is stated that the schizoid person may, "under certain circumstances, reveal painful feelings regarding

TABLE 4.1
DSM-IV Diagnostic Criteria for Schizoid
and Avoidant Personality Disorders

Schizoid Personality	Avoidant Personality
A pervasive pattern of detachment from social relationships and a restricted range of expression of emotions in interpersonal settings, beginning by early adulthood and present in a variety of contexts, as indicated by four (or more) of the following:	A pervasive pattern of social inhibition, feelings of inadequacy, and hypersensitivity to negative evaluation, beginning by early adulthood and present in a variety of contexts, as indicated by four (or more) of the following:
1. Neither desires nor enjoys close relationships, including being part of a family	1. Avoids occupational activities that involve significant interpersonal contact, because of fears of criticism, disapproval, or rejection
2. Almost always chooses solitary activities	2. Is unwilling to get involved with people unless certain of being liked
3. Has little, if any, interest in having sexual experiences with another person	3. Shows restraint within intimate relationships because of the fear of being shamed or ridiculed
4. Takes pleasure in few, if any, activities	4. Is preoccupied with being criticized or rejected in social situations
5. Lacks close friends or confidants other than first-degree relatives	5. Is inhibited in new interpersonal situations because of feelings of inadequacy
6. Appears indifferent to the praise or criticism of others	6. Views self as socially inept, personally unappealing, or inferior to others
7. Shows emotional coldness, detachment, or flattened affectivity	7. Is unusually reluctant to take personal risks or to engage in any new activities because they may prove embarrassing

his/her social isolation" (p. 695). Thus, for the first time, the DSM has seemed to be acknowledging something more than emotional flatness and emptiness in the schizoid individual.

PSYCHOANALYTIC UNDERSTANDING

Akhtar (1987) and Gabbard (2000) reviewed psychoanalytic contributions to the understanding of the schizoid personality. It is principally the work of British object relations analysts that formed the underpinnings of the psychoanalytic perspective. Fairbairn (1954) took the lead in describing the schizoid as an individual who displays an attitude of omnipotence, emotional aloofness, and preoccupation with fantasy and inner reality. Fairbairn believed that schizoid individuals retreat because of a fear that their intense neediness would harm others. Winnicott (1965) viewed the schizoid personality as a variant of "false-self" organization. He believed that behind the façade of compliance, the schizoid harbored more intense anxieties about self-cohesion and bodily integrity. Guntrip (1968) elaborated upon the work of Fairbairn and described the schizoid as

> feeling cut off, shut off, out of touch, feeling apart or strange, of things being out of focus or unreal, of not feeling one with people, or of the point having gone out of life, interest flagging, things seeming futile and meaningless, all describe in various ways this state of mind. Patients call it "depression," but it lacks the heavy, black, inner sense of brooding, of anger or guilt, which are not difficult to discover in classic depression.... Depression is object-relational. The schizoid person has renounced objects, even though he still needs them. (pp. 17–18)

Guntrip (1968) indicated that the more people cut themselves off from human relationships, the more they are driven back into highly charged fantasies of internal object relationships. Most importantly, Guntrip said that the schizoid individual feels extremely insecure and lost when separated from his love objects, but swallowed and engulfed when reunited. Therefore, schizoid people may cling to others for security, but quickly attempt to break away for freedom and independence.

Khan (1963, 1974, 1983) traced this oscillating relational style to a peculiar mother–child relationship. On the one hand, the mother repeatedly failed in her ability to provide a protective shield or buffer for the child, leading to what Khan (1963) called "cumulative trauma" of relational deprivation. Yet, through close physical contact and indulgences, the mother maintained a "symbiotic omnipotence" that discouraged involvement with other objects. Khan (1963) described the consequences from the oscillating pattern of "cumulative trauma" and "symbiotic omnipotence" as pseudocompliance, self-sufficiency, intellectualization, withdrawal, autoeroticism, magical thinking, secret optimism, and oversensitivity.

Several unifying themes emerge in the contributions of the British School. First, there is more to the schizoid individual than meets the eye. Emotional detachment and social isolation notwithstanding, these are people with rich internal lives, intense emotional needs, fears, and fantasies. In other words, there is an inherent contradiction between the overt detachment and emotional constriction, on the one hand, and the intense covert needs and fears, on the other. Second, the schizoid person has experienced a maternal relationship that was both intensely dependent and emotionally depriving. Later analytic writers developed both themes further by elaborating how schizoid individuals lack an integrated sense of self and remain dependent on external objects for self-cohesion (Jacobson, 1964; Mahler, 1968).

Akhtar (1987) synthesized the opposing aspects of the schizoid personality by describing both overt and covert manifestations in six areas of psychosocial functioning: self-concept; interpersonal relations; social adaptation; love and sexuality; ethics, standards, and ideals; and cognitive style. Thus, according to Akhtar (1987),

> The schizoid individual is "overtly" detached, self-sufficient, absent-minded, uninteresting, asexual, and idiosyncratically moral while "covertly" being exquisitely sensitive, emotionally needy, acutely vigilant, creative, often, perverse, and vulnerable to corruption. (p. 510)

Kernberg (1976) included the schizoid personality among the "lower level" personality organizations, which are based on a number of ego weaknesses and primitive defenses. In particular, the presence of splitting creates schisms in the sense of self, making it difficult to integrate disparate, and sometimes contradictory, representations of self and other.

From a psychoanalytic perspective, the avoidant and schizoid personalities are two sides of the same coin, one overt, the other covert. Slightly different from the perspective Kretschmer (1925), who viewed these as two subtypes of schizoid personality, the integrated psychoanalytic perspective views the schizoid as a fragmented, borderline-level individual, whose lifelessness and detachment remain split apart from intense neediness and hypersensitivity.

Encapsulated Secondary Autism and the Second Skin

In her work with psychotic children, Tustin (1972) developed the concept of "encapsulated secondary autism" to describe the defensive retreat into isolation and detachment ("encapsulation") as a means of protecting the self from panic associated with unbearable bodily separateness. Although not talking specifically about the concept of schizoid personality, Tustin described how the depressed and vulnerable mother may not provide sufficient protection for her child to manage the anxiety of separateness.

Encapsulation is essentially a defense against the terror of premature separation. Encapsulation gives rise to a rigid character structure in which the individual defensively retreats into a shell or develops a "thick skin" to hide his or her hypersensitivity. Tustin (1972) called these children "crustaceans." They become detached from others and overly dependent upon established routines, which are experienced as protective wrappings that help ensure bodily survival. This need to preserve sameness lies at the root of the autistic child's repetition of the same patterns of behavior.

Although Tustin (1972) was talking about childhood autism and psychosis, her descriptions resonate with Akhtar's (1987) integrated psychoanalytic understanding of schizoid personality. Tustin's views are useful because they bring the schizoid concept closer to the phenomenon of higher functioning autism and Asperger's syndrome.

RESEARCH FINDINGS

There has been relatively little research on the assessment of schizoid personality disorder with the Rorschach. Costello (1989) provided a case study of an individual hospitalized in a "therapeutic community for alcoholics" (p. 322) who completed the 16PF (Karson & O'Dell, 1976), Minnesota Multiphasic Personality Inventory (MMPI) Locus of Control Scale (Rotter, 1966), and Rorschach. The latter was administered and scored using the Beck scoring system (Beck, Beck, Levitt, & Molish, 1961). The following results were obtained: M:Sum C = 2:2, F% = 68.4, Lambda = 2.17, F+% = 92.3, and Populars = 10. The second author of this chapter (S. K. H.) rescored the responses (listed in the appendix of the case study) using the Comprehensive System. The following results were obtained: FT = 1, FM = 2, M = 2, CF = 1, FC = 2, H = 0, (H) = 1, A = 11, (A) = 2, Ad = 2, An = 1, (2) = 8, a:p = 1:3, MOR = 2, FABCOM 1 = 2, DV = 2, Hh = 1, and Art = 1. Furthermore, the patient's 16PF was consistent with a schizoid profile, and his MMPI Welsh code was 2″ 70 81′ 5364–/9:F–/KL:. Some of his responses included percepts of cartoon characters and insects. Oral themes also were observed (e.g., cartoon characters watering a plant, insects arguing, puppies begging, and a moth that was "bad about eating clothes," p. 325), which included themes of unsatisfying and potentially threatening relationships.

Khadavi, Wetzler, and Wilson (1997) evaluated manic inpatients, paranoid schizophrenics, and schizoaffective inpatients on the Rorschach, including an evaluation of patients' scores on the Schizoid–Affective Rating Scale (Carsky & Bloomgarden, 1980). On this scale, content is scored for "schizoid or schizophrenic themes [that] are nonconventional (e.g., a mask of war), bizarre (e.g., female organs with teeth), other worldly (e.g., two people from Mars), unreal (e.g., weird face), impersonal (e.g., walls between people), and without boundaries (e.g., figures blending into shadows)" (p. 369). No significant differences were observed among groups. Unfortunately, there seems to be little published research to evaluate the reliability and validity of this scale. It also is unclear whether this scale is meant to assess schizoid, schizotypal, and schizophrenic thinking and content differentially, given the ambiguous language used by the authors and the manual. (This problem may reflect, in part, the lack of diagnostic differentiation in the DSM at the time the manual was assembled.)

Most of the research on the assessment of schizoid personality disorder has been conducted in three domains: (a) its distinctiveness and relationship to schizophrenia spectrum disorders, (b) semistructured interviews, and (c) neurologic functioning. These are discussed in turn.

As noted earlier, the characterization of schizoid personality disorder has evolved in the DSM nomenclature. Of note is its relation to the schizophrenia spectrum disorders. Gunderson, Siever, and Spaulding (1983) have suggested that the transmission of negative schizophrenia symptoms may account, in part, for the development of a schizoid personality disorder. Battaglia, Bernardeschi, Franchini, Bellodi, and Smeraldi (1995) reported that the risk for schizoid personality disorder was significantly higher in schizotypal probands than in control subjects. They concluded that schizoid personality disorder and schizophrenia may lie along a continuum of schizophrenic illness, consistent with the conclusions of Siever and Kendler (1987). However, this issue is far from settled (Kalus, Bernstein, & Siever, 1995). For instance, schizoid personality disorder can be differentiated from schizotypal and borderline personality disorder on a composite scale of schizoid features created from several measures of schizoid personality (Raine, 1987).

Several diagnostic interviews can be used to assess schizoid personality disorder including the Structured Interview for DSM-IV Personality Disorders (Pfohl, Blum, & Zimmerman, 1995), the Personality Disorder Examination (Loranger, 1988), the International Personality Disorder Examination (Lornager, 1999), and the Structured Clinical Interview for DSM-IV Axis II Disorders (First, Gibbon, Spitzer, Williams, & Benjamin, 1997). Rogers (2001) has reviewed the psychometric properties of these instruments in detail. Some of these findings are highlighted. First, there has not been a wide body of research on the DSM-IV version of these measures. Thus, it is somewhat difficult to judge the utility of their present form. Second, across the various editions of these measures, evidence for the interrater and test–retest reliabilities has been varied (Dreessen, Hildebrand, & Arntz, 1998; Riso, Klein, Anderson, Ouimette, & Lizardi, 1994; Zimmerman, Pfohl, Coryell, Stangl, & Corenthal, 1988). Third, the validity of these measures has been suspect. The Structured Interview for DSM-IV Personality Disorder (SIDP) has had low to moderate correlations with self-report measures of personality disorders (e.g., MMPI personality disorder scales), with correlations among cluster A personality disorders ranging between .21 and .41. In four studies, concurrent validity coefficients between the Personality Disorder Examination (PDE) and SCID-II for cluster A personality disorders ranged between .08 and .28, and in another four studies, the validity coefficients between the PDE and Personality Diagnostic Questionnaire–Revised (Hyler, 1994; Hyler & Reider, 1987) ranged between .08 and .28. Finally, one study has suggested that there is poor external validity for the Personality Interview Questionnaire—II (precursor to the Personality Diagnostic Questionnaire-IV [PDQ-IV]). Widiger, Mangine, Corbitt, Ellis, and Thomas (1995) found that the schizoid personality disorder did not correlate with any "schizoid prototypic acts" (p. 249).

There is some evidence for the utility of other self-report measures of schizoid personality disorder. Coolidge and Merwin (1992) evaluated the psychometric properties of the Coolidge Axis II Inventory, which was based on DSM-III-R criteria. The Cronbach alpha for the schizoid scale was .73, but the correlation with this scale and the Millon Clinical Multiaxial Inventory–II (MCMI-II) Schizoid scale was .22. However, this poor finding may be attributable to the fact that schizoid personality disorder was not diagnosed for any individuals in this study. A principal components analysis of their measure yielded three factors, with dependent and schizoid loading most heavily on factor three. In this case, the dependent factor loading was .91, whereas the schizoid loading was –.94. Coolidge and Merwin's (1992) findings also are consistent with the findings of West, Rose, & Sheldon-Keller, (1994), who differentiated schizoid and dependent individuals by their attachment types: schizoid and dependent, respectively. Hicklin and Widiger (2000) evaluated the Somwaru and Ben-Porath (1995) revisions to the MMPI Personality Disorder Scales (Morey, Waugh, & Blashfield, 1985). They found positive correlations between this the schizoid scale and the MCMI-III schizoid scale ($r = .79$) and the PDQ-IV ($r = .71$). Internal consistency reliabilities also were good ($r = .85$).

The final domains within which schizoid personality disorder has been assessed are the cognitive and neurologic domains. Neuchterlein et al. (2002) evaluated neurocognitive deficits in first-degree relatives of schizophrenics using data from the UCLA Family Study. Results from measures of continuous performance, encoding and efficient visual search, sequential visual conceptual tracking, vocabulary, and DSM-III-R schizotypal personality disorder symptoms were combined to derive seven factors, including one they labeled as "schizoid symptoms." This factor was independent of the negative and positive schizotypy and cognitive disorganization factors. Cuesta, Peralta, and Zarzuela (2001) evaluated psychiatric inpatients admitted for a psychotic episode. In contrast to Neuchterlein et al. (2002), they found that the schizoid dimension of the Personality Assessment Schedule (Tyrer, 1988; Tyrer & Johnson, 1996) was positively correlated with both memory and executive functioning dimensions on several neuropsychological tests, including the Wechsler Adult Intelligence Scale and the Wisconsin Card Sorting Task.

In summary, little research has been conducted to investigate Rorschach variables associated with schizoid personality disorder. The assessment research to date appears to indicate that schizoid personality disorder may fall within a biologic spectrum of schizophrenic illness. Diagnostic interviews appear to have mixed findings regarding their validity, and neurocognitive deficits may be related to schizoid personality traits. Because these findings are equivocal, it seems that further evaluation of the Rorschach may yield additional information that would improve the assessment of schizoid personality disorder.

The case that follows illustrates the contradictions inherent in the schizoid concept and the diagnostic confusion that comes from efforts to separate the syndrome into two separate diagnostic categories.

CASE EXAMPLE: MR. PAXTON

Mr. Paxton was referred for psychoanalytic consultation from the outpatient clinic where he had been seen off and on for several years. He had been seeing a psychiatrist, who had prescribed antidepressant medication for chronic sleep difficulties, depression, and irritability. The long-standing nature of his complaints prompted the referral for consultation.

Since retiring from the postal service 10 years earlier at the age of 45, Mr. Paxton had felt "lost" and dissatisfied with his life. He complained of feeling "adrift," underachieving, frequently depressed, and unable to accomplish anything. Although he had retired after 25 years in the postal service working at solitary jobs that involved little interaction with others, he expressed extreme dissatisfaction with himself and disappointment in how his life had turned out. Despite supportive therapy, which he attended irregularly, and antidepressant medication, he continued to feel enormously frustrated. He was not gainfully employed, living only on a small government pension, which was barely sufficient to meet his needs. Mr. Paxton worked part-time, without monetary compensation, at a "friend's" convenience store and felt frustrated with his difficulties following through with his perpetual attempts to get a "real" full-time job.

Over the past 20 years, he had tried to take classes, always dropping out after a few days or weeks. Even while working at the convenience store, he combed the classified ads for job openings and kept detailed files of information about those jobs that showed potential. However, when one of his many job applications was accepted, he typically never showed up, only to begin his search all over again the next day.

Mr. Paxton was the only child of parents who divorced when he was 2 years old. His father died of cancer in the 1970s, and his mother had to be placed in a nursing home about the time he retired from the postal service. His relationship with his father had always been distant. He felt that his father was never involved in his life and provided nothing for him. His mother, by contrast, had been very close, yet paradoxically quite distant, and he referred to their relationship as "two islands" of separate existence. He indicated that she worked hard in a factory to provide for his physical needs, but believed she was overwhelmed by work and child-care responsibilities. He remembered how she used to carry him everywhere, but rarely talked to him.

When he became a teenager, she found herself unable to manage his behavior by herself. Because he had gotten into some trouble in school, she arranged to have him admitted to the state hospital for roughly 18 months. He later attended high school, eventually graduating and enlisting in the military. Mr. Paxton served a brief tour on active duty, then left the military and began working for the postal service.

Mr. Paxton had never married and felt that he had never had any friends. His closest relationship was with Mrs. G, a woman several years older than he who, besides his mother, had been the only other person in his life for the past 25 years. Although their relationship was initially sexual, this had lasted a few short months, after which their relationship became platonic and nonsexual. Mrs. G was a widow who owned the convenience store where he worked. She prepared all of his meals and did his laundry. In return, he worked for her without pay.

Mr. Paxton shared his ultimate concern that he would die alone. He had a vision of living by himself, as he had always done, and dying in a small apartment somewhere. He said that he hated his dreary and empty life, the boring sameness and absence of social connections. However, as much as he berated himself for his lonely and bleak existence, he boasted that he felt comfortable living alone and being unattached to anyone.

Mr. Paxton lived in the house wherein he had been born. Until his mother had grown severely demented, the two had lived together as "two islands." He tended to his house, but spent as little time there as possible. When not working at Mrs. G's store, he would drive around town, going from one coffee shop to another, rarely engaging in small talk with the waitresses or other customers. On occasion, he would develop a passing interest in one of the waitresses. However, nothing ever came of this.

Every few years, Mr. Paxton would purchase a new wardrobe, only to wrap his new clothes in plastic and keep them in the basement. Although he would periodically check on them, he was unable to put them on and wear them. His explanation of this inability was vague and repetitive. The clothes just did not "feel" right to him. Or more significantly, he did not feel right in them. Instead, each day, he donned the same outfit, a pair of neatly creased, but very tight, jeans and a snug jean jacket. He described how his jean jacket, in particular, provided him with a layer, something to come between his skin and the outside environment, which made him feel comfortable. He agonized over what to do when the weather changed and it became unbearably warm.

Mr. Paxton did not express fears about rejection or disapproval in particular. In fact, he said that as much as he wanted to change and be able to connect with people, he would fight every effort, including those of the analyst, to get him to change and give up what for him was the security of his isolation and detachment. His words often were evocative and almost poetic: "I've found myself a home and you're not gonna destroy it. That's where the resistance to changing is. I've established this in my head and will fight to death to hold onto what's mine."

Having tried other forms of supportive therapy, he expressed strong motivation to begin a psychoanalytic process. Once analysis began, themes of "lifelessness" and "coming alive" were evident. The patient's questions about whether he was a man or machine, living or dead inside, reflected a parallel countertransference experience in which I either felt keenly interested in and connected to him or, conversely, dreaded the lifeless, repetitive quality of the analytic hours.

Tustin (1972) addressed the "man or machine" issue by describing how many autistic children "seem to feel that they are an inanimate thing teetering on the edge of becoming alive and human. To become alive and human is frightening, because, as such, they could get hurt and die " (p. 44).

During one exchange about his growing attachment to and dependence on me, Mr. Paxton wondered if I was trying to take the place of a surrogate father for him. I invited his thoughts, and he protested that this was "ludicrous" because he was too old for this. Then he added, "I could just be suspicious that in the sense that you'd [he always referred to himself in the third person] be wary of someone trying to do that. Maybe subconsciously you'd want someone to do that, but there'd be a lack of trust of someone doing that and you'd hold them at arm's length. The bottom line is that there'd be a conflict between wanting it and not wanting it."

Rorschach Findings

The discussion of the Rorschach findings is organized according to key aspects of ego functioning, self, and object relations.

Affect and Controls Clusters. A surprising degree of inner turmoil and emotional perturbation is evident from Mr. Paxton's Structural Summary. Although both D and Adj D were 0, Mr. Paxton is experiencing significant subjective distress associated with painful feelings of loneliness, self-loathing, and dysphoria. Despite his efforts to manage his feelings on an intellectual level, Mr. Paxton vacillates ineffectively between thoughtless emotional reactivity, on the one hand, and thinking without emotion, on the other. That is, he has an ambitent problem-solving style. Perhaps going from one extreme to the other makes him rather unpredictable, with it never being clear whether he will respond in a thoughtful or emotional manner. When he experiences affect, he feels things intensely. His feeling states are diffuse and poorly integrated. Containment of strong feelings is a problem, as Mr. Paxton may have trouble regulating and modulating his emotional intensity (CF = 4).

Mr. Paxton's Rorschach is full of evidence to suggest that control of anger is an ongoing struggle. Six S responses and two AG special scores indicate a substantial amount of unmetabolized aggression and negativity. His second response to Card I shows how he may struggle to cloak his aggression behind a genteel and almost obsequious manner. After giving the response of a "stealth aircraft," Mr. Paxton "hopes" that he isn't "boring" the examiner "to death." His words reveal both the dangerous impulse and efforts to ward this off, as he feels compelled to check with the examiner to make sure that his silent anger has not caused harm.

The appearance of his "stealth aircraft" response and "boring you to death" comment follow Mr. Paxton's opening response to Card I (and the Rorschach), which thematically depicts the lifelessness that remains after something that is both vital and protective has been violently taken away. His initial morbid response of a skull with flesh "stripped away" evokes a profound sense of both deadening bleakness and great vulnerability. The outer covering and source of liveliness has been "stripped away," adding to the sense of traumatic vulnerability and lack of adequate protection. All that remains without this protective covering is a drying skull, something dead and lifeless. That his "stealth aircraft," complete with "cockpit" and "weapons," should occur after his opening morbid content (MOR) response suggests a defensive flight from vulnerability and loss to a more distant world of things—powerful and dangerous things that can kill you. No longer is he left with either the trauma of having his protection and security stripped away or the lifeless aftermath. Instead, Mr. Paxton identifies with the power and ominous threat of death and destruction. The vulnerability of his "stripped away" status is replaced by robotic strength and power.

In his next response to Card I, Mr. Paxton retreats even further from the painful vicissitudes of vulnerability and aggression and into a more remote and isolated personal landscape. His response of "the reflection of a landmass" suggests another means of distancing himself from threatening turmoil. A reflection of something so inanimate indicates not only being cut off from others, but an exquisite sense of isolation. What defines his landmass is "all of the empty open space around it." We find a similar sequence of going from a traumatically exposed and damaged image on card IV (response 16) to a distant view of a landmass (Card VII, response 19).

Mediation, Ideation, and Processing Clusters. Ego strength is suggested by an absence of severe signs of illogical thinking. Although some special scores occur, these are benign (level 1), and at most, suggest a slight looseness to Mr. Paxton's thinking in more unstructured situations. In terms of reality testing, the arousal of strong affect seems to have a negative effect on his ability to form accurate impressions and distinguish internal from external reality. His minus form level response to Card VIII reflects this regressive shift in reality testing when affect is stirred.

Nonetheless, certain psychic strengths are suggested by the presence of a moderate Lambda and balanced a:p ratio. Signs of mental flexibility and openness to experience contrast with clinical and historical data suggesting great inflexibility and difficulty shifting sets. As such, the presence of these markers may signal a hidden potential to be open to different perspectives. Furthermore, there is evidence that Mr. Paxton is motivated to grasp complex concepts and strive to higher levels of functioning. However, the W:M ratio suggests that Mr. Paxton's grasp may exceed his actual reach, sowing the seeds for feelings of discouragement and disappointment about the gap between aspiration and accomplishment.

Part of the difficulty may be Mr. Paxton's tendency to retreat from adaptive problem-solving efforts into fantasy, as suggested by his $M^P > M^a$. Instead of effectively translating his ambitions into action plans, Mr. Paxton escapes into fantasy. Here, he may console himself with fantasies of how he may suddenly someday change or how someone else will come along and deliver him from his distress. Either way, little forward movement occurs in the real world.

Self-Perception and Interpersonal Clusters.
Mr. Paxton's reflected landmass response suggests a degree of self-absorption that cuts him off and makes it difficult for him to have his needs met and empathize with other people. It is interesting that following his first three responses to Card I, he associates with something not fully human. He produces an M^P percept of a headless woman frozen in motion. Special emphasis is given to the "heavy dress or gown" she is wearing. She is stretching up, but cannot be fully human and alive because she has no head. Like his Card III response describing the front part of a tuxedo, his headless woman comes close to being a set of clothes, or outer coverings, without a person inside.

Despite Mr. Paxton's defensive efforts either to indulge in fantasies of power and strength or to view himself as an island, in need of no one else, his Rorschach reveals an embattled sense of self. His vista response suggests that his self-absorption may reflect a great deal of self-loathing and harsh self-criticism. His multiple MOR responses, depicting the "stripping" or "ripping" away of skin or outside covering, suggest not only a sense of being left unprotected and overexposed, but also a sense of having one's protective layering violently taken away. All that is left behind is the wreckage of something either dead or terribly damaged.

These MOR responses, depicting the aftermath of aggression, are highly reminiscent of Tustin's (1972) discussion of encapsulated secondary autism and the "second skin phenomena" (Bick, 1968). Encapsulation and reliance on a second skin binds the vulnerable sense of self that feels threatened by a traumatic and premature separation, the absence of an emotionally attuned and responsive mother, and the consequent failure to internalize maternal soothing and holding functions.

Encapsulation, as a protection against the dangerous and threatening outside world, has a rigidifying effect on the character. Schizoid individuals such as Mr. Paxton may become overly dependent on established routines, which they experience as protective wrappings that ensure bodily survival. These "crustaceans" hide their oversensitivity beneath a hardened outer shell or thick skin. Mr. Paxton's ever present tight-fitting jeans and jacket are a kind of "second skin," without which he feels exposed and insecure. Interestingly, response 26 is a "some type of crustacean."

The "man–machine" dilemma, previously described, is reflected by a number of scores and responses. The H: (H)+Hd+(Hd) index indicates a limited capacity to identify with real people. Internalizing part- and non-human objects (e.g., Hd, Ad) occurred more readily than the internalization of soothing and sustaining representations of real people (pure H). Several responses reveal a condensation of animate and inanimate, human and nonhuman features. For example, response 13 is a bat. However, reference to the bat's wings as "hinged" conveys a subtle mechanization. Further compounding this incongruity is the fact that this also is a texture response. The bat is "furry." Thus, the subtle oddity of this response juxtaposes something that is coldly mechanical with a craving for contact. Likewise, Mr. Paxton's aircraft wreckage response to Card VI (response 18) shows the interpenetration of the concepts of machine and living tissue. It should be noted that this was not given a special score because the outer coverings of aircraft are sometimes referred to as "skins."

Mr. Paxton demonstrates a surprising capacity to form connections (good M's and GHR > PHR). However, closeness seems accompanied by aggression. On Card II (response 7), two animals are touching nose to nose, but the animals turn out to be bloodied wolves that have been fighting. On Card III, he sees two people pulling something apart. The figures are in conflict. According to Mr. Paxton, "They are sharing something or they don't want to share something." This response is highly reminiscent of Mr. Paxton's words regarding whether to let the analyst become more important to him (described earlier).

A significant number of texture responses reveal a hidden neediness that belies Mr. Paxton's apparent aloofness and self-sufficiency. The cat response (Card IV, response 12) also is furry, but it is skinned, laid out, and has had its skull removed. A craving for contact is associated with a painful sense of vulnerability and loss. Nowhere is this theme more evident than in Mr. Paxton's third response to Card III (response 10) of "fetuses with umbilical cords attached to them. There is the head curled up like this one. This is the umbilical cord, and it looks like it's bloody from the color."

A vital connection has been threatened or damaged. The response that follows this vivid depiction of disrupted symbiosis is a "whirlpool." At least five times, Mr. Paxton makes reference to inanimate movement in this response, suggesting that powerful anxiety is unleashed in the context of threats to his primary attachments.

Despite his agitated neediness, Mr. Paxton leaves us with a distant and isolated image of himself. Ending the Rorschach, he signs out with "these look like two islands." Empty space surrounds two small details, which exist apart from everything else.

Mr. Paxton's Rorschach reveals a startling degree of emotional complexity and intensity in a man who feels both comforted and cursed by being a loner. The extent of highly charged affect, fantasy, neediness, and conflict remains encapsulated beneath the thick crust of his protective schizoid layering. To minimize anxiety, Mr. Paxton wrapped himself in a second skin made up of a monotonous daily routine, maintaining chronic interpersonal isolation and detachment, sticking close to his childhood home, and wearing his tight jeans and jacket. Together, these formed a collective buffer against a tantalizing but terrifying world. Mr. Paxton was not a hermit, who lived alone and never crossed the path of another human being. On the contrary, he often was around people, but always at an extremely great distance, watching but never coming too close. He once poignantly described himself as a "dead star," trying to seek warmth by passing close to the warmth of the sun.

Viewing him diagnostically as an avoidant rather than schizoid personality may satisfy DSM criteria, but it seems to oversimply the nature of his anxiety and internal world. Earlier anxieties, more basic than the affects of shame, embarrassment, fear of rejection, or disapproval, were in operation. More primitive fears of annihilation made Mr. Paxton keep his distance and stick to his deadening routine.

Tustin (1972) commented that it is more possible to help "crustacean" children than the "amoebas," a term she reserved for "passive, flaccid children," perhaps similar to Kretschmer's (1925) empty anaethetic–schizoid subtype. The "crustaceans," by contrast, have tried to manage threats of annihilation through encapsulation: "The tragedy is that it may result in their being permanently cut off from ordinary life and people because they have an extraordinary outside shell instead of an ordinary inside breast" (p. 54).

Over the course of three years, Mr. Paxton completed more than 500 hours of psychoanalysis. The day-to-day analytic discourse was character- ized by an oscillation between his deadening ruminations about his symp- toms and the boring sameness of his life, on the one hand, and his growing capacity to reflect on the lack of meaning in his life, his terror of changing, and his intensely ambivalent longings for closer relationships on the other.

Although Mr. Paxton said that he had grown more comfortable around people, there were few significant changes in his relational world outside of the analysis. He continued to struggle with inhibitions around going into a dangerous world and connecting with others. However, at the time he de- cided to terminate therapy, he had secured a full-time job as a janitor and felt enthused about going to work every day. Although he continued to view himself as a loner, Mr. Paxton said that he had begun to feel more alive inside. He said that he felt as though there was a "fresh breeze" blowing through his head, giving him greater clarity of focus: "It just feels like an ice jam is starting to break up and the water is beginning to flow through. I ba- sically feel more comfortable in my own skin."

Whereas the focus of this chapter is on a case study of an individual with schizoid personality disorder, a large body of research on the Rorschach assessment of schizoid personality disorder is needed. First, a large sam- ple of schizoid individuals is needed to generate a normative sample to substantiate the single-case findings described in this chapter. Because schizoid individuals rarely seek treatment, such a task likely will be diffi- cult to accomplish. However, published case studies and attempts to pro- vide group data for schizoid personality disorder would be useful in providing clinicians and researchers with some guidance on the Ror- schach patterns commonly observed in such individuals.

Second, research on the utility of the Rorschach for assessing schizoid personality disorder in comparison with other instruments is needed to demonstrate the incremental validity of the Rorschach for detecting and characterizing schizoid personality disorder over that of self-report mea- sures and clinical interviews. Given the detached and aloof lifestyle of many schizoid individuals, and the common perception that schizoid indi- viduals live in an autistic-like psychic state, the Rorschach has much poten- tial to elucidate the rich, internal emotional life experienced by such patients. Such elucidation may provide clinicians with some insight into treatment planning with schizoid individuals.

Because of the similarities between schizoid and avoidant personalities, a third area of important research would focus on the ability of the Ror- schach to differentiate schizoid and avoidant personalities. There is an important reason to believe that this might be a fruitful task. As noted earlier, the schizoid individual is overtly indifferent to social relationships and many of life's pleasures, whereas the avoidant individual is anxious about social contact and desperately desires it. Although both types of individuals may appear withdrawn and reserved, the Rorschach may detect that avoidant personalities have a higher level of social interest via a greater number of human contents, whereas schizoid persons may have less human content and a greater reliance on fantasy. Reliance on a clinical interview or self-report measures for this task, however, may be of equivocal validity (as discussed earlier).

REFERENCES

Akhtar, S. (1987). Schizoid personality disorder: A synthesis of developmental, dynamic, and descriptive features. *American Journal of Psychotherapy, 61*, 499–518.

American Psychiatric Association. (1968). *Diagnostic and statistical manual of mental disorders* (2nd ed). Washington, DC: American Psychiatric Association.

American Psychiatric Association. (1980). *Diagnostic and statistical manual of mental disorders* (3rd ed). Washington, DC: American Psychiatric Association.

American Psychiatric Association. (1987). *Diagnostic and statistical manual of mental disorders* (3rd ed.–Revised). Washington, DC: American Psychiatric Association.

American Psychiatric Association. (1994). *Diagnostic and statistical manual of mental disorders* (4th ed.). Washington, DC: American Psychiatric Association.

American Psychiatric Association. (2000). *Diagnostic and statistical manual of mental disorders* (4th ed. Text Revision). Washington, DC: American Psychiatric Association.

Battaglia, M., Bernardeschi, L., Franchini, L., Bellodi, L., & Smeraldi, E. (1995). A family study of schizotypal disorder. *Schizophrenia Bulletin, 21*, 33–45.

Beck, S. J., Beck, A. G., Levitt, E. E., & Molish, H. B. (1961). *Rorschach's Test: I. Basic Processes.* New York: Grune & Stratton.

Bick, E. (1968). The experience of skin in early object relations. *International Journal of Psychoanalysis, 49*, 484–486.

Carsky, M., & Bloomgarden, J. W. 1980). *A manual for scoring affective and schizotypal responses on the Rorschach.* Unpublished manuscript.

Coolidge, F. L., & Merwin, M. M. (1992). Reliability and validity of the Coolidge Axis II Inventory: A new inventory for the assessment of personality disorders. *Journal of Personality Assessment, 59*, 223–238.

Costello, R. M. (1989). Schizoid personality disorder: A rare type in alcoholic populations. *Journal of Personality Disorders, 3*, 321–328.

Cuesta, M. J., Peralta, V., & Zarzuela, A. (2001). Are personality traits associated with cognitive disturbance in psychosis? *Schizophrenia Research, 51*, 109–177.

Dreesen, L., Hildebrand, M., & Arntz, A. (1998). Patient–informant concordance for Structured Clinical Interview for DSM-III-R Personality Disorder (SCID-II). *Journal of Personality Disorders, 12*, 149–161.

Fairbairn, W. R. D. (1954). *An object relations theory of personality.* New York: Basic Books.

First, M. B., Gibbon, M., Spitzer, R. L., Williams, J. B. W., & Benjamin, L. S. (1997). *The structured clinical interview for DSM-IV Axis II disorders*. Washington, DC: American Psychiatric Association.

Gabbard, G. O. (2000). *Psychodynamic psychiatry in clinical practice*. Washington, DC: American Psychiatric Press.

Gunderson, J. G., Siever, L. J., & Spaulding, E. (1983). The search for a schizotype: Crossing the border again. *Archives of General Psychiatry, 40*, 15–22.

Guntrip, H. J. S. (1968). *Schizoid phenomena, object-relations, and the self*. New York: International Universities Press.

Hicklin, J., & Widiger, T. A. (2000). Convergent validity of alternative MMPI-2 personality disorder scales. *Journal of Personality Assessment, 75*, 502–518.

Hyler, S. E. (1994). *Personality diagnostic questionnaire-4 (PDQ-4)*. Unpublished test, New York State Psychiatric Institute.

Hyler, S. E., & Reider, R. O. (1987). *Personality diagnostic questionnaire-revised (PDQ-R)*. New York: Authors.

Jacobson, E. (1964). *The self and the object world*. New York: International Universities Press.

Kalus, O., Bernstein, D. P., & Siever, L. J. (1995). Schizoid personality disorder. In W. J. Livesley (Ed.), *The DSM-IV personality disorders* (pp. 58–70). New York: Guilford.

Karson, S., & O'Dell, J. W. (1976). *A guide to the clinical use of the 16PF*. Champaign, IL: Institute for Personality and Ability Testing.

Kernberg, O. (1976). *Object relations theory and clinical psychoanalysis*. New York: Jason Aronson.

Khadavi, A., Wetzler, S., & Wilson, A. (1997). Manic indices on the Rorschach. *Journal of Personality Assessment, 69*, 365–275.

Khan, M. M. R. (1963). The concept of cumulative trauma. *Psychoanalytic Study of the Child, 18*, 286–306.

Khan, M. M. R. (1974). *The privacy of the self*. New York: International Universities Press.

Khan, M. M. R. (1983). *The hidden selves*. New York: International Universities Press.

Kretschmer, E. (1925). *Physique and character*. New York: Harcourt Brace.

Loranger, A. W. (1988). *Personality disorder examination (PDE) manual*. Yonkers, NY: DV Communications.

Loranger, A. W. (1999). *International personality disorder examination (IPDE) manual*. Odessa, FL: Psychological Assessment Resources.

Mahler, M. S. (1968). Autism and symbiosis: Two extreme disturbances of identity. In *The selected papers of Margaret Mahler* (Vol. I). New York: International Universities Press.

Millon, T. (1969). *Modern psychopathology: A biosocial approach to maladaptive learning and functioning*. Philadelphia: W.B. Saunders.

Millon, T. (1974). *Abnormal behavior and personality*. Philadelphia: W.B. Saunders.

Millon, T. (1981). *Disorders of personality: DSM III, Axis II*. New York: John Wiley.

Millon, T. (1996). *Disorders of personality and beyond*. New York: John Wiley.

Morey, L. C., Waugh, M. H., & Blashfield, R. K. (1985). MMPI scales for DSM-II personality disorders: Their derivation and correlates. *Journal of Personality Assessment, 49*, 245–251.

Nuechterlein, K. H., Asarnow, R. F., Subotnik, K. L., Fogelson, D. L., Payne, D. L., Kendler, K. S., et al. (2002). The structure of schizotypy: Relationships between neurocognitive and personality disorder features in relatives of schizophrenic patients in the UCLA Family Study. *Schizophrenia Research, 53,* 121–130.

Pfohl, B., Blum, N., & Zimmerman, M. (1995). *The structured interview for DSM-IV personality: SIDP-IV.* Iowa City: University of Iowa.

Raine, A. (1987). Validation of schizoid personality scales using indices of schizotypal and borderline personality disorder in a criminal population. *British Journal of Clinical Psychology, 26,* 305–309.

Riso, L. P., Klein, D. N., Anderson, R. L., Ouimette, P. C., & Lizardi, H. (1994). Concordance between patients and informants on the personality disorder examination. *American Journal of Psychiatry, 151,* 568–573.

Rogers, R. (2001). *Handbook of diagnostic and structured interviewing.* New York: Guilford.

Rotter, J. B. (1966). Generalized expectancies for internal vs. external control of reinforcement. *Journal of Consulting and Clinical Psychology, 43,* 56–67.

Siever, L. J., & Kendler, (1987). An interim evaluation of DSM-III categories of paranoid, schizoid, and schizotypal personality disorder. In G. Tischler (Ed.), *Diagnosis and classification in psychiatry.* Cambridge, England: Cambridge University Press.

Somwaru, D. P., & Ben-Porath, Y. S. (1995, March). *Development and reliability of MMPI-2–based personality disorder scales.* Paper presented at the 30th Annual Workshop and Symposium on Recent Developments in Use of the MMPI-2 and MMPI-A. St. Petersburg Beach, FL.

Tustin, F. (1972). *Autism and childhood psychoses.* London: Science House.

Tyrer, P. J. (1988). *Personality disorder. Diagnosis, management, and course.* London: Wright.

Tyrer, P. J., & Johnson, T. (1996). Establishing the severity of personality disorder. *American Journal of Psychiatry, 153,* 1593–1597.

West, M., Rose, S., & Sheldon-Keller, A. (1994). Assessment of patterns of insecure attachment in adults and application to dependent and schizoid personality disorders. *Journal of Personality Disorders, 8,* 249–256.

Widiger, T. A., Mangine, S., Corbitt, E. M., Ellis, C. G., & Thomas, G. V. (1995). *Personality disorder interview-IV.* Odessa, FL: Psychological Assessment Resources.

Winnicott, D. W. (1965). *The maturational process and the facilitating environment.* New York: International Universities Press.

Zimmerman, M., Pfohl, B., Coryell, W., Stangl, D., & Corenthal, C. (1988). Diagnosing personality disorder in depressed patients: A comparison of patient and informant interviews. *Archives of General Psychiatry, 45,* 733–737.

Free Association	Inquiry
Card I	
1. Looks like the head of something to me. It looks like a skull. Like cattle or a steer or something like that. Eyes, mouth, and ears. Like a frontal view of a skull that's basically it. Can you turn it or do you have to look at it this was. (It's up to you).	1. The eyes and the ears. This is the front of the skull. This is the back here. Looks like flesh has been stripped away from it, and this is just the drying skull. There are the eye sockets, and this is the mouth. This would be the nasal area. (Dry?) Looks like that's it. It's dead. (What about it?) The shape of it is what I am trying to get at.
2. Or, it could be a futuristic aircraft. Wings and body mostly. This could be the cockpit. Weapons here and exhaust. I don't see anything else.	2. Body and wings. Weapons here in the front. This is the tail. Something like a stealth aircraft. You see them all the time. I hope this isn't boring you to death. (You have concerns about this?) I wonder if it sounds plausible. (Stealth?) The shape of it. The angles and wide body.
3. Or it could be a landmass. If it was a landmass it would be like it was reflected off a mirror.	3. See the reflection of that mass in the mirror. (What about it looks like a landmass?) The borders of it. This could be the dividing line. This could be the mirror. This here looks like the surrounding sea. (Sea?) Because of all the empty open space around it.
4. Middle part could be a body of a woman. This could be her hands stretched up but no head.	4. This being the upper area waist line. She's wearing a heavy dress or gown or something like this. This being the belt buckle here. Hands sticking up, holding her hands like that (A heavy dress?) The fullness through the body looks like one of those dresses from way back in the past. (Buckle?) Just because it's in the middle. Just above the hips.
Card II	
5. Again, this could be an aircraft in the middle, and this red back here could be the exhaust. This is part of the cockpit.	5. Futuristic type aircraft. Nose, main body, the wings. This is the tail, and this the exhaust. (What about it made it look like that?) Because it looks like streaks through the black and gives me the impression of exhaust or fire coming out of the tail pipe here.

6. This could be two animals here. The dark spots. This is the muzzle. Two dogs. Wolfs, nose to nose. Red spots mean they've been fighting. This could be the blood.

6. Two dogs or wolves touching nose to nose. This looks like fighting because it looks like blood here on them. (What about blood?) It just looks like blood, like they're fighting. The color of it. The way it's smeared and dried. (Dried?) Looks like someone has taken it and smeared it with their hand.

7. This part here could be like a steeple of a building. That's all.

7. It also looks like a church. This looks like the body of the building. Roof here. The path or lane here. The sidewalk leads up to the entrance. This would be the body of the steeple.

Card III
8. This could be two different people pulling something apart down here.

8. Here, two heads, body pulling like this and this is all the body. This is the head. It looks like they're pulling this way. I can't connect it with this in the middle, how it relates to them. This is a conflict going on where they are sharing something or they don't want to share something.

9. Or it could be the front part of a tuxedo or suit. This could be the bow tie, the red. This could be the body or the suit, the lapels here.

9. This is the shirt area and this the bow tie. (Tuxedo?) The first thing that struck me is the tie. It's a bow tie and that usually goes with that. As far as the rest of the suit, it's the color. It's black with a white shirt and some have a red tie with them.

10. These two areas here look like, I'll say they look like fetuses with umbilical cords attached to them.

10. There is the head curled up like this one. This is the umbilical cord, and it looks like it's bloody from the color.

11. These here look a little bit like a bowl or something in motion like a whirlpool. That's about it.

11. A whirlpool from the bowl shape. Like a mixing bowl, the deal in the middle. Looks like it's turning to me. It's in motion because it looks streaked and gives me the impression of motion. It looks like it's turning. It gives the impression to be at least like it's moving.

12. Looks like one of those cartoon monsters, real tall. Japanese like. Body, feet, arms, and head.

12. One of those Japanese type monsters (What about it made it looks like that?) Because of the height. Looks like standing there and looking up at it. This is the feet. This is the body. Mostly the shape of it. Like a Japanese print. Rough. I don't want to call it cheap looking. Poor quality because it's ragged looking. If you've ever seen those Japanese movies the special effects are not very good.

13. This way it looks almost bat like. Wings, head, claws, and tail. Spine running down the middle. I believe that's about it.

13. Wing, head, claws. Wings are hinged at the point. They are bat shaped or close to it. There could be a body that almost looks furry. (What about it made it look like that?) These areas, it's darker than this area, so it looks like it's hairy and this area would be hairless. Just plain skin.

Card IV
14. From both angles, it looks a lot like a butterfly. The legs and antennas.

14. Basically a Monarch butterfly. They have protrusions through the back. This would be the head with antennas.

15. This area here looks like a face, the nose, forehead, and mouth.

15. Forehead, nose, and mouth. Both identical facing opposite each other. An ordinary man's face. Nose was large. Had a man's profile.

Card VI
16. This looks like something that's been skinned. It's been dried and stretched out. The skin of some kind of a cat or something. This is its head and this is the skin around its skull.

16. Dried and laid out, some type of cat. If you skinned it and took the skull out, it looks like this. Head, nose, the body of the thing. (What about the skin?) The nose of the cat looks furry. These are the whiskers (Furry?) The color. The texture of it. It's a skinned animal.

17. If you want to go to an extreme, some type of a plant. This is the bust. This is the root system. This is the main root. This is the taproot here.

17. Like a bush, some type of bush. This is the main root and the taproot's all along the side. Looks like it's been sculpted. What do they call it? Looks like it's been manicured and shaped artificially.

18. Or it could be the wreckage of something. An aircraft. This would be the skin. I think that's about it.

18. Piece of the back of the skin. Top of the aircraft. It's been either burned, ripped away from the main body of the aircraft. It could have been a panel section because it ripped evenly all the way around. It looks like it's been burned because of the discoloration. (What about this?) Like smoke and heat. Like fire. It's burned because of the charring, dark, real dark, like it's been exposed to high temperatures. Its shape is rounded like a fuselage.

Card VII

19. This could be a landmass, right here and this could be like the bay or even the sea. This could be the river leading into it.

19. This is the landmass. This is the entrance to the bay. (What about it made it look like that?) Different coloration. Like the topography of a map. Shows different colors like the darker stands for different elevations. This was the river from the landmass that feeds into it.

20. This could be like those cartoon Indian heads. This could be the feathers. This is part of the body and the chest area. It believe that's it.

20. Feathers, head, mouth, body. Shape of a head like it's a comical figure. The feather here.

Card XIII

21. This could be like you see in biology class. Something has been cut open.

21. Fish or a frog. (Where?) All laid out like this. The entrails all of this here. This area would be the spine and bony areas. (What about it?) The color of it. The shape of it too. Like I say, the bony area. Like a central nervous system.

22. From this angle, it looks like a cat that is climbing on both sides. It's climbing up the cliffs.

22. This could be the rocky area. Like climbing over a rocky area. Legs, body. (What about the rocks?) Because of the position they are in. This leg is higher, and they are climbing.

23. This has a little bit of a resemblance to a starfish. Five sides. A head.

23. Five pointed sides. The head isn't well pronounced.

25. This looks like some type of rock formations, like a mountain. This area right through here.

25. It's uneven. It's craggy. Different shades for different rock. The pinnacle.

Card IX

26. This here again looks like some type of lobster, crustacean with the feet.

26. Some type of crustacean. Main body. (What about it?) Mainly the top shape. This would be the feet.

27. This area, the green area, looks a little bit like the pelvic area of a person.

27. This would be the pelvic area. (What about it?) Just this open space and the shape.

28. This looks almost like it's anatomical like it's lungs. I think that's about it.

28. These two here. Lung-like shapes.

Card X
29. I keep seeing creatures. These look like some type of crab. These two blue ones.

29. It just struck me as the body and the legs around it.

30. These two down here look like hydrates. Some sort of water insect.

30. Long legs in the shape of a body.

31. This area again looks like some type of skeleton from a creature.

31. A crustacean, like a skeleton or something (What about it?) Because of the ribs here. The spine, the body part. Something like a man. The way this is turned. Turned in like that.

32. These two look like islands.

32. They're shaped like islands.

RORSCHACH SEQUENCE OF SCORES FOR MR. PAXTON

Card	Resp	Loc (DQ)	Loc N	Determinants (FQ)	(2)	Content(s)	P	Z	Special Scores
I	1.	WSo	1	Fo		Ad		3.5	MOR, DV
	2.	Wo	1	Fu		Sc		1.0	
	3.	WS+	1	Fru		Ls		4.0	
	4.	Do	4	Mpo		Hd			INC, MOR, PHR
II.	5.	DS+	5	ma.CFo		Sc, Fi		4.5	
	6.	D+	1	FMa.CFo	(2)	A, Bl		3.0	AG, GHR
	7.	DdS+		Fu		Sc		4.5	
III.	8.	D+		Mao	(2)	H	P	3.0	AG, GHR
	9.	DdS+		FC'.FC-		Cg		4.5	
	10.	Do	2	Mp.CFu	(2)	H, Bl			MOR, GHR
	11.	Do	7	mau		Hh			
IV.	12.	Wo	1	FDo		(H)	P	2.0	GHR
	13.	Wo	1	FTo		A		2.0	DV
V.	14.	Wo	1	Fo		A	P	1.0	
	15.	Dd+		Mpo	(2)	Hd		5.0	PHR
VI.	16.	Wo	1	FTo		A	P	2.5	MOR
	17.	Wo	1	Fo		Bt		2.5	
	18.	Wo	1	C'Fu		Sc		2.5	MOR
VII.	19.	WS+	1	VFu		Ls		4.0	
	20.	Do	2	Fo	(2)	(Hd)	P		GHR
VIII.	21.	Wo	1	CF-		Ad		4.5	MOR
	22.	W+	1	FMao	(2)	A	P	4.5	
	23.	Wo	1	F-		A		4.5	
	24.	Ddo	1	Fu		A			
IX.	25.	Do	4	FYu		Ls			
	26.	Do	1	Fu		A			
	27.	Do	1	F-		An			
	28.	Do	4	F-	(2)	An			
X.	29.	Do	1	Fo	(2)	A	P		
	30.	Do	7	Fo	(2)	A			
	31.	Do	8	Fu		An			
	32.	Do	13	Fu	(2)	Ls			

Location Features	Determinants		Contents	Approach
	Blends	*Single*		
	FM.CF	M = 3	H = 2	I: WS.W.WS.D
Zf = 19	FC'.FC	FM = 1	(H) = 1	II: DS.D.DdS
ZSum = 63.0	M.CF	m = 2	Hd = 2	III: D.DdS.D.D
Zest = 63.0		FC = 0	(Hd) = 1	IV: W.W
		CF = 1	Hx = 0	V: W, Dd
W = 13		C = 0	A = 10	VI: W.W.W
D = 15		Cn = 0	(A) = 0	VII: WS.D
W+D = 28		FC' = 0	Ad = 2	VIII: W.W.W.Dd.D
Dd = 4		C'F = 1	(Ad) = 0	IX: D.D.D
S = 6		C'= 0	An = 3	X: D.D.D.D
		FT = 2	Art = 0	
Developmental Quality		TF = 0	Ay = 0	*Special Scores*
+ = 9		T = 0	Bl = 2	Lv 1 Lv 2
o = 23		FV = 0	Bt = 1	DV = 2x1 = 0x2
v = 0		VF = 1	Cg = 1	INC = 1x2 = 0x4
v/+ = 0		V = 0	Cl = 0	DR = 0x3 = 0x6
		FY = 1	Ex = 0	FAB = 0x4 = 0x7

Form Quality

	FQx	MQual	W+D
+	= 0	= 0	= 0
o	= 15	= 3	= 14
u	= 12	= 1	= 10
-	= 5	= 0	= 0
none	= 0	= 0	= 0

	Contents (cont.)	Special Scores (cont.)
	YF = 0	ALOG = 0x5
	Y = 0	CON = 0x7
	Fr = 1	Raw Sum 6 = 3
	rF = 0	Wgtd Sum 6 = 4
	FD = 1	
	F = 15	
	(2) = 10	AB = 0 GHR = 3
	Fd = 0	AG = 2 PHR = 4
	Fi = 1	COP = 0 MOR = 6
	Ge = 0	CP = 0 PER = 0
	Hh = 1	PSV = 0
	Ls = 4	
	Na = 0	
	Sc = 4	
	Sx = 0	
	Xy = 0	
	Id = 0	

111

Ratios, Percentages, and Derivations

Core

R = 32	L = .88

EB = 4:3.5	EA = 7.5	EBPer = N/A
eb = 4:6	es = 10	D = 0
	Adj es = 9	Adj D = 0

FM = 2	SumC' = 2	SumT = 2
m = 2	Sum V = 1	Sum Y = 1

Affect

FC: CF+C = 1:3
Pure C = 0
SumC':WSumC = 2:3.5
Afr = .60
S = 6
Blends:R = 3:32
CP = 0

Interpersonal

COP = 0   AG = 2
GHR: PHR = 3:4
a:p = 5:3
Food = 0
Sum T =2
Human Cont = 6
Pure H =2
PER = 0
Isol Indx = .16

Ideation

a:p = 5:3	Sum6 = 3
Ma:Mp = 1:3	Lv2 = 0
2AB+Art+Ay = 0	WSum6 = 4
MOR = 6	M- = 0
	M none = 0

Mediation

XA% = .84
WDA% = .86
X-% = .16
S- = 1
P = 7
X+% = .47
Xu% = .38

Processing

Zf = 19
W:D:Dd = 13:15:4
W:M = 13:4
Zd = 0.0
PSV = 0
DQ+ = 9
DQv = 0

Self-Perception

3r+(2)/R = .41
Fr+rF = 1
SumV = 1
FD = 1
An+Xy = 3
MOR = 6
H:(H)+Hd+(Hd) = 2:4

PTI = 0   *DEPI = 6   CDI = 1   S-CON = 6   HVI = No   OBS = No

Rorschach Assessment of Schizotypal Personality Disorder

Dana Deardeuff Foley
Veteran Affairs Medical Center, Oklahoma City

"Odd" and "eccentric" are the most common words associated with schizotypal personality disorder (SPD). As with all personality disorders, this disorder is characterized by a chronic and long-standing impairment in psychosocial functioning that not only is maladaptive, but also causes functional impairment (Skodol et al., 2002). This difficulty typically is recognized by adolescence or early adulthood (American Psychiatric Association [APA], 2000). The primary difficulties experienced by the patient with SPD are cognitive and perceptual distortions, behavioral eccentricities, and interpersonal difficulties.

The term "schizotypal" was first used by Rado in the 1950s in a paper delivered to the New York Academy of Medicine. This concept was later defined and expanded by Rado (1953) in an address to the American Psychiatric Association. He differentiated the theory of a "genotype," or the inherited cause of a disorder, from that of the "phenotype," the expressed outcome. He abbreviated the term "schizophrenic phenotype" to "schizotype." Rado theorized that regardless of the psychosis expression, there often are underlying traits present in many patients for their life span, beginning even in childhood. He defined the "schizotypal organization" as the psychodynamic traits characteristic of the schizotype.

Rado (1953) noted that the basic organization of schizotype patients was grossly inadequate, in that such individuals had an "integrative pleasure deficiency." The ability to experience pleasure or pleasurable emotions is a motivational force, and this "zest for life" drives performance. Rado noted that schizotypes had deficits in their ability to experience pleasure, thus decreasing their level of functioning. Because the schizotype would be cognizant of these inadequacies in interacting with others and his deficits in experiencing emotions, his desire to have fulfilling relationships would not be met. This then set the stage for a lifelong series of unmet needs and relationship difficulties attributable to these inadequacies, which created the conditions for a self-fulfilling prophecy. Rado believed that for some individuals, this difficulty led to a psychological decompensation, which could manifest itself as schizophrenia.

Meehl (1962) further postulated that the inherited element, "schizotaxia," may develop into the schizotype (defined by Rado) if encouraged or supported by the social learning history of the individual. For example, a person with schizotaxia who is exposed to an aversive or neglectful childhood would be more likely to progress to the schizotype. Otherwise, Meehl postulated that the schizotaxia may never manifest itself. Meehl noted that the strongest social learning predictor of schizophrenic decompensation resides in the schizophrenogenic mother. Patients with the schizophrenogenic mother then may develop schizophrenia, or the less severe, more compensated diagnosis of schizotypy. He noted that all schizotaxics become schizotypic in personality organization, but that other factors influence their degree of psychological organization. For example, those in a poor social regime with the schizophrenogenic mother are more likely to decompensate completely to schizophrenia. Meehl believed the four schizotype source traits included cognitive slippage, anhedonia, ambivalence, and interpersonal aversiveness.

The diagnosis of SPD was not included in diagnostic classification, however, until the *Diagnostic and Statistical Manual of Mental Disorders*, 3rd Edition (DSM-III; APA, 1980). Before the classification, SPD patients were most likely labeled "borderline, latent, or ambulatory schizophrenia" (Carr, Schwartz, & Fishler, 1989). Moreover, SPD was the first personality disorder defined partially by its relationship to schizophrenia (Siever, Bernstein, & Silverman, 1995). The essential features of this personality disorder were defined in the DSM-III (APA, 1980) as "various oddities of thought, perception, speech, and behavior that are not severe enough to meet the criteria for schizophrenia." Although a patient with SPD could develop psychotic symptoms, the symptoms were considered to be transient and occurred during extremely stressful periods.

In the DSM-III (APA, 1980), the original diagnosis required four of the following symptoms: magical thinking, ideas of reference, social isolation, recurrent illusions, odd speech, inadequate rapport attributable to constricted or inappropriate affect, suspiciousness or paranoid ideation, and social anxiety. The diagnosis was relatively unchanged in the DSM-III-R (APA, 1987), which required five of the symptoms and added the following criterion: "behavior or appearance that is odd, eccentric or peculiar." The disorder described in DSM-IV Text Revision (DSM-IV-TR; APA, 2000) is largely unchanged (Table 5.1).

TABLE 5.1

DSM-IV-TR Criteria for Schizotypal Personality Disorder

A. A pervasive pattern of social and interpersonal deficits marked by acute discomfort with, and reduced capacity for, close relationships, as well as by cognitive or perceptual distortions and eccentricities of behavior, beginning by early adulthood and present in a variety of contexts, as indicated by five (or more) of the following:

1. Ideas of reference, excluding delusions of reference

2. Odd beliefs or magical thinking that influences behavior and is inconsistent with subcultural norms (e.g., superstitiousness, belief in clairvoyance, telepathy, or "sixth sense"; in children and adolescents, bizarre fantasies or preoccupations)

3. Unusual perceptual experiences, including bodily illusions

4. Odd thinking and speech (e.g., vague, circumstantial, metaphoric, over-elaborate, or stereotyped)

5. Suspiciousness or paranoid ideation

6. Inappropriate or constricted affect

7. Behavior or appearance that is odd, eccentric, or peculiar

8. Lack of close friends or confidants other than first-degree relatives

9. Excessive social anxiety that does not diminish with familiarity and tends to be associated with paranoid fears rather than negative judgments about self

B. Does not occur exclusively during the course of schizophrenia, a mood disorder with psychotic features, another psychotic disorder, or a pervasive developmental disorder.

Note. If criteria are met before the onset of schizophrenia, add "premorbid" (e.g., "schizotypal personality disorder [Premorbid])."

Two of the most prominent personality disorder theorists (Kernberg, 1967; Millon, 1969) view SPD as one of the most severe personality disorders. Both view the internal personality dynamics of these individuals as so impaired that it interferes with their ability to obtain the social connectedness and support desperately needed to reinforce or bolster their own failing defenses.

There are many dimensions to the SPD construct. Meehl's (1962) original four schizotype source traits are very similar to the factors found more recently to describe SPD. Venables (1995) described four factors of SPD: positive schizotypy (cognitive–perceptual deficits), negative schizotypy (introverted anhedonia), social anxiety, and psychoticism/nonconformity. He noted that the two most common factors, positive schizotypy and negative schizotypy, were related to the negative and positive symptoms used to describe schizophrenia.

More recent research also indicates that SPD may be a multidimensional construct with different subtypes based on these factors (Fossati et al., 2001;

MacDonald, Pogue-Geile, Debski, & Manuck, 2001; Torgersen et al., 2002; Weinstein & Graves, 2001). Fossati et al. (2001) found three latent classes of symptoms that could account for the covariation in the DSM-IV SPD criteria, which supports the idea that the SPD construct is multidimensional. The class descriptions were as follows: (a) no close friends or confidants, odd thinking, suspiciousness, and inappropriate affect; (b) ideas of reference, magical thinking, unusual perceptual experiences, and suspiciousness; and (c) suspiciousness, ideas of reference to a lesser degree and no close friends. These authors found that almost all their subjects belonged to class a, characterized by interpersonal difficulties, withdrawal, and aloofness. However, class c yielded the strongest diagnostic efficiency for SPD and included the qualities of odd thinking, aloofness, social withdrawal, and excessive social anxiety. These characteristics also are consistent with those found in other studies (Kendler, McGuire, Gruenberg, & Walsh, 1995; Torgersen, 1984) that found these characteristics most commonly in the relatives of probands with schizophrenia.

Carr et al. (1989) noted that before the introduction of the SPD diagnosis, the clinical descriptors of this population were viewed as mild or subacute forms of schizophrenia. In fact, SPD is more common in first-degree relatives of patients with schizophrenia (APA, 2000). More recently, there appears to be some suggestion that SPD is on a continuum of difficulties labeled the "schizophrenia spectrum" (Waldeck & Miller, 2000). This spectrum typically includes schizophrenia and other psychotic disorders found on Axis I as well as the cluster A personality disorders found on Axis II. In this continuum, the diagnosis of schizophrenia would be at the extreme end of the spectrum. There is some question about linking Axis I diagnoses on a spectrum with Axis II disorders, because the current system does not easily accommodate this (Siever et al., 1995). However, the research is supportive of such a link.

RESEARCH ON SCHIZOID PERSONALITY DISORDER AND SCHIZOPHRENIA

Several studies have investigated the relationship of SPD to relatives of probands with schizophrenia. Torgersen, Onstad, Skre, Edvardsen, and Kringlen (1993) found a higher rate of SPD in co-twins and relatives of schizophrenic probands, even in the absence of shared environmental experiences. Kendler et al. (1993) reported that SPD was five times more likely to occur in relatives of probands with schizophrenia than in their controls. Their study yielded a 1.4% prevalence of SPD in the normative sample, and in the relatives of schizophrenia probands the prevalence was 6.9%. These authors concluded that SPD has a strong familial relationship to schizophrenia.

Many researchers conceptualize the disorder as related to schizophrenia (Coleman, Levy, Lenzenweger, & Holzman, 1996; Eckblad & Chapman, 1983; Kendler, 1985; Kendler, Masterson, Ungaro, & Davis, 1984; Kernberg, 1984; Siever et al., 1991, 1995; Torgersen et al., 1993; Trestman et al., 1995). Coleman et al. (1996) found that schizotypic individuals scored much the same on the Thought Disorder Index (Solovay et al., 1986; described later) as schizophrenic individuals and their first-degree relatives. These authors determined that the quality of thought disorder in schizotypic individuals is very similar to that of schizophrenic individuals. Likewise, Trestman et al. (1995) found that SPD patients evidenced difficulties in their cognitive performance on the Wisconsin Card Sorting Test and Trail-Making, Part B. These difficulties were similar to those of patients with schizophrenia. Furthermore, patients with SPD scored between the normative sample and the patients with schizophrenia.

Torgersen et al. (2002) compared SPD patients who were co-twins or first-degree relatives with a diagnosis of schizophrenia, SPD patients who did not have relatives with schizophrenia, patients with other disorders who had no relatives with SPD or schizophrenia, and a control sample with no psychiatric diagnosis and no familial history of SPD or schizophrenia. On the basis of their findings and descriptors of the sample, Torgersen et al. (2002) found that there is a genetic core of schizotypy related to schizophrenia. Patients with SPD scored higher than control subjects on all schizotypal feature measures. The SPD patients with a family history of schizophrenia scored higher than their SPD counterparts without a family history of schizophrenia on inadequate rapport and odd communication, the negative schizotypy features. However, the SPD patients without a family history of schizophrenia scored higher than the SPD patients with family history of schizophrenia on the positive schizotypy features including ideas of reference, suspiciousness/paranoid ideations, and social anxiety/ hypersensitivity to criticism. They also scored higher on the borderline features of self-damaging acts, chronic anger/hostility, free-floating anxiety, and sensitivity to rejection. These borderline features were found exclusively in SPD patients outside the schizophrenia family spectrum. Nonschizophrenic monozygotic co-twins of schizophrenics more commonly evidenced inadequate rapport, odd communication, social isolation, and delusions/hallucinations. Torgersen et al. (2002) concluded that the genetic core of SPD in families with schizophrenia consisted of inadequate rapport, odd communication, social isolation, and delusions/hallucinations. The genetic core for the SPD in families without schizophrenia comprised illusions, depersonalization/ derealization, and magical thinking.

A study by Siever et al. (1995) also supports the strong link between SPD and schizophrenia. These authors noted that SPD is found more frequently than schizophrenia in the probands of schizophrenics. Furthermore, they reported that SPD is more common among the biologic relatives of patients with schizophrenia than among the adoptive relatives, suggesting a genetic or biologic link. Patients with SPD also tend to respond favorably to treatment similar to that used for the schizophrenia patient (e.g., neuroleptics).

THE DYNAMICS AND SYMPTOMS OF SCHIZOTYPAL PERSONALITY DISORDER

The following description of SPD dynamics and symptoms is based on several key papers in the literature (Kendler, 1985; Kernberg, 1984; Meehl, 1990; Millon, 1996; Torgersen, 1995; Torgersen et al., 2002). Because personality structure lies on a continuum of adaptability, the schizotypal personality tends to be on the more maladaptive end of that continuum, evidencing less adaptability to societal norms. The psychological state of SPD patient's often is tenuous, at times bordering on psychotic. During the stressful and decompensated periods, the patient with schizotypal personality may evidence bizarre behavior, brief psychotic symptoms, and paranoia. These episodes typically occur when their already impaired coping capacity is overwhelmed. At these times, they may evidence delusional thought processes and bizarre behaviors, yet these psychotic symptoms are not present long enough for a diagnosis of schizophrenia or another psychotic disorder on Axis I. The eccentric thoughts of these patients are more enduring and static, whereas a psychotic episode diagnosed on Axis I tends to be more transient and resolves for some time. Therefore, the diagnosis of SPD requires the cognitive and perceptual distortions to be present outside the period of a psychotic episode.

Even when not overwhelmed, individuals with schizotypal personality have great difficulty coping with everyday demands. They are characteristically unable to behave within societal norms. Subsequently, other people perceive them as odd or eccentric and have difficulty relating to them effectively. The inability to relate effectively to other people causes increased anxiety, resulting in increased difficulty coping and interacting with others. This creates an endless cycle in which SPD patients are unable to get their needs met and unable to interact with others effectively. Consequently, they feel wholly incompetent to "fit in." They have difficulty recognizing or learning from their own mistakes, and then cannot make the changes necessary to alter this cycle. The anxiety they feel in social settings does not decrease over time or with familiarity, as with other types, in which there is remission. Therefore, they prefer to remain withdrawn and isolated in an effort to reduce their own anxiety levels.

Patients with SPD have difficulty integrating effectively in society. This isolation further complicates their ability to recognize and effectively learn societal norms that might help them find a niche in life. They remain on the periphery, unable to test their odd or eccentric beliefs effectively against reality. They typically have few, if any, close relationships outside those with immediate family members. Therefore, no feedback loop about interpersonal relationships or their interpersonal style is available to them.

Patients with SPD typically behave in a very eccentric fashion. They often have unusual beliefs that are not considered normal within their society. However, it is important to classify their unusual beliefs within their cultural background. Schizotypal personalities typically present themselves and behave without regard the societal expectations. They often dress in a very idiosyncratic manner and pay little attention to the details of their appearance. They commonly are seen as unkempt. Their speech often is filled with unusual verbalizations. Such behaviors are readily observable to other people in the environment, and thus, patients with SPD tend to "stick out" as unusual. Although they are capable of transitory accomplishments, SPD patients rarely can sustain the efforts necessary to make major achievements (Millon, 1996). They often lack desire to achieve or recognition of the need to achieve.

Patients with schizotypal personality commonly have difficulty with emotions. Millon (1996) noted that the SPD patient tends to have either constricted or inappropriate affect, and both are consistent with the emotional difficulties that accompany the disorder. At times the SPD patients may appear aloof, isolated, and lack affective expression. At other times, they may have intense affect, likely in response to fear of rejection or humiliation. At times they may display odd or unusual affect for a given situation, such as laughing or smiling when the matter at hand is very serious.

DIAGNOSTIC DIFFERENTIATION

Many important differential diagnostic considerations are involved in the diagnosis of SPD. The schizotypal personality bears some similarity to the avoidant, paranoid, schizoid, and borderline personality disorders as well as schizophrenia. Patients with SPD share social detachment and restricted affect with the schizoid and paranoid personalities. However, those disorders do not evidence the perceptual and cognitive distortions found in schizotypal patients. These patients share the social anxieties often found with the avoidant patient, but do not have their fear of rejection that is predominant with avoidant individuals.

Although SPD and borderline personality disorder (BPD) have some overlap in symptoms and presentation, research still recognizes these as two separate diagnoses (Carr, 1987; Carr et al., 1989). Frequently, BPD involves the transient psychotic symptoms commonly found in the schizotypal patient, but these tend to be based on emotional regulation difficulty rather than the more enduring, psychotic-like or bizarre characteristics of the schizotypal patient. In contrast, SPD patients are more likely to display blatantly psychotic symptoms when under stress or overwhelmed, not in response to emotional dysregulation. The more enduring unusual behaviors and cognitions of the SPD patient are static and independent of their emotional state, whereas the unusual behaviors and cognitions of the BPD patient are more dependent on and related to their emotional state (Siever et al., 1995). The schizotypal patient can be differentiated from the BPD patient best by the eccentric cognitions and behaviors that occur over long periods.

Cognitive slippage or subtle thought disorder appear to be hallmarks of SPD (Meehl, 1990). In fact, odd thinking is one of the most distinguishing features of SPD (Fossati et al., 2001). Patients with SPD also tend to have greater functional impairment than patients with other personality disorders. Skodol et al. (2002) found that SPD and BPD patients were three times more likely to have only a high school diploma, to be employed less frequently, to be rated as more functionally impaired by both interviewers and their own self-rating. These researchers further concluded that with measures other than interviewer ratings, SPD and BPD patients scored the highest on impairment, removing any possible interviewer bias.

As noted previously, another common diagnostic differentiation is with schizophrenia. The patient with SPD may display blatantly psychotic symptoms, but these symptoms are more transient in SPD patients than in patients with schizophrenia. Schizophrenics also have overt psychotic symptoms over the course of their illness, whereas SPD patients typically evidence such symptoms when under stress.

Similarly, because patients with SPD evidence ideas of references, it is important to distinguish those symptoms from corresponding delusions commonly seen with delusional disorder. It is important to remember in the diagnostic differentiation that the personality disorders on Axis II are, by nature, a chronic, life-long pattern of interaction, as opposed to symptoms that emerge suddenly or later in life and those that may be more episodic and circumscribed.

THE RORSCHACH
AND SCHIZOTYPAL PERSONALITY DISORDER

The Rorschach Inkblot Method (RIM) has historically been used effectively to assess thought disturbances and personality characteristics. The

RIM can more readily assess and define thought disturbance beyond many self-report measures (Holzman, Shenton & Solovay, 1986; Solovay et al., 1986). Specifically, the RIM is a very complex problem-solving task that challenges patients to use their resources—perceptual, cognitive, and affective—to develop a response to the task (Perry, Minassian, Cadenhead, Sprock, & Braff, 2003). Evidence of disturbed thought processes, both the more severe associated with schizophrenia and the less severe that characterize SPD, will be readily assessable by evaluating cognitive content and perceptual accuracy, as well as the individual's management of affectively toned stimuli. In contrast, more structured assessment tools such as self-report measures, structured interviews, and forced-choice questionnaires are less sensitive to the mild or moderate thought disturbances found with SPD because SPD patients may contain or mask their cognitive oddities, or may describe their functioning in a more benign manner under the structure of direct questions, as opposed to the unstructured RIM task.

Early efforts at using the Rorschach to assess thought disturbance is reported by Solovay et al. (1986). On the basis of Rapaport, Gill, and Schafer's (1968) work, Solovay et al. (1986) created the Thought Disorder Index (TDI), which distinguishes 23 qualitative categories for thought disturbance weighted along a continuum of severity.

The primary use of the RIM is not to achieve DSM-IV-TR (APA, 2000) text revision diagnostic classification (Exner, 2003; Weiner, 2000, 2003). As Carr et al. (1989) asserted, many structured and semistructured interviews can be used to define information from a patient in direct correlation with the DSM-IV-TR (APA, 2000) text revision criteria. Rather, the RIM is best used to describe personality characteristics (Exner, 2003; Weiner, 2003).

Using the diagnostic descriptors of SPD, there are some obvious expectations of results on the Structural Summary of Comprehensive System (Exner, 2003). The SPD patient has very confused and poorly integrated responses (Millon, 1996). The primary SPD characteristic of cognitive and perceptual oddities/distortions likely will produce significant differences in the Ideation and Mediation clusters between the non-patient and the schizotypal patient. This is likely to be evident in the patient's perceptual accuracy on the RIM. The SPD patient would be expected to evidence an elevation on X–% and a decrease in X+%, but not to the same degree expected of a patient with schizophrenia. In fact, research supports this idea. Exner (1986) found that patients with SPD have a lower X+% than the normative sample (69% vs. 80%), but the X+% is not as low as that seen in the schizophrenic sample (54%). Likewise, Erdberg (2003) and Exner (1986) found that patients with SPD likely will have an X–% greater than that seen in the normative sample (18% vs. 6%), but lower than that seen in the schizophrenic sample (31%). These perceptual accuracy factors also would decrease Form Appropriate Extended (XA%) and Form Appropriated Common Areas (WDA%) in comparison with the normative sample, but these percentages would be higher than that found in the schizophrenia sample.

Cognitive slippage, observed consistently in the SPD population, was described from very early conceptualization of the disorder. This symptom is likely to be reflected in the special scores on the RIM. Patients with SPD tend to evidence odd speech, which then may be found in an increased number of deviant verbalizations and deviant responses. At times their, speech is very unusual and egocentric. The SPD patient also would have more special scores, but is not as likely to show the same level of severity as the schizophrenic, and not as likely to be so bizarre that a level 2 special score is warranted. Although SPD patients are less likely to have level 2 special scores on the RIM (Erdberg, 2003; Exner, 1986), they can evidence the disordered thinking processes at a lower level than seen in the schizophrenic sample. With the confused quality of their cognition and perceptions, Millon (1996) asserts that SPD patients should be more likely to have incongruous combinations and fabulized combinations. Exner (1986) also reported that SPD patients do have more special scores ($M = 5.6$) in the nonpatient sample ($M = 1.6$) or the BPD sample ($M = 3.4$), but fewer than the schizophrenic sample ($M = 7.3$).

Patients with SPD tend to give an adequate number of responses and to have lambda values within the normal range (Erdberg, 2003). One would expect schizotypal patients to be introversive ($M >$ WsumC), in some cases pervasively so, because they tend to problem solve by processing information internally and are likely unable to use a trial and error approach to solve problems. Research indicates that patients with SPD tend to have an introversive style, such that they prefer to use ideation in problem solving, as opposed to a more action-oriented or behavioral style (Erdberg, 2003; Exner 1986). For some, this introversive style is likely to be pervasive and inflexible. Ambitent protocols are not uncommon.

Patients with SPD tend to show less vulnerability to stress and disruption, as evidenced by D scores of 0 or greater (Erdberg, 2003; Exner, 1986). This finding is likely attributable to the decreased amount of stress that these individuals permit in their lives, often by withdrawing and avoiding stressful situations. Thought distortion also may serve a defensive function. They tend to keep their emotions controlled, thus reducing the impact of emotions on their functioning. This finding also suggests that their Form color ratio would not evidence a higher level of unmodulated emotion.

Fantasy tends to be used actively for patients with SPD, which also can be associated with their use of magical thinking. Fantasy, as opposed to real interaction with other people, is preferred for SPD patients because their interactional styles are likely to be problematic. This characteristic is likely to elevate Passive Human Movement (Mp) for this population (Carr et al., 1989; Exner, 1986).

Schizotypal patients evidence serious difficulties in interpersonal relationships. Consequently, they are likely to have some differences from the normative sample in the Interpersonal Cluster on the Comprehensive System (Exner, 2003). Their internal representation of themselves and others typically is distorted and unrealistic, such that they have fewer whole human responses and more human detail or fictional human responses (Erdberg, 2003). This also represents an effort to distance themselves from others because of their interpersonal deficits. At times, they also may evidence greater distortion in human movement responses, elevating (M–) more than that seen in the normative sample (Exner, 2003). This is evidence of their significant inadequacies in the social realm. Because their perceptions tend to be unusual and confused, they may have percepts that are scored with both the cooperative and aggressive movements (Erdberg, 2003).

The Ego Impairment Index (EII; Perry & Viglione, 1991) was developed to provide an additional measure of psychological disturbance based on perceptual and thought disturbance. It comprises the sum of six weighted subcomponents from the RIM Comprehensive System: Distorted Form (FQ–), Human Movement Distorted Form (M–), Weighted Sum Special Scores (WSum6), Critical Contents, Poor Human Experience (PHR), and Good Human Experience (GHR). The EII has been studied with many patient populations, but has been particularly useful with schizophrenia spectrum disorders. The EII correlates positively with several measures of psychotic thought processes, such as the Magical Ideation Scale, selected subscales of the Minnesota Multiphasic Personality Inventory-2, and the Brief Psychiatric Rating Scale (Perry et al., 2003). In one study, Perry et al. (2003) evaluated patients with a schizophrenia spectrum disorder using the EII. They found that patients with SPD had a moderately higher EII ($M = 0.61$) than the normative sample ($M = 0.35$), but did not score as high as the patients with schizophrenia (outpatient $M = 0.92$; inpatient $M = 1.21$).

Cadenhead, Perry, and Braff (1996) studied visual backward masking (VBM), a measure of information processing, in SPD patients. The VBM task presents a stimulus, such as a letter or symbol, along with a masking stimulus at varying intervals in an attempt to disrupt the processing of the target stimulus. Over time, this disruption normalizes for most subjects. Cadenhead et al. (1996) found that patients with SPD show impairment in VBM along a continuum, with those who have more SPD symptoms showing greater deficits in VBM. The VBM scores were found to correlate significantly ($r = -0.78$) with the EII scores. The authors speculated that the VBM deficits in the SPD population reflected the underlying perceptual–cognitive deficits also found with EII scores in this patient population.

Most of the research on testing data appears to support the theory that SPD is related to schizophrenia, but that it is at the moderate level of the continuum, with schizophrenia being the extreme of the continuum. Exner (1986) found that the personality characteristics of SPD patients on the RIM are similar to those of patients with schizophrenia in many aspects, but less severe. Thus, he concluded that a possible label for SPD was "borderline schizophrenic." However, Edell (1987) found that patients with schizophrenia, SPD, and BPD were indistinguishable in quantity and quality of thought disorder on the RIM. Edell did note, however, that the most disorganized responses were largely restricted to the schizophrenia sample.

CASE EXAMPLE: MR. MATSON

Mr. Matson, a 40-year-old, divorced, White male, was referred for psychological testing to assist with diagnosis and treatment planning by his individual therapist. His parents brought Mr. Matson for evaluation because they were concerned about his mental health. He agreed to enter treatment somewhat reluctantly. He had been followed for individual therapy for four sessions. Born in a moderate-size city in the Midwest, Mr. Matson was raised by his biologic parents until they divorced when he was 14 years old. Mr. Matson's father was physically abusive to him, his two siblings, and his mother. After the divorce, Mr. Matson reported that he "raised himself" because his mother had to work two jobs.

Mr. Matson attended a local high school, but was not very active in school. He had a 3.0 grade point average and did not have any academic difficulties. Mr. Matson reported that he has always been "a loner" and did not have many friends in high school. Although he wanted to have close friends, Mr. Matson believed he did not "fit in" with any social group. Instead, he was busy at home with his pet rabbits.

After high school, Mr. Matson joined the military to "get away" and travel. He was in the infantry, but never served in combat. Mr. Matson noted that he did well in the military because it was easy to know what was expected of him, yet, did not make many friends there.

After completing his term of service, Mr. Matson went to work in a large manufacturing plant as a "sorter," where he was working at the time of the assessment. He found this to be very tiring work, but had been successful at it. He did not have much opportunity to make friends at work because he worked on a production line. In his spare time, he liked to work on electronic equipment.

Mr. Matson was married once to a woman he met overseas. They were married for about 11 years, but divorced because of "frequent arguments." She was from Korea and had moved to the United States with Mr. Matson. While married, they did not participate in many social activities, which was a source of conflict. He reported that she could not "handle" his mental problems and felt unable to connect with him. She also was frustrated with his inability to sustain social contacts. At the time of his assessment, Mr. Matson was living alone and had no social contact outside his work.

Mr. Matson began having some symptoms of depression about 14 years before testing and had regular episodes of depression. He reported feeling lonely at times. He had difficulty expressing his emotions and decreased interest in his activities. Mr. Matson reported that he never had auditory or visual hallucinations. However, he did report his belief that the radio stations played special love songs just for him. He also noted that sometimes when he changed the channel on the radio, the same song would be playing on another channel, which further emphasized this "special message" from his perspective. He reported that sometimes he felt a little paranoid about people at work because he believed they stared at and talked about him. This was particularly noticeable to Mr. Matson when he entered a room and it seemed that others stopped talking.

Mr. Matson presented for the assessment in dirty jeans and a tight golf shirt that looked a few sizes too small. His hair was uncombed, and he was unshaven. Mr. Matson walked with an odd gait, almost galloping down the hall. He engaged in conversation easily, but evidenced more anxiety during the testing administration. His speech was clear and coherent, although he was tangential at times. On a few occasions, he appeared to be excessively verbal and used some words in an inappropriate fashion. He evidenced little depression during the testing, but did use humor often, particularly when his anxiety level increased.

Mr. Matson's RIM results are presented in Table 5.2. Mr. Matson gave a valid protocol with 20 responses, and did not appear to be overly defensive (L = 0.54). The constellation indices did not show any significant disturbances (Depression Index, Coping Deficit Index, Rorschach Suicide Constellation, Hypervigilance Index, and Obsessive style Index). However, he did have a Perceptual Thinking Index (PTI) of 2, suggesting that he had some difficulty in his thinking. His results were not positive for any of the other constellations.

As commonly seen in the patient with SPD, Mr. Matson was pervasively introversive, thus preferring to use his own ideation in problem solving and thinking things through before taking action. He had few organized resources to manage life's stressors, but also had few stressors. Subsequently, his D score and adjusted D score both were zero, indicating that he was not currently overwhelmed by stress.

The Ideation cluster also was consistent with results commonly seen with SPD. Mr. Matson tended to be passive, preferring for others to take charge and make decisions (a:p of 4:6). He also engaged in excessive use of fantasy ($M^a : M^p = 1 : 4$). His Sum6 was 6, which was elevated, but not to a significant degree. Likewise, his weighted WSum6 was 13, evidencing some difficulties in his thought processes, but not to the extent of an actively psychotic patient. Mr. Matson's special scores tended to congregate in the less pathologic category of the special scores (e.g., deviant verbalizations and deviant responses). He did have one fabulized combination, but it was a level 1. Mr. Matson also had two M– scores, indicating significant distortion in interpersonal relationships. The Ideational cluster highlighted the moderate degree of impairment in his thinking and his passive and disorganized way of interpreting experience.

As with many patients with a diagnosis of SPD, Mr. Matson had a significant level of disturbance in his Mediation cluster. He evidenced a significant number of unusual perceptions (Xu% = 0.25) and a significant number of cognitive distortions (X–% = 0.30). Most of his FQ– responses occurred on color cards, thus indicating an increased capacity for distortion when emotions were involved. He was able to pick up on obvious cues in the environment and perceive common responses, as evidenced by his five popular responses. His protocol was lower than the normative sample in his perceptual accuracy (XA% = 0.70; WDA% = 0.67). These findings are consistent with the unusual, and often distorted, perceptions found in the SPD population.

Additional information on the Affective cluster indicated that Mr. Matson was able to modulate his emotions. However, he also was more likely to distort those perceptions as well. His Affective ratio was somewhat low (0.54), indicating a desire to withdraw from or avoid emotional stimuli. Mr. Matson also appeared to be fairly angry, with five Space(S) responses. He also had two S– responses, indicating significant distortion, with anger and some paranoia or suspiciousness.

Mr. Matson's perception of himself generally was adequate, although it likely was based on inaccurate data, misperceptions, or distortions. His Egocentricity Index was in the average range (0.35), and he did not have any reflections. As noted, patients with SPD tend to have fewer pure H responses, indicating difficulty interacting with others in an accurate and realistic fashion. Accordingly, Mr. Matson had one pure H response.

Mr. Matson's Interpersonal cluster also showed some deficits in functioning. He had few interactive movement responses (cooperative or aggressive), and no T responses, thus indicating that he did not expect interaction or comfort with others. His PHR exceeded his GHR, indicating some difficulty with interpersonal relationships, manifested as a tendency to be ineffective in relationships with others. When Poor Human Representation is greater than Good Human Representation, the patient is more likely to have maladaptive and ineffective interpersonal relationships. Mr. Matson's PHR responses were also more likely to include a form quality distortion, suggesting further difficulties in his interpersonal relationships, with significant interpersonal distortions.

In summary, Mr. Matson's protocol evidenced many of the RIM features found in SPD. Overall, he appeared to be functioning at an adequate level, with little elevation in the constellations. His functioning appeared to be egosyntonic because he was not distressed or uncomfortable in his current state. He had a distorted, unrealistic, and unusual perception of the world. He tended to think things through without acting, and did not appear to have any flexibility in this approach when situations demanded immediate action. He did not allow himself the ability to validate his internal ideation. He relied on fantasy because he could not have effective interpersonal relationships that would meet his needs. He was likely to appear unusual or odd to other people. His protocol evidenced the cognitive–perceptual difficulties seen in the SPD patient, but at a lower elevation than that commonly seen in the schizophrenia patient.

At least three broad domains in the assessment of SPD with the RIM require further evaluation. First, a large normative sample of SPD patients is needed for empirical verification of the RIM patterns and trends proposed in this chapter. Furthermore, more published case studies, such as the case described in this chapter, would contribute to the understanding of SPD and its assessment.

Second, as noted previously, the literature and research are highly suggestive of a genetic link between SPD and schizophrenia. As such, it would be beneficial to evaluate the ability of the Rorschach to assist in the differential diagnosis of SPD and schizophrenia. For that matter, a comparison of SPD with other cluster A personality disorders and other schizophrenia spectrum disorders (e.g., schizoaffective disorder) is warranted, to determine the ability of the Rorschach to aid in differential diagnosis.

Third, because the core symptoms of SPD involve odd communication, suspicious or paranoid ideation, and social isolation, further quantification of these characteristics with the RIM could be particularly helpful. For instance, it would be of great utility to evaluate Ideation, Mediation, and Processing clusters with measures of communication efficiency, clarity, and precision. Also, a study of social interaction and isolation within a well-designed laboratory setting would provide support for the RIM's external validity in assessing social isolation. Even better, ratings of social isolation and social contact from clinicians could be compared with the Interpersonal cluster variables to evaluate the external validity of this measure for psychiatric patients.

Finally, because the RIM is not as susceptible to censoring and self-presentation bias as self-report and interview measures can be, a study investigating the incremental validity of the RIM for assisting in the diagnosis of

SPD would be particularly beneficial. It may be that the RIM more readily
and efficiently detects SPD than more commonly used assessment techniques such as self-report measures and clinical interviews.

REFERENCES

American Psychiatric Association. (1980). *Diagnostic and statistical manual of mental disorders* (3rd ed.). Washington, DC: American Psychiatric Association.
American Psychiatric Association. (1987). *Diagnostic and statistical manual of mental disorders* (3rd ed. Rev.). Washington, DC: American Psychiatric Association.
American Psychiatric Association. (2000). *Diagnostic and statistical manual of mental disorders* (4th ed. text revision). Washington, DC: American Psychiatric Association.
Cadenhead, K., Perry, W., & Braff, D. (1996). The relationship of information-processing deficits and clinical symptoms in schizotypal personality disorder. *Biological Psychiatry, 40,* 853–858.
Carr, A. (1987). Borderline defenses and Rorschach responses: A critique of Lerner, Albert, and Walsh. *Journal of Personality Assessment, 51,* 349–354.
Carr, A., Schwartz, F., & Fishler, A. (1989). The diagnosis of schizotypal personality disorder by use of psychological tests. *Journal of Personality Disorders, 3,* 36–44.
Coleman, M., Carpenter, J., Waternaux, C., Levy, D., Shenton, M., Perry, J., et al. (1993). The Thought Disorder Index: A Reliability Study. *Psychological Assessment, 5,* 336–342.
Coleman, M., Levy, D., Lenzenweger, M., & Holzman, P. (1996). Thought disorder, perceptual aberrations, and schizotypy. *Journal of Abnormal Psychology, 105,* 469–473.
Eckblad, M., & Chapman, L. (1983). Magical ideation as an indicator of schizotypy. *Journal of Consulting and Clinical Psychology, 51,* 215–225.
Edell, W. (1987). Role of structure in disordered thinking in borderline and schizophrenic disorders. *Journal of Personality Assessment, 51,* 23–41.
Erdberg, P. (2003, March). *Rorschach assessment of personality disorders.* Symposia at the meeting of the Society for Personality Assessment, San Francisco, CA.
Exner, J. (1986). Some Rorschach data comparing schizophrenics with borderline and schizotypal personality disorders. *Journal of Personality Assessment, 50*(3), 455–471.
Exner, J. (2003). *The Rorschach: A Comprehensive System: Volume 1. Basic foundations* (4th ed.). New York: John Wiley.
Fossati, A., Maffei, C., Battaglia, M., Bagnato, M., Donati, D., Donini, M., et al. (2001). Latent class analysis of DSM-IV schizotypal personality disorder criteria in psychiatric patients. *Schizophrenia Bulletin, 27,* 59–71.
Holzman, P., Shenton, M., & Solovay, M. (1986). Quality of thought disorder in differential diagnosis. *Schizophrenia Bulletin, 12,* 360–372.
Kendler, K. (1985). Diagnostic approaches to schizotypal personality disorder: A historical perspective. *Schizophrenia Bulletin, 11,* 538–553.
Kendler, K., Masterson, C., Ungaro, R., & Davis, K. (1984). A family history study of schizophrenia-related personality disorders. *American Journal of Psychiatry, 141,* 424–427.

Kendler, K., McGuire, M., Gruenberg, A., O'Hare, A., Spellman, M., & Walsh, D. (1993). The Roscommon family study III: Schizophrenia-related personality disorders in relatives. *Archives of General Psychiatry, 50,* 781–788.

Kendler, K., McGuire, M., Gruenberg, A., & Walsh, D. (1995). Schizotypal symptoms and sign in the Roscommon family study: Their factor structure and familial relationship with psychotic and affective disorders. *Archives of General Psychiatry, 52,* 296–303.

Kernberg, O. (1967). Borderline personality organization. *Journal of the American Psychoanalytic Association, 15,* 641–685.

Kernberg, O. (1984). *Severe personality disorders: Psychotherapeutic strategies.* New Haven, CT: Yale University Press.

MacDonald, A., Pogue-Geile, M., Debski, T., & Manuck, S. (2001). Genetic and environmental influences on schizotypy: A community-based twin study. *Schizophrenia Bulletin, 27,* 47–58.

Meehl, P. (1990). Toward an integrated theory of schizotaxia, schizotypy, and schizophrenia. *Journal of Personality Disorders, 4,* 1–99.

Meehl, P. E. (1962). Schizotaxia, schizotypy, schizophrenia. *American Psychologist, 17,* 828–838.

Millon, T. (1969). *Modern psychopathology.* Prospect Heights, IL: Waveland Press.

Millon, T. (1996). *Disorders of personality DSM-IV and beyond.* New York: John Wiley.

Perry, W., Minassian, A., Cadenhead, K., Sprock, J., & Braff, D. (2003). The use of the Ego Impairment Index across the schizophrenia spectrum. *Journal of Personality Assessment, 80,* 50–57.

Perry, W., & Viglione, D. (1991). The Ego Impairment Index as a predictor of outcome in melancholic depressed patients treated with tricyclic antidepressants. *Journal of Personality Assessment, 56,* 487–501.

Rado, S. (1953). Dynamics and classification of disordered behavior. *American Journal of Psychiatry, 110,* 406–416.

Raine, A. (1991). The SPQ: A scale for the assessment of schizotypal personality based on DSM-III-R criteria. *Schizophrenia Bulletin, 17,* 555–564.

Rapaport, D., Gill, M., & Schafer, R. (1968). The Rorschach test. In R. Holt (Ed.), *Diagnostic psychological testing* (pp. 268–463). New York: International Universities Press. (Original published 1945)

Siever, L., Amin, F., Coccaro, E., Bernstein, D., Kavoussi, R., Horvath, T., et al. (1991). Plasma homovanillic acid in schizotypal personality disorder. *American Journal of Psychiatry, 148,* 1246–1248.

Siever, L., Bernstein, D., & Silverman, J. (1995). Schizotypal personality disorder. In J. Livesley (Ed.), *The DSM-IV personality disorders* (pp. 71–90). New York, NY: Guilford.

Skodol, A., Gunderson, J., McGlashan, T., Dyck, I., Stout, R., Bender, D., et al. (2002). Functional impairment in patients with schizotypal, borderline, avoidant, or obsessive-compulsive personality disorder. *American Journal of Psychiatry, 159,* 276–283.

Solovay, M. R., Shenton, M. E., Gasperretti, C., Coleman, M., Kestenbaum, E., Carpenter, J. T., & Holzman, P. S. (1986). Scoring manual for Thought Disorder Index (revised version). *Schizophrenia Bulletin, 12,* 483–496.

Torgersen, S. (1984). Genetic and nosological aspects of schizotypal and borderline personality disorder: A twin study. *Archives of General Psychiatry, 41,* 546–554.

Torgersen, S. (1995). Commentary on paranoid, schizoid, and schizotypal personality disorders. In J. Livesley (Ed.), *The DSM-IV personality disorders* (pp. 91–102). New York: Guilford.

Torgersen, S., Edvardsen, J., Oien, P., Onstad, S., Skre, I., Lygren, S., et al. (2002). Schizotypal personality disorder inside and outside the schizophrenic spectrum. *Schizophrenia Research, 54,* 33–38.

Torgersen, S., Onstad, S., Skre, I., Edvardsen, J., & Kringlen, E. (1993). "True" schizotypal personality disorder: A study of co-twins and relatives of schizophrenia probands. *American Journal of Psychiatry, 150,* 1661–1667.

Trestman, R., Keefe, R., Mitropoulou, V., Harvey, P., deVegvar, M., Lees-Roitman, S., et al. (1995). Cognitive function and biological correlates of cognitive performance in schizotypal personality disorder. *Psychiatry Research, 59,* 127–136.

Venables, P. (1995). Schizotypal status as a developmental stage in studies of risk for schizophrenia. In A. Raine, T. Lencz, & S. Mednick, (Eds.), *Schizotypal personality* (pp. 107–134). New York: Cambridge University Press.

Waldeck, T. & Miller, L. (2000). Social skills deficits in schizotypal personality disorder. *Psychiatry Research, 93,* 237–246.

Weiner, I. B. (2000). Using the Rorschach properly in practice and research. *Journal of Clinical Psychology, 56,* 435–438.

Weiner, I. B. (2003). *Principles of Rorschach interpretation* (2nd ed.). Mahwah, NJ: Lawrence Erlbaum Associates.

Weinstein, S., & Graves, R. (2001). Creativity, schizotypy, and laterality. *Cognitive Neuropsychiatry, 6,* 131–146.

Free Association	Inquiry
Card I 1. That looks like a thing that doesn't exist, like a bug of some kind.	1. It has antennae, body.
2. The whole thing looks like an angel, but it doesn't have a head.	2. The dark wings here and the body, but the head is missing.
3. The whole thing looks like a bat.	3. The body here, the wings here; there are spots on the wings here and here.
Card II 4. That looks like a face.	4. See the face here, the eyes; this part is the mouth; the cheeks here and here, and the red hat on top. He looks flustrated. (What made it look flustrated?) Just the way the eyes and the mouth are shaped.
5. That part looks like a dog.	5. Right here is the head, the nose, and ears are here, and then this is his tail. He's got feet here and here, just a dog.
6. This looks like a rocket ship blasting off.	6. This part here looks like the rocket ship; you can see the red exhaust coming out the back. I don't know, just looks like a rocket ship to me.
7. These could be two pigs sitting up.	7. I can see two pigs here and here, and it looks like they're sitting up looking at each other like this.
Card III 8. Okay, this looks like a, two women at home exercising.	8. These figures are probably people because they have heads, noses. (What made it look like exercising?) They're in such an unusual position, because they're bent over and the hands are holding on to that exercise equipment.
Card IV 9. This looks like a pelvis.	9. It's black and shaped like a pelvis, or at least what I think it would look like.
Card V 10. That looks like two buffalos charging at each other.	10. See here and here are the buffalo. They are hitting each other, ramming their heads together.

Card VI

11. A tanned animal hide.

11. Because it's tanned with its whiskers on, its nose and the whiskers that come off its face (points). It's got the midriff like a hamster or donkey, and it has skin that comes out here and here (points) where the skin came off the legs.

12. (v) A monster face.

12. Here's his head and his eyes and his chin. He looks like he's staring off in space, the top of his head has been cut off because there's nothing up there (points).

Card VII

13. Two people staring away from each other.

13. Right here and right here, two people looking away, like they are trying not to see each other, like nu'uh.

Card VIII

14. That looks like bobcats.

14. Right here is one and here is one. They have legs here, here, here and here, and that's the head.

Card IX

15. It looks like this white part is a cow head.

15. The white part is wider here like a head and here's the nostrils and here's the tongue, like on the cartoons how the head is shaped funny, the cartoon animals always look different than real ones; it's weird how they draw them; I wonder how they learn to do that.

16. That's two sea horses, just looking at each other.

16. See here and here? They are sea horses because here's the head and the little body and they are looking at each other as they float along.

17. That part could also be the top part of a person. See the green spine?

17. See here how you just see the green spine? There are the shoulders and the waist; he's just standing there but there's no head or legs, just the, what do you call that, I don't know, but that's what it looks like.

Card X

18. The turquoise blue part is crabs.

18. You can tell they are crabs because they have a lot of legs and a big claw, with some seaweed hanging off them (What made it look like seaweed?) Just the way it hangs there.

19. That kind of looks like a bug crawling.

19. Just right here, crawling, here's its body and its antennae sticking out.

20. It looks like a bug stuck in some seaweed.

20. Just here and this is the seaweed.

RORSCHACH SEQUENCE OF SCORES FOR MR. MATSON

Card	Resp	Loc (DQ)	Loc N	Determinants (FQ)	(2)	Content(s)	P	Z	Special Scores
I	1.	Do	4	Fo		A			DR
	2.	Wo	1	FYo		(Hd)		1.0	GHR
	3.	WSo	1	Fo		A	P	3.5	
II	4.	WS+	1	FC-		Hd,Hh		4.5	DV,PHR
	5.	Ddo	99	Fu		A			
	6.	DS+	5	FC.mao		Sc,Fi		3.0	
III	7.	D+	6	Mp-	(2)	A		3.0	FAB,PHR
	8.	D+	1	Mao	(2)	H,Id	P	3.0	GHR
IV	9.	Ddo	99	FC'u		An			
V	10.	W+	1	FMao	(2)	A		2.5	AG,PHR
VI	11.	Wo	1	Fo		Ad	P	2.5	DV
	12.	Wo	1	Mpu		Hd		2.5	MOR,PHR
VII	13.	D+	3	Mp-	(2)	Hd		3.0	DV,PHR
VIII	14.	Do	1	Fo	(2)	A	P		
IX	15.	DSo	8	Fu		Ad		5.0	DR
	16.	D+	3	FMpu	(2)	A		4.5	
	17.	DSo	8	Mp.CF-		Hd		5.0	PHR
X	18.	D+	1	Fo	(2)	A,Bt	P	4.5	
	19.	Do	3	FMa-		A			
	20.	Dv	10	FMp-		A,Bt			

Location Features	Determinants Blends	Single	Contents	Approach
		M = 4	H = 1	I: D.W.WS
Zf = 14	FC.m	FM = 4	(H) = 0	II: WS.Dd.DS.D
ZSum = 47.5	M.CF	m = 0	Hd = 4	III: D
Zest = 45.5		FC = 1	(Hd) = 1	IV: Dd
		CF = 0	Hx = 0	V: W
W = 6		C = 0	A = 10	VI: W.W
D = 12		Cn = 0	(A) = 0	VII: D
W+D =18		FC' = 1	Ad = 2	VIII: D
Dd = 2		C'F = 0	(Ad) = 0	IX: DS.D.DS
S = 5		C'= 0	An = 1	X: D.D.D
		FT = 0	Art = 0	
Developmental Quality		TF = 0	Ay = 0	Special Scores
+ = 8		T = 0	Bl = 0	Lv 1 Lv 2
o = 11		FV = 0	Bt = 2	DV = 3x1 = 0x2
v = 1		VF = 0	Cg = 0	INC = 0x2 = 0x4
v/+ = 0		V = 0	Cl = 0	DR = 2x3 = 0x6
		FY = 1	Ex = 0	FAB = 1x4 = 0x7

	Form Quality					
	FQx	MQual	W+D	YF = 0	Fd = 0	ALOG = 0x5
+	= 0	= 0	= 0	Y= 0	Fi = 1	CON = 0x7
o	= 9	= 1	= 9	Fr = 0	Ge = 0	Raw Sum 6 = 6
u	= 5	= 1	= 3	rF = 0	Hh = 1	Wgtd Sum 6 = 13
-	= 6	= 2	= 6	FD = 0	Ls = 0	
none	= 0	= 0	= 0	F = 7	Na = 0	AB = 0 GHR = 2
				(2) = 7	Sc = 1	AG = 1 PHR = 6
					Sx = 0	COP = 0 MOR = 1
					Xy = 0	CP = 0 PER = 0
					Id = 1	PSV = 0

Ratios, Percentages, and Derivations

Core

R =	20	L = .54

EB =	5:2	EA =	7	EBPer = 2.5
eb =	5:2	es =	7	D = 0
		Adj es = 7		Adj D = 0

FM =	4	SumC' = 1	SumT = 0
m =	1	Sum V = 0	Sum Y = 1

Affect

C: CF+C = 2:1
Pure C = 0
SumC':WSumC = 1:2
Afr = .54
S = 5
Blends:R = 2:20
CP = 0

Interpersonal

COP = 0   AG = 1
GHR: PHR = 2:6
a:p = 4:6
Food = 0
Sum T = 0
Human Cont = 6
Pure H = 1
PER = 0
Isol Indx = .10

Ideation

a:p =	4:6	Sum6 = 6
Ma:Mp = 1:4		Lv2 = 0
2AB+Art+Ay =0		WSum6 = 13
MOR = 1		M- = 3
		M none = 0

Mediation

XA% = .70
WDA% = .67
X-% = .30
S- = 2
P = 5
X+% = .45
Xu% = .25

Processing

Zf = 14
W:D:Dd = 6:12:2
W:M = 6:5
Zd = +2.0
PSV = 0
DQ+ = 8
DQv = 1

Self-Perception

3r+(2)/R = .35
Fr+rF = 0
SumV = 0
FD = 0
An+Xy = 1
MOR = 1
H:(H)+Hd+(Hd) = 1:5

PTI = 2   DEPI = 3   CDI = 3   S-CON = 3   HVI = No   OBS = No

III

CLUSTER B
PERSONALITY DISORDERS

Rorschach Assessment of Antisocial Personality Disorder and Psychopathy

James L. Loving
Private Practice, Philadelphia, Pennsylvania

Alan J. Lee
Private Practice, Hamilton, New Jersey

Assessment of individuals with antisocial or psychopathic personalities presents a number of challenges, including concerns about malingering, deception, and other deviant response sets; poor insight; overt defensiveness; difficult interpersonal styles; and possibly a heightened risk for violence Because these individuals often are encountered in forensic or correctional settings, these psychological and interpersonal obstacles are likely to be magnified by situational variables (e.g., high-stakes evaluation contexts, with obvious or subtle secondary gains; possible adversarial examinee–examiner dynamics). In these cases, assessment requires a reliance on multiple data sources, including not only a standard interview, but also an emphasis on behavioral observations, collateral records and interviews, and convergent psychological testing data. The Rorschach Inkblot Method may play a highly useful role within this integrative assessment approach.

Not surprisingly, the Rorschach assessment of antisocial personality disorder (ASPD) has received as much attention—theoretical, empirical, and critical—in the literature as any of the other personality disorders. This chapter provides an overview of the available conceptual and empirical literature. It includes specific reference to the use of the Rorschach in forensic settings, emphasizing a conservative, integrative approach to interpretation that should be thoroughly defensible in relevant referral situations. At the same time, the discussion notes areas of research that have thus far been less well validated but hold promise for clinical practice. These concepts are applied to an illustrative case example, and the chapter concludes with a look at the future of Rorschach assessment with this clinical population.

ASPD AND PSYCHOPATHY: OVERLAPPING BUT DISTINCT CONSTRUCTS

Psychopathy, or psychopathic personality, and its *Diagnostic and Statistical Manual of Mental Disorders* (DSM) counterpart, ASPD (American Psychiatric Association [APA], 2000), are closely related but distinct constructs. Because these terms are sometimes (incorrectly) treated as synonymous, a brief discussion of their similarities and differences is necessary.

Psychopathy has a long and convoluted history. At times, the condition has been overinclusive to the point of encompassing an amazing assortment of individuals with dysfunctional or perverse behaviors. At other times, the term has been narrowed to a much more homogeneous construct. The modern concept of psychopathy is tied to the conceptual work of Cleckley (1941), who spelled out and illustrated a list of behavioral and interpersonal attributes that he believed to be displayed by the prototypical psychopath. These included antisocial behavior, lack of remorse or sincerity, superficial charm, and an absence of distress or major neurotic or psychotic symptoms. Current descriptions of psychopathy typically include not only the individual's persistently irresponsible, rule-flouting behavior, but also his emotional disengagement and his aggressively narcissistic interpersonal stance.

Earlier versions of the DSM (e.g., APA, 1968) delineated ASPD using criteria that captured the essence of psychopathy. However, because of a desire to improve the reliability of the diagnosis, later DSM iterations have moved toward criteria that are almost exclusively behavioral, with a relative underemphasis on the underlying personality characteristics that are presumably at the core of the condition. The current criteria (Table 6.1) also are heavily weighted toward delinquent and illegal behaviors, so much so that it has been estimated (Hare, 1991) that up to 75% of correctional populations meet the criteria for ASPD. For the same reason, outside legal and correctional settings, some unknown proportion of individuals possesses psychopathic interpersonal and emotional features but fails to meet ASPD diagnostic criteria. Along these lines, several critical authors (Kernberg, 1992; Millon & Davis, 1996) have argued that ASPD has "drifted" so far from the traditional notion of psychopathy that it now encompasses a markedly different subset of people, and in fact no longer identifies any unique, coherent construct. The juvenile precursor of ASPD, conduct disorder, has a parallel history and has been the subject of similar lines of criticism.

TABLE 6.1

Modern Diagnostic Criteria for Antisocial Personality Disorder (APA, 2000)

A. Pervasive pattern of disregard for and violation of the rights of others, occurring since the age of 15 years, as indicated by three (or more) of the following:

     1. Failure to conform to social norms and lawful behaviors

     2. Deceitfulness

     3. Impulsivity or failure to plan ahead

     4. Irritability and aggressiveness

     5. Reckless disregard for the safety of self or others

     6. Consistent irresponsibility with respect to work or honoring of financial obligations

     7. Lack of remorse

B. Age of at least 18 years

C. Evidence of conduct disorder with onset before the age of 15 years

D. Occurrence of antisocial behavior not exclusively during the course of schizophrenia or a manic episode

As they are currently defined, ASPD and conduct disorder encompass a fairly wide range of individuals who repeatedly engage in illicit and irresponsible behavior. To illustrate, Rogers, Duncan, Lynett, and Sewell (1994) calculated that more than a half million combinations of diagnostic criteria allow for a diagnosis of ASPD, ranging from relatively innocuous combinations of behavior to much more disturbed and aggressive behaviors. Most psychopathic adults qualify for an ASPD diagnosis, but most ASPD adults do not exhibit a fully crystallized psychopathic personality. An antisocial individual, for example, may continually act out because of impulse control deficits, but also may possess a degree of the superego development and attachment capacity that are strikingly absent with true psychopathy. Some evidence has accumulated to suggest that primary psychopathy exists as a qualitatively distinct taxon (Harris, Rice, & Quinsey, 1994), although it also has been recommended that, in a practice setting, the condition should be treated as existing along a continuum of severity (Gacono, Loving, & Bodholdt, 2001). In this way, some antisocial individuals might be viewed as more severely psychopathic than others, insofar as they possess more numerous and more severe personality characteristics of the prototypical psychopath.

Partly in response to the shortcomings of ASPD taxonomy, Hare (1980, 1991, 2003) developed an instrument for assessing traditional psychopathy: The Psychopathy Checklist—Revised (PCL-R). This instrument is an evaluator rating scale that derives data from a detailed clinical interview and an in-depth review of collateral information. The PCL-R includes not only behavioral items, but also items that make up the interpersonal and affective factors of traditional psychopathy (Cooke & Michie, 2001). The instrument has been subjected to extensive empirical study, as well as a recent expansion of its normative data (Hare, 2003). This research base has supported the reliability and validity of psychopathy, as measured by the PCL-R, and has found the condition to be strongly associated with a wide variety of important outcomes in forensic samples (see Hare, 2003, for a review). Of most importance, PCL-R psychopathy has been identified as the single best predictor of future violence for various samples (Hemphill, Hare, & Wong, 1998; Steadman, et al., 2000). The presence of ASPD probably is most notable in nonforensic settings, where base rates are low. In forensic settings, however, findings have not shown the ASPD diagnosis to be predictive of violence or other key behavioral outcomes, as PCL-R psychopathy has. This lack of predictive validity is especially important, because clinicians and court officials inaccurately tend to infer a dismal treatment prognosis based on ASPD diagnosis (Lyon & Ogloff, 2000).

The distinctions between ASPD and psychopathy have been muddied by the text descriptions offered in the DSM-IV Text Revision (2000) and its earlier versions. The diagnostic criteria of ASPD are largely behavioral and do not correspond directly with traditional psychopathy, but in the narrative text, features of prototypical psychopathy are included as "associated features" of ASPD. The text commingles the two terms as though they are fully interchangeable, then suggests applying inferences from the PCL-R literature to the ASPD diagnosis, as in the following statement:

> Lack of empathy, inflated self-appraisal, and superficial charm are features that have been commonly included in traditional conceptions of psychopathy that may be particularly distinguishing of the disorder and more predictive of recidivism in prison or forensic settings where criminal, delinquent, or aggressive acts are likely to be nonspecific. (APA, 2000, p. 703)

In cases wherein the diagnostic criteria for ASPD are met, there is a risk of overinferring the presence of interpersonal and affective psychopathic features, and also of overestimating the individual's risk for violence or recidivism. Conceptually, ASPD and psychopathy are phenomenologically the same (e.g., evidencing an egocentric sense of self as well as object relations marked by aggression, predation, and a survival orientation). The reader must view research on ASPD with caution, however, because samples may be overinclusive, including some individuals who are behaviorally antisocial but not truly psychopathic.

ROLE OF THE RORSCHACH IN THE ASSESSMENT OF ASPD AND PSYCHOPATHY

Detecting the presence and severity of psychopathy is vital to many evaluations, in part because the disorder may have direct implications for treatment amenability and prognosis, as well as risk for violence, malingering, and other forms of problematic behavior. When an examinee has a known history of antisocial behavior, in-depth assessment can help determine to what degree this behavior has been fueled by underlying psychopathic personality features, as compared with other factors (e.g., substance abuse, impulse control deficits, self-destructive behavior perpetuated by other forms of psychopathology). Psychopathy and ASPD can exist with comorbid psychiatric conditions and intellectual limitations, with antisocial features uniquely coloring these conditions and vice versa.

Unfortunately, assessment becomes potentially complicated when issues of ASPD or psychopathy arise. Individuals whose personalities fall along the antisocial spectrum are notorious for both their reliance on deception and their lack of insight. Multimethod assessment becomes especially important, and in the context of this approach, the Rorschach may play a useful role in providing convergent or divergent data, so that conclusions are as robust and confident as possible.

As Meloy and Gacono (2000) have pointed out, during a thorough assessment of an antisocial individual, the Rorschach can provide increased depth and breadth of information, beyond what may be gleaned from other methods. In their words,

> What begins as a gross categorization of chronic antisocial behavior (DSM-IV) moves to a determination of the degree of psychopathic disturbance using the PCL-R. It is further refined through the Rorschach to measure the internal structure and dynamics of the particular patient. (p. 238)

Rorschach assessment can help to identify the presence of psychopathy, but it is arguably more useful for enriching the understanding of the examinee's unique strengths, weaknesses, and triggers that may increase his risk for acting out.

Forensic Applications

Although slightly off the main topic of this chapter, the use of the Rorschach in forensic contexts deserves specific discussion because it is in these settings that issues of antisociality and psychopathy most often become relevant. Also, in forensic contexts, instruments such as the Rorschach are most likely to receive close professional scrutiny. The clinician who applies the Rorschach to forensic cases needs to maintain a working knowledge of the current empirical and professional literature. A full discussion of this area is too parenthetical for inclusion here, but is available elsewhere (Gacono, Evans, & Viglione, 2002).

To summarize a few key points, it has been persuasively argued that the Rorschach is a commonly used, generally accepted tool that meets relevant admissibility standards. However, each of these points has been criticized on various grounds, so the clinician needs to remain aware of the evolving literature. For instance, McCann (1998) argued that the Rorschach meets contemporary legal and professional standards for admissibility. This position has been elaborated and debated in a series of articles by Grove and Barden (1999; Grove, Barden, Garb, & Lilienfeld, 2000) and Ritzler, Erard, and Pettigrew (2000a, 2000b).

Depending on the specific legal standard at hand, an issue often relevant to admissibility is whether a data source is generally accepted within the field. The Rorschach is widely taught at the graduate level (Mihura & Weinle, 2002) and remains among the most pervasively used assessment instruments in clinical settings (Archer & Newsom, 2000; but see also Piotrowski, Belter, & Keller, 1998). This finding also has been seen in forensic settings (Piotrowski, 1996), although in a recent survey (Lally, 2003), a sample of 64 American Board of Professional Psychology (ABPP) forensic psychology diplomates reported using the Rorschach infrequently, and rated it at levels below "acceptable" for six of six referral questions commonly encountered in criminal court. It remains to be seen whether Lally's findings reflect trends over time, difference in subject selection across studies, or other factors.

When admissibility patterns have been studied more directly, the court typically has been welcoming of Rorschach testimony. For example, Weiner, Exner, and Sciara (1996) reported survey data for clinicians who had collectively presented Rorschach results in more than 7,900 federal and state court cases. According to their reports, Rorschach testimony was serious challenged or excluded altogether in fewer than 0.1% of the cases. Similarly, Meloy, Hansen, and Weiner (1997) conducted a search of appeals court citations involving the Rorschach spanning the previous five decades. In 194 cases, the Rorschach was important enough to warrant mention in appellate court decisions, but it was challenged in only 10% of those cases. In cases wherein Rorschach testimony had been excluded, this usually was because of invalid procedures or applications rather than psychometric problems inherent in the instrument. It would be helpful to investigate the possible impact of more recent legal standards and the debate in the professional literature on these positive findings. To this end, one recent pilot study (Owens, Patrick, Packman, & Greene, 2004) replicated the Weiner et al. (1996) survey findings and found very preliminary evidence that the Rorschach continues to be welcome in the post-Daubert courtroom. Additional replications will be necessary in the coming years.

As is the case with most available psychological instruments, the Rorschach does not provide data that directly address specific psycholegal questions. However, it may provide rich descriptive information about the examinee, which adds convergent data in support of relevant conclusions. For example, it may be inappropriate to rely routinely on the Rorschach when the psycholegal question involves a subject's competency to stand trial, but in a complicated situation wherein the functional deficits at issue involve psychotic symptoms, the Rorschach could be one source of test data that portrays the individual as someone who does in fact exhibit gross perceptual distortions and disturbed thought processes, as compared with someone whose perceptual accuracy and thinking are relatively intact, with evidence instead of psychopathic traits and situational malingering. If the Rorschach is used as one component of a thoughtfully integrated multimethod assessment, and there is a direct conceptual link between Rorschach data and relevant psycholegal issues, inclusion of the instrument should be not only defensible, but also quite useful.

THE RORSCHACH LITERATURE

Returning to the specific assessment of antisocial and psychopathic personalities, the Rorschach should not be seen as an instrument that can directly or unilaterally diagnose ASPD or detect psychopathy. It can, however, provide information about personality traits and behavioral tendencies that, when coupled with corroborating data, support the presence of psychopathy.

The use of the Rorschach to assess psychopathy dates as early as the work of Lindner in 1943. Investigating the Rorschach records of incarcerated criminals whose diagnosis by prison psychiatric staff, identified them as either psychopathic or nonpsychopathic, Lindner found that the test protocols of psychopaths showed explosive, impulsive, asocial features, as well as generally superficial interpersonal relations. Another notable early contributor was Schafer (1948), who found the Rorschach effective in detecting the "chief personality features" of psychopathy. He asserted that, despite their tendency to generate "flat and bland" protocols, these individuals consistently demonstrate several characteristic structural features, such as a lack of shading responses (representing a corresponding absence of anxiety), a predominance of color over form (associated with conspicuous aggressiveness and impulsiveness), and numerous vaguely articulated whole responses (reflecting poor analytic and integrative abilities). In addition to many structural findings, Schafer outlined the interpersonal style he expected psychopathic characters to display during testing. In his experience, these individuals were likely to put up a pretentious, transparent front of excessive compliance, representing an attempt to disguise underlying shallow, primitive, and disdainful feelings toward the examiner.

More recently, various authors have investigated variables that exist within the Rorschach's Comprehensive System (Exner, 2003) as they relate to psychopathy and related conditions. In a conceptually useful article, Weiner (1991) described a study involving adjudicated and nonadjudicated adolescents and adults with a DSM-III-R diagnosis of ASPD. Selected Rorschach variables from these subjects were compared with the adult nonpatient norms used at the time (Exner, 1986). On the basis of both existing theory and the results of his study, Weiner presented a model incorporating various Rorschach indices into the assessment of psychopathy and criminality. He proposed that certain test variables correspond to underlying superego deficits and by definition reveal the presence of psychopathic features. At the same time, other variables relate to ego impairments, so that their presence predicts the demonstration of social maladjustment and the commitment of criminal behaviors that result in arrest. Specifically, Weiner asserted that the collective presence of four test findings ($T = 0$; $COP = 0$; pure $H < 2$; $S > 2$) is strongly indicative of psychopathic personality. Furthermore, he stated that 12 test indices associated with ego impairment (EB = ambient; $L > .99$; $Zd < -3.0$; $X + \% < .61$; $X-\% > .19$; $P < 4$; $Mp < Ma$; $p > a+1$; $CDI > 3$; $CF + C > FC + 1$; Pure $C > 0$; $FD = 0$) are predictive of unsuccessful criminal behavior (i.e., the commitment of criminal behavior resulting in arrest).

Exner (2003) cited two earlier studies that investigated reflection responses, wherein "sociopaths" or "imprisoned character disorders diagnosed with antisocial personality" produced more reflections than comparison groups, presumably providing evidence of increased self-absorption in these antisocial samples. In a study by Exner (cited in Exner & Weiner, 1995), adolescents who had been assigned DSM-III conduct disorder yielded Rorschach results that deviated from normative samples in ways that suggested diminished openness to interpersonal closeness, expectations for positive interactions, or interest in people (i.e., producing virtually no T, COP, or pure H scores, respectively). In the conduct disorder sample, other indices were further suggestive of interpersonal distance, wariness, and vigilance (positive Hypervigilence Index and elevated Isolation Index).

Kaser-Boyd (1993) compared the Rorschachs of battered women who had murdered their partners with the Comprehensive System normative data available at the time (Exner, 1986). As part of her discussion,

Kaser-Boyd noted a small subsample of "sociopathic female perpetrators" among her examinees. Like the majority of the women studied, the sociopaths tended to produce brief, constricted protocols characterized by an extratensive style and poor affect modulation. Unlike the nonsociopathic group members, however, they demonstrated much better reality testing and active, rather than passive, ideation. Not surprisingly, Rorschach analyses of potentially antisocial but overly diverse groups, such as adolescent murderers (Greco & Cornell, 1992) or Kaser-Boyd's (1993) undifferentiated sample of violent battered women, have not generally yielded substantial findings when comparisons have been made with "normal" populations. Characteristic test patterns have a greater likelihood of emerging when more homogeneous, meaningful groups are studied (see Gacono et al., 2001, for a more detailed discussion and additional examples).

By far the most comprehensive application of the Rorschach to psychopathy and related conditions was undertaken by Gacono and Meloy (1994) whose work culminated in their widely cited book, *The Rorschach Assessment of Aggressive and Psychopathic Personalities*. Earlier, Meloy (1988) had offered detailed, conceptually embedded hypotheses as to the Rorschach variables expected to be illustrative of psychopathy. In several studies that followed, Gacono, Meloy, and various colleagues investigated the Rorschach findings among subgroups of antisocial, conduct-disordered, and / or psychopathic samples, with the latter distinguished using the PCL-R or its predecessor, the PCL.

Gacono (1990) tested the hypothesis (Kernberg, 1975; Meloy, 1988) that individuals with dominant antisocial features are organized at the borderline level of personality organization. Using the PCL, he categorized a group of male ASPD inmates ($n = 33$) as either psychopathic or nonpsychopathic. Gacono noted that his "nonpsychopathic" subgroup was composed mostly of individuals who had earned moderate PCL scores, so they would be more precisely described as moderately psychopathic. Using several Rorschach research scales (Cooper & Arnow, 1986; Kwawer, 1980; Lerner & Lerner, 1980) and an independent measure of narcissism, he discovered high measures of borderline-level defensive operations and object relations, as well as a high prevalence of narcissism, in both ASPD groups. Gacono concluded that his findings supported Kernberg's original assertions about the presence of pathologic (or malignant) narcissism in the antisocial individuals studied. Gacono and Meloy (1992) later expanded on these findings using a larger sample.

More support for the presence of heightened narcissism among psychopaths was obtained through another study investigating psychopathic in comparison with moderately psychopathic ASPD-diagnosed criminals (Gacono, Meloy, & Heaven, 1990; $n = 42$). As a group, the psychopathic subjects exhibited higher levels of narcissism (high Fr), defensive omnipotence (high PER), and pathologic self-focus (high Egocentricity Index) relative to their less psychopathic ASPD counterparts.

Next, Gacono and Meloy (1991) examined patterns of attachment and anxiety in adult ASPD males (n = 42), again differentiating psychopathic from moderately psychopathic inmates using the PCL. Psychopaths were seen as exhibiting interpersonal detachment (low T) and a lack of diffuse anxiety (low Y). Also, D and AdjD scores showed a nonsignificant trend in the direction of less discomfort (higher D and AdjD) for the psychopathic group. Perhaps surprisingly, no difference was revealed between the two groups with respect to the frequency of vista (V), a variable associated with negative, painful introspection. The authors interpreted the presence of V in psychopaths as indicative of "failed grandiosity" or self-pity in response to being incarcerated. Separately, Gacono and Meloy (1992) compared Rorschachs of psychopathic and nonpsychopathic ASPD-diagnosed inmates (combined n = 60) with Comprehensive System (Exner, 1986) adult normative data. Psychopaths displayed elevated scores that the authors associated with narcissism (Fr), omnipotent defensiveness (PER), and grandiose aspirations (W:M). Also found among the psychopathic subjects was evidence of interpersonal detachment (low T) and a lack of interest in people as whole, real beings (low pure H), as well as unrealistic, pessimistic expectations for interpersonal exchanges (high Hd and low COP).

To test the hypothesis that psychopathic personalities represent an aggressive variant of narcissistic personality disorder, Gacono, Meloy, and Berg (1992) evaluated the Rorschach protocols of four subject groups: psychopathic and nonpsychopathic ASPD felons, as well as noninstitutionalized adults with a diagnosis of narcissistic personality disorder or borderline personality disorder. As compared with the clinically narcissistic group, the psychopathic ASPD group demonstrated comparably high rates of narcissism (high Fr and Egocentricity Index), but significantly less anxiety (fewer Y) and less capacity for attachment (fewer T). Also notable were the results for the nonpsychopathic ASPD inmates, who displayed significantly less narcissism than the psychopathic inmates and narcissistic personalities, as well as considerably higher levels of anxiety and attachment capacity than the psychopaths. Gacono, Meloy, and Bridges (2000) compared selected Rorschach variables in non–sexually offending psychopaths with those in sexual homicide perpetrators and nonviolent pedophiles (n =109). Their psychopathic subgroup differed from the other two subgroups by producing less evidence of interpersonal interest and attachment (Pure H, T), and less evidence of distress. A later study by Huprich, Gacono, Schneider, and Bridges (2004) found that psychopaths and psychopathic sexual homicide perpetrators had higher levels of oral dependency and aggression special scores that occurred together in their Rorschach protocols. Collectively, these two studies support Kernberg's

(1992) and Meloy's (1988) ideas that psychopaths are aggressivelyoriented variations of a narcissistic personality disorder.

A number of authors have investigated the Rorschach literature in the context of adolescents identified as conduct disordered or psychopathic. Weber, Meloy, and Gacono (1992) found that adolescents with conduct disorder produce less T, less H, and more Y than a comparison group of dysthymic adolescents ($n = 78$). Loving and Russell (2000) examined the Rorschach data of violent juveniles categorized as low, moderate, or high in terms of psychopathy, using the youth version of the PCL (since published as Forth, Kosson, & Hare, 2003). In that study ($N = 66$), the high psychopathy sample produced higher Fr and lower T than their less psychopathic counterparts. When Smith, Gacono, and Kaufman (1997) similarly compared the Rorschachs of psychopathic and nonpsychopathic adolescents with conduct disorder ($n = 45$), they discovered significantly higher mean Egocentricity Index scores in their psychopathic group. They also found a nonsignificant trend in the expected direction with respect to reflections, but no other significant differences in terms of the variables discussed in this presentation. Other Rorschach studies of conduct disorder or psychopathic juveniles have shown mixed or negative results (Archer & Krishnamurthy, 1997). Additional research would help to determine whether this speaks to the ineffectiveness of the Rorschach with this specific population or to the heterogeneity of antisocial adolescent samples, in which psychopathy may be imprecisely assessed and may not yet be fully crystallized.

In recent years, research attention has focused on investigating various extended aggression variables, first discussed in depth by Meloy and Gacono (1992). As described in their initial article, they counterintuitively discovered that psychopathic samples and other groups known to be violent actually produced lower Aggressive Movement (AG) than comparison groups. On the basis of their findings, they suggested that the presence of high AG may relate to the experience of egodystonic aggression. This was in contrast to the earlier conclusion that AG was associated with potential for aggressive acting out. Meloy and Gacono (1992) argued that psychopaths produce fewer AG scores than the average because they tend to discharge their aggressive impulses immediately instead of experiencing them internally. As a separate but compatible explanation, the lack of aggressive movement may be a by-product of the overall lack of interaction seen among factors in the typical psychopath's protocol. That is, AG responses often occur in the context of explicit interaction between two or more characters, and this type of interaction is grossly lacking in the symbolized object relations of many psychopathic examinees.

Gacono and Meloy's (1992) findings led them to develop new categories of aggressive responses that they believed would more accurately and comprehensively allow for the expression of various aggression-related experiences. Table 6.2 lists these variables, with scoring criteria and response examples. Extending the seminal work of these authors, Baity and Hilsenroth (1999, 2002; Baity, McDaniel, & Hilsenroth, 2000) have investigated the extended aggression scores, paying particular attention to the Aggressive Content (AgC) score. On the basis of their findings, these scores appear to be reliably coded, only partially overlapping, and related to internal representations of and possibly real-world expressions of aggression. Baity and Hilsenroth (1999) noted that "the aggression variables do appear useful in providing clinical information about internal representations, interpersonal relations, and maladaptive functioning" (p. 108). In particular, elevated AgC has been associated with the presence of ASPD, and AgC also has been regularly observed in psychopaths, sexual homicide perpetrators,

TABLE 6.2

**Extended Aggression Variables: Scoring Criteria and Examples
(adapted with permission from Meloy & Gacono, 1992)**

Variable	Scoring Criteria	Examples
Aggressive movement (AG; see Exner, 2003)	Any movement response in which the action is clearly aggressive	"It's two people pulling a crab apart"
Aggressive Content (AgC)	Any content (except content coded as popular) that is popularly perceived as predatory, dangerous, malevolent, injurious, or harmful	"It's a gun"
Aggressive Potential (AgPot)	Any response in which an aggressive act is getting ready to occur	"Two little alien creatures … these crab creatures are going to lop their heads off"
Aggressive Past (AgPast)	Any response in which an aggressive act has occurred or the object has been the target of aggression	"Looks like a bug here; someone used a drill press on him"
Sado-Masochism (SM)	Any response in which devalued, aggressive, or morbid content is accompanied by pleasurable affect expressed by the subject	"Two bears attacking this butterfly and doing a high-five" or "A lady dancing and she got her head blown off" with pleasurable laughter from examinee

and pedophiles (Huprich et al., 2004). For AgC and the other extended variables, specific cutoff scores and interpretive implications have yet to be explored sufficiently in the published literature. However, Mihura and her colleagues (Mihura & Nathan-Montano, 2001; Mihura, Nathan-Montano, & Alperin, 2003) have recently begun to explore the correlates of the various extended scores, so that a more differentiated understanding of their separate meanings can be found.

As the Rorschach has been subjected to criticism in recent years, the most vocal group of critical authors has focused a segment of their attention on the assessment of psychopathy. A detailed discussion of specific issues is beyond the scope of this chapter, but can be found in a series of articles and reply articles published elsewhere (see Wood, Lilienfeld, Garb, & Nezworksi, 2000; then Gacono, Loving, & Bodlholdt, 2001; and Wood, Lilienfeld, Nezworski, & Garb, 2001).

On the basis of their earlier findings, Meloy and Gacono (2000) summarized several Comprehensive System data points expected to typify the Rorschach of a prototypical psychopath. These are adapted and presented in Table 6.3. Although this collection of values can best be described as conceptual guideposts for hypothesis generation, several of their findings have been supported through the accumulation of literature over the past decade. Other findings (e.g., cognitive triad variables) deserve further research attention.

CASE ILLUSTRATION: MR. APPLE[1]

Mr. Apple was referred to the second author (A. J. L.) for evaluation via court order, for a description of his psychological and emotional functioning, especially as it may have related to his risk for violence and other behaviors that could compromise his ability to care for his newborn child. Now in his early 50's, Mr. Apple had never married, but had fathered seven children from four different relationships. His newborn child was the product of his current 5-year relationship, although he had spent most of that time period incarcerated and had been released only 10 months prior to this evaluation. By his own account, he had little involvement with his six other children.

Although he initially described a fairly typical childhood, Mr. Apple later revealed that his parents had separated when he was 8 years old after his father's repeated domestic violence toward his mother, as well as ac-

---

[1]Excellent case illustrations of Rorschach assessment with psychopathy and ASPD are found throughout Gacono and Meloy (1994). Case illustrations are collected in Meloy, Acklin, Gacono, Murray, and Peterson (1997), and one is found in Weiner (2003).

TABLE 6.3

Selected Comprehensive System Data From a Prototypical Psychopath
(adapted from Meloy & Gacono, 2000)

Cluster	Variable	Value
Validity and approach	Responses	21
	Lambda	> 0.99
Controls and affect	D and AdjD	0
	FC: CF+C	1: 4 (Pure C > 0)
	Afr	< 0.50
	T	0
	Y	0
	S	> 2
Interpersonal perceptions	H: (H)+Hd+(Hd)	2: 2.5
	COP	0
	AG	0
	Sx	1
Self-perception	Fr	1
	PER	> 2
	W:M	> 3:1
Cognitive triad	X+%	0.54
	X–%	0.22
	M–	1
	WSum6	17

counts of his mother's infidelity. He described his father as punitive and strict, but alternatively overly lax, uninvolved, apathetic, and irresponsible. Mr. Apple noted that his own behavioral and attitude problems were in contrast to the conduct of his two high-functioning older siblings. He described sensing from an early age that he was an outsider, and he had often engaged in purposefully defiant, oppositional, and negativistic behaviors across settings. He described some recurring juvenile delinquency history. Although he purported good academic potential, he openly acknowledged that his behavioral problems had interfered with his school functioning.

After high school, Mr. Apple had enlisted in the military, but had been dishonorably discharged shortly thereafter, for reasons he declined to discuss. His adult work history primarily involved numerous hands-on labor jobs, with most of these being relatively brief and unstable. This also included one stint as a part-time substance abuse counselor, although he had apparently never sought the training required to pursue this position on a formalized basis.

Mr. Apple's employment had been interrupted by five separate and lengthy prison sentences and numerous brief periods of jail detention. His charges included multiple drug-related offenses, possession of a weapon, aggravated assault, burglary, fraud/forgery, terroristic threats, shoplifting, numerous violations of parole and probation, motor vehicle violations, nonpayment of child support, and resisting of arrest. In short, he reported more than two dozen arrests and nearly as many convictions.

Mr. Apple's medical history was noncontributory, and he had never been prescribed psychotropic medications. He described a history of poly-substance abuse throughout much of his adult life, centering on his use of cocaine and heroin, as recent as his latest incarceration that had begun roughly 5 years before this evaluation. He had previously been in two residential drug programs, including one during his most recent incarceration. Otherwise, he denied any history of psychiatric treatment, or any prominent mood disturbance other than recent depressive experiences, which were manifested through irritability and explosiveness.

During the evaluation, Mr. Apple presented as a bulky and muscular African American male who appeared younger than his chronological age might suggest. He described his mood as sad, related to recent events contributing to the evaluation, but he in fact evidenced very superficial affect and sometimes chuckled as he reminisced about his life history. Overall, he appeared detached from his self-reported emotions, and instead related in an overly intellectualized manner. He presented as remarkably arrogant and self-assured. He often made reference to his age and connected this to a sense of life wisdom. He was smooth and engaging, often trying playfully to ingratiate himself with the examiner and addressing him with the overly comfortable "Doc." He proclaimed a sense of uniqueness, for instance, seeming to brag as he recounted his lengthy legal history. Screening of intelligence-related abilities revealed no evidence of gross deficits on either the Wechsler Abbreviated Scale of Intelligence (WASI; FSIQ-2 = 90) or the Bender Visual-Motor Gestalt Test. Mr. Apple's responses to the Personality Assessment Inventory (PAI) rendered an interpretively useful protocol (ICN, INF, NIM, PIM all within normal limits), with no significant elevations on the clinical scales, although his Aggression (AGG) subscale was slightly elevated (T = 69), with Aggressive Attitude (AGG-A) at T = 70 and Antisocial Behavior (ANT-A) T = 71. The PAI thus provided some useful data, but did not do justice to Mr. Apple's rich behavioral history.

Much of the literature has encouraged the utility of conjointly using self-report inventories and unstructured techniques such as the Rorschach to assess ASPD and psychopathy (Acklin, 1993; Ganellen, 1996; Lee, 1995;

Lovitt, 1993; Weiner, 1993). The authors concurred that Mr. Apple clearly exceeded DSM-IV diagnostic criteria for ASPD, and although the PCL-R was not formally scored for the purposes of this evaluation, the authors agreed that the examinee had exhibited, through his known history and his interpersonal behaviors at evaluation, the variety and severity of affective, interpersonal, and behavioral features that would likely place him at or near the PCL-R's traditional cutoff for a high psychopathy level. Mr. Apple's Rorschach also yielded clinical information that helped explicate his historical information, observations, and other test data. His Rorschach raw responses (see Appendix A) were coded initially by the second author (A. J. L.) at the time of the evaluation and later were recoded by the first author (J. L. L.) to provide a reliability check. His Sequence of Scores and Structural Summary are displayed at the end of the chapter. The following discussion centers on Comprehensive System–based interpretation, with an incorporation of extended aggression variables and other aforementioned concepts Specific hypotheses are first derived from the Rorschach, then placed into context, using outside information from the literature and from Mr. Apple's other data sources.

Validity and Approach

Mr. Apple was productive but simplistic in his overall approach. He produced a valid number of responses ($R = 25$), which is slightly higher than the mean R values for Comprehensive System adult nonpatients and various Gacono and Meloy (1994) antisocial samples. However, his high Lambda ($L = 1.78$) suggests a marked style of oversimplifying incoming information, which is expected to impinge on his performance throughout the protocol.

Self-Perception and Interpersonal Perception

Mr. Apple showed evidence of a chronic and recurring pattern of difficulty meeting life's demands (CDI = 5). Analysis of his positive CDI content shows a relative lack of psychological resources (low EA) despite his adequate intellectual functioning The positive CDI also reflected elements of his poor interpersonal functioning, including low COP and AG (0), low Sum T (0), and high Isol/R (0.28), all collectively suggestive of social disengagement. Interestingly, Mr. Apple produced a Food response, which is traditionally interpreted in terms of oral dependency and unmet needs, which might drive him to seek gratification. This finding, which is atypical except in younger children, seems in contrast to the aforementioned signs of interpersonal detachment. Speculatively, although Mr. Apple often is distant and detached, he is not without interpersonal urges and needs. This likely results in a sense of tension between his urges and needs, and discomfort in appropriately seeking others out for whole, mutual, and reciprocal relationships. If Fd is associated with dependency needs, it is additionally interesting that his response ("filleted meat") includes coding related to a sense of damage (MOR) and brief cognitive slippage. The response also is scored with AgPast, a finding observed elsewhere with psychopathic individuals (Huprich et al., 2004).

Mr. Apple's Rorschach data suggest an interpersonal stance that is not only distant (T = 0), but also defensive or even authoritarian (PER = 3). His overall interest in others tends to be lacking (SumH = 4). When he does consider the people around him, he may not be able to view them as whole, real objects with needs independent of his own (pure H = 1). This stance may be related to a lack of expectations for positive, mutually agreeable interactions (COP = 0). Interestingly, Mr. Apple's AG value also is not elevated. If AG is associated with expectations for aggressive interactions, its absence may initially seem counterintuitive for an individual with his extensive history of anger management problems and overt violence. In actuality, as discussed earlier, this finding is consistent with antisocial samples who produce less AG than comparison groups. For Mr. Apple, his aggression has become egosyntonic to the extent that there is no significant intrapsychic tension or manifestations of AG in his protocol.

Considering Gacono and Meloy's (1992) extended aggression categories, Mr. Apple yielded four rather striking AgC responses (i.e., Dracula, Nazi insignia, volcano, the Predator), as well as two AgPast responses (i.e., bloody head of someone who "caught it bad," filleted meat cut in half). Aggression may have a more prominent place in Mr. Apple's internal world than an AG = 0 suggests, including speculatively a preoccupation with aggression and power (AgC), as well as a possible sense of having been the victim of unfair and unjust experiences (AgPast). Sequence analysis also is noteworthy, in that Mr. Apple began his Rorschach protocol with two AgC responses before a seeming effort to compensate for such aggressive representations by his third response of "angels." This sequence is perhaps not dissimilar to the psychodynamic defense mechanism of undoing. His first two responses (i.e., Dracula, Nazi insignia) also reflect some degree of intellectualization, rationalization, and psychological distancing, as suggested by AB and Ay codes. His first three responses include strong indications for PER scoring, suggesting his excessive reliance on his personal experiences to justify his early responses as he entered into this novel Rorschach experience. This likely has ramifications for analogous behaviors when he encounters novel situations in daily life.

In terms of self perception, Mr. Apple's protocol shows signs of underlying painful self-inspection (V = 1), poor self-evaluation (Egocentricity

Index = 0.28), and a sense of pessimism and being damaged (MOR = 3) or even victimized (AgPast = 2). In his case, Vista may reflect a situational sense of failed grandiosity that has surfaced in light of recent circumstances, including removal of his newborn child from his care. His sense of pessimism seems to reflect his characteristic view that he has been the victim of an unjust or unfair society, attitudes that are not uncommon among correctional and criminal populations. Mr. Apple's self-concept also includes indications of identification with the aggressor, as evidenced by his resonance with aforementioned percepts, not the least of which is "the Predator."

Capacity for Control and Affect

Again, Mr. Apple's positive CDI is a salient finding, which speaks to long-standing coping deficits and a poor prognosis for healthier adjustment, although he does not experience excessive distress (D and AdjD = 0), and does not possess age-expectable psychological resources (EA = 4.5) for managing affective irritation and situational demands. In both authors' anecdotal experience, many individuals who have spent substantial periods in incarcerated or institutionalized settings seem particularly prone to produce low EA.

Shedding light on vague self-descriptions, Mr. Apple shows evidence of significant mood-related difficulties (positive DEPI). Whereas some elements of his affective disruption may be situational in nature (e.g., V = 1), others suggest more stable predispositions. Mr. Apple's usual preference is to withdraw from emotionally charged situations (Afr = 0.39). He is much less willing than most to process and manage his emotions and is more likely to approach emotional situations in a detached, superficial, and intellectualized manner to avoid the affective impact of the same (IntellIndex = 8). Still, when he is confronted by inescapable emotions, he tends to lose cognitive constraint rather quickly (FC:CF+C = 0:2), and at times becomes rather explosive in his emotional displays (pure C = 1). In Mr. Apple's case, any experience of painful affect is likely to be fleeting because he discharges his emotions through immediate externalizing displays.

Cognitive Triad

Mr. Apple's high Lambda style (L = 1.78) signifies a rather constricted and rigid approach to taking in information, which likely impinges on the information he is able to use for decision making. He appears unable or unwilling to see the nuances and subtle details of situations, and instead receives information in a hasty, haphazard manner (Zd = −8.0) that prevents him from making well-informed decisions. Despite these liabilities, he continues to strive to accomplish far more than his resources seemingly permit

(W:M = 12:2). This may be a manifestation of the <u>unrealistically grandiose</u> <u>expectations</u> that many antisocial and psychopathic individuals present, <u>despite a lack of resources to fulfill them</u>. A remarkable degree of fluidity and immaturity was also suggested in Mr. Apple's processing (DQv = 10), suggesting that he may be at risk for regressive, immature behaviors unless he experiences external structure and boundaries.

Mr. Apple's Rorschach reveals no compelling signs of gross perceptual inaccuracies (X–% = 0.16, PTI = 0), although he does tend to respond to situations in an unconventional fashion. Instead of making conventional decisions, he prefers to offer his own idiosyncratic responses (X+% = 0.44; Xu% = 0.28), a finding that has been seen within antisocial and psychopathic samples (Gacono & Meloy, 1992). Importantly, when situations are well defined, Mr. Apple is capable of providing highly conventional responses (P = 8; WDA% = 0.73). The possibility of serious thinking problems is raised (Sum6 = 8; WSum6 = 17), but inspection of Mr. Apple's specific special score responses reveals no extreme oddities. Instead, these answers are composed only of Level 1 DVs and DRs, which appear to have stemmed from his need to demonstrate his uniqueness, self-proclaimed wit, and superiority through his expressions ("I was a great fan of the movie Papillion"; also misuses of "substance," "tendrils," and "voluminous").

Rorschach Data in Context

The preceding descriptions should be seen as hypotheses, needing further corroboration from extratest data. Although the Rorschach portrayal of Mr. Apple is rich and potentially useful, the examiner should expect to be challenged as to the validity of resultant interpretations, especially in areas wherein the empirical support is especially lacking. Several variables have been associated with psychopathy, but would benefit from additional replication so that conclusions can be offered with more confidence. In the meantime, the evaluator would be wise to implement the Rorschach as one component of a conservative, thoughtfully integrated assessment battery, in which Rorschach data points are tied closely to known observed behaviors and known history.

Both Weiner (1991) and Meloy and Gacono (2000) proposed sets of variables tied conceptually and empirically to psychopathic personality. Although it must be noted that these combinations of findings have not received sufficient empirical support to be deemed a sensitive or specific diagnostic constellation, these collections of variables might be seen as a second comparison point for antisocial individuals or examinees in forensic settings That is, after interpreting via the available Comprehensive System nonpatient norms, it might be useful to perform a simple qualitative comparison of the examinee's findings with those of known psychopathic samples. Conceptually, this approach would assist in assessing for the presence of psychopathy, but it also would allow the evaluator to identify points of departure from the prototypical psychopathic protocol, so that all "associated features" of the condition are not prematurely applied to the unique examinee. If psychopathy is viewed as existing along a continuum of severity, it stands to reason that many individuals will demonstrate a partial symptoms presentation rather than a fully crystallized manifestation of the condition. The presence or absence of specific findings may directly inform treatment and planning decisions.

Mr. Apple clearly met three of the four test findings Weiner (1991) proposed as collectively suggestive of psychopathic personality (T = 0; COP = 0; H < 2), and he was on the margin of the fourth (S > 2). Additionally, he met several of the ego deficit–related criteria proposed by Weiner (e.g., EB = ambitent; Zd < −3.0; CDI > 3; CF+C > FC+1; FD = 0) as predictive of unsuccessful criminal behaviors. Mr. Apple's history of multiple arrests, convictions, and incarcerations certainly are in line with the Weiner criteria. Meloy and Gacono's (2000) proposed findings of the prototypical psychopathic individual (Table 6.3) also are very well represented in Mr. Apple's case. However, perhaps just as noteworthy are the areas in which his protocol differed from the data points conceptually expected in psychopathy. As one example, Mr. Apple showed evidence of mood-related discomfort and possible depressive indicators (e.g., positive DEPI; SumV = 1; MOR = 4). Perhaps this suggests inroads for intervention, although Rorschach data and known history suggest that Mr. Apple is prone to engage in immediate externalization and complex defensive operations instead of confronting or working through his unpleasant emotional experiences.

Second, his narcissistic personality features appear to be ambivalent and bolstered by brittle defenses, although social interactions would lead the observer to infer a much more entrenched and oblivious narcissistic presentation. This hypothesis provides another small glimmer of prognostic hope, but simultaneously raises concerns as to specific triggers that might provoke his acting out (i.e., interactions in which his tenuous grandiosity is threatened).

Third is the contrast between Mr. Apple's usual inclination to act in idiosyncratic ways and his capacity to choose very conventional responses when expectations are extremely clear. This speaks to types of situations in which his behavior has the best likelihood for remaining stable and appropriate.

Overall, the reported case illustrates both the nomothetic and idiographic utility of the Rorschach of an individual who meets DSM-IV diagnostic criteria for ASPD and psychopathy on the PCL-R. Not unexpectedly, the Rorschach produced useful information that was not elicited by other instruments, even well-validated and reliable measures such as the PAI. The Rorschach provided remarkably useful descriptive data regarding the ASPD subject's functioning such as personality organization, interpersonal functioning and object relations, affective and emotional style and controls, perceptual–mediational and thought processes, self-concepts, and attitude. The Rorschach provided information that both converged and diverged from prototypical data of ASPD and psychopathic individuals as delineated in an ever-increasing body of research. The convergence of data along conceptually related constructs and the empirically derived information about ASPD or psychopathic individuals' Rorschach helps to confirm the presence of this ASPD disorder and the constellation of psychopathic symptoms and traits. Perhaps of equal or greater importance, the divergence of such Rorschach data provides especially meaningful idiographic information about an individual's functioning for tailoring specific treatment or management needs.

In this case analysis of Mr. Apple, one of the principal recommendations returned by the first author to the referral source was that Mr. Apple not be supported as an independent caregiver to the young child. The Rorschach, of course, provided only indirect and convergent evidence for this conclusion. His history of emotional modulation problems, impulsivity, poor relationships style, lack of empathy stemming, and ego-syntonic views of aggression, when coupled with other historical information, provided fairly compelling support as to his chronic and entrenched antisocial traits and the risk he posed to his young child. Interestingly, in Mr. Apple's case, PAI findings were relatively benign, providing little indication of his severe character pathology or behavioral concerns. However, this contrast between the self-report PAI and the Rorschach, especially when considered in the context of Mr. Apple's known background, provided a useful comparison of the difference between how Mr. Apple views himself and how he manifests his traits on the complex perceptual–mediation tasks of the Rorschach. Mr. Apple's affective discomfort on the Rorschach provided some perhaps unexpected deviation from a prototypical psychopathic Rorschach protocol, in this case probably signaling his sense of failed grandiosity, and helped to further understanding of his probably situational and transient willingness to work with authorities in seeking the return of this young child. However, the Rorschach and other data sources contributed to the examiner's opinion as to the likely chronic nature of Mr. Apple's difficulties and the poor prognosis for change. Nonetheless, when various rehabilitative and management recommendations were presented by authorities to Mr. Apple as avenues for working toward possible reunification, he indicated his unwillingness to engage in the recommended programming and surrendered his parental rights.

Many Rorschach variables have been conceptually related to the emotional, interpersonal, and behavioral dimensions of psychopathy, and a subset of these variables has been borne out through empirical study. To date, none have enjoyed extensive replication (or at least enough to satisfy critics of the Rorschach), and additional research is needed to determine where the instrument is especially strong or weak for its intended purposes. Currently, attention appears to be turning toward Gacono and Meloy's (1992) extended aggression variables, and this will ideally help to identify useful cutoff values for all the extended variables, and to elucidate the psychological dimensions associated with each. Beyond this collection of variables, however, it will be beneficial for researchers to return attention to the variables that are already incorporated in the Comprehensive System. This includes additional replication of the aforementioned variables within well-defined (i.e., PCL-R–defined) psychopathic samples. Investigation of more broadly defined antisocial subgroups (e.g., individuals with a diagnosis of ASPD or conduct disorder) may be of interest, but should be interpreted cautiously, because there is a risk of nonsignificant findings being attributed erroneously to the inadequacy of the instrument itself.

Even in its current state, the available literature clearly provides some useful conceptual guidelines for Rorschach assessment in cases of suspected or relevant psychopathy. When psychopathy is at issue, the Rorschach may help to assess its presence and severity. Even when the condition's presence (or absence) has already been established, the Rorschach can be helpful for gaining a more idiographic understanding of the person, including (a) areas of particular strength and treatment amenability, as compared with areas of weakness contributing to risk; and (b) the presence of comorbid conditions that enrich the full understanding of the person and his or her varied needs. So long as the Rorschach is viewed in the conservative, integrative manner outlined in this chapter—that is, as a generator of rich, descriptive hypotheses to be integrated always with outside sources of information—its inclusion in the assessment battery is expected to be highly defensible in clinical and forensic contexts. At the same time, it remains necessary for clinicians to keep abreast of the ever-evolving literature as it moves forward.

REFERENCES

Acklin, M. W. (1993). Integrating the Rorschach and the MMPI in clinical assessment: Conceptual and methodological issues. *Journal of Personality Assessment, 60,* 125–131.

American Psychiatric Association. (1968). *Diagnostic and statistical manual of mental disorders* (2nd ed.). Washington, DC: American Psychiatric Association.

American Psychiatric Association. (2000). *Diagnostic and statistical manual of mental disorders* (4th ed., text revision). Washington, DC: American Psychiatric Association.

Archer, R., & Krishnamurthy, R. (1997). MMPI-A and Rorschach indices related to depression and conduct disorder: An evaluation of the incremental validity hypothesis. *Journal of Personality Assessment, 69*(3), 517–533.

Archer, R., & Newsom, C. (2000). Psychological test usage with adolescent clients: Survey update. *Assessment, 7*(3), 227–235.

Baity, M., & Hilsenroth, M. (1999). Rorschach aggression variables: A study of reliability and validity. *Journal of Personality Assessment, 72*, 93–110.

Baity, M., & Hilsenroth, M. (2002). Rorschach Aggressive Content (AgC) variable: A study of criterion validity. *Journal of Personality Assessment, 78*, 275–287.

Baity, M., McDaniel, P., & Hilsenroth, M. (2000). Further exploration of the Rorschach Aggressive Content (AgC) variable. *Journal of Personality Assessment, 74*, 231–241.

Cleckley, H. (1941). *The mask of sanity.* St. Louis, MO: Mosby.

Cooke, D., & Michie, C. (2001). Refining the construct of psychopathy: Towards a hierarchical model. *Psychological Assessment, 13*(2), 171–188.

Cooper, S., & Arnow, D. (1986). An object relations view of the borderline defenses: A Rorschach analysis. In M. Kissen (Ed.), *Assessing object relations phenomena* (pp. 143–171). New York: International Universities Press.

Exner, J. (1986). *The Rorschach: A comprehensive system: Volume 1. Basic foundations* (2nd ed.). New York: John Wiley.

Exner, J. (2003). *The Rorschach: A comprehensive system: Volume 1. Basic foundations* (4th ed.). New York: John Wiley.

Exner, J., & Weiner, I. (1995). *The Rorschach: A comprehensive system: Volume 3. Assessment of children and adolescents* (2nd ed.). New York: John Wiley.

Forth, A., Kosson, D., & Hare, R. (2003). *The Psychopathy Checklist: Youth Version technical manual.* Toronto: Multi-Health Systems.

Gacono, C. (1990). An empirical study of object relations and defensive operations on antisocial personality disorder. *Journal of Personality Assessment, 54*(3 & 4), 589–600.

Gacono, C. B., Evans, B., & Viglione, D. (2002). The Rorschach in forensic practice. *Journal of Forensic Psychology Practice, 2*(3), 33–53.

Gacono, C., Loving, J., & Bodholdt, R. (2001). The Rorschach and psychopathy: Toward a more accurate understanding of the research findings. *Journal of Personality Assessment, 77*(1), 16–38.

Gacono, C., & Meloy, J. R. (1991). A Rorschach investigation of attachment and anxiety in antisocial personality disorder. *Journal of Nervous and Mental Disease, 179,* 546–552.

Gacono, C., & Meloy, J. R. (1992). The Rorschach and the DSM-III-R antisocial personality: A tribute to Robert Lindner. *Journal of Clinical Psychology, 48,* 393–485.

Gacono, C., & Meloy, J. R. (1994). *The Rorschach assessment of aggressive and psychopathic personalities.* Hillsdale, NJ: Lawrence Erlbaum Associates.

Gacono, C., Meloy, J. R., & Berg, J. (1992). Object relations, defensive operations, and affective states in narcissistic, borderline, and antisocial personality disorder. *Journal of Personality Assessment, 59*(1), 32–49.

Gacono, C., Meloy, J. R., & Bridges, M. (2000). A Rorschach comparison of psycho-paths, sexual homicide perpetrators, and pedophiles: Where angels fear to tread. *Journal of Clinical Psychology, 56*(6), 757–777.

Gacono, C., Meloy, J. R., & Heaven, T. (1990). A Rorschach investigation of narcis-sism and hysteria in antisocial personality disorder. *Journal of Personality Assess-ment, 55,* 270–279.

Ganellen, R. (1996). *Integrating the Rorschach and MMPI-2 in personality assessment.* Mahwah, NJ: Lawrence Erlbaum Associates.

Greco, C., & Cornell, D. (1992). Rorschach object relations of adolescents who com-mitted homicide. *Journal of Personality Assessment, 59*(3), 574–583.

Grove, W., & Barden, R. (1999). Protecting the integrity of the legal system: The ad-missibility of testimony from mental health experts under Daubert/Kumho analyses. *Psychology, Public Policy, and Law, 5*(1), 224–242.

Grove, W., Barden, R., Garb, H., & Lilienfeld, S. (2000). Failure of Rorschach Compre-hensive System–based testimony to be admissible under the Daubert–Joiner–Kumho standard. *Psychology, Public Policy, and Law, 8*(2), 216–234.

Hare, R. (1980). A research scale for the assessment of psychopathy in criminal pop-ulations. *Personality and Individual Differences, 1,* 111–117.

Hare, R. (1991). *The Hare Psychopathy Checklist—Revised.* Toronto: Multi-Health Sys-tems.

Hare, R. (2003). *Hare Psychopathy Checklist—Revised* (2nd ed.). Toronto: Multi-Health Systems.

Harris, G., Rice, M., & Quinsey, V. (1994). Psychopathy as a taxon: Evidence that psy-chopaths are a discrete class. *Journal of Consulting and Clinical Psychology, 62*(2), 397–397.

Hemphill, J., Hare, R., & Wong, S. (1998). Psychopathy and recidivism: A review. *Le-gal and Criminological Psychology, 3,* 139–170.

Huprich, S., Gacono, C., Schneider, R., & Bridges, M. (2004). Rorschach oral depend-ency in psychopaths, sexual homicide perpetrators, and pedophiles. *Behavioral Sciences and the Law, 22,* 1–12.

Kaser-Boyd, N. (1993). Rorschachs of women who commit homicide. *Journal of Per-sonality Assessment, 60*(3), 458–470.

Kernberg, O. (1975). *Borderline conditions and pathological narcissism.* New York: Aronson.

Kernberg, O. (1992). *Aggression in personality disorders and perversions.* New Haven, CT: Yale University Press.

Kwawer, J. (1980). Primitive interpersonal modes, borderline phenomena, and Ror-schach content. In J. Kwawer, A. Sugarman, P. Lerner, & H. Lerner (Eds.), *Border-line phenomena and the Rorschach test* (pp. 89–105). New York: International Universities Press.

Lally, S. (2003). What tests are acceptable for use in forensic evaluations? A survey of experts. *Professional Psychology: Research and Practice, 34*(5), 491–498.

Lee, A. (1995). *Relationship between the Rorschach and Minnesota Multiphasic Personal-ity Inventory-2 in schizophrenic individuals.* Unpublished doctoral dissertation, In-stitute for Graduate Clinical Psychology, Widener University, Chester, Pennsylvania.

Lerner, P., & Lerner, H. (1980). Rorschach assessment of primitive defenses in bor-
    derline personality structure. In J. Kwawer, A. Sugarman, P. Lerner, & H. Lerner
    (Eds.), *Borderline phenomena and the Rorschach test* (pp. 257–274). New York: Inter-
    national Universities Press.
Lindner, R. (1943). The Rorschach test and the diagnosis of psychopathic personal-
    ity. *Journal of Criminal Psychopathology, 1,* 69–93.
Loving, J., & Russell, W. (2000). Selected Rorschach variables of psychopathic juve-
    nile offenders. *Journal of Personality Assessment, 75*(1), 126–142.
Lovitt, R. (1993). A strategy for integrating a normal MMPI-2 and dysfunctional
    Rorschach in a severely compromised patient. *Journal of Personality Assessment,
    60,* 141–147.
Lyon, D., & Ogloff, J. (2000). Legal and ethical issues in psychopathy assessment. In
    C. Gacono (Ed.), *The clinical and forensic assessment of psychopathy: A practitioner's
    guide* (pp. 139–174). Mahwah, NJ: Lawrence Erlbaum Associates.
McCann, J. (1998). Defending the Rorschach in court: An analysis of admissibility
    using legal and professional standards. *Journal of Personality Assessment, 70*(1),
    125–144.
Meloy, J. R. (1988). *The psychopathic mind: Origins, dynamics, and treatment.*
    Northvale, NJ: Aronson.
Meloy, J. R., Acklin, M., Gacono, C., Murray, J., & Peterson, C. (Eds.). (1997). *Contem-
    porary Rorschach interpretation.* Mahwah, NJ: Lawrence Erlbaum Associates.
Meloy, J. R., & Gacono, C. (1992). The aggression response and the Rorschach. *Jour-
    nal of Clinical Psychology, 48*(1), 104–114.
Meloy, J. R., & Gacono, C. (2000). Assessing psychopathy: Psychological testing
    and report writing. In C. Gacono (Ed.), *The clinical and forensic assessment of psy-
    chopathy: A practitioner's guide.* (pp. 231–249). Mahwah, NJ: Lawrence Erlbaum
    Associates.
Meloy, J. R., Hansen, T., & Weiner, I. (1997). Authority of the Rorschach: Legal cita-
    tions during the past 50 years. *Journal of Personality Assessment, 69*(1), 53–62.
Mihura, J., & Nathan-Montano, E. (2001). An interpersonal analysis of Rorschach
    aggression variables in a normal sample. *Psychological Reports, 89,* 617–623.
Mihura, J. Nathan-Montano, E., & Alperin, R. (2003). Rorschach measures of aggres-
    sive drive derivatives: A college student sample. *Journal of Personality Assess-
    ment, 80*(1), 41–49.
Mihura, J., & Weinle, C. (2002). Rorschach training: Doctoral students' experiences
    and preferences. *Journal of Personality Assessment, 79*(1), 39–52.
Millon, T., & Davis, R. (1996). *Disorders of personality: DSM-IV and beyond* (2nd ed.).
    New York: John Wiley.
Owens, S., Patrick, K., Packman, W., & Greene, R. (2004, March). *Is the Rorschach still
    welcome in the courtroom?* Poster presented at the annual meeting of the Society
    for Personality Assessment, Miami, FL.
Piotrowski, C. (1996). Use of the Rorschach in forensic practice. *Perceptual and Motor
    Skills, 82*(1), 254.
Piotrowski, C., Belter, R., & Keller, J. (1998). The impact of "managed care" on the
    practice of psychological testing: Preliminary findings. *Journal of Personality As-
    sessment, 70*(3), 441–447.

Ritzler, B., Erard, R., & Pettigrew, G. (2000a). Protecting the integrity of Rorschach expert witnesses: A reply to Grove and Barden (1999) regarding the admissibility of testimony under Daubert/Kumho analyses. *Psychology, Public Policy, and Law, 8*(2), 201–215.

Ritzler, B., Erard, R., & Pettigrew, G. (2000b). A final reply to Grove and Barden: The relevance of the Rorschach Comprehensive System for expert testimony. *Psychology, Public Policy, and Law, 8*(2), 235–246.

Rogers, R., Duncan, J., Lynett, E., & Sewell, K. (1994). Prototypical analysis of antisocial personality disorder. *Law and Human Behavior, 18,* 471–484.

Schafer, R. (1948). *The clinical application of psychological tests: Diagnostic summaries and case studies.* New York: International Universities Press.

Smith, A., Gacono, C., & Kaufman, L. (1997). A Rorschach comparison of psychopathic and nonpsychopathic conduct disordered adolescents. *Journal of Clinical Psychology, 53,* 289–300.

Steadman, H., Silver, E., Monahan, J., Appelbaum, P., Robbins, P., Mulvey, E., Grisso, T., Roth, L., & Banks, S. (2000). A classification tree approach to the development of actuarial violence risk assessment tools. *Law and Human Behavior, 24,* 83–100.

Weber, C., Meloy, J. R., & Gacono, C. (1992). A Rorschach study of attachment and anxiety in inpatient conduct disordered and dysthymic adolescents. *Journal of Personality Assessment, 58*(1), 16–26.

Weiner, I. (1991). Conceptual issues in the Rorschach assessment of criminality and antisocial personality. *Rorschachiana, 17,* 31–38.

Weiner, I. (1993). Clinical considerations in the conjoint use of the Rorschach and the MMPI. *Journal of Personality Assessment, 60,* 148–152.

Weiner, I. (2003). *Principles of Rorschach interpretation* (2nd ed.). Mahwah, NJ: Lawrence Erlbaum Associates.

Weiner, I., Exner, J., & Sciara, A. (1996). Is the Rorschach welcome in the courtroom? *Journal of Personality Assessment, 67*(2), 422–424.

Wood, J., Lilienfled, S., Garb, H., & Nezworski, T. (2000). The Rorschach test in clinical diagnosis: A critical review, with a backward look at Garfield (1947). *Journal of Clinical Psychology, 56,* 395–430.

Wood, J., Lilienfeld, S., Nezworski, T., & Garb, H. (2001). Coming to grips with negative evidence for the Rorschach: A comment on Gacono, Loving, and Bodholdt; Ganellen; and Bornstein. *Journal of Personality Assessment, 77*(1), 48–77.

RORSCHACH PROTOCOL FOR MR. APPLE

Free Association	Inquiry
Card I 1. Bat, stuff connected to Dracula.	1. Because of the wings, symmetrical, I come up when Dracula was big. The charcoal gray. It denotes mystery and foreboding.
2. Could be some insignia, Nazi stuff.	2. I have a fascination with World War II, and the players and Germany. The Nazis had the lightning bolts on it. (What made it look like an insignia?) Shapes of these lightning bolts.
3. Could be angels, with the wings.	3. The wings. When we were kids we'd make snow angels in the snow. The fact that this is basically symmetrical.
Card II 4. The red could symbolize...the way it's splashed it could be blood or paint.	4. Yeah, could be head of a bear or...the red pretty much is the color of blood...the guy caught it bad. (Head?) Just the blood, more than the head, really.
5. Pathway going up into there maybe.	5. The dark and light. The light at the end of the tunnel, and we as humans are drawn to light.
6. Crater or volcano.	6. Craters and volcano when dormant, they have lakes in them. This could be the outer rim, inside is a crater lake.
Card III 7. Red guy in the middle could be a butterfly.	7. Looks like a butterfly. (Butterfly?) The wings and the substance in the middle.
8. Two people holding whatever these two are.	8. Could be in some type of posture, dancers.
Card IV 9. This looks like the Predator, Abominable Snowman, Yeti.	9. Bigfoot or Yeti, something kind of ominous and powerful. (Ominous and powerful?) It seems to be so big, dark, and foreboding.
Card V 10. Again, the bat theme.	10. Batty. (Batty?) Yeah, the symmetrical ears, feet, two wings.
11. Butterfly, again.	11. I'm predisposed to butterflies...I was a great fan of the movie Papillion...a symbol of butterfly, of peace...the peace-love generation. (Butterfly?) The wings.

12. Could be an animal pelt, too.	12. Animal pelt...because it looks like a rug that...Native Americans might have done this to an animal for a rug or clothing. (Pelt?) This, the shapes of these.
Card VI 13. This definitely looks like another pelt thing.	13. This here might not fit. (Pelt?) From these cut out like this.
14. Something animal or insect.	14. Because of the tendrils out here. (Tendrils?) These things.
15. Filleted meat.	15. The same...the fact that you cut it in half and probably the illusion of much more thicker and voluminous. (Thicker and voluminous?) Before it's split.
Card VII 16. Could be smoke.	16. The blotchy look.
17. Clouds.	17. Wispy around the edges, something in the middle, something possibly on fire.
18. Genies coming out of lamp as twins.	18. Twin genies, wispy look.
Card VIII 19. Something with colorful stuff, this could be animals here hanging on to a ship mast.	19. Nice colors...I'm appreciative of colors...it's symmetrical.
Card IX 20. Could be a flower, what kind I don't know.	20. The base of it, more of it, the stamen.
21. Shape suggests a whole lot...green area could be elephants.	21. Trunk action here with ears, rest of the body, too, it's vague.
Card X 22. These guys could be crabs.	22. Seaworthy sea stuff. (Crabs?) From these legs.
23. These are map parts, plots on a map.	23. Different parts, shapes, plots on a map.
24. Animal looking guys.	24. From these guys' shapes.
25. They look like crabs.	25. The leggy crabs.

RORSCHACH SEQUENCE OF SCORES FOR MR. APPLE

Card	Resp	Loc (DQ)	Loc N	Determinants (FQ)	(2)	Content(s)	P	Z	Special Scores
I	1.	Wo	1	C'Fo		A, Ay	P	1.0	AB, PER (AgC)
	2.	WSo	1	Fu		Ay		3.5	PER (AgC)
	3.	Wo	1	Fu		(H)		1.0	PER, GHR
II	4.	Ddv	99	C		Bl			MOR, DR (AgPast)
	5.	Ddv	99	VFu		Ls			
	6.	DdSv	99	Fu		Na			(AgC)
III	7.	Do	3	Fo		A			DV
	8.	D+	9	Mao	(2)	H, Id	P	3.0	GHR
IV	9.	Wo	1	C'Fo		(H)	P	2.0	GHR (AgC)
V	10.	Wo	1	Fo		A	P	1.0	
	11.	Wo	1	Fo		A	P	1.0	DR, AB, PSV
	12.	Wv	1	Fu		Ad, Ay			
VI	13.	Dv	1	Fo		Ad	P		
	14.	Do	1	Fu		A			DV
	15.	Dv	1	F-		Fd			MOR, DV (AgPast)
VII	16.	Wv	1	Y		Fi			
	17.	Wv	1	Y		Cl, Fi			MOR
	18.	W+	1	Mp.YFo	(2)	(H), Ay	P	2.5	GHR
VIII	19.	W+	1	FMp.CFu	(2)	A, Sc	P	4.5	FAB, DR
IX	20.	Wv	1	Fo		Bt			
	21.	Do	1	F-	(2)	A			
X	22.	Do	1	Fo	(2)	A	P		DV
	23.	Dv	9	F-		Ge			
	24.	Do	8	F-	(2)	A			
	25.	Do	7	Fo	(2)	A			

STRUCTURAL SUMMARY FOR MR. APPLE

Location Features	Determinants		Contents	(Extended AG
	Blends	Single		Scores*)
	M.YF	M = 1	H = 1	
Zf = 9	FM.CF	FM = 0	(H) = 3	(AG = 0)
ZSum = 19.5		m = 0	Hd = 0	(AgC = 4)
Zest = 27.5		FC = 0	(Hd) = 0	(AgPot = 0)
		CF = 0	Hx = 0	(AgPast= 2)
W = 12		C = 1	A = 10	(SM = 0)
D = 10		Cn = 0	(A) = 0	
W+D = 22		FC' = 0	Ad = 2	*Not included in CS
Dd = 3		C'F = 2	(Ad) = 0	
S = 2		C' = 0	An = 0	
		FT = 0	Art = 0	
Developmental Quality		TF = 0	Ay = 4	Special Scores
+ = 3		T = 0	Bl = 1	Lv 1 Lv 2
o = 12		FV = 0	Bt = 1	DV = 4x1 = 0x2
v = 10		VF = 1	Cg = 0	INC = 0x2 = 0x4
v/+ = 0		V = 0	Cl = 1	DR = 3x3 = 0x6
		FY = 0	Ex = 0	FAB = 1x4 = 0x7
Form Quality		YF = 0	Fd = 1	ALOG = 0x5

	FQx	MQual	W+D		
				Y = 2	CON = 0x7
+	= 0	= 0	= 0	Fr = 0	Raw Sum 6 = 8
o	= 11	= 2	= 11	rF = 0	Wgtd Sum 6 = 17
u	= 7	= 0	= 5	FD = 0	
-	= 4	= 0	= 4	F = 16	AB = 2 GHR = 4
none	= 3	= 0	= 2	(2) = 7	AG = 0 PHR = 0
				Sc = 1	COP = 0 MOR = 3
				Sx = 0	CP = 0 PER = 3
				Xy = 0	PSV = 1
				Id = 1	

Contents (continued): Fi = 2, Ge = 1, Hh = 0, Ls = 1, Na = 1

STRUCTURAL SUMMARY FOR MR. APPLE (CONTINUED)

Ratios, Percentages, and Derivations

Core

R = 25   L = 1.78

EB = 2:2.5   EA = 4.5   EBPer = N/A
eb = 1:6   es = 7   D = 0
    Adj es = 5   Adj D = 0

FM = 1   SumC' = 2   SumT = 0
m = 0   Sum V = 1   Sum Y = 3

Affect

FC: CF+C = 0:2
Pure C = 1
SumC':WSumC = 2:2.5
Afr = .39
S = 2
Blends:R = 2:25
CP = 0

Interpersonal

COP = 0   AG = 0
GHR: PHR = 4:0
a:p = 1:2
Food = 1
Sum T = 0
Human Cont = 4
Pure H = 1
PER = 3
Isol Indx = .28

Ideation

a:p = 1:2   Sum6 = 8
Ma:Mp = 1:1   Lv2 = 0
2AB+Art+Ay = 8   WSum6 = 17
MOR = 3   M- = 0
    Mnone = 0

Mediation

XA% = .72
WDA% = .73
X-% = .16
S- = 0
P = 9
X+% = .44
Xu% = .28

Processing

Zf = 9
W:D:Dd = 12:10: 3
W:M = 12 : 2
Zd = -8.0
PSV = 1
DQ+ = 3
DQv = 10

Self-Perception

3r+(2)/R = .28
Fr+rF = 0
SumV = 1
FD = 0
An+Xy = 0
MOR = 3
H:(H)+Hd+(Hd) = : 3

PTI = 0   *DEPI = 6   *CDI = 5   S-CON = 7   HVI = No   OBS = No

Rorschach Assessment
of Borderline Personality Disorder

Joni L. Mihura
University of Toledo

A well-defined, consensual understanding of borderline personality has been a long time in the making. In 1938, Stern first used the term "borderline" in reference to patients who appeared to occupy the border between neurosis and psychosis. Many subsequent early writings explored the idea of a core or latent psychosis (Hoch & Polatin, 1949; Zilboorg, 1941), more aptly called borderline schizophrenia (and later classified as schizotypal personality disorder; Spitzer, Endicott, & Gibbon, 1979).

The imprecise use of borderline diagnostic criteria was challenged in Knight's (1953) seminal discussion of "borderline states." He emphasized the borderline patient's tendency to regress in unstructured settings (psychoanalysis and during unstructured tests such as the Rorschach), wherein their ego weaknesses and difficulty working in a therapeutic alliance made it necessary to modify the typical psychoanalytic treatment structure. Kernberg's (1967) seminal article described borderline personality organization from an object relations/ego psychology perspective. Similar to Stern's (1938) original conceptualization, borderline personality organization was described as a personality level between neurotic and psychotic, which included all severe types of personality disorder. Three main borderline personality organization characteristics were (a) identity diffusion, (b) primitive defenses (e.g., splitting and projective identification), yet (c) generally intact reality testing. Grinker, Werble, and Drye (1968) provided the first empirically based borderline personality criteria: identity disturbance, anaclitic relationships, depression attributable to loneliness, and salient expressed anger.

Based on a review of this and other literature, Gunderson and Singer (1975) proposed borderline features that have greatly influenced the current understanding of borderline personality disorder (BPD). These major BPD descriptors included intense and negative affect, impulsivity, social maladaptation, brief psychotic experiences, loose thinking on unstructured tests such as the Rorschach, and relationships that vacillate between superficiality and intense dependency. From this literature review, Gunderson and colleagues developed the Diagnostic Interview for Borderlines (DIB; Gunderson, Kolb, & Austin, 1981), which showed good differential diagnostic potential (Gunderson & Kolb, 1978). Seven criteria from the DIB, plus an unstable identity criterion from Kernberg (1967) and Grinker et al. (1968), helped to form the eight *Diagnostic and Statistical Manual of Mental Disorders,* 3rd Edition (DSM-III; American Psychiatric Association [APA], 1980) criteria for BPD (Spitzer et al., 1979). The DSM-III BPD essential features emphasized "instability" in a variety of areas (interpersonal, mood, self-image). The DSM-IV (APA, 1994) retained these same basic eight criteria and added a ninth criterion to assess unstable cognition (Table 7.1).

BORDERLINE PERSONALITY DISORDER: MAJOR FEATURES

Because the DSM-IV BPD criteria can result in 126 possible combinations for a BPD diagnosis, it is important to determine its core or main compo-

TABLE 7.1

Borderline Personality Disorder: Summary of DSM-IV Criteria

A pervasive pattern of instability of interpersonal relationships, self-image, affects, and marked impulsivity (characterized by five or more of the following criteria):

1. Frantic efforts to avoid real or imagined abandonment

2. Unstable and intense interpersonal relationships that alternate between extremes of idealization and devaluation

3. Identity disturbance

4. Self-damaging impulsivity

5. Suicidal or self-mutilating behavior

6. Affective instability due to marked mood reactivity

7. Chronic feelings of emptiness

8. Inappropriate, intense anger or difficulty controlling anger

9. Transient, stress-induced paranoid ideation or severe dissociative symptoms

Note. Table was derived from the DSM-IV (APA, 1994, p. 654).

nents. Overall, much of the research using DSM criteria finds three major BPD components (Blais, Hilsenroth, & Castlebury, 1997; Sanislow, Grilo, & McGlashan, 2000; Sanislow et al., 2002): (a) unstable identity/interpersonal relationships, (b) affective instability, and (c) behavioral instability or aggressive impulsivity. Cognitive content and processes are embedded in many of these categories (e.g., cognitive shifts in one's view of self and others), although the DSM-IV criterion 9 more specifically addresses the cognitive disturbances of paranoia and dissociation.

Therefore, BPD is discussed in the following sections with regard to four major categories: (a) unstable identity/interpersonal relationships, (b) (negative) affective instability, (c) behavioral instability (self-destructive aggressive impulsivity), and (d) cognitive instability (psychotic-like thinking). In addition to a discussion of BPD based on the major DSM criteria, other potentially helpful descriptors are discussed, including three descriptors suggested by Skodol et al. (2002): primitive defenses, transitional object relatedness, and regression proneness.

Unstable Identity/Interpersonal Relationships (Self and Other)

Research investigating BPD suggests that early maladaptive interpersonal experiences—childhood sexual abuse, other forms of abuse and neglect, disturbed parental bonding and attachment, invalidating and inconsistent parenting—are important etiological factors (Nickell, Waudby, & Trull, 2002; Yen et al., 2002; Zanarini et al., 2000). Relatedly, critical to understanding the borderline personality diagnosis and conceptualization are the interpersonal dynamics stemming from the major object needs of BPD individuals to maintain an intact sense of self. For example, the BPD person's intense fears of being alone or abandoned stem from their problems with object constancy wherein others are used to maintain a stable and real sense of self. These object constancy or true object relatedness problems often are understood as separation–individuation or separation–abandonment conflicts (Mahler, Pine, & Bergman, 1975; Perry & Cooper, 1986; Reich & Zanarini, 2001) and transitional object relatedness (Cardasis, Hachman, & Silk, 1997; Modell, 1963; Winnicott, 1953).

As such, the BPD ego is not well integrated, but characterized by splitting of self- and other-representations that are experienced episodically as alternating between good (satisfying/sustaining) and bad (frustrating/destructive) (Kernberg, 1967; Perry & Cooper, 1986). Therefore, the BPD sense of self is unstable, marked by rapidly shifting feelings about the self that include feeling unreal and empty, as well as potentially nonexistent when a major object relationship ends (Wilkinson-Ryan & Westen, 2000). As a way to stay connected to the major object and, therefore, reality, the BPD client uses projective identification—a covert means of control or manipulation that intrapsychically maintains a connection to the major object (Kernberg, 1967; Perry & Cooper, 1986). In projective identification, the person projects a part self- or object-representation on the other, treats the other as if she or he were this projection, who then may unconsciously identify with the projection and act in accordance. The content of these projections fall into good (idealized: rescuing, sustaining) and bad (devalued: neglectful, abusive) categories.

When real or fantasized separations or disconnections occur, this evokes devaluation of the previously idealized object. These devaluing and destructive attacks are experienced as originating from the other (projected), wherein the BPD client maintains a masochistic view of the self as a helpless victim, with resultant intense anger directed at self and others (Zanarini et al., 1998). Although to the outside observer the BPD's need for the other is clear, awareness of the intensity of this need can be frightening and potentially destabilizing to the BPD person. Therefore, the BPD person may deny the full intensity of his or her dependency needs, and instead report hostile avoidance (Sack, Sperling, Fagen, & Foelsch, 1996).

Affective Instability (Emotional Dysregulation)

Affect for the BPD individual is negative, intense, and unstable. Anger is a key component of the affective instability. It may be accompanied by devaluation of others (especially the BPD individual's major objects) and/or projected. The BPD affect typically fluctuates between negative affect states (i.e., anger, irritability, anxiety, depression, dysphoria). These unstable affect states do not, however, typically include the euphoric or grandiose states seen with the bipolar disorders and are marked more by anger and anxiety (Henry et al., 2001; Koenigsberg et al., 2002). The intense and inordinate anger can be understood as an attempt to maintain contact with and control the needed object, and to relatedly maintain a real sense of self. Depression is a less discriminating negative affect, and can be understood as the BPD person's conviction of his or her inherent and global badness (which can become extreme as in being "evil"). The more sustained dysphoric qualities are related to an inner sense of emptiness, which helps to distinguish BPD from major depression (Rippetoe, Alarcon, & Walter-Ryan, 1986; Westen et al., 1992).

Behavioral Instability/Impulsivity

Likely because of both nature and nurture (New & Siever, 2002; White, Gunderson, Zanarini, & Hudson, 2003), impulsivity (especially aggressive impulsivity) appears to be a major component of BPD. The BPD person is often prone to periods of self-destructive and aggressive impulsivity (e.g., substance abuse, sexual promiscuity, self-mutilation, suicide attempts or gestures). These impulsive behaviors may serve the dual purpose of warding off the panic and disintegration attributable to loss of the major object and attempting to make contact with the lost object or new sustaining objects. For example, substance abuse is common with BPD (Trull, Sher, Minks-Brown, Durbin, & Burr, 2000). Imbibing the substance both numbs the anxiety and serves as a temporary object, whereas the effects of the substance may pave the way for object connections (e.g., impulsive sexual encounters). Additionally, self-mutilation and suicide attempts often are preceded and accompanied by real and fantasized interactions with others (Brown, Comtois, & Linehan, 2002; Welch & Linehan, 2002), as the anger and rage at the abandoning object is turned toward the internalized bad part–object. These self-destructive impulsive acts (e.g., self-harm behaviors, suicidality) are more frequent for BPD patients with a history of abuse (Brodsky, Malone, Ellis, Dulit, & Mann, 1997; Sansone, Gaither, & Songer, 2002).

Cognitive Instability

Often, BPD cognitive disturbances are manifest because of difficulties maintaining a relationship with reality in unstructured or stressful situations. These largely transient cognitive disturbances include dissociation and paranoia, and occasionally other types of transient quasi-psychotic experiences. Only fairly recently, a DSM-IV criterion was added to assess cognitive instability regarding transient, stress-induced brief paranoid or dissociative (e.g., depersonalization) experiences. The "stress" in this situation typically is a loss of contact with a major object, mainly when the loss is felt to be essential and irreversible. Other transient quasi-psychotic experiences (e.g., thought insertion, thought control, visual and auditory hallucinations) also are associated with BPD (Dowson, Sussams, Grounds, & Taylor, 2000), although the reality of these beliefs and sensory experiences typically is more tenuous than with blatant psychosis. Some theorists and researchers consider these brief psychotic or dissociative experiences in the context of object loss to be pathognomic of BPD (Skodol et al., 2002). These past psychotic experiences also have been found to predict repeated BPD hospitalizations (Hull, Yeomans, Clarkin, & Goodman, 1996), which suggests that psychotic-like thinking may present a particular vulnerability for BPD.

RORSCHACH RESEARCH
ON BORDERLINE PERSONALITY DISORDER

Previous reviews of the relationship between BPD and Rorschach scales have been published (Gartner, Hurt, & Gartner, 1989; Wood, Lilienfeld, Garb, & Nezworski, 2000; Zalewski & Archer, 1991). However, several important BPD/Rorschach empirical studies have been published since the most recent of these reviews. Furthermore, none of these reviews specified the search strategy used to locate studies, and only one used exclusion criteria for methodological problems (Wood et al., 2000). Therefore, the following section describes the current review's methodology and briefly compares its content with that of previous published reviews.

The current review focuses on Rorschach scales relevant to a DSM BPD diagnosis, as well as a psychodynamic understanding of BPD, as described in the previous sections. A PsycINFO search was conducted on November 30, 2003, for articles and chapters published between 1980 and 2003 using the search terms [borderline personality disorder (subject) or borderline states (subject) or borderline (abstract)] and [Rorschach (subject or abstract)]. From these search results, empirical studies were reviewed that assessed adult BPD or BPD traits by the DSM (DSM-III, DSM-III-R, or DSM-IV; American Psychiatric Association, 1980, 1987, 1994), Gunderson's Diagnostic Interview for Borderlines (DIB; Gunderson et al., 1981; DIB-R; Zanarini, Gunderson, Frankenburg, & Chauncey, 1989), or BPD self-report scales using DSM or DIB definitions (e.g., Personality Assessment Inventory; Morey, 1991). Study results were excluded when the methodology was judged to include criterion contamination (e.g., diagnosis was not made blind to Rorschach data or Rorschachs were not scored blind to BPD diagnosis) or a low sample size per analysis ($N < 30$). Although the search strategy located 52 Rorschach borderline empirical studies with adults, only 18 met the preceding inclusion criteria and were believed to be studies with the most solid methodology. Notably, the methodology significantly improved over time, with 85% of the studies published between 1997 and 2003 meeting the inclusion criteria, as compared with only 18% published between 1981 and 1996.[1]

A comparison of the 18 studies in this review with the previously mentioned reviews showed that none were included in Gartner et al.'s (1989) review and that one was included in Zalewski and Archer's (1991) review. Most of the currently reviewed studies were more recently published, and the other studies in these reviews did not meet the current study inclusion criteria. Wood et al. (2000) used study exclusion criteria for BPD diagnosis and criterion contamination, but their criteria differed from the current criteria by including no sample size criterion, including child and adolescent samples, and including studies with potential scoring bias (i.e., the study's first author, who would not be blind to study hypotheses, administered and scored the Rorschachs, a potential problem also noted by Wood et al. [2000]), and excluding studies with a diagnosis based on chart reviews (that excluded Rorschach results). There was an overlap of six studies between

---

[1]For a copy of more detailed review methodology (including a list of excluded studies) contact the author.

the current 18 studies and the 10 studies in Wood et al. (2000). The 16 non-overlapping studies were attributable to inclusion/exclusion criteria differences (7 studies), more recently published studies (7 studies), and two studies not located by the undefined search strategy of Wood et al. (2000).

For the following BPD–Rorschach empirical review, critical efforts were made to include both significant and nonsignificant findings. Interestingly, the review identified mostly non-Comprehensive System (Exner, 2003) scales. In the subsequent sections, response productivity (R) and Lambda findings are discussed, followed by sections grouped according to four BPD characteristics: unstable identity/interpersonal relationships, affective instability, behavioral instability/impulsivity, and cognitive instability. In the critical evaluation of these studies, areas in which empirical support is strong, weak, or not documented are highlighted. Accordingly, these findings suggest ways in which empirical evaluation of the Rorschach and BPD can be developed.

Response Productivity and Lambda

Overall, mean BPD Rorschach R does not appear to differ from that of most other diagnostic groups or normal subjects (Bornstein, Hilsenroth, Padawer, & Fowler, 2000; Hilsenroth, Fowler, & Padawer, 1998; Hilsenroth, Fowler, Padawer, & Handler, 1997; Hirshberg, 1989; but see Skinstad, Troland, & Mortensen, 1999). There is little research on Lambda levels in BPD protocols, and none comparing BPD and normal protocols. No Lambda differences were found between BPD and mixed personality disorder (PD) protocols (Skinstad et al., 1999), and BPD, neurotic, and psychotic protocols did not differ in terms of high Lambda levels (> 1.5) (Burla, Ferracuti, & Lazzari, 1997). In general, BPD protocols are not likely distinguishable by R from those for normal subjects or most other diagnostic groups. No clear conclusions can be made for Lambda.

Unstable Identity and Interpersonal Relationships

Major BPD characteristics on the Rorschach are expected to include a level of personality organization between neurotic and psychotic, characterized by transitional object relations and separation–individuation conflicts. Primitive defenses include splitting and projective identification. Interpersonal relationships are marked by vacillations between primitive idealization and devaluation, covert manipulation and control, masochism, and a dependency that denies neediness.

Personality Organization. The Mutuality of Autonomy Scale (MOA; Urist, 1977) assesses level of personality organization, with the most mature level characterized by mutuality and autonomy (MOA Level 1) and pathological levels characterized by control and destructiveness (MOA Levels 5–7). Pathological MOA levels have been related consistently to borderline personality, including both DSM BPD criteria and borderline traits (Blais, Hilsenroth, Castlebury, Fowler, & Baity, 2001; Blais, Hilsenroth, Fowler, & Conboy, 1999; Mihura, Nathan-Montano, & Alperin, 2003). They have been shown to predict BPD diagnostic criteria over and above the Minnesota Multiphasic Personality Inventory–2 (MMPI-2) BPD scale (Blais et al., 2001). Higher MOA scores are related to borderline features of unstable relationships and self-destructive impulsivity, such as suicidal behavior, self-mutilating behaviors, and self-reported self-destructive impulses (Blais et al., 1999; Fowler, Hilsenroth, & Nolan, 2000; Mihura et al., 2003). Therefore, research suggests that the MOA is a valid and informative measure of the quality of borderline personality object relations. These scores also seem to capture the borderline personality style of interpersonal control and manipulation that is accompanied by self-destructive behaviors.

Two Rorschach scales have been studied that assess borderline personality conflicts in terms of separation–individuation: the Separation-Individuation Scale (S-I; Coonerty, 1986) and the Symbiotic Phenomena Content Scale (SPCS; Hirshberg, 1989). In each of these cases, BPD protocols contained more Rorschach scores indicating separation conflicts, as compared with other groups. Coonerty (1986) found higher S-I Total scores in BPD than in schizophrenic protocols. In line with Mahler's theory (e.g., Mahler et al., 1975), BPD protocols contained higher S-I Rapprochement scores, but lower Preseparation (psychotic) scores than schizophrenic protocols (as well as higher S-I Narcissism scores, but not higher S-I Differentiation scores). Using the SPCS (which is similar to the MOA), Hirshberg (1989) also found higher Separation scores in BPD than in non-BPD protocols in an eating disordered sample. Therefore, on both the S-I and SPCS, there is support for more separation conflicts in BPD protocols.

The Transitional Object Scale (TOS; Greenberg, Craig, Seidman, Cooper, & Teele, 1987), based on a Winnicottian (1953; Modell, 1963) view of borderline personality, also is supported as a measure of BPD. The TOS is related to BPD diagnosis, and higher in BPD than in antisocial PD and schizophrenic protocols (Cooper, Perry, Hoke, & Richman, 1985; Greenberg et al., 1987). The TOS also is related to current transitional object usage, unstable identity and interpersonal relationships (i.e., splitting), and treatment regressions. However, in the study of Cooper et al. (1985), the difference between BPD and antisocial PD protocols was not significant when TOS scores were controlled for R. Therefore, a caution is given that TOS scores may be confounded with R.

Splitting and Projective Identification. There are two Rorschach measures of splitting and projective identification: one in the Lerner Defense Scales (LDS; Lerner & Lerner, 1980) and the other in the Rorschach Defense Scales (RDS; Cooper, Perry, & Arnow, 1988). Research has found RDS and LDS Splitting scores significantly related to BPD and unrelated to antisocial PD (Blais et al., 1999; Cooper et al., 1988). In addition, LDS Splitting scores were negatively related to narcissistic PD (Blais et al., 1999). Burla et al. (1997)[2] found a trend for higher LDS Splitting scores in BPD than in neurotic (anxiety and somatoform disorders) protocols. Research has found less support for the ability of LDS Splitting scores to differentiate BPD from histrionic PD and psychotic disorders. Specifically, Blais et al. (1999) found that LDS Splitting scores also were significantly related to histrionic PD criteria, and Burla et al. (1997) found no significant LDS Splitting differences between BPD and psychotic protocols. Research has shown that LDS Splitting scores are associated with DSM BPD criteria of unstable relationships and feeling empty (Blais et al., 1999), and these scores are higher for BPD patients who self-mutilate (Fowler et al., 2000). RDS Splitting scores have been associated with splitting of self and other images, feeling empty, and crises regressions (Cooper et al., 1988).

There is some evidence that LDS and RDS measures of projective identification are not specifically related to a DSM BPD diagnosis (Blais et al., 1999; Cooper et al., 1988). However, LDS Projective Identification scores were found to be higher in BPD than in neurotic, but not psychotic, protocols (Burla et al., 1997). In fact, two studies conducted by different researchers found no instances of LDS Projective Identification scores in neurotic protocols (Burla et al., 1997; Lerner & Lerner, 1982).

Consistent with splitting and projective identification occurring more specifically in borderline personality organization (vs. BPD), patients with both borderline and schizotypal traits scored significantly higher on LDS Splitting and Projective Identification than either neurotics or schizophrenics (Lerner, Albert, & Walsh, 1987; Lerner & Lerner, 1982[3]). Therefore, research suggests that Rorschach splitting and projective identification scores are particularly consistent with what would be expected for patients with borderline personality organization, whereas splitting scores may be more indicative of a DSM BPD diagnosis.

---

[2]The LDS analyses of Burla et al. (1997) were conducted using frequencies of the simple presence or absence of a score per protocol, reducing the power for their analyses. Also, for LDS defenses with scoring levels (e.g., Devaluation Idealization), the typical total defense score was not computed. Therefore, the only LDS results presented from their study are LDS defenses without scoring levels (i.e., Splitting and Projective Identification).

[3]Studies such as these that included schizotypal traits in the BPD diagnostic criteria are not included in the main 18 reviewed studies.

Devaluation and Idealization, Masochism, and Dependency.
There is good support for a relationship between Rorschach devaluation
measures and BPD. Both LDS and RDS Devaluation scores were related to
DSM BPD diagnostic criteria, and LDS Devaluation scores predicted BPD
diagnostic criteria over and above the MMPI-2 BPD scale (Blais et al., 1999;
Blais et al., 2001; Cooper et al., 1988). Findings show LDS Devaluation
scores are unrelated to narcissistic, antisocial, and histrionic PD criteria
(Blais et al., 1999), and that RDS Devaluation scores are unrelated to antisocial PD (Cooper et al., 1988). Findings also show that LDS Devaluation
scores are related to the DSM BPD criteria of unstable relationships, affective instability, and suicidal behavior (Blais et al., 1999), and that they are
higher for BPD patients who self-mutilate than for those who do not
(Fowler et al., 2000). Higher RDS Devaluation scores are related to poorer
treatment outcome for BPD (Cooper, Perry, & O'Connell, 1991). These Rorschach devaluation findings are consistent with what would be expected
for the BPD diagnosis, as well as the unique personal and interpersonal
dysfunction created by high levels of devaluation.

In contrast to devaluation scores, neither RDS nor LDS Idealization scores
have been found related specifically to BPD diagnosis (Cooper et al., 1988;
Hilsenroth et al., 1997). However, LDS Idealization scores were found to be
higher in BPD protocols than in those for normal subjects, antisocial PD, and a
sample of DSM Cluster A PDs, but not narcissistic PD or a sample of DSM
Cluster C PDs (Hilsenroth et al., 1997). Hilsenroth et al. (1997) found that LDS
Idealization scores were related to the DSM-IV narcissistic PD criterion 2: "unlimited fantasies of success." Fowler et al. (2000) found that LDS Idealization
scores were higher in the protocols of BPD patients who self-mutilated.

Two Rorschach scores may capture masochistic traits (self as victim) in
BPD: the Comprehensive System (CS) Morbid (MOR) response and
Gacono and Meloy's (1994) Aggressive Past (AgPast) response, which is
similar to MOR but does not code for dysphoric content. Baity and
Hilsenroth (1999) found that, using stepwise regression with several Rorschach aggression scores, MOR was most positively associated with DSM
BPD criteria and negatively associated with DSM antisocial PD criteria
(AgPast did not enter their model). However, Skinstad et al. (1999) did not
find higher MOR levels in BPD than in mixed PD protocols. Mihura et al.
(2003) did not find AgPast related to the overall level of self-reported borderline traits in college students, but did find that AgPast was related to the
borderline traits of unstable relationships and self-destructive impulsivity.
Therefore, MOR responses may be more likely in BPD protocols, whereas
AgPast may indicate a type of masochism not specifically related to BPD.

The Rorschach Oral Dependency scale (ROD; Masling, Rabie, &
Blondheim, 1967) has good support as an implicit measure of dependency

(Bornstein, 1999). Both high and low scores are problematic. High scores suggest an excessively needy overdependency, and low scores suggest counterdependency. Interestingly, ROD scores are found to be low for BPD outpatients, yet high for BPD inpatients, as compared with BPD outpatients and other diagnostic groups (Blais et al., 1999; Bornstein et al., 2000). Moreover, ROD scores were found to predict DSM BPD criteria over and above the MMPI-2 BPD scale (Blais et al., 2001). It is not clear whether the BPD inpatient–outpatient discrepancies on the ROD are attributable to state or trait differences, for example, whether dependency needs are attributable more to the breakdown of BPD defenses or more to stable differences between BPD inpatients and BPD outpatients. However, the high ROD scores of BPD inpatients suggest that the intensity of their dependency needs may be destabilizing, whereas BPD outpatients may function relatively more stably by defending successfully against these needs.

Regarding the BPD attachment needs, extant research does not support a direct relationship between tactile attachment needs as measured by the Rorschach (Texture score; T) and DSM BPD criteria (Blais, Hilsenroth, & Fowler, 1998). Because research suggests that T's are less common for people with childhood sexual abuse (Leavitt, 2000; Leavitt & Labott, 1996; Owens, 1984), it is possible that BPD patients with childhood sexual abuse histories defensively shut off their awareness of tactile attachment needs. However, this does not exclude the presence of T responses in the protocols of BPD patients with childhood sexual abuse. Hypothetically, because these tactile attachment needs may be experienced or expressed in self-destructive ways, the T responses of BPD patients may contain signs of anger or self-destructiveness (e.g., AG or Devaluation scores), although no research has addressed this hypothesis.

Affective Instability

Major BPD affective instability characteristics include intense, unstable negative affect states consisting of anger, severe anxiety, and depression with a sense of badness. Dysphoria with a sense of emptiness may constitute the more stable affect experience.

Anger.   There are no CS measures that assess primitive types of aggression or anger. It is unclear whether the CS AG score typically will be higher in BPD protocols. However, Skinstad et al. (1999) did find higher AG levels in alcoholics with a diagnosis of BPD than in those with mixed PD. Mihura et al. (2003) did not find AG related to borderline traits in college students. Their findings showed that AG was related to a more general measure of anger and aggressive attitude. Research suggests that AG may be a measure of ego-dystonic versus ego-syntonic anger (Mihura &

Nathan-Montano, 2001; Mihura et al., 2003). Therefore, high rates of AG in BPD protocols may indicate an intolerable degree of ego-dystonic anger.

Other Rorschach scales are more specifically designed to measure primitive aggression or anger. Holt's (1977) primitive aggression score (most severe, A1) was found related to DSM BPD total criteria, but not DSM antisocial, narcissistic, or histrionic total criteria (Blais et al., 1999). Higher A1 scores also have been found for BPD patients who self-mutilate (Fowler et al., 2000). The more socialized type of aggression in Holt's A2 score may be related to BPD, but this area needs more solid research. Holt's A1 score seems related mainly to aggressive or self-destructive acting out rather than anger per se (Blais et al., 1999).

Unstable Negative Affect.   Lower color form levels (CF, C vs. FC) are generally considered to assess unmodulated emotion. However, these scores are not specific to the negative affective instability seen in BPD. Rorschach studies show mixed results for the relationship between BPD and chromatic color scores (e.g., Blais et al., 1998; Burla et al., 1997; Mihura et al., 2003). High levels of color responses in general are more likely to represent a histrionic PD protocol (Blais et al., 1998). However, given that the unstable affective states in BPD are characterized by negative affect, it seems likely that a BPD protocol would contain signs of anger or aggression (e.g., A1, A2, AG, or Devaluation scores) to accompany these lower color form levels. Regarding negative affective instability specifically, Blais et al. (1999) found that LDS Devaluation was related to this BPD criterion.

Depression and Dysphoria.   There are no CS Rorschach scores that specifically capture the type of depression and dysphoria seen in BPD. The CS Depression Index (DEPI) criteria do not seem to capture the particular angry and empty nature of the BPD depressive experience, although there is some evidence that DEPI is higher in BPD than in neurotic (anxiety and somatoform) disorders, but not in mixed PD or psychotic protocols (Burla et al., 1997; Skinstad et al., 1999). For the BPD empty depressive experiences, Rorschach splitting and projection measures show significant associations with a sense of emptiness (Blais et al., 1999; Cooper et al., 1988), although there is no extant research to determine whether these scores are specifically related to BPD depression or dysphoria.

There is less conclusive evidence of other BPD negative affect states as measured by the Rorschach, because the research in this area is scarce. Higher levels of negative affect states (e.g., C', V, Y, Color-Shading Blends) might be expected in BPD protocols than in those of normal samples, but sound research studies are needed in this area.

Behavioral Instability/Impulsivity

It is expected that BPD behavioral instability or impulsivity would be particularly characterized by self-destructive impulsive behaviors. However, there are no CS Rorschach scales specific to self-destructive impulsive behaviors. Although general impulsivity may be indicated by low D and AdjD scores and less form in color responses (Pantle, Ebner, & Hynan, 1994), there is insufficient research to support these as measures of BPD impulsivity. However, as reported earlier, there are non–CS Rorschach scales that are theoretically and empirically related to self-destructive impulsivity, particularly MOA, LDS Splitting and Devaluation, and Holt's A1 (Blais et al., 1999; Fowler et al., 2000; Mihura et al., 2003). Although not investigated in a BPD sample, there is some evidence that a combination of Gacono and Meloy's (1994) AgPast and Aggressive Potential (AgPot) is related to borderline traits and generally aggressive and self-destructive impulses, including suicidal impulses and self-damaging impulsivity (Mihura et al., 2003). Therefore, BPD self-destructive impulsive behaviors may be more likely given pathological MOA scores, higher LDS Splitting and Devaluation scores, Holt's A1 scores, or an elevated AgPast+AgPot score.

Cognitive Instability

Major BPD characteristics related to cognitive instability include transient, stress-induced paranoid and/or dissociative experiences. Sustained psychosis is not characteristic of BPD, although psychotic-like thinking is likely and related to repeated hospitalizations.

Psychosis and Psychotic-Like Thinking. There is a certain type of BPD thinking disturbance in Rorschach protocols that is consistent with BPD and borderline personality organization.[4] BPD protocols are found to have higher Schizophrenia Index (SCZI) levels than those of normal subjects, Cluster C PDs, and mixed PDs, similar to Cluster A PDs, yet lower than psychotics (Burla et al., 1997; Hilsenroth et al., 1998; Skinstad et al., 1999). However, Burla et al. (1997) found no differences in SCZI between BPDs and neurotics (anxiety and somatoform disorders). Findings have shown that BPD protocols are particularly less likely than psychotic protocols to meet all six SCZI criteria (Hilsenroth et al., 1998). Regarding specific criteria, psychotic protocols are more likely to meet SCZI-3, -4, and -5 criteria than BPD protocols (Hilsenroth et al., 1998). That is, as compared with

---

[4]There was no published research on BPD with the newer CS Perceptual-Thinking Index (PTI) that replaced the SCZI, nor the WA% and WDA% scales when this chapter was written.

BPD protocols, psychotic protocols show predominantly very poor reality testing (FQ–), more bizarre thought disorder, and more instances of thought disorder in general. On the Thought Disorder Index (TDI; Johnston & Holzman, 1979), Harris (1993) found that BPD protocols had more overall thinking disturbance than those of a mixed PD group. No BPD or mixed PD protocols had the most bizarre level of TDI scores (Level 1.0). On CS measures of reality testing (X+%, X–%), BPD protocols have shown more reality testing problems than those of normal subjects, similar to the protocols of neurotics and other PDs, but either equivalent or indicative of less impairment than psychotics protocols (Burla et al., 1997; Hilsenroth et al., 1998; Skinstad et al., 1999).

Therefore, BPD protocols may show more psychotic-like thinking disturbances (CS Cognitive Special Scores and TDI total scores) than those for normal subjects and all PDs but Cluster A, but less clearly psychotic thinking than psychotic protocols. Regarding reality testing (X+%, X–%), BPD protocols likely will show more impairment than those for normal subjects, and either equivalent or less impairment than psychotic protocols.

Paranoia.   Cooper et al. (1988) found that RDS Projection scores were positively related to BPD. Furthermore, as expected for BPD paranoia when the major object is experienced as absent, RDS Projection scores were related to crisis regressions (Cooper et al., 1988) and poorer treatment outcome (Cooper et al., 1991). The findings of Stuart et al. (1990) with the Concept of the Object Scale (COS; Blatt, Brenneis, Schimek, & Glick, 1976) are consistent with higher levels of paranoia in BPD patients. On the COS Content of Interaction scale, BPD patients reported more malevolent human interactions than depressed patients and normal controls. Therefore, higher levels of RDS Projection scores and COS malevolent content scores may indicate a stronger propensity for paranoia in BPD patients.

Dissociation.   No Rorschach dissociation measures were investigated in the BPD analyses on which this review is based.[5] Two Rorschach dissociation measures are Labott's and Wagner's signs (Labott, Leavitt, Braun, & Sachs, 1992; Wagner, Allison, & Wagner, 1983), although these scales are more typically used to assess for dissociative identity disorder. The Trauma Content index (TC/R; Armstrong & Loewenstein, 1990) may be helpful in predicting dissociation, although it is unclear whether TC/R elevations are more specifically attributable to past trauma instead of dissociation (Kamphuis, Kugeares, & Finn, 2000). However, a dissertation by

---

[5]Some studies compared their samples with Exner's (1986) BPD group, which was excluded from this review because of potential criterion contamination.

Delany (1996) found that high dissociating BPD patients had higher TC scores than low dissociating BPD patients.

CASE EXAMPLE: MS. SHAHEEN

This case study uses the Rorschach protocol of Ms. Shaheen, a 36-year-old, single, Lebanese female inpatient. At the time of testing, Ms. Shaheen was pursuing a doctorate in linguistics and had worked as a translator and interpreter. She currently was experiencing conflicts regarding her ability to obtain her doctorate, largely related to difficulty finishing her dissertation. She had a history of both outpatient and inpatient treatment and had been diagnosed with BPD by multiple sources. Ms. Shaheen's Rorschach was administered originally by a male psychologist during one of her hospitalizations after an overdose.

As an important note, the selection criteria for the current case were (a) a case with which the author was not familiar before scoring and interpreting the protocol and (b) a reliable BPD diagnosis. This case was not chosen because it contained all the previously discussed Rorschach scores.

Ms. Shaheen's Rorschach was rescored by the present author using the most current CS scoring (Exner, 2003) and the previously discussed non-CS scales (none of these were originally scored).[6] These non-CS scores (and published scoring guidelines) are the MOA scale (Holaday & Sparks, 2001; Urist, 1977), the TOS (Greenberg et al., 1987), LDS Splitting, Projective Identification, Devaluation, and Idealization scores (Lerner & Lerner, 1980), AgPot and AgPast (Gacono & Meloy, 1994), Holt's (1977) primary and secondary aggression scores (A1 & A2), the COS (Blatt et al., 1976), and the TC/R (Armstrong & Loewenstein, 1990).

Ms. Shaheen's Rorschach results are presented at the end of the chapter, and the Structural Summary with non-CS scores in the last column. Table 7.2 presents Ms. Shaheen's CS scores and the major non-CS scores deemed important for BPD assessment, along with her results on these scores and comparative mean scores (most are based on the mean from BPD samples), followed by a concise interpretation of these scores in the last column. Therefore, the Table 7.2 scores are not mean normative scores, but the scores that might be expected for a BPD protocol or the BPD symptoms for the scale.

---

[6]To be useful for clinical application, only those non-CS scales are presented that have (a) published scoring rules that appear adequate for use as scoring guidelines and (b) some evidence of published mean scores (BPD or nonclinical) for comparative purposes.

TABLE 7.2

Major BPD-Rorschach Scores: Rorschach Scale, Comparison Mean Scores, Current Case Scores, and Interpretation

Rorschach Scale	Comparison Score[a]	Case Score	Interpretation[b]
Unstable relationships/unstable identity			
MOA-PATH	1.8	**5**	**Unstable relationships**
TOS	4.5	**7**	**Unstable relationships; identity disturbance**
LDS Splitting	0.7	**1**	**Unstable relationships; feeling empty**
LDS Devaluation	6.9	2	Unstable relationships (due to devaluing)
LDS Idealization	4.2	3	Unstable relationships (due to idealizing)
MOR	2.1	1	Masochism
ROD/R	.25	**.25**	**Heightened dependency needs**
	.11	--	Defensive counterdependency
Negative and unstable affect			
AG	1.1	**5**	**Anger**
Holt A2	5.7	**7**	**Anger**
LDS Devaluation	6.9	2	Negative affective instability
Self-destructive impulsivity			
MOA-PATH	2.4 (vs 1.1)	**5**	**Suicidal behaviors; self-mutilating behaviors; self-damaging impulsivity**
LDS Devaluation	8.1 (vs 5.5)	2	Suicidal behaviors; self-mutilating behaviors
LDS Splitting	1.2 (vs .13)	1	Self-mutilating behaviors
LDS Idealization	6.1 (vs 1.9)	3	Self-mutilating behaviors
Holt A1	1.5 (vs .43)	0	Self-mutilating behaviors; impulsivity
AgPot+AgPast	2.8	**4**	**Aggressive, suicidal, and self-damaging impulsivity**
Cognitive instability			
SCZI	3.4	3	Psychotic-like thinking and perceptions
SCZI=6	Not 6	3	SCZI=6, more likely psychotic
Sum6/WSum6	5.7/18.1	**15/49**	**Instances of psychotic-like thinking**
X+%	.51	**.30**[c]	**Distorted perceptions**
COS Content	2.1	**2**[c]	**Paranoid ideation**
TC/R	.46 (vs .24)	**.45**	**Dissociative states**

[a]Comparison scores are based on (a) the mean or combined mean for the BPD group(s) in the related research study/studies (except the self-destructive impulsivity variables and TC/R): MOA-PATH (Fowler et al., 2000); TOS (Greenberg et al., 1987); LDS Splitting and Devaluation (Fowler et al., 2000); LDS Idealization (Fowler et al., 2000; Hilsenroth et al., 1997); MOR (Baity & Hilsenroth, 1999; Skinstad et al., 1999); ROD/R (Bornstein et al., 2000; Fowler et al., 2000); SCZI (Hilsenroth et al., 1998; Skinstad et al., 1999); Sum6/WSum6 and X+% (Skinstad et al., 1999); COS Content (Stuart et al., 1990); (b) the mean score for the particular BPD characteristic: the first five self-destructive impulsivity variables are BPD self-mutilating vs non self-mutilating groups (Fowler et al., 2000) and TC/R is from high vs low BPD dissociative groups (Delany, 1996), or (c) 1 SD > M in a nonclinical group for AgPot+AgPast (Mihura et al., 2003).
[b]Bolded interpretations are considered significant for interpretation based on the case score vs the comparison score.
[c]Lower scores on these variables reflect more of the personality characteristic.

Test Validity and Test-Taking Attitudes and Behaviors

Ms. Shaheen's Rorschach was valid for interpretation with R = 20 and Lambda = .25. Although her R was within the normal range, examiner prompts on both Cards I and II may have led to a compliant response set of two per card. Her low Lambda level suggests that she was engaged in the testing and perhaps a little too prone to become absorbed in her experiences. Behaviorally, she was somewhat resistant, but complied with testing. Her testing comments suggest critical evaluations of her own performance, heightened by her perception of the examiner's influence or status (e.g., Card II: "I told you, I'm not functioning well!"; Card IX: "You scare me" [Examiner: "Why?"] "When I see a PhD I get scared.... I need to get my PhD" [repeats twice]).

Major BPD–Rorschach Scale Case Results

Ms. Shaheen's Rorschach results (Table 7.2) are consistent with several major BPD characteristics. Her scores on three Rorschach scales with virtually no scoring overlap (MOA-PATH [composite score of MOA levels 5 + 6 + 7], TOS, LDS Splitting) indicate a pattern of unstable and intense interpersonal relationships. However, her specific LDS Idealization and Devaluation scores are not particularly high, suggesting that these interpersonal defenses may be less characteristic of her unstable relationships. Her TOS and LDS Splitting scores, respectively, suggest an identity disturbance and chronic feelings of emptiness. Her dependent need for others (ROD/R) is problematically high, consistent with what would be expected for BPD inpatients. She likely has significant problems with intense and frequent anger (AG, A2). Her results are not consistent with affective instability, although only one scale with a BPD mean score of 1 was used (LDS Devaluation).

On self-destructive impulsive behaviors, Ms. Shaheen's scores are most consistent with BPD suicidality and generally self-damaging impulsive behaviors (MOA-PATH, AgPot), but less consistent with BPD self-mutilating impulsive behaviors (LDS Splitting, Devaluation, and Idealization; A1). Ms. Shaheen apparently has much difficulty in the area of cognitive instability, and her scores are consistent with general BPD psychotic-like thinking (Sum6, WSum6, X+%) and repeated hospitalizations. She may have instances of paranoid ideation (COS Content of Interaction) and dissociation (TC/R).

Expanded Rorschach BPD Case Interpretation

The following Rorschach case interpretation is based on further interpretation of the previously discussed BPD Rorschach scores, as well as general personality and psychopathology interpretations from CS scores.

Identity/Interpersonal Relationships. Ms. Shaheen's personality organization is consistent with that of borderline personality organization and BPD (MOA-PATH, TOS). Her object relations are characterized by malevolent control and influence (all five MOA-PATHs are Level 5), with potential physical attack lurking in every relationship (e.g., [R = response #] R2, R7, R18–R20). She likely has a highly unsuccessful transitional object relatedness (e.g., TOS, PHR:GHR) and her yearning for close attachments (T) is fraught with aversion and aggressive fears (R7). Her need for others is likely high (ROD/R, T), but so aversive to her and frightening to admit that it is a major conflict. Ms. Shaheen may be particularly unlikely to connect consciously her interpersonal needs to her resultant BPD symptoms (FD = 0). She is capable of seeing positive, cooperative, and mutual interpersonal interactions (COP, MOA1), although these may be of a more regressively playful nature that would not bode well for real mature love relationships (R3, R13, R14, R16, TOS). However, this playful nature may bode well for therapy with a clinician attuned to these playful transitional capacities and needs. Excluding intimate relationships, therefore, she likely is able to relate to others in a way that is at least superficially engaging and endearing. She appears to be interested in others (Pure H) and not naturally inclined to interpersonal isolation (Isolation Index). But, she frequently feels empty and has difficulty seeing herself and others in a whole, continuous, integrated sense (LDS Splitting). Specifically, she may split her perceptions of others into aggressive/attacking versus supporting/dependent, with distorted perceptions of what constitutes support (R18; FQ– on support figure who is "supporting the fight"). Ms. Shaheen may get into relationships that feel like a stranglehold on her emerging self (R7; LDS Projective Identification). She may have difficulty taking perspective on and mutually discussing benign but anxiety-provoking interpersonal situations in a way that is not threatening (FD; R4 & R15; PERs; R17 comments).

With regard to her sense of self and identity, it appears that Ms. Shaheen is floundering (TOS). She does not appear to have a pathological sense of self as a victim (MOR), nor a markedly narcissistic one (Fr+rF = 0). Her negative self-view is more likely internalized as a belief that her purpose in life is over if she gives up her aggressive identity and related behaviors (R6 content interpretation, "bombs" whose "function is over and ... dying out" [AgC,[7] MOR]). Her general emotional sense of self may be experienced as bodily concerns that are alternatingly intellectualized and projected (R12, R15, & R17; C' and C responses, Art). Although Ms. Shaheen's perception of herself and others is based largely on real experiences [H:(H)+Hd+(Hd)], her sexual needs may be met by autistic, idealizing fantasy (R13).

---

[7]AgC = Aggressive Content (Gacono & Meloy, 1994) and likely indicates an aggressive identity (Baity & Hilsenroth, 2002; Mihura et al., 2003).

Affect. Ms. Shaheen has particularly marked difficulty with anger (AG, A2), which is less attributable to primitive aggression (A1), but more attributable to how pervasive aggression is in her thinking, the degree to which it disrupts her relationships with others, and how frequently it is expressed in impulsive action (AG with three Ms and all the PHRs; AgPot, no Y). She appears to have difficulty modulating her emotions in general (FC < CF+C), which are likely either somaticized or aggressively acted out (CF w/AgC+AgPot and An). Regarding depression, she experiences emotional pain from holding back her negative emotions, which she unsuccessfully tries to intellectualize (C' responses with Art and Hx). However, she does not appear to suffer from an endogenous, guilty depression (DEPI), but more likely experiences a reactive depression accompanied by a chronic, empty dysphoria in which she perceives the world as a confusing, dangerous, and anxiety-provoking place (LDS Splitting, WSum6, all aggressive scores, comments to examiner, "scared" by percepts). It also is possible that she suffers from some trauma-related anxiety symptoms (war-related memory intrusions in R4, R6, R8).

Ms. Shaheen is not easily spontaneous in emotional situations (Afr), but likely feels her behaviors are driven by others' coercion (MOA-PATH, LDS Projective Identification, testing comments and compliance with R). All in all, Ms. Shaheen probably has limited instances of good, peaceful experiences in emotional situations, and instead is focused on either bodily concerns or impending aggression (R's on Cards VIII to X). However, she may have some relatively good instances in emotional situations in which she can be playful, although articulation of her emotions in these situations seems to elude her (R16).

Behavior/Impulsivity. Although Ms. Shaheen on the surface appears to have good psychological resources (EA, D and AdjD), these resources are pervasively compromised (PHR with all Ms and CFs). Although her inclination is to plan before taking action (introversive), her thinking is disrupted regularly by confusion and distortions and is colored by aggression (M's with Special Scores, LDS primitive defenses, poor FQ, and aggressive scores). In light of her achievement- and action-oriented drives (W:M, Ma:Mp, PhD student), her inability to direct her behaviors effectively toward her goals likely plagues her sense of competence. Instead, her behavior frequently is chaotic, punctuated with aggressive impulsivity (M's with Special Scores, AgPot's). There also is a danger of self-damaging impulsivity (MOA-PATH; AgPot + AgPast; FC < CF+C).

Cognition. Ms. Shaheen's thinking is quite confused, with several instances of circumstantial thinking (WSum6, DR's). Her thinking disturbance is predominantly not bizarre (Sum6 Level 1 vs. Level 2). Her reality testing is not pervasively compromised as in psychosis, but more unconventional and idiosyncratic (Xu% > X–%). Her slips into more severe reality testing disturbance largely occur after she experiences strong need states (3 out of 4 FQ– preceded by FMa's). Ms. Shaheen probably has occasional instances of fairly severe paranoid ideation when she is engaged in splitting and devaluing the other, viewing the other as engendering dangerous, competitive fights instead of supporting her (R18: COS Content1 w/M-, LDS Splitting [fighting/supporting] and Devaluation, FAB1). In subsequent interpersonal situations, she appears to perseverate on and displace this primitive conflictual theme and may engage in a convoluted mental battle with the other (R19; LDS Devaluation, FAB1 [close to FAB2], "fighting w/their heads"). This interpersonal theme and related thinking disturbance may complicate the completion of her dissertation and related work with her mentor. Finally, there is some evidence that Ms. Shaheen may dissociate at times (TC/R). Her dissociation may have some basis in trauma memories, but may be induced more generally by extended periods of seemingly unresolvable intense anger (TC responses, including five AG's).

The preceding review and case study is intended to provide an overview of what to expect in a BPD Rorschach protocol, including why (BPD conceptualization, BPD-Rorschach research) and how (BPD-Rorschach case study). The Rorschach is not designed to determine the BPD diagnosis (this is the job of the DSM interview), but Rorschach results can help to provide a dynamic understanding of the particular BPD person's personality characteristics. Although every person with BPD is not expected to show all the BPD-Rorschach signs (similar to the DSM BPD criteria), the foregoing research review helps us understand the types of Rorschach scores most characteristic of a BPD protocol. Some guidelines suggesting the expected levels for these BPD-Rorschach scores are provided (Table 7.2), but more research is needed to provide a normative base for the non-CS scores.

REFERENCES

American Psychiatric Association. (1980). *Diagnostic and statistical manual of mental disorders* (3rd ed.). Washington, DC: Author.

American Psychiatric Association. (1987). *Diagnostic and statistical manual of mental disorders* (3rd ed., revised). Washington, DC: Author.

American Psychiatric Association. (1994). *Diagnostic and statistical manual of mental disorders* (4th ed.). Washington, DC: Author.

Armstrong, J. G., & Loewenstein, R. J. (1990). Characteristics of patients with multiple personality and dissociative disorders on psychological testing. *Journal of Nervous and Mental Disease, 178,* 448–454.

Baity, M. R., & Hilsenroth, M. J. (1999). Rorschach aggression variables: A study of reliability and validity. *Journal of Personality Assessment, 72,* 93–110.

Baity, M. R., & Hilsenroth, M. J. (2002). Rorschach Aggressive Content (AgC) variable: A study of criterion validity. *Journal of Personality Assessment, 78,* 275–287.

Blais, M, A., Hilsenroth, M. J., & Castlebury, F. D. (1997). Content validity of the DSM-IV borderline and narcissistic personality disorder criteria sets. *Comprehensive Psychiatry, 38,* 31–37.

Blais, M. A., Hilsenroth, M. J., Castlebury, F., Fowler, J. C., & Baity, M. R. (2001). Predicting DSM-IV cluster B personality disorder criteria from MMPI-2 and Rorschach data: A test of incremental validity. *Journal of Personality Assessment, 76,* 150–168.

Blais, M. A., Hilsenroth, M. J., & Fowler, J. C. (1998). Rorschach correlates of the DSM-IV histrionic personality disorder. *Journal of Personality Assessment, 70,* 355–364.

Blais, M. A., Hilsenroth, M. J., Fowler, J. C., & Conboy, C. A. (1999). A Rorschach exploration of the DSM-IV borderline personality disorder. *Journal of Clinical Psychology, 55,* 563–572.

Blatt, S. J., Brenneis, C. B., Schimek, J. G., & Glick, M. (1976). Normal development and psychopathological impairment of the concept of the object on the Rorschach. *Journal of Abnormal Psychology, 85,* 364–373.

Bornstein, R. F. (1999). Criterion validity of objective and projective dependency tests: A meta-analytic assessment of behavioral prediction. *Psychological Assessment, 11,* 48–57.

Bornstein, R. F., Hilsenroth, M. J., Padawer, J. R., & Fowler, J. C. (2000). Interpersonal dependency and personality pathology: Variations in Rorschach Oral Dependency scores across Axis II disorders. *Journal of Personality Assessment, 75,* 478–491.

Brodsky, B. S., Malone, K. M., Ellis, S. P., Dulit, R. A., & Mann, J. J. (1997). Characteristics of borderline personality disorder associated with suicidal behavior. *American Journal of Psychiatry, 154,* 1715–1719.

Brown, M. Z., Comtois, K. A., & Linehan, M. M. (2002). Reasons for suicide attempts and nonsuicidal self-injury in women with borderline personality disorder. *Journal of Abnormal Psychology, 111,* 198–202.

Burla, F., Ferracuti, S., & Lazzari, R. (1997). Borderline personality disorder: Content and formal analysis of the Rorschach. In I. B. Weiner (Ed.), *Rorschachiana XXII: Yearbook of the International Rorschach Society* (pp. 149–162). Ashland, OH: Hogrefe & Huber.

Cardasis, W., Hachman, J. A., & Silk, K. R. (1997). Transitional objects and borderline personality disorder. *American Journal of Psychiatry, 154,* 250–255.

Coonerty, S. (1986). An exploration of separation-individuation themes in the borderline personality disorder. *Journal of Personality Assessment, 50,* 501–511.

Cooper, S. H., Perry, J. C., & Arnow, D. (1988). An empirical approach to the study of defense mechanisms: I. Reliability and preliminary validity of the Rorschach defense scales. *Journal of Personality Assessment, 52,* 187–203.

Cooper, S. H., Perry, J. C., Hoke, L., & Richman, N. (1985). Transitional relatedness and borderline personality disorder. *Psychoanalytic Psychology, 2,* 115–128.

Cooper, S. H., Perry, J. C., & O'Connell, M. (1991). The Rorschach Defense Scales: II. Longitudinal perspectives. *Journal of Personality Assessment, 56,* 191–201.

Delany, D. (1996). High and low dissociative patients with accompanying borderline personality symptoms: Differences on the Rorschach test. (Doctoral dissertation, University of Missouri, 1996). *Dissertation Abstracts International, 56,* 4633.

Dowson, J. H., Sussams, P., Grounds, A. T., & Taylor, J. (2000). Association of self-reported past "psychotic" phenomena with features of personality disorders. *Comprehensive Psychiatry, 41,* 42–48.

Exner, J. E. (1986). Some Rorschach data comparing schizophrenics with borderline and schizotypal personality disorders. *Journal of Personality Assessment, 50,* 455–471.

Exner, J. E. (2003). *The Rorschach: A comprehensive system: Volume 1. Basic foundations and principles of interpretation* (4th ed.). New York: John Wiley.

Fowler, J. C., Hilsenroth, M. J., & Nolan, E. (2000). Exploring the inner world of self-mutilating borderline patients: A Rorschach investigation. *Bulletin of the Menninger Clinic, 64,* 365–385.

Gacono, C. B., & Meloy, J. R. (1994). The aggression response. In C. B. Gacono & J. R. Meloy (Eds.), *The Rorschach assessment of aggressive and psychopathic personalities* (pp. 259–278). Hillsdale, NJ: Lawrence Erlbaum Associates.

Gartner, J., Hurt, S. W., & Gartner, A. (1989). Psychological test signs of borderline personality disorder: A review of the empirical literature. *Journal of Personality Assessment, 53,* 423–441.

Greenberg, R., Craig, S., Seidman, L., Cooper, S., & Teele, A. (1987). Transitional phenomena and the Rorschach: A test of a clinical theory of borderline personality organization. In J. S. Grotstein, M. F. Solomon, & J. A. Lang (Eds.), *The borderline patient: Emerging concepts in diagnosis, psychodynamics, and treatment* (pp. 83–94). Hillsdale, NJ: Analytic Press.

Grinker, R., Werble, B., & Drye, R. (1968). *The borderline syndrome: A behavioral study of ego functions.* New York: Basic Books.

Gunderson, J. G., & Kolb, J. E. (1978). Discriminating features of borderline patients. *American Journal of Psychiatry, 135,* 792–796.

Gunderson, J. G., Kolb, J. E., & Austin, V. (1981). The diagnostic interview for borderline patients. *American Journal of Psychiatry, 138,* 896–903.

Gunderson, J. G., & Singer, M. T. (1975). Defining borderline patients: An overview. *American Journal of Psychiatry, 132,* 1–10.

Harris, D. (1993). The prevalence of thought disorder in personality-disordered outpatients. *Journal of Personality Assessment, 61,* 112–120.

Henry, C., Mitropoulou, V., New, A. S., Koenigsberg, H. W., Silverman, J., & Siever, L. J. (2001). Affective instability and impulsivity in borderline personality and bipolar II disorders: Similarities and differences. *Journal of Psychiatric Research, 35,* 307–312.

Hilsenroth, M. J., Fowler, J. C., & Padawer, J. R. (1998). The Rorschach Schizophrenia Index (SCZI): An examination of reliability, validity, and diagnostic efficiency. *Journal of Personality Assessment, 70,* 514–534.

Hilsenroth, M. J., Fowler, J. C., Padawer, J. R., & Handler, L. (1997). Narcissism in the Rorschach revisited: Some reflections on empirical data. *Psychological Assessment, 9,* 113–121.

Hirshberg, L. M. (1989). Rorschach images of symbiosis and separation in eating-disordered and in borderline and nonborderline subjects. *Psychoanalytic Psychology, 6,* 475–493.

Hoch, P., & Polatin, P. (1949). Pseudoneurotic forms of schizophrenia. *Psychiatric Quarterly, 23,* 248–276.

Holaday, M., & Sparks, C. L. (2001). Revised guidelines for Urist's Mutuality of Autonomy scale (MOA). *Assessment, 8,* 145–155.

Holt, R. R. (1977). A method for assessing primary process manifestations and their control in Rorschach responses. In M. A. Rickers-Ovsiankina (Ed.), *Rorschach psychology* (2nd ed., pp. 375–420). Huntington, NY: Krieger.

Hull, J. W., Yeomans, F., Clarkin, J. Li, C., & Goodman, G. (1996). Factors associated with multiple hospitalizations of patients with borderline personality disorder. *Psychiatric Services, 47,* 638–641.

Johnston, M. H., & Holzman, P. S. (1979). *Assessing schizophrenic thinking: A clinical and research instrument for measuring thought disorder.* San Francisco: Jossey-Bass.

Kamphuis, J. H., Kugeares, S. L., & Finn, S. E. (2000). Rorschach correlates of sexual abuse: Trauma content and aggression indexes. *Journal of Personality Assessment, 75,* 212–224.

Kernberg, O. (1967). Borderline personality organization. *Journal of the American Psychoanalytic Association, 15,* 641–685.

Knight, R. P. (1953). Borderline states. *Bulletin of the Menninger Clinic, 17,* 1–12.

Koenigsberg, H. W., Harvey, P. D., Mitropoulou, V., Schmeidler, J., New, A. S., Goodman, M., et al. (2002). Characterizing affective instability in borderline personality disorder. *American Journal of Psychiatry, 159,* 784–788.

Labott, S. M., Leavitt, F., Braun, B. G., & Sachs, R. G. (1992). Rorschach indicators of multiple personality disorder. *Perceptual and Motor Skills, 75,* 147–158.

Leavitt, F. (2000). Texture response patterns associated with sexual trauma of childhood and adult onset: Developmental and recovered memory implications. *Child Abuse and Neglect, 24,* 251–257.

Leavitt, F., & Labott, S. M. (1996). Authenticity of recovered sexual abuse memories: A Rorschach study. *Journal of Traumatic Stress, 9,* 483–496.

Lerner, H., Albert, C., & Walsh, M. (1987). The Rorschach assessment of borderline defenses: A concurrent validity study. *Journal of Personality Assessment, 51,* 334–348.

Lerner, H. D. & Lerner, P. M. (1982). A comparative study of defensive structure in neurotic, borderline, and schizophrenic patients. *Psychoanalysis and Contemporary Thought, 5,* 77–115.

Lerner, P. M., & Lerner, H. D. (1980). Rorschach assessment of primitive defenses in borderline personality structure. In J. S. Kwawer, H. D. Lerner, P. M. Lerner, & A. Sugarman (Eds.), *Borderline phenomena and the Rorschach test* (pp. 257–274). New York: International Universities Press.

Mahler, M. S., Pine, F., & Bergman, A. (1975). *The psychological birth of the human infant: Symbiosis and individuation.* New York: Basic Books.

Masling, J. M., Rabie, L., & Blondheim, S. H. (1967). Obesity, level of aspiration, and Rorschach and TAT measures of oral dependence. *Journal of Consulting Psychology, 31,* 233–239.

Mihura, J. L., & Nathan-Montano, E. (2001). An interpersonal analysis of Rorschach aggression variables in a normal sample. *Psychological Reports, 89,* 617–623.

Mihura, J. L., Nathan-Montano, E., & Alperin, R. J. (2003). Rorschach measures of aggressive drive derivatives: A college student sample. *Journal of Personality Assessment, 80,* 41–49.

Modell, A. H. (1963). Primitive object relationships and the predisposition to schizophrenia. *International Journal of Psychoanalysis, 44,* 282–292.

Morey, L. C. (1991). *Personality Assessment Inventory: Professional manual.* Odessa, FL: Psychological Assessment Resources.

New, A. S., & Siever, S. L. (2002). Neurobiology and genetics of borderline personality disorder. *Psychiatric Annals, 32,* 329–336.

Nickell, A. D., Waudby, C. J., & Trull, T. J. (2002). Attachment, parental bonding, and borderline personality disorder features in young adults. *Journal of Personality Disorders, 16,* 148–159.

Owens, T. H. (1984). Personality traits of female psychotherapy patients with a history of incest: A research note. *Journal of Personality Assessment, 48,* 606–608.

Pantle, M. L., Ebner, D. L., & Hynan, L. S. (1994). The Rorschach and the assessment of impulsivity. *Journal of Clinical Psychology, 50,* 633–638.

Perry, J. C., & Cooper, S. H. (1986). A preliminary report on defenses and conflicts associated with borderline personality disorder. *Journal of the American Psychoanalytic Association, 34,* 863–893.

Reich, R. D., & Zanarini, M. C. (2001). Developmental aspects of borderline personality disorder. *Harvard Review of Psychiatry, 9,* 294–301.

Rippetoe, P. A., Alarcon, R. D., & Walter-Ryan, W. G. (1986). Interactions between depression and borderline personality disorder: A pilot study. *Psychopathology, 19,* 340–346.

Sack, A., Sperling, M. B., Fagen, G., & Foelsch, P. (1996). Attachment style, history, and behavioral contrasts for a borderline and normal sample. *Journal of Personality Disorders, 10,* 88–102.

Sanislow, C. A., Grilo, C. M., McGlashan, T. H. (2000). Factor analysis of the DSM-III-R borderline personality disorder criteria in psychiatric inpatients. *American Journal of Psychiatry, 157,* 1629–1633.

Sanislow, C. A., Grilo, C. M., Morey, L. C., Bender, D. S., Skodol, A. E., Gunderson, J. G., et al. (2002). Confirmatory factor analysis of DSM-IV criteria for borderline personality disorder: Findings from the Collaborative Longitudinal Personality Disorders Study. *American Journal of Psychiatry, 159,* 284–290.

Sansone, R. A., Gaither, G. A., & Songer, D. A. (2002). The relationships among childhood abuse, borderline personality, and self-harm behavior in psychiatric inpatients. *Violence and Victims, 17,* 49–56.

Skinstad, A. H., Troland, K., & Mortensen, J. K. (1999). Rorschach responses in borderline personality disorder with alcohol dependence. *European Journal of Psychological Assessment, 15,* 133–142.

Skodol, A. E., Gunderson, J., Pfohl, B., Widiger, T. A., Livesley, W. J., & Siever, L. J. (2002). The borderline diagnosis I: Psychopathology, comorbidity, and personality structure. *Biological Psychiatry, 51,* 936–950.

Spitzer, R. L., Endicott, J., & Gibbon, M. (1979). Crossing the border into borderline personality and borderline schizophrenia: The development of criteria. *Archives of General Psychiatry, 36,* 17–24.

Stern, A. (1938). Psychoanalytic investigation of and therapy in the borderline group of neuroses. *Psychoanalytic Quarterly, 7*, 467–489.

Stuart, J., Westen, D., Lohr, N., Benjamin, J., Becker, S., Vorus, N., et al. (1990). Object relations in borderlines, depressives, and normals: An examination of human responses on the Rorschach. *Journal of Personality Assessment, 55*, 296–318.

Trull, T. J., Sher, K. J., Minks-Brown, C., Durbin, J., & Burr, R. (2000). Borderline personality disorder and substance use disorders: A review and integration. *Clinical Psychology Review, 20*, 235–253.

Urist, J. (1977). The Rorschach test and the assessment of object relations. *Journal of Personality Assessment, 41*, 3–9.

Wagner, E. E., Allison, R. B., & Wagner, C. F. (1983). Diagnosing multiple personalities with the Rorschach: A confirmation. *Journal of Personality Assessment, 47*, 143–149.

Welch, S. S., & Linehan, M. M. (2002). High-risk situations associated with parasuicide and drug use in borderline personality disorder. *Journal of Personality Disorders, 16*, 561–569.

Westen, D., Moses, M. J., Silk, K. R., & Lohr, N. E., Cohen, R., & Segal, H. (1992). Quality of depressive experience in borderline personality disorder and major depression: When depression is not just depression. *Journal of Personality Disorders, 6*, 382–393.

White, C. N., Gunderson, J. G., Zanarini, M. C., & Hudson, J. I. (2003). Family studies of borderline personality disorder: A review. *Harvard Review of Psychiatry, 11*, 8–19.

Wilkinson-Ryan, T., & Westen, D. (2000). Identity disturbance in borderline personality disorder: An empirical investigation. *American Journal of Psychiatry, 157*, 528–541.

Winnicott, D. W. (1953). Transitional objects and transitional phenomena. *International Journal of Psychoanalysis, 34*, 89–97.

Wood, J. M., Lilienfeld, S. O., Garb, H. N., & Nezworski, M. T. (2000). The Rorschach test in clinical diagnosis: A critical review, with a backward look at Garfield (1947). *Journal of Clinical Psychology, 56*, 395–430.

Yen, S., Sr., Shea, M. T., Battle, C. L., Johnson, D. M., Zlotnick, C., Dolan-Sewell, R., et al. (2002). Traumatic exposure and posttraumatic stress disorder in borderline, schizotypal, avoidant and obsessive–compulsive personality disorders: Findings from the Collaborative Longitudinal Personality Disorders Study. *Journal of Nervous and Mental Disease, 190*, 510–518.

Zalewski, C., & Archer, R. P. (1991). Assessment of borderline personality disorder: A review of MMPI and Rorschach findings. *Journal of Nervous and Mental Disease, 179*, 338–345.

Zanarini, M. C., Frankenburg, F. R., DeLuca, C. J., Hennen, J., Khera, G. S., & Gunderson, J. G. (1998). The pain of being borderline: Dysphoric states specific to borderline personality disorder. *Harvard Review of Psychiatry, 6*, 201–207.

Zanarini, M. C., Frankenburg, F. R., Reich, D., B., Marino, M. F., Lewis, R. E., Williams, A. A., et al. (2000). Biparental failure in the childhood experiences of borderline patients. *Journal of Personality Disorders, 14*, 264–273.

Zanarini, M. C., Gunderson, J. G., Frankenburg, F. R., & Chauncey, D. L. (1989). The revised Diagnostic Interview for Borderlines: Discriminating BPD from other Axis II disorders. *Journal of Personality Disorders, 3*, 10–18.

Zilboorg, G. (1941). Ambulatory schizophrenias. *Psychiatry, 4*, 149–155.

RORSCHACH PROTOCOL FOR MS. SHAHEEN

Free Association	Inquiry

Card I

1. Something that flies. I don't know...a fly...a bee. (See anything else in there?)

1. Here, see, it's the anatomy; here's the body of the bee or the fly; here, this is the wings.

2. Could be a bird ... it scares me anyway.

2. The same thing you know. The body, the wings but what scares me is the two, these two here ... because I once had the nightmare that an eagle was strangling me (client continues story about eagle dream at age 8). I thought it more like a bee or a fly because the head isn't big enough, but it looks like an eagle because of its hands clutching.

Card II

What is it? I don't know. (Take your time, no hurry). I told you, I'm not functioning well! (You're doing fine. I just want to know what it looks like to you).

3. Maybe two baby animals playing with something.

3. Two pigs playing with these red things above, standing on their hind feet; you know, they seem to be happy. (Happy?) Yeah. I think they're happy. (What makes it look like that?) See here, they're smiling; it's a curve.

E: Mmm, good.
S: What are you waiting for?
E: What else do you see?
S: I don't see anything else ... should I see another thing?
E: Everyone sees more than one thing.
S: I don't have to do the whole thing?
E: No, doesn't have to be the whole thing.

196

4. Because you could take this white part in it ... looks like a warplane ... it could be real or a toy. I don't know.

4. This is the white part. And it's this part (D3) that makes it look like a warplane because it's coming at a very high speed. I've seen them coming at night. (Coming at high speed?). The red thing ... the fuel coming out. It's burning and the nozzle, it's pointed. To me, it looks like a warplane.

Card III

5. Two people in ... I don't know what the word is ... that's another thing, my brain doesn't do English (Try your best). I'm losing my English. I don't know the word. They're making this thing come up and down like this (demonstrates blanket toss) and they're folding it over this thing, like, have a blanket and throwing it up.

5. This is the blanket they're carrying, and they're flopping the orange thing up and down by doing this to the blanket (demonstrates).

6. These two things on the sides in the red— you could think of them as fireworks, but also as bombs.

6. Yes, fireworks or bombs—after they've exploded. (Help me see). You know. This looks like the end of the firework—it exploded and it died down. This is how it looks then. Same with a shell. This is how it looks after it explodes. (I'm still not sure I see it as you do). Fireworks, they go up in the air, explode out in this shape, and come back down in this shape—same thing with a shell. It's like their function is over and they are dying out. I hate this kind of testing.

Card IV

7. It's ugly! It's so ugly it reminds me of some bear, or a chimpanzee walking. (see below #8 for continued response)

7. This is the ugliest. Probably a chimpanzee, you know, because of the tail—a bear has no tail you know. (Ugly?) Ugly—very ugly picture. (What makes it look ugly?) Maybe the furry quality I feel here in the different shades of black here. The furry quality. It's also walking as if to attack ... it's under attack, it's about to attack.

(7. cont.) It can't be a bear. It must be a chimpanzee because of the tail … I don't know about the arms but they are. What sort of test is that?

8. These two things scare me. I don't know why. They kind of look like guns don't they?

8. These two, they're like M-16's. (Scare you?). Yeah, because of the civil war in Lebanon everybody was carrying one and if you weren't carrying one like me … but I know how to shoot one.

Card V

9. Oh, that's also ugly! They're all symmetrical. That's all I can say. Since they're symmetrical, this could be … it could be … if you took a lot of ink and folded it on the paper, it would come up like this.

9. An inkblot, yeah—you could say that of any of them, all of them look like that. I said it particular to this one because I don't think of anything really but a butterfly…I did say butterfly, right? I hate butterflies, flies, anything like that. I hate all flies—of course it's ugly, what's nice about it … it's somewhat scary too … maybe because it's all black. These edges, too. It's creepy.

10. Otherwise I think it's a butterfly.

10. Body, wings, and I hate butterflies. I used to be scared of them, but not anymore.

Card VI

11. (v) A flower of some sort.

11. It could be a flower. Can you see that? (Help me.) These are the petals, this is the pistol … here these could be some leaves. (Pistol?) Pistol, pistol, I didn't mean the gun pistol (on and on about forgetting biology) and this is the center of flower that gives insects the pollen grains.

12. (v) It also looks like an x-ray of the abdomen or something of the back.

12. Yeah I thought this could be the vertebrae. The back of the bone, the bone of the back (traces). This one … it's also the colors! It has the colors of an x-ray (Colors?) Shades of gray. (Where?) This part (points to center) but even the other sides, but it's as if you're testing for this thing—yes.

Card VII
13. (Frowns) Shit. (softly, long pause) two mermaids.

13. Head, a bust, and the tails. Their tails are connected so they're playing with each other. I think it's another happy picture like the pig ones ... it's happy because there's companionship because they can do things together.

14. Or ... two puppies jumping on rocks.

14. This would be the puppies, and this would be the rocks. Again, it's a happy picture. (Help me see the puppies). Heads, ears, bodies, tails, front feet on the rocks, something like that. I don't know.

Card VIII
15. I'd say this comes from a medical book...teaching about the human anatomy.

15. Yeah, it's typical of what you'd find in an encyclopedia under human anatomy. It's the colors that remind me of it. Maybe an encyclopedia, not a medical book...or a dictionary. (see below #16 for continued response)

16. Or like two cats. This could be cats playing with, I don't know, just this.

16. Cats, pink, the two pink parts—cats playing with this gray and blue part but I don't know what this gray and blue part is. (Continues #15) The spinal cord, the kidneys, the abdomen, see here and here ... I don't know ... it's clearer.

Card IX
17. There's something I think could come from a medical book ... I don't know, and really don't know what else. (very long pause).

17. You scare me. (Why?) When I see a Ph.D., I get scared. The same thing, the colors, the symmetry, the vertical thing in the middle as if it's the spinal cord. I need to get my Ph.D. (repeats twice).

18. This could be two people fighting with each other and below them it could be the people supporting each side or holding them. These green things are upholding the orange things so it's like supporting the person who's fighting.

18. This is how they're fighting as if these are swords. (I'm not sure I see it as you do). The ones in real light orange are weapons; the ones in dark orange are the hands carrying the weapons.

Card X
I wasn't good at all …
  but anyway. (Why do
  you say that?)
  Because I think so.

19. Why are they all so
    symmetrical, even?
    Again it looks like
    two people fighting.

19. These are their bodies, their heads, and they're fighting
    with their heads here. There, they were fighting with
    their hands (I'm not sure I see it as you do). In that one.
    This one they're fighting with their heads. They have
    helmets on. Their weapon … is the vertical thing, the
    vertical gray thing.

20. This could be two
    ugly birds.

20. Oh yeah, small birds, small birds. This is their eyes. This
    is their beaks. (Eyes?; Subject points). (Beaks?; Subject
    points). They're quarreling. They're angry at each other.
    (Ugly?) I think because they're gray again … otherwise
    everything else is color. The expression is very ugly. The
    expression on their faces is very ugly. They're out to get
    one another.

RORSCHACH SEQUENCE OF SCORES FOR MS. SHAHEEN

Card	Resp	Loc (DQ)	Determinants (FQ)	(2)	Content(s)	P	Z	Special Scores	Non-Comprehensive System Scores
I	1.	Wo	Fu		A		1.0	INC1,DR1,AG,ALG,PHR	LDS Projective ID,AgC,A2,MOA5,TC,TOS
	2.	Wo	FMao		A		1.0	INC1,PHR	MOA2,TOS,ROD
II	3.	W+	Ma-	(2)	A, Id, Hx		4.5	PER	AgC.AgPot,A2
	4.	DS5+	ma.CFo		Sc, Fi		4.5		MOA1,COS Content3
III	5.	D1+	Ma.mpu	(2)	H, Hh, Id	P	4.0	DV2,COP,PHR	AgC.AgPast,A2,TC
	6.	D2o	mpu	(2)	Ex			MOR	
IV	7.	Wo	FMa.TFu		A		2.0	DR1,AG,PHR	TOS.AgPot,A2,MOA5,TC
	8.	D4o	F-	(2)	Sc			DR1	TOS,A2,AgC
V	9.	Wv	FC'u		Art			DR1	TOSx2
	10.	Wo	Fo		A	P	1.0	DR1	
VI	11.	Wo	Fu		Bt		2.5	DR1	ROD
	12.	Wo	FC'-		Xy		2.5	DR1	TOS
VII	13.	W+	Mau	(2)	(H), Sx		2.5	ALG,COP,PHR	LDS Idealization3,MOA1,ROD,COS Content3,TC
	14.	W+	FMao	(2)	A, Ls				MOA2
VIII	15.	Wo	CFo		Art, An		4.5	PER	TC
	16.	Dd99+	FMao	(2)	A, Id	P	3.0		MOA2
IX	17.	Wo	CF-		An		5.5		TC
X	18.	D+	Ma-	(2)	H, Sc	P	2.5	AG,COP,FAB1,PHR	LDS Splitting, LDS Devaluation1,AgC,A2,MOA5,COS Content1,TC
	19.	Dd21+	Mau	(2)	H, Id, Sc		4.0	AG,FAB1,PSV,PHR	LDS Devaluation1,AgC,A2,MOA5,COS Content1,TC
	20.	DS8+	Ma.CFu	(2)	A, Hx		6.0	AG,FAB1,PHR	AgC,AgPot,A2,MOA5,RODx2,TC

STRUCTURAL SUMMARY FOR MS. SHAHEEN

Location Features

Zf = 17
ZSum = 53.5
Zest = 56.0

W = 12
D = 6
W+D = 18
Dd = 2
S = 2

Developmental Quality
+ = 9
o = 10
v = 0
v/+ = 1

Form Quality

	FQx	MQual	W+D
+	= 0	= 0	= 0
o	= 6	= 0	= 5
u	= 9	= 4	= 8
-	= 5	= 2	= 5
none	= 0	= 0	= 0

Determinants

Blends
ma.CFo
Ma.mpu
FMa.TFu
Ma.C'Fu

Single

M	= 4	FY	= 0
FM	= 3	YF	= 0
m	= 1	Y	= 0
FC	= 0	Fr	= 0
CF	= 2	rF	= 0
\C	= 0	FD	= 0
Cn	= 0	F	= 4
FC'	= 2	(2)	= 10
C'F	= 0		
C'	= 0		
FT	= 0		
TF	= 0		
T	= 0		
FV	= 0		
VF	= 0		
V	= 0		

Contents

H	= 3	Fi	= 1
(H)	= 1	Ge	= 0
Hd	= 0	Hh	= 1
(Hd)	= 0	Ls	= 1
Hx	= 2	Na	= 0
A	= 8	Sc	= 4
(A)	= 0	Sx	= 1
Ad	= 0	Xy	= 1
(Ad)	= 0	Id	= 4
An	= 2		
Art	= 2		
Ay	= 0		
Bl	= 0		
Bt	= 1		
Cg	= 0		
Cl	= 0		
Ex	= 1		
Fd	= 0		

Approach

I:	W.W
II:	W.DS
III:	D.D
IV:	W.D
V:	W.W
VI:	W.W
VII:	W.W
VIII:	W.Dd
IX:	W.D
X:	Dd.DS

Special Scores

	Lv 1	Lv 2
DV	= 0 x1	= 1x2
INC	= 2x2	= 0x4
DR	= 7x3	= 0x6
FAB	= 3x4	= 0x7
ALOG	= 2x5	
CON	= 0x7	

Raw Sum 6 = 15
Wgtd Sum 6 = 49

AB	= 0	GHR	= 0
AG	= 5	PHR	= 8
COP	= 3	MOR	= 1
CP	= 0	PER	= 2
		PSV	= 1

Ratios, Percentages, and Derivations

Core			*Affect*		*Interpersonal*		
R = 20	L = .25		FC: CF+C	= 0:3	COP = 3	AG = 5	
			Pure C	= 0	GHR: PHR	= 0:8	
EB = 6:3.0	EA = 9.0	EBPer = 2.0	SumC':WSumC	= 3:3	a:p	= 11:2	
eb = 7:4	es = 11	D = 0	Afr	=.43	Food	= 0	
	Adj es = 9	Adj D = 0	S	= 2	Sum T	= 1	
			Blends:R	= 4:20	Human Cont	= 4	
FM = 4	SumC' = 3	SumT = 1	CP	= 0	Pure H	= 3	
m = 3	Sum V = 0	Sum Y = 0	PER	= 2			
			Isol Indx	= .10			

Ideation				*Mediation*		*Processing*		*Self-Perception*	
a:p	= 11:2	Sum6	= 15	XA%	= .75	Zf	= 17	3r+(2)/R	= .50
Ma:Mp	= 6:0	Lv2	= 1	WDA%	= .72	W:D:Dd	= 12:6:2	Fr+rF	= 0
2AB+Art+Ay	= 2	WSum6	= 49	X-%	= .25	W:M	= 12:6	SumV	= 0
MOR	= 1	M-	= 2	S-	= 0	Zd	= -2.5	FD	= 0
		Mnone	= 0	P	= 4	PSV	= 1	An+Xy	= 3
				X+%	= .30	DQ+	= 9	MOR	= 1
				Xu%	= .45	DQv	= 1	H:(H)+Hd+(Hd)	= 3:1

PTi = 2	DEPI = 3	CDI = 1		S-CON = 4	HVI = No	OBS = No
(SCZI = 3)						

8

Rorschach Assessment of Histrionic Personality Disorder

Mark A. Blais
Matthew R. Baity
*Massachusetts General Hospital
and Harvard Medical School*

Hysteria is one of the oldest and most significant psychiatric conditions. Clear descriptions of hysteria have been found in both ancient Greek and Egyptian medical texts (Veith, 1977). Hysteria was the principal psychiatric condition that confronted Freud as he struggled to understand (and treat) mental illnesses. It was his clinical experiences with hysteria that provided the starting point for the development of psychoanalysis (Breuer & Freud, 1895/1957). Given its long history and prominence in psychiatric medicine, it is not surprising that the Rorschach Inkblot Method should also be associated with hysteria.

The traditional psychoanalytic formulations of hysteria, and later "hysterical character," have focused on repressed sexuality, excessive and shallow emotionality, and an overdeveloped fantasy life (Fenichel, 1945). Shapiro (1965) expanded this formulation by emphasizing the cognitive features of hysteria, namely the global, diffuse, and impressionistic cognitive style associated with the disorder. Although the concept of hysteria has undergone revision and evolution over the years, Histrionic Personality Disorder (HPD) continues to be a recognized psychiatric condition, represented in of the formal nomenclature of the *Diagnostic and Statistical Manual of Mental Disorders* (4th ed. [DSM-IV]; American Psychiatric Association [APA], 1994).

Although HPD is not among the most prevalent personality disorders, it is sufficiently common in both clinical and nonclinical samples that clinicians should be familiar with its presentation and diagnostic criteria, and should consider it in their differential diagnosis. For example, Blais & Norman (1997) found that 12% of a large sample of primarily personality disordered patients qualified for a HPD diagnosis. Torgersen, Kringlen and Cramer (2001) reported that 2% of subjects from a large non–treatment-seeking community sample met criteria for HPD.

The original DSM (APA, 1952) made no mention of hysteria, but did contain a condition termed "emotionally unstable personality," which resembled hysteria. In the second edition of the DSM (DSM-II; APA, 1968), hysterical personality was separated from hysterical neuroses and recognized as a disorder in its own right. The work of Lazare and colleagues (Lazare, 1970; Lazare, Klerman, & Armor, 1966, 1970) helped to clarify the descriptive features of the disorder and more firmly established the syndrome of histrionic personality (Pfohl, 1995). In a series of factor analytic studies, Lazare and colleagues identified aggression, emotionality, exhibitionism, egocentricity, sexual provocativeness, dependency, and obstinacy as the primary traits of hysterical personality. Lazare's findings provided much of the empirical support for the diagnostic criteria used to identify the DSM-III-R (APA, 1987) version of HPD.

With HPD's core features of "pervasive and excessive emotionality and attention-seeking behavior" (p. 655, APA, 1994), the DSM-IV version of HPD can be seen as reflecting a blend of both the psychoanalytic conceptualization of the hysterical character (Easser & Lesser, 1965) and Lazare's empirical trait findings. Interestingly, one of the revisions of the HPD diagnostic algorithm for the DSM-IV involved increasing the number of criteria needed for making the diagnosis from four to five. One study that explored the impact of this change found that significantly fewer patients qualified for the DSM-IV HPD diagnosis than for the DSM-III-R HPD diagnosis (Blais, Hilsenroth, & Castlebury, 1997). However, there is no evidence to suggest that patients who fall one criterion short of the DSM-IV HPD diagnosis (but would have qualified for the DSM-II-R diagnosis) are any less functionally impaired. Therefore, it also is important for clinicians to diagnose subclinical features of HPD for patients who have histrionic personality features or traits.

The eight DSM-IV HPD criteria (Table 8.1) can be reorganized (rationally) to reflect three deeper psychological processes (latent variables) that appear to underlie the behavioral manifestations of the disorder. These deeper processes are covert dependency needs (criteria 7 and 8), an excessive reliance on attention from others to regulate self-esteem (criteria 1, 2, and 4) and emotional dysregulation (criteria 3, 5, and 6). In addition to describing the observable features of HPD, these psychological processes likely account for

TABLE 8.1
DSM-IV HPD Criteria Set

1. Is uncomfortable when not the center of attention

2. Engages is interactions that often are characterized by inappropriately sexually seductive or provocative behavior

3. Displays rapidly shifting and shallow expressions of emotions

4. Uses physical appearance to draw attention to self

5. Has style of speech that is excessively impressionistic

6. Shows self-dramatization, theatricality, and exaggerated expression of emotion

7. Is highly suggestible

8. Considers relationships to be more intimate than they actually are

Note. Adapted from the DSM-IV (APA, 1994, pp. 657–658).

the strong empirical and clinical association of HPD with its neighboring disorders in the cluster B spectrum: borderline (BPD) and narcissistic (NPD) personality disorders (Blais, McCann, Benedict & Norman, 1997; Blais & Norman, 1997). For example, the presence of excessive and labile emotionality links HPD to BPD, whereas exclusive reliance on others to provide self-esteem is a feature characteristic of both HPD and NPD.

By focusing on these underlying psychological processes, clinicians can more meaningfully link the descriptive HPD criteria to the latent psychological and personality structures tapped by Rorschach variables. One of the unresolved theoretical issues related to HPD is the degree to which dependency needs underlie or motivate the behavior of HPD patients. Two theorists in particular, Millon (1996) and Horowitz (1991), assign primary importance to dependency needs. However, the DSM-IV (APA, 1994) criteria do not directly identify interpersonal dependency as part of the behavioral manifestation of HPD. As demonstrated in the following discussion, Rorschach assessment and research findings have been informative in this dispute.

RORSCHACH AND HISTRIONIC PERSONALITY DISORDER

The Rorschach Inkblot Method has had a long clinical association with the psychiatric diagnostic category of hysteria. In fact, Hermann Rorschach has provided us with his interpretation of the protocol for a 30-year-old woman with a diagnosis of hysterical neurosis. In his interpretation, Rorschach noted that the patient's record was coarctated, containing only 10 responses. This was thought to reflect the subject's reliance on defensive repression. He also noted a "marked tendency toward color answers, that is, more extratensive than introversive features" (Rorschach, 1921/1942, p. 143). In addition he thought the protocol reflected significant color shock and an inability to formulate responses to the color cards that he termed "marked avoidance of color."

Beginning with Rorschach's writings, color responses have been associated with emotional functioning. Because of this association, Rorschach (1921/1942) thought that his test had a unique ability to tap into the patient's affective functioning:

> The test gives orientation as to the affective status of the subject. It gives information as to the stability or instability, strength or weakness of feelings, the intensivity or extensivity of the affective reactions, the control or lack of control over the reactions, the suppression or freedom of the reactions. (pp. 97–98)

Furthermore, he wrote, "The absolute number of color responses is a good measure of affective lability" (Rorschach, 1921/1942, p. 98). Later, Schachtel (1966) focused on the passive and reactive stance in relation to the blot and the task (saying, "What might this be?") taken by the patient in producing color responses. For Schachtel, color-dominated responses (CF & C) indicated that a patient was struck by and passively reacting to external stimuli rather than actively taking in and cognitively working over the stimuli, as suggested by form-dominated color responses (FC). While not linked to hysterical personality in his original writing, it is easy to understand how the Rorschach indications described by Schachtel (emotional reactivity, expressiveness, and a passive reactive stance in relation to the external environment) have historically been related to HPD because these traits are pronounced features of this disorder.

In his classic text on applied psychological testing, Schafer (1948) provided a detailed review of the protocol from a case with a diagnosis of hysteria. Schafer indicated that in the typical record of a hysteric, SumC should exceed M, and M should not exceed 2. SumC should be composed predominant of (CF + C) > FC. Following Rorschach, he suggested that a hysteric's record tends to be brief, with a low R signaling the predominant use of repression. Along these same lines, Schafer noted that rejection of one or more cards was common among individuals with a hysterical style. Schafer thought these patients also should produce fewer W and Dd (DR's in Rapaport's system) responses than expected, relying instead more heavily on the obvious D areas of the blot. Schafer speculated that the presence of excessive anatomy content in the hysteric's record may indicate a preoccupation with conversion symptoms, whereas excessive sexual content may signal sexual symptoms.

Beck's (1952) description of a hysteric patient's protocol is very similar to Schafer's. Both authors considered SumC > M, low R, and a decreased number of M responses as primary markers of a hysteric presentation. Similarly, both authors indicated that an excess of either anatomy or sexual content responses also may be found in the record of patients with hysteria. Interestingly, Beck was consistent with Rorschach's earlier observation when he reported that many hysterics would produce a low affective ratio (Afr in the Comprehensive System [CS]) in addition to manifesting signs of affective lability (CF+C). This combination, according to Beck, was indicative of patients who had shallow, but unpredictable, explosive emotional reactions. These core features also are found with HPD, as discussed earlier.

Shapiro (1965) used Rorschach findings to illuminate the cognitive features of the hysterical style. Drawing heavily on his Rorschach assessment experience, he defined the typical hysteric cognitive style as vague, global, diffuse, and impressionistic. For him, these cognitive features were reflected in the hysterics' excessive use of color on the Rorschach (indicating a passive/impressionistic approach to the task), and by the difficulty these patients have managing the inquiry phase of the test. Shapiro noted that when asked to justify his responses during the inquiry phase of the test, a patient with hysteria appeared to be caught off guard and to evidence considerable trouble explaining "What made the blot look like that?" As a result of this difficulty, form responses typically dominated (higher lambda in the CS) the record, as well as responses with vague developmental quality (DQ vague in the CS; Exner, 2003).

RORSCHACH STUDIES ASSESSING HISTRIONIC PERSONALITY DISORDER

Unfortunately, only a limited number of empirical studies have explored the relation of Rorschach variables to the DSM-IV HPD. Blais, Hilsenroth, and Fowler (1998) evaluated the relation between preselected Rorschach variables and the DSM-IV HPD criteria. The Rorschach variables chosen by Blais et al. (1998) included FC+CF+C (sum color, measuring emotionality), T (texture, a measure of immature dependency; Marsh & Viglione, 1992), R (number of responses, a measure of repression) and DEN (Lerner's [1991] measure of defensive denial). This study also evaluated the ability of these Rorschach variables to distinguish HPD from BPD and NPD. The results indicated that both FC+CF+C and T were strongly and specifically correlated with HPD. In addition, these two Rorschach variables were significantly correlated with seven of the eight HPD criteria. The total Rorschach color responses (FC+CF+C) was correlated positively with HPD criteria numbers 2, 3, 4 and 5, whereas the texture responses were correlated positively with criteria numbers 1, 5, 6, 7 and 9 (Blais et al., 1998).

These findings suggest that emotionality, emotional expression, and immature dependency needs are strongly associated with these prototypic HPD behaviors. Interestingly, the Rorschach measure of defensive denial (Lerner, 1991), although not correlated with the DSM-IV HPD criteria, was significantly associated with the Minnesota Multiphasic Personality Inventory–2 (MMPI-2) Hysteria scale. The authors argued that the differential relationship found between DEN and both the MMPI-2 Hy scale and DSM-IV HPD criteria raised questions regarding the extent to which the current DSM-IV criteria behaviorally capture the important feature of denial long associated with HPD. Interestingly, although the clinical literature almost universally considered a low number of responses to be a marker of repression, and subsequently hysteria, no significant association between R and HPD criteria were found.

In a follow-up study, Blais, Hilsenroth, Castlebury, Fowler, and Baity (2001) explored the incremental validity of Rorschach variables relative to MMPI-2 personality disorder scales (Colligan, Morey, & Offord, 1994; Morey, Waugh, & Blashfield, 1985) for predicting DSM-IV cluster B criteria. In this study, two Rorschach variables (FC+CF+C and T) added incrementally to the MMPI-2 HPD scales in identifying DSM-IV HPD criteria. In fact, when both the MMPI-2 scales and the Rorschach variables were entered simultaneously into the regression equation, only the Rorschach variables were independent predictors of the DSM-IV HPD criteria. The results from this study directly support the findings on HPD and the Rorschach in the Blais et al. (1998) study, which furthers the link between these variables and the DSM-IV disorder while reinforcing the importance of considering both emotional expression and covert immature dependency in the assessment of HPD.

Bornstein (1998) used the Rorschach Oral Dependency scale (ROD; Masling, Rabie, & Blondheim, 1967) to explore the relationship of covert and overt dependency needs in HPD. The ROD scale is composed of content linked through psychoanalytic theory to oral dependency needs. The ROD content consists of food and drinks, food sources, food objects, food providers, passive food receivers, food organs, supplicants, nurturers, gifts and gift givers, good luck symbols, oral activity, passivity and helplessness, pregnancy, reproductive anatomy, and negation of oral percepts (e.g., "a man with no mouth"). In this study, college students completed the Interpersonal Dependency Inventory (IDI, a self-report measure of dependency; Hirschfeld et al., 1977) and the Personality Diagnostic Questionnaire-Revised (PDQ-R, a self-report measure of the DSM-III-R personality disorders; Hyler, Skodol, Kellman, Oldham, & Rosnick, 1990), then wrote two responses to Rorschach Cards I, II, III, VIII, and X. These written Rorschach responses were scored according Masling's (1986) ROD criteria. Bornstein found that PDQ-R HPD scores were strongly associated with Rorschach ROD scores but not with the IDI. Bornstein interpreted these findings as supporting the idea that patients with HPD use psychological defenses such as displacement, denial, and repression to keep their underlying dependency needs out of awareness. Interestingly, Bornstein also found that dependent personality disorder (DPD) was significantly correlated with both the ROD and the IDI, suggesting that DPD patients may be more aware of their dependency needs than HPD patients.

Although the empirical studies are limited in number, the findings are impressively consistent. All three studies indicated that HPD is associated with high levels of unrecognized (likely unconscious) dependency needs, and that these traits are not adequately captured with standard self-report instruments. In addition, Rorschach color responses were strongly associated with HPD in two studies, and provided diagnostic value that exceeded corresponding MMPI-2 scales. Together, these findings point to the importance of using a multimethod approach in assessing patients for HPD (Hilsenroth, Handler, & Blais, 1996). At its best, assessment research should inform both clinical practice and theory. The consistent findings with regard to the role of unconscious dependency needs in HPD patients support the theoretical formulations of Millon (1996) and Horowitz (1991) and suggest that the DSM-IV HPD criteria set could be improved with the inclusion of criteria that more directly identify this feature.

SUMMARY OF RESEARCH AND CLINICAL LITERATURE

Table 8.2 summarizes the findings from the authors' review of both the clinical and research literature. As already discussed with the empirical findings, the clinical literature is surprisingly consistent. Almost all the clinical writers are in agreement that hysteria and HPD are associated with Rorschach findings of low R, decreased M, SumC > M, and increased CF+C. Empirical studies support the utility of SumC in identifying HPD patients, but do not support low R as a marker of this condition. A number of the clinical writers have emphasized the tendency of patients with hysteria to produce anatomy or sexual content responses, but this has not been studied empirically in HPD patients. The empirical literature also has identified covert dependency needs (T, ROD) as strongly associated with the DSM-III-R and DSM-IV versions of HPD, but this motivation is not emphasized in the Rorschach clinical literature. In summary, a great deal of consistency exists between the clinical and empirical investigations of HPD. Despite the strong overlap between theory and research to date, very little research has been published in this arena, leaving a relatively wide-open field for future explorations.

TABLE 8.2
Rorschach Variables Related to Histrionic Personality Disorder

Rorschach Variables	Clinical Literature	Empirical Literature
Low R	HR, RS, SB	
FC+CF+C	HR	Blais et al., 1998
		Blais et al., 2001
SumC > M	HR, RS, SB	
CF+C > FC	RS & SB	
Texture		Blais et al., 1998
		Blais et al., 2002
Elevated DQ v & v/+	DS	
Elevated F%	DS	
Low affect ratio	SB	
DEN		Blais et al., 1998
ROD		Bornstein, 1998
Card rejections	RS	
Anatomy content	RS & SB	
Sexual content	RS & SB	

Note. HR, Rorschach (1921/1942); RS, Schafer (1948); SB, Beck (1952); DS, Shapiro (1965); DEN, denial in the Lerner Defense Scale (Lerner, 1991); ROD, Rorschach Oral Dependency scale (Masling, Rabie, & Blonheim, 1967).

CASE ILLUSTRATION: MRS. ZUCKER

Mrs. Zucker, an attractive 38-year-old, twice-divorced white female was admitted to a medical unit from the emergency ward after she reportedly attempted suicide by ingesting 10 mg of Valium. She took the pills in response to hearing that her most recent ex-husband planned to remarry. "I can't believe he would do this to me and our son. What will I do without him?" she said repeatedly when interviewed. After taking the overdose, she induced vomiting and called an ambulance to take her to the "the world's greatest hospital." Her presentation in the Emergency Department was remarkable for an acute change in mental status showing confusion, disorientation, and the presence of multiple vague neurologic symptoms (muscle weakness, dizziness, odd somatosensory experiences).

Mrs. Zuker's two-day hospital course was medically unremarkable, as were the results of blood and neurologic evaluations. A review of written records showed that this patient was called difficult and demanding, according to the nursing staff, who wrote that "her every wish needed their immediate attention or she would fly into theatrics." However, the medical resident found her to be "an interesting case ... charming at times," and was considering becoming her primary care physician.

This case concluded with no physical etiology for her neurologic symptoms, and she was started on an antidepressant for suspected depression. A psychiatric consultation was requested to rule out conversion disorder as the cause of her physical symptoms. Given her presentation, a combined neuropsychological and personality assessment was requested by the consulting psychiatrist.

Additional history indicated that Mrs. Zucker was an unemployed advanced practice nurse who lived alone with her 10-year-old son. She received alimony and child-support from her second husband, whom she described as a "near famous cardiologist who everyone here has heard of." Although divorced for nearly 4 years, she still referred to him as "my husband." She qualified her unemployed status by saying that she loved her work as a nurse, but that she was too exacting and skilled for many of the doctors with whom she worked. Although she had no definitive diagnoses, she did produce a long list of physicians with whom she had consulted regarding her varying ailments. Included on the list were the names of many prominent psychiatrists, all of whom she said were "wonderful" but failed to "hold her" in treatment.

The medical record indicated that Mrs. Zucker had experienced seizures after the birth of her son. The current status of her seizure disorder was unclear, but her reported physical condition had worsened over the years with increased fatigue and lethargy. These symptoms were particularly pronounced when her husband finished his residency and went full-time into academic medicine. He often worked, "100's of hours a week, leaving me alone to care for my beautiful boy," she said. She was medically hospitalized about that time for suspected lupus, but no diagnosis was fully established. More recently, her symptom picture included dizziness, headaches, and memory problems, all of which seemed to develop during the time leading up to the divorce. After the divorce, the patient's life centered on caring for her son and trying to manage her physical ailments. She had not worked outside the home for 7 to 8 years.

Testing indicated that Mrs. Zucker's measured intelligence was somewhat unevenly developed and within the average to high-average range. Her Wechsler Adult Intelligence Scale, 3rd Edtion (WAIS-III) showed a full-scale IQ of 106, a verbal IQ of 112, and a performance IQ of 98. Her weakest scores occurred on the Picture Completion and Information subtests, for which she obtained scaled scores of 6 and 8, respectively. On these tests, she had trouble being specific and exact with her answers. "Anything could be missing," she said repeatedly during the Picture Completion subtest. Her performance across a battery of standard neuropsychological tests was quite variable, but all her scores fell within the average to high-average range, and no consistent recognizable pattern of deficits was noted.

Mrs. Zucker's MMPI-2 (Butcher, Dahlstrom, Graham, Tellegen, & Kaemmer, 1989) profile was valid (L = 57, F = 58; K = 43) with the two highest scale elevations shown by scales 3 (hysteria) and 1 (hypochondriasis), respectively. Interestingly, both the Conversion V (scales 1 and 3 elevated at T-scores of 80 and 89, respectively, and scale 2 at 60) and the Scarlett O'Hara V were quite pronounced: T (scale 4) = 60, T (scale 5) = 30, and T (scale 6) = 70) in her profile. The Conversion V configuration suggested that Mrs. Zucker converts psychological distress into more acceptable physical complaints. According to Greene (1999), individuals with the 3–1 code type "characteristically develop physical symptoms when under stress," and these symptoms often are related to obvious secondary gain. Groth-Marnat (1997) wrote that for individuals with a 3–1 code type, "interpersonal relationships will be superficial, with extensive repression of hostility, and often their interactions will have an exhibitionistic flavor" (p. 265). Not surprisingly, patients with this code type often receive diagnoses of passive–aggressive and/or histrionic personality disorder on Axis II (Groth-Marnat, 1997). The Scarlett O'Hara V is indicative of hostility and anger indirectly expressed. These individuals with Scarlett O'Hara V tend to be demanding, dependent, and possessed of an inordinate need for affection. They have great difficulty forming close relationships, primarily because they lack the ability to take responsibility for their own faults (Groth-Marnat, 1997). When scale 3 is the highest elevated scale, the patient will be superficially sociable, egocentric, and blind to hostile impulses (Greene, 1999; Groth-Marnat, 1997). Overall, the description provided by the MMPI-2 profile was strongly consistent with a DSM-IV diagnosis of HPD for Mrs. Zucker.

The Rorschach was given and scored according to the Comprehensive System (Exner, 2003), and the Rorschach Interpretation Assistance Program version 5.00 (Exner & Weiner, 2003) was used to generate and interpret the Structural Summary. The record was valid (R = 17 and L = .70), and there were no card rejections. Among the Rorschach indices, the results for both the Depression Index and the Coping Deficit Index were positive. Together, these two indices point to episodes of affective disturbances (likely depression) and chronic difficulties effectively functioning in the interpersonal environment. Mrs. Zucker's EA was lower than expected (3.5), and although she technically had an ambient style, she clearly was leaning toward being extratensive (EB = 1:2.5). Her perceptual accuracy was adequate (XA% = . 88; WDA% = . 88). However, her endorsement of conventional reality could be considered more apparent than real, because her preference to be unique and different from others was clear in her record (Xu%=44). Her perceptual style was vague and impressionistic (DQv & v/+ = 3), but she also was an overincoporater (Zd = 3.5). Together, these findings suggest that Mrs. Zucker felt unsure and uncertain about decisions and had little consistency in problem-solving approaches.

Mrs. Zucker's WSumC was weighted toward undercontrolled expression of emotions (CF = 2; C = 1). The presence of two C's further suggests the presence of painful negative affect (anxiety and depression) that reduces her ability to experience pleasure. Interestingly, her Afr was low, indicating her reluctance to become involved in emotionally arousing situations. As such, she appeared to fulfill Beck's (1952) requirement for the presence of shallow emotional experiences and labile emotional reactions (CF+C > FC and low Afr). Her four S responses indicated strong oppositional tendencies along with chronic anger and resentment that she displayed toward people and the world in general. Although multiple S responses have not traditionally been associated with HPD, this finding is consistent with this patient's MMPI-2 profile, particularly the Scarlett O'Hara V (indirect expression of hostility and anger).

Interpersonally, Mrs. Zucker's profile suggests that she has adequate interest in others and appears to have the ability to develop close intimate relationships (GHR:PHR = 4:0). However, she also experiences considerable interpersonal neediness at a level that shows dependency desires as more immature (T = 2). The combination of her immature dependency and her oppositional tendencies are likely to lead to intense interpersonal relationships that are transient, chronically conflicted, and tumultuous. Her self-image is generally negative (Egocentricity Index = 0.29) and tends to be based on external comparisons in which she feels she does not measure up (M = 1, suggesting limited introspection). The presence of two sexual content responses suggest that sexuality plays a role in regulating her self-image, her relationships, or both.

Overall, Mrs. Zucker's Rorschach protocol, although perhaps not prototypic of HPD, was marked by many of the research and clinical findings that have been associated with this condition. In particular, her greater affectivity (FC+CF+C < M), her tendency toward undermodulated expressions of affect (CF+C > FC), and her marked dependency and interpersonal neediness (T) all are consistent with the research and clinical literature. Additional signs of HPD present in the record were her somewhat reduced R (17), low Afr, and elevated sexual content (Sx = 2). Her idiosyncratic perceptual style (Xu% = 44) is a nonspecific sign of a personality disorder. Although clinicians might entertain a diagnosis of narcissistic personality disorder based upon the clinical presentation, history, and MMPI-2 profile, the fact that Fr+rF is 0 and either an FV or FD determinant is absent seems to argue against this diagnosis. The Rorschach finding least consistent with HPD in this protocol was the presence of four S responses. This level of chronic anger would be considered atypical of HPD patients and is somewhat more suggestive of a borderline level of psychopathology (Blais & Bistis, 2004). It is possible that Mrs. Zucker's multiple S responses are a reflection of the deeper underlying psychological construct shared by BPD and HPD and, in part, is responsible for the empirical association so often reported between these conditions (Blais & Norman, 1997). Overall, it was though that the weight of the test data, both projective and self-report data, along with Mrs. Zucker's clinical presentation best supported a provisional diagnosis of major depression and HPD.

Hysteria and HPD are interesting and complex conditions that have fascinated medical practitioners for thousands of years. The prevalence of HPD, along with its tendency to be misdiagnosed, suggests that assessment psychologists should be well acquainted with the typical features of this disorder. The area in the assessment of HPD that seems to be lacking, yet has the most promise, is further examination of how the features of HPD (both conscious and unconscious) are expressed on the Rorschach. Much of the clinical and theoretical groundwork has been laid, as discussed in this chapter. Empirical studies to date have shown a great deal of consistency in both the research realm, and early theoretical writings. However, research in this area cannot remain stagnant. The DSM alone does not provide the breadth and depth of information that can be obtained from a thorough psychological assessment. As with any disorder, no single assessment instrument or approach appears to be sufficient for making a diagnosis of HPD. Rather a multimethod approach (self-report, clinician ratings, and projective data) seems to serve this function best (Ganellen, 1996; Hilsenroth et al., 1996). Given that Rorschach data has been found to have incremental validity in the prediction of DSM-IV HPD criteria, the inclusion of this data could be considered critical for describing a patient's affective style and degree of emotional control, as well as the unconscious dependency needs that motivate much of the HPD patient's overt behavior.

REFERENCES

American Psychiatric Association. (1952). *Diagnostic and statistical manual of mental disorders* (1st ed.). Washington, DC: Author.

American Psychiatric Association. (1968). *Diagnostic and statistical manual of mental disorders* (2nd ed.). Washington, DC: Author.

American Psychiatric Association. (1987). *Diagnostic and statistical manual of mental disorders* (3rd ed., Revised). Washington, DC: Author.

American Psychiatric Association. (1994). *Diagnostic and statistical manual of mental disorders* (4th ed.). Washington, DC: Author.

Beck, S. J. (1952). *Rorschach's test: Advances in interpretation.* New York: Grune & Stratton.

Blais, M., & Bistis, K, (2004). Projective assessment of borderline psychopathology. In M. Hilsenroth & D. Segal (Eds.), *Comprehensive handbook of psychological assessment: Volume 2 personality assessment* (pp. 485–499). Hoboken, NJ: John Wiley.

Blais, M. A, Hilsenroth, M. J., & Castlebury, F. (1997). The psychometric characteristics of the cluster B personality disorders under DSM-III-R and DSM-IV. *Journal of Personality Disorder, 11,* 270–278.

Blais, M. A., Hilsenroth, M. J., Castlebury, F., Fowler, J. C., & Baity, M. R. (2001). Predicting DSM-IV cluster B personality disorder criteria from MMPI-2 and Rorschach data: A test of incremental validity. *Journal of Personality Assessment, 76,* 150–168.

Blais, M. A., Hilsenroth, M. J., & Fowler, J. C. (1998). Rorschach correlates of the DSM-IV histrionic personality disorder. *Journal of Personality Assessment, 70,* 355–364.

Blais, M. A., McCann, J. T., Benedict, K. B., & Norman, D. K. (1997). Toward an empirical/theoretical grouping of the DSM-III-R personality disorders. *Journal of Personality Assessment, 11,* 191–198.

Blais, M. A., & Norman, D. K. (1997). A psychometric evaluation of the DSM-IV personality disorders criteria sets. *Journal of Personality Disorders, 11,* 168–176.

Bornstein, R. F. (1998). Implicit and self-attributed dependency needs in dependent and histrionic personality disorders. *Journal of Personality Assessment, 71,* 1–14.

Breuer, J., & Freud, S. (1895/1957). *Studies in hysteria.* (Standard ed., Vol. 2). London: Hogarth Press.

Butcher, J., Dahlstrom, W., Graham, J., Tellegen, A., & Kaemmer, B. (1989). *MMPI-2: Manual for administration and scoring.* Minneapolis: University of Minnesota Press.

Colligan, R., Morey, L., & Offord, K. (1994). The MMPI/MMPI-2 personality disorder scales: Contemporary norms for adults and adolescents. *Journal of Clinical Psychology, 50,* 168–200.

Easser, B., & Lesser, S. (1965). Hysterical character and psychoanalysis. *Psychoanalytic Quarterly, 34,* 390–405.

Exner, J. E. (2003). *The Rorschach: A comprehensive system: Volume 1. Basic foundations* (4th ed.). New York: John Wiley.

Exner, J. E., & Weiner, I. B. (2003). Rorschach Interpretation Assistance Program: Version 5 (RIAP5) [Computer software]. Lutz, FL: Psychological Assessment Resources, Inc.

Fenichel, O. (1945). *The psychoanalytic theory of neurosis.* New York: W. W. Norton.

Ganellen, R. J. (1996). Integrating the Rorschach and the MMPI-2 in Personality Assessment. Mahwah, NJ: Lawrence Erlbaum Associates.

Gorth-Marnat, G. (1997). *Handbook of psychological assessment.* New York: John Wiley.

Greene, R. (1999). *The MMPI-2/MMPI an interpretive manual* (2nd ed.). Boston: Allyn and Bacon.

Hilsenroth, M., Handler, L., & Blais, M. (1996). Assessment of narcissistic personality disorder: A multimethod review. *Clinical Psychology Review, 16,* 655–683.

Hirschfeld, R. M. A., Klerman, G. L., Gough, H. G., Barrett, J., Korchin, S. J., & Chodoff, P. (1977). A measure of interpersonal dependency. *Journal of Personality Assessment, 41,* 610–618.

Horowitz, M. J. (1991). *Hysterical personality style and the histrionic personality disorder.* Northvale, NJ: Aronson.

Hyler, S. E., Skodol, A. E., Kellman, D., Oldham, J. M., & Rosnick, L. (1990). Validity of the Personality Diagnostic Questionnaire—Revised: Comparison with two structured interviews. *American Journal of Psychiatry, 147,* 1043–1048.

Lazare, A. (1971). The hysterical character in psychoanalytic theory. *Archives of General Psychiatry, 25,* 131–137.

Lazare, A., Klerman, G., & Armor, D. (1966). Oral, obsessive and hysterical personality patterns, *Archives of General Psychiatry, 14,* 624–630.

Lazare, A., Klerman, G., & Armor, D. (1971). Oral, obsessive, and hysterical personality patterns: Replication of factor analysis in an independent sample. *Journal of Psychiatric Research, 7,* 275–279.

Lerner, P. (1991). *Psychoanalytic theory and the Rorschach.* Hillsdale, NJ: Analytic Press.

Marsh, A., & Viglione, D. (1992). A conceptual validation study of the texture response on the Rorschach. *Journal of Personality Assessment, 58,* 571–579.

Masling, J. M. (1986). Orality, pathology, and interpersonal behavior. In J. M. Masling (Ed.), *Empirical studies of psychoanalytic theories* (Vol. 2, pp. 73–106). Hillsdale, NJ: Lawrence Erlbaum Associates.

Masling, J. M., Rabie, L., & Blondheim, S. H. (1967). Obesity, level of aspiration, and Rorschach and TAT measures of oral dependence. *Journal of Consulting Psychology, 31,* 233–239.

Millon, T. (1996). *Disorders of personality: DSM-IV and beyond.* New York: John Wiley.

Morey, L., Waugh, M., & Blashfield, R. (1985). MMPI scales for the DSM-III personality disorders: Their derivation and correlates. *Journal of Personality Assessment, 49,* 245–251.

Pfohl, B. (1995). Histrionic personality disorder. In W. J. Livesley (Ed.), *The DSM-IV personality disorders* (pp. 173–192). New York: Guilford.

Rorschach, H. (1921/1942). *Psychodiagnostics.* Berne: Hans Huber.

Schachtel, E. (1966). *Experiential foundation of Rorschach's test.* New York: Basic Books.

Schafer, R. (1948). *The clinical application of psychological tests.* New York: International Universities Press.

Shapiro, D. (1965). *Neurotic styles.* New York: Basic Books.

Torgersen, S., Kringlen, E., & Cramer, V. (2001). The prevalence of personality disorders in a community sample. *Archives of General Psychiatry, 58,* 590–596.

Veith, I. (1977). Four thousand years of hysteria. In M. Horowitz (Ed.), *Hysterical personality* (pp. 58–79). New York: Jason Aronson.

RORSCHACH SEQUENCE OF SCORES FOR MRS. ZUCKER*

Card	Resp	Loc (DQ)	Loc No	Determinants (FQ)	(2)	Content(s)	P	Z	Special Scores
I	1.	WS+	1	FC'o		A	P	4.0	
	2.	Wo	1	Fo		(H), Sx		1.0	GHR
	3.	WS+	1	Fu		Id		3.5	
II	4.	Do		FMao	(2)	A			
	5.	DS+		FC'		An		4.5	
	6.	Dv		FTu	(2)	Cl			
III	7.	D+		Mao	(2)	H, Sx, Cg	P	3.0	AG,GHR
IV	8.	Wv/+	1	FTu		Fd		4.0	
V	9.	Wo	1	Fo		A	P	1.0	
VI	10.	Do		Fo		A			
VII	11.	Do		Fu		A			
VII	12.	Do		Fo	(2)	H	P		GHR
VIII	13.	Do		FMao	(2)	A	P		
	14.	Dv		CFu		Bt			
IX	15.	Wo	1	F-		Cg		4.5	
IX	16.	WS+	1	FCu		(Ad)		5.5	PER
X	17.	Do		CFu		(H)			GHR

* Free Association and Inquiry are not available for this individual.

Location Features	Determinants	Contents	Approach
	Blends		

Location Features

Zf = 9
ZSum = 31.0
Zest = 27.5

W = 7
D = 10
W+D = 17
Dd = 0
S = 4

Developmental Quality
+ = 5
o = 9
v = 1
v/+ = 2

Determinants

Blends

Single
M = 1
FM = 2
m = 0
FC = 1
CF = 2
C = 0
Cn = 0
FC' = 2
C'F = 0
C' = 0
FT = 2
TF = 0
T = 0
FV = 0
VF = 0
V = 0
FY = 0
YF = 0
Y = 0
Fr = 0
rF = 0
FD = 0
F = 7
(2) = 5

Form Quality

	FQx	MQual	W+D
+	= 0	= 0	= 0
o	= 8	= 1	= 8
u	= 7	= 0	= 7
-	= 2	= 0	= 2
none	= 0	= 0	= 0

Contents

H = 2
(H) = 2
Hd = 0
(Hd) = 0
Hx = 0
A = 6
(A) = 0
Ad = 0
(Ad) = 1
An = 1
Art = 0
Ay = 0
Bl = 0
Bt = 1
Cg = 2
Cl = 1
Ex = 0
Fd = 1
Fi = 0
Ge = 0
Hh = 0
Ls = 0
Na = 0
Sc = 0
Sx = 2
Xy = 0
Id = 1

Approach

I: WS.W.WS
II: D.DS.D
III: D
IV: W
V: W
VI: D.D
VII: D
VIII: D.D.W
IX: WS
X: W

Special Scores

	Lv 1	Lv 2
DV =	0x1	= 0x2
INC =	0x2	= 0x4
DR =	0x3	= 0x6
FAB =	0x4	= 0x7
ALOG =	0x5	
CON =	0 x7	

Raw Sum 6 = 0
Wgtd Sum 6 = 0

AB = 0   GHR = 4
AG = 1   PHR = 0
COP = 0   MOR = 0
CP = 0   PER = 1
          PSV = 0

STRUCTURAL SUMMARY FOR MRS. ZUCKER (CONTINUED)

Ratios, Percentages, and Derivations

Core

R = 17   L = .70

EB = 1:2.5   EA = 3.5   EBPer = N/A
eb = 2:4   es = 6   D = 0
Adj es = 6   Adj D = 0

FM = 2   SumC' = 2   SumT = 2
m = 0   Sum V = 0   Sum Y = 0

Affect

FC: CF+C = 1:2
Pure C = 0
SumC':WSumC = 2:2.5
Afr = .42
S = 4
Blends:R = 0:17
CP = 0
PER = 1
Isol Indx = .18

Interpersonal

COP = 0   AG = 1
GHR: PHR = 4:0
a:p = 3:0
Food = 1
Sum T = 2
Human Cont = 4
Pure H = 2

Ideation

a:p = 3:0   Sum6 = 0
Ma:Mp = 1:0   Lv2 = 0
2AB+Art+Ay = 0   WSum6 = 0
MOR = 0   M- = 0
M none = 0

Mediation

XA% = .88
WDA% = .88
X-% = .12
S- = 1
P = 5
X+% = .47
Xu% = .41

Processing

Zf = 9
W:D:Dd = 7:10:0
W:M = 7:1
Zd = +3.5
PSV = 0
DQ+ = 5
DQv = 2

Self-Perception

3r+(2)/R = .29
Fr+rF = 0
SumV = 0
FD = 0
An+Xy = 1
MOR = 0
H:(H)+Hd+(Hd) = 2:2

PTI = 0   *DEPI = 5   *CDI = 4   S-CON = 5   HVI = 1   OBS = 1

9

Rorschach Assessment of Narcissistic Personality Disorder

Leonard Handler
University of Tennessee

Mark J. Hilsenroth
Adelphi University

Narcissistic personality disorder (NPD) was first included as a diagnostic category in the *Diagnostic and Statistical Manual of Mental Disorders*, 3rd ed. (DSM-III; American Psychiatric Association, 1980), largely because of widespread interest in the theoretical and clinical concepts of narcissism by psychodynamic psychotherapists (Kernberg, 1970, 1975; Kohut, 1971, 1977; Pulver, 1970; Stolorow, 1975; Teicholz, 1978). According to Kernberg (1975), the essential characteristics of the NPD individual "center on pathological self-love, pathological object love, and pathological super-ego" (p. 35). Pathological self-love is seen in the NPD's self-centeredness, grandiosity, self-absorption, excessive self-reference, exhibitionistic tendencies, a sense of superiority, recklessness, and "a discrepancy between their inordinate ambitions and what they can achieve" (p. 35). Yet, the NPD individual has an inordinate need to be loved and admired. The NPD patient often places extreme value on physical attractiveness, power, wealth, looking good, and intellectual pretentiousness. These patients need and seek admiration from others, and they demonstrate emotional shallowness, especially in relationships. Although feelings of grandiosity often are evident, they frequently alternate with feelings of insecurity and inferiority. Kernberg (1975) emphasized that pathological object love is manifested by extreme envy. The NPD individual devalues others who threaten his or her status, in attempts to deny feelings of envy.

The NPD individual has little interest in the lives of other people and often expresses contempt toward others. Kernberg (1975) stated: "Unconsciously it manifests as a 'spoiling' maneuver consisting of incorporating what comes from others and simultaneously devaluating what has been incorporated" (p. 36). Typically, NPDs exploit others and, as can be seen from recent news regarding illegal actions of some corporate executives, their excessive greed is reflected in their wish to "steal or appropriate what others have" (p. 36). Their emotional life is shallow, and they have little genuine empathy for others. They feel restless and bored unless their self-regard is being actively nourished (Lerner, 1998).

Although the NPD individual idealizes people, this approach is temporary at best, often quickly changing to devaluation. Thus, for example, Kernberg (1975) stated: "The patients' unconscious seem to experience those around them first as idols, and then as enemies or fools" (p. 36). Thus, their relationship with others is quite precarious; they do not commit to others, and they have difficulty empathizing with others. This inability leads them often to be quite hurtful and insensitive toward others and their needs; they often act in a thoughtless, and frequently cruel, manner.

Superego problems are exhibited in the NPD's inability to experience differentiated forms of depression, such as remorse, sadness, and self-exploration. These patients exhibit severe mood swings when their grandiose efforts fail or they do not get the desired admiration from others, or if they receive criticism, which shatters their grandiosity. In this regard, Kernberg (1975) viewed their self-esteem as regulated by shame rather than by guilt. Values are focused on protection of self-esteem. The NPD person needs, courts, and covets external admiration. Cooper (1998) indicated that the NPD demonstrates a "damaged capacity for emotional ties to others, damaged capacity for sustained pleasure in one's own activities, damaged capacities for mourning and sadness, and inner feelings of deadness and boredom" (p. 60).

The justification for regarding NPD as an independent diagnostic entity with features distinguishable from other personality disorders has been a matter of some controversy (Loranger, Oldham, & Tulis, 1982; Perry & Vaillant, 1989; Pope, Jonas, Hudson, Cohen, & Gunderson, 1983; Siever & Klar, 1986). In fact, almost no empirical work focusing exclusively on NPD had been conducted until the late 1980s. In their review of data concerning DSM-III-R (American Psychiatric Association, 1987) descriptors of NPD, Gunderson, Ronningstam and Smith (1991), stated: "[NPD] remains a disorder about which there has been little empirical evidence and around which basic questions of description, clinical utility, and validity still remain" (p. 167). In the decade since this statement was made, several attempts have been made to add to the diagnostic literature for NPD (Blais, Hilsenroth, & Castlebury, 1997a, 1997b).

DSM IV-TR DIAGNOSTIC CRITERIA
FOR NARCISSISTIC PERSONALITY DISORDER

The DSM-IV-TR (American Psychiatric Association, 4th edition, Text Revision, 2000) cites the following criteria for an NPD diagnosis: "A pervasive pattern of grandiosity (in fantasy or behavior), need for admiration, and lack of empathy, beginning by early adulthood and present in a variety of contexts, as indicated by five or more of the following:

1. Has a grandiose sense of self-importance (e.g., exaggerates achievements and talents, expects to be recognized as superior without commensurate achievements)
2. Is preoccupied with fantasies of unlimited success, power, brilliance, beauty, or ideal love
3. Believes that he or she is 'special' and unique and can only be understood by, or associate with, other special high-status people (or institutions);
4. Requires excessive admiration
5. Has a sense of entitlement (i.e., unreasonable expectations of especially favorable treatment or automatic compliance with his or her expectations)
6. Is interpersonally exploitative (i.e., takes advantage of others to achieve his or her own ends)
7. Lacks empathy: is unwilling to recognize or identify with the feelings and needs of others
8. Is often envious of others or believes that others are envious of him or her
9. Shows arrogant behaviors or attitudes." (p. 717)

ARE THERE TWO SUBTYPES OF NPD?

Some theorists believe there are two subtypes of NPD. Akhtar and Thompson (1982), Cooper (1981), Cooper and Ronningstam (1992), Gabbard (1989), Masterson (1981), and Wink (1991) describe what they believe to be two distinct subtypes of NPD: the aforementioned type described in the DSM-IV-TR as the loud, ostentatious, self-centered braggart, and the shy, timid, seemingly inhibited individual, who hardly fits the usual DSM description of narcissism. However, there has been no research supporting the validity of NPD subtypes. More than likely these so-called subtypes actually describe differences in style of self-presentation rather than significant subtype differences. Nevertheless, it is helpful to examine these differences in style of self-presentation to demonstrate the extremes in overt behavior of the NPD patient. When the fantasies of NPD patients with varied self-presentations are explored, a variety of underlying narcissistic characteristics may be present. The patients with shy or passive self-presentations typically carry on most of their narcissistic activities in fantasy and are too inhibited to expose their fantasies to public view. They appear on the surface to be very empathic because others mistake their shy presentation as genuine interest.

Akhtar (1989) compared the two presentation styles of NPD, calling them "overt" and "covert." Whereas the overt NPD style includes grandiose and entitled behavior, the covert NPD often is morose, with feelings of self-doubt and shame. The covert NPD presentation style often is characterized by an inability to depend on and trust others. Whereas the NPD patient with an overt style often is socially charming and successful, the self-presentation of the NPD patient with a covert style typically is aimless, with shallow vocational commitment. Such patients possess a dilettante-like attitude, often with chronic boredom and multiple but superficial interests. With the covert style of presentation, the NPD patient often shifts values to gain favor. Their covert presentation style typically is limited to trivia and shows impaired capacity for learning new skills. On the other hand, those patients with an overt style often are impressively knowledgeable, decisive, opinionated, and typically quite articulate.

Thus, whereas the NPD individual may be loud and arrogant, he or she also may be subdued and introverted. The individual's vulnerability in self-esteem makes him or her very sensitive to narcissistic injury from criticism or failure. Such patients may or may not show the vulnerability outwardly, but such "injuries" may haunt them, often for long periods, leaving them feeling humiliated, degraded, shamed, hollow, and empty. Although the reaction of the NPD individual to such injury may be rage or defiant counterattack, he or she may instead withdraw in shame or assume a posture of humility to mask and protect the grandiosity. In some cases the NPD individual is a high achiever because of his or her overwhelming ambition and confidence. However, sometimes achievement is poor. The NPD individual may avoid taking risks for fear that his or her risk taking or assertive attempts may result in failure, causing more narcissistic injury. In such patients one sees withdrawal, depression, shame, and humiliation. Whereas the overt self-presentation style of the NPD individual often can be identified in interviews, the NPD person who presents as "quiet" is much more difficult to detect in interviews and in self-presentation. Indeed, the diagnosis of NPD often is quite difficult from observations and even from interview. However, projective tests such as the Rorschach often are quite capable of contributing to the diagnosis of NPD.

TWO PSYCHOANALYTIC THEORIES OF NARCISSISM

A number of authors within the psychoanalytic community have written extensively about narcissism and disorders of the self (Jacobson, 1964;

Kernberg, 1970, 1975; Kohut, 1971, 1977; Pulver, 1970; Stolorow, 1975; Teicholz, 1978). In particular the work of Otto Kernberg and Heinz Kohut have occupied the attention of the psychoanalytic community. These authors have developed a theoretical substrate of narcissism that includes the structural organization of the self, damaged self-esteem, primitive affects, object representations, and grandiosity. Kernberg sees this narcissistic patient as organized on the borderline level, whereas Kohut sees such patients as closer to the neurotic end of the pathology continuum. Kernberg's theory of narcissism focuses around a disturbance in object relations, whereas Kohut saw the problem as focused around a disturbance in the cohesive self (Lerner, 1988).

Kernberg (1975) emphasized the role of intrapsychic conflict in pathological narcissism and specific disturbances in object relations (Lerner, 1998). This conflict model incorporates the infant's experience of external objects as a basis for elaborating the drives and defenses that shape the child's internal reality. As the child matures, these affects and cognitions separate into libidinal and aggressive, positive and negative components, partly as a function of the experiences of gratification and frustration with the object world. These components develop into mental representations reflecting the infant's experience of interactions with its environment. These self and object representations, now infused with affective meaning, separate along the dimension of actual and idealized representations, which ultimately find expression as contents in the ego and superego, respectively. Kernberg theorized that if this normal process of differentiation breaks down or collapses, the result will be a pathological re-fusion of actual and idealized self and object representations.

This structural breakdown is thought to be the result of unmanageable aggression, which overwhelms the developing ego as it struggles to integrate the increasing differentiation of its representational contents. When confronted by painful interactions with its caretakers, the infant tries to reclaim its libidinal investment in them. In addition, the infant's unmet dependency needs require it to protect these object representations from the primitive aggressive impulses. To accomplish this task the infant erects two principal defenses, projection and excessive splitting, to mitigate the anxiety this conflict generates. The intense aggression is in part projected out of the internal world onto the external one, further exacerbating the infant's experience of crippling anxiety as it struggles to avoid the "bad external objects." In the effort to preserve the weakened remnants of the "good objects" as defensive bulwarks against the "bad objects," splitting intensifies, with good and bad, self and object representations existing in relatively isolated states. This lack of integration manifests itself in a compromised self-concept, which operates in conjunction with an equally impaired concept of others. Not only is the structural integrity of the self weakened, but its predominantly negative affect adversely affects the capacity for positive self-regard. Subsequently, these enfeebled actual and ideal self-representations use increasingly more primitive manifestations of grandiosity to shield the ego from the painful experiences and rageful reactions to an unrewarding object world. For Kernberg (1975) these intrapsychic manifestations lead to the use of grandiosity, a major part of the constellation of defenses against aggression that characterize pathological narcissism.

In contrast to Kernberg, Kohut (1971, 1977) ultimately abandoned intrapsychic conflict as etiologically central in favor of experiential deficit as the pivotal variable in narcissistic pathology. For Kohut, narcissistic pathology is viewed as the final end product of the parents' unsuccessful attempts to support the infant's grandiose and idealizing needs. To relieve feelings of helplessness, the infant requires the parent to serve as an object that can perform psychological tasks such as tension management and self-esteem regulation (a selfobject), which the infant is unable to accomplish for itself.

In the course of normal development, the parent reinforces the infant's immersion in its imagined omnipotence by empathically "mirroring" its grandiosity. In addition, the parent must also effectively serve as a container for the infant's primitive idealizations of the parent. This idealization allows the infant to fuse with the omnipotent selfobject and thereby ward off the threat of disorganization and feelings of helplessness. The parents' capacity to serve as effective selfobjects provides an environment that allows the infant gradually to internalize the functions the parents have performed. These conditions, which include empathic responsiveness tempered by optimal frustration, permit the infant sufficient time and resources to develop a cohesive sense of self that is capable of mastering individuation. However, should the interpersonal environment become unresponsive to the infant's needs, pathological self-development will ensue.

In the instance of empathic failure, the infant's normal grandiosity remains arrested at an infantile stage. The failure to echo empathically the infant's omnipotence and grandiosity undermines the sense of efficacy upon which the cohesive self and a positive self-regard rest. As the infant matures, these unmet primitive demands are split off from the developing ego. This split-off archaic grandiosity remains and is not integrated into actual or idealized representations, but continues to demand narcissistic recognition throughout adulthood.

A second type of environmental failure occurs if the selfobject is too disillusioning to provide a powerful idealizable selfobject with which the infant can then fuse. Painful disillusionment with the parental selfobjects will be expressed as an inner emptiness, accompanied by deflated self-esteem. In these circumstances, the child will continue to seek idealized parental surrogates into adulthood, desiring fusion to enhance the fragile self.

With either of these environmental failure types, the development of a cohesive sense of the self is thwarted, and consequently remains structurally unintegrated and affectively impoverished. Lerner (1998) described a picture of the narcissist from Kohut's (1971, 1977) case material as a person who lacks a cohesive self, and who is "excessively self-conscious and self-preoccupied, who experience[s] continuous feelings of vulnerability, who defend[s] against lowered feelings of self-esteem with grandiosity, and who experience[s] a particular type of depressive affect involving feelings of depletion, emptiness, and nonexistence" (p. 257). Kohut painted a picture of these patients as lacking enthusiasm and zest, and having feelings of subjective deadness (Lerner, 1998).

The theoretical differences between these two authors is focused on the search for the postulated explanatory mechanisms of the structural impairment. The conflict model attributes this severely compromised self-development to frustrating, painful experiences with the object world (Kernberg 1975, 1984). As a consequence, the child pathologically develops excessive, unmanageable aggression, which limits his or her capacity to integrate self and object representations in a normal way. By contrast, the deficit model links pathological self-representations to early traumatic failure in normal development, in which primitive and grandiose self-representations remain arrested at an earlier stage of self-development (Kohut, 1971, 1977).

Central to the disagreement between the theoretical viewpoints of Kernberg (1975) and Kohut (1971, 1977) is the primacy of aggression in the etiology of pathological narcissism. For Kernberg, intense aggression is one of the fundamental determinants of pathological self-development, whereas Kohut viewed parental failures of empathy and idealization as the primary etiological agents in the deficit or arrest of the emerging self. Kohut also recognized "narcissistic rage" as a feature of this clinical syndrome, but he regarded its presence as secondary to primary failures in empathy and idealization. However, these aggressive components are primary for Kernberg; in his view the disappointments described by Kohut are defensive reactions by which the patient can rationalize his or her seething rage. Moreover, Kernberg considered the idealizing needs elaborated by Kohut as primitive defenses against the imagined destructive power of this rage (Kernberg, 1975).

Both Kernberg (1975) and Kohut (1971, 1977) emphasized the centrality of splitting as a defensive operation underlying narcissistic pathology. In each theory, splitting is viewed as a normal process in development, which becomes pathological when it is used extensively to generate negative, self and other representations from positive representations. However, each theory emphasizes a different function served by splitting. According to Kernberg, the child uses splitting *to protect significant others* from unmanageable aggression in reaction to frustrations with those significant others. However, Kohut (1971) understood splitting to be a defensive function *to protect the child* from frustrated needs for parental empathy and recognition.

Kohut and Kernberg disagreed on the etiological mechanisms that account for these maladaptive internal structures, but they agreed that there is a structural relationship between compromised self (and object) representations and impairment in the regulation of self-esteem. They agreed that problems with respect to regulating self-esteem are primary in narcissistic pathology, and that structural aspects of the self are causally implicated in these difficulties. They also agreed on the direct relationship between the self or self-representation and self-esteem, and on the dynamics underlying the grandiose façade and an entitled sense of self-importance that mask or defend the patient against unconscious feelings of inferiority, vulnerability, helplessness, and impoverished self-esteem.

Although the psychoanalytic community has viewed these two models as relatively independent of each other, it is clear that to do so would undoubtedly be an error. A review of these theoretical perspectives (Eagle, 1984) has shown that in fact a great deal of overlap exists between them. They have many of the same constructs, structures, and defining characteristics in common. In addition, Glassman (1988) empirically demonstrated that these models are not orthogonal, but exhibit a moderate association ($r = .44$) between the deficit and the conflict latent constructs.

DIFFERENTIATING NARCISSISTIC PERSONALITY DISORDER FROM OTHER PERSONALITY DISORDERS

Investigators have attempted to develop specific criteria on a number of assessment measures that may aid in the differentiation of NPD from other personality disorders. In particular, several of the phenomenological studies by Gunderson and Ronningstam (Gunderson, Ronningstam, & Bodkin, 1990; Ronningstam, 1988; Ronningstam & Gunderson, 1988, 1990, 1991) have focused on identifying characteristics of NPD patients, which has led to the development of the Diagnostic Interview for Narcissism (DIN). Although findings have shown self-report measures to be useful in the diagnosis of personality disorders generally (Blais, et al.,1997a, 1997b) and scales designed to assess NPD have received extensive use (Chatham, Tibbals, & Harrington, 1993; Colligan, Morey, & Offord, 1994; Millon, 1983, 1987; Morey, Waugh, & Blashfield, 1985; Wink & Gough, 1990), this chapter focuses on the use of the Rorschach in its ability to differentiate NPD from other clinical groups (Berg, 1990; Berg, Packer, & Nunno, 1993; Farris, 1988; Gacono & Meloy, 1994; Gacono, Meloy, & Berg, 1992; Gacono, Meloy,

& Heaven, 1990; Hilsenroth, Hibbard, Nash, & Handler, 1993; Hilsenroth, Fowler, Padawer, & Handler, 1997), and on the exploration of NPD traits and dynamics as illuminated by Rorschach findings.

Several authors also have called for research concerning the differential diagnosis and treatment of individuals with various forms of character pathology (Blatt & Lerner, 1983; Kernberg, 1975). All have stressed the importance of careful diagnostic assessment of these individuals, especially using psychological testing for treatment planning, management of transference, and countertransference issues. The ability to distinguish narcissistic pathology specifically would enable practicing clinicians to make more appropriate decisions in choosing treatment strategies for such persons. Identification of variables related to pathological expressions of narcissism is only a starting point, to be followed by the identification of those NPD features that are the most outstanding and important in differential diagnosis (Davis, Blashfield, & McElroy, 1993; Westen, 1997; Westen & Arkowitz-Westen, 1998; Westen, & Shedler, 1999a, 1999b, 2000). However, because narcissistic traits commonly occur in other personality disorders, there are a variety of opinions as to the clinical features and theoretical aspects of NPD (Kernberg, 1984; Millon & Davis, 1996; Pulver, 1970; Teicholz, 1978). Therefore, it is imperative that indices of narcissism be identified that can separate NPD individuals from related "dramatic" Cluster B personality disordered patients [antisocial (ANPD), borderline (BPD), and histrionic (HPD)] while differentiating unrelated (Cluster A and Cluster C) personality disorders (Holdwick, Hilsenroth, Blais, & Castlebury, 1998).

RESEARCH ON NARCISSISTIC PERSONALITY DISORDER WITH THE RORSCHACH

A number of studies have used the Rorschach in differential diagnostic research for NPD. Farris (1988) found that NPD patients had significantly higher cognitive–perceptual functioning and more responses indicative of body narcissism and phallic–oedipal issues than BPD patients. Moreover, BPD patients produced significantly more splitting, projective identification, and primitive object representations on the Lerner Defense Scales than narcissistic patients (Lerner & Lerner, 1980). Berg (1990) similarly investigated the difference between NPD and BPD patients and found that the BPD group demonstrated a significantly higher number of unusual percepts and splitting responses, as defined by the Rorschach Defense Scales (Cooper & Arnow, 1986), and less grandiosity than a NPD group.

Gacono et al. (1992) noted that psychopathic antisocial and NPD patients produced a similar number of reflection responses, as compared with nonpsychopathic antisocial (ANPD) patients, BPDs, and Exner's (1993) nonpatient males. The Egocentricity Index also yielded significant main effects findings. Psychopathic ANPD and NPD patients had significantly higher scores than nonpsychopathic ANPD patients on the Egocentricity Index as well as a high number of personalized responses. The BPD and psychopathic ANPD groups produced significantly more primitive object relations responses than the narcissistic patients, and a great deal of violent symbiotic separation and reunion themes in their content. Narcissistic patients produced significantly more primitive idealization responses than either the psychopathic or the nonpsychopathic ANPD group, and significantly more diffuse-shading (Y) and texture-shading (T) responses than the psychopathic antisocial comparison group (Gacano et al., 1992). Gacono et al. (1992) also found that the NPD group produced a large number of idealization responses (56%), a finding similar to that of Hilsenroth et al. (1993).

Hilsenroth et al. (1993) further investigated Rorschach differences in BPD and NPD patients with a clinical control group of Cluster C personality disorders by examining Rorschach content variables designed to assess defensive structures, aspects of aggression, and egocentricity. The BPD patients used primitive defensive structures (splitting and projective identification) to a greater degree and severity and had greater levels of aggression. The NPD patients had significantly higher levels of egocentricity than the BPD patients, and higher levels of idealization than the Cluster C group.

Berg et al. (1993) found that BPD and NPD patients produced a significantly greater number of object relational scores representing figures needing some external source of support than a schizophrenic group. That is, the object existed only insofar as it was an extension or reflection of another object. The BPD patients also produced significantly more object relational themes of severely imbalanced, malevolent, and engulfing relationships than the NPD patients. Rorschach protocols of the NPD group reflected difficulty relating to others on a mutually autonomous basis, thereby causing these patients to rely solely on need-satisfying relationships. These findings appear to highlight prior theoretical work concerning the character structure of patients with disorders of the self, as noted by Kohut (1971).

In summary, NPD patients develop higher levels of object representations, use fewer primitive or severe defenses (i.e., splitting and projective identification), generate less aggressive imagery, and develop more reflection and personalized responses than BPD patients or a majority of nonpsychopathic ANPD patients. Also, NPD patients produce more primitive idealized responses than nonpsychopathic ANPDs and Cluster C personality disorder patients. Thus, the Rorschach variables that have demonstrated utility of NPD diagnosis are an increased number of reflection, personalized, and idealization responses and an elevated Egocentricity Index.

Although the aforementioned research indicates that the Rorschach may be helpful in differentiating NPD patients from other clinical groups, Nezworski and Wood (1995) questioned the ability of the Rorschach to assess accurately pathologic manifestations of narcissism and related constructs such as self-focus or self-esteem. They reviewed the literature in an effort to investigate the relationship between the Egocentricity Index, described in *The Rorschach: A Comprehensive System* (Exner, 1969, 1973, 1974, 1978, 1986, 1991, 1993), and self-focus, self-esteem, narcissism, ego functioning, depression, antisocial sociopathy, and homosexuality.

Nezworski and Wood (1995) interpreted self-focus as a construct that "appears to be closely related to narcissism and involves a tendency to focus attention on the qualities and experiences of the self rather than those of the external world" (p. 191). They examined 22 Exner studies as well as 28 other articles and 9 dissertations. The authors suggested that these studies offer mixed results or demonstrate no relationship between the Egocentricity Index and such characteristics. Studies supporting a relationship between reflections and the diagnosis of NPD (Berg, 1990; Gacono et al., 1992) were criticized and largely discounted by these authors for basing diagnoses of narcissism on unspecified or circular (using Rorschach data) diagnostic criteria. Nezworski and Wood (1995) concluded by questioning the utility of the Egocentricity Index and, by extension, the Comprehensive System itself to assess NPD.

In his comment on the Nezworski and Wood (1995) article, Exner (1995) noted that the reviewers based their analyses and conclusions on an assumption that the Comprehensive System includes a formalized measure for narcissism (i.e., the Egocentricity Index), "a conclusion that would not be made by anyone thoroughly familiar with the system and its applications" (p. 200). Instead, Exner pointed to the reflection response as the more likely specific measure for narcissism, describing the Egocentricity Index as "a crude measure of self-concern or self-attention" (Exner, 1978, pp. 130–134) within a context of balance, with psychopathology suggested by either unusually low or high Egocentricity Index scores. Positing a direct one-to-one relationship between the Egocentricity Index and any particular personality characteristic, including self-esteem and self-concept, was criticized by Exner as "marked oversimplification."

Hilsenroth, Fowler, Padawer, and Handler (1997) investigated the extent to which the Rorschach is able to accurately identify pathological expressions of narcissism, contrasting a sample of 91 patients found to meet DSM-IV criteria for Axis II disorders and a control group of 50 nonclinical subjects on four Rorschach variables. These variables included the number of reflection, personalized, and idealization responses as well as the Egocentricity Index. The results indicated that these variables can be used effectively to differentiate pathologically narcissistic patients from a nonclinical sample as well as from Cluster A and Cluster C personality disorders, and that Rorschach variables can be used to aid in the differential diagnosis of NPD patients from within the DSM-IV Cluster B diagnoses. Reflection and idealization variables were found to be empirically related to the Minnesota Multiphasic Personality Inventory–2 (MMPI-2) NPD–Nonoverlapping Scale (both at $r = .31; p < .05$). In addition, the number of reflection responses a patient produced on his or her Rorschach protocol was significantly and positively related ($r = .33; p < .001$) to the patient's total number of DSM-IV criteria for NPD.

With regard to individual DSM-IV NPD criteria, production of a reflection response was found to be associated with fantasies of unlimited success, a sense of entitlement, a grandiose sense of self-importance, and arrogant/haughty behaviors. The Rorschach reflection variable was significantly related to DSM-IV NPD criteria associated with the intrapsychic or cognitive features pertaining to pathological narcissism, more so than to behavioral expressions. Although the idealization response score was not significantly related to the total number of DSM-IV NPD criteria, it was related to NPD criterion 2 (fantasies of unlimited success). Thus, the relationship of reflection and idealization responses to the more intrapsychic or internal characteristics of NPD suggest that the Rorschach may prove to be useful when used in tandem with other methods of assessment designed to assess more overt/behavioral expressions of NPD.

Additionally, the reflection and idealization variables were used for classification purposes in ways that are clinically meaningful in the diagnosis of NPD, indicating that selected Rorschach variables can be used effectively to differentiate pathologically narcissistic patients from a nonclinical sample as well as from Cluster A and Cluster C personality disorders. Furthermore, the Rorschach protocols of NPD patients contained a significantly higher number of personalized responses and a higher Egocentricity Index than the protocols of a nonclinical group. Whereas these variables provided some utility in the differentiation of NPD patients from the nonclinical group, they also differentiated many of the other clinical groups from the nonclinical sample. However, concerning the elevated Egocentricity Index in the NPD group, a post hoc analysis showed that it is *not* the number of pair responses that are the source of these group differences. Rather, it is the number of reflection responses that elevate the Egocentricity Index, a finding anticipated by Exner (1995) in his comment on the Nezworski and Wood (1995) review.

The number of personalized responses on the Rorschach also was found to be higher in the Rorschach protocols of the patients with antisocial personality disorder than in the protocols of other diagnostic groups (Gacono et al., 1992). In contrast, the Hilsenroth et al. (1997) sample of antisocial personality disorder subjects did not include the severe psychopaths and violent felons reported by Gacono and colleagues (Gacono & Meloy, 1994; Gacono et al., 1990; Gacono et al., 1992). Instead, these patients were more representative of those individuals likely to be served in an outpatient setting. The high number of reflection responses developed by the psychopathic antisocial personality disorder patients in past studies may be related to a very high incidence of comorbid NPD. In their expanded treatise on psychopathic patients, Gacono and Meloy (1994) indicated that a large number of these cases would meet DSM-III-R/IV criteria for NPD in addition to ANPD.

As indicated in the previous discussion, the most robust variables found to discriminate NPD patients from all other groups were the number of Rorschach reflection and idealization responses. The scores for these variables were significantly higher in the NPD group than in the nonclinical, Cluster A PD, and Cluster C PD groups. In contrast to the patients with other Cluster B personality disorders, the NPD patients had a significantly greater number of reflection responses than either the ANPD or BPD group, as well as a significantly greater incidence of idealization responses than the ANPD group. Given the importance of these two variables with regard to both their theoretical salience and their diagnostic utility, the implications of these two scores in relation to the diagnosis of NPD is discussed further.

The Hilsenroth et al. (1997) study supports past research on NPD patients (Gacano et al., 1992; Hilsenroth et al., 1993), in which idealization and reflection responses were found to occur frequently. These consistent findings suggest a link between pathological narcissism and the reflection response. Although the correlation between the number of reflection responses and the DSM-IV criteria for NPD is moderate ($r = .33; p < .003$), this does not exclude other formulations or interpretations of reflection responses (e.g., elevated self-esteem and self-focus; Exner, 1993; Greenwald, 1990; Sugarman, 1980; Weiner, 2003; or self-absorption; Viglione, 1990) as incompatible with the current findings. Reflection responses were not significantly related to other DSM-IV cluster B total criteria, a highly desirable finding for clinicians faced with questions of differential diagnosis.

The relationship of reflection and idealization responses to the more intrapsychic or internal characteristics of NPD suggests that the Rorschach may prove to be very useful when used in tandem with other methods of assessment designed to assess more overt/behavioral expressions of NPD. An assessment using measures that evaluate both the intrapsychic and the interpersonal/behavioral aspects of NPD is optimal and provides clinicians with a richer understanding of these patients. This multidimensional assessment may be especially salient given that recent authors have criticized the exclusive use of self-report inventories to assess NPD. These authors suggest that self-report instruments tend to be more direct in identifying narcissistic traits, and that they are therefore more likely to evoke defensive responses (Gunderson et al., 1990). These authors also state that NPD patients are particularly unable to view themselves in a realistic manner. Although interviews allow for the clinical observation of behavior, it is possible that this same criticism may also apply, at least in part, to semistructured interviews.[1]

The relationship between these Rorschach scores and the MMPI-2 NPD scales show some interesting relationships and nonrelationships between the two methods of assessment. Both idealization and reflection responses were related to the nonoverlapping version of the MMPI-2 NPD scale. This scale is composed of 14 items unique to the MMPI-2 NPD–Nonoverlapping Scale and is not used on any of the other 11 personality disorder scales developed by Morey and his colleagues (Colligan et al., 1994; Morey et al., 1985). This finding stands in contrast to the finding that there is no significant relationship between these Rorschach variables and the MMPI-2 NPD-Overlapping Scale, in which 17 other items (31 total) are duplicated in at least one other personality disorder scale. Collectively, the findings indicate that these Rorschach variables have a stronger relationship with a self-report measure designed exclusively to assess NPD than with a broader and longer scale that shares items with related personality disorder scales.

Furthermore, the diagnostic efficiency statistics of the reflection and idealization variables performed very well in distinguishing NPD from the other groups in the study. In a comparison of the NPD patients with the total sample, an important finding was that almost no individual correctly identified as not having NPD had one or more reflections or a total idealization score of 5 or more. In addition, the overall correct classification rate using these two criteria ranged from a low of .63 to a high of .83. This high probability for correct classification of NPD patients and non-NPD patients using the Rorschach criteria was fairly effective in making a diagnostic assignment of NPD. It appears that an examination of the reflection and idealization Rorschach variables can be useful in the diagnosis of NPD.

It is important to note that although the reporting of diagnostic performance statistics may provide more clinically relevant information than a

---

[1]Additionally, interviews have limitations of which clinicians should be well aware. Past research has indicated that clinicians may underestimate or minimize coexisting syndromes once the presence of one or two Axis II disorders have been recognized (Widiger & Frances, 1987). Unlike self-report inventories, which may include indices that detect intentional response dissimulation (faking), exaggeration of symptoms, random responding, and acquiensence or denial, clinical interviewers may be susceptible to active attempts at malingering. Assessment of personality disorder criteria may be difficult through direct inquiry, so it is questionable whether NPD patients would admit that they are egocentric, self-indulgent, inconsiderate or interpersonally exploitive. See the chapter by Dr. Huprich and Dr. Ganellen for a further discussion of this issue.

categorical analysis of group differences, this single sign approach is not truly clinically representative of the actual diagnostic decision-making processes. A responsible assessment process entails a multimethod approach evaluating various dimensions of functioning including test scores used in conjunction with information gathered from a patient's history, behavioral observations, and interaction with the clinician during the testing procedures (Benjamin, 1993; Leary, 1957; Phillips, 1992; Rapaport, Gill, & Schafer, 1945; Schafer, 1954; Sugarman, 1981, 1991). Therefore, it is not suggested that clinicians use the presence of one or more reflection responses on the Rorschach as an indication of NPD. To do so would yield a very concrete interpretation of the data presented in this discussion and would be clinically unsophisticated. What the Hilsenroth et al. (1997) data do suggest is that the presence of one or more reflection responses will be typical of outpatient populations who meet some of the DSM-IV criteria for NPD, but possibly not five of the nine criteria necessary for a positive diagnosis of NPD. Regarding this point, a mean of 3.4 NPD criteria were met by those in the clinical sample who produced one or more reflection responses. In addition, the presence of one or more reflection responses seems more strongly related to the patient's intrapsychic or cognitive characteristics than to the patient's behavioral expressions of NPD. Subsequently, the presence or absence of one or more reflection responses can aid clinicians in the diagnostic decision-making process within a comprehensive assessment battery.

Related to these issues, Gacono and Meloy (1994) made two very salient points with regard to the interpretation of the reflection response that deserve to be highlighted given the current discussion. First, a combined analysis of the structure, sequence, and content of a given reflection response can help to provide a clearer interpretation of meaning for a given individual (an ideographic approach) than the use of only one global hypothesis for the meaning of reflections (a nomothetic approach). Second, these authors keenly observed that one reflection, although unexpected in any protocol, should not lead to the immediate diagnosis of pathological narcissism. Instead, interpretive formulations of the reflection response, or any other potentially pathognomic indicator, should be evaluated in the context of the entire protocol and should not be interpreted in isolation from other structural (i.e., location, determinant, form quality) and content data. The interpretive approach outlined in this discussion is antithetical to "cookbook" formulations and will necessitate more work, training, and experience on the part of clinicians (Hilsenroth, Handler, & Blais, 1996).

In contrast to the conclusions offered by Nezworski and Wood (1995), the data from the Hilsenroth et al. (1997) study support and extend previous research using the Rorschach in the assessment of NPD (Berg, 1990; Berg et al., 1993; Farris, 1988; Gacono & Meloy, 1994; Gacono et al., 1992;

Hilsenroth et al., 1993). In addition, the findings show that the reflection and idealization variables are related to DSM-IV criteria and a self-report measure of narcissism. Also, the reflection (i.e., mirroring) and idealization responses represented two defensive operations that have been strongly associated with the theoretical literature concerning narcissistic character disorders (Kernberg, 1970, 1975, 1984; Kohut, 1971, 1977). These findings reflect converging lines of evidence and support the use of the Rorschach as a valuable instrument in the diagnosis of NPD. They also contribute to a conceptual understanding of narcissism and narcissistic pathology.

Blais, Hilsenroth, Castlebury, Fowler, and Baity (2001) examined the incremental validity of the MMPI-2 and the Rorschach in predicting DSM-IV Cluster B personality disorders. Despite the weak interrelationship observed between the two instruments, hierarchical regression analyses clearly indicated that both the Rorschach and MMPI-2 nonoverlapping personality disorder scales were meaningfully related to the DSM-IV cluster B criteria total scores. Both the Rorschach reflection response and the MMPI-2 NPD–Nonoverlapping Scale independently predicted the total number of DSM-IV NPD criteria assigned to subjects. The final adjusted R^2 for this regression equation was .35, indicating that together these scales accounted for more than one third of the total variance in the DSM-IV NPD criteria assignment. However, these scales were not themselves significantly correlated ($r = .18$). These findings are consistent with the observation that the best data from which to predict a criterion variable are those that are valid but not highly intercorrelated (Meehl, 1954). Collectively, they indicate that to a substantial degree, material present in a patient's self-report (the MMPI-2 data) and material demonstrated outside of a patient's awareness (Rorschach responses) reflect important components of the DSM-IV conception of narcissism and NPD. These data also provide further support for the importance of using a multimethod assessment procedure, particularly in the evaluation of personality functioning (Hilsenroth, Handler, & Blais, 1996).

RORSCHACH COMPREHENSIVE SYSTEM INTERPRETATION OF NARCISSISTIC PERSONALITY DISORDER PATHOLOGY

Although the presence of one or more reflection responses can indicate the presence of narcissism, such responses, by themselves, do not necessarily indicate pathological narcissism. In addition, it is necessary to consider an analysis of related self-perception and interpersonal variables of the Comprehensive System (Exner, 2003; Weiner, 2003). Although the validity research cited for these variables is not specific for NPD, the constellation of these variables in a protocol may provide support for the diagnosis of NPD. For example, Weiner (2003) stated that adaptive interpersonal relationships are characterized by the abilities (a) to sustain a reasonable level of interest, involvement, and comfort in interacting with other people (characterized by SumH, H:Hd+(H)+(Hd), and Isol/R), (b) to anticipate intimacy and security in these interpersonal interactions (characterized by SumT and HVI), (c) to balance collaboration and acquiescence with competitiveness and assertiveness in relating to other people (characterized by COP, AG, and a:p), and (d) to perceive people and social situations in an accurate and empathic manner (characterized by accurate M; see Exner, 2003). (p. 170)

Criterion (a) concerns the extent to which people are attentive to and feel comfortable in interpersonal relationships. Weiner (2003) stated: "Generally speaking, 'SumH < 4' indicates limited interpersonal interest in people and constitutes a personality liability" (p. 170). Concerning comfort in interpersonal relationships, Hd+(H)+(Hd) > H denotes identification deficiencies as well as "a maladaptive extent of social discomfort" (Weiner, 2003, p. 171; Exner, 2003). Weiner indicated that people with this imbalance in their human contents "typically experience uneasiness in dealing with people who are real, live, and fully functional" (p. 171). The Isolation Index (Isol/R), composed of contents devoid of people divided by R, is considered a good measure of interpersonal isolation (Exner, 2003). Weiner has indicated that an Isol/R score higher than .33 "should be taken as an index of either marked avoidance of social interaction or of markedly deficient opportunities for interpersonal contact" (p. 172).

Concerning measures of interpersonal relatedness (SumT and Hypervigilence Index [HVI]), it is important to note that individuals with no T in their records often feel uncomfortable when they are near people who give T responses because "they experience them as intrusive kinds of people who encroach on their privacy and personal space and have excessive expectations of physical and psychological closeness" (Weiner, 1998, p. 174). Weiner added, "T-less persons neither anticipate nor seek out intimate interpersonal relationships" (p. 174). For example, T-less protocols have been found in 72% of character disorders (Weiner, 1998). In a similar vein, an elevated HVI typically indicates interpersonal insecurity and hyperalertness of a paranoid nature, or, alternatively, a fear of interpersonal relations because they are potentially harmful to a person's self-esteem (Exner, 2003). Thus, for example, a very handsome narcissistic man with a high HVI could not approach very attractive women, the only kind he wanted to pursue, because he feared any rejection would result in his overwhelming sense of humiliation.

Weiner (1998) indicated that COP greater than 2 "is commonly associated with being regarded as likable and outgoing and being sought after as a friend or companion" (p. 178). On the other hand, the absence of COP indicates "a maladaptive deficiency in the capacity to anticipate and engage in collaborative activities with others." Such people tend to impress others "as being distant or aloof" and "in combination with an elevated Isol/R and a low SumH, lack of COP often indicates interpersonal avoidance and withdrawal" (pp. 178–179). Generally, an aggressive movement (AG) score greater than 2 indicates problematic interpersonal relationships. Weiner (1998) indicates that the preferred way to interpret AG responses is as "an indication of inclinations to display either verbal or nonverbal assertive behavior" (p. 169). To show that AG can be either aggressive or assertive, Weiner described two bears fighting as an example of aggressive AG and two men arm wrestling as an example of an assertive AG.

The final category, interpersonal empathy (i.e., being able to "put oneself into another's shoes," and to appreciate how they feel) provides further understanding of the interpersonal relatedness of the NPD patient. In this regard M+, Mo, and Mu responses identify empathic ability and M– responses indicate deficient empathic ability (Exner, 2003; Weiner, 1998). Weiner (1998) stated:

> Two or more accurately perceived M identifies adequate capacity for empathy, … whereas [M– > 1] … indicates impairment in social perception. The more M– responses there are in a record, the more likely and more severely the subject is likely to be having adjustment difficulties attributable in part to faulty perception of people in social interactions. (p. 182)

RORSCHACH CONTENT VARIABLES

Silverstein (1999) described indications of narcissism derived from content analysis of the Rorschach. He used various testing-of-the-limits approaches to obtain associations with the patients' percepts, which he believed is necessary often to identify the response as narcissistic. He explained that grandiosity is seen when patients endow their Rorschach responses with exaggerated power (e.g., "the greatest airplane known to man," "the most powerful force to destroy the planet," "a king sitting on his throne and looking over his kingdom" (p. 116). Because beneath this show of bravado is a lack of self-esteem, such responses often include negative consequences. Silverstein (1999) indicated that "the greatest airplane may have an association to a crash, or the powerful king is overthrown" (p. 117).

Other responses include an emphasis on majestic aspects, such as "the majestic takeoff of a spaceship," indicating the patient's wish to be admired, or "a lion described as strong or with a good mane" (Silverstein, 1999; p. 118). Another example comes from a 37-year-old male patient who saw a "stealth bomber" on Card V, and elaborated the response as "broad wide wings, the sleekness of it, the principle that it's an undetectable surveillance, suggesting that it is the best of its kind and most powerful" (p. 118). Silverstein added, "The response conveys a desire to be admired for its sleek looks" (p. 118). Fantasies of greatness or power often coexist with responses indicating vulnerability or weakness. For example, the stealth bomber response was followed by "a microorganism." Silverstein explained, "In the psychopathology of self-disorders, patients often give responses depicting powerful, buoyant imagery, such as the space shuttle or the stealth bomber, followed by indications of an underlying devalued self" (pp. 118–119).

Another important point made by Silverstein (1999) is that NPD patients give responses to sustain optimal self-esteem at any cost. For example, a patient gave the following response to Card II: "Looks like I've been working on my car and I banged my fingers again, and the dirt and grease and blood" (p. 119). In the Inquiry he added, "If someone's bleeding like that, why don't you get up and do something about it, but like if it's me, I'd just as soon get the job done; it's obviously been bleeding for a while, and I'd just keep working right through it" (p. 119). This response, noted Silverstein, indicates that "whether bravado, grandiosity, invulnerability, or sheer brute tenacity, the response of this man dramatically conveyed the price that he paid for walling off the intensity of the affect surrounding threats to self-esteem" (p. 120).

One chief manifestation of a self-disorder is "depression with its associated problems of emptiness, chronic boredom, or disillusionment with life, expressed in the form of self-deprecation" (Silverstein, 1999, p. 128). For example "two bison, small horns and a head, irregularly shaped legs," and "two bear rugs with just one arm" demonstrate the self-deprecation of narcissistic individuals in their weakness and sense of being inferior or damaged. Another example comes from a 16-year-old girl who was hospitalized because of a suicide attempt. On Card I she saw "a dog, a Brittany Spaniel, a puppy, looks dead or sick or unhappy, just kind of there, no emotion" (Silverstein, 1999, pp. 138–139).

Arnow and Cooper (1988) have also applied Kohut's formulations about NPD to the Rorschach. Given that the testing situation is one in which the patient's primary needs are expressed, and in which these needs typically are frustrated and not met, the assessor can view the patient's responses in three interpretive dimensions: the state of the self, the role of archaic self-objects, and anticipations regarding new objects. Following the work of Kohut and Wolf (1978), Arnow and Cooper (1988) described syndromes seen in the assessment setting: "the understimulated self," "the overstimulated self," "the fragmented self," and "the overburdened self." The person with an understimulated self "craves stimulation to ward off feelings of inner deadness associated with an unresponsive self-object" (Lerner, 1991, p. 258), which results in very active attempts to seek stimulation, or the opposite, the empty depression that lies beneath the frantic search. Sometimes both are seen in the same protocol, depending upon the patient's interpretation of his or her relationship with the examiner. Lerner (1991) gives the example of such responses: "the Mardi Gras," "colorful sea scene," and "a brilliantly colored galaxy" (p. 258). The empty depression is seen in themes of barrenness, deadness, and desolation.

Individuals with an overstimulated self, in an attempt to entertain the examiner, have Rorschach contents that include themes of accomplishment and performance (e.g., dancing bears). Lerner (1991) stated, "Ordinary percepts are elevated to special productions through elaborate embellishments. The fantastic creations, for these individuals, are not in the service of self-enhancement; rather, they derive from a need to comply with the imagined expectations of the other" (p. 259). Patients with fears of fragmenting give responses in which there is concern about the integrity of objects or preoccupations, reflecting hypochondriacal concerns. This also is seen in such images as "a broken vase" or "pieces of a puzzle" (Arnow & Cooper, 1988, p. 65).

The overburdened self is the result of a failure to merge with an omnipotent, soothing selfobject, with the result that "the self does not develop the capacity to soothe itself or protect itself from being traumatized by the spreading of emotions, especially ... anxiety" (Lerner, 1991, p. 259). Therefore, the object relations of this person are related to the danger of exposing the self to any interactions that threaten the person's ability to modulate affect. Rorschach responses given by such individuals express their apprehension concerning emotional control, such as, "A volcano on the inside but it's frozen over on the top where no one would guess what's on the inside" (Arnow & Cooper, 1988, p. 66).

EXAMINER–PATIENT INTERACTION

The interaction of NPD patients with the examiner may vary considerably, depending on their self-presentation. For example, omnipotent and grandiose NPD patients demonstrate their compelling need to be special and to be treated as such. They often are difficult to schedule, and often ask for special considerations. Lerner (1988) indicated that their test responses "are not offered with the intent of conveying meaning or sharing an experience." Rather, their responses are prompted by "the desire to impress the examiner as well as to create a product they feel will do justice to their inflated sense of self" (p. 277).

On the other hand, some NPD patients present themselves as undefended in the area of self-esteem. These patients are more resistant. They see the Rorschach "as a laborious, onerous task in which nothing they produce will be good enough" (p. 277). Not only will the relationship of these NPD patients with the examiner be different, but the content of their responses often will reflect this self-presentation. In the first case, the responses often are self-aggrandized percepts, whereas in the latter group, themes of deficiency, damage, and inadequacy are offered.

In addition, the need to be mirrored by the examiner may take several different forms. Many of these patients work very hard to impress the examiner with their intellectual ability and their creativity, so they will earn the examiner's recognition and admiration. They may attempt to use humor to impress and entertain the examiner. Thus, Arnow and Cooper (1988) stated: "When an examiner experiences the patient's Rorschach as a performance and feels either lectured to or entertained, it is likely that the patient has assumed a role in order to maximize the supply of mirroring" (p. 55).

For many NPD patients the examiner's "neutral" position is experienced by the patient as deficient mirroring. The results of this experience vary. Some patients become mildly frustrated, or openly irritated. Some become bored and withdraw investment in the task, whereas others become suspicious. "Often during inquiry one senses withdrawal of interest and sullen fury as it becomes even more clear that the examiner fails to offer even a hint of acclaim for the patient's performance" (p. 56). Sometimes, the NPD patient looks to the examiner as a powerful idealized object, using blatant flattery in the process. In some instances, the examiner and the test as well are devalued, perhaps to ward off possible disappointment by the idealized object.

Before beginning the case study, it is important to note the necessity of obtaining multiple and diverse assessment information before concluding that a particular person fits any DSM diagnosis. Nevertheless, because the focus in the discussion is on the Rorschach, only Rorschach data are illustrated and discussed.

The presented case study is drawn from the clinical sample used in the study by Hilsenroth et al. (1997). All the protocols in this study were evaluated as part of a larger project investigating DSM-IIIR and DSM-IV personality disorders in clinical outpatients (Blais, et al., 1997a; Castlebury, Hilsenroth, Handler, & Durham, 1997; Hilsenroth et al., 1996). All the participants in this study were drawn from an archival search of files at a university-based outpatient psychological clinic, accomplished by an exhaustive search of approximately 800 cases seen over a 7-year period. The presence or absence of symptoms was determined by a retrospective review of patient records, which included an evaluation report, session notes (including reports of history, symptoms, and relevant topics in the first 12 weeks of therapy), and 3-month treatment summaries. Information regarding patient identity, diagnosis, and test data, including the Rorschach, were appropriately masked or made unavailable to the raters. High interrater agreement for the presence or absence of a personality disorder was established (Kappa = .90). The kappa value for presence or absence of NPD was also .90.

CASE EXAMPLE: MR. NORTON

Mr. Norton was positive for five of the DSM NPD criteria identifying narcissistic personality disorder: grandiosity; fantasies of unlimited success, power, brilliance, and beauty; sense of entitlement; interpersonal exploitation; and lack of empathy. In addition, subsequent clinical data indicated that he also was positive for three additional criteria: belief that he or she is "special," requirement for excessive admiration, and arrogant behaviors or attitudes.

Mr. Norton, a 33-year-old man originally from Texas, came to an outpatient community clinic because of "severe depression, lack of motivation, and a desire to get my life on the right track." He had spent some time in jail for writing bad checks, and he was a compulsive gambler. Seen at the clinic for 14 sessions, he returned to the clinic 2 years later. He saw a different therapist the second time, but remained for only six sessions.

The patient's interaction with both therapists was consistent with his NPD diagnosis. For example, he refused to adhere to the therapeutic frame, refused to pay his bill, canceled appointments at the last minute, or did not show up for appointments. In both therapies, he quit because he was asked to pay his bill and was rather angry with both therapists for asking him to comply with the previously agreed-upon treatment frame (e.g., attending appointments on a regular weekly basis, payment of fees).

The case record indicates that Mr. Norton became "rageful" with the first therapist for not providing him with immediate "help." He felt it was his right to be provided help, and angrily demanded that the therapists "make" him stop his illegal activities, but gloated over his ability to get away with them. He demanded that one therapist "fix" him. The case record indicates that he became angry when the therapist brought up the issue of his overdue bill, becoming outraged that he was expected to pay for therapy. He stated that he "could not believe" the therapist wanted to be paid, knowing he had "such severe problems." Rather, he felt he deserved special consideration because he had so many problems and because they were so severe. Although he threatened to "walk out" during one session when the fees were mentioned, he did not do so. However, he rejected the therapist's offer to lower the fees, and he did not return for additional sessions.

The patient reported a very poor work history. He stated that he quit jobs because he felt "they were beneath" him, or because he "could not get along" with his employer. He stated that he was fired from other jobs because he "showed little interest and motivation." Mr. Norton reported that he had few friends and was rather isolated from people. Both therapists indicated that he appeared alternately grandiose and debased, demonstrating a great deal of overconcern with his appearance. He told the therapists that he felt he was special and different from others because he had a specific talent in the arts and because he was "extremely intelligent." In one session, he became irritated when the therapist described the session as an hour, when in fact it was only 50 minutes long, adding that he felt "cheated."

According to the therapists, the patient demonstrated extreme oversensitivity about people's reactions to him and sought constant attention and reassurance from others. They described Mr. Norton as treating them in a manner that was "irresponsible, egocentric, and very impulsive." He aroused anger and discomfort in the therapists, neither of whom made any positive comments in the record about him, other than that he could be witty and charming on occasion.

Mr. Norton's Rorschach record contained three reflections, consistent with narcissistic issues and self-preoccupation. This finding is consistent with the self-centered approach reported by his therapists. According to Weiner (2003), people with numerous reflection responses tend to be "arrogant." They "assign a higher priority to their own needs and interests than to those of others …. They characteristically externalize responsibility for their failures … and blame any difficulties they encounter on the actions of others. They approach life situations with an air of superiority and a sense of entitlement" (pp. 160–161). This description seemed to characterize the patient's reported interactions with his two therapists and with his description of his relationships with others.

Weiner (2003) added that with respect to adjustment difficulties, the selfishness, self-admiration, sense of entitlement, and externalization of responsibility result in "problematic interpersonal relationships, … and they elicit negative reactions from people who find the narcissist's lack of humility and infrequent altruism objectionable and offensive" (p. 161). This was certainly the case with Mr. Norton. He reported that he had few friends and had trouble holding a job. In addition, he blamed his friends for getting him into legal trouble, without considering his own motivation.

Mr. Norton had five M responses in his record, two of which were minus and two others with unusual form quality. The ratio of good human response to poor human response (GHR:PHR) was 2:5, also indicating ineffective and maladaptive interpersonal behavioral patterns. Exner (2003) indicated that such people have "interpersonal histories that are marked by conflict and/or failure" (p. 511). The GHR and PHR values for this patient are quite disparate, suggesting an increased likelihood that his interpersonal behavior will be ineffective and be viewed by others as unfavorable.

Indeed, the patient's behavior with the two therapists and his reported failures in relationships validate this interpretation.

The content of the M responses is important because it reveals the patient's attitude in his relationships. For example, on Card II, Response 3, Mr. Norton described seeing "two alien people ... like ET, communicating by touching hands ... communicating by more than a mouth." On Card II, Response 5, he described seeing "two more people ... standing in weird positions, maybe surrounded by fire ... most humans couldn't stand like that—it might be physically impossible unless you're a contortionist." Both of these responses, although reflecting the patient's interpersonal alienation, and despite the pain they reflect, also can be scored as Idealization on the Lerner Defense Scale (Lerner, 1998). These responses represent perceptions of beings with special powers and abilities. In particular, they suggest special powers to communicate and to be known. Whereas they may be seen as defending against feelings of debasement, they may, in addition, relate to the patient's desire for people, especially the therapist, to intuit his needs and gratify them. Likewise, the skills of a contortionist would be quite useful in extracting himself from the precarious legal and interpersonal situations in which he is involved.

On Card VI Mr. Norton saw "two angry people, grouches, facing away from each other, looking in opposite directions," and on Card X, he saw "a child throwing a temper tantrum," which describes the two therapists' experience of him. These percepts, especially given that all but one of his M responses were unusual or minus form quality, and that two had associated AG scores, reflect the patient's inability to relate cordially and empathically with others, leading to poor social and interpersonal adjustment. This finding suggests that the patient may misjudge the attitudes and intentions of others and probably forms inaccurate impressions of situations in relationships (Weiner, 2003). Therapy notes clearly support this hypothesis, both in the therapy relationships and in the patient's life as well. Weiner (2003) noted that such adjustment leads to inappropriate responding in social situations, which also is reported in the patient's record. Mr. Norton described having interpersonal adjustment difficulties in all phases of his life. For example, counter to what may be expected, he viewed himself as giving "too much" in a relationship. He stated that he likes to be the one who gives, yet he feels resentful when giving to others. Although it is possible that his giving is a control and distancing issue, it also is quite possible that this "giving" percept is a distortion of his interpersonal relationships. These problematic M responses coupled with Mr. Norton's AG responses and evidence of several perceptual idiosyncrasies (S–%, X–%, Xu%, F+%), if not distortions, suggest that he would display his inappropriate behavior in a verbal or nonverbal manner (Weiner, 2003). In this regard, the possibilities for pleasant interpersonal relationships are undermined by his seeing the world as a malevolent place, anticipating adversarial and antagonistic interactions, and behaving in an inordinately aggressive, belligerent, or domineering manner. This indeed describes the patient's reported attitude in his relationship with both therapists.

Another important Rorschach variable to consider in the diagnosis of NPD is the presence or absence of T, in conjunction with the other aforementioned variables. The absence of T is said to indicate a person's impairment in forming close attachments with other people, and aversion to intimacy, probably leading to adjustment difficulties (Weiner, 2003). Certainly, the clinic therapy records support Mr. Norton's expectation of being harmed by close, trusting relationships with others. He also reportedly viewed himself as a victim in his relationship with both therapists, reflecting his interpersonal insecurity and hyperalertness to danger.

Although the patient seemed attentive to others (SumH = 6), only two of the responses were H. The others were one (H) and three Hd responses, suggesting that the patient did not find comfort in interpersonal relationships, leading to the risk of "a maladaptive pattern of withdrawn and avoidant behavior that may culminate in interpersonal isolation [and] social disinterest and discomfort" (Weiner, 1998, p. 163). Indeed, the patient reported that he often avoids relationships because they always prove to be painful. In addition, his one COP response reflects quasi-human forms and unusual perceptual qualities.

The content of some of the patient's responses, in addition to the aforementioned M examples, also is useful in making the determination of NPD, along with the analysis of the Rorschach Comprehensive System variables described earlier. The patient's grandiosity can be seen from his response to Card VII: "some sort of head gear, looks like for a man, a Roman emperor." On Card IX, the patient saw "a very fancy stage costume for a Broadway production for a musical, for a female of course. Bow on top and puffed sleeves, the ornateness and colors." In similar fashion, he described his percept of "a chantilly lamp, elaborately shaped and so colorful" on Card VIII. These responses illustrate the patient's exhibitionistic need to be the center of attention. His grandiosity was noted by the examiner, who commented in her report: "He attempts to be a large presence in the room."

As mentioned in the introduction to the case study, to make an accurate diagnosis of NPD, it is important to use multitrait measures and multiple methods of data collection (e.g., self-report measures, projective measures, interview data, observation, information from referral and other sources; see Hilsenroth et al., 1996). The reader is also referred to Handler and

Meyer (1998) and Handler and Clemence (2003) for a more detailed discussion of multitrait–multimethod assessment.

A similar approach is necessary for valid Rorschach interpretation, in general, and for the diagnosis of NPD in particular. While there is no single Rorschach variable that by itself defines NPD, or any other DSM diagnosis, reflection responses and, to a lesser extent, idealization responses, have received the most empirical support in the literature concerning assessment for the construct of narcissism, as opposed to NPD, per se. Certainly, the aggregate analysis of various Rorschach Structural Summary variables is important, especially the following: the self-esteem variables (Fr+rF, 3r+(2)/R); measures relating to positive self-regard (V, MOR); self-awareness (FD); a measure of a stable sense of identity [H:Hd+(H)+(Hd)], measures of interpersonal interest, involvement, and comfort (SumH, H:Hd+(H)+(Hd), ISOL); measures relating to interpersonal intimacy and security (SumT, HVI); measures related to the balance between interpersonal collaboration and acquiescence with competitiveness and assertiveness (COP, AG, a:p); and the ability to be interpersonally empathic (accurate M; Weiner, 2003). In addition, an analysis of the content of the responses is important, along with an evaluation of the patient's style of responding and the quality of his or her interaction with the examiner. For additional information concerning other individual NPD variations in Rorschach findings, the reader is referred to excellent chapters by H. Lerner (1988), P. Lerner (1988), Arnow and Cooper (1988), and Silverstein (1999). Attempts to avoid the complex aggregation and integration of data, along with a consideration of the research supporting each variable, may lead to serious and misleading errors in evaluation.

REFERENCES

Akhtar, S. (1989). Narcissistic personality disorder: Descriptive features and differential diagnosis. *Psychiatric Clinics of North America, 12*, 505–530.

Akhtar, S., & Thompson, J. (1982). Overview: Narcissistic personality disorder. *American Journal of Psychiatry, 139*, 12–20.

American Psychiatric Association. (1980). *Diagnostic and statistical manual of mental disorders* (3rd ed.). Washington, DC: Author.

American Psychiatric Association. (1987). *Diagnostic and statistical manual of mental disorders* (3rd ed., rev.). Washington, DC: Author.

American Psychiatric Association. (1994). *Diagnostic and statistical manual of mental disorders* (4th ed.). Washington, DC: Author.

American Psychiatric Association. (2000). *Diagnostic and statistical manual of mental disorders* (4th ed., Text Revision; TR). Washington, DC: Author.

Arnow, D., & Cooper, S. (1988). Toward a Rorschach psychology of the self. In H. Lerner & P. Lerner (Eds.) , *Primitive mental states and the Rorschach* (pp. 53–70). New York: International Universities Press.

Benjamin, L. (1993). *Interpersonal diagnosis and treatment of personality disorders.* New York: Guilford.

Berg, J. (1990). Differentiating ego functions of borderline and narcissistic personalities. *Journal of Personality Assessment, 55,* 537–548.

Berg, J., Packer, A., & Nunno, V. (1993). A Rorschach analysis: Parallel disturbance in thought and in self/object representation. *Journal of Personality Assessment, 61,* 311–323.

Blais, M., Hilsenroth, M., & Castlebury, F. (1997a). Psychometric characteristics of the cluster B personality disorders under DSM-III-R and DSM-IV. *Journal of Personality Disorders, 11,* 270–278.

Blais, M., Hilsenroth, M., & Castlebury, F. (1997b). The content validity of the DSM-IV borderline and narcissistic personality disorder criteria sets. *Comprehensive Psychiatry, 38,* 31–37.

Blais, M., Hilsenroth, M., Castlebury, F., Fowler, J., & Baity, M. (2001). Predicting DSM-IV Cluster B personality disorder criteria from MMPI-2 and Rorschach data: A test of incremental validity. *Journal of Personality Assessment, 76,* 150–168.

Blatt, S., & Lerner, H. (1983). The psychological assessment of object representations. *Journal of Personality Assessment, 47,* 7–28.

Castlebury, F., Hilsenroth, M., Handler, L., & Durham, T.(1997). The use of the MMPI-2 Personality Disorder Scales in the assessment of DSM-IV antisocial, borderline, and narcissistic personality disorders. *Assessment, 4*(2), 155–168.

Chatham, P., Tibbals, C., & Harrington, M. (1993). The MMPI and the MCMI in the evaluation of narcissism in a clinical sample. *Journal of Personality Assessment, 60,* 239–251.

Colligan, R., Morey, L., & Offord, K. (1994). The MMPI/MMPI-2 personality disorder scales: Contemporary norms for adults and adolescents. *Journal of Clinical Psychology, 50,* 168–200.

Cooper, A. (1981). Narcissism. In S. Arieti, H. Keith, & H. Brodie (Eds.), *American Handbook of Psychiatry* (Vol 4., pp. 297–316). New York: Basic Books.

Cooper, A. (1998). Further developments in the clinical diagnosis of narcissistic personality disorder. In E. Ronningstam (Ed.), *Disorders of narcissism: Diagnostic, clinical and empirical findings* (pp. 53–74). Washington, DC: American Psychiatric Association.

Cooper, A., & Ronningstam, E. (1992). Narcissistic personality disorder. *American Psychiatric Press Review of Psychiatry, 11,* 80–97.

Cooper, S., & Arnow, D. (1986). An object relations view of the borderline defenses: A review. In M. Kissen (Ed.), *Assessing object relations phenomena* (pp. 143–171). New York: International Universities Press.

Davis, R., Blashfield, R., & McElroy, R. (1993). Weighting criteria in the diagnosis of a personality disorder: A demonstration. *Journal of Abnormal Psychology, 102,* 319–322.

Eagle, M. (1984). *Recent developments in psychoanalysis: A critical evaluation.* New York: McGraw-Hill.

Exner, J. (1969). Rorschach responses as an index of narcissism. *Journal of Personality Assessment, 33,* 324–330.

Exner, J. (1973). The self-focus sentence completion: A study of egocentricity. *Journal of Personality Assessment, 37,* 437–455.

Exner, J. (1974). *The Rorschach: A comprehensive system: Volume 1. Basic foundations.* New York: John Wiley.

Exner, J. (1978). *The Rorschach: A comprehensive system: Volume 2. Current research and advanced interpretation.* New York: John Wiley.

Exner, J. (1986). *The Rorschach: A comprehensive system: Volume 1. Basic foundations* (2nd ed.). New York: John Wiley.

Exner, J. (1991). *The Rorschach: A comprehensive system: Volume 2. Current research and advanced interpretation.* (2nd ed.). New York: John Wiley.

Exner, J. (1993). *The Rorschach: A comprehensive system: Volume 1. Basic foundations* (3rd ed.). New York: John Wiley.

Exner, J. (1995). Comment on Narcissism in the Comprehensive System for the Rorschach. *Clinical Psychology: Science and Practice, 2,* 200–206.

Exner, J. (2003). *The Rorschach: A comprehensive system: Volume 1. Basic foundations* (4th ed.). New York: John Wiley.

Farris, M. (1988). Differential diagnosis of borderline and narcissistic personality disorders. In H. Lerner & P. Lerner (Eds.), *Primitive mental states and the Rorschach* (pp. 299–338). New York: International Universities Press.

Gabbard, G. (1989). Two subtypes of narcissistic personality disorder. *Bulletin of the Menninger Clinic, 53,* 527–532.

Gacono, C., & Meloy, J. (1994). *The Rorschach assessment of aggressive and psychopathic personalities.* Hillsdale, NJ: Lawrence Erlbaum Associates.

Gacono, C., Meloy, J., & Berg, J. (1992). Object relations, defensive operations, and affective states in narcissistic, borderline and antisocial personality disorder. *Journal of Personality Assessment, 59,* 32–49.

Gacono, C., Meloy, J., & Heaven, T. (1990). A Rorschach investigation of narcissism and hysteria in antisocial personality disorder. *Journal of Personality Assessment, 55,* 270–279.

Glassman, M. (1988). Kernberg and Kohut: A test of competing psychoanalytic models of narcissism. *Journal of the American Psychoanalytic Association, 36,* 597–625.

Greenwald, D. (1990). An external construct validity study of Rorschach personality variables. *Journal of Personality Assessment, 55,* 768–780.

Gunderson, J., Ronningstam, E., & Bodkin, A. (1990). The Diagnostic Interview for Narcissistic Patients. *Archives of General Psychiatry, 47,* 676–680.

Gunderson, J., Ronningstam, E., & Smith, L. (1991). Narcissistic personality disorder: A review of data on DSM-III-R descriptions. *Journal of Personality Disorders, 5,* 167–177.

Handler, L., & Meyer, G. (1998). The importance of teaching and learning personality assessment. In L. Handler & M. Hilsenroth (Eds.), *Teaching and learning personality assessment* (pp. 3–30). Mahwah, NJ: Lawrence Erlbaum Associates.

Handler, L., & Clemence, A. (2003). Education and training in psychological assessment. In J. Graham & J. Naglieri (Eds.), *Handbook of psychology: Assessment* (Vol. 10, pp. 181–209). New York: John Wiley.

Hilsenroth, M., Fowler, C., Padawer, J., & Handler, L. (1997). Narcissism in the Rorschach revisited: Some reflections on empirical data. *Psychological Assessment, 9,* 113–121.

Hilsenroth, M., Handler, L., & Blais, M. (1996). Assessment of narcissistic personality disorder: A multimethod review. *Clinical Psychology Review, 16,* 655–684.

Hilsenroth, M., Hibbard, S., Nash, M., & Handler, L. (1993). A Rorschach study of narcissism, defense, and aggression in borderline, narcissistic and cluster C personality disorders. *Journal of Personality Assessment, 60,* 346–361.

Holdwick, D., Hilsenroth, M., Blais, M., & Castlebury, F. (1998). Identifying the unique and common characteristics among the DSM-IV antisocial, borderline, and narcissistic personality disorders. *Comprehensive Psychiatry, 39,* 277–286.

Jacobson, E. (1964). *Self and the object world.* New York: International Universities Press.

Kernberg, O. (1970). Factors in the psychoanalytic treatment of narcissistic personalities. *Journal of the American Psychoanalytic Association, 18,* 51–85.

Kernberg, O. (1975). *Borderline conditions and pathological narcissism.* New York: Aronson.

Kernberg, O. (1984). *The treatment of severe character disorders.* New Haven: Yale University Press.

Kohut, H. (1971). *The analysis of the self.* New York: International Universities Press.

Kohut, H. (1977). *The restoration of the self.* New York: International Universities Press.

Kohut, H., & Wolf, E. (1978). The disorders of the self and their treatment: An outline. *International Journal of Psycho-Analysis, 59,* 413–425.

Leary, T. (1957). *Interpersonal diagnosis of personality.* New York: Ronald.

Lerner, H. (1988). The narcissistic personality as expressed through psychological tests. In H. Lerner & P. Lerner (Eds.), *Primitive mental states and the Rorschach* (pp. 257–298). New York: International Universities Press.

Lerner, P. (1988). Rorschach measures of depression, the false self, and projective identification in patients with narcissistic personality disorders. In H. Lerner & P. Lerner (Eds.), *Primitive mental states and the Rorschach* (pp. 71–94). Madison, CT: International Universities Press.

Lerner, P. (1998). *Psychoanalytic perspectives on the Rorschach.* Hillsdale, NJ: The Analytic Press.

Lerner, P., & Lerner, H. (1980). Rorschach assessment of primitive defenses in borderline personality structure. In J. Kwawer, H. Lerner, P. Lerner, & A. Sugarman (Eds.), *Borderline phenomena and the Rorschach test* (pp. 257–274). New York: International Universities Press.

Loranger, A., Oldham, J., & Tulis, E. (1982). Familial transmission of DSM-III borderline personality disorder. *Archives of General Psychiatry, 39,* 795–799.

Masterson, J. (1981). *The narcissistic and borderline disorders.* New York: Brunner/Mazel.

Meehl, P. (1954). *Clinical versus statistical prediction.* Minneapolis: University of Minnesota Press.

Millon, T. (1983). *Millon clinical multiaxial inventory manual.* Minneapolis: National Computer Systems.

Millon, T. (1987). *Millon clinical multiaxial inventory manual* (2nd ed.). Minneapolis: National Computer Systems.

Millon, T., & Davis, R. (1996). Disorders of personality: DSM IV and beyond (2nd ed.). Oxford, England: Wiley.

Morey, L., Waugh, M., & Blashfield, R. (1985). MMPI scales for DSM-III personality disorders: Their derivation and correlates. *Journal of Personality Assessment, 49,* 245–251.

Nezworski, T., & Wood, J. (1995). Narcissism in the Comprehensive System for the Rorschach. *Clinical Psychology: Science and Practice, 2,* 179–199.

Perry, J., & Vaillant, G. (1989). Personality disorders. In H. Kaplan & B. Sadock (Eds.), *Comprehensive textbook of psychiatry* (Vol 2., 5th ed., pp. 1352–1383). Baltimore: Williams & Wilkins.

Phillips, L. (1992). A commentary on the relationship between assessment and the conduct of psychotherapy. *Journal of Training and Practice in Professional Psychology, 6,* 46–52.

Pope, H., Jonas, J., Hudson, J., Cohen, B., & Gunderson, J. (1983). The validity of DSM-III borderline personality disorder. *Archives of General Psychiatry, 40,* 23–30.

Pulver, S. (1970). Narcissism: The term and the concept. *Journal of the American Psychoanalytic Association, 18,* 319–341.

Rapaport, D., Gill, M., & Schafer, R. (1945). *Diagnostic psychological testing* (Vol. 1). Oxford, England: Year Book Publishers.

Ronningstam, E. (1988). Comparing three systems for diagnosing narcissistic personality disorder. *Psychiatry: Journal for the Study of Interpersonal Processes, 51,* 300–311.

Ronningstam, E., & Gunderson, J. (1988). Narcissistic traits in psychiatric patients. *Comprehensive Psychiatry, 29,* 545–549.

Ronningstam, E., & Gunderson, J. (1990). Identifying criteria for narcissistic personality disorder. *American Journal of Psychiatry, 147,* 918–922.

Ronningstam, E., & Gunderson, J. (1991). Differentiating borderline personality from narcissistic personality disorder. *Journal of Personality Disorders, 5,* 225–232.

Schafer, R. (1954). *Psychoanalytic interpretation in Rorschach testing.* New York: Grune & Stratton.

Siever, L., & Klar, H. (1986). A review of DSM-III criteria for the personality disorders. In A. Frances & R. Hales (Eds.), *American Psychiatric Association Annual Review* (Vol. 5, pp. 99–301). Washington, DC: American Psychiatric Association.

Silverstein, M. (1999). Self psychology and diagnostic assessment: Identifying self-object functions through psychological testing. Mahwah, NJ: Lawrence Erlbaum Associates.

Stolorow, R. (1975). Toward a functional definition of narcissism. *International Journal of Psycho-Analysis, 56,* 179–185.

Sugarman, A. (1980). The borderline personality organization as manifested on psychological tests. In J. Kwawer, H. Lerner, P. Lerner, & A. Sugarman (Eds.), *Borderline phenomena and the Rorschach test* (pp. 39–57). New York: International Universities Press.

Sugarman, A. (1981). The diagnostic use of countertransference reactions in psychological testing. *Bulletin of the Menninger Clinic, 45,* 473–490.

Sugarman, A. (1991). Where's the beef? Putting personality assessment back into personality assessment. *Journal of Personality Assessment, 56,* 130–144.

Teicholz, J. (1978). A selective review of the psychoanalytic literature on theoretical conceptualizations of narcissism. *Journal of the American Psychoanalytic Association, 26,* 831–861.

Viglione, D. (1990). Severe disturbance or trauma-induced adaptive reaction: A Rorschach child case study. *Journal of Personality Assessment, 55,* 280–295.

Weiner, I. (1998). *Principles of Rorschach interpretation.* Mahwah, NJ: Lawrence Erlbaum Associates.

Weiner, I. (2003). *Principles of Rorschach interpretation* (2nd ed.). Mahwah, NJ: Lawrence Erlbaum Associates.

Westen, D. (1997). Divergences between clinical and research methods for assessing personality disorders: Implications for research and the evolution of Axis II. *American Journal of Psychiatry, 154,* 895–903.

Westen, D., & Arkowitz-Westen, L. (1998). Limitations of Axis II in diagnosing personality pathology in clinical practice. *American Journal of Psychiatry, 155,* 1767–1771.

Westen, D., & Shedler, J. (1999a). Revising and assessing Axis II, Part I: Developing a clinically and empirically valid assessment method. *American Journal of Psychiatry, 156,* 258–272.

Westen, D., & Shedler, L. (1999b). Revising and assessing Axis II: Part II: Toward an empirically based and clinically useful classification of personality disorders. *American Journal of Psychiatry, 156,* 273–285.

Westen, D, & Shedler, J. (2000). A prototype-matching approach to diagnosing personality disorders toward DSM-V. *Journal of Personality Disorders, 14*(2), 109–126.

Widiger, T., & Frances, A. (1987). Interviews and inventories for the measurement of personality disorders. *Clinical Psychology Review, 7,* 49–75.

Wink, P. (1991). Two faces of narcissism. *Journal of Personality and Social Psychology, 61,* 590–597.

Wink, P., & Gough, H. (1990). New narcissism scales for the California Psychological Inventory. *Journal of Personality Assessment, 54,* 446–462.

Free Association	Inquiry
Card I 1. Oh my, what if you see nothing? (Take your time). I see an animal's face. I wouldn't know what animal though.	1. Here are the eyes, nose mouth, and ears. (The whole thing?) I just see a face, the chin is right here.
(Most people see more than one thing). Oh really? Oh, wonderful...hmmm (turned card around and looked). I certainly see an animal's face, but I don't see anything else.	
2. It might resemble a bat, a flying bat, but I don't remember what bat's looks like. I'm not caught up on my animals.	2. Maybe looks like a bat. (Flying?) Looks like wing span and bat has small head like that. Looks like wings are open.
Card II 3. Oh my girl (laughed). Well, it's two alien people communicating with each other, some sort...might have bodies...might be touching hands. Now I see that.	3. Halfway down looks like feet. They're the eyes and eyebrows. (Communicating?) Not verbally, like ET communicating with more than a mouth. Right here. They're communicating by touching hands. I don't know what the red part is.
4. (v) Looking at it this way looks like a creature or animal. I see eyes, nose, weird mouth part coming out of head.	4. Here are the tentacles coming out of the mouth, or horns, or whatever. (Eyes?) Some creatures' eyes are lower.
(Turned card). I don't see anything else...I don't know what that red thing would be.	

254

Card III

5. Two more people and what are they doing? Looks like they're...I don't know, standing in weird positions maybe surrounding a fire or something. Maybe red is supposed to be fire. All are mirror images of each other, must be identical then.

5. The black part, head, chest, hands, feet (points). (People?). Just weird, different; females. Most humans couldn't stand like that—it might be physically impossible unless you're a contortionist. Might be warming hands on fire, very possible. (Fire?) Flames and this is fire.

6. (v) Some type of crustacean. Claws and two big old eyes, that's what it is. It's got claws, pincers. I don't know what the red means. Is there a meaning for the red and black? (Whatever you like). This is the same as the last one. The normal way it looks like people and upside down it looks like a creature.

6. Here's the claws and pincers. The whole thing except for the two red parts. (Heart?) The part that's in red and in the center of the body. I know some crustaceans have it directly in the center.

Card IV

7. No red this time. Maybe some sort of tree. I can see distinct, no vague, form of a tree or tree-like figure. I don't see a creature in this one. If they're supposed to be the same, I certainly don't see it in this one.

7. Here's the tree trunk, and the rest are just foliage. (Foliage?) Just looks like it might be a tree trunk, it's kind of far-fetched.

8. It could be a waterfall maybe...not like that, but shower-like thing that water comes down. Like you see in the center of malls or something.

8. Same place as tree. This might be the places that shoots water up, and this is water falling down. (Falling down?) Kind of like a spray that goes up and comes down. I don't believe I see anything else.

Card V
9. That's a bat, more so than the other one was like. It's a bat, both ways, upside down and normal.

9. The whole thing, just the way the thing looks.

10. (Turns card a number of times). This is far-fetched, three synchronized swimmers. I guess, four, four sets of legs.

10. Four sets of legs, like synchronized swimmers. I saw legs and looks like it could be swimmers. I am just sure it's a mirror image of each other, so I thought that's what it was. (Legs?) Just looks like legs.

11. Might be some sort of butterfly not native to America. The wing span and antenna are foreign to the U.S.

11. Upside down, big wins and antennas, looks like a butterfly's body.

Card VI
12. Might be hand-held fan. A fan used to fan yourself, an old antique one.

Card VI
12. This is the handle, and you hold it right here and fan yourself. (Antique?) Looks old-looking, not normal shaped fan. (Old?) Not contemporary shape.

13. (v) Or it might be a flower.

13. Looks like it might be the shape of flower and leaves. Not necessarily this part.

14. Or a lampshade, a very unusual lampshade.

14. This part is the lamp, light bulb, and shade.

15. (v) OK, now I see two angry people, two people-grouches facing away from each other— head to head looking in opposite directions. I can see grouchy looks on faces and long noses.

15. Here are the eyes, high forehead, mouth, long nose, chin. (Grouchy?). Look on the face, and since they're facing away from each other.

(Turns card). I don't see anything else. (Looks closely).

256

16. (>) I can see the side of a snake that has swallowed a huge gigantic something or other…one third of its looks like a snake. I know it's far-fetched.

16. The whole thing. Two side things look like snake eyes, the long shape. (Swallowed?) Just has a weird shape like it swallowed something odd-shaped.

Card VII

17. (Turns card back and forth). Either way, looks like some sort of head gear. Looks like for a man, a Roman emperor or something.

17. Looks like maybe headgear made of steel or something. The shape.

18. (v) Looks like a hat for an exotic dancer or something.

18. All this would be feathers, just extra space.

19. Could be maybe a piece of glassware…a weird-shaped bowl, very weird-shaped.

19. Right here is opening, and the whole thing is a weird-shaped bowl, and you put something inside it this way.

Card VIII

20. I see a mountain range. Mountain top with colorful foliage in front of it.

20. Green and orange and red. (Foliage?) Just colors and the fact that it's on a mountain. (Front?) Mountain's in the back

21. Two shapes on the side look like creatures of some sort, maybe climbing a mountain. Who knows?

21. Here are the head, legs, tails. (Climbing?) Only because of the picture.

22. (v) This way it's a flower with different colors.

22. The top part are leaves or something. Just the color.

23. (v) Or a chantilly lamp. I believe that's what they are called.

23. It's so elaborately shaped and so colorful.

24. (>) This way it's neat. This animal that I saw earlier is climbing. Bottom part is a reflection. This creature, maybe a bobcat, is roaming this area, and the bottom part is reflection on the water.

24. Right here is the top part, and everything else is image on the water. (Bobcat?) I don't know. (Roaming?) Goes up and feet are moving. (Mountain?) Green part looks like mountain and fall colors of trees below it.

25. (v) I want to say these two things remind me of tear drops. I don't see a face, but they remind me of tear drops. Just tears, a flowing stream looks like a lot of tears.

25. This is the only part, tear drops falling, descending. I don't see a face. I don't know why I said that.

Card IX
26. (v) Well, looks like maybe a very fancy stage costume for a Broadway production for a musical for a female of course. Bow on top and puffed sleeves, green part on top and there.

26. Here are the bow, puffed sleeves, bottom of dress. (Costume?) The ornateness and the colors. Look of colors on Broadway. Maybe hands on hips. It's a costume.

27. (v) Just somewhat of a volcano exploding. Red part up here looks like maybe...the red part doesn't look like a volcano.

27. This center part is going up and then this comes out. The center and red part. Coming up out of here and shooting off. I don't see anything else.

Card X
28. (v) If all things are together, a hand held fan—looks like a handle to it, if held together. I don't know what I am trying to say.

28. This is the handle, and all this is the fan. Just this is the handle, and the rest is a colorful fan.

29. (v) Lamp shade.

29. Here is where the bulb goes, and here is the shade.

30. (v) I see a face—eyes, nose, mouth, maybe evil connotation.

30. All this part. Looks like it's evil. Whole thing, look in the eyes.

31. Or fireworks display. Sky is full of fireworks.

31. Just all the colors are spread out so far.

32. Or a child throwing a temper tantrum in the bedroom.

32. Only because everything is so spread out. Child is sitting in the middle of the floor throwing things. The child's not there, but everything is all over the room.

33. Could be the bottom of the ocean. Some of the shapes look like creatures—different sea life, colored plants, rocks or something. Maybe spreading out coral formations.

33. Yellow and green are some type of sea plants and that's coral. These are crabs.

RORSCHACH SEQUENCE OF SCORES FOR MR. NORTON

Card	Resp	Loc (DQ)	Loc No	Determinants (FQ)	(2)	Content(s)	P	Z	Special Scores
I	1.	WSo	1	Fo		Ad		3.5	
	2.	Wo	1	FMao		A	P	1.0	
II	3.	D+	6	Mau	(2)	(H)		3.0	GHR, COP
	4.	DSo	5	F-		(A)		4.5	
III	5.	W+	1	Mp.CF.Fro		H, Fi	P	5.5	GHR
	6.	Do	1	FCu		A			
IV	7.	Wv	1	Fo		Bt			
	8.	Wv	1	mau		Na			
V	9.	Wo	1	Fo		A	P	1.0	
	10.	Wo	1	Fr.Ma-		Hd		1.0	PHR
	11.	Wo	1	Fo		A	P	1.0	
VI	12.	Wo	1	Fo		Art		2.5	
	13.	Wo	1	Fu		Bt		2.5	
	14.	Wo	1	F-		Hh, Sc		2.5	
	15.	D+	1	Mpu	(2)	Hx, H		2.5	AG, PHR
	16.	Wo	1	F-		A		2.5	
VII	17.	Wo	1	Fu		Ay, Cg		2.5	
	18.	Wo	1	Fu		Cg, Art		2.5	
	19.	Wo	1	Fu		Hh		2.5	
VIII	20.	Dv	6	FC.FDo		Ls			
	21.	Do	1	FMao	(2)	A, Ls	P		
	22.	Wv	1	CFo		Bt			
	23.	Wo	1	FCu		Hh, Art		4.5	PSV
	24.	W+	1	FMa.FC.Fro		A, Na	P	4.5	PHR
IX	25.	Do	1	mp-	(2)	Hd			
	26.	Wo	1	FCu		Cg		5.5	
	27.	Wo	1	ma-		Ex		5.5	
X	28.	Wo	1	FC-		Art		5.5	
	29.	Wo	1	F-		Hh, Sc		5.5	
	30.	DdSo	30	F-		Hd, Hx		6.0	PHR
	31.	Wv	1	C		Ex			
	32.	W+	1	Ma-		Hx, Hh		5.5	AG, PHR
	33.	Wo	1	FCo		Na, A		5.5	

Location Features	Determinants		Contents	Approach
	Blends	*Single*		
	M.CF.Fr	M = 3	H = 2	I: WS.W
Zf = 25	Fr.M	FM = 2	(H) = 1	II: D.DS
ZSum = 88.5	FC.FD	m = 3	Hd = 3	III: W.D
Zest = 84.5	FM.FC.Fr	FC = 5	(Hd) = 0	IV: W.W
		CF = 1	Hx = 3	V: W.W
W = 25		C = 1	A = 8	VI: W.W.W.D.W
D = 7		Cn = 0	(A) = 1	VII: W.W.W
W+D = 32		FC' = 0	Ad = 1	VIII: D.D.W.W.W.D
Dd = 1		C'F = 0	(Ad) = 0	IX: W.W
S = 3		C' = 0	An = 0	X: W.W.DdS.W.W.W
		FT = 0	Art = 4	
Developmental Quality		TF = 0	Ay = 1	*Special Scores*
+ = 5		T = 0	Bl = 0	Lv 1 Lv 2
o = 23		FV = 0	Bt = 3	DV = 0x1 = 0x2
v = 5		VF = 0	Cg = 3	INC = 0x2 = 0x4
v/+ = 0		V = 0	Cl = 0	DR = 0x3 = 0x6
		FY = 0	Ex = 2	FAB = 0x4 = 0x7
		YF = 0	Fd = 0	ALOG = x5

Form Quality			
	FQx	MQual	W+D
+	= 0	= 0	= 0
o	= 12	= 1	= 12
u	= 10	= 2	= 10
-	= 10	= 2	= 9
none	= 1	= 0	= 1

Contents (cont.)	Special Scores (cont.)	
Y = 0	CON = 0x7	
Fr = 0	Raw Sum 6 = 0	
rF = 0	Wgtd Sum 6 = 0	
FD = 0		
F = 14	AB = 0	GHR = 2
(2) = 4	AG = 2	PHR = 5
Sc = 2	COP = 1	MOR = 0
Sx = 0	CP = 0	PER = 0
Xy = 0		PSV = 1
Id = 0		

Fi = 1
Ge = 0
Hh = 5
Ls = 2
Na = 3

STRUCTURAL SUMMARY FOR MR.NORTON

Ratios, Percentages, and Derivations

Core

			Affect	*Interpersonal*
R = 33	L = .74		FC: CF+C = 7:3	COP = 1 AG = 2
			Pure C =	GHR: PHR = 2:5
EB = 5:7	EA = 12	EBPer = N/A	SumC':WSumC = 0:7	a:p = 9:2
eb = 6:0	es = 6	D = +2	Afr =0.74	Food = 0
	Adj es = 4	Adj D = +3	S =3	Sum T = 0
			Blends:R = 4:33	Human Cont = 6
FM = 3	SumC' = 0	SumT = 0	CP = 0	Pure H = 2
m = 2	Sum V = 0	Sum Y = 0	PER = 0	
			Isol Indx = .33	

Ideation

		Mediation	*Processing*	*Self-Perception*
a:p = 9:2	Sum6 = 0	XA% = .67	Zf = 25	3r+(2)/R = .39
Ma:Mp = 4:1	Lv2 = 0	WDA% = .69	W:D:Dd = 25:7:1	Fr+rF = 3
2AB+Art+Ay = 5	WSum6 = 0	X-% = .30	W:M = 25:4	SumV = 0
MOR = 0	M- = 2	S- = 2	Zd = +4.0	FD = 0
	Mnone = 0	P = 5	PSV = 0	An+Xy = 0
		X+% = .36	DQ+ = 5	MOR = 0
		Xu% =	DQv = 5	H:(H)+Hd+(Hd) = 2:3

PTI = 3   DEPI = 3   CDI = 1   S-CON = 2   HVI = 3   OBS = 0

262

IV

CLUSTER C
PERSONALITY DISORDERS

IV

Rorschach Assessment
of Avoidant Personality Disorder

Ronald J. Ganellen
Northwestern University

The conceptualization and diagnostic criteria for avoidant personality disorder (APD) first appeared in the *Diagnostic and Statistical Manual of Mental Disorders*, 3rd Edition (DSM-III) (American Psychiatric Association [APA], 1980; Frances, 1980). Although earlier theorists had described characteristics related to APD, this diagnosis was not formally included in the diagnostic nomenclature before the DSM-III. For instance, some of the dynamics of this disorder were suggested in Fenichel's (1945) description of the phobic character—a tense, apprehensive, fearful person who exhibits a general inhibition across a wide range of activities (Frances & Widiger, 1987). Others in the analytic tradition had written about individuals who exhibit a conflict about getting involved with others, and whose behavior shifts between a desire to develop relationships and a desire to avoid relationships. These are the dynamics associated with the analytic view of a schizoid character. Guntrip (1968), for instance, referred to the approach–avoidance conflict schizoid individuals experience as the "in–out" paradigm.

Millon (1981) argued that psychodynamic theorists, such as Guntrip, did not distinguish between two types of individuals who avoid developing close interpersonal relationships and tend to be behaviorally awkward and inhibited in social interactions. Millon contrasted the history and dynamics of individuals who have limited contact with others because their interest in becoming involved with others is low with those of individuals who want to be involved with others, but have difficulty developing relationships because of the anxiety they experience in social interactions. According to Millon's conceptualization, a diagnosis of schizoid personality disorder (SZPD) should be applied to individuals in the former group, whereas, a diagnosis of APD should be applied to the latter group.

Proponents of the Five-Factor Model of personality have located DSM-IV (APA, 1994) criteria for APD on specific dimensions of this model (Widiger, Trull, Clarkin, Sanderson, & Costa, 2002). They characterize APD as involving low scores on Extraversion and high scores on Neuroticism. In addition to elevations in these primary dimensions, the Five-Factor Model also predicts that avoidant individuals will have elevated scores on the Neuroticism facets of Self-Consciousness, Anxiety, and Vulnerability, and low scores on the Extraversion facets of Assertiveness and Excitement Seeking. Widiger et al. (2002) explained that this pattern of predicted scores accounts for the social inhibitions and cautious style typical of avoidant individuals. Preliminary studies of these hypotheses have been supported empirically (Dyce & O'Connor, 1998; Huprich, 2003; Reynolds & Clark, 2001; Trull, Widiger, & Burr, 2001; Wilberg, Urnes, Friis, Pedersen, & Karterud, 1999).

Some writers have pointed out both the importance and the difficulty of distinguishing between APD and SZPD in clinical settings (Livesley & West, 1986; Trull, Widiger, & Frances, 1987). Widiger, Mangine, Corbitt, Ellis, and Thomas (1995) observed that differentiating the two was problematic using DSM-III-R criteria because of item overlap in the diagnostic criteria. For example, in the DSM-III-R, the description of an individual who "has no close friends or confidants (or only one)" was included in the criteria for both APD and SZPD. This item was deleted from the criteria for APD in the DSM-IV because the item did not contribute to diagnostic clarity, and did not accurately reflect the dynamics of APD, which involves both an intense desire for close relationships and distress at not being able to develop these relationships.

From the perspective of the Five-Factor Model, both SZPD and APD involve significant social introversion. However, the Five-Factor Model predicts that the two differ in the nature of the introversion, consistent with Millon's (1981) theory. Widiger et al. (2002) posited that SZPD is characterized by low levels of Warmth, which individuals manifest behaviorally by being cold and distant, and low levels of Positive Emotions, which reflects low levels of interest in and limited capacity to experience satisfaction from interpersonal interactions. In contrast, these authors noted that the pattern exhibited by individuals with APD demonstrate that they are able to express affection and experience a sense of warmth and pleasure when they have contact with people, although they often are behaviorally cautious and inhibited about expressing emotions.

OVERLAP OF AVOIDANT PERSONALITY
DISORDER AND SOCIAL PHOBIA

One difficulty clinicians often encounter in clinical settings involves differentiating APD from generalized social phobia. Reich (2001), for instance, argued that according to the empirical evidence, social phobia and APD cannot be distinguished on the basis of either symptoms or response to treatment. The overlap between the two disorders may occur, in part, because there is considerable overlap in the DSM-IV diagnostic criteria for both disorders. It also is possible that there is a high degree of comorbidity for APD and generalized social anxiety disorder or social phobia. The DSM-IV recognizes that these are not mutually exclusive disorders and directs clinicians to apply both diagnoses when appropriate.

Some writers have suggested that differentiation of APD from generalized social phobia is facilitated by obtaining a detailed history and giving careful attention to the developmental trajectory of social difficulties. For instance, Widiger et al. (1995) asserted that a history of pervasive, generalized social timidity, avoidance, and insecurity in relating to others that has been present since late childhood or early adolescence is more likely attributable to a personality disorder than to a social phobia.

Widiger et al. (1995) also pointed out that individuals with APD often are bothered by a generalized negative self-image, as indicated by criterion 6 of the DSM-IV ("views self as socially inept, personally unappealing, or inferior to others"). In contrast, individuals with a social phobia frequently feel confident in areas of their life unrelated to social interactions and question themselves only when they are engaged in a situation related to their specific phobic fears. This was apparent in the case of a man the author treated for a generalized social phobia who was fearful of being the focus of attention in large groups. He was confident about his capabilities to manage work responsibilities and to provide appropriate support for his older, physically infirm parents, but sought treatment because he became paralyzed by anxiety as he anticipated standing at the front of the congregation on his wedding day and then greeting well-wishers in a receiving line after the ceremony. Whereas individuals with social phobia are bothered by feelings of self-consciousness and embarrassment related to specific types of situations, APD is characterized by a more fundamental sense of inadequacy and worthlessness that contributes to generalized inhibitions about participating in social situations.

Other writers have speculated that the high degree of comorbidity between APD and generalized social phobia suggests that the two have a common genetic basis (Alpert, Uebelacker, McLean, & Nierenberg, 1997; Reich, 2002). Partly on the basis of these findings, some theorists have suggested that social phobia and APD may represent different points on a spectrum of disorders involving social anxiety (Reich, 2001; Schneider, Blanco, Antia, & Liebowitz, 2002).

Several family studies provide data consistent with the hypothesis that APD and social phobia are variants of the same disorder rather than independent disorders. For instance, one family study examined the rates of social phobia and APD among relatives of probands with and those without generalized social phobia. Stein et al. (1998) found markedly higher risks for both generalized social phobia and APD in the former than in the latter group, suggesting a shared genetic vulnerability for both disorders.

An epidemiologic study that examined familial patterns of social phobia, APD, and social anxiety in the general population also suggested that APD and social phobia share a common biologic basis (Tillfors, Furmark, Ekselius, & Fredrikson, 2001). This study found that the presence of either social phobia or APD alone was associated with two- to three-fold increase in risk of social anxiety. The risk for social anxiety was not increased by a combination of the two disorders or the severity of symptoms. Similar to the assertions made by other authors, Tillfors et al. (2001) suggested that social phobia and APD may be variants of a more general dimension of social anxiety rather than separate disorders. If this is the case, then findings that individuals with social phobia exhibit significant impairment in both normal social and occupational functioning (Lochner et al., 2003) also may apply to APD as both involve a persistent fear of situations in which an individual may be exposed to the scrutiny of others that results in either avoidance of social situations or enduring social situations with considerable anxiety, which interferes with behavior or causes discomfort.

These studies highlight some of the conceptual and practical difficulties clinicians face when attempting to differentiate between APD and generalized social phobia. Some authors suggest that these are two independent disorders that can be distinguished on the basis of clinical presentation and history. Others take the position that given considerable overlap in diagnostic criteria, high rates of comorbidity, and evidence suggesting a shared biologic vulnerability, it may be more parsimonious to view APD and generalized social anxiety as variations of a common dimension involving social anxiety.

There are several implications of these varying perspectives for clinical practice. Clinicians should be aware that APD and generalized social phobia frequently co-occur. According to the DSM-IV, an individual can be given both an Axis I diagnosis of generalized social phobia and an Axis II diagnosis of APD if appropriate. Following the guidelines suggested by Widiger et al. (1995), clinicians should carefully examine the clinical history, age of onset, estimations of self-worth, and chronicity of symptoms of social anxiety in an effort to determine whether one diagnosis is appropriate or whether both should be assigned. Particular attention should be given to the extent of the link between anxiety about social interactions and more generalized feelings of inadequacy and worthlessness.

CLINICAL FEATURES
OF AVOIDANT PERSONALITY DISORDER

Specific criteria required to make a diagnosis of APD are contained in the DSM-IV. Instead of reviewing these criteria, the following section discusses several central psychological dimensions associated with APD. These features are related to the diagnostic criteria, often to more than one criterion, but are not as specific as the criterion contained in the DSM-IV.

According to the DSM-IV, APD is characterized by a "pervasive pattern of social inhibition, feelings of inadequacy, and hypersensitivity to negative evaluation" affecting an individual's functioning in wide range of social situations, which started during or before early adulthood (APA, 1994, p. 62). For instance, in social situations individuals with APD usually prefer to stay in the background while letting others do the talking, have trouble initiating conversations with people they do not know well, and feel awkward, self-conscious, and unsure of themselves. Typically, they are reluctant to call attention to themselves by speaking up or being the center of attention.

Fear of Negative Evaluation

The diagnostic criteria and clinical descriptions of APD emphasize the extent to which involvement in and avoidance of contact with others in social and occupational settings is influenced by an individual's fears of criticism, disapproval, and rejection. This is explicitly stated in criterion 1 of the DSM-IV, which involves avoidance of occupational activities for fear of criticism, disapproval, or rejection, and in criteria 2 to 4 of DSM-IV, which involve hesitation to participate in social activities for fear of criticism, rejection, or humiliation.

Whereas hypersensitivity to criticism and disapproval is a central feature of APD, it is not specific to APD, because individuals with both dependent personality disorder (DPD) and narcissistic personality disorder (NPD) also are quite sensitive to disapproval. Widiger et al. (1995) stated that, for APD, apprehensions about being criticized usually also involve worries about rejection, whereas, for NPD, approval and disapproval usually produce an inflated or deflated sense of self-worth without necessarily provoking concerns about social rejection. The reactions of the NPD individual to criticism reflects a fragile self-esteem that shifts depending on whether others respond with affirmation and admiration or in a negative, critical, or indifferent manner. Avoidant individuals differ from individuals with NPD in that they are not motivated by an excessive need for attention and do not covet and seek admiration. Furthermore, whereas narcissistic individuals are likely to protest criticisms or rebukes with an attitude of outrage and anger and to deny shortcomings suggested by others, individuals with APD characteristically are quick to accept blame when things do not go smoothly and to view any misunderstanding, confusion, or hassle with others as confirmation that they are stupid, foolish, and worthless.

Widiger et al. (1995) pointed out that the presence or absence of fears of criticism, disapproval, and rejection is particularly important in differentiating among APD, SZPD, and schizotypal personality disorder (STPD). Whereas both APD and SZPD individuals avoid social interactions, the motivation for APD is fear of negative evaluations and the resulting distress. In contrast, individuals with SZPD characteristically are indifferent to and unconcerned about how others view them. Although individuals with STPD may acknowledge that they are bothered by social anxiety, the discomfort they experience often is associated with unrealistic, paranoid fears rather than concerns about appearing incompetent, unattractive, or undesirable.

It is characteristic of individuals with either APD or DPD to be concerned about and sensitive to criticism and disapproval. However, Widiger et al. (1995) stressed that the most recent revision of criteria for DPD does not identify sensitivity to criticism as a central feature of the disorder. For example, they noted that although one criterion for DPD in the DSM-III-R was that of being "easily hurt by criticism or disapproval," this item was not included in the DSM-IV criteria for DPD. Instead, the DSM-IV emphasizes a pervasive need of these individuals for care, and for reliance on others, as well as their willingness to take a compliant, submissive role, and their vulnerability to feeling helpless and uncertain without advice from others. Widiger et al. (1995) commented that individuals with DPD view expressions of approval and disapproval as signs that show whether another person is willing to provide support. Stated differently, they emphasized that in contrast to individuals with DPD, who interpret approval as an indication that another person cares enough about them to provide the help, reassurance, and guidance they need, individuals with APD view approval as a commentary on their worth.

Negative Self-Image

The aforementioned apprehensive worry and fear about others' reactions that characterizes APD coexists with feelings of inadequacy. For instance, avoidant individuals may be reluctant to approach another person not only because they are uncertain how the other person will react, but also because of a conviction that others will find them boring, unattractive, or uninteresting. This underscores the extent to which low self-esteem and a tendency to be self-critical are a central feature of APD. Their ability to interact naturally and freely with others can be constrained either because they feel self-conscious and foolish or because of a fear that they will be embarrassed and humiliated.

Widiger et al. (1995) observed that for some individuals, concerns about being socially inept, unattractive, or inferior to others may be exaggerated, whereas for others, these concerns may be realistic. These researchers cautioned clinicians to consider whether individuals who say they are awkward with others or unappealing in some way may be appraising themselves accurately. For instance, individuals with a marked physical deformity attributable to cerebral palsy may be realistic if they say most people their age are turned off by their appearance and avoid them. Widiger et al. (1995) suggested that an individual's belief that he or she is socially inept, personally unappealing, or inferior to others should be viewed as a sign of APD only if the clinician determines that the belief is inaccurate, exaggerated, or pervasively influences the individual's self-image and willingness to be socially active.

Emotional Constriction

The concerns that individuals with APD have about themselves and how others respond to them contribute to a tendency to be self-conscious and inhibited. Their careful, cautious, constricted manner of expressing themselves may affect their involvement in both casual social interactions and more personal relationships. In casual interactions, avoidant persons tend to be quiet, withdrawn, and inhibited. They may be reluctant to express their opinions and feelings, even to others with whom they have established a relationship, because of their fears that they will be ridiculed or shamed if they do. This is the basis for DSM-IV criterion 3: a tendency to hold back on revealing personal information or expressing intimate feelings for others, such as people with whom they have a romantic relationship.

When the diagnostic criteria for APD were revised for the DSM-IV, an effort was made to differentiate APD more cleanly from a generalized social phobia (Millon, 1991). Whereas one criterion in the DSM-III-R involved reticence in social situations for fear of appearing foolish, the DSM-IV version of this item specifies "restraint within intimate relationships because of the fear of being shamed of ridiculed." Note that this change involves a shift from anxiety and inhibitions experienced in social situations generally, such as a fear of public speaking, to inhibitions within close personal relationships. This reflects an attempt to differentiate between anxiety about performing in public, which is more characteristic of a social phobia, and anxiety that interferes with the ability to express oneself in a comfortable, free, spontaneous manner even with familiar people. Note, however, that an individual with APD may feel tense, awkward, and inhibited both in public and in close relationships, whereas an individual with generalized social phobia may be anxious and fear humiliation in both public performance situations and interaction with others socially. This underscores the aforementioned difficulty distinguishing between APD and generalized social phobia.

This tendency to be cautious and inhibited in intimate relationships is not specific to APD. Widiger et al. (1995), for instance, described individuals with DPD as similarly tending to express themselves in a tentative manner and "holding back" on their feelings. Whereas dependent individuals control what they say to avoid jeopardizing a relationship with a person on whom they depend, individuals with APD are motivated primarily by fears of being shamed or humiliated if they express themselves more openly. The fear of appearing foolish, ridiculous, or unworthy of attention drives avoidant individuals to "tread lightly" and try to avoid saying anything that will attract negative attention and make them feel awkward, self-conscious, or embarrassed.

Negative Affect

As described earlier, it is characteristic of individuals with APD to worry and feel self-conscious frequently about how they appear to others, to be apprehensive about how others will react to them, and to be preoccupied with concerns about disapproval, criticism, and rejection. They ruminate about what others think of them and whether they are succeeding or failing in social situations. Their concerns are not restricted to interactions with persons with whom they already have some actual social relationship, such as friends or coworkers, but can occur in relation to strangers they may never see again. For instance, individuals with APD may worry that they appear incompetent, awkward, or unsophisticated to a waiter taking their order in a restaurant, or wonder if they sound stupid, shallow, or boring to a stranger sitting close enough to overhear what they say during a casual conversation.

These features of APD suggest that individuals with the disorder are vulnerable to feeling worried, unhappy, and distressed. Although they may not meet DSM-IV criteria for a mood or anxiety disorder, they often are tense, ill at ease, and discouraged about their relationships with others.

Consistent with this suggestion, research suggests that there is a high rate of comorbidity between APD and Axis I anxiety and mood disorders (Alpert et al., 1997: Docherty, Fiester, & Shea, 1986; Millon & Kotik, 1985).

It should be noted that the association between APD and difficulties with mood and anxiety may have been increased when criteria were revised for the DSM-IV. For instance, Widiger et al. (1995) noted that criterion 4 was changed from "easily hurt by criticism or disapproval" in the DSM-III-R to "is preoccupied with being criticized or rejected in social situations" in the DSM-IV. They point out that this change raised the threshold for this criterion from a vulnerability to criticism and rejection to a history of anticipating, worrying, and ruminating about disapproval and rejection.

RORSCHACH INDICES
OF AVOIDANT PERSONALITY DISORDER

No empirical investigations have identified a configuration of Rorschach scores characteristic of APD. According to the clinical description of the psychological features central to the APD discussed earlier, the following Rorschach variables conceptually are particularly relevant to assessment of APD. It should be clearly stated that the following discussion is speculative and theory-driven rather than based on data. Research is needed to assess the relationship between the theoretically relevant scores subsequently discussed and the central features of APD discussed earlier. It should be noted also that significant values for any of these variables are not unique to APD. However, Rorschach findings may be useful for investigating the specific concerns and difficulties experienced by an individual with APD.

Introversion

As discussed earlier, introversion is a key feature of APD. Several Rorschach data points may provide indications of introversion and discomfort in social situations. As indicated earlier, in contrast to SZPD, individuals with APD are interested in people, but experience considerable discomfort. Thus, it might be predicted that schizoid and avoidant individuals would differ on the number of responses produced with human content. Individuals with SZPD would be expected to have a low number of human content responses consistent with less than expected interest in others (SumH < 4). In contrast, avoidant individuals would be expected to produce either an average or an elevated number of responses with human content. If they produce an average value for human content, one would expect that they would produce more part-human than whole-human content responses. This pattern reflects discomfort in social situations and uneasiness in interaction with others. An elevated number of human content responses frequently is associated with a sense of mistrust and wary preoccupation about others.

The predicted Rorschach profile of APD also is expected to have an abnormal value for Texture (T). Given their discomfort in social interactions, their uncertainty about whether others will respond to them in a concerned, accepting manner, and their mistrust of others, many avoidant individuals are likely to have 0 in their records. This is consistent with their tendency to open up slowly to others unless certain of acceptance, and their preference to be less self-revealing than most others. Stated differently, the absence of T shows the avoidant individual's preference to remain distant and detached in relationships. However, some avoidant individuals may produce an elevated value for T because they experience a sense of emotional deprivation, loneliness, and disappointment about the absence of closeness with others. An elevated number of T responses should be interpreted in this fashion only if there is no history of recent losses in the individual's life.

The tendencies for individuals with APD to be introverted, to feel uncomfortable in many social situations, and to avoid social interactions also may be related to elevated scores on the Isolation Index. A high score on the Isolation Index often signals limited involvement in social interactions, a marked avoidance of interpersonal situations, and feelings of loneliness or alienation.

People who feel uncomfortable in social situations who keep a distance from others, and who do not anticipate positive responses from others often produce fewer than expected cooperative movement responses (COP) on the Rorschach. Individuals with low values for COP generally are not gregarious or outgoing and tend to remain on the sidelines in social gatherings. Their behavior and attitudes may give others the impression that they are distant, uninvolved, and disinterested in being part of social activity. Given these descriptions, it is reasonable to predict that individuals with APD would produce a low number of COP responses.

Negative Self-Concept

As discussed earlier, it is characteristic of individuals with APD to be troubled by insecurities and self-doubts, and to anticipate that others will criticize or reject them. From a Rorschach perspective, concerns about self-image and feelings of inadequacy are likely to be manifested by low scores on the Egocentricity Index $(3r+(2)/R < .33)$. Individuals who produce scores in this range evaluate themselves as less competent and attractive than others, think poorly of themselves, and often feel worthless and inferior.

A negative self-concept also can be identified by an elevated number of Morbid responses (MOR > 2). This indicates that an individual holds negative attitudes about him- or herself. In some cases, an elevated number of MOR responses specifically indicates that individuals have negative views of their bodies and feel unattractive and physically undesirable.

In addition, an elevated number for Form Dimension (FD > 2) or Vista (V > 0) responses also reflects negative self-evaluations and self-recriminations. This is particularly likely to be the case if Vista is elevated in the absence of a clear history denoting a recent failure or setback. Whereas some individuals produce one or more Vista responses if they are self-critical about a recent setback, individuals who produce an elevated number of Vista responses without a history of a clear-cut failure tend to be chronically dissatisfied with themselves, sometimes to the point of viewing themselves as incompetent, inadequate, and worthless. Because it is characteristic of individuals with APD to depreciate and denigrate themselves, it is likely that their Rorschach protocols will include elevated values for MOR, FD, and V in addition to low scores on the Egocentricity Index

The question might be raised whether individuals with APD may also produce a positive score on the Hypervigilance Index (HVI) given their hypersensitivity to criticism. Exner (1993) developed the HVI to identify individuals who are wary, watchful, and suspicious of others, characteristics that can be seen as associated with high levels of sensitivity to criticism. Whereas some features of the HVI are conceptually related to aspects of an avoidant style, others are not. For example, individuals with both a positive HVI and an avoidant style who feel vulnerable when relating to others, are apprehensive about negative interactions and try to anticipate them, and have a mistrustful view of other people (e.g., T = 0; H content > 6).

However, a high score on the HVI also indicates a specific style of information processing that involves an attempt to take stock and make sense of as much information as possible in an effort to detect signs of threats (e.g., Zf > 12; Zd > +3.5). This is not necessarily true of avoidant individuals. Furthermore, those individuals who produce a positive HVI tend to be overly concerned with protecting their personal space and are most comfortable when they feel in control of an interpersonal interaction. As discussed earlier, individuals with an APD are apprehensive when they are with others because they fear being criticized, ridiculed, or rejected, rather than because of a need to maintain control and to prevent others from intruding into their personal space. Thus, whereas indicators of interpersonal mistrust and discomfort would be expected in the Rorschach protocols of individuals with APD (as discussed earlier), one would not expect routinely to find a positive HVI in their protocols.

Emotional Constriction

The emotional constriction characteristic of APD may be identified by the Rorschach in several ways. A tendency to be inhibited about expressing emotions may be seen when the Constriction Ratio shows that a greater number of responses involved achromatic color than chromatic color (C' ≥ WSumC). This finding identifies individuals who tend to hold in their feelings to the point they may be described as being emotionally "bottled up."

A second Rorschach indicator of inhibition in expressing emotions is a low score on the Affective Ratio (Afr < .46). Individuals with low Afr scores are uncomfortable in situations that involve an open exchange of emotions. Their discomfort occurs as a reaction to direct expression of feelings regardless of whether the feelings are positive or negative. As a result, individuals who produce a low score on the Afr withdraw from emotionally charged interactions, including expressions of warmth and affection, and are reluctant to reveal their inner thoughts and feelings to others. As a result, others may view them as emotionally distant and reserved.

A third Rorschach indicator of emotional inhibition is an unweighted FC:CF+C ratio in which the value for FC exceeds the value for CF+C (e.g., when the value of FC is at least twice the value of CF+C and the value for pure C is zero). This finding identifies an individual who is restrained in expressing emotions to the point of appearing emotionally detached, remote, and hard to get to know. It is reasonable to predict that scores on the Constriction Ratio, Afr, or FC:CF+C will capture the self-consciousness, inhibition, and discomfort in expressing personal information that is characteristic of individuals with APD.

Emotional Distress

Although the DSM-IV does not specifically identify emotional distress as one of the clinical features required for a diagnosis of APD, avoidant individuals frequently experience considerable emotional distress, which may be subclinical in nature, and often develop comorbid mood or anxiety disorders, as discussed earlier. The vulnerability to emotional distress characteristic of APD may be reflected on several Rorschach variables. For instance, the relatively persistent worry, discouragement, and concerns about failing that trouble individuals with APD are likely to be manifested by an Adjusted D of –1. For the reasons discussed earlier, this is likely to occur in part because of elevated scores on C' and V. An Adjusted D score in this range is hypothesized to reflect the chronic sense of distress, self-dissatisfaction, and apprehensive worry experienced by avoidant individuals.

A score of 5 or higher on the Depression Index (DEPI) also is likely to be produced by some individuals with APD. Whereas in some instances, an elevated score on the DEPI is a sign of a mood disorder, scores in this range also can reflect a vulnerability to react to difficulties in life with considerable emotional distress (Exner, 2003; Weiner, 2003). The potential for the APD individual repeatedly to feel disappointed, moody, tense, anxious, dejected, or unhappy is likely to be associated with an elevated score on the DEPI.

Another Rorschach variable associated with negative mood is the Coping Deficit Index (CDI). As described by Exner (2003), a positive CDI often is produced by individuals who have difficulties establishing and maintaining satisfying social relationships because of their deficits in social skills and lack sensitivity to others. Individuals with APD who have problems relating to others comfortably (albeit problems developing warm, rewarding relationships), occur not because of social skills deficits, but because these individuals are inhibited, self-conscious, and emotionally constricted. Thus, it is reasonable to expect that some individuals with APD will have a high CDI, but this should not be expected in most cases of APD.

Several other indices of emotional distress are likely to be found in the Rorschach protocols of individuals with APD. These variables are considered more speculative than the aforementioned variables and should be viewed with skepticism until empirical research investigates their association with APD. For instance, it is reasonable to anticipate higher than expected values for the right side of the eb in the Rorschachs of individuals with APD. The common thread among variables that fall on the right side of the eb (C', V, T, and Y) is that all involve shading and are related to different types of distressing affect. The implications from several of these responses have been discussed previously. However, individuals who produce a greater than expected value when these shading variables are summed tend to be troubled by negative affect, even if they do not display distress overtly or do not report feeling tense, apprehensive, self-critical, or discouraged.

As discussed earlier, individuals with APD typically approach social situations with a desire to be liked and accepted by others while being bothered at the same time by apprehensions and fears that they will be criticized or ignored and end up feeling inadequate and unwanted. Even when things are going smoothly with others, they tend to anticipate negative outcomes, such as feeling embarrassed and ashamed. The tendency to respond to situations with a painful mixture of conflicting feelings often is manifested on the Rorschach by an elevated number of Color- Shading blend responses. Thus, there is good reason to expect that avoidant individuals will produce more Color-Shading blends than nonpatients.

CASE EXAMPLE: MR. ANDERS

Mr. Anders, a 36-year-old, single, White computer programmer, recently began seeing a therapist because of worry and a sense of dissatisfaction with his life. He reported being sporadically anxious, unhappy, and distressed since childhood. In particular, he recalled worrying a great deal about how he fit in socially as a youngster and being concerned that he did not make friends easily. He also mentioned becoming quite anxious and worried when his parents went out in the evenings because he feared they might not return.

Mr. Anders reported that he was teased by other children during grade school because he was chubby and because of his behavior. He explained that he often tried to get attention by acting in inappropriate ways, such as trying to kiss girls. Although Mr. Anders developed friendships as he got older, it bothered him that he was not more popular, and that he often felt tongue-tied when he attempted to talk to girls he thought were attractive.

Mr. Anders stated that during college, he dated one woman for 4 years. During that time, he had few friends and described himself as a loner. He married his girlfriend after they graduated from college. A year later, they divorced. When asked about this, he explained that his wife frequently complained that he did not communicate with her and questioned his interest because he never told her he thought she was attractive. When asked how he reacted to the divorce, Mr. Anders replied that he was relieved because he often had felt guilty when his wife expressed unhappiness. Although he very much wanted to make her happy, he thought his wife expected him to be someone he was not and felt pressured by her to be involved in ways that seemed forced, awkward, and uncomfortable.

Mr. Anders did not date for several years after the divorce. At the time he sought therapy, he had been dating a woman for about 5 months. He was pleased with the way their relationship was progressing. He commented that she came from a large family and had a wide circle of friends. He worried whether her family and friends would like and accept him and acknowledged that, if given the choice, he would rather not have to meet them.

Mr. Anders had concerns about his future at work. He had received positive responses while working as a programmer, and his supervisor had given him more responsibility. Mr. Anders added that these responsibilities involved overseeing the work of others and participating in meetings with clients. He felt quite uncomfortable in these situations, often thinking he did not know what to say, and worried about embarrassing himself. He stated that after these situations occur, "I kick myself for looking like a fool. My girlfriend wants me to get ahead, to show them I deserve a promotion. Given my druthers, I'd be much happier spending my 8 hours working away in my cubicle. Heck, I'd work 10 hours a day instead of 8 if I didn't have to talk to those people. Don't think she'd like that, though."

When asked about his current mood, Mr. Anders replied that his outlook is more positive than in the past, although he often questions whether he is a "loser" when things go wrong, either at work or socially. His sleep, appetite, and level of energy were normal. He continued to be interested in and able to enjoy activities. He often had difficulty concentrating when working on tasks at work, and denied any suicidal intent or ideation.

Rorschach Findings

Rorschach data indicate that Mr. Anders currently is tense, worried, and unhappy (DEPI = 6; CDI = 5; D Score = –2). His unhappiness most likely relates to difficulties establishing and maintaining satisfying relationships (CDI = 5) and persistent doubts about his self-worth (3R+2/R = .30). In general, Mr. Anders functions best in familiar situations that have clearly spelled out guidelines for acceptable and unacceptable behavior, but has difficulty responding effectively to unexpected problems (Adj D Score = –1; CDI = 5). He has limited personal resources on which to draw when he has to handle situations for which he is not prepared and easily becomes "rattled" and upset (EA = 3.5; Adj D = –1; CDI = 5). In such situations he often feels inadequate, helpless, and unsure of what to do (3r+2/R = .30). These feelings of powerlessness may be so intense that Mr. Anders becomes paralyzed by self-doubts and uncertainty about whether he is able to handle the situation on his own (Y = 4). The self-doubts and tendency to feel helpless contribute to the difficulties Mr. Anders experiences at work and in social interactions.

Mr. Anders characteristically tries to keep upsetting feelings under control by maintaining a rather cerebral, intellectualized stance (2AB+Art+Ay = 7, SumC', WSumC = 4:0.5). He usually is more comfortable responding to situations by focusing on abstract or theoretical issues rather than by acknowledging his own personal reactions. This allows him to remain detached from troubling feelings that might otherwise overwhelm and disorganize him. Given this style, Mr. Anders may express himself in a somewhat academic, "bookish" manner. Although this may impress some people who value his investment in academic pursuits, other people may perceive Mr. Anders as emotionally restrained, detached, or unable to express himself spontaneously.

In general, Mr. Anders is a rather shy, introverted man who is troubled by self-doubts and questions about his worth (3r+2/R = .30, MOR = 3). His reactions to many situations often revolve around ways in which he feels inadequate and inferior to others. Given his tendency to become absorbed in his own thoughts, he also is likely to be troubled by self-critical rumination (EB = 3:0.5; 2AB+Art+Ay = 7, 3R+2/R = .30). This suggests Mr. Anders frequently anticipates being humiliated, ridiculed, or criticized by others, and can get "locked" into repetitive, self-denigrating thoughts about his actions and ways in which he feels he failed. Because of his poorly developed social skills (CDI = 5), and lack of confidence, he may be nervous, inhibited, and apt to act awkwardly with others. Mr. Anders may even consider avoiding social situations that involve people he does not know well given the discomfort he often experiences during social interactions.

At the same time that Mr. Anders approaches social encounters with apprehension, he also has strong desires to be involved with others ($T = 2$). He very much wants to be liked and accepted by others and to have close, warm bonds with them. However, Mr. Anders is bothered by a chronic sense of loneliness and persistent frustration about his relationships (Isolation Index = .35). He may be quite sensitive to rejection, and anxiously questions whether other people truly like him and want to be with him. These concerns likely developed in response to his painful experiences as a youngster in which he felt excluded, unwanted, and socially undesirable.

It may be difficult for Mr. Anders to be alone because this kindles painful feelings of loneliness and memories of times when he felt left out (Isolation Index = .35, DEPI = 6). His reactions also involve an undercurrent of anger and resentment, which color how he reacts to others ($S = 4$). There is a possibility that, at times, Mr. Anders may feel so desperate to be involved with other people that his behavior has a "driven," compulsive quality (FM = 0; $T = 2$). At these times, it may be more important for him to avoid being alone than to consider whether he is selecting an appropriate partner. This suggests some risk that others may take advantage of Mr. Anders, or that he may get involved in unrewarding relationships.

Rorschach findings correspond with Mr. Anders' description of his difficulties in many respects and identify areas to be addressed in psychotherapy. These include efforts to improve his social skills, increase his sense of self-worth while decreasing his sensitivity to feeling criticized and rejected, strengthen feelings of competence and self-confidence, and address his tendency to avoid social interactions. For instance, it would be useful for Mr. Anders to discuss specific interactions in detail to help himself understand the situation clearly, recognize different ways he could respond, and increase his awareness of how his actions affect other people. He also may find it useful to identify and examine the conflict he experiences concerning his need for contact with others, on the one hand, and his tendency to avoid or hold back in interactions, on the other. The possibility that Mr. Anders' judgment about the people with whom he becomes involved is undermined by his need to be involved also should be considered during the course of treatment.

REFERENCES

Alpert, J. E., Uebelacker, L. A., McLean, N. E., Nirenberg, A. A., et al. (1997). Social phobia, avoidant personality disorder, and atypical depression: Co-occurrence and clinical implications. *Psychological Medicine, 27,* 627–633.

American Psychiatric Association. (1980). *Diagnostic and statistical manual of mental disorders* (3rd ed.). Washington, DC: Author.

American Psychiatric Association. (1994). *Diagnostic and statistical manual of mental disorders* (4th ed.). Washington, DC: Author.

Docherty, J. P., Fiester, S. J., & Shea, T. (1986). Syndrome diagnosis and personality disorder. In A. Frances & R. Hales (Eds.), *Psychiatry update: The American Psychiatric Association annual review* (Vol. 5, pp. 315–355). Washington, DC: American Psychiatric Press.

Dyce, J. A., & O'Connor, B. P. (1998). Personality disorders and the five-factor model: A test of facet-level predictions. *Journal of Personality Disorders, 12,* 31–45.

Exner, J. E. (1993). *The Rorschach: A comprehensive system, Volume 1* (3rd ed.). New York: John Wiley.

Exner, J. E. (2003). *The Rorschach: A comprehensive system, Volume 1* (4th ed.). New York: John Wiley.

Fenichel, O. (1945). *The psychoanalytic theory of neurosis.* New York: Norton.

Frances, A. J. (1980). The DSM-III personality disorders section: A commentary. *American Journal of Psychiatry, 137,* 1050–1054.

Frances, A. J., & Widiger, T. A. (1987). A critical review of four DSM-III personality disorders: Borderline, avoidant, dependent, and passive-aggressive. In G. Tischler (Ed.), *Diagnosis and classification in psychiatry* (pp. 269–289). New York: Cambridge University Press.

Guntrip, H. (1968). *Schizoid phenomena, object relations, and the self.* New York: International Universities Press.

Huprich, S. K. (2003). A SCID-II evaluation of NEO-PI-R profiles of veterans with personality disorders. *Journal of Personality Disorders, 17,* 33–44.

Livesley, W. J., & West, M. (1986). The DSM-III distinction between schizoid and avoidant personality disorders. *American Journal of Psychiatry, 31,* 59–61.

Lochner, C., Mogotsi, M., du Toit, P. L., Kaminer, D., Niehaus, D. J., Stein, D. J. (2003). Quality of life in anxiety disorders: A comparison of obsessive compulsive disorder, social anxiety disorder, and panic disorder. *Psychopathology, 36,* 255–262.

Millon, T. (1981). *Disorders of personality: DSM-III: Axis II.* New York: John Wiley.

Millon, T. (1991). Avoidant personality disorder: A brief review of issues and data. *Journal of Personality Disorders, 5,* 353–362.

Millon, T., & Kotik, D. (1985). The relationship of depression to disorders of personality. In E. Beckham & W. Leber (Eds.), *Handbook of depression* (pp. 700–744). Homewood, IL: Dorsey Press.

Reich, J. (2001). The relationship of social phobia to avoidant personality disorder. In S. G. Hofmann & P. Dibartolo (Eds.), *From social anxiety to social phobia: Multiple perspectives* (pp. 148–161). Needham Heights, MA: Allyn & Bacon.

Reynolds, S. K., & Clark, L. A. (2001). Predicting dimensions of personality disorder from domains and facets of the Five-Factor Model. *Journal of Personality, 69,* 199–222.

Schneider, F. R., Blanco, C., Antia, S., & Liebowitz, M. R. (2002). The social anxiety spectrum. *Psychiatric Clinics of North America, 25*(4), 757–774.

Stein, M. B., Chartier, M. J., Hazen, A. L., Kozak, M. V., Tancer, M. E., Lander, S., et al. (1998). A direct-interview family study of generalized social phobia. *American Journal of Psychiatry, 155,* 90–97.

Tillfors, M., Furmark, T., Ekselius, L., & Fredrikson, M. (2001). Social phobia and avoidant personality disorder as related to parental history of social anxiety: A general population study. *Behavior Research & Therapy, 39,* 289–298.

Trull, T. J., Widiger, T. A., & Burr, R. (2001). A structured interview for the assessment of the five-factor model of personality: Facet-level relations to the Axis II personality disorders. *Journal of Personality, 69,* 175–198.

Trull, T. J., Widiger, T. A., & Frances, A. J. (1987). Covariation of avoidant, schizoid, and dependent personality disorder criteria sets. *American Journal of Psychiatry, 144,* 767–771.

Weiner, I. B. (2003). *Principles of Rorschach Interpretation* (2nd ed.). Mahwah, NJ: Lawrence Erlbaum Associates.

Widiger, A. T., Mangine, S., Corbitt, E. M., Ellis, C. G., & Thomas, G. V. (1995). *Personality Disorder Interview-IV: A semistructured interview for the assessment of personality disorders.* Odessa, FL: Psychological Assessment Resources.

Widiger, T. A., Trull, T. J., Clarkin, J. F., Sanderson, C., & Costa, P. T. (2002). A description of the DSM-IV personality disorders with the Five-Factor Model of personality. In P. T. Costa & T. A. Widiger (Eds.), *Personality disorders and the Five-Factor Model of personality.* Washington, DC: American Psychological Association.

Wilberg, T., Urnes, O., Friis, S., Pedersen, G., & Karterud, S. (1999). Borderline and avoidant personality disorders and the Five-Factor Model of personality: A comparison between DSM-IV diagnoses and NEO-PI-R. *Journal of Personality Disorders, 13,* 226–240.

RORSCHACH PROTOCOL FOR MR.ANDERS

Free Association	Inquiry

Card I

1. Uh...it looks like a bat, sort of.

1. Well, I guess this is the body. These are the wings, a tail of some kind. That's pretty much it.

2. Or three people dancing? In some weird way. That's about it.

2. Yeah. All right. That looks like her head. This one in the middle's closest to me. That looks like her dress. The line is one the separation between two legs. This is her waist, it narrows to her waist. Actually, now I see something else. (Stick with what you saw originally). O.K. These are two women or two witches on the side. These are their capes and their black witches' hats. (Capes?) Like they're flying up in the air, as if they're dancing or twirling.

Card II

3. (Long pause. Pt. shakes his head). I have no...It reminds me of some picture I've seen in a book on fractile mathematics. That's about it.

3. Yeah. I don't know. (What about the card looks like that?) This part reminds me of that. It's symmetrical. (Help me see it). It's mainly this. That's pretty much all I could make of it at the time.

Card III

4. It looks like two monkeys at some kind of a...two female monkeys. I don't know, with a butterfly in the middle. And two fetuses or embryos on the side here.

4. These are the two apes. Their heads, kind of shaped like apes. Like a leg. You can see only one leg because you're looking from the side. There's something in the middle, the butterfly. There are their arms. (Looking from the side?) Well, looking at their profiles. Like two monkeys. Can't see both legs. Because one leg covers up the other. (You mentioned a butterfly). Well, two wings. Kind of symmetrical shape to the butterfly. Then I said something about these. (You saw fetuses or embryos). Yeah. The umbilical cord here. (What about it looks like a fetus?) Well, it's attached to an umbilical cord, and it's kind of amorphous. Maybe a slight head here.

Card IV
5. It looks like a bear rug.

5. Yeah. This kind of looks like its head. And the rest of it is its body. These are its legs. Obviously doesn't look exactly like a bear. Sort of close. It looked kind of fuzzy in a way. Like fur. (Fuzzy?) The fur. The ink made it...because it's different levels of darkness, of blacks. Made it look furry.

Card V
6. It looks like a bat.

6. Well, these are its wings. And antennae, although I don't think bats have antennae. Head, legs. Although I don't know if bats have legs. Probably not. And it's black.

7. Or a butterfly. That's about all I see.

7. Yeah. The antennae. And its wings. Some kind of legs. That's pretty much it.

Card VI
8. Again it looks like a rug. The skin of some animal laid out on the floor. A rug.

8. Yeah. Well, this looks kind of furry around here. This looks like the edge of the body. This looks furry as well, although I don't know what part it would be. (What makes it look furry?) Just the way you have little...little areas that seem dark or lighter.

9. Or, maybe, like down the middle is a smooshed snake. That's it.

9. Yeah. Up here. There's two eyes. Its back bone, vertebrae. Spinal cord. (You said it was smooshed). Yeah, because it's flattened out. (And you mentioned the back bone). Looks like a white, a very thin white line goes down there. It looks like a bone of some kind, or I imagined it to be.

Card VII
10. It looks like a very abstract drawing of two girls looking at each other. And...that's it.

10. Yeah. Well, this could be a feather in their hair for decoration. Their hair is kind of put up in some kind of a bun. Their foreheads, recesses of the eyes, nose, mouth, the upper part of their bodies. I don't know what these are, maybe some rocks. (I'm not sure what you meant when you said the recesses of their eyes). Yeah. Well, the forehead goes in. It goes in. (Goes in?) It's a profile. The shape of the face in profile.

Card VIII

11. Oh, we've got some color...It looks like some rug. Some kind of animal skin rug on the floor, with two badgers on each side.

11. Yeah. Yeah. These two things look like badgers. Or two rodents of some kind. Its legs, head, tail. Only see three legs, like one is missing. (You also said an animal skin rug). There. Just that it was flat. Flat and kind of symmetrical. That's all I could see.

12. And maybe again, a lot of these looks like some kind of fractile math drawing.

12. Yeah. It just reminded me of that. Up top here. At the very top. (I'm not sure I see it). Just reminded me of some pictures I'd seen in a book. It looked kind of fuzzy but there was some kind of symmetry.

13. Or maybe a cut-out of a human body I saw last week at the museum. Kept under glass. That's about all I can see.

13. Yeah. I guess I thought of it because I was there last weekend. They have some slices of a human body put in glass. (Show me where you're looking). All over except the badger maybe. (What about the card looked the human body?) It looks -- this could be the spinal cord here. These could be various organs of the human body. (Organs?) Yeah, they do. (You said it's under glass?) No. No. Not this. That's how it was at the museum.

Card IX

14. Uh...I see some antlers coming out at the top. Maybe by some branches.

14. Right here. Just sticking out. And it's kind of whitish, light orange. Becomes kind of whitish.

15. The rest doesn't make...Wait a minute. I think I see some eyes.

15. Yeah, I see two eyes here. Looks like a rodent. Two eyes, nose, teeth. Sort of like a beaver. (I'm not sure I see that). Right here. Looks like two little nostrils. Right here. Two eyes, nose. You know how the teeth of a beaver stick out over the mouth. (Over the mouth?) Yeah. Like a beaver. The teeth kind of go outside, over the mouth.

16. Yeah. Maybe. like...yeah. Maybe like a chest and two shoulders. And that's all I can think of. Some eyes, a nose. Some sort of face of a rodent of some kind. A beaver.

16. Yeah. Look in here. A human. One shoulder, the other shoulder. The chest and maybe the neck of a person. It's kind of rounded. Kind of muscular, looks like here's a concentration of color. Here its white, one indicating a space, a light between the arm and body. Like bright sunlight. (A concentration of color?) It's pink. In the pink, the color is concentrated. (You said the pink looks muscular). It reminds me of pictures I've seen in books. The way the shoulders are round it looks like a man with strong shoulders.

Card X

17. Looks like a spider of some kind.

17. Yeah. Two spider-like animals here. I guess spiders have eight legs. Don't know if they do, but something along that line.

18. I see two eyes, a mustache, a nose.

18. Here are the two eyes, a nose, a mustache here. It curls at the end, like people wore at one time. (You said it curls at the end?) Like the way people wore it at one time. (What about the card looks like that?) Here. (Points). Goes down and comes up.

19. Maybe another set of eyes. The shape of a head with a helmet on.

19. Up here. (I'm not sure I see it). I don't know. The way the eyes are positioned relative to the helmet on a head. The dark concentration here. That looks like a helmet. Shaped like in those samurai movies.

20. Two little creatures talking to each other. I don't know what they are. These creatures here. And that's it.

20. Yeah. On top. Looks like two little creatures. These are the eyes here. They have some kind of arms, legs, tails. (You said they're talking to each other?) Yeah, or communing. Something like that.

RORSCHACH SEQUENCE OF SCORES FOR MR. ANDERS

Card	Resp	Loc (DQ)	Loc No	Determinants (FQ)	(2)	Content(s)	P	Z	Special Scores
I	1.	Wo	1	Fo		A	P	1.0	
	2.	W+	1	Ma.FY.ma.FC'+	(2)	H,(H),Cg		4.0	COP,GHR
II	3.	Dv	4	F-		Art			PER
III	4.	Wo	1	FDo	(2)	A, An		5.5	FAB
IV	5.	Wo	1	FTo		Ad		2.0	MOR
V	6.	Wo	1	FC'o		A	P	1.0	DR
	7.	Wo	1	Fo		A	P	1.0	
VI	8.	Wo	1	FTo		Ad	P	2.5	
	9.	Do	5	FC'o		A			MOR
VII	10.	D+	2	Mpo	(2)	Art, Hd, Ls	P	3.0	GHR
VIII	11.	W+	1	Fu	(2)	A, Ad, Bt	P	4.5	MOR
	12.	Ddv	24	F-		Art, Na			PER
	13.	Do	6	Fu		An, Art			PER
IX	14.	Ddo	34	FYu		Ad, Bt			DV
	15.	DdSo	99	FDu		Ad		5.0	
	16.	DSo	6	FY.FC'.FCu		Hd, Art, Na		5.0	PER,PHR
X	17.	Do	1	Fo	(2)	A	P		
	18.	DSo	2	Fu		Hd, Ay			PHR
	19.	DdS+	22	FY-		Hd, Cg, Ay		4.5	PHR
	20.	D+	8	Mpo	(2)	(A)		4.0	GHR

STRUCTURAL SUMMARY FOR MR. ANDERS

Location Features	Determinants	Contents	Approach
	Blends		

Location Features

Zf = 13
ZSum = 43.0
Zest = 41.5

W = 8
D = 8
W+D = 16
Dd = 4
S = 4

Developmental Quality
+ = 5
o = 13
v = 0
v/+ = 2

Form Quality

	FQx	MQual	W+D
+	= 1	= 1	= 1
o	= 10	= 2	= 10
u	= 6	= 0	= 4
-	= 3	= 0	= 1
none	= 0	= 0	= 0

Determinants

Blends
M.FY.m.FC'
FY.FC'.FC

Single
M = 2
FM = 0
m = 0
FC = 0
CF = 0
C = 0
Cn = 0
FC' = 2
C'F = 0
C' = 0
FT = 2
TF = 0
T = 0
FV = 0
VF = 0
V = 0
FY = 2
YF = 0
Y = 0
Fr = 0
rF = 0
FD = 2
F = 8
(2) = 6

Contents

H = 1
(H) = 1
Hd = 4
(Hd) = 0
Hx = 0
A = 7
(A) = 1
Ad = 6
(Ad) = 0
An = 2
Art = 5
Ay = 2
Bl = 0
Bt = 2
Cg = 2
Cl = 0
Ex = 0
Fd = 0
Fi = 0
Ge = 0
Hh = 0
Ls = 1
Na = 2
Sc = 0
Sx = 0
Xy = 0
Id = 0

Approach

I: W.W
II: D
III: W
IV: W
V: W.W
VI: W.D
VII: D
VIII: W.Dd.D
IX: Dd.DdS.DS
X: D.DS.DdS.D

Special Scores

	Lv 1	Lv 2
DV =	0x1	= 0x2
INC =	0x2	= 0x4
DR =	1x3	= 0x6
FAB =	1x4	= 0x7
ALOG =	0x5	
CON =	0x7	

Raw Sum 6 = 2
Wgtd Sum 6 = 7

AB = 0   GHR = 3
AG = 0   PHR = 3
COP = 1 MOR = 3
CP = 0   PER = 4
         PSV = 0

Rorschach Assessment
of Dependent Personality Disorder

Robert F. Bornstein
Gettysburg College

During the past 50 years, there have been more than 600 published studies of trait dependency and dependent personality disorder (DPD). Research in both areas has been—and continues to be—strongly influenced by psychoanalytic theory, particularly object relations models of personality and psychopathology (Bornstein, 1993, 2005). Despite their shared psychodynamic roots, however, the constructs of trait dependency and DPD have diverged somewhat in recent years. Contemporary research on trait dependency has focused on the variability in dependent behavior across different situations and settings (Pincus & Wilson, 2001), and on identifying adaptive and maladaptive features of dependent personality traits (Bornstein & Languirand, 2003). Research on DPD has taken a very different route, with most studies in this area assessing the comorbidity of DPD with other Axis I and Axis II disorders or the moderating effects of DPD on psychotherapy process and outcome (Bornstein, 1997).

As trait dependency and DPD evolve in response to accumulating research findings and changes in the diagnostic nomenclature, techniques for assessing these constructs are evolving as well. This chapter discusses the Rorschach Inkblot Method (RIM) for assessment of the dependent personality, drawing upon studies of trait dependency and DPD. The discussion begins with a description of the convergences and divergences between these two constructs. The discussion then moves to RIM assessment of the dependent personality, with a primary focus on the most well-established, widely used RIM dependency test: the Rorschach Oral Dependency (ROD) scale (Masling, Rabie & Blondheim, 1967). After a review of evidence regarding the validity and utility of the ROD scale, strategies for the effective use of ROD data in clinical and research settings are outlined, and suggestions are offered for future work in this area.

TRAIT DEPENDENCY AND DPD: CONVERGENCES AND DIVERGENCES

Contemporary conceptualizations of trait dependency emphasize four core components (Bornstein, 1996a; Pincus & Gurtman, 1995): (a) cognitive (i.e., a perception of oneself as weak and ineffectual, coupled with the belief that others are powerful and potent), (b) motivational (i.e., a marked need for guidance, support, and reassurance from others), (c) behavioral (i.e., use of relationship-facilitating self-presentation strategies to strengthen ties to potential caregivers), and (d) emotional (e.g., fear of abandonment, performance anxiety). Studies suggest that cognitive structures (i.e., self and object representations) are a key element in the dependent personality, and that they play a central role in shaping dependency-related motivations, behaviors, and affective responses (see Bornstein, 1996a, for a discussion of this issue).

Unlike contemporary models of trait dependency, the *Diagnostic and Statistical Manual of Mental Disorders*, 4th Edition, Text Revision (DSM-IV-TR) DPD criteria (American Psychiatric Association [APA], 2000) emphasize dependency-related behavior and emotion, with no attention given to the cognitive underpinnings of dependent personality traits. Moreover, within the behavioral realm the DPD, symptom criteria focus almost exclusively on submissiveness and passivity, with minimal reference to the possibility of significant behavioral variation across context or situation. Thus, the core symptoms of DPD in the DSM-IV-TR include difficulty making decisions (symptom 1), expressing disagreement (symptom 3), and initiating projects and activities (symptom 4); needing others to assume responsibility for most areas of life (symptom 2), while going to great lengths to obtain nurturance and support (symptoms 5 and 7); and feeling uncomfortable when alone (symptom 6), yet preoccupied with fears of abandonment (symptom 8).

In summarizing the convergences and divergences between trait dependency and DPD, Bornstein (2005) noted that, although both constructs capture the fundamental need for nurturance and support that is central to a dependent personality orientation, trait dependency and DPD differ in four domains:

Intensity. Persons with DPD experience needs for nurturance and support that are stronger than those experienced by persons with subsyndromal levels of trait dependency.

Pervasiveness. In DPD, maladaptive dependency-related behavior is expressed indiscriminately across contexts and settings; trait dependency tends to be exhibited more prominently in some contexts than others.

Rigidity. Individuals with trait dependency are able to adapt their self-presentation strategies to fit current situational demands, whereas those with DPD have a more rigid (i.e., less flexible) coping style.

Dysfunction. Because of these intensity, pervasiveness, and flexibility differences, DPD tends to be associated with greater dysfunction and impairment than trait dependency.

RORSCHACH ASSESSMENT
OF THE DEPENDENT PERSONALITY

Although several variables in Exner's (1993, 2000) Comprehensive System (CS) are theoretically related to dependency (e.g., food, texture, passive human movement), no published studies have provided data linking these variables with observable indices of dependent behavior. The vast majority of studies in this area have examined relationships between ROD scores and various self-report, projective, and behavioral measures of dependency (Bornstein, 1996b, 1998b, 1999). The following sections discuss administration, scoring, and interpretation of the ROD scale; construct validity findings; ROD studies of trait dependency and DPD; and the links between ROD scores and CS variables.

RORSCHACH ORAL DEPENDENCY SCALE:
ADMINISTRATION, SCORING, AND INTERPRETATION

The ROD scale, borrowed almost entirely from Schafer's (1954) speculations regarding oral dependent content in RIM responses, was initially developed by Masling et al. (1967). A key strength of the ROD scale is the simplicity of its scoring and interpretation procedures. Because these procedures are highly standardized, clinicians and researchers can obtain useable ROD data with minimal training.

Rorschach Oral Dependency scores may be derived from existing (i.e., archival) RIM protocols, from individually administered RIM protocols collected in the standard manner, or from data collected using a group Rorschach administration (see Bornstein, 1996b, for detailed instructions regarding group ROD administration). When data are collected in groups, only Free Associations are used (there is no Inquiry in the group administration). When data are collected individually, ROD scores are derived pri-

BORNSTEIN

marily, although not exclusively, from material in the Free Association. Any oral dependent percept that emerges in the Free Association portion of the protocol is scored automatically, but Inquiry data are used to clarify Free Association information that is ambiguous with respect to ROD scoring. In other words, oral-dependent content that first emerges in the Inquiry is not scored, but when information in the Inquiry makes it clear that an ambiguous Free Association (e.g., "a pot") does in fact fit one of the ROD categories (e.g., when the respondent elaborates, "yes, a pot—they're using it to cook"), the original response is scored as oral dependent.

Regardless whether RIM data are collected individually or in groups, ROD scoring is based on a lexical strategy, and participants receive one point for each response that contains one or more percepts from the categories in Table 11.1. The number of responses containing at least one oral-dependent percept is divided by the total number of responses (i.e., R) to control for variations in response productivity.

To date, most ROD investigations involving nonclinical participants have used the group administration, whereas most investigations involving psychiatric inpatients and outpatients have used individually administered RIM protocols. To ascertain that ROD data collected using these two methods yield comparable results, Bornstein, Bonner, Kildow, and McCall (1997) compared the means and distributions of ROD scores collected individually and in groups. In two separate studies using different experimental designs, Bornstein et al. (1997) found that individual and group ROD administrations yielded comparable means and standard deviations. Skewness, kurtosis, and heteroscedasticity values confirmed that in both studies, individual and group ROD score distributions were highly similar.

Bornstein and Masling (2005) used meta-analytic techniques to pool the results of extant studies and derive clinical and nonclinical norms for the ROD scale. The mean proportion of oral-dependent imagery in studies of college students (N of independent samples = 21) was .13, with women and men producing identical ROD means in these investigations. The mean proportion of oral-dependent responses produced by psychiatric patients (N of independent samples = 11) was .11, with men ($M = .12$) producing slightly higher ROD scores than women ($M = .10$).

Typically, ROD scores range from .00 to about .40, and no firm cutoffs for identifying dependent and nondependent participants have been delineated for use in clinical and research settings. Researchers have used various strategies to identify dependent and nondependent participants (see Masling, Weiss, & Rothschild, 1968; Sprohge, Handler, Plant & Wicker, 2002, for examples). Some researchers use a simple mean or median split to select dependent and nondependent groups, whereas others include only the extreme high and low scorers (e.g., the highest and lowest 20%). Many clinicians and researchers use a dimensional approach, examining correla-

TABLE 11.1

**Categories of Scoreable Responses on the Rorschach
Oral Dependency (ROD) Scale**

Category	Sample Responses
1. Foods and drinks	Milk, whiskey, boiled lobster
2. Food sources	Restaurant, saloon, breast
3. Food objects	Kettle, silverware, drinking glass
4. Food providers	Waiter, cook, bartender
5. Passive food receivers	Bird in nest, fat or thin man
6. Begging and praying	Dog begging, person saying prayers
7. Food organs	Mouth, stomach, lips, teeth
8. Oral instruments	Lipstick, cigarette, tuba
9. Nurturers	Jesus, mother, father, doctor, God
10. Gifts and gift-givers	Christmas tree, cornucopia
11. Good luck objects	Wishbone, four-leaf clover
12. Oral activity	Eating, talking, singing, kissing
13. Passivity and helplessness	Confused person, lost person
14. Pregnancy and reproductive organs	Placenta, womb, ovaries, embryo
15. "Baby-talk" responses	Patty-cake, bunny rabbit, pussy cat
16. Negations of oral dependent percepts	No mouth, woman with no breasts

Note. In category 1, animals are scored only if they are invariably associated with eating (e.g., do not score *duck* or *turkey* unless food-descriptive phrases are used, such as *roast duck* or *turkey leg*). In category 3, *pot* and *cauldron* are scored only if the act of cooking is implied. In category 13, *baby* is scored only if there is some suggestion of passivity or frailness. In category 14, *pelvis*, *penis*, *vagina*, and *sex organs* are not scored. Originally published as Table 1 in R. F. Bornstein (1996), "Construct Validity of the Rorschach Oral Dependency Scale: 1967–1995" (*Psychological Assessment, 8*, 200–205). Reprinted by permission.

tions between ROD scores and scores on theoretically related measures (e.g., Duberstein & Talbot, 1993).

In using ROD scores to identify discrete groups of dependent and nondependent participants, it is important to use separate gender-based mean or median scores. Although the sample sizes in most studies are not sufficient to produce statistically significant gender differences, men do tend to obtain slightly higher ROD scores than women. These gender differences are small in magnitude, but the mean difference across clinical samples (.10 for women vs. .12 for men) actually represents a 20% shift in ROD score across gender. Thus, when Bornstein (1995) used meta-analytic techniques to synthesize all extant findings regarding gender differences in ROD scores, he found a modest but statistically significant effect size, with men obtaining higher ROD scores than women ($d = .17$; combined $z = 2.08$; $p < .02$).

CONSTRUCT VALIDITY OF THE ROD SCALE

Dozens of investigations have examined the construct validity of the ROD scale. The following sections summarize the findings regarding interrater, retest, and internal reliability, then discuss discriminant and convergent validity results.

Interrater Reliability

Interrater reliability in ROD scoring is uniformly excellent. When two raters unaware of each other's judgments independently score a set of ROD protocols, they typically agree on the scoring of 85 to 95% of percepts (Bornstein, Manning, Krukonis, Rossner & Mastrosimone, 1993; Weiss & Masling, 1970). Pearson correlation coefficients between the two sets of ratings usually exceed .90, regardless of whether data were collected from clinical or nonclinical participants (Gordon & Tegtemeyer, 1983; Juni, Masling & Brannon, 1979). When researchers calculate ROD reliability using Spitzer, Cohen, Fliess, and Endicott's (1967) kappa coefficient, which corrects for inflated reliability estimates that result from low score base rates, reliabilities greater than .80 usually are obtained (Duberstein & Talbot, 1993; O'Neill & Bornstein, 1990). Kappa coefficients in this range are acceptable for any psychological test, and are particularly high for a projective rating scale (Nunnally & Bernstein, 1994).

Retest Reliability

Only one study has assessed the retest reliability of ROD scores. Bornstein, Rossner, and Hill (1994) collected ROD protocols from a mixed-sex sample of college students on two separate occasions, with one third of the participants retested after 16 weeks, one third retested after 28 weeks, and the rest retested after 60 weeks. Comparable retest reliability coefficients were obtained for women and men in this study, with retest reliability (r) found to be .67 at 16 weeks, .48 at 28 weeks, and .46 at 60 weeks.

Internal Reliability

Two approaches have been used to assess the internal reliability of ROD scores. Bornstein, Hill, Robinson, Calabrese, and Bowers (1996) calculated coefficient alpha by collecting ROD scores from a large, mixed-sex sample of college students, then treating each Rorschach card as a single test item that could contribute to the total ROD score (Parker, 1983). This approach yielded ROD coefficient alphas of .61 for women and .62 for men.

Other investigations have assessed the relationship between the amount of oral (i.e., food- and mouth-related) and dependent imagery in participants' ROD protocols. These studies produced mixed results. One investigation (Bornstein et al., 1993) found significant, positive correlations between ROD dependency and orality scores in men ($r = .44$), and women ($r = .35$). However, two similar studies (Bornstein & Greenberg, 1991; Shilkret & Masling, 1981) found nonsignificant correlations between orality and dependency scores ($r = .01$ in the Bornstein and Greenberg study, and $r = -.06$ in the Shilkret and Masling study). When the correlation coefficients from these three studies are combined, the overall correlation between ROD orality and dependency scores is modest ($r = .10$).

Discriminant Validity

As is true for most psychological tests, researchers have devoted far more attention to convergent validity issues than to issues regarding the discriminant validity of the ROD scale (Bornstein, 1996b). However, several noteworthy findings have emerged in recent years. Gordon and Tegtemeyer (1983) and Bornstein and O'Neill (1997) found that ROD scores were unrelated to IQ scores in children and adults. Bornstein et al. (1994) found that ROD scores were unaffected by the number and severity of stressful life events experienced by participants during 16-, 28-, and 60-week intertest intervals. Bornstein, Rossner, Hill, and Stepanian (1994) found that ROD scores were unaffected by instructional manipulations in which participants were encouraged to present themselves as highly dependent or independent. These results suggest that the ROD scale is relatively immune from self-presentation effects. Finally, Bornstein, Bowers, and Bonner (1996) reported that ROD scores were unrelated to self-report masculinity and femininity scores.

Convergent Validity: Trait Dependency

Bornstein (1999) used meta-analytic techniques to assess the relationship between ROD scores and observable, measurable dependent behavior in all published studies in this area (N of independent samples $= 21$). Dependency-related behaviors in these investigations included suggestibility, social help-seeking, medical help-seeking, and perseverance in experimental tasks. Bornstein (1999) found an overall validity coefficient (r) of .37 (combined $Z = 8.49$; $p < .001$), which suggests that the ROD-dependent behavior link is robust and reliable. This criterion-referenced validity coefficient was larger than that obtained for every self-report dependency test except Beck, Epstein, Harrison, and Emery's (1983) Sociotropy-Autonomy Scale (for which $r = .46$).

Additional information regarding the convergent validity of the ROD scale may be found in Table 11.2, which summarizes the empirically established clinical correlates of ROD scores. As Table 11.2 shows, high ROD scores are associated with increased likelihood of eating disorders, alcohol abuse/dependence, depression, borderline personality disorder, and internalizing disorders in children. High ROD scores also are associated with an array of clinically relevant help- and support-seeking behaviors, with sensitivity to subtle interpersonal cues emitted by therapists, and with increased length of hospital stay (see Bornstein [1996b, 1999], and Bornstein and Masling [2005] for detailed descriptions of these studies).

Convergent Validity: DPD

Two studies have assessed the relationships between ROD scores and DPD symptoms or diagnoses. Bornstein (1998a) administered the ROD scale and the Personality Diagnostic Questionnaire—Revised (PDQ-R; Hyler et al.,

TABLE 11.2
Empirically Established Correlates of Rorschach
Oral Dependency (ROD) Scores in Clinical Participants

Clinical Correlate	Population	Magnitude (r)
Eating disorders	Inpatients–Outpatients	.23–.28
Alcohol abuse/dependence	Inpatients–Outpatients	.18–.58
Depression	Inpatients–Outpatients	.08–.50
Borderline personality disorder	Inpatients	.19
Internalizing disorders in children	Outpatients	.30
Help-seeking response set on the MMPI (i.e., high F and low K)	Inpatients	.29
Number of medical consultations	Inpatients	.51
Number of medication prescriptions	Inpatients	.25
Ability to infer therapist's attitudes and personal beliefs	Outpatients	.32
Length of hospital stay	Inpatients	.46

MMPI, Minnesota Multiphasic Personality Inventory

Note. Detailed descriptions of these studies along with references are provided by Bornstein (1996b, 1999), and Bornstein and Masling (2005). All statistics have been converted to correlation coefficients representing the magnitude of the relationship between ROD scores and outcome variables. For those cases in which multiple studies assessed an ROD–clinical correlate link, the range of correlation coefficients is provided.

1988) to a large, mixed-sex sample of college students, and found significant, positive correlations between ROD scores and PDQ-R scores in women (r = .30) and men (r = .35). When Bornstein (1998a) compared the mean ROD scores among participants who scored above the PDQ-R threshold for DPD, participants who scored above the threshold for one or more other personality disorders (PDs), and participants who did not score above any PD threshold, he found that DPD participants obtained significantly higher ROD scores (M = .16) than participants with other PDs (M = .12), or no PD (M = .09). The only other PD associated with elevated ROD scores was histrionic (M = .16).

In a follow-up study of 60 psychiatric inpatients and 58 outpatients, Bornstein, Hilsenroth, Padawer, and Fowler (2000) compared mean ROD scores across an array of PD groups. They found that inpatients with borderline PD (M = .27) obtained significantly higher ROD scores than participants in any other PD group, including borderline PD outpatients (M = .11) and a mixed group of dependent and avoidant PD outpatients (M = .20). Inpatients with psychotic disorders obtained a mean ROD score of .19, whereas the mean for narcissistic PD outpatients was .20, and that for antisocial PD outpatients was .12.

Convergent Validity: ROD-Comprehensive System Links

Only one investigation has assessed the links between ROD scores and CS variables theoretically related to dependency. Huprich, O'Neill, Bornstein, Kusaj, and Smith (2003) selected matched groups of 12 dependent and 12 nondependent psychiatric patients from a large heterogeneous sample on the basis of their ROD scores and compared these patients on 14 variables from Exner's (1993, 2000) Interpersonal Cluster (IC). Three IC variables (cooperative movement responses, M with pairs, and poor human responses) reliably distinguished dependent from nondependent patients. When Huprich et al. (2003) pooled all 14 effect sizes using meta-analytic techniques, they found an overall ROD–IC effect size (r) of .32.

Huprich et al.'s (2003) results are noteworthy in at least two respects. First, they suggest that dependent and nondependent patients do in fact differ on several theoretically related CS variables. Second, they indicate that although ROD scores covary to some degree with dependency-related CS scores, these two indices are in fact tapping distinct facets of personality and interpersonal functioning. Most of the variance in ROD scores is not accounted for by CS IC scores.

EFFECTIVE USE OF ROD DATA IN CLINICAL AND RESEARCH SETTINGS

When Bornstein (2002) used meta-analytic techniques to examine the relationship between ROD scores and scores on self-report measures of de-

pendency (N of independent samples = 11), he found that the mean
ROD–self-report test score correlation (r) was .29, with women (r = .30)
producing somewhat higher intertest intercorrelations than men (r = .24).
Clearly, RIM and self-report dependency scores assess different features of
dependency. Drawing from McClelland, Koestner, and Weinberger's
(1989) framework, Bornstein (2002) interpreted these findings to suggest
that ROD scores assess implicit (i.e., unconscious) dependency needs,
whereas self-report scores tap self-attributed dependency needs (i.e., dependency needs that a person acknowledges openly when asked).

The modest relationships between ROD and self-report dependency
scores suggest that clinicians and researchers can gain additional insight regarding patient functioning by combining and contrasting these scores.
Figure 11.1 presents a framework within which these scores may be integrated to yield unique information regarding an individual's underlying
and expressed dependency needs. As shown in the upper right and lower
left quadrants of Fig. 11.1, it is possible for a person to score high or low on
both measures, indicating convergence between the person's self-attributed and implicit dependency scores. The other two cells in Fig. 11.1 illustrate discontinuities between implicit and self-attributed dependency
needs. In one case (i.e., high projective dependency score coupled with low

SCORE ON OBJECTIVE DEPENDENCY TEST

		LOW	HIGH
SCORE ON PROJECTIVE DEPENDENCY TEST	**LOW**	Low Implicit Low Self-Attributed **Low Dependency**	Low Implicit High Self-Attributed **Dependent Self-Presentation**
	HIGH	High Implicit Low Self-Attributed **Unacknowledged Dependency**	High Implicit High Self-Attributed **High Dependency**

FIG. 11.1. Continuities and discontinuities between implicit and self-attributed
need states: A four-cell model. Originally published as Fig. 1 in R. F. Bornstein,
"Implicit and self-attributed dependency needs: Differential relationships to laboratory and field measures of help seeking" (*Journal of Personality and Social Psychology, 75,* 778–787). Reprinted by permission.

self-report dependency score), a person has high levels of implicit dependency needs, but does not acknowledge them. This person may be described as having unacknowledged dependency strivings. In the other case (i.e., low projective dependency score coupled with high self-report dependency score), the person has low levels of implicit dependency needs, but presents him- or herself as highly dependent. This individual may be described as having a dependent self-presentation.

As Bornstein (2002) noted, exploration of these test score discontinuities can reveal important information regarding an individual's personality structure and interpersonal style. For example, in Bornstein's (1998a) investigation (described earlier), college students with significant DPD symptoms obtained high scores on both the ROD scale and a widely used self-report measure of dependency, the Interpersonal Dependency Inventory (IDI; Hirschfeld et al., 1977). The students with significant histrionic PD symptoms, in contrast, obtained high ROD scores and low IDI scores. Using the four-cell model in Fig. 11.1, DPD students would be described as having high dependency, whereas histrionic PD students would be in the unacknowledged dependency quadrant.

CASE EXAMPLE

RIM Free Association and Inquiry data are presented from a 46-year-old female outpatient with a diagnosis of DPD. This patient met DPD criteria 3, 5, 6, 7, 8, and 9, and received comorbid diagnoses of major depressive disorder on Axis I, and narcissistic and borderline PDs on Axis II. Ms. Dixon was seen in weekly psychodynamic psychotherapy for 1 year, with mutually agreed-upon termination after remission of her depressive symptoms and significant improvement in interpersonal functioning. Because this patient was included in Hilsenroth, Fowler, and Padawer's (1997) clinical sample, information regarding diagnosis, psychological test administration, and scoring reliability is available in their article.

Of the 15 RIM percepts in Ms. Dixon's protocol, 6 (40%) were scored for ROD content. Her responses are highlighted in boldface, in both the Free Association and the Inquiry portions of the protocol (if inquiry data were used to assign a score). The ROD categories into which these responses were classified are as follows: response I/2—Food Organs (category 7), response II/3—Passivity and Helplessness (category 13), response III/5—Passivity and Helplessness (category 13), response VI/8—Food Organs (category 7), response VII/10—Good Luck Objects (category 11), and response IX/13—Oral Activity (category 12).

This protocol illustrates the types of responses that characterize different ROD subcategories, and the way that inquiry data may be used to clarify ambiguous free association data. In three of six oral dependent percepts (I/2, VI/8, and IX/13), oral-dependent content in the Free Association could be ascertained only via elaboration of the initial percept in the Inquiry portion of the protocol. Had these percepts not emerged initially in the Free Association, however, material in the Inquiry would not have resulted in ROD scores.

This protocol also is useful in illustrating responses that ought not be classified as oral dependent. For example, response IV/6 ("floppy-eared dog"), although unusual, does not meet the threshold for ROD category 15 (Baby-Talk Responses). Similarly, response X/15 ("the blue part with tails could be fish") does not qualify as oral dependent. Had Ms. Dixon described these fish as food in the inquiry, the response would have been coded in category 1 (Foods and Drinks). However, she elaborated the response as "a blue lobster on each side" rather than "a *steamed* blue lobster on each side." The latter response would have received a ROD score.

Several aspects of the Structural Summary data are noteworthy. First, despite the relatively small number of percepts, this patient produced two texture (T) responses, indicating the presence of strong underlying dependency needs. Both T responses occurred in percepts with vague developmental quality, and one (response II/3) occurred in conjunction with a morbid special score (MOR). These patterns suggest that this patient's underlying dependency strivings are coupled with strong negative affect, and with negative attitudes regarding body image and integrity. The patient's Depression Index score of 5 is consistent with her comorbid diagnosis of major depressive disorder.

It also is worth contrasting this protocol with the patterns described by Huprich et al. (2003) in their analysis of ROD–CS relationships. Consistent with the findings of Huprich et al., this patient's sole M response (response III/5) co-occurred with COP, and with a positive ROD score. Moreover, this response was classified into the ROD subcategory of Passivity and Helplessness. Although the number of cooperative movement responses, M with pairs, and poor human responses in this patient's protocol are not especially high, given that this protocol was quite brief, they are noteworthy.

The findings of Bornstein (1998a) and Bornstein et al. (2000) confirm that the ROD scale can be used to refine psychiatric diagnoses and increase diagnostic accuracy by differentiating ostensibly similar syndromes. However, as several researchers have noted, the RIM by itself is not a diagnostic tool, and should not be used to derive DSM diagnoses without other converging data (see Bornstein, 2001, and Weiner, 2000, for discussions of this issue). These limitations hold true for the ROD scale as well: It is useful for assessing dependency—but not for diagnosing DPD—in clinical and non-clinical participants.

Perhaps the best use of the ROD scale in inpatient and outpatient settings is for assistance in making clinical decisions regarding dependency-related behaviors. As the studies in Table 11.2 indicate, ROD scores can help predict consultation frequency, psychotropic medication use, treatment length, and other salient clinical variables. Because many behaviors predicted by the ROD scale influence treatment efficacy, duration, and cost, administration of this scale may be especially important in the current health care environment.

At present, the ROD scale is the RIM index of choice for assessment of dependency. However, several CS variables have potential utility in this area (Huprich et al., 2003), and continued research is needed to assess which of these CS indices, or CS score combinations, may be most effective in assessing dependency-related traits in clinical and nonclinical populations. Moreover, because the majority of ROD studies to date have assessed trait dependency rather than DPD, additional research is needed to ascertain the degree to which ROD scores and DPD symptoms covary in different populations and settings.

Without question, effective use of ROD data in clinical and research settings requires that these data be integrated with data derived from self-report dependency tests and diagnostic interviews (see Meyer, 1997, for a related discussion). Hirschfeld et al.'s (1977) IDI may be particularly useful in this regard because adequate inpatient and outpatient norms for the IDI scale are available, and numerous investigations have examined the convergences and divergences of ROD and IDI scores (see Bornstein, 2005, for a review). As findings continue to accumulate, IDI and ROD scores may prove useful in making other clinically relevant predictions (e.g., suicidality; Bornstein & O'Neill, 2000). Continued research on the clinical correlates of implicit and self-attributed dependency scores also may lead to improved DPD diagnostic criteria in future versions of the DSM.

REFERENCES

American Psychiatric Association. (2000). *Diagnostic and statistical manual of mental disorders* (4th ed., Text Revision). Washington, DC: Author.

Beck, A. T., Epstein, N., Harrison, R. P., & Emery, G. (1983). *Development of the Sociotropy-Autonomy Scale: A measure of personality factors in psychopathology.* Unpublished manuscript, University of Pennsylvania School of Medicine, Philadelphia.

Bornstein, R. F. (1993). *The dependent personality.* New York: Guilford.

Bornstein, R. F. (1995). Sex differences in objective and projective dependency tests: A meta-analytic review. *Assessment, 2,* 319–331.

Bornstein, R. F. (1996a). Beyond orality: Toward an object relations/interactionist reconceptualization of the etiology and dynamics of dependency. *Psychoanalytic Psychology, 13,* 177–203.

Bornstein, R. F. (1996b). Construct validity of the Rorschach Oral Dependency Scale: 1967–1995. *Psychological Assessment, 8,* 200–205.

Bornstein, R. F. (1997). Dependent personality disorder in the DSM-IV and beyond. *Clinical Psychology: Science and Practice, 4,* 175–187.

Bornstein, R. F. (1998a). Implicit and self-attributed dependency needs in dependent and histrionic personality disorders. *Journal of Personality Assessment, 71,* 1–14.

Bornstein, R. F. (1998b). Implicit and self-attributed dependency strivings: Differential relationships to laboratory and field measures of help-seeking. *Journal of Personality and Social Psychology, 75,* 778–787.

Bornstein, R. F. (1999). Criterion validity of objective and projective dependency tests: A meta-analytic assessment of behavioral prediction. *Psychological Assessment, 11,* 48–57.

Bornstein, R. F. (2001). Clinical utility of the Rorschach Inkblot Method: Reframing the debate. *Journal of Personality Assessment, 77,* 39–47.

Bornstein, R. F. (2002). A process dissociation approach to objective–projective test score interrelationships. *Journal of Personality Assessment, 78,* 47–68.

Bornstein, R. F. (2005). *The dependent patient: A practitioner's guide.* Washington, DC: American Psychological Association.

Bornstein, R. F., Bonner, S., Kildow, A. M., & McCall, C. A. (1997). Effects of individual versus group test administration on Rorschach Oral Dependency scores. *Journal of Personality Assessment, 69,* 215–228.

Bornstein, R. F., Bowers, K. S., & Bonner, S. (1996). Relationships of objective and projective dependency scores to sex role orientation in college student subjects. *Journal of Personality Assessment, 66,* 555–568.

Bornstein, R. F., & Greenberg, R. P. (1991). Dependency and eating disorders in female psychiatric inpatients. *Journal of Nervous and Mental Disease, 179,* 148–152.

Bornstein, R. F., Hill, E. L., Robinson, K. J., Calabrese, C., & Bowers, K. S. (1996). Internal reliability of Rorschach Oral Dependency Scale scores. *Educational and Psychological Measurement, 56,* 145–153.

Bornstein, R. F., Hilsenroth, M. J., Padawer, J. R., & Fowler, J. C. (2000). Interpersonal dependency and personality pathology: Variations in Rorschach Oral Dependency scores across Axis II diagnoses. *Journal of Personality Assessment, 75,* 478–491.

Bornstein, R. F., & Languirand, M. A. (2003). *Healthy dependency.* New York: Newmarket Press.

Bornstein, R. F., Manning, K. A., Krukonis, A. B., Rossner, S. C., & Mastrosimone, C. C. (1993). Sex differences in dependency: A comparison of objective and projective measures. *Journal of Personality Assessment, 61,* 169–181.

Bornstein, R. F., & Masling, J. M. (2005). The Rorschach Oral Dependency Scale. In R. F. Bornstein & J. M. Masling (Eds.), *Scoring the Rorschach: Seven validated systems.* Mahwah, NJ: Lawrence Erlbaum Associates.

Bornstein, R. F., & O'Neill, R. M. (1997). Construct validity of the Rorschach Oral Dependency (ROD) scale: Relationship of ROD scores to WAIS-R scores in a psychiatric inpatient sample. *Journal of Clinical Psychology, 53,* 99–105.

Bornstein, R. F., & O'Neill, R. M. (2000). Dependency and suicidality in psychiatric inpatients. *Journal of Clinical Psychology, 56,* 463–473.

Bornstein, R. F., Rossner, S. C., & Hill, E. L. (1994). Retest reliability of scores on objective and projective measures of dependency: Relationship to life events and intertest interval. *Journal of Personality Assessment, 62,* 398–415.

Bornstein, R. F., Rossner, S. C., Hill, E. L., & Stepanian, M. L. (1994). Face validity and fakability of objective and projective measures of dependency. *Journal of Personality Assessment, 63,* 363–386.

Duberstein, P. R., & Talbot, N. L. (1993). Rorschach oral imagery, attachment style and interpersonal relatedness. *Journal of Personality Assessment, 61,* 294–310.

Exner, J. E. (1993). *The Rorschach: A comprehensive system: Volume 1. Basic foundations* (3rd ed.). New York: John Wiley.

Exner, J. E. (2000). *A primer for Rorschach interpretation.* Asheville, NC: Rorschach Workshops.

Gordon, M., & Tegtemeyer, P. F. (1983). Oral-dependent content in children's Rorschach protocols. *Perceptual and Motor Skills, 57,* 1163–1168.

Hilsenroth, M. J., Fowler, J. C., & Padawer, J. R. (1997). Narcissism in the Rorschach revisited: Some reflections on empirical data. *Psychological Assessment, 9,* 113–121.

Hirschfeld, R. M. A., Klerman, G. L., Gough, H. G., Barrett, J., Korchin, S. J., & Chodoff, P. (1977). A measure of interpersonal dependency. *Journal of Personality Assessment, 41,* 610–618.

Huprich, S. K., O'Neill, R. M., Bornstein, R. F., Kusaj, C., & Smith, P. Q. (2003). Rorschach Interpersonal Cluster variables distinguish dependent from nondependent patients. *Individual Differences Research, 1,* 64–72.

Hyler, S. E., Rieder, R. O., Williams, J. B. W., Spitzer, R. L., Hendler, J., & Lyons, M. (1988). The Personality Diagnostic Questionnaire. *Journal of Personality Disorders, 2,* 229–237.

Juni, S., Masling, J. M., & Brannon, R. (1979). Interpersonal touching and orality. *Journal of Personality Assessment, 43,* 235–237.

Masling, J. M., Rabie, L., & Blondheim, S. H. (1967). Obesity, level of aspiration, and Rorschach and TAT measures of oral dependence. *Journal of Consulting Psychology, 31,* 233–239.

Masling, J. M., Weiss, L., & Rothschild, B. (1968). Relationships of oral imagery to yielding behavior and birth order. *Journal of Consulting and Clinical Psychology, 32,* 89–91.

McClelland, D. C., Koestner, R., & Weinberger, J. (1989). How do self-attributed and implicit motives differ? *Psychological Review, 96,* 690–702.

Meyer, G. J. (1997). On the integration of personality assessment methods: The Rorschach and MMPI. *Journal of Personality Assessment, 68,* 297–330.

Nunnally, J. C., & Bernstein, I. H. (1994). *Psychometric theory.* New York: McGraw-Hill.

O'Neill, R. M., & Bornstein, R. F. (1990). Oral dependence and gender: Factors in help-seeking response set and self-reported psychopathology in psychiatric inpatients. *Journal of Personality Assessment, 55,* 28–40.

Parker, K. C. H. (1983). A meta-analysis of the reliability and validity of the Rorschach. *Journal of Personality Assessment, 47,* 227–231.

Pincus, A. L., & Gurtman, M. B. (1995). The three faces of interpersonal dependency: Structural analysis of self-report dependency measures. *Journal of Personality and Social Psychology, 69,* 744–758.

Pincus, A. L., & Wilson, K. R. (2001). Interpersonal variability in dependent personality. *Journal of Personality, 69,* 223–251.

Schafer, R. (1954). *Psychoanalytic interpretation in Rorschach testing*. New York: Grune & Stratton.

Shilkret, C. J., & Masling, J. M. (1981). Oral dependence and dependent behavior. *Journal of Personality Assessment, 45*, 125–129.

Spitzer, R. L., Cohen, J., Fliess, J. L., & Endicott, J. (1967). Quantification of agreement in psychiatric diagnosis. *Archives of General Psychiatry, 17*, 83–87.

Sprohge, E., Handler, L., Plant, D. D., & Wicker, D. (2002). A Rorschach study of oral dependence in alcoholics and depressives. *Journal of Personality Assessment, 79*, 142–160.

Weiner, I. B. (2000). Using the Rorschach properly in practice and research. *Journal of Clinical Psychology, 56*, 435–438.

Weiss, L. R., & Masling, J. M. (1970). Further validation of a Rorschach measure of oral imagery: A study of six clinical groups. *Journal of Abnormal Psychology, 76*, 83–87.

Free Association	Inquiry

Card I

1. Looks like a bat or something eerie.

1. The way it's spread way out, this part the wings on each side. (Spread out?) It looks like the wings spread out on each side. (Eerie?) It just does, the whole appearance, it doesn't look natural. Maybe a demon or something you'd see on Ghostbusters.

2. It looks like a **pumpkin face**.

2. **The eyes and the mouth**. They're carved in the shape you would carve a pumpkin face. It's centered like eyes, the mouth, and a part in the center that could be a nose. It's a lit jack-o-lantern. It's light inside.

Card II

3. It looks like **an animal that's been squashed by a car**. That could be blood, and animal fur.

3. Because it's red, it looks like blood. It looks like it's lying flat on the ground, there's not much under it, it looks like it's been flattened. As far as the blood, the bottom part looks splashed. The dark part just looks like animal fur (touches card).

4. The top part of the dark color could be something ancient, something you would see in ruins. Something that was built a long time ago.

4. This looks like the top of a building you would see in ruins, it just looks like the shape of it. It looks like something ancient, not modern, very old. It looks like something similar to the ruins in Tulum, Mexico.

Card III

5. It looks like two people facing each other, **maybe twins that have a common bond**.

5. The top part could be an arched back, their legs and their head. And it looks like they are both holding onto something that connects. It could be a game. It looks like some kind of stool that has cushions on it. They may be talking to each other.

Card IV

6. It looks like a floppy eared dog. The top part does.

6. On each side it looks like its ears, in front the whole thing. I'm looking at it from behind. It looks like it's sitting flat on the floor with its legs out. It looks like it's watching and looking at something. It looks funny like a dog.

Card V

7. It looks like some kind of flying animal, like a bat possibly.

7. The wings are widespread, little feet hanging down and it has a head on top. It's flying because its legs are higher than the wings, and they're hanging down and not touching the ground.

Card VI

8. **It looks like a cat that's been gutted at the end of the day.** It looks like I do at the end of the day.

8. This reminds of a cartoon I saw. When you go to work in the morning, the cat looked real nice. And at the end of the day he looks like this, flattened out. **The top part does look like a cat head with ears and the long fur on its cheeks.** When I say gutted I do not mean literally, but mentally drained.

Card VII

9. Clouds, dark clouds.

9. The top part could be floating in the air. They look soft but dark. (Soft?) The soft look as it gets lighter. Parts of it are dark, and as it gets lighter it's a fluffy look. (Float?) It just looks light, like it could float. It doesn't look flat like it's lying on something.

10. It looks like it's kind of separated, **like the wishbone in a chicken.**

10. It looks like it has a bone in the middle that could be pulled in the middle like a wishbone. It's the shape of a wishbone. It's not exactly like a piece of chicken with a wishbone, but it could be.

Card VIII

11. It looks like the colors in a painting. A piece of art.

11. The colors are soft like a flower, or colors you would put in a painting. It could be the shape of two animals holding onto something like a tree, pulling on each side. The top part is the tree. They're standing on a rock on one foot. (Tree?) It looks like the top part of a pine tree. It looks like the shape of a rock, not the color.

12. It looks like a flower.

12. The whole thing looks like colors in flowers. The outside looks like petals, maybe an iris. These are the little things that go up in the middle of an iris.

Card IX
13. **This looks like a flower too, in full bloom, an exotic plant**.

13. **It looks similar to a man eating plant**. Something that would grab your hand if you put it down in the middle. This is the part that has blossomed out. The top part has blossomed out. It also has petals and leaves that branch out. It definitely looks exotic, not a domestic plant. Not an ordinary flower. The whole plant looks exotic because of the colors and the way it's shaped.

Card X
14. This could be a building in Russia, maybe not the colors, but the shape. Or Japan, yeah, more like Japan.

14. The way that the top is made, it looks like a building in Japan. Really, the whole shape of it. The blue parts and yellow parts could be lights, the orange part could be flowers, and the green part at the bottom is a tree. Mostly the pink and brown is the building. It's the colors that makes it look like a flower.

15. The blue part with tails could be fish.

15. It looks like a blue lobster on each side. The shape of it looks like a lobster.

RORSCHACH SEQUENCE OF SCORES FOR MS. DIXON

Card	Resp	Loc (DQ)	Loc No	Determinants (FQ)	(2)	Content(s)	P	Z	Special Scores
I	1.	Wo	1	FMao		(A)	P	1.0	
	2.	WSo	1	FYu		(Hd)		3.5	
II	3.	Wv	1	CF-.TF-		A. Bl			MOR
	4.	Dv	4	FC'u		Ay			MOR, PER
III	5.	D+	1	Mau	(2)	H. Hh	P	3.0	COP
IV	6.	Do	7	FMpo		A			
V	7.	Wo	1	FMao		A	P	1.0	
VI	8.	Wo	1	Fu		(A), Hx		2.5	MOR, DR2, PER
VII	9.	Wv	1	T.mp		Cl			
	10.	Do	4	F-		Ad			
VIII	11.	Wo	1	FC.FMau	(2)	Art, Na, A	P	4.5	
	12.	Wo	1	FCo		Bt		4.5	
IX	13.	Wo	1	FCo		Bt		5.5	
X	14.	Wo	1	FC-		Sc, Bt		5.5	DR1
	15.	Do	1	FCu	(2)	A			

STRUCTURAL SUMMARY FOR MS. DIXON

Location Features	Determinants		Contents	Approach
	Blends	Single		
		M = 1	H = 1	I: W.W
Zf = 9	CF.TF-	FM = 3	(H) = 0	II: W.D
ZSum = 31.0	FC.FMau	m = 0	Hd = 0	III: D
Zest = 27.5	T.mp	FC = 4	(Hd) = 1	IV: D
		CF = 0	Hx = 1	V: W
W = 10		C = 0	A = 5	VI: W
D = 5		Cn = 0	(A) = 2	VII: W.D
W+D = 15		FC' = 1	Ad = 1	VIII: W.W
Dd = 0		C'F = 0	(Ad) = 0	IX: W
S = 1		C' = 0	An = 0	X: W.D
		FT = 0	Art = 1	
Developmental Quality		TF = 0	Ay = 1	Special Scores
+ = 1		T = 0	Bl = 1	Lv 1 Lv 2
o = 11		FV = 0	Bt = 3	DV = 0x1 = 0x2
v = 3		VF = 0	Cg = 0	INC = 0x2 = 0x4
v/+ = 0		V = 0	Cl = 1	DR = 1x3 = 1x6
		FY = 1	Ex = 1	FAB = 0x4 = 0x7

Form Quality

	FQx	MQual	W+D		
+	= 0	= 0	= 0	YF = 0	ALOG = 0x5
o	= 5	= 0	= 5	Y = 0	CON = 0x7
u	= 6	= 1	= 6	Fr = 0	Raw Sum 6 = 2
-	= 3	= 0	= 3	rF = 0	Wgtd Sum 6 = 9
none	= 1	= 0	= 1	FD = 0	
				F = 2	AB = 0 GHR = 2
				(2) = 3	AG = 0 PHR = 1
				Sc = 1	COP = 1 MOR = 3
				Sx = 0	CP = 0 PER = 2
				Xy = 0	PSV = 0
				Id = 0	

Contents (additional):
Fd = 0
Fi = 0
Ge = 0
Hh = 1
Ls = 0
Na = 1

Ratios, Percentages, and Derivations

Core			*Affect*	*Interpersonal*
R = 15	L = .15		FC: CF+C = 5:1	COP = 1 AG = 0
			Pure C = 0	GHR: PHR = 2:1
EB = 1:3:5	EA = 4.5	EBPer = 3.5	SumC':WSumC = 1:3.5	a:p = 4:2
eb = 5:4	es = 9	D = -1	Afr = .50	Food = 0
	Adj es = 9	Adj D = -1	S = 1	Sum T = 2
			Blends:R =3:15	Human Cont = 2
FM = 4	SumC' = 1	SumT = 2	CP = 0	Pure H = 1
m = 1	Sum V = 0	Sum Y = 1		PER =2
				Isol Indx = .47

Ideation		*Mediation*	*Processing*	*Self-Perception*
a:p = 4:2	Sum6 = 2	XA% = .73	Zf = 9	3r+(2)/R = .20
Ma:Mp = 1:0	Lv2 = 1	WDA% = .73	W:D:Dd = 10:5:0	Fr+rF = 0
2AB+Art+Ay=2	WSum6 = 9	X-% = .20	W:M = 10:1	SumV = 0
MOR = 3	M- = 0	S- = 0	Zd = +3.5	FD = 0
	Mnone = 1	P = 4	PSV = 0	An+Xy = 0
		X+% = .33	DQ+ = 1	MOR = 3
		Xu% = .40	DQv = 3	H:(H)+Hd+(Hd) = 1:1

PTI = 0   DEPI = 5   CDI = 4   S-CON = 6   HVI = 0   OBS = 0

Obsessive–Compulsive Personality Disorder

Robert B. Schneider
VA Northern California Health Care System–Martinez

Freud's enduring cultural influence is readily apparent in the ubiquity of his once-radical psychoanalytic terminology in everyday speech. One of the best such examples is the commonplace use of the term "anal" to describe obsessive–compulsive personality traits. Indeed, psychoanalytic theory offered the first systematic description and explanation of this personality style. Freud (1908/1963) contended that anal character is distinguished by the three core features of *orderliness* (with particular concern for bodily cleanliness and task conscientiousness), *obstinacy* (stubbornness and defiance), and *parsimony* (excessive frugality). The theory held that these traits were rooted in problematic toilet training, with associated conflicts over power, control, and anger, during the anal stage (McWilliams, 1994; Mitchell & Black, 1995). Fenichel (1945), making a symptomatic/characterologic distinction that persists today in the *Diagnostic and Statistical Manual of Mental Disorders,* differentiation of obsessive–compulsive disorder (OCD) and obsessive–compulsive personality disorder (OCPD), thought that anal character traits, although often accompanied by repetitive thoughts and ritualistic behaviors, represented not merely periodic regression but a true developmental arrest (Pollak, 1987; Simon & Meyer, 1990). The contrast noted by Gabbard (2000) and Pollak (1987) between the ego dystonic obsessions and compulsions of OCD and the ego syntonic nature of OCPD traits seems to lend support to such an etiologic distinction.

Neoanalytic theorists, primarily Sullivan (1956), have shifted emphasis to the interpersonal origins of characterologic obsessiveness. Sullivan focused on obsessive–compulsives' deep feelings of insecurity stemming from confusing early experiences of parental rejection and maltreatment concealed by a facade of caring. In such an environment, the child, who accordingly learns to veil anger and other negative emotions, develops a pervasive need for both self-control and environmental order. This anxious orientation engenders characteristic "security operations" of reflexive emotional constriction, euphemistic verbal expression, pedantic concern with rules, and perfectionism. Salzman (1968) has similarly stressed the core concern with the controlling of both self and the environment that arises from underlying feelings of helplessness (Simon & Meyer, 1990). Gabbard (2000), echoing the analytic emphasis on reaction formation, displacement, undoing, and isolation of affect in the anal character, asserts that outwardly controlled OCPD patients harbor a "reservoir of rage" toward their emotionally unavailable, morally exacting parents.

While deemphasizing drives, conflicts, and developmental arrests, Shapiro (1965) both echoed and modified Freud's earlier triadic view of anal character in his examination of three central features of the obsessive–compulsive's global "style" of functioning: rigidity, distortion of the experience of autonomy, and loss of reality. According to Shapiro, the first and third features are primarily cognitive phenomena. That is, obsessive–compulsives tend to focus narrowly on some task or idea, thereby substantially closing off their minds to broader perspectives and alternative views. Additionally, in their joyless, moralistic perseveration, they deprive themselves of both intuitive, impressionistic experiences in life and any real affective attachment to the beliefs they dogmatically hold. As Schafer (1954) put it, such persons lack "emotional conviction."

The second feature concerns the experience of being relentlessly "driven." That is, in order to achieve adequate autonomy, obsessive–compulsives feel they must go beyond normal volition and be deliberate in everything they do—omnipotent in their emotional and mental self-control and earnestly teleologic in all activity. Will is not exercised in the service of wants and needs so much as it is used to monitor and control those impulses carefully. The classical analytic view identifies an unduly harsh superego as the central problem. Fairbairn's concept of a hypertrophic antilibidinal ego—an overdeveloped attachment to internalized "rejecting objects" arising in an interpersonally chilly and unsatisfying early environment (Fairbairn, 1952; Mitchell & Black, 1995)—also seems to capture the pervasive "tense deliberateness" (Shapiro, 1965) of obsessive–compulsive functioning. In the inward focus on cold but vitally important objects, emotional excitement and spontaneity may come to feel like dangerous rebelliousness, whereas grimly persistent, anhedonic industriousness brings a sense of safety.

The essential elements of these neoanalytic, interpersonal, and protocognitive conceptualizations all are present in DSM-IV-TR's (American

Psychiatric Association, 2000) diagnostic criteria for obsessive–compulsive personality disorder (OCPD). Following both Freud's and Shapiro's conceptualizations, DSM-IV-TR defines OCPD triadically as "a pervasive pattern of preoccupation with orderliness, perfectionism, and mental and interpersonal control, at the expense of flexibility, openness, and efficiency" (p. 729). For an OCPD diagnosis, this pattern must be indicated by at least four of the following eight (paraphrased) criteria: (a) preoccupation with details, rules, lists, and order; (b) perfectionism that impedes task completion; (c) excessive devotion to work, with a paucity of social/leisure activities; (d) moral rigidity and overconscientiousness; (e) inability to discard worn-out or worthless objects; (f) difficulty delegating tasks or collaborating; (g) miserliness; and (h) stubbornness.

Notably, the first criterion and the last two constitute Freud's anal–character triad. Most of the criteria reflect Shapiro's (1965) descriptions, and the enunciation of the disorder's three central features includes the Sullivanian focus on OCPD's interpersonal dimension. Although OCPD is distinguished by a core concern with orderliness and control, this need clearly manifests itself in multiple domains of functioning.

RESEARCH ON THE ASSESSMENT OF OBSESSIVE–COMPULSIVE PERSONALITY DISORDER

Empirical research on OCPD has been limited. As Simon and Meyer (1990) note, older factor-analytic studies (Hill, 1976; Lazare, Klerman, & Armor, 1966; Torgersen, 1980) suggested a distinctive constellation of traits in OCPD. However, more recent empirical studies examining prediction of OCPD with the NEO Personality Inventory-Revised (Huprich, 2003; Reynolds & Clark, 2001; Trull, Widiger, & Burr, 2001) have yielded a conspicuous lack of support for facet-level predictions of OCPD, as compared with other personality disorders (PDs). Some incongruence between contemporary dimensional personality assessment (e.g., based on the Five-Factor Model [FFM]) and the categorical DSM system seems to exist in the case of OCPD. Research to date certainly suggests that FFM-derived measures such as the NEO-PI-R may not do a very good job of assessing the central features of OCPD as delineated by DSM.

Other recent research on OCPD has tended to occur in three main areas: cognitive style, psychosocial functioning, and comorbidity with Axis I disorders, particularly anxiety and depression. Notably, virtually all OCPD research has used self-report instruments, diagnostic interviews, or both, and many studies have used nonclinical college samples. Such methods, although certainly valuable, may lack the means to detect less conscious and more clinically significant aspects of the disorder. For example, self-reports and interviews may not detect the finer nuances of defensive functioning and object relations that seem critical to an understanding of OCPD, which is preeminently concerned with rigid control of both the self and the relational environment. Including projective measures such as the Rorschach, which may be able to elucidate such crucial unconscious aspects of personality functioning as affect management and interpersonal relatedness, holds the potential to enrich greatly current cognitively focused OCPD assessment and research.

The cognitive studies to date examine primarily attentional processes in OCPD. Gallagher, South, and Oltmanns (2003) investigated obsessive–compulsives' difficulty tolerating uncertainty when facing an ego-threatening experience (in this study, a cognitive ability test). Using the Personality Diagnostic Questionnaire-4 (Hyler, 1994), the authors identified three groups of undergraduates: those meeting criteria for OCPD, those meeting criteria for avoidant PD, and those meeting no criteria for any PD. As compared with normal subjects and avoidants, obsessive–compulsives more actively sought information about the task beforehand, and more feedback about their performance afterward. Overall, they reported significantly higher levels of "dispositional monitoring" (attending to potential environmental threats) than the other groups. The authors concluded that obsessive–compulsives tend to be quite active in their efforts to reduce disquieting ambiguity. This finding suggests that threat-oriented perfectionism in OCPD does not always result in inaction and procrastination or preclude adaptive functioning.

On the other hand, Starcevic (1990) offered extensive clinical observations (although without empirical support) that in more primitive, incapacitating forms of OCPD, the core sense of vulnerability may become somatically focused, leading to the development of hypochondriasis. A more recent review (Smith & Benjamin, 2002) of research on functional impairment in various PDs provides empirical support for this link. Findings have shown OCPD to be twice as likely as other PDs to coexist with somatoform disorders. In somaticizing OCPD, increased activity to meet the perceived threat may take shape as repetitive medical help-seeking. Such a phenomenon, which seemingly resembles the concept of "active dependency" (Bornstein, 1995), suggests the possibility of an anaclitic dimension in OCPD, which generally has been seen as a predominantly introjective type of psychopathology (Blatt & Shichman, 1983).

Sacco and Olczak (1996) suggested that an obsessive cognitive style may be adaptive, depending on context. Using a psychoanalytically oriented self-report measure, the Lazare-Klerman Trait Scale (Lazare et al., 1966), with undergraduates, the investigators delineated groups high for either obsessiveness (comprising the traits of rigidity, parsimony, perseverance, emotional constriction, severe superego, and orderliness) or its traditionally conceived opposite personality style, hystericism (comprising emotionality, aggression, oral aggression, sexual provocativeness, egocentricity, and exhibitionism). The groups were then given the Breskin Rigidity Test (Breskin, 1968) and a modified Stroop Color Word Test (Stroop, 1935) as measures of cognitive flexibility and attentional capacity.

The authors found that persons with obsessive tendencies display more cognitive rigidity but not greater attentional capacity than persons with hysterical traits. However, consistent with Shapiro's (1965) observations, the obsessive group showed no superiority in academic aptitude, but somewhat higher levels of academic (high school and college) achievement. Thus, although cognitive rigidity may compromise affective and interpersonal functioning by sharply limiting emotional spontaneity, impressionistic enjoyment of experience, and relational warmth, it may be associated with one salient compensation: an intellectual tenacity that facilitates academic success. An older physiologic study (Smokler & Shevrin, 1979) found evidence of left hemisphere predominance in obsessive individuals and contrasting right-hemisphere predominance in histrionic persons, suggesting the possibility that obsessive individuals experience greater reliance on language and logic. In moderation, then, obsessive–compulsive tendencies may be a personality strength, but in "full-blown" OCPD, an unbalanced strength becomes a weakness.

A recent study using large clinical samples attempted to demarcate this boundary of maladaptiveness. Skodol et al. (2002) compared psychosocial impairment in selected "severe" PDs (schizotypal from Cluster A and borderline from Cluster B), ostensibly milder PDs (avoidant and OCPD from Cluster C), and major depression. All the groups were identified initially through diagnostic interviews (the Structured Clinical Interview for DSM-IV Axis I Disorders, Patient Edition [First, Spitzer, Gibbon, & Williams, 1996], and the Diagnostic Interview for DSM-IV Personality Disorders [Zanarini, Frankenburg, Sickel, & Yong, 1996]), with the classifications then supported by either the self-report Schedule for Nonadaptive and Adaptive Personality (Clark, 1993) or an independent clinician's rating. Psychosocial functioning in multiple domains (e.g., employment, household duties, academic performance, interpersonal relationships, recreation) for the groups then was assessed by interviewers using the Longitudinal Interval Follow-up Evaluation-Baseline Version (Keller et al., 1987) and by the self-report Social Adjustment Scale (Weissman & Bothwell, 1976). The groups also were assessed for global functioning in three ways: global satisfaction, global social adjustment, and DSM-IV's Axis V Global Assessment of Functioning (GAF).

In general, OCPD patients exhibited the lowest levels of impairment among the groups, especially in work and education. However, almost 90% of the OCPD patients had "moderate or worse" impairment in at least one area, or had a GAF below 60. Furthermore, they showed only a narrow superiority to the other groups in global satisfaction, consistent with the theoretical view that a gnawing perfectionism is central to OCPD. Thus, although OCPD may be a more "moderate" PD, both psychosocial impairment and subjective distress may be significant. It is worth noting that in this study, all information about functional impairment was obtained from the patients themselves. Given the hallmark perfectionism of OCPD, obsessive–compulsives may have found it harder than persons in other groups to admit to difficulties in certain valued areas of performance (e.g., work and education) or in general functioning. As noted earlier, projective measures may be less susceptible to such minimization in the assessment of OCPD impairment.

The third area of research in which OCPD has been included is comorbidity of PDs with Axis I pathology. Given the chronic tension and disappointment-inducing perfectionism of OCPD, it is not surprising that most findings concern anxiety and depression. In their review of studies from 1981 to 1995 examining comorbidity of PDs and major depression among both inpatients and outpatients, Corruble, Ginestet, and Guelfi (1996) found that for Cluster C PDs and depression, comorbidity findings varied widely, except in the case of OCPD: Consistently high rates (up to 20%) of co-occurrence were found. As the authors noted, a wide variety of semistructured interviews and self-report measures were used in these studies.

In another review article, Bienvenu and Stein (2003) reported a significant relationship between Cluster C traits and Axis I anxiety disorders, including social phobia, OCD, and PTSD. More specifically, OCPD traits and neuroticism were significantly elevated in first-degree relatives of persons with a diagnosis of OCD. The authors noted that relative genetic and environmental influences are not determinable in such studies, but on the basis of previous suggestions that heritability of anxiety disorders is limited (and consistent with dynamic–interpersonal explanations of OCPD's origins), they argue for the importance of environmental factors in a potential common developmental pathway for OCD and OCPD.

Rees, Hardy, and Barkham (1996), using a structured interview, the Personality Disorder Examination (Loranger, Susman, Oldham, & Russakoff, 1985), to identify Cluster C PDs in outpatients, suggested that obsessive–compulsive personality traits may be more strongly related to anxiety than to depressive symptoms as described in the DSM system and measured by the self-report Beck Depression Inventory (Beck, Ward, Mendelson, Mock, & Erbaugh, 1961) and a structured interview combining the Present State Examination (Wing, Cooper, & Sartorius, 1974) and the Diagnostic Interview Schedule (Robins, Helzer, Croughan, & Ratliff, 1981). They found that persons with OCPD traits, especially the factor termed "stubborn insistence on getting their own way," appear vulnerable to high levels of autonomic arousal and decision-impeding cognitive inefficiency, which may be more related to anxiety than to depression. As the authors noted, however, the outpatients in their samples were relatively high-functioning, with some depressive symptoms, but not severely impaired at the time the study was conducted. Thus, links between OCPD and major depressive symptoms may not have been assessed adequately.

Nonetheless, an important OCPD–anxiety link is further suggested by Pollak's (1987) wide-ranging review of the clinical and empirical literature on the long-controversial relationship between OCPD and OCD. Pollak concluded that although the two disorders appear to be distinct, and OCPD traits seem to be neither necessary nor sufficient factors for the development of OCD, premorbid obsessive–compulsive traits do seem more likely than other personality patterns in OCD. The reverse relationship—childhood OCD symptoms in persons later diagnosed with OCPD—has not been supported empirically. Although the etiologic relationship between the two disorders remains elusive—it is not clear, for example, whether the disorders share a common set of genetic or environmental influences—the finding of premorbid OCPD traits in up to 50% of persons diagnosed with OCD appears to support the psychodynamic idea that the Axis I disorder may develop when characterologic defenses fail in some way and a more acute, egodystonic need for ritualistic control erupts (Fenichel, 1945; Millon, 1981).

In a more recent review of empirical studies investigating the possible links between OCD, OCPD, and anorexia nervosa (AN), Serpell, Livingstone, Neiderman, and Lask (2002) reported consistent evidence of OCD–AN comorbidity, and growing, if widely varying, findings (ranging from 3.3% to 60%) of comorbidity between OCPD and AN, both of which are characterized by rigid self-control and obsessional thinking. These researchers also reported somewhat inconsistent findings in family studies of OCPD–OCD comorbidity, but stated that according to recent evidence, a subtype of OCD—one focused on compulsive checking rather than on compulsive washing—may be strongly linked to obsessive–compulsive personality traits. Little etiology-clarifying research (e.g., twin and adoption studies and longitudinal studies) on the relationships between these three disorders has been conducted to date.

Collectively, these studies suggest important cognitive, behavioral, and emotional aspects of OCPD, but they do not examine comprehensive, multidimensional assessment. Empirical studies have focused mainly on separate features of obsessive–compulsive functioning in a variety of domains. How might such disparate dimensions be more integratively assessed? If Shapiro (1965), supported to some extent by recent research, is accurate about the core cognitive aspect of the obsessive–compulsive "style," assessment should focus on the OCPD individual's environmental scanning, perception, and interpretation, and needs to be capable of detecting his or her central concern with orderliness. At the same time, neoanalytic work and DSM-IV criteria suggest that the impact of this rigid control orientation on emotion, self-perception, and interpersonal functioning also should be closely examined. Moreover, given obsessives' stringent ways of managing affect, optimal assessment would be able to circumvent these defenses to illuminate hidden anger, anxiety, and depression. The Rorschach Comprehensive System (CS), with its multidomain clusters of personality functioning—including what Exner (2003) calls the "cognitive triad" of the processing, mediation, and ideation clusters—seems well-suited to this cognitively focused, but affectively and interpersonally informed, task. Indeed, the clinical literature suggests that OCPD's constellation of traits, which might be called the "many faces of rigidity," can be detected on the Rorschach in terms of affect, perception of self and others, and characteristic thinking patterns, but most distinctively in terms of environmental processing.

THE RORSCHACH PROTOCOL
OF OBSESSIVE–COMPULSIVE PERSONALITY DISORDER

Systematic inquiry into Rorschach assessment of OCPD, although much less voluminous than work with some other PDs (notably those of Cluster B), is by no means new. Two decades before the advent of the CS, Schafer (1954) made a significant psychoanalytic contribution to Rorschach assessment of the obsessive–compulsive personality. Focusing on a cluster of characteristic defenses—regression, isolation (and intellectualization), reaction formation, and undoing—he described how an obsessive–compulsive protocol should look.

Schafer (1954) delineated a number of Rorschach markers of obsessive–compulsive tendencies, involving content, location, determinants, and test-taking behavior, that translate quite directly to CS measurement. Expected content includes anal themes and imagery (although hostile and messy images may be "prettied up" or followed by themes of solicitousness and control in an "undoing" effort), machines or machine-like human behavior (paralleling the obsessive–compulsive's own mechanistic functioning), and intellectualizing preoccupation with abstractions and arcana of the arts and sciences. Pervasive reaction formation, primarily against dependency and hostility, also may yield themes of autonomy and conscientiousness within the protocol. Location markers include focus on small blot details (reflecting perceptual conservatism and avoidance of stressful decision making in less clear-cut synthesized responses) and potentially elevated S (perhaps resulting from painstaking scrutiny of the blots or sullen opposition to being tested). Expected determinants include an affect-controlling emphasis on form over color and shading (although the latter two may be brought in "to be thorough and dutiful"), with generally good form quality indicating cautious avoidance of impressionistic responding; and a relatively high M (suggesting a capacity for reflection aided by affect isolation, which "may neutralize the dangers" of introspection), with resulting introversive tendencies. In test-taking behavior, one may expect to see an aloof and possibly pompous "observer" who may, despite apparent emotional detachment from the task, produce a relatively high R for such reasons as conscientiousness and eagerness to please, performance anxiety, intellectual vanity and exhibitionism, or even anger-driven, "anal-expulsive" verbal messiness (e.g., unnecessarily verbose descriptions, images involving feces or dirt, objects or material in disarray) provoked by the humiliatingly evaluative context.

Schafer (1954) noted that markedly different responses may occur when defenses fail. For instance, despite heavy use of reaction formation, aggressive impulses may, in times of stress, "infiltrate" the protocol. Such stress may be quite high in clinical contexts and during the ambiguous Rorschach itself. Schafer's caveats must be kept in mind in attempts to identify a prototypical OCPD protocol. Clearly, it is important to address the degree to which the putative exemplar's ego defenses seem intact at the time of testing.

Schafer's (1954) observations lack the empirical backing of CS-based studies. His analysis also is, at times, so flexibly idiographic that nomothetic clarity is sacrificed to some extent. Still, his thorough exploration provides an influential historical prelude to CS examination of OCPD. Moreover, although Schafer stressed the need to look beyond what he called the "psychological hieroglyphics" of scores alone (imagery themes and test-taking behavior are equally vital, he argued) for adequate Rorschach interpretation (Viglione, Brager, & Haller, 1991), many of his observations about OCPD and the Rorschach appear consistent with Exner's empirical, norm-based research.

Given OCPD's venerable history as a theoretical construct, it is surprising that, aside from Exner's work, so little empirical Rorschach research has been conducted to investigate it. In one of the very few such studies, Kates (1950) compared patients with "anxiety reactions" (apparently generalized anxiety disorder, in DSM-IV terms) to obsessive–compulsive patients (possibly with OCD or OCPD; the patients appear to have qualities of both). Kates (1950) found notable differences between the two groups. Obsessive–compulsives gave many more Rorschach responses than anxiety-reaction patients, suggesting a "greater need to demonstrate … adequacy." Anxiety-reaction patients were significantly more likely to reject cards and obtained a higher global maladjustment score. Kates hypothesized that obsessive–compulsives may have rather effective defenses against overt anxiety, as well as a "drive for completeness" in many situations, a speculation supported by the recent evidence for intolerance of uncertainty (Gallagher et al., 2003). They also gave more Dd responses, possibly reflecting greater meticulousness, and used more color. Kates concluded that despite much "inner tension," obsessive–compulsive defenses against anxiety are effective enough to permit some experience of affect, albeit in a carefully controlled manner. Such conclusions are consistent with the long-standing dynamic view of OCPD as a relatively high-functioning PD, with a "common and 'classic' neurotic-level organization" (McWilliams, 1994).

In CS assessment, obsessive–compulsive tendencies can be measured by the Processing cluster, and by the index composed substantially of Processing variables: the Obsessive Style Index (OBS). The OBS was created in 1990 during cross-validation of the Schizophrenia Index (SCZI) and the Depression Index (DEPI) in studies that included a comparison group comprising both OCPD patients and persons with compulsive behaviors. Six variables (in four possible combinations) correlated strongly with obsessive–compulsive tendencies: Dd > 3; Zf > 12; Zd > +3.0; Populars > 7; FQ+ > 1 (or > 3 in two of the combinations), and X+% > 0.89 (Exner, 1993, 2001, 2003). Of these, FQ+ and X+% were most heavily weighted (Exner, 2003).

Since the original 1990 studies, research with the OBS seems to have been minimal. Exner's 2003 revision of his principal text adds little to his 1993 discussion of the OBS. Still, the OBS appears to have a low false-positive rate (Ganellen, 1996), and despite the inclusion of both OCD and OCPD patients in the original studies, it seems to be a solid Rorschach marker of obsessive–compulsive tendencies. A positive OBS suggests marked perfectionism, preoccupation with details, cautious environmental processing, and indecisiveness (Exner, 2003), as well as difficulty expressing feelings (Ganellen, 1996).

As the OBS suggests, OCPD protocols should include an elevated number of details, especially unusual ones. The inherent formlessness of the inkblots may provoke considerable psychological discomfort in obsessive–compulsives. Clinical literature suggests that OCPD individuals may attempt to "neaten" the task in one of two main ways. As Shapiro (1965) and McWilliams (1994) note, with their characteristic narrowed focus, these individuals may provide a large number of precisely delineated D and, especially, Dd responses. Alternatively, they may try hard to combine parts meaningfully: A need to impose order on the chaos of the blots may underlie their typically high level of organizational activity (Zf > 12; Zd > +3.0). "Overincorporation" (Zd > +3.0) is related to meticulousness, inefficiency, and pained indecision about those environmental elements that are critical and those that are not (Weiner, 2003; Wilson, 1994). In addition, obsessive–compulsives may provide lengthy, elaborate form responses in an effort to get the description of the percept "just right." Notably, an elevation in FQ+

responses is a core criterion for a positive OBS.[1] High R also may result from a combination of compliance and perfectionism (Kates, 1950; Schafer, 1954), although extremely angry or anxious patients may, consistent with the Freudian notion of anal retentiveness, produce a stingily brief record. A rambling "overinclusiveness of thinking," perhaps resulting from an unconscious wish to obscure one's own emotions and even stultify potentially critical interlocutors with an "anesthetizing cloud" of words (Gabbard, 2000), raises the potential for Deviant Responses (DR). Finally, obsessive–compulsives are likely to exhibit good form quality (X+%) and an elevated number of Populars, consistent with their typically intact reality testing and perceptual conservatism.

In the Processing cluster, along with perfectionistic overincorporation, other strong OCPD indicators may be seen. In the W:D:Dd ratio, unusual details (Dd) may predominate. On the other hand, an urge to be both impressively thorough and neat may elevate W, possibly resulting in suggestions of overambitiousness in the W:M ratio. Given the distinguishing perfectionism of OCPD, which may place a nagging ambitiousness at odds with more mundane detail focus, it would not be surprising to see such a case of "reach exceeding grasp." Finally, some perseverative (PSV) responses are likely, especially if the OCPD patient also exhibits OCD symptoms.

Effortful, inefficient processing may have an impact on Mediation and Ideation, the two related clusters in the "cognitive triad" (Exner, 2003). Painstaking processing should nonetheless be accompanied by generally good form quality (high XA%, WDA%, and X+%; low X–%) and marked conventionality in perception, reflected in an elevated number of Populars and below-average Xu%. Theory and clinical work also suggest that OCPD's concealed anger may "infiltrate" the protocol if defenses begin to fail (Gabbard, 2000; Schafer, 1954). Thus, S– may be elevated for more distressed OCPD patients.

In the Ideation cluster, two potential OCPD markers stand out. One of the most salient indicators should be a markedly elevated Intellectualization Index. Although the intellectualization defense is not unique to OCPD, theoretical, clinical, and empirical observations converge on the expectation that this index will be conspicuously high for obsessive–compulsives (Gabbard, 2000; Schafer, 1954; Sullivan, 1956; Weiner, 2003). The other major OCPD variable in this cluster is the a:p ratio. Obsessive–compulsives are most fundamentally concerned with control, as virtually all authors agree. Accordingly, they are likely to exhibit rigidly "active" and narrowed thinking in their relentless need to preempt potential threats to their psychological equi-

---

[1]This suggests that clinicians' widespread undercoding of FQ+ (Wilson, 1994) may impede the Rorschach's potentially significant contribution to OCPD diagnosis in clinical practice.

librium. For this prototypically introjective character disorder (Blatt & Shichman, 1983), "maladaptive single-mindedness" (Wilson, 1994) generates tireless but constrained mental activity, perhaps centrally focused on reducing disquieting environmental ambiguity (Gallagher et al., 2003). At the same time, obsessive–compulsive persons are unlikely to indulge much in fantasy, an activity that requires too much relaxation of "tense deliberateness" (Shapiro, 1965). Thus, Ma should predominate over Mp.

In their core problem-solving and stress-management strategies, obsessive–compulsives tend to rely heavily on rumination, painstakingly considering and reconsidering options. Their seemingly indefatigable mentation, however, may not be especially productive or effective, particularly for decision making (Gabbard, 2000; Shapiro, 1965). This chronic, paralytic stewing over decisions suggests that obsessive–compulsives probably will appear on the Rorschach as introversive, perhaps pervasively so. However, an introversive style is not a certainty. In the most recent nonpatient adult standardization sample (Exner, 2001), the eight protocols (1% of the total) with a positive OBS included five introversives, one extratensive, and two ambitents. Among outpatients, of the 44 (8%) with a positive OBS, there were 35 introversives, two extratensives, six ambitents, and one with an avoidant style. As McWilliams (1994) notes, the linking of "obsessive" and "compulsive" tendencies in OCPD is heuristically useful and, more importantly, reflects their common etiology according to psychodynamic theory. However, whereas both thinking and doing may be used excessively as a way to avoid emotion, one of the two may be much more heavily used than the other. In the characteristic indecisiveness of OCPD, a desperate press to "do something" may impinge on rumination as anxiety builds. Thus, on the Rorschach, although OCPD is most likely to yield an introversive style, for some obsessive–compulsives, a vacillation between enervating, hair-splitting rumination and a frustration-fueled urge to act may result in ambitence.

A similar tension between the need to be environmentally vigilant and the desire for relief from such painful pressure may result in either very high or very low Lambda. OCPD is characterized by uncannily well-balanced ambivalence (Gabbard 2000; Shapiro, 1965). Weiner (2003) provides a vivid contrast between persons who are insufficiently open to experience (high Lambda) and those who are excessively open (low Lambda). However, his neat dichotomy may not capture the phenomenology of OCPD, which in terms of experiential openness, consists of the "worst of both worlds": a narrow viewpoint, but also a tormenting, visceral uncertainty—a lack of "emotional conviction"—about the rightness of that rigid perspective (Schafer, 1954). Driven by this uncertainty to scrutinize their world from every possible angle, overincorporative obsessive–compulsives are likely to exhibit an "inability to back away" from stimuli (Exner,

1993), and to produce a below-average Lambda. Although extreme situational defensiveness on the Rorschach may produce a high Lambda, the typical OCPD defenses are likely to be regularly permeable: Anxiogenic rumination and intrusive, affectively hued thoughts may repeatedly assault the defensive perimeters of intellectualizing self-control. Although this experience of impingement is chronically stressful, the obsessive–compulsive's sense of control is paradoxically fed by the tension, which is registered as a reassuring vigilance. Thus, adjusted D may well equal 0 or even be positive. However, markers of more debilitating situational stress, likely to be experienced during Rorschach testing and during the acute psychological difficulties that often occasion clinical assessment, may be elevated (Y, m, negative D). The apparent comorbidity of OCPD with anxiety disorders (American Psychiatric Association, 2000; Bienvenu & Stein, 2003; Rees et al., 1996) suggests that Y in particular may be markedly elevated.

Extreme affective distress in OCPD generally is kept at bay reasonably well by a constellation of defenses, particularly isolation and intellectualization. One strong negative emotion that may be somewhat more accessible in certain contexts (e.g., power relations in occupational hierarchies) is anger, particularly righteous indignation (McWilliams, 1994). On the Rorschach, especially if the examinee feels humiliated or resentful about being tested, S may be moderately elevated. Characteristic emotional avoidance should yield a low Affective Ratio (Afr), and emotion experienced is likely to be well controlled (FC:CF+C should be 2:1 or higher). A reversal in this ratio, or the presence of pure C, is unlikely. During times of crisis, however, in obsessive–compulsives with poorer ego development, such volatility is possible. More likely, increased stress will be accompanied by elevations in C', which generally should be high in obsessive–compulsives, for whom psychological "biting of the tongue" tends to be chronic. Blends, particularly those involving both color and shading, should be elevated, reflecting OCPD's strenuous mental wrestling with both environmental ambiguity and emotional ambivalence (Gabbard, 2000; Weiner, 2003). The implicit pessimism of OCPD may flare into overt depressive symptoms during times of crisis, as comorbidity studies suggest (Corruble et al., 1996). Thus, the Depression Index also may be positive.

In OCPD, as in depressive PD, such affective distress is likely to be related to negative self-perception (McWilliams, 1994). The hallmark perfectionism of OCPD tends to produce a chronic, rather global, sense of dissatisfaction with oneself (Skodol et al., 2002). Experience, perceived continually through a lens calibrated to detect potential failure, may over time come to feel like an endless series of disasters narrowly averted. Thus, despite a tolerable (although tense) homeostasis when life circumstances seem under adequate control, a heavier onslaught of external stressors or a developmental transition such as a "midlife crisis" can produce collapse of self-esteem (Gabbard, 2000). In a clinical context, then, obsessive–compulsive persons should show elevations on Rorschach markers of dysphoria related to negative self-appraisal. In times of crisis, Vista and morbid content (MOR) should be markedly elevated, and the Egocentricity Index may be even lower than usual for OCPD, as guilt and shame over perceived failure destroy defensive "private vanity" about holding oneself to exceptionally high standards (McWilliams, 1994). Even in distress, obsessive–compulsives' strong ruminative tendencies should yield some use of Form Dimension (FD), but insight is likely to be pessimistically skewed: V, MOR, or both may cluster around these responses. As Exner (2003) notes, such self-scrutiny is to be expected for most persons during crises or difficult life transitions. In OCPD, however, gloomy self-examination may be especially harsh and depressogenic. The possible link between OCPD and somatically focused Axis I pathology such as hypochondriasis and anorexia nervosa (Serpell et al., 2002; Smith & Benjamin, 2002; Starcevic, 1990) suggests that this gloomy rumination may involve elevated body concern (An+Xy). Especially in more "primitive" forms of OCPD, this gut-level sense of oneself as deeply damaged will be accompanied by fear of genuine intimacy, with its inherent risks of derogation and disappointment. Thus, an elevation of part-human over whole-human percepts on the Rorschach is likely. Likewise, animal content may be elevated, with the urge to seek reassurance about oneself constrained by the need for a "sure thing" in that quest.

Although a diagnosis of OCPD may have less direct interpersonal implications than some other DSM-IV PDs whose very names reflect their pervasive relational aspects (e.g., dependent, avoidant, narcissistic, antisocial), an obsessive–compulsive's Rorschach is likely to yield several salient Interpersonal cluster results. Tightly controlled but periodically "infiltrating" anger, perhaps originating in recurrent early experiences of caregivers' veiled hostility (McWilliams, 1994; Schafer, 1954; Sullivan, 1956), may generate an above-average number of aggressive (AG) responses. Weariness related to the rigid maintenance of anger control may yield MOR in conjunction with AG. A reflexive mistrust of others may inhibit cooperative (COP) responses. Yet, obsequiousness as a defense against anger (a reaction formation that seems especially likely in the assessment context) should elicit some affiliative impulses. Thus, both AG and COP may be seen, possibly in counterbalanced (simultaneous or alternating) fashion. This may signal an anxious effort at undoing and a precarious id–superego balance (Schafer, 1954), although it has been argued that a mixture of AG and COP can be adaptive in competitive vocations and hierarchical organizational structures (Weiner, 2003). Consistent with the interpersonal chilliness and rigid autonomy of OCPD, overt impulses to reach out to others for help, support, and contact should be suppressed (low T), and primitive dependency needs (Fd) should generally be absent. This is not to say, of course, that human relationships are unimportant to obsessive–compulsives. In fact, OCPD, with its mildly paranoid tendencies (Blatt & Shichman, 1983), is centrally concerned with the views, opinions, and potential actions of others. Thus, human content may be rather plentiful, and the Isolation Index probably will be in the normal range. As discussed earlier, however, a paucity of pure H may be seen, and the ratio of good human responses to poor human responses (GHR:PHR) may suffer accordingly. Finally, an anxious need to justify percepts may elevate personalized responses (PER).

The following case illustrates the Rorschach assessment of OCPD, in this example, with coexisting depression. Although the presence of an Axis I disorder complicates the clinical picture, it indicates what might be expected in actual practice when, as many authors (Corruble et al., 1996; Gabbard, 2000; Schafer, 1954) suggest, obsessive–compulsive defenses fail.[2]

CASE EXAMPLE: MR. IRWIN

Mr. Irwin is a 67-year-old married white male referred by his internist for assessment of his level of depression and psychological adjustment after cardiovascular problems that required angioplasty and insertion of a pacemaker. These procedures had frightening complications. Mr. Irwin had life-threatening fluid accumulation in his chest, and while undergoing emergency intervention, he had overheard staff speaking solemnly about the possibility that he might die. Although he recovered, he reported being permanently shaken by this "graphic reminder of my mortality." Since the experience, he reported a preoccupation with death and had ceased any planning for the future. He reported no vegetative depressive symptoms and denied any suicidal ideation. However, along with preoccupation about death, he reported increased difficulty concentrating, as well as much doubt about his coping abilities since his medical scare.

Mr. Irwin reported some rather chronic difficulties as well, including marital friction for many years. He stated that felt dissatisfied with his wife but stuck with her. He stated that he could not recall the last time they had sexual relations, as this situation predated his medical problems by many years. He reported frequent irritability toward his wife, especially in recent months, with surges of intense anger when she showed concern for his physical health or questioned his decisions. He also reported some mutual

---

[2]The author thanks Ronald J. Ganellen, PhD (1996) for his generosity in permitting the re-presentation of this case from his book, *Integrating the Rorschach and the MMPI-2 in Personality Assessment*. Some of Dr. Ganellen's observations have been integrated into this chapter's case discussion.

violence (slapping and pushing), with his wife being injured (reportedly accidentally) on one occasion when objects were thrown. He had no history of arrests or legal problems.

Mr. Irwin, a self-described liberal, holding a master's degree in political science, had worked for many years in a government job, primarily enforcing civil rights policies. He reportedly had received many commendations for his high-quality work and described warm relationships with coworkers. After his retirement (which had occurred about 7 years before his assessment), he stayed active with part-time work, most recently at a community service center in a position for which he was recruited because of his community reputation and connections. Mr. Irwin complained of poor management at the center, suggesting that he could do much better.

Mr. Irwin described a discrepancy between his self-image and the opinions others seemed to have of him. He felt that he was seen as a friendly, confident, effective leader, and he had enjoyed much support from friends and acquaintances during his recent medical ordeal. At the same time, however, he described a chronic, internal "silent debate" about making even minor decisions, involving much agonized rumination. Although aware of the ineffectiveness of such endless stewing, he stated that he did not seem able to stop. He also reported feeling rigid and robotic, without emotions, much of the time. He stated that these longstanding tendencies had led to depression when he was in his 20's. Although ensuing psychotherapy reportedly helped somewhat, he stated that his ruminative tendencies and decision-making difficulty had persisted his whole life.

Mr. Irwin's Rorschach exemplifies the protocol of a distressed obsessive–compulsive person in many striking ways. His protocol is brief (R = 15), but extremely effortful. A number of his responses involve carefully elaborated form descriptions (FQ+ = 5), which contribute heavily to his positive OBS. This dramatically high number of FQ+ responses is especially striking given his low R. His Rorschach performance brings to mind the solemn self-importance of the perfectionistic $M*A*S*H$ character Charles Emerson Winchester, who said of his painstaking surgical work, "I do one thing at a time; I do it very well; and then I move on." Inspection of Mr. Irwin's OBS also shows overincorporative tendencies (Zd = +3.5) and notable care and conservatism in his perceptions (P = 9; X+% = 0.93). Mr. Irwin's OBS is positive in three of the four possible ways. Consistent with his self-reported ongoing "silent debate," he appears to have marked obsessive and perfectionistic tendencies.

Mr. Irwin's "cognitive triad" (Processing, Mediation, and Ideation clusters) also exhibits OCPD hallmarks, although some expected findings are absent (which may be attributable in part to the brevity of his protocol). Although he does not show the expected preoccupation with small, unusual details, Mr. Irwin nonetheless seems to work hard to make sense of the blots by systematically perceiving relationships between parts (W > D+Dd; DQ+ = 8; Zd = +3.5). As mentioned earlier, Mr. Irwin shows the expected good form quality (high XA%, WDA%, X+%; low X–%). In fact, he displays marked perceptual conventionality (P = 9), perhaps reflecting a strong sense of social propriety.

In his Ideation cluster, several variables stand out, possibly suggesting some "downstream" cognitive effects of the heavy effort Mr. Irwin makes in processing blot stimuli. As expected, Mr. Irwin's Intellectualization Index is quite high (3 standard deviations above the nonpatient mean). This defense against strong emotion is consistent with his description of himself as "robotic," and with his report about his marriage, which seems to lack much emotionality except that generated by anger. Mr. Irwin's a:p ratio also is consistent with an obsessive–compulsive style. The 7:2 ratio suggests a rigidly narrow viewpoint, to which he is likely to cling doggedly. This does not appear to have caused him as much interpersonal difficulty with friends and coworkers as might be expected. It may be that in his workplace, relative homogeneity in political sentiment among fellow social activists minimizes interpersonal friction that might otherwise result from Mr. Irwin's dogmatism. When challenged, however (e.g., when his wife questions his decisions), Mr. Irwin appears to be much less congenial. He may well exemplify the brittleness of conviction in OCPD discussed by Schafer (1954) and Shapiro (1965). In addition, he exhibits some mild cognitive peculiarity (WSum6 = 13). This is mainly attributable to his three DRs, which are consistent with the overreliance on profuse verbalization to defend against psychological pain in OCPD (Gabbard, 2000; Sullivan, 1956). This circumstantiality, and the looseness of association suggested by his FABCOM, may represent unwonted mental carelessness in his current distressed state, or possibly a defensive brief detachment from the task (Exner, 2003; Wilson, 1994). Nonetheless, Mr. Irwin shows minimal propensity to seek such relief through fantasy (Ma:Mp = 3:1).

Mr. Irwin's extremely low Lambda seems typical of OCPD. The need to scrutinize things from as many angles as possible permits coloring of his perceptual world by affective nuances. Consistent with his self-reported brooding about mortality and his agonizing over even small decisions, Mr. Irwin, despite his inveterate intellectualization, seems unable to avoid rumination, especially about emotionally upsetting matters. His problem-solving style (EB) is ambitent, further suggesting excessive vacillation in his decisions. He seems to harbor dour and possibly bitter feelings (SumC' = 2). He may ponder an issue endlessly; then, having failed to reach a satisfying conclusion, he may act precipitously. Such spasmodic pseudoresolution, coupled with helpless feelings in the face of increasing concentration problems (m = 3) and mounting anxiety (SumY = 5), may fuel his periodic violence toward his wife. Although, like most obsessive–compulsives, he does not appear to suffer a chronic stress overload (AdjD = 0), he appears to be feeling unusually distressed (D = –1) in the wake of his control-shattering medical scare.

Mr. Irwin's positive Depression Index is consistent with his self-reported depressive symptoms of pessimism, preoccupation with death, anhedonia, concentration problems, and low self-confidence. Despite his aversion to emotions (Afr = 0.25), he appears to have significant trouble modulating affect (FC:CF+C = 2:3; pure C = 1), and to be caught up currently in a maelstrom of dysphoria (blends:R = 8:15, with shading heavily present). Perhaps epitomizing his defensive struggle is his response to Card IX, in which the attempt of "hope" (the orange) to surmount "foreboding" (the green) becomes a life or death battle (red blood). Accordingly, intellectualization (AB, Art) fails to prevent the violent eruption of emotional material (pure C, Bl). Reflecting his demoralizing preoccupation with his own mortality, he does not currently seem to be feeling angry (S = 1) so much as downcast and depleted (V = 1; MOR = 3; m = 3; Y = 5). Within this general mood of dejection, he may make rather naive and hollow attempts to assert a brighter outlook (CP = 1, with the color projection accompanying an anxiety-ridden m^a, YF response, and coming immediately after an FY response accompanied by MOR).

As expected when an obsessive–compulsive sinks into depression, Mr. Irwin's current collapse seems strongly linked to damaged self-perception. Surprisingly, his Egocentricity Index is above average. It seems that Mr. Irwin still regards himself rather highly, possibly indicating his career success's enduring buffer against low self-esteem. However, both his history of violence and several self-perception markers on his Rorschach suggest that this mild grandiosity may be largely defensive. He appears to have some capacity for introspection and insight (FD = 1), but, consistent with his long-standing "silent debate," it often may be pessimistically skewed and accompanied by a wearying sense of his own defectiveness (V = 1; MOR = 3). Surprisingly, given his recent medical problems, he does not show much bodily concern (An+Xy = 0). This suggests that he may have relatively well-developed defenses and thus does not typically somaticize psychological concerns (Starcevic, 1990). Nonetheless, his insecurities may make it somewhat difficult for him to relate to others as whole, autonomous human beings (H:[H]+Hd+[Hd] = 3:3). Such difficulties are consistent with his marital distress, particularly its lack of sexual intimacy, which in turn fits with the psychoanalytic emphasis on pregenital sexual squeamishness in anal character (Schafer, 1954).

Mr. Irwin's interpersonal profile is in fact somewhat mixed. Consistent with his history of relational harmony at work, he appears to have some empathic capacity (M = 4) and generally good social skills (GHR:PHR = 5:1). His less than optimal H:(H)+Hd+(Hd) ratio and his immaturity suggested by high animal content (7), however, indicate that this social adaptiveness may not carry over to truly intimate relationships. The nice, confident guy at work may be much surlier and more defensive at home. Accordingly, he displays expected ambivalence in his expectations of relationships, anticipating both cooperation and aggressiveness (AG = 2; COP = 2) in an alternating sequence. Notably, he generally attributes aggressiveness to animals and cooperation to humans, consistent with an obsessive–compulsive's moral prudishness. He also exhibits the characteristic "undoing" of anal aggression described by Schafer (1954) (e.g., in response 3, he questions the plausibility of his percept after describing a bloody fight between elephants). Unsurprisingly, this habitually self-reliant "leader" does not appear to reach out to others much for support (SumT = 0; Fd = 0), although he certainly does not shun social contact (Isolation Index = 0.13; Human Content = 6). Overall, as suggested by the dichotomy between his self-doubt and others' apparent admiration of him, and between his harmony at work and strife at home, Mr. Irwin's interpersonal functioning appears superficially adequate, but much poorer at a more intimate level. Notably, such a contrast is entirely consistent with Sullivan's (1956) description of the prototypical obsessive–compulsive's early family environment, in which a veneer of pleasantness chronically conceals significant distress and dysfunction.

In summary, as the preceding case example is intended to illustrate, the obsessive–compulsive personality appears to have a fairly distinctive Rorschach "signature," which includes an inefficiently high level of organizational activity; perfectionistic attention to form, which may be painstakingly described; perceptual conservatism; ideational rigidity; an introversive or ambitent problem-solving style; affective constraint, with vigorously restrained anger; brittle self-esteem; somewhat immature yet not grossly pathological object relations; and a sharp contrast between generally tense stability and marked situational distress, especially feelings of anxiety, helplessness, and failure.

Despite evidence of the Rorschach's validity provided by this profile, surprisingly little empirical research has been conducted with the Rorschach on OCPD. Among the seemingly fruitful studies to be done on the cognitive, emotional, and interpersonal distinctiveness of OCPD on the Rorschach, the interpersonal dimension seems especially in need of further investigation. There is an incongruity between the heavy theoretical emphasis on OCPD's relational origins (Sullivan, 1956) and the comparatively scant attention to interpersonal factors in CS assessment of obsessive–compulsive tendencies. This de-emphasis may be attributable in part to the "generality" problem with the CS's Interpersonal cluster. As Exner (2003) states, "Rorschach hypotheses about an individual's interpersonal functioning must be based on a higher degree of inference than is necessary for some of the other CS clusters," and are "often more general than might be desired" (p. 489). Research on more specific behavioral correlates of Interpersonal cluster variables (e.g., the rather global human representational variables PHR and GHR, which thus far have been examined primarily in connection with psychotic disorders and depression) may provide a more nuanced understanding of obsessive–compulsives' relational functioning in comparison to persons with other psychological problems.

Among the putative "signature" markers of OCPD, there appears to be a particular need for further research investigating the OBS. Examining the capacity of the OBS to differentiate OCPD from OCD and from the other Cluster C PDs seems especially important because of the mixed OCD–OCPD sample in the original research. To address this problem, as well as the methodologic issue of potential overlap of OCD, OCPD, and the other Cluster C PD's in Axis I and II comorbidity studies, it seems crucial to compile a large normative data set for OCPD. The use of well-validated self-report measures and semistructured interviews with large samples to identify OCPD and its related disorders, and then comparison of these groups on the Rorschach, will provide some direction on how to differentiate and characterize these related diagnostic groups further. It also may yield the sort of informational gestalt that becomes available when implicit and self-attributed tendencies are examined together (Bornstein, 2002; Ganellen, 1996; McClelland, Koestner, & Weinberger, 1989). Emergent differences in unconscious functioning (e.g., ego defenses and object relations) might then be examined in conjunction with overt distress and observable dysfunction to gain a clearer, more differentiated picture of psychological disorders in which chronic anxiety and tension are similarly prominent, but not necessarily for similar reasons.

REFERENCES

American Psychiatric Association. (2000). *Diagnostic and statistical manual of mental disorders* (4th ed., text revision). Washington, DC: Author.

Beck, A. T., Ward, C. H., Mendelson, M., Mock, J., & Erbaugh, J. (1961). An inventory for measuring depression. *Archives of General Psychiatry, 4,* 561–571.

Bienvenu, O. J., & Stein, M. B. (2003). Personality and anxiety disorders: A review. *Journal of Personality Disorders, 17,* 139–151.

Blatt, S. J., & Shichman, S. (1983). Two primary configurations of psychopathology. *Psychoanalysis and Contemporary Thought, 6,* 187–254.

Bornstein, R. F. (1995). Active dependency. *Journal of Nervous and Mental Disease, 183,* 64–77.

Bornstein, R. F. (2002). A process dissociation approach to objective–projective test score interrelationships. *Journal of Personality Assessment, 78,* 47–68.

Breskin, S. (1968). Measurement of rigidity, a non-verbal test. *Perceptual and Motor Skills, 27,* 1203–1206.

Clark, L. A. (1993). *Schedule for Nonadaptive and Adaptive Personality* (SNAP). Minneapolis, MN: University of Minnesota Press.

Corruble, E., Ginestet, D., & Guelfi, J. D. (1996). Comorbidity of personality disorders and unipolar major depression: A review. *Journal of Affective Disorders, 37,* 157–170.

Exner, J. E., Jr. (1993). *The Rorschach: A comprehensive system: Volume 1. Basic foundations* (3rd ed.). New York: John Wiley.

Exner, J. E., Jr. (2001). *A Rorschach workbook for the comprehensive system* (5th ed.). Asheville, NC: Rorschach Workshops.

Exner, J. E., Jr. (2003). *The Rorschach: A comprehensive system* (4th ed.). Hoboken, NJ: John Wiley.

Fairbairn, W. R. D. (1952). *An object-relations theory of the personality.* New York: Basic Books.

Fenichel, O. (1945). *The psychoanalytic theory of neurosis.* New York: W.W. Norton.

First, M. B., Spitzer, R. L., Gibbon, M., & Williams, J. B. W. (1996). *Structured Clinical Interview for DSM-IV Axis I Disorders, Patient Edition* (SCID-P). New York: New York State Psychiatric Institute, Biometrics Research.

Freud, S. (1908/1963). Character and anal eroticism. In P. Reiff (Ed.), *Collected papers of Sigmund Freud* (Vol. 10). New York: Collier.

Gabbard, G. O. (2000). *Psychodynamic psychiatry in clinical practice* (3rd ed.). Washington, DC: American Psychiatric Press.

Gallagher, N. G., South, S. C., & Oltmanns, T. F. (2003). Attentional coping style in obsessive–compulsive personality disorder: A test of the intolerance of uncertainty hypothesis. *Personality and Individual Differences, 34,* 41–57.

Ganellen, R. J. (1996). *Integrating the Rorschach and the MMPI-2 in personality assessment.* Mahwah, NJ: Lawrence Erlbaum Associates.

Hill, A. B. (1976). Methodological problems in the use of factor analysis: A critical review of the experimental evidence for the anal character. *British Journal of Medical Psychology, 49,* 145–159.

Huprich, S. K. (2003). Evaluating NEO Personality Inventory-Revised profiles in veterans with personality disorders. *Journal of Personality Disorders, 17,* 33–44.

Hyler, S. E. (1994). *Personality Diagnostic Questionnaire-4* (PDQ-4). New York: New York State Psychiatric Institute.

Kates, S. L. (1950). Objective Rorschach response patterns differentiating anxiety reactions from obsessive–compulsive reactions. *Journal of Consulting Psychology, 14,* 226–229.

Keller, M. B., Lavori, P. W., Friedman, B., Nielsen, E., Endicott, J., McDonald-Scott, P., & Andreasen, N. C. (1987). The Longitudinal Interval Follow-Up Evaluation: A comprehensive method for assessing outcome in prospective longitudinal studies. *Archives of General Psychiatry, 44,* 540–548.

Lazare, A., Klerman, G. L., & Armor, D. J. (1966). Oral, obsessive, and hysterical personality patterns: An investigation of psychoanalytic concepts by means of factor analysis. *Archives of General Psychiatry, 14,* 624–630.

Loranger, A. W., Susman, V. L., Oldham, J. M., & Russakoff, L. M. (1985). *Personality Disorder Examination (PDE): A structured interview for DSM-III-R personality disor-*

ders. White Plains, NY: New York Hospital-Cornell Medical Center, Westchester Division.

McClelland, D. C., Koestner, R., & Weinberger, J. (1989). How do self-attributed and implicit motives differ? *Psychological Review, 96*, 690–702.

McWilliams, N. (1994). *Psychoanalytic diagnosis*. New York: Guilford.

Millon, T. (1981). *Disorders of personality, DSM-III: Axis II*. New York: John Wiley.

Mitchell, S., & Black, M. (1995). *Freud and beyond: A history of modern psychoanalytic thought*. New York: Basic Books.

Pollak, J. (1987). Relationship of obsessive–compulsive personality to obsessive–compulsive disorder: A review of the literature. *Journal of Psychology, 121,* 137–148.

Rees, A., Hardy, G. E., & Barkham, M. (1996). Covariance in the measurement of depression/anxiety and three cluster C personality disorders (avoidant, dependent, obsessive–compulsive). *Journal of Affective Disorders, 45,* 143–153.

Reynolds, S. K., & Clark, L. A. (2001). Predicting dimensions of personality disorder from domains and facets of the five-factor model. *Journal of Personality, 69,* 199–222.

Robins, L., Helzer, J. E., Croughan, J., & Ratliff, K. S. (1981). National Institute of Mental Health Diagnostic Interview Schedule: Its history, characteristics, and validity. *Archives of General Psychiatry, 38,* 381–389.

Sacco, J. M., & Olczak, P. V. (1996). Personality and cognition: Obsessivity, hystericism, and some correlates. *Journal of Social Behavior and Personality, 11,* 165–176.

Salzman, L. (1968). *The obsessive personality: Origins, dynamics, and therapy*. New York: Science House.

Schafer, R. (1954). *Psychoanalytic interpretation in Rorschach testing*. New York: Grune & Stratton.

Serpell, L., Livingstone, A., Neiderman, M., & Lask, B. (2002). Anorexia nervosa: Obsessive–compulsive disorder, obsessive–compulsive personality disorder, or neither? *Clinical Psychology Review, 22,* 647–669.

Shapiro, D. (1965). *Neurotic styles*. New York: Basic Books.

Simon, K. M., & Meyer, J. (1990). Obsessive–compulsive personality disorder. In A. T. Beck & A. Freeman (Eds.), *Cognitive therapy of personality disorders* (pp. 309–332). New York: Guilford.

Skodol, A. E., Gunderson, J. G., McGlashan, T. H., Dyck, I. R., Stout, R. L., Bender, D. S., et al. (2002). Functional impairment in patients with schizotypal, borderline, avoidant, or obsessive–compulsive personality disorder. *American Journal of Psychiatry, 159,* 276–283.

Smith, T. L., & Benjamin, L. S. (2002). The functional impairment associated with personality disorders. *Current Opinion in Psychiatry, 15,* 135–141.

Smokler, I. A., & Shevrin, H. (1979). Cerebral lateralization and personality style. *Archives of General Psychiatry, 36,* 949–954.

Starcevic, V. (1990). Relationship between hypochondriasis and obsessive–compulsive personality disorder: Close relatives separated by nosological schemes? *American Journal of Psychotherapy, 44,* 340–347.

Stroop, J. R. (1935). Studies of interference in serial verbal reactions. *Journal of Experimental Psychology, 6,* 643–661.

Sullivan, H. S. (1956). *Clinical studies in psychiatry*. New York: Norton.

Torgersen, S. (1980). The oral, obsessive, and hysterical personality syndromes. *Archives of General Psychiatry, 37,* 1272–1277.

Trull, T. J., Widiger, T. A., & Burr, R. (2001). A structured interview for the assessment of the Five-Factor Model of Personality: Facet-level relations to the Axis II personality disorders. *Journal of Personality, 69,* 175–198.

Viglione, D. J., Brager, R., & Haller, N. (1991). Psychoanalytic interpretation of the Rorschach: Do we have better hieroglyphics? *Journal of Personality Assessment, 57,* 1–9.

Weiner, I. B. (2003). *Principles of Rorschach interpretation* (2nd ed.). Mahwah, NJ: Lawrence Erlbaum Associates.

Weissman, M., & Bothwell, S. (1976). The assessment of social adjustment by patient self-report. *Archives of General Psychiatry, 33,* 1111–1115.

Wilson, S. (1994). *Interpretive guide to the comprehensive Rorschach system* (5th revision). Laguna Beach, CA: Author.

Wing, J. K., Cooper, J. E., & Sartorius, N. (1974). *The measurement and classification of psychiatric symptoms.* Cambridge: Cambridge University Press.

Zanarini, M. C., Frankenburg, F. R., Sickel, A. E., & Yong, L. (1996). *The Diagnostic Interview for DSM-IV Personality Disorders* (DIPD-IV). Belmont, MA: McLean Hospital.

Free Association	Inquiry

Card I

1. An exotic butterfly.

1. That's not it. (The first thing you said you saw was an exotic butterfly). Oh, yes. Right. The two drawings on the side look like gigantic, gauzy wings that butterflies have, with the black veins. Not veins, the connecting ribs. And the little tiny feelers. Not feelers, antennas. (Gauzy?) Because you can see they're translucent. (Translucent?) Lighter in some parts than other parts. (You said the wings looked gigantic). Well, when you look at the whole thing, it seems to be over half, occupies over half the space. I looked at the middle as the body, and the two side things as larger than the body.

2. You can see more than one thing in them? (Most people see more than one thing). At first blush, an exotic butterfly. On the other hand, two figures both look like women. Some kind of statues. Like winged figures sort of holding onto each other. Arms flying out. In the middle is another figure sort of holding them.

2. Yes. Two arms flying out. This is where they're holding each other. In the center is another figure holding them together in a unified fashion. If you can differentiate between the light and dark parts, here are the legs and torso and arms of the middle figure, and the winged figures are holding onto the arm. (Light and dark parts?) Here, in the center, looks like some kind of clothing, and the body inside the light.

Card II

3. (Laughs) At first blush, these look like two elephants. They're sort of meeting with their trunks. Looks like they're fighting over something. The red splotch looks like blood. As strange as it is, seems like baby elephants. Don't have tusks. Maybe not elephants, pygmy animals fighting over something.

3. Yeah. Then I changed my mind. (The first thing you saw was two elephants). These two things extending look like tusks. That made it look like elephants. (Fighting?) Because of the red splotches. Then I saw they didn't have tusks, so how can they make each other bleed?

4. On the other hand, it could be sort of like a dance. Clapping of the hands. I don't know what the red spots mean. Have no idea of how to fit that into what I see.

4. That's right. (Show me where you were looking). Well, it's like (subject claps hands) two dancers coming together and hitting hands and back away and come together. Like folk dancers. Again, I can't make out what the red blotches are.

Card III
5. Well, these are two male figures. They're doffing their hats to each other, and in between is a red bow. I haven't the foggiest idea what it means, but it's a red bow.

5. Here's one male figure and the other. This is their hats down here, like old- fashioned top hats or bowler hats. The way people used to greet each other, I gather. (Top hats?) Well, I first thought it could be beaver hats because they're round. Round and furry. (Furry?) Well, it's not, it's a regular outline of the hats. If beaver, would be more irregular. Fur can't be completely, can look straggly. (Then you mentioned a red bow). Couldn't figure it out. Couldn't tell if part of a background or a woman walking away with an old-fashioned dress and bow in the back. Or a woman walking towards them with a bow in the front.

6. Maybe that stuff in the background of the two men doffing their hats...um...I don't know, but it looks like dead cats. Not dead. Looks like some kind of decoration.

6. I said dead cats, then I changed my mind. But at first thought, dead cats being hurled out of the window. (Show me that). See the tail, and they look lifeless. The heads are still. Cats are pretty lively. (Decoration?). No, don't see that.

Card IV
7. Oh, something like an ogre out of a child's story, sitting on his throne. Awaiting his retinue. He's sort of immobile. His feet are huge and enormous. His body is chunky. His arms are very weak. So, I guess he's dependent on his retinue. Looks like an ogre from a children's story. I don't think he has much of a brain, has a very small head.

7. That's right! The whole thing is an ogre. This is the throne he's sitting on. (You mentioned his feet are huge). Well, these are the shoes, the wider part are shoes or boots. Relative to the body they look enormous, much closer to you than the body. That's the pants the shoes fit into. (And he has a small head). Yes. This is the head here. Sits on top of this ruff or collar. Can just see the little nose and head.

Card V

8. This is a butterfly. A beautiful butterfly. Huge butterfly! Probably in Africa or some exotic, tropical place. And it's flying and... I guess some bird of prey will see this butterfly and destroy her. Or some predator.

8. Yes. That's right. (Exotic?) Here's the wings, spread, and antenna, body. Sort of a mottled thing, the dark and light. It's the biggest butterfly I've ever seen! From Africa, because I gather butterflies are bigger in tropical climates, bigger there than in a northern climate, such as here.

Card VI

9. A combination of things. This is a bearskin.

9. It is flat, legs of bear, or the skin of him. It looked tawny like a bearskin. Like a brown bear. It looks like it had been split here. Like a bearskin in position by a hearth. (Tawny?) The different shadings. (Split?) Here. It's darker in the center, lighter there. It reminds me of a picture I've seen.

10. Somehow, it looks like a rocket taking off! (laughs) Yeah. That's what it is, it's the burst of flame from a rocket taking off into space. Once again, engaging in some fruitless mission NASA is engaged in. There, it's taking off with a roar. This is the red flame in back, taking off.

10. Here's the spaceship. All of this, the bearskin becomes the flame billowing out from it. This is the nose of the spaceship. (You mentioned the red flame in back). Well, this looks like the red, the dark looks like a dark red, the flame and everything.

Card VII

11. Could see many things. These could be clouds. It looks like fleecy, soft clouds, if you're lying on peaceful green grass, looking up, or a meadow, and you can make whatever you want out of the clouds. Somehow it appears very peaceful and calming.

11. Yes. The whole thing. The whole thing looked gauzy, fleecy like clouds do. Gauzy because of the shading. (Peaceful and calming?) No violent activity. It's sort of, at most, sort of floating. At the least, sort of static.

336

12. There's two women's faces, facing each other with hair in an upsweep.

12. Here's one and here's one. Facing each other. (Hair?) This is hair in an upsweep.

Card VIII
13. (Shakes head). Damned if I know! Well, this is a ... a decorative piece of some sort. On each side is a bear. In the middle it's sort of an Indian work. I suppose, not knowing symbols Indians know, it tells the story of a particular individual. His symbol is the bear, which I understand Indians have. Tells the story of his tribe. It's very colorful. It's a saga of some sort.

13. That's right. On each side is two bears. And my association was Indian, Native American, let's be politically correct, are always described in terms of being close to nature, knowing how to live with nature. They adopt animal symbols. Then I thought, what has to be in the middle, the bears symbolize a man or a tribe. And in the middle is the saga of the individual or tribe. I can't make out what that story would be. It's like hieroglyphics, except Indian-style.

Card IX
14. Part of an abstract drawing or painting. By an artist that uses almost watercolors. The different colors are reflecting different moods. Like the greenish hue or aqua is one of forbidding or foreboding. The orange is showing hope. It's on top of the foreboding, something you look forward to. The bottom is the red, red blood, I guess, of people having those feelings.

14. Yes. The green was forbidding or foreboding. Orange was of, I guess I associated it with a sunrise. Associated sun with hope. Maybe that's the story of life -- the struggle between two opposite poles.

Card X

15. It looks like sea life. Crabs, shrimp, and lobster, all at the bottom of the sea, living out their lifespan. What do you call, what's on the bottom that everything eats? There are kelp and crab. These may be fishermen's hooks at top and two undistinguished something, sea urchins, are the bait. It looks like a colorful display of sea life that a scuba diver may see.

15. That's right. Here are the crab and the shrimp. This looks like a lobster. I have never seen one, but I'm not great on lobster. For some reason the word "kelp" sprang to mind. Maybe using kelp to catch lobsters. I know in reality they use pots to catch lobster, but this has nothing to do with reality. Here are some, looks like plankton other sea life feeds on. It looks like a graphic scene of sea life, even with the interference of man!

RORSCHACH SEQUENCE OF SCORES FOR MR. IRWIN

Card	Resp	Loc (DQ)	Loc N	Determinants (FQ)	(2)	Content(s)	P	Z	Special Scores
I	1.	Wo	1	FV.FC'+		A	P	1.0	
	2.	W+	1	Ma.FYo	(2)	(H), H, Cg		4.0	COP, GHR
II	3.	D+	1	FMa.CFo	(2)	A, Bl	P	3.0	AG, MOR, DR, PHR
	4.	W+	1	Mao	(2)	H		4.5	COP, GHR
III	5.	D+	1	Ma.CF+	(2)	H, Cg	P	4.0	DR, GHR
	6.	Do	2	mao	(2)	A			MOR, AG
IV	7.	W+	1	Mp.FD+		(H), Hh	P	4.0	GHR
V	8.	Wo	1	FMa.FY+		A	P	1.0	
VI	9.	Do	1	FYo		Ad	P		MOR, PER
	10.	W+	1	ma.YF+		Sc, Fi		2.5	CP
VII	11.	WSv/+	1	mp.C'F.YFo		Cl		4.0	
	12.	Do	1	Fo	(2)	Hd	P		GHR
VIII	13.	W+	1	FCo	(2)	Art, A	P	4.5	AB
IX	14.	Wv/+	1	C		Art, Bl			AB
X	15.	W+	1	FCo	(2)	A	P	5.5	DR, FAB

339

STRUCTURAL SUMMARY FOR MR. IRWIN

Location Features	Determinants Blends	Single	Contents	Approach
		M = 1	H = 3	I: W.W
Zf = 11	FV.FC'	FM = 0	(H) =2	II: D.W
ZSum = 38.0	M.FY	m = 1	Hd = 1	III: D.D
Zest = 34.5	FM.CF	FC =2	(Hd) = 0	IV: W
	M.CF	CF = 0	Hx = 0	V:W
W = 10	M.FD	C = 1	A = 6	VI: D.W
D = 5	FM.FY	Cn = 0	(A) = 0	VII: WS.D
W+D = 15	m.YF	FC' = 0	Ad = 1	VIII: W
Dd = 0	m.C'F.YF	C'F = 0	(Ad) = 0	IX:W
S = 1		C'= 0	An = 0	X:W
		FT = 0	Art = 2	

Developmental Quality

+ = 8		TF = 0	Ay = 0
o = 5		T = 0	Bl = 2
v = 0		FV = 0	Bt = 0
v/+ = 2		VF = 0	Cg = 2
		V = 0	Cl = 1

Special Scores

Lv 1	Lv 2
DV = 0x1	= 0x2
INC = 0x2	= 0x4
DR = 3x3	= 0x6
FAB = 1x4	= 0x7
ALOG = 0x5	
CON = 0x7	

Form Quality

	FQx	MQual	W+D		
+	= 5	= 2	= 5	FY = 1	
o	= 9	= 2	= 9	YF = 0	
u	= 0	= 0	= 0	Y= 0	Raw Sum 6 = 4
-	= 0	= 0	= 0	Fr = 0	Wgtd Sum 6 = 13
none	= 1	= 0	= 1	rF =0	

FD = 0	Hh = 1	AB = 2 GHR= 5
F = 1	Ls = 0	AG = 2 PHR = 1
(2) =8	Na = 0	COP = 2 MOR = 3
	Sc = 1	CP = 1 PER = 1
	Sx = 0	PSV = 0
	Xy = 0	
	Id = 0	

340

STRUCTURAL SUMMARY FOR MR. IRWIN CONTINUED

Ratios, Percentages, and Derivations

Core

R = 15	L = .07	
EB = 4:4.5	EA = 8.5	EBPer =N/A
eb = 5:8	es = 13	D = -1
	Adj es = 7	Adj D = 0
FM = 2	SumC' = 2	SumT =0
m = 3	Sum V = 1	Sum Y = 5

Affect

FC: CF+C =2:3
Pure C = 1
SumC':WSumC = 2:4.5
Afr = .25
S = 1
Blends:R = 8:15
CP = 1

Interpersonal

COP = 2   AG = 2
GHR: PHR = 5:1
a:p = 7:2
Food = 0
Sum T = 0
Human Cont = 6
Pure H = 3
PER = 1
Isol Indx = .13

Ideation

a:p = 7:2	Sum6 = 4
Ma:Mp = 3:1	Lv2 =0
2AB+Art+Ay = 6	WSum6 = 13
MOR = 3	M- = 0
	Mnone = 0

Mediation

XA% = .93
WDA% = .93
X-% = .00
S- = 0
P = 9
X+% = .93
Xu% = .00

Processing

Zf = 11
W:D:Dd = 10:5:0
W:M = 10:4
Zd = +3.5
PSV =0
DQ+ = 8
DQv = 0

Self-Perception

3r+(2)/R = .53
Fr+rF = 0
SumV = 1
FD = 1
An+Xy = 0
MOR = 3
H:(H)+Hd+(Hd) = 3:3

PTI = 1   DEPI = 5   CDI = 1   S-CON = 5   HVI = No   OBS = Yes

V

OTHER PERSONALITY DISORDERS

Rorschach Assessment of Passive–Aggressive Personality Disorder

Barry Ritzler
Galit Gerevitz-Stern
Long Island University

Passive–aggressive personality disorder (PAPD) is described as "a pervasive pattern of negativistic attitudes and passive resistance to demands for adequate performance in social and occupational situations that begins by early adulthood and that occurs in a variety of contexts" (American Psychiatric Association [APA], 2000, p. 733). In early versions of the *Diagnostic and Statistical Manual of Mental Disorders* (DSM) (i.e., DSM-II, APA, 1969), PAPD was labeled as negativistic personality disorder because of the degree to which individuals showed pervasive oppositionality in their thoughts, feelings, behaviors, and interpersonal relationships. A list of the DSM-IV-Text Revision (APA, 2001) diagnostic criteria is provided in Table 13.1.

The studies of passive–aggressive personality disorder (PAPD) in the DSM and empirical literature have had mixed, and sometimes contradictory, findings. McCann (1988) reviewed the PAPD construct and concluded that part of the problem with this diagnostic category was its changing diagnostic criteria. He suggested that the then recent DSM-III-R (APA, 1987) PAPD criteria promised more reliable diagnoses. However, even after the publication of DSM-IV-Text Revision (APA, 2001) and revised diagnostic criteria, it is uncommon to find and assign PAPD as a diagnosis to patients in clinical settings. Perhaps this is attributable to the very nature of the diagnosis, whereby individuals passively resist seeking help and entering treatment? Nevertheless, PAPD has received relatively less attention in the empirical literature than other Axis II disorders. This is especially true for studies of PAPD and the Rorschach. Most studies of

TABLE 13.1
DSM-IV-Text Revision Research Criteria
for Passive–Aggressive Personality Disorder[a]

A. A pervasive pattern of negativistic attitudes and passive resistance to demands for adequate performance, beginning by early adulthood and present in a variety of contexts, as indicated by four (or more) of the following:

    1. Passively resists fulfilling routine social and occupational tasks

    2. Complains of being misunderstood and unappreciated by others

    3. Is sullen and argumentative

    4. Unreasonably criticizes and scorns authority

    5. Expresses envy and resentment toward those apparently more fortunate

    6. Voices exaggerated and persistent complaints of personal misfortune

    7. Alternates between hostile defiance and contrition

B. Does not occur exclusively during major depressive episodes and is not better accounted for by dysthymic disorder.

[a]Taken from APA (2001), pp. 734–735.

PAPD have focused on "objective," self-report, or observer-report measures. The findings from these studies are reviewed, and the utility and validity of the PAPD diagnosis are discussed.

ASSESSING PASSIVE–AGGRESSIVE PERSONALITY DISORDER WITH SELF- AND INFORMANT REPORTS

Millon Clinical Multiaxial Inventory

Early studies on the Passive–Aggressive scale of the Millon Clinical Multiaxial Inventory (MCMI ; Millon, 1983, 1987, 1994) produced mixed results about the scale's validity. Craig, Verinis, and Wexler (1985) compared alcoholics with opium addicts on the original MCMI. They found that alcoholics scored higher on the Passive–Aggressive scale than opium addicts, but also scored higher on several other personality disorder scales.

A more recent study by Fernandez-Montalvo, Landa, Lopez-Goni, Loria, and Zarzuela (2002) evaluated MCMI-II profiles of 70 alcoholics. They found this scale, along with three others, to be significantly higher than the profiles of nonalcoholic patients. Another MCMI-II study compared 26 inpatients with borderline personality disorder profiles with 42 other psychiatric inpatients (Torgersen & Alnaes, 1990). The Passive–Aggressive scale was one of six that differentiated the two groups.

Other studies also question the validity and sensitivity of the MCMI in assessing PAPD. Widiger and Sanderson (1987) found low convergent validity for the MCMI in a sample of 42 psychiatric inpatients with a diagnosis of DSM-III personality disorders. McCann, Flynn, and Gersh (1992) also found no correspondence between the Passive–Aggressive scale of the MCMI and a DSM-III diagnosis of PAPD. Rather, they found the Passive–Aggressive scale to be correlated with many other personality disorder diagnoses. Lall (1995) evaluated the relationship between suicidal ideation and psychopathology in a study of military personnel. The Passive–Aggressive scale of the MCMI was one of nine scales that were significantly higher for the suicidal ideation group ($n = 42$) than for the nonsuicidal group ($n = 89$). Similar results were obtained when the MCMI-III was evaluated in suicidal inpatients. Craig and Bivens (2000) found that suicide attempters ($n = 68$) scored significantly higher on the Passive–Aggressive scale and seven other personality disorder scales than 340 nonsuicidal patients. Also, Joiner and Rudd (2002) recently reported that the MCMI-III Passive–Aggressive scale was significantly higher for a sample of 250 patients deemed to be at risk for suicide than for those not at risk.

The MCMI has shown better specificity in studies that have focused on other psychological problems. For instance, Berman and McCann (1995) found that displacement, as assessed on the Defense Mechanism Inventory (Gleser & Ihilevich, 1979), was significantly associated with the Passive–Aggressive scale. King (1998) reported that the Passive–Aggressive and Antisocial scales of the MCMI-II were the best indicators of university-level academic performance deficits in a sample of 32 students. This scale also was elevated more frequently among young adult males with chronic authority conflicts than among women, older males, and those with other conflict issues (Vereycken, Vertommen, & Corveleyn, 2002).

Collectively, these findings suggest that the MCMI may not be specific in assessing PAPD, but may be associated more with related features of various types of psychopathology and psychological problems. There are several possibilities to account for these findings. First, as noted by Widiger and Sanderson (1987), the MCMI may be providing information about passive–aggressive tendencies and not PAPD per se. Second, given the dynamics of their psychopathology, PAPD patients may not accurately report their passive–aggressive tendencies on the MCMI. Third, as noted by McCann (1988), PAPD individuals may not be aware of their defensiveness and passive–aggressive behaviors, and thus may inaccurately report their own behavior. Fourth, also noted by McCann (1988), inconsistent diagnostic criteria in the DSM system and inconsistencies in assessing PAPD may not allow for a consistent and accurate assessment of the PAPD. At the very least, it appears that the MCMI Passive–Aggressive scale may be sensitive in detecting overall level of psychopathology.

MMPI AND MMPI-2

Most of the studies conducted with the Minnesota Multiphasic Personality Inventory (MMPI) and the MMPI-2 have found associations between scales 2, 4, and/or 7 and passive–aggressive traits. Even more specifically, several MMPI studies have found relationships between passive–aggressive characteristics and alcoholism (Nerviano & Gross, 1983). A pattern within these studies is described by Overall (1973), who found that alcoholics were characterized by a 2–4–7 code type and described as "depressive, with passive–aggressive features."

MMPI Personality Disorder Scales

The MMPI Personality Disorder scales were created by Morey, Waugh, and Blashfield (1985), who combined rational and empiric keying strategies to create scales based on DSM-III descriptions of personality disorders, including PAPD. To create the PAPD scale, 14 items were assembled. Initial analyses in a sample of 475 psychiatric patients provided promising results for content validity and internal consistency. However, attempts to replicate the scales were not as supportive. Schuler, Snibbe, and Buckwalter (1994) found no evidence to support the validity of the Passive–Aggressive scale despite substantial support for many other of the original scales.

Inspection of the 14 PAPD items may help to explain the lack of findings. Only 5 of the 14 items appear to have face validity and are scored in the "true" direction. Because the scale overall has low face validity and individuals with PAPD tend to deny problems with frustration and anger, it is possible that they do not provide accurate responses to the items. Alternatively, the Passive–Aggressive scale simply may not be valid.

OTHER SELF-REPORTS
AND SEMISTRUCTURED INTERVIEWS

Coolidge and Merwin (1992) developed the Coolidge Axis II Inventory, a "true–false" interview that assesses personality disorders. They found preliminary support for the reliability of the PAPD scale, but only a modest concordance rate (50%) with DSM-III personality disorders. Although the measure was validated only on 24 patients with personality disorders, it did correlate highly with the MCMI-II Passive–Aggressive Scale ($r = .86$).

Some studies have used interview methods to assess PAPD. Klein (2003) evaluated patients and informants with the Personality Disorder Examination (PDE; Loranger, 1988) and three outcome measures of depression, global function, and social adjustment. Klein found that patient reports of passive–aggressive symptoms were not associated with any of the independent ratings from the outcome measures, whereas informant reports significantly predicted all three measures. Klein (2003) suggested that informant reports may have greater validity than patient reports, especially in the case of passive–aggressive personality disorder.

Driessen, Veltrup, Wetterling, John, and Dilling (1998) assessed 250 psychiatric patients who had a comorbid alcohol dependency diagnosis using the Composite International Diagnostic Interview (Peters et al., 1996) and the International Personality Disorder Examination (Loranger et al., 1994). They found that these patients had a relatively high number of passive–aggressive characteristics, as compared with nonalcoholic patients.

Axelrod, Widiger, Trull, and Corbett (1997) evaluated the relationship of self-report and diagnostic interview measures of PAPD in the Five-Factor Model (FFM; Costa & McCrae, 1992; Trull & Widiger, 1997) to scores on the Personality Diagnostic Questionnaire-Revised (PDQ-R; Hyler & Rieder, 1987) and the MMPI Personality Disorder scales. Combining the PDQ-R and MMPI Personality Disorder scales into a composite score, Axelrod et al. (1997) found a significant correlation between the composite score and the semistructured interview for PAPD on the FFM interview, but no relationship between the FFM self-report and the PAPD composite scale. These findings suggest that the mechanism used to assess PAPD is an important factor for identifying and assessing PAPD. That is, ratings made by interviewers may more readily detect PAPD than self-reports made by patients themselves.

Other studies with the PDQ-R have been reported in the literature, although their conclusions are somewhat limited. For instance, Yeung, Lyons, Waternaux, and Faraone (1993) assessed first-degree relatives of 194 patients with psychiatric disorders. They found a significant number of passive–aggressive characteristics (not personality disorders per se) in the relatives.

PROJECTIVE TESTS

Thematic Apperception Test

Few studies have evaluated PAPD or passive–aggressive characteristics in clinical or nonclinical populations with the Thematic Apperception Test (TAT). Wolowitz and Shorkey (1969) evaluated 10 paranoid schizophrenics, 10 nonparanoid schizophrenics, and 20 patients characterized as passive–aggressive. These researchers found that passive–aggressive patients had more passive–aggressive themes in their stories, as determined by external raters. Interestingly, another study evaluated the stimulus pull of Thematic Apperception Test (TAT) cards. Goldfried and Zax (1965) asked undergraduates to provide dimensional ratings of all 30 TAT cards on 10 bipolar adjective scales. They found that some of the cards had a definite "pull" for passive–aggressive content. However, they did not attempt to use the TAT to identify individuals with passive–aggressive characteristics.

In the light of many mixed results regarding the assessment of PAPD, there is legitimate concern as to whether the disorder exists at all or should be regarded as an important dimension of personality organization. However, because some studies suggest that PAPD can be assessed reliably and validly, and because individuals with PAPD may not appear as regularly for psychological treatment as individuals with other disorders, the syndrome may be worth further study.

Rorschach Studies

Very few Rorschach studies have been conducted to investigate PAPD and its related characteristics. In part, the reason for this may be that such patients are seldom available in sufficient numbers for study. Others, too, may not have considered the Rorschach to be a useful tool for studying the disorder.

Wiener (1956) suggested that passive–aggressive personality characteristics are associated with oral fixation. He investigated this hypothesis in a clinical sample and found that patients who met criteria for PAPD and alcoholism gave significantly fewer hostile oral images on the Rorschach and more positive oral imagery (e.g., "cotton candy" vs. "a biting monster"). Unfortunately, the design of the study made it impossible to determine whether the differences are more related to passive–aggressive characteristics, alcoholism, or both.

In the only other published study that mentions the Rorschach and PAPD, Abram, Meixel, Webb, and Scott (1976) evaluated obese patients before jejuinoileal bypass surgery with the Rorschach, Wechsler Adult Intelligence Scale (WAIS), Bender–Gestalt, MMPI, and Tennessee Self-Concept Scale. They found that 9 of the 34 patients evaluated had moderate levels of passive–aggressive characteristics. However, no specific information was provided about how the passive–aggressive characteristics were identified with the personality measures used in the study.

EXPECTED RORSCHACH PATTERNS
FOR PASSIVE AGGRESSIVE PERSONALITY DISORDER

As noted earlier, few studies have been performed with the Rorschach and individuals with a diagnosis of PAPD. Consequently, the following discussion is speculative and should be considered as such. Research to evaluate these hypotheses is needed before any further conclusions can be drawn about Rorschach patterns of individuals with a diagnosis of PAPD. Nevertheless, the Rorschach appears to provide meaningful information in the assessment of PAPD, especially since research on self-reports and observer-reports of PAPD have yielded mixed findings on the validity of the measures.

The Rorschach patterns proposed in the following discussion are based on the DSM-IV Text Revision (APA, 2001) description and criteria for PAPD (see Table 13.1). This description notes that "the essential feature (of PAPD) is a pervasive pattern of negativistic attitudes and passive resistance to demands for adequate performance in social and occupational situations" (p. 790). In the Comprehensive System, such attitudes are associated with White Space (S) responses. Exner (2000) proposed that individuals with more than three S responses are "disposed to be more negativistic or oppositional toward the environment than are most people" (p. 106). Furthermore, in the Comprehensive System, passive personality styles are associated with a ratio of passive movement > active movement +1 (p > a + 1). Of this finding, Exner (2000) proposed that "the individual generally will assume a more passive, [although not necessarily submissive] role in interpersonal relations" (p. 313).

The DSM-IV Text Revision of PAPD adds that individuals with the disorder "are often overtly ambivalent ... wavering indecisively (in) an intense conflict between dependence on others and the desire for self-assertion (and poor) self-confidence despite a superficial bravado. They foresee the worst possible outcome for most situations" (p. 790). Emotional ambivalence in the Comprehensive System is associated with color-shading blends. As proposed by Exner (2003), color-shading blends that exclude diffuse shading indicate "a trait-like feature by which the subject often is confused by emotion and may frequently experience both positive and negative feelings about the same stimulus situation" (p. 504). Such emotional wavering and ambivalence also is associated with an ambitent Erlebnistypus ratio (M:WSumC). According to Exner (2003), ambitents' "failure to develop a consistent preference or style in their coping behaviors seems to lead to less efficiency and more vacillation" (p. 413). This can be further detected in Rorschach markers of dependency (i.e., food responses) and "a desire for self-assertion," seen in unusual form quality responses (FQu). Exner (2003) stated that FQu responses "can signal an excessive commitment to the self and an unwillingness to adhere to the standards of conventionality" (p. 471). Such features also are detected by the Personalization (PER) response because individuals with elevations on this variable tend to be "overly authoritarian or argumentative when interpersonal situations appear to pose challenges to the self" (p. 527).

Poor self-confidence can be assessed with the Egocentricity Index. Low scores on this variable "signal a marked sense of dissatisfaction with oneself" (Exner, 2003, p. 506). Likewise, the characteristic pessimism seen in such individuals can be detected in elevated Morbid (MOR) responses. "If the value of MOR is 3 or higher, it is very likely that the thinking of the subject is marked frequently by a pessimistic set in which relationships are viewed with a sense of doubt and/or discouragement" (p. 478).

The DSM-IV Text Revision also specifies that the PAPD diagnosis should be made with caution in the presence of a major depressive episode or dysthymic disorder. Consequently, as significant problems with depression and affect are detected by the Depression Index (Exner, 2003), a positive Depression Index would contradict the presence of PAPD and its related characteristics.

In summary, PAPD is hypothesized to be characterized by the following Comprehensive System variables: relatively high scores on S, Food, FQu, PER, and MOR; relatively low scores on the Egocentricity Index; p > a + 1; an ambitent personality style (M approximately equal to WSumC); and emotional ambivalence (color-shading blends ≥ 1).

CASE EXAMPLES

The proposed Comprehensive System profile for PAPD is illustrated by two case examples taken from the archives of the Rorschach Workshops Incorporated, with the permission of Dr. John Exner.

Case 1: Mr. Albert

Mr. Albert is a 21-year-old male who was evaluated after his dismissal from a prestigious university for academic failure. His mother sought the assessment through a psychologist at the manufacturing plant where she works as a secretary.

Mr. Albert received good grades in high school and was somewhat active in various sporting activities. He dated some, but never maintained a relationship for an extended time. At the time of testing, he had a girlfriend who lived in another state. They spoke about two to three times per week by telephone and saw each other once every month.

Mr. Albert believes that he can do nothing right from his father's perspective. He describes his mother as "too interested and involved in what I am doing." Mr. Albert believes that some of these problems are the results of following in the footsteps of his older brothers (by 10 years). That is, he believes that his parents seldom recognize his more modest achievements, as compared with those of his highly accomplished brother.

On the WAIS-R, Mr. Albert attained a full-scale IQ of 120 (verbal = 123; performance = 118). He stated that before testing, he had no idea what he wanted to do with his future and was not sure he wanted to return to college. He could not explain why he failed, but indicated that he would welcome any help he could receive from the psychologist. First Viewing, Inquiry, Sequence of Scores, and the Structural Summary for Mr. Albert are provided at the end of the chapter.

Case 2: Mr. Bixby

Mr. Bixby is a 40-year-old male who was assessed as part of a claim for disability benefits from the Veterans Administration. He had been receiving a

20% disability stipend for the past 18 years for a ruptured spinal disk. He also reports that he has been experiencing flashbacks for the past few years from his Vietnam combat experience. While in Vietnam, Mr. Bixby served in a motor supply unit that came under heavy fire on several occasions. He also was involved in handling shipments of Agent Orange and believes he may have been exposed to dangerous levels of the chemical.

Mr. Bixby graduated from high school with above-average grades, but flunked out of college after three semesters. He enlisted in the Army and was sent to Vietnam after basic training. After suffering the ruptured disk, he was given an honorable medical discharge. He returned to the states, re-entered college, and graduated at the age of 25 years with a Bachelor's degree in criminal justice. He married a woman he met in college, but was divorced 3 years later. He has held several jobs related to his college training. He lost one job when the company cut back on employees in his specialty area, but his work performance has been generally adequate.

Mr. Bixby has been dating a woman regularly, but has no marriage plans. He admits to a problem with alcohol, but says his drinking has never cost him his job and has not interfered with relationships, with the exception of his first marriage. In that case, he reports that his wife left him having complained of his heavy drinking. Currently, he complains of frequent fatigue and is afraid he may have "latent leukemia" resulting from his Agent Orange exposure. The results of yearly tests for bone cancer have been negative. He has participated in several organized protests by Vietnam veterans seeking compensation for Agent Orange exposure. First Viewing, Inquiry, Sequence of Scores, and Structural Summary for Mr. Bixby are at the end of the chapter.

Table 13.2 presents the critical PAPD profile results from the Comprehensive System for both cases. An asterisk identifies results indicative of what was hypothesized for PAPD.

Both individuals are significant on p > a + 1 and S > 2. Neither individual was positive on Depression Index nor suppressed on the Egocentricity Index, which was the only hypothesized variable not in the anticipated direction. Seven of the 10 hypothesized variables were observed for at least one of the cases. On 4 of the 10 variables, Mr. Albert and Mr. Bixby differed. Mr. Albert was ambitent, whereas Mr. Bixby was extratensive (M < WSumC). Mr. Bixby had more PER ($n = 5$) and MOR ($n = 4$) responses, whereas Mr. Albert did not (0 and 1 respectively). Also, Mr. Albert had more FQu responses (41%) whereas Mr. Bixby did not (11%).

Very few assessment studies have been conducted on a sample of individuals specifically identified as passive–aggressive. Extant studies have detected passive–aggressive characteristics in heterogeneous samples (e.g.,

TABLE 13.2

Critical Passive–Aggressive Comprehensive System Variables
for Case Examples

Variable	Case 1	Case 2
Space	4*	3*
Food content	2*	4*
Form quality u (%)	41*	11
Personalizations	0	5*
Egocentricity Index	.45	.61
p > a + 1	3/11	3/7*
Problem-solving style	Ambitent*	Extratensive
Color-shading blends	1*	2*
Depression Index	No	No

*Results consistent with hypothesized passive–aggressive profile.

alcoholics), but few have examined PAPD per se. Specific scales (self-report and interviews) have been developed to assess passive–aggressive personality, but to date, validation studies have been equivocal. The proposed profiles of PAPD on the Rorschach may hold promise for assessing PAPD or passive–aggressive personality characteristics. However, the scarcity of patients with these characteristics likely will make Rorschach studies difficult.

Future research would benefit by systematically assessing passive–aggressive characteristics with DSM criteria. Studies using MMPI-2, MMPI Personality Disorder scales, and MCMI with individuals who have passive–aggressive characteristics would be helpful in further elucidating the association between such characteristics and external validity indicators. The relationship of these scales to the selected Rorschach variables is needed both to validate and elucidate the relationship of projective and nonprojective measures to each other. For instance, measures of PAPD from the Five-Factor Model yield different results for the same individual (Axelrod et al., 1997), suggesting that the method by which PAPD and characteristics are assessed is an important factor to consider in detecting such features. Given that the Rorschach is an implicit measure of personality (McClelland, Koestner, & Wienberger, 1989), it may do an even better job in detecting real-world passive aggressive features that are not subject to conscious control. Obviously, this issue is seminal in assessment of the passive–aggressive construct. The two reported case examples suggest that the Rorschach may be a useful method for identifying and validating the passive–aggressive personality as a discrete type of psychological difficulty.

REFERENCES

Abram, H., Meixel, S., Webb, W., & Scott, H. (1976). Psychological adaptation to je-juinoileal bypass for morbid obesity. *Journal of Nervous and Mental Disease, 162,* 151–157.

American Psychiatric Association. (1969). *Diagnostic and statistical manual of mental disorders* (3rd ed.). Washington, DC: Author.

American Psychiatric Association. (1987). *Diagnostic and statistical manual of mental disorders* (3rd ed.). Washington, DC: Author.

American Psychiatric Association. (2000). *Diagnostic and statistical manual of mental Disorders* (4th ed., Text Revision). Washington, DC: Author.

Axelrod, S., Widiger, T., Trull, T., & Corbett, E. (1997). Relations of Five-Factor Model antagonism facets with personality disorder symptomatology. *Journal of Personality Assessment, 69,* 297–313.

Berman, S., & McCann, J. (1995). Defense mechanisms and personality disorders: An empirical test of Millon's theory. *Journal of Personality Assessment, 64,* 132–144.

Coolidge, F., & Merwin, M. (1992). Reliability and validity of the Coolidge Axis II Inventory: A new inventory for the assessment of personality disorders. *Journal of Personality Assessment, 59,* 223–228.

Costa, P. T., Jr., & McCrae, R. R. (1992). *The NEO PI-R Professional Manual.* Odessa, FL: Psychological Assessment Resources.

Craig, R., & Bivens, A. (2000). MCMI-III scores on substance abusers with and without histories of suicide attempts. *Substance Abuse, 21,* 155–161.

Craig, R., Verinis, S., & Wexler, S. (1985). Personality characteristics of drug addicts and alcoholics on the Millon Clinical Multiaxial Inventory. *Journal of Personality Assessment, 49,* 156–160.

Driessen, M., Veltrup, C., Wetterling, T., John, U., & Dilling, H. (1998). Axis I and Axis II comorbidity in alcohol dependence and the two types of alcoholism. *Alcoholism: Clinical and Experimental Research, 22,* 77–86.

Exner, J. (2003). *The Rorschach: A comprehensive system: Volume I* (4th ed.). New York: John Wiley.

Exner, J. (2000). *A primer for Rorschach interpretation.* Asheville, NC: Rorschach Workshops.

Fernandez-Mantalvo, J., Lander, N., Lopez-Goni, J., Lorea, I., & Zarzuela, A. (2002). Personality disorder in alcoholics: A descriptive study. *Revista de Psicopatologia y Psicologia Clinica, 7,* 215–225.

Gleser, G., & Ihilevich, D. (1979). Personality factors and ego defenses. *Academic Psychology Bulletin, 1,* 171–179.

Goldfried, M., & Zax, M. (1965). The stimulus value of the TAT. *Journal of Projective Techniques and Personality Assessment, 29,* 46–57.

Hyler, S., & Rieder, R. (1987). *PDQ-R: Personality Diagnostic Questionnaire— Revised.* New York: New York State Psychiatric Institute.

Joiner, T., & Rudd, M. (2002). The incremental validity of passive aggressive personality symptoms rivals or exceeds that of other personality symptoms in suicidal outpatients. *Journal of Personality Assessment, 79,* 161–170.

King, A. (1998). Relations between MCMI-II personality variables and measures of academic performance. *Journal of Personality Assessment, 71,* 253–268.

Klein, D. N. (2003). Patients' versus informants' reports of personality disorders in predicting 7½ year outcome in outpatients with depressive disorders. *Psychological Assessment, 15,* 216–222.

Lall, R. (1995). Prototypal personality traits of military personnel with suicide ideation on the Millon Clinical Multiaxial Inventory-II. *Dissertation Abstracts International, 56*(1-b), 0529.

Loranger, A., Sartorious, N., Andreoli, A., & Berger, P. (1994). The composite international diagnostic interview. *Archives of General Psychiatry, 51,* 215–224.

Loranger, A. W. (1988). *Personality Disorder Examination (PDE) manual.* Yonkers, NY: DV Communications.

McCann, J. (1988). Passive–aggressive personality disorder: A review. *Journal of Personality Disorders, 2,* 170–179.

McCann, J., Flynn, P., & Gersh, D. (1992). MCMI-II diagnosis of borderline personality disorder: Base rates versus prototypic items. *Journal of Personality Assessment, 58,* 105–114.

McClelland, D., Koestner, R., & Wienberger, J. (1989). How do self-attributed and implicit motives differ? In F. Halisch & J. van den Bercken (Eds.), *International perspectives on achievement and motivation.* (pp. 259–289). Bristol, PA: Swetz & Zeitlinger.

Millon, T. (1983). *Millon clinical multiaxial inventory manual.* Minneapolis: National Computer Systems.

Millon, T. (1987). *Millon clinical multiaxial inventory.* Minneapolis: National Computer Systems.

Millon, T. (1994). *MCMI-III manual.* Minneapolis: National Computer Systems. Morey, L., Waugh, M., & Blashfield, P. (1985). MMPI scales for DSM-III personality disorders: Their derivation and correlates. *Journal of Personality Assessment, 49,* 245–251.

Nerviano, V., & Gross, H. (1983). Personality types of alcoholics on objective inventories: A review. *Journal of Studies on Alcohol, 44,* 837–851.

Overall, J. (1973). MMPI personality patterns of alcoholics and narcotic addicts. *Quarterly Journal of Studies on Alcoholism, 34,* 104–111.

Peters, L., Andrews, G., Cottler, L., Chatterji, S., et al. (1996). The International Personality Disorder Examination. *International Journal of Methods in Psychiatric Research, 6,* 167–174.

Schuler, C., Snibbe, J., & Buchwalter, J. (1994). Validity of the MMPI personality disorder scales (MMPI-PD). *Journal of Clinical Psychology, 50,* 220–227.

Torgersen, S., & Alnaes, R. (1990). The relationship between the MCMI personality scales and DSM-III, Axis II. *Journal of Personality Assessment, 55,* 698–702.

Trull, T., & Widiger, T. (1997). *Structured interview for the Five-Factor Model of personality (SIFFM).* Odessa, FL: Psychological Assessment Resources.

Vereycken, J., Vertommen, H., & Corveleyn, J. (2002). Authority conflicts and personality disorders. *Journal of Personality Disorders, 16,* 41–51.

Widiger, T., & Sanderson, C. (1987). The convergent and discriminant validity of the MCMI as a measure of the DSM-III personality disorders. *Journal of Personality Assessment, 51,* 228–242.

Wiener, G. (1956). Neurotic depressives' and alcoholics' oral Rorschach percepts. *Journal of Projective Techniques, 20,* 453–455.

Wolowitz, H., & Shorkey, C. (1969). Power motivation in male paranoid children. *Psychiatry: Journal for the Study of Interpersonal Processes, 32,* 459–466.

Yeung, A., Lyons, M., Waternaux, C., & Faraone, S. (1993). Empirical determination of thresholds for case identification: Validation of the Personality Diagnostic Questionnaire–Revised. *Comprehensive Psychiatry, 34,* 388–391.

RORSCHACH PROTOCOL FOR MR. ALBERT

Free Association	Inquiry
Card I 1. Oh my goodness, kind of like an angel at first. (Most people see more than one thing, take your time).	1. When I first looked at it, first I saw wings over here, just a general first glance, just looked like kind of an angel. (Help me to see it like you do). Well, the wings and the body here, like an angel.
2. Looks like a couple of winged somethings on the end carrying somebody up. Looks like a person with two heads and just 2 arms. (Chuckles). Are you waiting on me? (It's up to you).	2. Looks like these might be angels right here and maybe their wings on the side. They are holding this person up like this, looks like it could be Jesus, except he has two heads up there, and this looks like he's holding his hands up in the air.
3. There's a little face in there too I see, I guess	3. Yes ma'am, looks like two eyes and mouth right here, some sort of strange face, see here (circles center area).
4. Actually it looks like a wolf, kind of. That's about all I can get.	4. Right, um, it's the nose right here and his ears and his eyes or maybe a fox, I think I meant to say fox, wolf or fox, just his face.
Card II 5. Two kids playing pat-a-cake (laughs)	5. Just looks like they are sitting here kneeling and got their hands up here touching, like playing pat-a-cake. I didn't really see a head for the kids, they are probably turned away and the heads are behind the body the way you see it here.
6. Sort of looks like there is a butterfly right there. That's about all I...	6. This looks like a butterfly right here. (What about it makes it look like a butterfly?) Just the shape, the wings, and the body.
Card III Am I allowed to turn it up? (It's up to you).	

7. (v) Kind of looks like a monster right here with a bowtie on.	7. With his hands raised in the air. (I'm not sure I see it like you do). Here is body right here, and there is little bowtie and arms raised in the air there, and two big bug eyes and mouth right here, you can't see any legs.
8. This way it looks like two, ah, …two ladies holding onto something in the middle.	8. This is the heads. Coming down here is their chest, that's why I said it looks like ladies. Looks like these are the arms right here and holding onto… looks like a head, looks like holding onto an alien head. It looks like maybe they have on high-heels, big kneecaps. (An alien head?) Just, you know, pictures we see basically with really big eyes right there, like the head of an alien.
9. Couple of guitars out here.	9. Yes, right there. Just looks like kind of like the shape of a guitar.
Card IV 10. Looks like Godzilla laying down and big feet and tail	10. It looks like just laying down up the page, like this was feet sticking out here, and his tail right there, and like arms cut off or something. Maybe has arms, I don't know.
11. (v) Kind of looks like a weed when you turn it up too.	11. Just looks like a dandelion weed just growing up out of the ground. (Help me see it like you do). The way shape of blot is, kind of folded over looks like a leaf folding over on itself. (Folding over on itself?) The difference in color, light on top and the shadow on the rest, stuff like that, like the leaf is folded.
Card V 12. Like ah, a moth.	12. Just like wings coming out right here and like antennae and his little tail right there.
13. (v) And a bat Yes, that's a bat it.	13. Just looks like it has wings right there and it has a head.
Card VI 14. (<) Kind of looks like a fish if you turn it on its side.	Card VI 14. I mean that just looks like his teeth right here and dorsal fin and a fin on the bottom and little tail back here.
15. (<) Maybe a weird guitar.	15. (Remember, I need to see it like you do). Just a funky shape right here, and you have the neck of the guitar coming up here.
16. (v) Maybe a space age plane or something, I don't know.	16. Like this is the body and wings and nose of a plane right here.

Card VII
17. Looks like two little girls looking at each other with their hands and everything, and they got little dresses on them.

17. Heads right here, ponytails sticking up and looks like hands off to side like, like this (demonstrates), and they got little dresses on. (I'm not sure about the dresses). Well, the lower part doesn't have much shape, like it would be a dress.

18. (v) Upside down it also looks like two little girls but backs are to each other. They are turning around looking at each other.

18. Right, just looks like hair up here, the face and cheek kind of turning around eyes, hands down by side, bottoms sticking out, and there is their legs.

Are these standard inkblots? (Yes). Everyone has same ones? (Yes).

Card VIII
19. (Chuckles to self). Couple of parrots sitting in tree.

19. I just saw those two things on the side and kind of looked like a parrot. (A parrot?) I just see head, and there's his back and feathers, and maybe that's his feet, and there is his tail. (You said sitting in a tree?) That's…he's not flying, so I guess hanging onto a tree or something. (Can you help me see the tree?) I just said a tree, I don't really see a tree, but the center might be one.

20. Or a couple of geckos climbing a mountain or something on the side.

20. Just looks like it might be a lizard or something, there's his tail and legs. (Mountain?) Just in the middle, that weird shape in middle

21. (v) Maybe some sort of war mask worn by an Indian or something, I don't know.

21. Just looks like this part down here is the mouth, and these are like eye holes or something. (You said a war mask). All the colors make me think of that.

Card IX
These are getting pretty weird (chuckles).

22. Looks kind of like there is a vase or something on a platform in the middle with all that green and orange stuff around it but I...

22. Just the...in the very middle, looks like the shape of a glass or something sitting on this red platform, and that was about it, I didn't figure anything else out. (You said green and orange stuff around it). Looks like it's just there and covering it up or something, I don't know what it is. (Covering it up?) Just that it looks like the shape of a glass here but the colors are covering part of it so you can't see it. Something is covering it partly. (And the glass or vase?) Just the shape, the coloring of it and shading of it, kind of light and then it gets darker down here at the bottom.

23. Either that or modern art.

23. Yes, that was joke really, it looks like something a painter would paint and let you figure it out. (I'm not sure why it looks like that?) Just all the colors, just splotches of color.

Card X
Can I see individual things in here? (It's up to you).

24. I see a couple of crabs.

24. That's here, two blue crabs right here and looks like they are holding green pea pods in their hands.

25. A flower or flowers.

25. Two yellow flowers here.

26. Some chilis.

26. Two reddish brown chilis, here and here. They have that sort of chili shape to them.

27. Green caterpillars.

27. Right here looks like hanging onto something in the middle, I don't know what.

28. And two really big chilis, like you cook with.

28. Right here. (I'm not sure how they look like big chilis). Just the shape of them, they look like that.

29. And I see a little...I don't know what these things are, you know how little helicopter like seeds that come down, that's what I'm trying to say.

29. I think it's a maple seed, I don't know. (What makes it look like that?) Just the shape, it looks exactly like it.

RORSCHACH SEQUENCE OF SCORES FOR MR. ALBERT

Card	Resp	Loc (DQ)	Loc No	Determinants (FQ)	(2)	Content(s)	P	Z	Special Scores
I	1.	Wo	1	Fo		(H)		1	GHR
	2.	W+	1	Ma-pu		(H),H,Ay		4	COP,GHR
	3.	DdSo	99	F-		Hd		3.5	PHR
	4.	WSo	1	Fo		Ad		3.5	
II	5.	D+	6	Ma-	(2)	Hd		3	COP, PHR
	6.	Do	3	Fo		A			
III	7.	DdS+	99	Mp-		(Hd),Cg		4	PHR
	8.	D+	1	Mp-	(2)	H, (Hd)	P	3	FAB, PHR
	9.	Do	2	Fu	(2)	Sc			
IV	10.	Wo	1	FMp.FDo		(Ad)		2	MOR
	11.	Wo	1	mp.FVo		Bt		2	
V	12.	Wo	1	Fo		A		1	
	13.	Wo	1	Fo		A	P	1	PSV
VI	14.	Wo	1	F-		A		2.5	
	15.	Wo	1	Fu		Sc		2.5	
	16.	Wo	1	Fo		Sc		2.5	
VII	17.	W+	1	Mpo		H,Cg	P	2.5	GHR
	18.	W+	1	Mpo	(2)	H		2.5	GHR
VIII	19.	W+	1	FMp-	(2)	A,Bt		4.5	
	20.	W+	1	FMau	(2)	A,Ls		4.5	
IX	21.	WSo	1	FCu		(Hd),Ay		4.5	GHR
	22.	W+	1	CF.FD.FYo		Bt, Hh		5.5	
	23.	Wv	1	C		Art			
X	24.	D+	1	FMp.FCo	(2)	A,Bt	P	4	INC
	25.	Dv	15	CFo	(2)	Bt			
	26.	Do	7	FCu	(2)	Fd			
	27.	D+	10	FC.FMpo	(2)	A,Id		4	
	28.	Do	9	Fo		Bt			

STRUCTURAL SUMMARY FOR MR. ALBERT

Location Features	Determinants		Contents	Approach
	Blends	Single		
	FM.FD	M = 6	H = 4	I: W.W.DdS.WS
Zf = 22	m.FV	FM = 2	(H) = 2	II: D.D
ZSum = 67.5	CF.FD.FY	m = 0	Hd = 2	III: DdS.D.D
Zest = 73.5	FM.FC	FC = 2	(Hd) = 3	IV: W.W
	FC.FM	CF = 1	Hx = 0	V: W.W
W = 17		C = 1	A = 7	VI: W.W.W
D = 9		Cn = 0	(A) = 0	VII: W.W.
W+D = 26		FC' = 0	Ad = 1	VIII: W.W.WS
Dd = 2		C'F = 0	(Ad) = 1	IX: W.W
S = 4		C' = 0	An = 0	X: D.D.D.D.D
		FT = 0	Art = 1	
Developmental Quality		TF = 0	Ay = 2	Special Scores
+ = 11		T = 0	Bl = 0	Lv 1 Lv 2
o = 16		FV = 0	Bt = 6	DV = 0x1 = 0x2
v = 1		VF = 0	Cg = 0	INC = 1x2 = 0x4
v/+ = 0		V = 0	Cl = 0	DR = 0x3 = 0x6
		FY = 0	Ex = 0	FAB = 1x4 = 0x7
		YF = 0	Fd = 1	ALOG = 0x5
Form Quality		Y = 0	Fi = 0	CON = 0x7
		Fr = 0	Ge = 0	Raw Sum 6 = 2

Form Quality

	FQx	MQual	W+D
+	= 0	= 0	= 0
o	= 15	= 2	= 15
u	= 6	= 1	= 6
-	= 6	= 3	= 4
none	= 1	= 0	= 1

rF = 0	Hh = 0	Wgtd Sum 6 = 6
FD = 0	Ls = 1	
F = 11	Na = 0	AB = 0 GHR = 5
(2) = 11	Sc = 3	AG = 0 PHR = 4
	Sx = 0	COP = 2 MOR = 1
	Xy = 0	CP = 0 PSV = 1
	Id = 0	

Ratios, Percentages, and Derivations

Core			Affect	Interpersonal
R = 28	L = .65		FC: CF+C = 4:3	COP = 2 AG = 0
			Pure C = 1	GHR: PHR = 6:4
EB = 6:5.5	EA = 11.5	EBPer = N/A	SumC':WSumC = 0:5.5	a:p = 3:9
eb = 5:2	es = 7	D = +1	Afr = .56	Food = 1
	Adj es = 7	Adj D = +1	S = 4	Sum T = 0
			Blends:R = 5:28	Human Cont = 11
FM = 4	SumC' = 0	SumT = 0	CP = 0	Pure H = 4
m = 1	Sum V = 1	Sum Y = 1		PER = 0
				Isol Indx = .25

Ideation		Mediation	Processing	Self-Perception
a:p = 3:9	Sum6 = 2	XA% = .75	Zf = 22	3r+(2)/R = .38
Ma:Mp = 2:5	Lv2 = 0	WDA% = .81	W:D:Dd = 17:9:2	Fr+rF = 0
2AB+Art+Ay =3	WSum6 = 6	X-% = .21	W:M = 17:6	SumV = 1
MOR = 1	M- = 3	S- = 2	Zd = -6.0	FD = 2
	Mnone = 0	P = 4	PSV = 1	An+Xy = 0
		X+% = .54	DQ+ = 11	MOR = 1
		Xu% = .21	DQv = 1	H:(H)+Hd+(Hd) = 4:7

PTI = 1   DEPI = 3   CDI = 2   S-CON = 5   HVI = Yes   OBS = No

Free Association	Inquiry
Card I I know it should look like something but it doesn't. (Take your time.	
1. Maybe hands, these two little things up here (tries to turn card). (I think if you'll look a bit longer, you'll probably find something else, too).	1. It looks like when you hold them up, like this (demonstrates), just the hands and the rest of wrists maybe, you can't see the rest of the person, just two hands being held up.
2. Well, (laughs) these white parts could be ghost figs, these two.	2. Like in the cartoons, just a like a couple of ghosts you know, with the white sheets or whatever they sure have that gives shape to them.
Card II 3. It looks like two wild bears in some kind of fight to the death, I guess.	3. The red parts remind me of the blood. They have it on their heads and feet, and there's some blotches of it on their bodies too, see the red here (points). They're on their hind legs and they're pushing at each other, with their arms up here.
Can I turn it? (Whatever you like).	
4. (v) Now it reminds me of infected bone and tissue.	4. The grey part would be the bone, the white is the marrow, the bone is turning grey. Bones that are infected get like that, and the red is the inflammation caused by the infection.
Card III 5. Two monkeys. I don't know what the red looks like, but the grey looks like monkeys holding something, some food I guess.	5. The long legs and the arms and the shape of the head, it's kind of an exaggerated human form like advanced primates. They're holding something between them -- coconuts or whatever they eat.

364

6. (v) That center red could lungs.

6. They're shaped like that, and they are red like lungs have little blood vessels in them to carry the oxygen. They get all clogged up if you have lung cancer. I remember that from a biology course I took once.

Card IV
7. Well these look like boots, so I guess it could be a figure lying down on the ground.

7. A human I guess. He has big feet, so it's probably a man. First, I saw the boots here (points), just the shape of them. Then these look like legs, it's in a perspective you are looking from the feet, he's lying down and its foreshortened. It reminds me of a homeless guy I saw in DC when we did the march there. He was lying down like this, passed out.

Card V
8. A silhouette of a butterfly, I don't think a butterfly would be black, so it's the silhouette of one.

8. It's the shape, like flying, flapping its wings. See how (points) they go out.

9. It could be a bat, too. I don't know if a bat has antennae like butterflies.

9. He's flying also, the wings are the same. It's all the same as the butterfly, but now the black is right, bats are black. The only difference is that bats fly fast and make noise, like screech, and butterflies are quiet. I saw a TV program about them. A lot looked like this.

Card VI
Oh, another tough one, let me see…

10. The top reminds me of a palm tree. It has the palms sticking out like blowing in a wind.

10. This is the trunk and the palms, but they look very straight, usually they are graceful. They flow more than these, these are just sticking out, like they're blowing in a strong wind, like a gale.

Card VII
11. Somebody looking into a mirror and seeing her reflection.

11. Well, they're the same almost. This one looks a little more blurry (right side), the darkness of it around the edges is more pronounced, and the edges on this one are more precise (left side). See this would be the real one, and this (left) is the mirror image -- the nose and chin and the hair.

Card VIII
12. Two little mice, like just born. They're trying to stand up.

12. I've seen them in the lab when I took psychology. They don't have fur. They're just all pink like this with their little legs, like they're trying to stand or walk. They're very slow at first.

13. The bottom looks like some internal organ, I don't know which one though.

13. It's very colorful. I don't know what organ, but from the color, I'd guess something in the lower parts, and it has a toughness about it, the way the colors vary in the shades, maybe a ligament. It's actually got two colors, orange and pink.

Card IX
14. These top things could be lobsters. Yeah, they're orange, like after you cook them.

14. They have that color, its too light I think, but it's the right color, and they have pointed heads. These would be the claws. They're cooked, ready to eat.

15. This pink looks like cotton candy. I use to get it at the fair when I was a kid.

15. It's just the ends, each one looks like a ball of pink cotton candy. You know, they used to swirl it on a cardboard stick.

Card X
16. (v) A couple of sea horses that look like they've been battered up.

16. They have that shape but thy look pretty limp there, like they're dead or all beat up. They're probably dead 'cause they're green. I think they're red or brown when they are alive.

17. Two bugs sniffing around this thing, something in between them.

17. Well, they have antennae. They're on their back legs like they were sniffing this thing. Whatever it is probably something that they eat, I don't know.

18. If you add this white part, it looks like you are looking down somebody's throat. You can see their tonsils.

18. Well, the grey is like the roof of the mouth, and the white is the opening and back in there you can see their tonsils. This pink is like part of the inside of the mouth, you know, like it's pink inside, and the blue part is the jaw, see here (carefully outlines).

RORSCHACH SEQUENCE OF SCORES FOR MR.BIXBY

Card	Resp	Loc (DQ)	Loc No	Determinants (FQ)	(2)	Content(s)	P	Z	Special Scores
I	1.	Do	1	Mpo		Hd			PHR
	2.	DdSo	30	FC'o	(2)	(H)			GHR
II	3.	W+	1	FMa.CFo	(2)	A,Bl		4.5	AG,INC,MOR, PHR
	4.	WSv/+	1	C'F.CF-		An		4.5	MOR
III	5.	D+	1	FMpo	(2)	A,Fd		3.0	
	6.	Do	3	FCo		An			DR, PER
IV	7.	W+	1	Mp.FDo		H,Cg	P	4.0	PER, GHR
V	8.	Wo	1	FC'.FMpo		(A)		1.0	
	9.	Wo	1	FMa.FC'o		A	P	1.0	DR, PER
VI	10.	Do	3	mpu		Bt			
VII	11.	D+	1	Mp.Fr.FYo		Hd	P	3.0	GHR
VIII	12.	Do	1	FMa.FCo	(2)	A	P		PER
	13.	Dv	2	CF.YF-		An			
IX	14.	Do	3	FCu	(2)	Fd,A			MOR
	15.	Do	4	CFo	(2)	Fd			PER
X	16.	Do	4	FCo	(2)	A			MOR
	17.	D+	11	FMp0	(2)	A,Fd		4.0	
	18.	DdSo	99	FD.CF-		Hd,An		6.0	PHR

367

STRUCTURAL SUMMARY FOR MR. BIXBY

Location Features	Determinants		Contents	Approach
	Blends	Single		
	FM.CF	M = 1	H = 1	I: D.DdS
Zf = 9	CF.CF	FM = 2	(H) = 1	II: W.WS
ZSum = 31.0	M.FD	m = 1	Hd = 3	III: D.D
Zest = 27.5	FC'.FM	FC = 3	(Hd) = 0	IV: W
	FM.FC'	CF = 1	Hx = 0	V: W.W
W = 5	M.Fr.FY	C = 0	A = 7	VI: D
D = 11	FM.FC	Cn = 0	(A) = 1	VII: D
W+D = 16	CF.YF	FC' = 1	Ad = 0	VIII: D.D
Dd = 2	FD.CF	C'F = 0	(Ad) = 0	IX: D.D
S = 3		C' = 0	An = 4	X: D.D.DdS
		FT = 0	Art = 0	

Developmental Quality

+ = 5	
o = 11	
v = 1	
v/+ = 1	

	TF = 0	Ay = 0	Special Scores

Form Quality

	FQx	MQual	W+D
+	= 0	= 0	= 0
o	= 13	= 3	= 12
u	= 2	= 0	= 2
-	= 3	= 0	= 2
none	= 0	= 0	= 0

Single (cont.)	Contents (cont.)	Special Scores (cont.)	
T = 0	Bl = 1		Lv 1 Lv 2
FV = 0	Bt = 1	DV =	0x1 = 0x2
VF = 0	Cg = 1	INC =	1x2 = 0x4
V = 0	Cl = 0	DR =	2x3 = 0x6
FY = 0	Ex = 0	FAB =	0x4 = 0x7
YF = 0	Fd = 4	ALOG = 0x5	
Y = 0	Fi = 0	CON = 0x7	
Fr = 0	Ge = 0	Raw Sum 6 = 3	
rF = 0	Hh = 0	Wgtd Sum 6 = 8	
FD = 0	Ls = 0		
F = 0	Na = 0	AB = 0 GHR = 3	
	Sc = 0	AG = 1 PHR = 3	
(2) = 8	Sx = 0	COP = 0 MOR = 4	
	Xy = 0	CP = 0 PER = 5	
	Id = 0	PSV = 0	

STRUCTURAL SUMMARY FOR MR. BIXBY (CONTINUED)

Ratios, Percentages, and Derivations

Core
R = 18	L = .00	
EB = 3:7	EA = 10	EBPer = 2.3
eb = 7:6	es = 13	D = -1
	Adj es = 12	Adj D = 0
FM = 6	SumC' = 4	SumT = 0
m = 1	Sum V = 0	Sum Y = 2

Affect
FC: CF+C = 4:5
Pure C = 0
SumC':WSumC = 4:7
Afr = .64
S = 3
Blends:R = 9:18
CP = 0

Interpersonal
COP = 0   AG = 1
GHR: PHR = 3:3
a:p = 3:7
Food = 4
Sum T = 0
Human Cont = 5
Pure H = 1
PER = 5
Isol Indx = .06

Ideation
a:p = 3:7	Sum6 = 3
Ma:Mp = 0:3	Lv2 = 0
2AB+Art+Ay = 0	WSum6 = 8
MOR = 4	M- = 0
	Mnone = 0

Mediation
XA% = .83
WDA% = .88
X-% = .17
S- = 2
P = 4
X+% = .72
Xu% = .11

Processing
Zf = 9
W:D:Dd = 5:11:2
W:M = 5:3
Zd = +3.5
PSV = 0
DQ+ = 11
DQv = 1

Self-Perception
3r+(2)/R = .61
Fr+rF = 1
SumV = 0
FD = 2
An+Xy = 4
MOR = 4
H:(H)+Hd+(Hd) =1:4

PTI = 1   DEPI = 4   CDI = 3   S-CON = 6   HVI = No   OBS = No

Rorschach Assessment
of Depressive Personality Disorder

Steven K. Huprich
Eastern Michigan University

The Diagnostic and Statistical Manual of Mental Disorders, 4th Edition (DSM-IV) (American Psychiatric Association [APA], 1994) describes depressive personality disorder (DPD) as

> a pervasive pattern of depressive cognitions and behaviors beginning by early adulthood and present in a variety of contexts, as indicated by five or more of the following: (1) usual mood is dominated by dejection, gloominess, cheerlessness, joylessness, unhappiness; (2) self-concept centers around beliefs of inadequacy, worthlessness, and low self-esteem; (3) is critical, blaming, and derogatory toward self; (4) is brooding and given to worry; (5) is negativistic, critical, and judgmental toward others; (6) is pessimistic; (7) is prone to feeling guilty or remorseful. (p. 733)

Although DPD recently has been proposed for inclusion in the DSM, it also has been a construct of interest for some time (reviewed in Huprich, 1998). Schneider (1958) described the individual with depressive personality as quiet, serious, constantly pessimistic, and lacking the capacity to have fun. Laughlin (1956) characterized depressive personalities as (a) being overserious, overconscientious, and dependable; (b) having an increased vulnerability to letdown and disappointment, which arises from early disappointments in child–parent relationships; (c) denying overt levels of hostility; (d) being rigid, meticulous, and perfectionistic; and (e) having a masochistic orientation, involving excessively high standards for self and others, angry attitudes toward self and others, including a need for punishment of those who fail to meet the excessively high standards (including oneself).

Berliner (1966) equated the depressive personality with moral masochism. Here, the individual has a strong desire to be loved and cared for, yet also feels substantial disappointment and hatred toward loving people who cannot really be trusted to provide such support. Thus, his or her efforts at seeking interpersonal gratification are associated with pain and suffering and the need to be punished. The desire for punishment is unconscious aggression the individual feels toward disappointing others that cannot be expressed directly and is subsequently directed toward the self. Similar descriptions of the masochistic tendency in depressive personalities are posited by Kernberg (1984, 1987, 1990) and Simons (1987).

Kahn (1975) and Bemporad (1973, 1976) have emphasized dependency features in depressive personalities. They observed that such individuals have low self-esteem, which tends to deteriorate when others become frustrating; tendencies toward dependency (in place of autonomy) in relationships; chronic guilt because of their excessive hostility toward loving objects; and tendencies toward masochistic relationships and self-denigration.

Biologically oriented researchers and theorists describe DPD as falling on a continuum of affective disorders. Klein and colleagues (Klein, 1990, 1999; Klein & Miller, 1993; Klein & Shih, 1998) and Akiskal (1989, 1997) argued that DPD is the product of a biologically determined temperament that predisposes to mood disorders, an argument that stems from the ideas of Kretschmer (1925) and Kraepelin (1921). Klein, Akiskal, and colleagues report high rates of comorbidity of Axis I mood disorders in first-degree relatives of individuals with a diagnosis of DPD. Klein (1999) also reported that rates of DPD are higher in relatives of individuals with dysthymia than in relatives of controls.

The proposal of DPD as a diagnostic category has not been without controversy. Some have argued that DPD is a variant of affective illness and not a personality disorder per se (Klein, 1999; Ryder & Bagby, 1999). It also has been suggested that the degree of overlap between DPD and dysthymia does not permit a clinically or empirically supported differentiation (Ryder & Bagby, 1999). Yet, as discussed later, several studies have supported the differentiation of DPD from dysthymia and other mood and personality disorders. Likewise, a growing body of evidence supports the validity of DPD as a disorder of personality.

RESEARCH ON THE ASSESSMENT OF DPD

Two broad arenas of research have investigated the DPD construct. One such body of research has examined the rates of overlap and differentiation of DPD from dysthymia and other mood disorders. This research has been conducted with both psychiatric patients (Hirschfeld & Holzer, 1994; Klein, 1990; Klein & Shih, 1998; McDermutt, Zimmerman,& Chelminski, 2003; Phillips et al., 1998) and undergraduate students meeting criteria for DPD and dysthymia (Huprich, 2000, 2001b; Klein & Miller, 1993). Overall, results indicate that, despite overlap with similar mood disorders, DPD can be differentiated. That is, not all individuals with a diagnosis of DPD meet the criteria for dysthymia, and vice versa. Across these studies, the rate of overlap averages about 50% (Huprich, 2001a), with the range of overlap falling between 19% (Klein & Miller, 1993) and 73% (Klein, 1999).

Regarding the differentiation of DPD and dysthymia, Huprich (2001b) predicted that nonclinical undergraduates classified as having a depressive personality (based on scores from a diagnostic interview) would have greater impairment in object relations than those classified as dysthymic or a control subject. Using the Social Cognition and Object Relations Scale (Westen, 1995) to assess object relations, Huprich (2001b) found that depressive personalities had more simplistic representations of others than dysthymic and control participants. He also found that dysthymic and DPD participants had more negative affective representations of others. Using the same sample, Huprich (2000) compared Five-Factor model (FFM; Costa & McCrae, 1992; Widiger, Trull, Clarkin, Sanderson, & Costa, 1994) profiles of DPD individuals with those of dysthymics. He found that the DPD group had significantly higher levels of angry hostility and self-consciousness, and significantly lower levels of extraversion, gregariousness, and openness than the dysthymic group. Huprich concluded that these findings are consistent with the theoretical understanding of DPD.

Another body of research has focused on personality traits and psychosocial variables proposed to be associated with DPD. Using Schneider's (1958) description to classify individuals as having DPD, Klein (1990) found that depressive personalities were more self-critical, showed less extraversion, had greater stress reactivity, and harbored more negative attributions than those without depressive personality. Hartlage, Arduino, and Alloy (1998) reported that depressive personalities were more likely to experience feelings of counterdependency, a sense of being burdened, low self-esteem, and high self-criticism, as compared with other patients who have mood disorders. They suggested that these traits are independent of state depression and may distinctively characterize DPD.

Huprich (2003a) assessed DPD in Veteran psychiatric outpatients. Using the Depressive Personality Disorder Inventory (DPDI; Huprich, Margrett, Barthelemy, & Fine, 1996; Huprich, Sanford, & Smith, 2002) to classify individuals as having DPD, he found that, as hypothesized, DPD patients had significantly greater levels of depression, perfectionism, alienation, and insecure attachment, as well as concerns about making mistakes, believed their parents to be more critical and less supportive, believed their friends to be unsupportive, and doubted their actions more often as compared with psychiatric controls. Correlational analyses indicated that, after controlling for state-like depression, the DPDI remained correlated with all the afore-mentioned variables except low social support from friends and doubts about actions. Huprich (2003a) concluded that these findings support pre-vious theoretical speculation about the development of DPD, namely, that experiences of loss and perfectionistic orientations toward self and other help account for the development of DPD.

As noted earlier, the FFM has been evaluated for its ability to assess de-pressive personality (Costa & McCrae, 1992). Widiger et al. (1994) pre-dicted that depressive personalities would show higher ratings for anxiety, depression, and self-consciousness and lower ratings for tenderminded-ness than normal control subjects. Some studies have found empirical sup-port for the first three facet-level predictions among samples of individuals meeting criteria for DPD (Dyce & O'Connor, 1998, Huprich, 2000, 2003b). These three studies also found other facets that characterize depressive per-sonality disorder, including low levels of positive emotions, gregarious-ness, assertiveness, achievement striving, actions, and trust. Not only are these findings convergent, but they also are consistent with many conceptualizations of DPD.

RELATED RORSCHACH RESEARCH

It should first be noted that there is no published study on DPD and the Rorschach. This is not surprising given the relative newness of the DPD category and its proposed status in DSM-IV (APA, 1994). As such, related research is briefly discussed, along with its implications for assessing de-pressive personality disorder.

Perhaps the most relevant variable to begin with is the Depression Index (DEPI), because it consists of many variables hypothesized to characterize DPD: Vista, Form Dimension, White Space, Color-Shading Blends, Egocen-tricity Index, Affective Ratio, Blends, Sum Shading, Achromatic Color, Morbid, Cooperative Movement, Intellectualization Index.[1] The DEPI was created to differentiate depressive and nondepressive patients (Exner, 1986). Although it did correctly identify 70% of patients with dysthymia or major depression, the false-positive rates were high, ranging up to 30%. Further research on the DEPI indicated that its ability to identify adults (Ball, Archer, Gordon, & French, 1991; Carlson, Kula, & St. Laurent, 1997;

---

[1]These variables are reflected in the current DEPI (Exner, 2003) and are different from those in an earlier version (Exner, 1986).

Viglione, Brager, & Haller, 1988) and adolescents (Archer & Gordon, 1988; Carter & Dacey, 1996; Lipovsky, Finch, & Belter, 1989) with depressive disorders was poor. As such, a revised DEPI was created, which was associated with a more accurate hit rate (Exner, 1993). The false-positive rate ranged between 3% (for nonpatient adults) and 19% (for schizophrenics). However, subsequent research with this revised version also failed to produce similarly favorable results (Ball et al., 1991; Exner, 2003; Krishnamurthy & Archer, 2001; Meyer, 1993). Thus, Exner (2003) has now suggested that positive DEPI values are best interpreted as "representing an affective problem" (p. 312) rather than indicating that the individual has a specific diagnosis.

A closer look at the development of the DEPI may help to explain its poor performance. Exner (1993) noted that changing the definitions and the breadth of symptoms entailed in mood disorders in the creation of the DSM-III led to very different conceptualizations of mood disorders than those reported beforehand. To accommodate these changes, Exner (1993) grouped depressed individuals into three clusters: (a) those with emotional distress; (b) those with pessimistic cognitions, lethargy, and self-defeating behaviors; and (c) those who feel helpless. (Despite this clustering, depressed patients in Exner's samples often have had features of all three clusters). Exner then created the revised DEPI by combining the first two groups and compared the results against those for the third group (i.e., helpless).[2] Whereas his discriminant functions for the first two groups yielded strong hit rates, the same equation, when applied to the helpless group, did poorly. Therefore, it could be that the failure of the DEPI to assess Axis I depressive disorders is related to the complex admixture of symptoms depressed patients report, which contributes to the shrinkage phenomena at cross-validation (Dies, 1995). Exner (1993) has appeared even to recognize this possibility. He has cited Wiener (1989), who noted that there are 256 possible combinations of symptoms that could classify someone as meeting the criteria for the DSM-III-R definition of dysthymia.

The nature of the variables that compose the DEPI also may shed light on why the DEPI fails to detect Axis I depression. Many variables on the DEPI index have long-term temporal stability. Some of these variables (and their 3-year stability coefficients) are Vista (.81), Egocentricity Index (.87), Affective Ratio (.90), Animal Movement (.72), Texture (.87), and Achromatic Color (.67). Thus, these variables appear to assess trait-like phenomena. Interestingly, most DEPI research has been conducted with individuals meeting criteria for major depression. Because DPD is, by definition, a stable

---

[2]Whereas dysthymics have been included in some research samples, they often have been combined for individuals with more transient mood disorders. Of course, no research has evaluated Rorschach protocols of patients with DPD.

construct (and verified to be so empirically; Klein & Shih, 1998), and because many depressive disorders remit over time, it is possible that DEPI scores actually may be more closely aligned to DPD than to Axis I depressive disorders. That is, they may be assessing DPD traits, some of which are seen in state-like features of Axis I depression, but eventually remit when the depressive episode has finished. Future research should address this issue further to evaluate the utility of the DEPI in assessing DPD.

THE RORSCHACH PROTOCOL
OF DEPRESSIVE PERSONALITY DISORDER

This section discusses the expected pattern of findings on the Rorschach for a prototypical patient with DPD. These are discussed by cluster and key variables. It should be noted that these patterns are meant to be descriptive and not diagnostic, because diagnosis is a task accomplished by clinicians after they have reviewed all relevant data (Meyer et al., 1998; Weiner, 2003).

Not surprisingly, DPD protocols are remarkable for their predominance of Vista (V), Achromatic Color (C'), and White Space (S) responses. Patients with DPD are negativistic, ruminative, and critical of self and others (APA, 1994; Huprich, 1998, 2000, 2003a, 2003b). Looking with an "eye of perfectionism" toward themselves and others, DPD patients predominantly perceive the bad aspects of life's experiences. As such, their records should show an elevated number of V responses. White space (S) responses are suggestive of oppositionality, and when S exceeds 2, an individual likely harbors anger and resentment toward others who have failed to meet his or her expectations (Weiner, 2003). The individual with DPD is believed to have experienced early interpersonal loss and disappointment with caregivers and meaningful others. This disappointment becomes pervasive, leading to the expectancy that others are disappointing. An examination of human content responses may show a number of co-occuring S responses. Achromatic color (C') responses also may be elevated in patients with DPD. Individuals meeting criteria for DPD have elevated levels of depressive affect (Huprich, 2003a, 2003c; Klein, 1999), a point also noted by DSM-IV (APA, 1994). As such, C' responses should be observed.

Also within the Affect cluster, DPD patients are likely to have Sum C' ≥ WSumC. Although responsive to emotional material (seen not only in WSumC but also in the Affective Ratio), individuals with DPD are more likely to report dysphoric affect. However, caution is warranted here because C' is not as stable as many other variables that assess affect (3-year retest reliability is reported at $r = .67$; Exner, 1999). Thus, an individual with DPD who is not clinically or significantly depressed may not display this pattern of results.

Overall, DPD individuals are relatively constricted in the expression of much affect except for that which is negative and are not likely to have pure C types of responses. They also may have as many blends as the normative sample, or perhaps more, because their negativity and pessimism likely colors their world, so that relatively straightforward percepts (e.g., "a bat") are cast in a dysphoric light (e.g., "The shades of dark gray reminded me of a bat you would see at Halloween"). Again, however, some caution is warranted here because the number of blends in a protocol has shown some fluctuation in a 3-year period ($r = .67$; Exner, 1999).

The relationship of DPD to the DEPI variable deserves special consideration. As discussed earlier, findings have shown the DEPI to be equivocal in detecting depression. In fact, Exner (2003) stated, "Positive DEPI values are probably best interpreted as representing an affective problem rather than specifically equating positive values with diagnostic categories" (p. 312). However, many of the variables hypothesized to be associated with DPD (V, S, C', Color-Shading blends, 3r+2/R, blends, and the Intellectualization and Isolation Indices; see later) are components of the DEPI. If all these variables were elevated as suggested, the DEPI would equal 6. Thus, it would not be surprising to find the DEPI positive. However, given the mixed findings with this variable, as well as the relative instability of C' and the number of blends (Exner, 1999), such a marker should be considered tentative at best. On a related note, the Coping Deficit Index (CDI), was a direct outgrowth of revisions to the DEPI (Exner, 1999) and reflects a sense of helplessness commonly observed in individuals with limited coping resources. Given the DPD person's propensity toward depression and dysphoria, the CDI may be elevated during interpersonal crises or periods of disappointment or frustration.

Within the Self-Perception cluster, many variables are of relevance to the assessment of DPD. Given DPDs' low self-esteem and tendencies toward negative self-regard, the Egocentricity Index should be relatively low, and the number of V responses should be elevated. Exner (2003) and Weiner (2003) reported that $3r+(2)/R$ is a relatively stable trait and indicates pervasive problems in striking a healthy balance in self-focus and other focus. Patients with DPD often become excessively self-focused on their negativity (i.e., elevated Vistas) or on the disappointment they perceive from others. As Weiner (2003) noted, elevated Vs, in conjunction with a low Egocentricity Index ($3r + 2/ R$), is indicative of chronic, recurring depression. Also within this cluster, DPD patients may be expected to have FD > 2 and Human detail > Human content. Although FD responses indicate more objective means of self-evaluation, Weiner (2003) observed that when FD > 2, the individual may be self-evaluating and self-focused to a fault, so that every minor flaw is observed. The H:Hd+(H)+(Hd) ratio may be very telling about the interpersonal relatedness of an individual with DPD. Given the characterization of DPD individuals as having strong needs for interpersonal relatedness (Bemporad, 1973, 1976; Kahn, 1975), it may be that their relationships are focused on obtaining their interpersonal needs without becoming too close. Thus, Hd, (H), and (Hd) may predominate over H. Likewise, animal content may be greater than human content, reflecting the DPD patient's discomfort with closeness while seeking a relationship that is safer and less likely to disappoint.

Within the Interpersonal cluster, DPD patients are likely to have few, if any, cooperative movement responses (COPs), but may have elevated aggressive movement (AG), given their expectation that they will be hurt by others. Gacono and Meloy's (1992) aggressive special scores may be particularly useful with such patients. These four scores are labeled Aggressive Content, Aggression Past, Aggressive Potential, and Sadomasochistic Aggression. Of interest are the Aggression Past and Aggressive Potential scores. Responses are scored if a percept is described where an aggressive act has just occurred (e.g., "Here's a bear who's been shot"—Aggression Past) or is about to happen (e.g., "That's a monster that is gearing up to attack his prey"—Aggressive Potential). In this case, it would be expected that DPD patients may provide Aggression Past and Aggressive Potential responses. Both types of responses are indicative of the individual's expectation that others can and will hurt him or her, reflecting his or her preoccupation with loss and disappointment from others.

Texture (T) responses are not likely to be observed in DPD protocols. Weiner (2003) stated that the absence of T responses in protocols does not necessarily mean that individuals "avoid interpersonal relationships.... However, their relationships tend to be distant and detached, rather than close and intimate" (p. 174). He adds that T-less individuals neither anticipate nor seek out relationships, and tend to be uncomfortable around others.

In the Controls cluster, DPD individuals are likely to have adequate psychological resources. Their current affective state may lead to elevations in the D score, and given their chronic affective turmoil and problems with self-perception and interpersonal relationships, their Adjusted D score may be negative. However, DPD traditionally has been conceptualized as a "higher level" personality disorder (Kernberg, 1984, 1990). Specifically, DPD individuals tend to function adequately on a day-to-day basis. Although chronically unhappy, pessimistic, and self-critical, they are not so impaired as to have serious problems with impulse control or to have serious affective dysregulation that would require hospitalization. Rather, they are individuals who have accepted their fate that life is disappointing (Millon, 1996). To the extent that DPD individuals have come to associate gratification with intrapsychic suffering and interpersonal guardedness (Berliner, 1966; Kernberg, 1984; 1987, 1990; Simons, 1987), they will live a life that is miserably stable.

Depressive personality disorder is not associated with lapses in reality testing or perceptual inaccuracy. Thus, Mediation, Ideation, and Processing clusters are not anticipated to show marked elevations or suppressions. However, DPD individuals often are viewed as serious-minded and hard-core realists (APA, 1994; Kernberg, 1984, 1987, 1990; Millon, 1996). As a "higher-level" personality disorder, DPD is characterized by the use of intellectualization and repressive defenses. Thus, the Intellectualization Index is expected to be elevated. Additionally, past research has found that DPD individuals have perfectionistic features (Hartlage et al., 1998; Huprich, 2003a; Klein, 1990). These features include excessive criticism of self and others. Thus, the DPD individual may produce a greater than expected number of Dd responses, reflecting the patient's careful efforts not to miss anything in the inkblots that could disappoint the examiner and lead to potential rejection. She or he also may overincorporate (Zd > 3.0) in her or his effort to be thorough and complete. Alternatively, the DPD individual also may produce a greater than usual number of W responses, again suggestive of perfectionistic features that focus on the need to attend to the entire blot (Weiner, 2003). If the individual is not currently depressed, elevations in R also may be found. However, as depressive affect comes to be predominant, R actually may decrease.

The following case example shows a patient who appears to meet the DSM-IV criteria for DPD. This case was selected for two reasons. The protocol appears to have many features believed present in DPD, yet the patient is not a "textbook" case which reflects the reality of most clinical situations. Rather, he presents with an extensive history and set of presenting problems. Thus, this case presents both nomothetic features of DPD, as seen clinically and in the assessment of DPD with the Rorschach, as well as idiographic descriptors of the examinee. The author is grateful to Dr. Robert Schneider for providing this example.

CASE EXAMPLE: MR. MASEY

Mr. Masey is a 66-year-old Caucasian referred for psychological assessment after failing to respond to antidepressant and anxiolytic medication. He frequently referred to his psychiatric symptoms as "stupid" and "irrational," often blaming himself for having failed to overcome his problems. He also was remorseful about his history of two failed marriages, blaming himself for being a "double failure." However, he maintained contact with his children from these marriages and had a generally positive relationship with them. He also regularly commented on the punitive nature of God, and how much he felt sorry for those who had to endure God's judgment. At times, Mr. Masey became very angry with God, after which he indulged in self-retributions for being so "irrational."

Mr. Masey reported feeling lonely for most of his life and expressed reservations about opening up to someone concerning his past. Being a Veteran, he was particularly remorseful over his combat experience, in which many soldiers who reported to him died because of what he described as his own poor training for combat. His survivor guilt was notable, given that he frequently envisioned the faces of the killed men looking at him accusingly. Despite experiencing profound combat-related trauma, he denied any psychotic episodes or lapses in reality testing.

Mr. Masey grew up in an intact home with his parents and one sister (now deceased after committing suicide). He described his mother as a "hypochondriac" and his father as frequently absent and emotionally distant. He added that his father was a perfectionist who never provided praise, but was quick to criticize. As a result, Mr. Masey stated that he had to care for himself.

Mr. Masey sought treatment initially for posttraumatic stress disorder (PTSD). He regularly experienced flashbacks, fragmented memories of his combat experience, nightmares, a pervasive sense of hypervigilance, and an avoidance of war-related stimuli. He regularly commented on a sense of powerlessness he felt while in combat, much like the powerlessness he felt toward his unavailable mother. He also recognized a growing sense of anger he had toward himself, the government, and God. He saw his anger as a "duality." That is, it seemed to be directed toward himself and others.

Mr. Masey's Rorschach has many features typical of a depressive personality. Results suggest that his affective life is full of negativity, pessimism, hostility, and anxiety (elevations in C',V, S, Y). He has a high number of blends, indicative of emotional complexity often involving depression and/or anxiety. He is chronically angry (S = 2) and engages in an unusual amount of introspection that is negative and critical (V = 1; FD = 4). Interestingly, his DEPI results are positive, suggesting that he likely has problems with his affect. Although his Rorschach suggests that he currently is experiencing situational distress (D = –1), his long-term coping generally appears to be adequate (AdjD = 0; CDI, negative). As such, Mr. Masey is an individual with pervasive, chronic negativity and unusual self-inspection, which is very characteristic of an individual with DPD.

There also were some unexpected (unpredicted) results in the Affect cluster of Mr. Masey's Rorschach. He had more CF responses than what would be expected. Three of the four he reported were in the last three cards. Here, the affective stimulation appears to have been great. His CF responses are blended with markers of anxiety and unmet need states that involve excessive bodily concerns and a sense of being damaged. His perceptual accuracy here is severely compromised and, at the end, becomes based on his personal experience. It may be that such patterns reflect his ongoing PTSD conflicts. Once his PTSD has been adequately addressed, the frequency of his CF responses may decrease. Subsequently, he may have Sum C' > WSumC, which is expected in patients with depressive personalities. Furthermore, he may appear more ambitent or introversive in his problem-solving style at future testing.

Also unexpected was his positive Rorschach Suicide Constellation (S-CON). Although Mr. Masey did not report suicidal thinking, his current distress and lack of adequate coping resources put him at an increased risk for self-destruction. Given a family history of suicide, this finding is one of concern for the treating therapist.

Mr. Masey's self-perception is quite interesting. On the one hand, he engages in excessive self-focus that tends to be negative, self-critical, and laden with much concern about his bodily integrity and functioning ($V = 1$; $FD = 4$; $An + Xy = 3$; $MOR = 5$). On the other hand, he provided two reflection responses, which subsequently contributed to elevations on the Egocentricity Index. Consistent with this is a tendency to relate only to parts of people with whom he believes he can get his needs met ($H < (H) + Hd + (Hd)$).

At least three possibilities may account for these contradictory findings. First, Mr. Masey's narcissistic strivings may be indicative of his efforts to compensate for his poor self-esteem. That is, he may enact in a self-aggrandizing manner when faced with threats to his sense of self. Mr. Masey's therapist reported that Mr. Masey often pulled for validating comments as a way to bolster his fragile self-esteem. In fact, Mr. Masey frequently took a "holier-than-thou" attitude when feeling angry at others. His assumptions of self-righteousness, however, were quickly diminished by self-deprecation.

Second, the elevated reflections may be indicative of Mr. Masey's defensive efforts to ward off negative feelings when criticized by authority figures, similar to what he experienced with his father. The blend on Card IV is particularly suggestive of such anxiety and negativity experienced in the context of an authority figure simultaneously with efforts to maintain self-esteem (FY.FV.Fru).

Third, Mr. Masey's narcissistic strivings are not inconsistent with introjective depression and pathology. According to Blatt and Shichman (1983), individuals with introjective (self-critical) depression can vacillate between an introjective depressive and phallic narcissist orientation. The phallic narcissist is concerned with demonstrating his superiority and achievements, especially by way of his body. Mr. Masey's history indicates that he achieved some superiority by assuming a leadership position with a combat unit. However, Mr. Masey also reported that he was chronically negative and self-critical, an observation supported by his therapist. He also had excessive concerns about feeling damaged and physically weak ($MOR = 5$; $An + Xy = 3$). As such, Mr. Masey's reflection responses and unusually high regard for himself may be indicative of the tension he regularly experiences between a need to view himself more positively and the pervasive sense of his badness and imperfections.

Interpersonally, Mr. Masey has patterns of difficulties commonly observed in individuals with DPD. He tends not to see positive interaction occurring between people (COP = 0), and may even anticipate hostility or conflict (AG = 1). He also does not express dependency needs (T = 0, Food = 0), likely because of fears that others will disappoint him or be critical of him. Yet, Mr. Masey is not particularly isolated from human interaction (Isol/R is within a normal range). Rather, he tends to relate to people in ways not as threatening to his esteem that at the same time provide for him what he would like in relationships (A = 4, (H)+Hd+(Hd) = 4; H = 1).

Inspection of the cognitive triad indicates some typical patterns for the depressive personality. Mr. Masey clearly uses intellectualization (2AB +Art + Ay = 5). These processes were notable at the beginning of the assessment, in which a mixture of ideation, self-observation, and negativity coexisted (Mp.FD.FC'o and Art content). Most likely, Mr. Masey intellectualizes his negativity and self-observation as a way to distance himself from such adverse feelings. He also uses intellectualization when confronted with a stimulus invoking authority and parental themes (Card IV). Both art content and an abstract special score exist on Card IV, all the more demonstrating his need to protect himself from the images the card invokes. Finally, intellectualization is found with Card VII, for which movement (mp.Mp) and oppositionality (WS) play a predominant role in the response. This card also pulls for interpersonal relatedness, and it appears that, although Mr. Masey channels his resources into meaningful output (M), he may believe that such actions ultimately will be out of his control (passive movement, m).

Contrary to what was expected, Mr. Masey tended to underincorporate (Zd = –2.0), often processing the whole card in place of details. However, he also had an inordinate number of W responses (n = 13) for a 16-response record. This indicates that he is seeking to accomplish more than he can achieve (W:M = 13:3). Such achievement strivings may be related to his desires for perfectionism. Yet, although he sought to provide "complete" responses to the cards, he misses important elements of his stimulus field. Consequently, his Mediation also suffers. That is, although he was "complete" in his answer, he is incomplete in his ability to respond most adaptively to the demands of his environment and becomes somewhat inaccurate in his ability to perceive it.

Also remarkable for Mr. Masey is the finding of two PSV scores. A PSV can be suggestive of cognitive dysfunction, inflexibility, or preoccupation. In this case, the first PSV occurred with Card V, which fell on the heels of a potentially provocative Card IV. It could be that this PSV is exemplary of obsessive defenses and processing commonly found with depressive personalities (Huprich, 1998). The second PSV occurred between cards VIII and IX. There was an occurrence of CF.YF–, An, and Bl. In this case, it could be that the affective stimulation aroused in both cards signaled Mr. Masey's preoccupation with being damaged and anxious. It would not be surprising to learn that Mr. Masey experiences anxiety and maladaptive thoughts about his integrity under affectively provocative situations, perhaps deriving from his need to punish himself for feeling good things when he was supposedly responsible for his soldiers' deaths.

Depressive personality disorder can be assessed on the Rorschach. Many variables in the Structural Summary assess trait-like features of DPD. These features include pervasive negativity and pessimism, intellectualization, perfectionistic tendencies, and discomfort with interpersonal relationships. Consistent with past theory and research, a case is presented that demonstrates typical patterns of DPD on the Rorschach, as well as idiographic phenomena consistent with this individual's personal history. Further validation of these findings and the differential assessment of DPD from other mood disorders of varying degrees would be most welcome.

REFERENCES

Akiskal, H. S. (1989). Validating affective personality types. In L. Robbins & J. Barrett (Eds.), *The validity of psychiatric diagnosis* (pp. 217–227). New York: Raven Press.

Akiskal, H. S. (1997). Overview of chronic depressions and their clinical management. In H. S. Akiskal & G. B. Cassano (Eds.), *Dysthymia and the spectrum of chronic depressions* (pp. 1–34). New York: Guilford.

American Psychiatric Association. (1994). *Diagnostic and statistical manual of mental disorders* (4th ed.). Washington, DC: Author.

Archer, R. P., & Gordon, R. A. (1988). MMPI and Rorschach indices of schizophrenic and depressive diagnoses among adolescent inpatients. *Journal of Personality Assessment, 52,* 276–287.

Ball, J. D., Archer, R. P., Gordon, R. A., & French, J. (1991). Rorschach depression indices with children and adolescents: Concurrent validity findings. *Journal of Personality Assessment, 57,* 465–476.

Bemporad, J. R. (1973). New views on the psychodynamics of the depressive character. In S. Arieti (Ed.), *World biennial of psychiatry* (pp. 219–243). New York: Basic Books.

Bemporad, J. R. (1976). Psychotherapy of the depressive character. *Journal of the American Academy of Psychoanalysis, 4,* 347–352.

Berliner, B. (1966). Psychodynamics of the depressive character. *Psychoanalytic Forum, 1,* 244–251.

Blatt, S. J. (1974). Levels of object representation in anaclitic and introjective depression. *The Psychoanalytic Study of the Child, 29,* 107–157.

Blatt, S. J., & Shichman, S. (1983). Two primary configurations of psychopathology. *Psychoanalysis and Contemporary Thought, 6*, 187–254.

Carlson, C. F., Kula, M. L., & St-Laurent, C. M. (1997). Rorschach revised DEPI and CDI with inpatient major depressive and borderline personality disorder with major depression. *Journal of Clinical Psychology, 53*, 51–58.

Carter, C. L., & Dacey, C. M. (1996). Validity of the Beck Depression Inventory, MMPI, and Rorschach in assessing adolescent depression. *Journal of Adolescence, 19*, 223–231.

Costa, P. T., Jr., & McCrae, R. R. (1992). *The NEO PI-R Professional Manual*. Odessa, FL: Psychological Assessment Resources.

Dies, R. R. (1995). Conceptual issues in Rorschach research. In J. E. Exner, Jr. (Ed.), *Issues and methods in Rorschach research* (pp. 25–52). Hillsdale, NJ: Lawrence Erlbaum Associates.

Dyce, J. A., & O'Connor, B. P. (1998). Personality disorders and the Five-Factor Model: A test of facet-level predictions. *Journal of Personality Disorders, 12*, 31–45.

Exner, J. E. (1986). *The Rorschach: A comprehensive system: Volume 1. Basic Foundations* (2nd ed.). New York: John Wiley.

Exner, J. E. (1993). *The Rorschach: A comprehensive system: Volume 1. Basic Foundations* (3rd ed.). New York: John Wiley.

Exner, J. E. (1999). The Rorschach: Measurement concepts and issues of validity. In S. B. Embretston & S. L. Hershberger (Eds.), *The new rules of measurement*. Mahwah, NJ: Lawrence Erlbaum Associates.

Exner, J. E. (2003). *The Rorschach: A comprehensive system: Volume 1. Basic Foundations* (4th ed.). New York: John Wiley.

Gacono, C. B., & Meloy, J. R. (1992). *The Rorschach assessment of aggressive and psychopathic personalities*. Hillsdale, NJ: Lawrence Erlbaum Associates.

Hartlage, S., Arduino, K., & Alloy, L. B. (1998). Depressive personality characteristics: State dependent concomitants of depressive disorder and traits independent of current depression. *Journal of Abnormal Psychology, 107*, 349–354.

Hirschfeld, R. M. A., & Holzer, C. E. (1994). Depressive personality disorder: Clinical implications. *Journal of Clinical Psychiatry, 55*(Suppl), 10–17.

Huprich, S. K. (1998). Depressive personality disorder: Theoretical issues, clinical findings, and future research questions. *Clinical Psychology Review, 18*, 477–500.

Huprich, S. K. (2000). Describing depressive personality analogues and dysthymics on the NEO-Personality Inventory—Revised. *Journal of Clinical Psychology, 56*, 1521–1534.

Huprich, S. K. (2001a). The overlap of depressive personality disorder and dysthymia, revisited. *Harvard Review of Psychiatry, 9*, 158–168.

Huprich, S. K. (2001b). Object loss and object relations in the depressive personality. *Bulletin of the Menninger Clinic, 65*, 549–559.

Huprich, S. K. (2003a). Depressive personality and its relationship to depressed mood, interpersonal loss, negative parental perceptions, and perfectionism. *Journal of Nervous and Mental Disease, 191*, 1–7.

Huprich, S. K. (2003b). Testing facet level predictions and construct validity of depressive personality disorder. *Journal of Personality Disorders, 17*, 219–232.

Huprich, S. K. (2003c). Testing the theoretical underpinnings of major depression and depressive personality disorder. Unpublished manuscript. Ypsilanti, MI: Eastern Michigan University.

Huprich, S. K., Margrett, J. E., Barthelemy, K. J., & Fine, M. A. (1996). The Depressive Personality Disorder Inventory: An initial investigation of its psychometric properties. *Journal of Clinical Psychology, 52,* 153–159.

Huprich, S. K., Sanford, K., & Smith, M. (2002). Further psychometric evaluation of the Depressive Personality Disorder Inventory. *Journal of Personality Disorders, 16,* 255–269.

Kahn, E. (1975). The depressive character. *Folia Psychiatrica et Neurologica Japonica, 29,* 291–303.

Kernberg, O. F. (1984). *Severe personality disorders.* New Haven, CT: Yale University Press.

Kernberg, O. F. (1987). Clinical dimensions of masochism. In R. A. Glick & D. I. Meyers (Eds.), *Masochism: Current and psychotherapeutic contributions.* Hillsdale, NJ: Analytic Press.

Kernberg, O. F. (1990, May 16). *Differential diagnosis of the depressive–masochistic personality disorder.* Paper presented at the 143rd Annual Meeting of the American Psychiatric Association, New York, NY.

Klein, D. N. (1990). Depressive personality: Reliability, validity, and relation to dysthymia. *Journal of Abnormal Psychology, 99,* 412–421.

Klein, D. N. (1999). Depressive personality in relatives of outpatients with dysthymic disorder and episodic major depressive disorder and normal controls. *Journal of Affective Disorders, 55,* 19–27.

Klein, D. N. & Miller, G. A. (1993). Depressive personality in a nonclinical sample. *American Journal of Psychiatry, 150,* 1718–1724.

Klein, D. N., & Shih, J. H. (1998). Depressive personality: Associations with DSM-III-R mood and personality disorders and negative and positive affectivity, 30-month stability, and prediction of course of Axis I depressive disorders. *Journal of Abnormal Psychology, 107,* 319–327.

Kraepelin, E. (1921). *Manic–depressive insanity and paranoia.* Edinburgh, Scotland: E. & S. Livingstone.

Kretschmer, E. (1925). *Physique and character.* New York: Harcourt and Brace.

Krishnamurthy, R., & Archer, R. P. (2001). An evaluation of the effects of Rorschach EB style on the diagnostic utility of the Depression Index. *Assessment, 8,* 105–109.

Laughlin, H. P. (1956). *The neuroses in clinical practice.* Philadelphia: W. B. Saunders.

Lipovsky, J. A., Finch, A. J., Jr., & Belter, R. W. (1989). Assessment of depression in adolescents: Objective and projective measures. *Journal of Personality Assessment, 53,* 449–458.

McDermut, W., Zimmerman, M., & Chelminski, I. (2003). The construct validity of depressive personality disorder. *Journal of Abnormal Psychology, 112,* 49–60.

Meyer, G. J. (1993). The impact of response frequency on the Rorschach constellation incides and on their validity with diagnostic and MMPI-2 criteria. *Journal of Personality Assessment, 60,* 153–180.

Meyer, G. J., Finn, S. E., Eyde, L. D., Kay, G. G., Kubiszyn, T. W., Moreland, K. L., Eisman, E. J., & Dies, R. R. (1998). *Benefits and costs of psychological assessment in healthcare delivery: Report of the Board of Professional Affairs Psychological Assessment Workgroup, Part I.* Washington, DC: American Psychological Association.

Millon, T. (1996). *Disorders of personality* (2nd ed.). New York: Wiley-Interscience.

Phillips, K. A., Gunderson, J. G., Triebwasser, J., Kimble, C. R., Faedda, G., Lyoo, I. K., et al. (1998). Reliability and validity of depressive personality disorder. *American Journal of Psychiatry, 155,* 1044–1048.

Ryder, A. G., & Bagby, R. M. (1999). Diagnostic viability of depressive personality disorder: Theoretical and conceptual issues. *Journal of Personality Disorders, 13,* 99–117.

Schneider, K. (1958). *Psychopathic personalities.* London, England: Cassell.

Simons, R. C. (1987). Psychoanalytic contributions to psychiatric nosology: Forms of masochistic behavior. *Journal of the American Psychoanalytic Association, 35,* 583–608.

Viglione, D. J., Jr., Brager, R. C., & Haller, N. (1988). Usefulness of structural Rorschach data in identifying inpatients with depressive symptoms: A preliminary study. *Journal of Personality Assessment, 52,* 524–529.

Weiner, I. B. (2003). *Principles of Rorschach interpretation* (2nd ed.). Mahwah, NJ: Lawrence Erlbaum Associates.

Wiener, M. (1989). Psychopathology reconsidered: Depression interpreted as psychosocial transactions. *Clinical Psychology Review, 9,* 295–321.

Westen, D. (1995). *Social Cognition and Object Relations Manual.* Boston, MA: Harvard University.

Widiger, T. A., Trull, T. J., Clarkin, J. F., Sanderson, C., & Costa, P. T., Jr. (2002). A description of the DSM-IV personality disorders with the Five-Factor Model of personality. In P. T. Costa, Jr. & T. A. Widiger (Eds.), *Personality disorders and the five factor model of personality* (2nd ed., pp. 89–99). Washington, DC: American Psychiatric Press.

RORSCHACH PROTOCOL FOR MR.MASEY

Free Association	Inquiry
Card I 1. Right off hand, it looks like something out of Lord of the Rings. The dark-side figure that came after Gandolf, a winged creature. Hands here. Looks like the thing is either looking toward you or 180 degrees away from you.	1. Hands, pectoral muscles, torso here, head bent down as if toward you, and wings here. An evil being that dwelt under the mountains. (Evil?) The coloration. I associate darkness with evil.
2. A maple leaf that's been through a hell of a storm.	2. Yeah, jagged edges, stem here, a maple leaf will alays shred at the far end first.
Card II 3. Looks like there's been an explosion, something similar to a terrorist bomb. There's blood in there, a plaza, with destruction on either side of it.	3. Yes, like cities in Vietnam, ruins. Black suggests the opposite of good. It's like on TV. You see streets where bodies have been picked up, with blood everywhere. The red really strikes me. And this looks like a street leading up here, the dimension of it.
Card III 4. Upside down, it looks like part of a beetle. I don't know what the red would be, unless marking, but you have the exoskeleton, markings on the belly, forward arms, just ahead of the manacles and eyes here.	4. Yeah, forefeet here, eyes, manacles, exoskeleton partially here. You don't see the other legs. And red markings here.
Card IV 5. Oh, gosh! (Sigh). I can see many faces in there-nose, eyes, mouth,	5. Eyes, brows, hair of different shades, then the chin outlines here, here, and here, like an abstract painting if you will.

chin. Hidden, almost
shadowed back in there,
with mirror images of
them reflected here.
There are about six
different faces in there.
But I've seen the same
thing on my bathroom
wall and not just once,
either (laughs).

6. A shoe or boot on
either side, with a leg
and a foot—but missing
the torso and the rest of
the body.

6. Yeah, shoe or boot, with legs going up on either side. Just
the shape.

Card V
7. A bat.

7. Either a fruit bat or vampire bat. Long ears, wings.

8. Or a swallowtail
butterfly. The
swallowtail has these
little appendages.

8. Mm, hmm. Tail, antennae, wings.

9. Could be a fool
trying to hang-glide I
guess.

9. Yeah, if you ever saw a hang-glider from the top...kind of
in a harness on the thighs, with the legs sticking out. I'm a
pilot, and I always wanted to do that, but I never had the guts.

Card VI
10. That looks like a
napalm bomb that
exploded. I remember a
pilot in an F-4 Phantom.
That's what it looked
like. He was coming
right toward me.

10. The bomb explodes and makes a smoke plume that
extrudes on either side and the empty casing heads coming
right toward you. In our case, it flew over our right flank.
Mainly the shape reminds me of that.

Card VII
11. Oh boy! Sexy
pictures. I see four faces
here. These two seem to
be an adolescent or
child, with maybe a hat
or ponytail or a scarf
blowing up. It's like

11. Yeah, looks like the air is keeping the hair or scarf of
whatever it is up here. It looks innocent. But here, you have
the eye, nose, snarling mouth – an evil look, mainly the eyes
and mouth with almost a tooth here. Comic artists do this a
lot, you know—rounded nose equals innocence, pointed nose
equals evil. We picture Satan with horns and a pointed nose.

this is innocence here, and this is uninnocence down here, if I can use that horrible phrase. And these faces down here look like the opposite of those up here. I don't know what this would be down here unless it's the torso of this head. These have the eyes, the brown, the snarled mouth. Maybe the bust continues here. If you had a statue you'd have to have something to put them on in other words.

Card VIII

12. That looks like two lizards, but I don't know what it has to do with the rest of the shape.

12. Lizards walking, with an eye ridge here, though no tail.

13. That looks like water. Separating an animal stepping across some rocks from his mirror image, but if that's an animal, he's an ugly sucker.

13. Yeah, rocks, or maybe coral—the color—and his mirror image reflected here. Just an ugly shaped body.

14. Upside down, it looks like somebody's been blown apart. Lung area, chest cavity, there is always fatty tissue up here, guts down here, spinal column. You ever seen anybody blown apart? If you did, you'd never forget it, especially if they look at you, and they know they're dying (puts card

14. Lungs are very pink and pretty until they lose oxygen, like after an explosion. The blood inside your body turns many different colors, depending on oxygenation and bruising, and your intestines generally look a certain way depending on what you ate and the extent of digestion.

down). I don't like to
look at it, makes my
head hurt right back
here.

Card IX
15. This looks like the
lower portion of that
other one. It's really the
same thing, and I don't
want to look at it. (Puts
card down). I mean,
why do I see that ? The
red makes sense but not
the green. Maybe it's
the coagulation of blood,
but they shouldn't go
together. I've seen the
insides of so many men,
but I haven't seen the
soul there (crying).

15. Legs, guts, upper chest area. Your stomach is a pretty
pink too, but when you die things are starved for oxygen and
turn a terrible blue color-different shades.

Card X
16. My mind's fixed on
bodies now. I've got ten
of them laying in a boat.
Which one do you want
to look at? The
bronchial tubes here,
lungs here, the rest is
just splattered.

Card X
16. Yeah, splattered everywhere. You see the tubes, then the
pink lungs. Maybe this is the bladder area here, maybe vocal
chords here, just a splat.

RORSCHACH SEQUENCE OF SCORES FOR MR. MASEY

Card	Resp	Loc (DQ)	Loc No	Determinants (FQ)	(2)	Content(s)	P	Z	Special Scores
I	1.	Wo	1	Mp.FD.FC'o		(H), Art		1.0	GHR
	2.	WO	1	Fo		Bt		1.0	MOR
II	3.	WS+	1	C'F.CF.FDu		Bl, Sc		4.5	MOR
III	4.	Ddo	99	FC-		Ad			DV
IV	5.	Wo	1	FY.FV.Fru		Hd, Art		2.0	DR, AB, PHR
	6.	D+	6	Fo	(2)	Hd, Cg		4.0	PHR
V	7.	Wo	1	Fo		A	P	1.0	
	8.	Wo	1	Fo		A	P	1.0	PSV
	9.	W+	1	FD.Mpo		H, Sc		2.5	DR, PHR
VI	10.	W+	1	mma.FD.FC'u		Sc, Fi		2.5	PER
VII	11.	WS+	1	mp.Mpu	(2)	Hd, Cg, Art	P	4.0	DV, AG, GHR
VIII	12.	Do	1	FMau	(2)	A	P		
	13.	W+	1	FMa.FC.Fro		A, Na	P	4.5	DR
	14.	Wo	1	CF.YF-		An, Bl		4.5	MOR, DR
IX	15.	Wo	1	CF.YF-		An, Bl		5.5	PSV, MOR, DR, PER
X	16.	Wo	1	CF-		An		5.5	DV, MOR

391

Location Features	Determinants		Contents	Approach
	Blends	*Single*		
	M.FD.FC'	M = 0	H = 1	I: W.W
Zf = 14	C'F.CF.FD	FM = 1	(H) = 1	II: WS
ZSum = 43.5	FY.FV.Fr	m = 0	Hd = 3	III: Dd
Zest = 45.5	FD.M	FC = 1	(Hd) = 0	IV: W.D
	m.FD.FC'	CF = 1	Hx = 0	V: W.W.W
W = 13	m.M	C = 0	A = 4	VI: W
D = 2	FM.FC.Fr	Cn = 0	(A) = 0	VII: WS
W+D = 15	CF.YF	FC' = 0	Ad = 1	VIII: D.W.W
Dd = 1	CF.YF	C'F = 0	(Ad) = 0	IX: W
S = 2		C' = 0	An = 3	X: W
		FT = 0	Art = 3	
Developmental Quality		TF = 0	Ay = 0	*Special Scores*
+ = 6		T = 0	Bl = 3	Lv 1 Lv 2
o = 10		FV = 0	Bt = 1	DV = 3x1 = 0x2
v/+ = 0		VF = 0	Cg = 2	INC = 0x2 = 0x4
v = 0		V = 0	Cl = 0	DR = 5x3 = 0x6
		FY = 0	Ex = 0	FAB = 0x4 = 0x7
		YF = 0	Fd = 0	ALOG = 0x5
Form Quality		Y = 0	Fi = 1	CON = 0x7

	FQx	MQual	W+D		
+	= 0	= 0	= 0	Fr = 0	Ge = 0
o	= 7	= 2	= 7	rF = 0	Hh = 0
u	= 5	= 1	= 5	FD = 0	Ls = 0
-	= 4	= 0	= 3	F = 4	Na = 1
none	= 0	= 0	= 0	(2) = 3	Sc = 3

Raw Sum 6 = 8
Wgtd Sum 6 = 18

Sx = 0   AB = 1   GHR = 2
Xy = 0   AG = 1   PHR = 3
Id = 0   COP = 0   MOR = 5
         CP = 0   PER = 2
                  PSV = 2

Ratios, Percentages, and Derivations

Core

R = 16   L = .33

EB = 3:5   EA = 8.0   EBPer = 1.7
eb = 4:7   es = 11   D = -1
                Adj es = 8   Adj D = 0

FM = 2   SumC' = 2   SumT = 0
m = 2   Sum V = 1   Sum Y = 2

Affect

FC: CF+C = 2:4
Pure C = 0
SumC':WSumC = 3:5
Afr = .45
S = 2
Blends:R = 9:16
CP = 0

Interpersonal

COP = 0   AG = 1
GHR: PHR = 2:3
a:p = 3:4
Food = 0
Sum T = 0
Human Cont = 5
Pure H = 1
PER = 2
Isol Indx = .19

Ideation

a:p = 3:4   Sum6 = 8
Ma:Mp = 0:3   Lv2 = 0
2AB+Art+Ay = 5   WSum6 = 18
MOR = 5   M- = 0
                       Mnone = 0

Mediation

XA% = .75
WDA% = .80
X-% = .25
S- = 0
P = 5
X+% = .44
Xu% = .31

Processing

Zf = 14
W:D:Dd = 13:2:1
W:M = 13:3
Zd = -2.0
PSV = 2
DQ+ = 6
DQv = 0

Self-Perception

3r+(2)/R = .56
Fr+rF = 3
SumV = 1
FD = 4
An+Xy = 3
MOR = 5
H:(H)+Hd+(Hd) = 1:4

PTI = 1   *DEPI = 6   CDI = 3   *S-CON = 9   HVI = 3   OBS = 1

VI

PERSONALITY DISORDERS,
PSYCHOANALYTIC SCIENCE,
AND THE RORSCHACH

VI

15

Rorschach Assessment of Object Relations: The Personality Disorders

Paul M. Lerner
Private Practice, Camden, Maine

Clinicians and researchers alike are recognizing the crucial role of disturbed object relations in the development and expression of all types of psychopathology, including the personality disorders. This recognition, coupled with an appreciation of the distinction between internalized object relations and relations between the self and the object in the external world, has led Rorschach investigators (Blatt, 1990; Lerner, 1998; Mayman, 1967) to focus on the concept internal object relations, or on what Sandler and Rosenblatt (1962) have denoted the "representational world."

In suggesting that internal objects be considered as the contents of the unconscious, Melanie Klein laid the conceptual foundation for all subsequent explorations of the inner relationship between self and object. On the basis of her early work in child analysis, Klein (1926, 1927) introduced the concept of internal objects, which she described as inner fantasy images of the parents. In *Mourning and Melancholia*, Freud (1917) explained how lost actual objects were transformed gradually into inner presences. Klein extended this formulation by indicating that the "internal world of fantasy objects was a ubiquitous force in psychological life even when no actual loss had occurred" (Brown, 1996, p. 23).

Fairbairn (1952) extended Klein's notions concerning the formation of internal objects in several important and unique ways. As Grotstein (1991) noted, "His conception of endopsychic structures and their interrelationships imparted an anatomy and function to the internal world which is unparalleled in other theories, including Klein's, yet is congruent with her conceptions in other ways" (p. 37). Grotstein is hereby noting that by de-

397

scribing the structures (i.e., internal objects) that comprise the inner world and by outlining the functions they serve, Fairbairn (1952) specified several of Klein's formulations that heretofore had been somewhat elusive.

Since the pioneering writings of Klein and Fairbairn, a vast array of terms have been introduced to describe the cast of characters that assumedly inhabit the internal object world. A partial list would include self and object representations, internal objects, introjects, identifications, self-objects, autistic objects, symbiotic objects, good objects, and bad objects. Brown (1996), in his article, *A Proposed Demography of the Representational World*, suggested a map for organizing, interrelating, and locating these various concepts.

The following discussion first reviews Brown's demographic analysis of the representational world, with the intent of defining and describing the concept object representation. The discussion moves to the work of five Rorschach investigators, each of whom has used the concept of object representation to study object relations in various patient groups. As the work of these individuals is reviewed, including research scales several have developed, special attention is accorded findings related to patients with the diagnosis of personality disorder.

INTERNAL OBJECT RELATIONS

Both Kernberg (1976) and Ogden (1983) agreed that internal object relations units, consisting of unconscious self-representations and object representations, constitute the essential ingredients of psychic structure. Integrating the work of Kernberg and Ogden with the more recent writing of Hamilton (1995), Brown, (1996) outlined five characteristics of internal object relations units.

The first characteristic involves the degree of separateness between the representations of the self and the other. A continuum is visualized in which there is little differentiation between self and object at one pole, whereas at the opposite pole there is a clear and firm distinction between representations of the self and of the other. Mahler (1968), in particular, has outlined the stages through which self and object gradually and progressively become differentiated.

A second characteristic, emphasized by Kernberg (1982), is the affective link between self and object representations. In internal object relations units, the affective bind that links the self with the object may be positive or negative, benign or malignant (Blatt, Tuber, & Auerbach 1990), clear or confused, somatized (Krystal, 1988), or even nonexistent.

A third property is the cognitive level of representations. Blatt (1974) has written extensively of this dimension. Basing his discussion on an integration of psychoanalytic object relations theory with the developmental theories of Piaget and Werner, he describes how representations begin as vague, diffuse, sensorimotor experiences of pleasure and unpleasure, but then gradually expand and develop into well-differentiated, consistent, and relatively realistic representations of the self and object world. For Blatt, earlier forms of representation are based on action sequences associated with need gratification. Intermediate forms are based on specific perceptual and functional features, and more advanced forms are symbolic and conceptual.

A fourth characteristic is the level of ego functioning associated with each internal object relations unit. For instance, certain units may have a strong regressive element, as evidenced by the firmness of boundary between self and other and level of reality adherence. This aspect, besides drawing attention to defensive processes, also explains how meaning is generated within each of these units and clarifies Ogden's contention that internal objects have a relative mind of their own.

The fifth and final dimension according to Brown (1996) is the functional aspects of the mental representations. This refers to the psychic functions the mental representations serve within the individual's personality. For example, they provide self-soothing, bolster superego prohibitions, or enhance the individual's sense of identity.

In addition to outlining five dimensions along which object relations units may be understood, Brown (1996) also identified four general classes of internal object relations units.

One class is referred to as the "self in relation to autistic objects." This term is used "to denote the primarily sensory experience of the object which is leaned up against so to speak in order to achieve the earliest definition of self as bounded by the skin surface" (p. 31). Grotstein (1987) discussed how the autistic object provides a "sensory floor" upon which future self-development is based. Brown's term "autistic object" subsumes other related concepts, including sensation objects (Tustin, 1981), hard objects (Tustin, 1984), precursor objects (Gaddini, 1975), and confusional objects (Tustin, 1981).

A second class, more developmentally advanced, is the self in relation to symbiotic objects. According to Mahler, Pine, and Bergman (1975), in the second month, with the beginning awareness of the need-satisfying object, the infant enters the symbiotic phase. The inborn stimulus barrier begins to crack, and with a cathectic shift toward the sensoriperceptive periphery, the infant behaves and functions as though infant and mother are merged in an omnipotent dual unity encircled by a common protective shield. Symbiotic objects provide "a background of safety" (Sandler, 1960) from which the child progressively separates and individuates. Kohut (1977) has described a type of self–object relationship in which the object continues to be used later in development in a way similar to a symbiotic object. The relationship, according to Kohut, is one in which the self merges with the object so as to maintain a sense of self-cohesion and ward off disintegration.

A third class of object relations units is the self in relation to transitional internal objects. This refers to "a manner of self in relation to an object in which they are both joined and separated simultaneously" (Brown, 1996, p. 37). This type of relatedness is similar to what Mahler et al. (1975) described as "hatching" from the symbiotic relation, and Klein (1957) identified as occurring in the depressive position. Various authors (Kernberg, 1976) have introduced the term "introject" to denote the transitional internal object.

The final class, the self in relation to object representations, denotes the highest level of mental representation, the culmination of the formation of the representational world. Here, object representations are true symbols. That is, they represent the external object at a conceptual level and in a well-differentiated and realistic way. It should be noted that Brown (1996) is using the term "object representation" more narrowly than other authors. For instance, Blatt (1974), Kernberg (1976), and Mayman (1967) all use the term in a far broader way to include mental representations at all levels.

RESEARCH SCALES AND STUDIES

This section reviews the work of five writers, each of whom has contributed to the systematic study of the object representational construct by means of the Rorschach.

The Work of Mayman

A true pioneer in bringing a more phenomenologic and object relational dimension to Rorschach practice and research was Mayman. Using the specific theoretical contributions of Jacobon and Erickson and the test contributions of Schachtel, Mayman (1967) conceptualized object representations as templates or enduring internalized images of the self and of others around which the phenomenologic world is structured, and into which ongoing experiences of others are assimilated. It was Mayman's contention that Rorschach content, like the manifest content of dreams and early memories, was more than simply an embellished screen that concealed and hinted at deeper and more profound levels of unconscious meaning. He argued that manifest content in its own right could reflect levels of ego functioning, the relative capacity for object relations, and the nature of interpersonal strivings. According to Mayman (1967), "A person's most readily accessible object representations called up under such unstructured conditions tell much about his inner world of objects and about the quality of relationships with these inner objects toward which he is predisposed" (p. 17).

Mayman (1967) identified several dimensions for assessing the content of Rorschach response with the intent of answering the following questions:

> What kind of world does each person recreate in the inkblot milieu? What kinds of animate and inanimate objects come most readily to mind? What manner of people and things is he prone to surround himself with? Does he put together, for example, a peopleless world of inanimate objects; if so, which objects have special valence for him? Do they hint at a certain preferred mode of acting upon the world or of being acted upon by it? Are they, for example, tooth-equipped objects? Or, phallically intrusive objects? Decaying or malformed objects? (p. 17)

Besides attuning to the level of the psychosexual state and the degree of humanness in Rorschach responses, Mayman also considered the extent to which conflict or rage permeate the depiction of the other as well as expressions of the individual's vulnerability to separation and loss.

Overall then, Mayman (1977) viewed the Rorschach human response as a window through which one could see "important personal meaning" about "a person's capacity to establish empathic contact with another human being" (p. 244).

In an early study, Mayman (1967), grounded in these theoretical notions and committed to a clinical empathic–intuitive approach to projective test data, selected Rorschach protocols from the Menninger Psychotherapy Research Project and distilled from each record verbatim clusters of "content fragments" that he considered to be self-representations, object representations, and conflict representations. All patients were evaluated independently on the Health-Sickness Rating Scale (Lubersky, 1962), as well as on a wide range of other clinical variables. The Health-Sickness scale comprises a general description of the health–sickness dimension and a plethora of short case descriptions to anchor the scale points. Mayman examined the extent to which ratings of psychopathology, based exclusively on representational content gleaned from a Rorschach administered before treatment, corresponded to clinical ratings of psychopathology. Editing out all references to traditional Rorschach scores, such as form level or determinant, Mayman asked graduate students and interns to "immerse themselves" in each patient's Rorschach responses, to regard the imagery as a sample of the patient's inner world, and to assign a rating for the degree of psychopathology implicit in the representational content. Mayman found that these relatively inexperienced judges could successfully predict ratings on the basis of an independent psychiatric evaluation ($r = .86$). Most importantly, Mayman demonstrated that an object relational approach to Rorschach content correlated significantly with independent ratings of psychopathology. He also showed that comparatively inexperienced, clinically trained raters using a clinical methodology can make important contributions to research.

Mayman's seminal contributions to Rorschach research have spawned a number of object-representation scales and a host of construct-validity studies that have further refined the concept (Urist, 1973) and have extended the thematic analysis of object representations to manifest dreams (Krohn, 1974), to autobiographical data (Urist, 1973), and to studies assessing a person's capacity to enter into and benefit from insight-oriented psychotherapy (Hatcher & Krohn, 1980; Ryan, 1973). Different scales designed to evaluate object-representational levels as specific points on a developmental continuum have been applied and correlated across various data bases, including manifest dreams, the Rorschach, early memories, and health–sickness ratings (Krohn & Mayman, 1974). Collectively, these studies reflect Mayman's focal interest in thematic content; his unique and gifted clinical approach to projective data, which emphasizes the role of empathy and intuition; and his lifelong interest in variables related to psychoanalytic theory.

Mutuality of Autonomy Scale

Following upon Mayman's clinical methodology and integrating the theoretical formulations of Kernberg and Kohut, Urist (1973) investigated the multidimensional qualitative aspects of the object representational concept by correlating several Rorschach scale ratings of 40 adult inpatients, covering a wide spectrum of psychopathology, with independent ratings of written autobiographies. The specific scales developed by Urist were gauged to reflect the developmental ordering of stages in the unfolding of object relations along a number of overlapping dimensions, including mutuality of autonomy, body integrity, aliveness, fusion, thought disorder, richness and complexity, and differentiation and individuation. Urist found significantly high correlations among the various measures of object relations (Rorschach ratings and ratings of autobiographies) and interpreted this as indicating high consistency among self- and object representations across a wide range of sampled behavior.

Urist (1973) also demonstrated that object relations are not unidimensional areas of ego functioning. A factor analysis showed an important distinction between two related but separate structural underpinnings of object representations: an integrity factor, related to issues of self–other differentiation, stability, and consistency, and a boundary factor, related to developmental gradations in fusion–merger tendencies and in thought disorder associated with the inability to maintain a cognitive–perceptual sense of the boundary between self and other and between one object and another.

On the bases of this research, Urist (1977) developed the Mutuality of Autonomy Scale (MOAS), a measure reliant solely on Rorschach imagery to assess states in the child's shifting sense of self in relation to the mother. The MOAS is applied to all relationships (those of humans, animals, natural forces, and the like) expressed in Rorschach content. The series of scale points are not considered as discrete categories, but instead as differentiations along a continuous and coherent line of development. At the lower, more primitive end of the scale, is found Rorschach imagery that reflects themes of an undifferentiated, symbiotic fusion of body parts. At the next higher stage is found themes relating to the child's experience of self and mother, each as having physical proprietorship over his or her respective body. However, the body of one can be sensed as under the control of the other.

Themes of mirroring represent the third stage. Here, the child's relatedness involves the other being regarded as an extension of the child's own need state. Signs of differentiation appear in the fourth stage, but the prevailing anaclitic imagery indicates object relations on a predominantly need-satisfying basis. Higher scale points reflect movement toward object constancy, meaning that others are progressively viewed as separate and valued in their own right. The most advanced stage involves the capacity for empathy, the ability to invest in the subjective world of another while respecting the other's mutual autonomy. The scale, then, consists of the following seven ascending points: envelopment–incorporation, magical control–coercion, reflection–mirroring, anaclitic–dependent, simple interaction, collaboration–cooperation, and reciprocity–mutuality.

In his initial study, Urist (1977) applied the scale to the Rorschach records of 60 patients representing a wide range of psychopathology levels. Using therapist ratings and other clinical ratings as independent measures of object relations, Urist found that his scale correlated significantly with these ratings.

In contrast to the original study in which the scale was applied to the full Rorschach record, Urist and Shill (1982) applied the scale more narrowly to excerpted Rorschach responses, including responses in which a relationship was simply implied (e.g., "a run over cat"). In this study, independent ratings of object relations were obtained by applying a clinical version of the MOA to the clinical records of 60 adolescent inpatients and outpatients representing a broad spectrum of diagnoses. The authors reported significant correlations between the scale scores obtained from the Rorschach and those obtained from the confidential records.

Harder, Greenwald, Wechsler, and Ritzler (1984) found that the MOAS correlated significantly with ratings of psychopathology as assessed by a complex symptom–dimension checklist and independent diagnostic assessments based on the *Diagnostic and Statistical Manual of Mental Disorders,* 3rd Edtion (DSM-III; American Psychiatric Association, 1980) criteria. A mean MOA score based on only four Rorschach cards distinguished among schizophrenic, affective, and nonpsychotic conditions. More severe psychiatric disorders were associated with a more disturbed mean MOA score.

In a sample of acutely disturbed adolescent and young adult patients admitted to a long-term, intensive residential treatment facility, Blatt et al. (1990) reported that the mean MOA score correlated significantly with independent ratings of clinical symptoms and presence of thought disorder. Unexpectedly, however, the scale did not correlate with independent ratings of social behavior and interpersonal relationships. This pattern of results led the authors to question whether the scale primarily assesses object relations or, rather, a general level of psychopathology.

Although the question raised by the authors is quite important, it also is highly complex (Lerner 1998). Nonetheless, there is a more recent study that supports the MOAS as a measure of object relations. Using a sample of 57 outpatients, all of whom bore DSM-IV diagnoses, Ackerman, Hilsenroth, Clemence, Weatherill, and Fowler (2001) examined the convergent validity between the MOAS and the Social Cognition and Object Relations Scale (SCORS). The SCORS consists of eight variables scored on a 7-point global rating. Unlike the MOAS which is applied to Rorschach responses, the SCORS is applied to Thematic Apperception Test (TAT) stories. Support for the convergent validity between the two scales was obtained. As predicted, higher (benevolent–healthy) ratings on the SCORS were significantly related to level 1 ratings on the MOAS. For example, individuals who were rated on the SCORS as having positive expectations from relationships, revealed on the MOAS more differentiated self–other object representations.

To briefly recap, findings have demonstrated the scale to be effective in distinguishing among different psychiatric diagnostic entities. Scale scores have been related to independent ratings of psychopathology, clinical symptoms, and object relations. A question has been raised as to whether the scale primarily assesses object relations or severity of psychopathology. This is a complicated question, for as Lerner (1998) has noted, these variables are intertwined. Nevertheless, the scale appears to have good clinical and research utility. Further research with this instrument should continue to evaluate this utility, the incremental validity it provides over the Comprehensive System, and its assessment of psychopathology above and beyond typical DSM-IV categories.

Next, several studies are reviewed in which the scale has been applied to personality disordered groups. Building on the work of Kernberg (1975), Spear (1980) drew a distinction between two different types of borderline patients: the obsessive–paranoid borderline patient and the infantile–hysterical borderline patient. Later, Spear and Sugarman (1984) applied a modified version of the MOAS to the Rorschach protocols of groups representing each of these subtypes of borderline patients and a group of schizophrenic patients. The authors found that scale scores distinguished the two borderline groups from each other and the infantile–hysterical borderlines from the schizophrenics. Specifically, they found that the infantile–hysterical borderline patients functioned at a higher object-relations level, and that the obsessive–paranoid borderlines functioned at a lower level, closer to that of the schizophrenic patients.

Blais, Hilsenroth, Fowler, and Conboy (1999) investigated the borderline personality disorder diagnosis as defined in DSM-IV in a sample of university clinic outpatients. Using several psychoanalytically based assessment techniques, including the MOAS, the authors reported that clinical ratings of MOAS were the only ratings that correlated significantly with the total number of borderline symptoms. Furthermore, the investigators also found that the MOAS correlated with the DSM-IV borderline criteria involving unstable relationships and suicidal behavior.

Because of the scale's theoretical roots and the availability of other Rorschach measures of object relations devised for adult populations, the MOAS has received considerable currency in studies involving children with personality disorders.

Coates and Tuber (1988) used MOAS scores to explore and describe the internal object world of 14 male children diagnosed gender identity disorder. Each child had at least one MOAS scale score that indicated significant imbalances or destruction among interactive percepts on the Rorschach. This group had a total of 11 responses that suggested mutual, benign interaction, and of these, 9 of the percepts involved women. By contrast, of the 34 responses scored as malevolent, only 1 involved a woman and the remaining 33 involved males. Collectively, the findings showed a discernible pattern involving an idealization of the female and an attribution of malevolence to the male. The authors interpreted this pattern as indicating that children with gender identity disorder need to maintain a strong internal tie to the mother to protect her from their own rage. Although the source of the child's rage was not evident from the data, on theoretical grounds, it might be speculated that at some level the child sensed it was his mother who had feminized him.

In a follow-up study, Tuber and Coates (1989) compared the Rorschach records of 26 gender identity–disturbed (GID) boys with a control group of 18 subjects. In this study, the GID subjects produced significantly more malevolent interactions, as judged by the MOA scale, than the control subjects; had a median MOAS score in the malevolent range, as contrasted with the control subject's median score in the benign range; and had a distribution of MOAS scores that was significantly more disturbed than that of the control subjects.

Goddard and Tuber (1989) found that a group of boys meeting DSM-III-R criteria for separation anxiety disorder (SAD) had a significantly more disturbed mean MOAS score than a demographically matched control group. According to Tuber (1992), of importance in this study was the striking "congruence between the SAD child's clinging behavioral symptomatology and their clinging, leaning MOAS responses ... [providing] an important link between inner representations and manifest behavior" (p. 185).

Thomas (1987) investigated and compared the MOAS scores of the following three clinical groups: children with a DSM-III diagnosis of attention deficit disorder and hyperactivity, children with a diagnosis involving both an attention deficit disorder with hyperactivity and a borderline personality disorder, and children with a diagnosis of borderline personality disorder alone. The author found that in all three groups the modal MOAS scores were in the more disturbed range. Interestingly, the two groups of children with a diagnosis of attention deficit disorder with hyperactivity produced a higher proportion of scores in the disturbed range than the borderline group.

Meyer and Tuber (1989) explored the MOAS scores of 4- and 5-year-old children who each had an imaginary companion. Because the phenomenon of an imaginary companion simultaneously serves two functions, as a fantasized representation and as a "real" companion, it is of considerable interest to those studying object relations and object representations. The authors first compared the Rorschachs of these children with norms for similar-aged children provided by Ames, Metraux, Rodell, and Walker (1974). They found that the Rorschachs of the imaginary-companion group included five times as many human movement responses, more than four times as many animal movement responses, and eight times as many inanimate movement responses as the normative group provided by Ames et al. (1974).

To understand the nature of their object relations more fully, Meyer and Tuber (1989) next applied the MOAS to the entire range of movement responses of the imaginary-companion group. Important differences in the quality of MOAS scores were found depending on whether the rating involved human, animal, or inanimate movement. The scores involving human content were largely of a benign, reciprocal nature. Responses reflective of controlling or menacing interaction were far more prevalent in the animal movement responses. Moreover, MOAS responses expressing attacking or catastrophically violent interactions were associated exclusively with inanimate movement responses. According to these patterns of findings, it may be concluded that these children distance, displace, and disown highly charged conflictual feelings in their relationships. In keeping with the writings of Nagera (1969) and Fraiberg (1959), the glaring dichotomy between "good" human and "bad" animal and inanimate responses, as shown on the MOAS, indicates "that the imaginary companions serve simultaneously as a means of disowning 'bad' self representations while sustaining 'good' ones" (Meyer & Tuber, 1989, p. 166).

In summary, the MOAS has proven to be especially useful in depicting significant features of both normative and pathologic aspects of child personality. It differentiates between psychiatric and control samples in a predictable way and clarifies important features of the internal experience of children with a diagnosis of gender identity disturbance, separation anxiety disorder, and attention deficit disorder. Findings also have demonstrated it to be useful in articulating meaningful features in the inner experience of children who have imaginary companions.

Concept of the Object Scale

Building on their initial investigation of boundary disturbances, Blatt, Brenneis, Schimek, and Glick (1976) developed a highly comprehensive and sophisticated manual for assessing object representations in Rorschach records. Based on the developmental theory of Werner (1940) and ego psychoanalytic theory, the system calls for the scoring of human responses along three developmental dimensions: differentiation, articulation, and integration. Within each of these areas, categories have been established along a continuum based on developmental levels. Differentiation refers to the type of figure perceived, and to whether the figure is quasi-human detail, human detail, quasi human, or fully human. For the dimension of articulation, responses are scored according to the number and types of characteristics ascribed to the figure. The integration dimension of the response is scored in three ways: the degree of internality of the action, the degree of integration of the object and its action, and the integration of the interaction with another object. Responses also are scored along a content dimension of benevolence–malevolence.

In an initial study, Blatt et al. (1976) applied the scoring system to the Rorschach protocols of 37 normal subjects on four separate occasions over a 20-year period. The results from this longitudinal study showed that human responses on the Rorschach consistently change with development. More specifically, there was a marked and progressive increase in the number of well-differentiated, highly articulated, and integrated human figures. In addition, there was a significant increase in the attribution of activity that was congruent with important characteristics of the figures and an increase in the degree to which human objects were seen in constructive and positive interaction.

The Concept of the Object Scale has been applied to a wide range of psychopathology, including that of patients with a diagnosis of personality disorders. Blatt and Lerner (1983) used the scale to investigate the Rorschach records of several patients, each of whom was independently selected as a prototypic example of a specific clinical disorder. The authors not only found a unique quality of object representation for each of the disorders, but their findings based on Rorschach data also were remarkably congruent with clinical expectations.

A nonparanoid schizophrenic patient had the object representations in his Rorschach responses that were inaccurately perceived and at lower developmental levels of differentiation (i.e., quasi-human rather than full human figures). The representations were inappropriately articulated and seen as inert or involved in unmotivated activity. There was relatively little interaction between figures, and the Rorschach content was essentially barren.

For a narcissistic patient organized at a borderline level, the object representations as expressed on the Rorschach were found to deteriorate gradually with stress or simply with time. Intact, accurately perceived full human figures gave way to inaccurate, inappropriately articulated, quasi-human representations. Early responses had a superficially intact quality, and relationships between figures were depicted as benevolent and conventional. Yet action between figures lacked inner definition, and there was little meaning attributed to the action. In time, the concept of the object deteriorated in quality as the representations changed from full to quasi-humans or part-objects. Furthermore, the responses became progressively more inaccurately perceived and inappropriately elaborated.

The representations of a patient with a diagnosis of infantile character and anaclitic depressive features were accurately perceived and well differentiated, but minimally articulated. Interaction was perceived between figures, but this typically involved an active–passive transaction in which one figure was seen as vulnerable and in a relationship with a depriving, rejecting, undependable other.

In a seriously suicidal patient with an introjective depression characterized by deep feelings of self-criticism and guilt, there was oscillation between object representations at a high developmental level and seriously impaired representations in which the activity was destructive and had malevolent intent (Blatt, 1974).

Finally, in a patient diagnosed as hysteric, object representations were accurately perceived, well-differentiated, and highly articulated. The elaborations, however, involved superficial external and physical details rather than more internal or personal attributes. There was little internal sense of motivation or action between figures. Rather, things seemed simply to occur.

On the basis of their clinical analysis of these prototypic cases, Blatt and Lerner (1983) concluded that there are significant and consistent differences in the structure and content of object representations among patients with different types of psychopathology, and that object representations can be validly assessed through a systematic appraisal of human responses on the Rorschach. These clinical findings have been substantiated in a number of research studies involving various clinical groups, including depressives (Fibel, 1979), opiate addicts (Blatt et al., 1984), and anorexics (Sugarman, Quinlan, & Devenis, 1982).

Building upon the work of Blatt and Lerner (1983), subsequent investigators have used the Concept of the Object Scale to study impaired in object representations in borderline patients. Farris (1988), for instance, compared the Rorschach protocols of borderline patients with those of narcissistic patients. He found that the borderline subjects showed a significantly lower level of object differentiation, articulation, and integration than the narcissistic subjects.

Stuart et al. (1990) used the Concept of the Object Scale to compare the object relations of borderline inpatients with those of inpatient depressives and normal control subjects. The parts of the measure that assess the individual's experience of human action and interaction distinguished among the three groups. Separating the cognitive from the affective component of object relations, the authors found that the borderlines, compared with each of the other two groups, displayed a greater object-relational sophistication, saw human action as highly motivated, and had an overwhelming tendency to experience interpersonal relations as malevolent.

The most comprehensive study of impairments in level of object representation among borderline patients is represented in the work of Lerner and St. Peter (1984). These authors applied the Blatt scale to four groups: outpatient neurotics, outpatient borderlines, hospitalized borderlines, and hospitalized schizophrenics. Overall, strong support was found for the general proposition that impairments in level of object representation, as indicated by the assessment of the developmental–structural properties of human responses given to the Rorschach, show distinct patterns in groups differing in type and severity of psychopathology.

Several interesting and unexpected findings also emerged from Lerner and St. Peter's (1984) study. Subdividing the responses into those accurately perceived and those inaccurately perceived, the investigators found an inverse relationship between the developmental level of the concept of the object and degree of psychopathology. That is, the less severe the psychopathology was, the higher the developmental level of the patient's object concept. This inverse relationship, however, did not hold for the inaccurately perceived responses. Quite surprisingly, the hospitalized borderline group achieved the highest levels of human differentiation, articulation, and integration (i.e., for inaccurately perceived responses). Because response accuracy is taken as an indicator denoting quality of reality testing, this finding prompted the authors to question the relationship between reality testing and object relations. They then compared the protocols of the two borderline groups.

It was found that although the outpatient borderlines produced more accurate human responses than their hospitalized counterparts, their responses tended to involve quasi-human rather than whole-human figures. In other words, although the outpatient borderlines were able to perceive objects accurately (intact reality testing), their perceptions were accompanied by a distancing and dehumanizing of the object. The hospitalized borderlines, by contrast, were unable to distance their objects, and as a consequence, their reality testing suffered. If one conceptualizes the ability to distance and devalue objects as reflecting the defenses of splitting and primitive devaluation, and the inability to distance and devalue objects as indicating the absence or failure of these defenses, then the findings may be understood as supporting Kernberg's (1975) contention regarding the intimate relationship among quality of reality testing, the nature of the defensive structure, and the organization of internalized object relations.

Finally, in reviewing the thematic content of the human responses, the investigators found that the hospitalized borderline patients, in comparison with the three other groups, offered the most malevolent content and were the only group to produce inaccurately perceived malevolent responses. Conceptually, these patients may be understood in terms of their inability to defend against or escape from internal malevolent objects.

In summary, Blatt et al. (1976) have steadfastly maintained the significance of assessing impairments in object representations and the importance of their role in predisposing an individual to a particular form of psychopathology. On the basis of developmental theory and ego psychology, the authors devised a comprehensive scale for assessing object representations in Rorschach records. When applied to the individual protocols of prototypic cases, the scale yielded Rorschach findings that were highly consistent with clinical expectations. A review of findings regarding the borderline patient led to several interesting conclusions: (a) there is consistent evidence to suggest that the object representations of borderline patients are significantly more impaired and less developmentally advanced than those of neurotic and narcissistic patients; (b) from a structural perspective, the object representations of borderline patients are different from and more advanced than those of schizophrenic patients; and (c) from a thematic perspective, the object representations of more severely disturbed borderline patients are characterized by malevolence.

Coonerty's Scale of Separation–Individuation

The most direct application of Margaret Mahler's developmental theory to the Rorschach is found in the work of Coonerty (1986). Using the descriptions of Mahler et al. (1975) as a guideline, Coonerty developed a scale for identifying and categorizing Rorschach responses reflective of concerns and issues associated with the preseparation stage and each phase of the separation-individuation process. Referable to the preseparation phase are internal responses (e.g., blood, heart, lungs) and responses lacking boundaries (e.g., fabulized combinations). Rorschach imagery reflective of merging, engulfment, and hatching is considered indicative of concerns arising from the early differentiation subphase of separation–individuation. Themes related to the practicing subphase involve narcissistic concerns. Therefore, reflective Rorschach content includes mirroring responses, pairing responses, omnipotent responses, and insignificant creative responses. Percepts indicative of rapprochement issues include figures separating or coming together with resulting damage to one or both, figures engaged in a push–pull struggle, figures whose form changes, figures whose affect changes, and figures enmeshed and unable to separate.

Coonerty (1986) applied the scale to the Rorschach records of 50 borderline patients and 50 schizophrenic patients drawn from the testing files of a large teaching hospital. The subjects all were adult patients 18 to 65 years of age who met DSM-III criteria based upon initial screening evaluations, including a detailed psychological, medical, developmental, social, and psychiatric history. The scale was established as reliable on the basis of a 96% agreement in scoring between two raters. As predicted, the borderline group produced significantly more responses reflective of separation–individuation themes than the schizophrenic group, whereas the schizophrenics produced significantly more preseparation responses.

Van-Der Keshet (1988) applied Coonerty's scale to the Rorschachs of clinical anorexics, anorexic ballet students, nonanorexic ballet students, and normal control subjects. The clinical anorexic group was further subdivided into those patients manifesting restrictive characteristics and those exhibiting bulimic symptoms. A comparison of the various groups on the scale showed several interesting findings. Although no main effect was found among the groups for the preseparation scale, several significant findings were obtained for the separation–individuation scores. Bulimic anorexics produced significantly more engulfment responses than any of the other groups. Mirroring responses distinguished the anorexic ballet students from each of the other groups. Moreover, the control subjects produced significantly fewer rapprochement responses than the other four groups. The overall pattern of results not only lent construct validity to Coonerty's scale, but also demonstrated the scale's usefulness in highlighting significant dynamic configurations associated with specific clinical groups.

Support for Van-Der Keshet's (1988) findings, specifically those related to bulimic anorexics, is provided in a study by Parmer (1991). The Rorschachs of 13 bulimic female undergraduate students, ranging in age from 18 to 21 years, were compared with the protocols of a matched nonbulimics groups on several measures, including Coonerty's scale. The bulimics offered significantly more differentiation subphase responses involving merging, engulfment, and hatching themes than the control subjects.

Coonerty's scale also has been applied to the treatment situation. Horner and Diamond (1996) reported that in a group of borderline outpatients, scale scores distinguished the patients who prematurely terminated psychotherapy from those who continued. The patients who dropped out offered a preponderance of responses with a narcissistic theme. Specifically, such responses outnumbered responses with a rapprochement theme four to one. By contrast, the patients who continued in treatment provided a relatively even distribution of scores across all themes, with an even ratio of narcissism to higher level rapprochement themes.

Diamond, Kaslow, Coonerty, and Blatt (1990) used a modified version of Coonerty's original scale to evaluate changes in self- and object representations consequent to long-term psychodynamic inpatient treatment. The authors extended the scale by adding two higher developmental levels (object constancy and intersubjectivity) and also by elaborating existing scale points. The revised scale was applied to the Rorschachs of four patients assessed at both admission and discharge. Shifts toward higher levels of separation–individuation and intersubjectivity were observed in each case, and the changes noted on the basis of Rorschach data paralleled those obtained on the Object Representation Inventory, a 10-point scale for rating descriptions of self and significant others.

Although compared with other measures it has received limited currency, Coonerty's (1986) Scale of Separation–Individuation has proven to be effective in differentiating borderline and schizophrenic patients and in highlighting important developmental issues in relation to bulimic individuals. It also has been shown to identify borderline patients who prematurely leave treatment and to reflect internal changes associated with long-term treatment.

Borderline Interpersonal Relations Scale

To study early disturbances in the object relations of borderline patients, Kwawer (1980) devised a Rorschach scale consisting of various points that represent level of relatedness stages in the unfolding of selfhood through differentiation from a primarily mothering figure. Underlying the scale is the proposition that borderline pathology recapitulates stages of symbiotic relatedness and other primitive modes of unity and disunity. Narrower in scope than the Mutuality of Autonomy Scale because of its emphasis on more primitive modes of object relating, Kwawer's scale also relies exclusively on Rorschach content.

An initial stage, "narcissistic mirroring," includes responses in which mirrors or reflections play a prominent role. Responses at this level are understood as indicating a heightened state of self-absorption in which the other is experienced solely as an extension of the self and used for the exclusive purpose of mirroring or enhancing the self. A second stage, "symbiotic merger," consists of responses that reflect a powerful push toward merger, fusion, and reuniting. A third stage of interpersonal differentiation is found in separation and division responses. The Rorschach imagery at this stage is reminiscent of the biology of cell division reflected in the following response: "These two things appear to have been once connected but broke apart." The fourth and final stage, "metamorphosis and transformation," is reflective of a very early and rudimentary sense of self. At this stage, incipient selfhood is manifest in themes of one-celled organisms, fetuses, and embryos.

In pilot work, Kwawer (1980) found that the Rorschach records of 16 borderline patients could be significantly distinguished from those of a matched control group on the basis of the scoring categories. More specifically, each of the borderline patients offered at least one scoreable response, and this was not the case with the control subjects.

The most extensive application of Kwawer's scale is found in the work of Gacono and Meloy (1994). In an attempt to describe the inner workings of the aggressive and psychopathic personalities, the authors collected Rorschach data on the following antisocial groups: conduct-disordered adolescents; antisocial personality–disordered males, with and without schizophrenia; antisocial adult females; and male and female sexual homicide perpetrators.

Overall, the combined results of the entire project indicated that each of these groups relates to others in primitive ways, and that Kwawer's (1980) scale is sensitive to these more primitive modes. Such a finding supports Kernberg's (1976) contention that antisocial disorders, from an interpersonal perspective, may be considered subvariants of the borderline personality organization. The prevalence, across all groups, of the narcissistic mirroring category may be taken as indicating that these individuals relate to others in a narcissistic way, are highly self-absorbed, and have been insufficiently mirrored. A similarity in category order and usage was found between the adolescent conduct-disordered males and the adult antisocial personality–disordered males. This finding has important prognostic and developmental implications. Among those who commit sexual homicide, the most frequently used of the Kwawer categories was boundary disturbance. This suggests that in addition to five other factors identified by Meloy, Gacono, and Kenney (1994) as implicated in the act of sexual homicide should be added disturbances in maintaining the boundary between self and other.

DISCUSSION

The past several decades have witnessed dramatic shifts in psychoanalytic theory. An earlier interest in drives, energy, and structures has given way to a more contemporary concern with self, object relations, experience, and subjective meanings. In concert with this evolution in theory has been movement away from an experience-distant metapsychology couched in a mechanistic framework of impersonal constructs and movement toward an experience-near clinical theory. Each of the scales reviewed in this chapter not only is based in psychoanalytic theory, but also reflects this conceptual shift.

Despite these shifts in theoretical emphasis, what has remained basic to psychoanalytic theory is recognition of the distinction among internal object relations, the internal world, and relations between the self and the object in the external world. This, too, is reflected in these scales, particularly, in the formulations underlying the scales' development and in the ways that findings are interpreted and discussed.

Because these scoring systems are based in psychoanalytic theory, they make use of diagnostic classification systems that differ in important ways from the more commonly used DSM system. For the psychoanalytic clinician and researcher, DSM-IV presents serious limitations (Francis & Cooper, 1981; Kernberg, 1984). Like its more immediate predecessors, almost total emphasis is accorded that which is observable and can be described, with little attention paid to underlying and more invisible structures and dynamics. From a psychoanalytic perspective, such an approach cannot conceptualize individuals who present marked contradictions between external and internal spheres of functioning.

In addition, each DSM edition has made use of a categorical schema rather than a dimensional or contextual one. By definition, different types of psychopathology are viewed as discrete and discontinuous, and the distinction between normalcy and pathology is considered as one of kind, not as one of degree. The attempt to negotiate this by assigning dual or multiple diagnoses with the implied premise that each diagnosis signifies a distinct disturbance is antithetical to the psychoanalytic clinician who views various external expressions (e.g. symptoms, complaints) as arising from a common internal source.

Because of these difficulties, together with the consideration that the DSM scheme does little to inform a more dynamic form of treatment, as noted, the psychoanalytically informed investigator uses alternative diagnostic schemes such as those of Fenichel (1945) and Kernberg (1970). Kernberg's diagnostic system involves assessing patients along two relatively independent dimensions. The first dimension consists of a descriptive characterlogic diagnosis in terms of character structure. Representative and commonly encountered character structures include the hysterical character, the obsessive compulsive character, the narcissistic personality, the schizoid personality, and so on. For a fuller description of these character structures and others as well as a discussion of the concept of character, the reader is referred to Lerner (1998).

Recognizing that a descriptive characterlogic diagnosis is necessary but not sufficient, Kernberg (1970) outlined a second dimension. Referred to as "levels of personality organization," this dimension involves a systematic appraisal of underlying psychological structures. The specific structures assessed include level of instinctual development, signs of ego weakness, quality of internalized object relations, level of superego development, and ego identity. Each of these structures is placed on a continuum ranging from higher level to intermediate level to lower level.

Kernberg's (1976) classification system has been described for the following reason. A careful reading of the studies included in this review will show that many, regardless of scale, included a group of borderline patients. Although the investigators selected their sample of borderline patients on the basis of DSM criteria, they were not viewing the borderline concept from that more descriptive perspective. Rather, they were viewing the concept from a Kernbergian vantage point. For Kernberg (1975), borderline does not constitute a characterlogic diagnosis, but instead, falls along this second dimension and represents an intermediate level of personality organization sandwiched between a higher neurotic level and a lower psychotic level.

According to Kernberg (1975), borderline pathology, as representative of the intermediate level of personality organization, is characterized by a predominance of oral conflicts; the presence of ego weaknesses including low anxiety tolerance, interferences in reality testing, and impulsivity; and identity diffusion. In addition, borderline individuals use more primitive defenses, which include splitting, devaluation, and projective identification; present a more punitive and less integrated superego; and engage in chaotic and unstable object relations based on an internal object relations world pervaded by splits.

The investigations reviewed in this chapter embraced a number of different clinical populations including borderline patients, antisocial personalities, anorexic patients, gender-disturbed children, and children with separation disorders. Despite differences in presentation, the collective findings, when viewed in the context of Kernberg's theory and his notion of borderline pathology, indicate that these individuals share several common structural features. Their external object relations tend to be conflictual and unstable, are on a need-gratifying or threatening basis, and are pervaded by a need to control. Their internal object world evidences impaired object representations, an inability to integrate positive and negative aspects of the object, and struggles tolerating ambivalence.

Before this chapter is concluded an important cautionary note must be struck. Significant shifts in psychoanalytic theory have been described, especially the movement away from a more experience-distant theory concerned with energy and forces and the movement toward a more experience-near theory that emphasizes relationships and meanings. In this discussion, the focus has been almost exclusively on the concept object relations. Nonetheless, in psychoanalytic theory, object relations are not considered in isolation. Instead, they are seen as intimately related to virtually all other aspects of personality. For example, woven through the work of Blatt et al. (1976) is the core proposition that underlying psychopathology are impaired object representations, and that the nature of the impairment predisposes the individual to a specific type of psychological disorder. Implicit in this proposition is the notion that the quality and nature of object representations are related to symptoms and lines of regression (i.e., quality of affective and cognitive disturbances).

Along these same lines, Kernberg (1976) has noted, in what he references as his "object-relations-centered model of development," that internalized object relations serve a crucial organizing factor for both ego and superego development. Here, for instance, the basis of superego development is seen as the early internalization of parental reprimands (i.e., the punishing parent) and parental approvals (i.e., the loving parent). Conversely, for individuals who exhibit major deficits in superego functioning (i.e., antisocial personality, sociopathic personality) one can infer major disturbances in their internalized object relations.

The centrality of object relations in personality development and functioning is particularly evident in newer conceptualizations of defense. Whereas earlier theories of defense emphasized their role in regulating and modulating impulses and affects, more recent theories draw attention to the role of defense in object relations. The work of Melanie Klein (1926) is representative of this line of theorizing, especially her concept of projective identification. Klein described projective identification as a "defensive process in which parts of the self and internal object are split off and projected into an external object. Because the object is not felt to be separate, but rather is identified with the projected parts, the process affords possession of and control over the object" (Segal, 1973, p. 27).

Also representative of this new view of defense is the work of Modell (1984). In suggesting that defenses directly mediate affect between objects,

Modell placed defense in a new context—a two-person context. He contended that "affects are the mediums through which defenses against objects occur" (p. 41). Once affects are linked to objects, "the process of instinct-defense becomes a process of defense against objects" (p. 41). The individual, as it were, masters affects by controlling the object who stirs or carries the affect.

The formulation that internalized object relations are not isolated phenomena, but rather, a decisive organizing factor in personality development, has highly significant clinical and research implications. If object relations constitute a thread that weaves through the fabric of development, then with regard to clinical assessment, object relations may be considered as an intervening variable that allows the assessor to infer to other areas of development (Lerner, 1998). In other words, from an assessment of object relations one also may infer affect development, superego development, mode of defense, and even cognitive development. Furthermore, because treatment involves various types of relationships, object relations again may be used as an intervening variable linking Rorschach findings with treatment planning.

From a research perspective, the studies reviewed in this chapter indicate that there are reliable and valid methods available for the systematic assessment of object representations and internalized object relations. Understandably, much of the research to date has involved the use of these measures to study and compare impairments in object relations among groups differing in levels of psychopathology. The procedures developed, however, also provide the means for investigating a wide range of theoretical formulations. For example, because innovative Rorschach scales have been developed for assessing other dimensions of personality including defense (Lerner & Lerner, 1980), ego impairment (Perry & Viglione, 1991), and the structuring of experience (Peebles, 1975), a point has been reached that now calls for an interrelating of these scales across different clinical and normal populations. Then too, because internalized object relations and the representational world emerge from the interaction of cognitive, affective, interpersonal, and social forces, they may be regarded as core structures for investigating the multitude of factors that influence normal psychological growth, the impairments that eventuate in psychopathology, and the changes that result from treatment.

With shifts in emphasis in psychoanalytic theory, newer concepts such as object representations and internalized object relations have gained greater currency in both the psychoanalytic and assessment literatures. Because these concepts are less removed from the clinical situation and closer to clinical data, they lend themselves to operationalizing in a way the older and more abstract concepts did not.

The research reviewed in this chapter indicates that there are reliable and valid scales for systematically assessing and investigating object representations and internalized object relations. Four conceptually based scoring systems are presented and discussed. The combined findings support the proposition that the constructs object representations and internalized object relations are enduring dimensions of personality organization. Both conceptually and clinically, they are considered as important sources for providing meaningful information about the developmental level of personality more broadly. Such a formulation points to further directions that future research ought to take.

REFERENCES

Ackerman, S., Hilsenroth, M., Clemence, A., Weatherill, R., & Fowler, C. (2001). Convergent validity of Rorschach and TAT scales of object relations. *Journal of Personality Assessment, 77,* 295–306.

American Psychiatric Association (1980). *Diagnostic and statistical manual of mental disorders* (3rd ed.). Washington DC: American Psychiatric Association.

American Psychiatric Association. (1994). *Diagnostic and statistical manual of mental disorders* (4th ed.). Washington, DC: American Psychiatric Association.

Ames, L., Metraux, R., Rodell, J., & Walker, R. (1974). *Child Rorschach responses* (2nd ed.). New York: Bruner/Mazel.

Blais, M., Hilsenroth, M., Fowler, J., & Conboy, C. (1999). A Rorschach exploration of the DSM-IV borderline personality disorder. *Journal of Clinical Psychology, 55,* 563–572.

Blatt, S. (1974). Levels of object representation in anaclitic and introjective depression. *The Psychoanalytic Study of the Child, 29,* 107–157.

Blatt, S. (1990). The Rorschach: A test of perception or an evaluation of representation. *Journal of Personality Assessment, 55,* 394–416.

Blatt, S., Berman, W., Bloom-Feshbach, S., Sugarman, A., Wilber, C., & Kleber, H. (1984). Psychological assessment in opiate addicts. *Journal of Nervous and Mental Disease, 172,* 156–165.

Blatt, S., Brenneis, C., Schimek, J., & Glick, M. (1976). A developmental analysis of the concept of the object on the Rorschach. Unpublished manuscript, Department of Psychology, Yale University, New Haven, CT.

Blatt, S., & Lerner, H. (1983). The psychological assessment of object representation. *Journal of Personality Assessment, 47,* 7–28.

Blatt, S., Tuber, S., & Auerbach, J. (1990). Representation of interpersonal interactions on the Rorschach and level of psychopathology. *Journal of Personality Assessment, 54,* 711–728.

Brown, L. (1996). A proposed demography of the representational world. *Melanie Klein and Object Relations, 14,* 21–60.

Coates, S., & Tuber, S. (1988). The representation of object relations in the Rorschachs of extremely feminine boys. In H. Lerner & P. Lerner (Eds.), *Primitive mental states and the Rorschach* (pp. 647–664). Madison, CT: International Universities Press.

Cohen, C., & Sherwood, V. (1991). *Becoming a constant object*. Northvale, NJ: Jason Aronson.

Coonerty, S. (1986). An exploration of separation–individuation themes in the borderline personality disorder. *Journal of Personality Assessment, 50,* 501–511.

Diamond, D., Kaslow, N., Coonerty, S., & Blatt, S. (1990). Changes in separation-individuation and inter-subjectivity in long-term treatment. *Psychoanalytic Psychology, 7,* 363–397.

Fairbairn, W. (1952). *Psychoanalytic studies of the personality.* London: Tavistock.

Farris, M. (1988). Differential diagnosis of borderline and narcissistic personality disorder. In H. Lerner & P. Lerner (Eds.), *Primitive mental states and the Rorschach* (pp. 199–238). Madison, CT: International Universities Press.

Fenichel, O. (1945). *Psychoanalytic theory of neurosis.* New York: Norton.

Fibel, B. (1979). *Toward a developmental model of depression: Object representation and object loss in adolescent and adult psychiatric patients.* Unpublished doctoral dissertation, Department of Psychology, University of Massachusetts, Amherst, MA.

Fraiberg, S. (1959). *The magic years.* New York: Scribners.

Francis, A., & Cooper, A. (1981). Descriptive and dynamic psychiatry: A perspective of DSM-III. *American Journal of Psychiatry, 137,* 1050–1054.

Freud, S. (1917). Mourning and melancholia. *Standard Edition, 14,* 237–260.

Gacono, C., & Meloy, J. R. (1994). *The Rorschach assessment of aggressive and psychopathic personalities.* Hillsdale, NJ: Lawrence Erlbaum Associates.

Gaddini, R. (1975). The concept of transitional object. *Journal of the Academy of Child Psychiatry, 4,* 731–736.

Goddard, R., & Tuber, S. (1989). Boyhood separation anxiety disorder. *Journal of Personality Assessment, 53,* 239–252.

Grotstein, J. (1987). *Schizophrenia as a disorder of self-regulation and interactional regulation.* Presented at the Boyer House Foundation Conference "The Regressed Patient," San Francisco, CA.

Grotstein, J. (1991). An American view of the British psychoanalytic experience: Psychoanalysis in counterpoint. *Melanie Klein and Object Relations, 9,* 1–62.

Hamilton, N. (1995). Object relation units and the ego. *Bulletin of the Menninger Clinic, 59,* 416–426.

Harder, D., Greenwald, D., Wechsler, S., & Ritzler, B. (1984). The Urist mutuality of autonomy scale as an indicator of psychopathology. *Journal of Clinical Psychology, 40,* 1078–1082.

Hatcher, R., & Krohn, A. (1980). Level of object representation and capacity for intensive psychotherapy in neurotics and borderlines. In J. Kwawer, H. Lerner, P. Lerner, & A. Sugarman (Eds.), *Borderline phenomena and the Rorschach test* (pp. 299–320). New York: International Universities Press.

Horner, M., & Diamond, D. (1996). Object relations development and psychotherapy dropout in borderline outpatients. *Psychoanalytic Psychology, 13,* 205–224.

Kernberg, O. (1970). A psychoanalytic classification of character pathology. *Journal of the American Psychoanalytic Association, 18,* 800–822.

Kernberg, O. (1975). *Borderline conditions and pathological narcissism.* New York: Jason Aronson.

Kernberg, O. (1976). *Object relations theory and clinical psychoanalysis.* New York: Jason Aronson.

Kernberg, O. (1982). Self, ego, affects, and drives. *Journal of the American Psychoanalytic Association, 30,* 893–917.

Kernberg, O. (1984). *Severe personality disorders.* New Haven: Yale Press.

Klein, M. (1926/1975). The psychological principles of early analysis. In *Love, guilt, and reparation* (pp. 128–138). New York: Delacorte Press.

Klein, M. (1927/1975). Symposium on child analysis. In *Love guilt, and reparation* (pp. 139–169). New York: Delacorte Press.

Klein, M. (1957/1975). Envy and gratitude. In *Envy and gratitude and other works: 1946–1963* (pp. 176–235). New York: Delacorte Press.

Kohut, M. (1977). *The restoration of the self.* New York: International Universities Press.

Krohn, A. (1974). Borderline empathy and differentiation of object representations: A contribution to the psychology of object relations. *International Journal of Psychoanalytic Psychotherapy, 3,* 142–165.

Krohn, A., & Mayman, M. (1974). Object representations in dreams and projective tests. *Bulletin of the Menninger Clinic, 38,* 445–466.

Krystal, H. (1988). *Integration and self-healing.* Hillsdale, NJ: The Analytic Press.

Kwawer, J. (1980). Primitive interpersonal modes, borderline phenomena, and the Rorschach test. In J. Kwawer, H. Lerner, P. Lerner, & A. Sugarman (Eds.), *Borderline phenomena and the Rorschach test* (pp. 89–106). New York: International Universities Press.

Lerner, P. (1998). *Psychoanalytic perspectives on the Rorschach.* Hillsdale, NJ: The Analytic Press.

Lerner, P., & Lerner, H. (1980). Rorschach assessment of primitive defenses in borderline personality structure. In J. Kwawer, H. Lerner, P. Lerner, & A. Sugarman (Eds.), *Borderline phenomena and the Rorschach test* (pp. 257–274). New York: International Universities Press.

Lerner, H., & St. Peter, S. (1984). Patterns of object relations in neurotic, borderline, and schizophrenic patients. *Psychiatry, 47,* 77–92.

Luborsky, L. (1962). Clinicians' judgments of mental health. *Archives of General Psychiatry, 7,* 407–417.

Mahler, M. (1968). *On human symbiosis and vicissitudes of individuation: Volume 1. Infantile psychosis.* New York: Basic Books.

Mahler, M., Pine, F., & Bergman, A. (1975). *The psychological birth of the human infant.* New York: Basic Books.

Mayman, M. (1967). Object representations and object relationships in Rorschach responses. *Journal of Projective Techniques and Personality Assessment, 31,* 17–24.

Mayman, M. (1977). A multidimensional view of the Rorschach movement response. In M. Rickers-Ovsiankina (Ed.), *Rorschach psychology* (2nd ed., pp. 229–250). Huntington, NY: Krieger.

Meloy, J. R., Gacono, C., & Kenny, L. (1994). A Rorschach investigation of sexual homicide. *Journal of Personality Assessment, 62,* 58–67.

Meyer, J., & Tuber, S. (1989). Intrapsychic and behavioral correlates of the phenomenon of imaginary companions in young children. *Psychoanalytic Psychology, 6,* 151–168.

Modell, A. (1984). *Psychoanalysis in a new context.* Madison, CT: International Universities Press.

Nagera, H. (1969). The imaginary companion: Its significance for ego development and conflict resolution. *The Psychoanalytic Study of the Child, 24,* 165–195.

Ogden, T. (1983). The concept of internal object relations. *International Journal of Psychoanalysis, 64,* 227–243.

Parmer, J. (1991). Bulimia and object relations: MMPI and Rorschach variables. *Journal of Personality Assessment, 56,* 266–276.

Peebles, R. (1975). Rorschach as self-system in the telophasic theory of personality development. In P. Lerner (Ed.), *Handbook of Rorschach scales* (pp. 71–136). New York: International Universities Press.

Perry, W., & Viglione, D. (1991). The Ego-Impairment Index as a predictor of outcome in melancholic depressed patients treated with tricyclic anti-depressants. *Journal of Personality Assessment, 56,* 487–501.

Ryan, E. (1973). *The capacity of the patient to enter an elementary therapeutic relationship in the initial psychotherapy interview.* Unpublished doctoral dissertation, Department of Psychology, University of Michigan, Ann Arbor, MI.

Sandler, J. (1960). The background of safety. *International Journal of Psychoanalysis, 41,* 352–356.

Sandler, J., & Rosenblatt, B. (1962). The concept of the representational world. *The Psychoanalytic Study of the Child, 15,* 128–162.

Segal, H. (1973). *Introduction to the work of Melanie Klein.* London: Hogarth Press.

Spear, W. (1980). The psychological assessment of structural and thematic object representations in borderline and schizophrenic patients. In J. Kwawer, H. Lerner, P. Lerner, & A. Sugarman (Eds.), *Borderline phenomena and the Rorschach test* (pp. 321–342). New York: International Universities Press.

Spear, W., & Sugarman, A. (1984). Dimensions of internalized object relations in borderline and schizophrenic patients. *Psychoanalytic Psychology, 1,* 113–130.

Stuart, J., Westen, D., Lohr, N., Benjamin, J., Becker, S., Vorus, N., & Silk, K. (1990). Object relations in borderlines, depressives, and normals: An examination of human responses on the Rorschach. *Journal of Personality Assessment, 55,* 296–318.

Sugarman, A., Quinlan, D., & Devenis, L. (1982). Ego boundary disturbance in juvenile anorexia nervosa. *Journal of Personality Assessment, 46,* 455–461.

Thomas, T. (1987). *A Rorschach investigation of borderline and attention deficit disorder children.* Paper presented to the Society for Personality Assessment, San Francisco, CA.

Tuber, S. (1992). Empirical and clinical assessments of children's object relations and object representations. *Journal of Personality Assessment, 58,* 179–197.

Tuber, S., & Coates, S. (1989). Indices of psychopathology in the Rorschachs of boys with severe gender identity disorder. *Journal of Personality Assessment, 57,* 100–112.

Tustin, F. (1981). *Autistic states in children.* Boston: Routledge and Keegan Paul.

Tustin, F. (1984). Autistic shapes. *International Review of Psychoanalysis, 11,* 279–290.

Urist, J. (1973). *The Rorschach test as a multidimensional measure of object relations.* Unpublished doctoral dissertation, Department of Psychology, University of Michigan, Ann Arbor, MI.

Urist, J. (1977). The Rorschach test and the assessment of object relations *Journal of Personality Assessment, 41,* 3–9.

Urist, J., & Shill, M. (1982). Validity of the Rorschach Mutuality of Autonomy Scale: A replication using excerpted responses. *Journal of Personality Assessment, 46,* 451–454.

Van-Der Keshet, J. (1988). *Anorexic patients and ballet students: A Rorschach analysis.* Unpublished doctoral dissertation, Department of Applied Psychology, University of Toronto, Toronto, Ontario.

Werner, H. (1940). *The comparative psychology of mental development.* New York: International Universities Press.

Westen, D. (1995). Social Cognition and Object Relations Scale: Q-sort for projective stories (SCORS-Q). Unpublished manuscript, Cambridge Hospital and Harvard Medical School, Cambridge, MA.

Rorschach Assessment of Personality Disorders: Applied Clinical Science and Psychoanalytic Theory

Marvin W. Acklin
John A. Burns School of Medicine
University of Hawaii at Manoa

Susan H. S. Li
James Tyson
Argosy University, Honolulu

The genius and enduring value of the Rorschach Test to the psychodiagnostician is its ability to speak in the aboriginal language of the mind. (Acklin & Oliveira-Berry, 1996)

The current *Diagnostic and Statistical Manual of Mental Disorders*, 4th Edition, Text Revision (DSM-IV-TR; American Psychiatric Association, 2000) defines personality traits "as enduring patterns of perceiving, relating to, and thinking about the environment and oneself that are exhibited in a wide range of social and personal contexts." Personality traits "characterize an individual's functioning" (p. 686). When these characteristic ways of experiencing and behaving become rigid, maladaptive, or otherwise dysfunctional, and the outcome is "significant functional impairment or subjective distress," they are defined as a personality disorder (p. 686). The DSM-IV-TR personality disorder criteria describe the enduring pattern as "pervasive involving cognition, affectivity, interpersonal functioning, or impulse control, across a broad range of personal and social situations, causing significant distress or impairment, and of stable or long-term duration." Assessment of personality disorders "requires an evaluation of the individual's long-term patterns of functioning" (p. 686) and "the particular personality features must be evident by early adulthood" (p. 686).

The DSM-IV conceptualization of personality and personality disorders is the outcome from a long tradition of thinking about personality development and functioning (McWilliams, 1994; Tyson & Tyson, 1990). This tradition originates in Freud's psychosexual stage and structural theories, developments in psychoanalytic ego psychology and characterologic theory, object relations theory, and, with the emphasis on standardization and psychometric acceptability, a shift toward the observable behavioral or interpersonal aspects of personality functioning and disorder. In the following sections, conceptual and methodologic issues important to consider in assessing personality disorders will be discussed. Psychoanalytic theory and the Rorschach Inkblot Test's contribution to understanding about an individual's subjective experience, personality organization, and disorders are presented. This information may be evaluated through both nomothetic and ideographic approaches within an integrated heteromethod approach to personality assessment. It is suggested that the Rorschach Inkblot Test is a valuable tool for capturing the internal psychodynamics of the individual and his or her personality organization, functioning, and experience.

PERSONALITY ASSESSMENT AND DIAGNOSIS: NATURE AND RATIONALE OF THE ASSESSMENT TASK

The American Psychological Association's (APA) Board of Professional Affairs established a Psychological Assessment Work Group and commissioned it (a) to evaluate contemporary threats to psychological and neuropsychological services and (b) to assemble evidence on the efficacy of assessment in clinical practice. In their report, Meyer et al. (2001) described the purposes and appropriate application of psychological assessments and provide a broad overview of testing and assessment validity. They described the scope and goals of psychological assessment as follows:

1. To describe current functioning, including cognitive abilities, severity of disturbance, and capacity for independent living
2. To confirm, refute, or modify the impressions formed by clinicians through their less structured interactions with patients
3. To identify therapeutic needs, highlight issues likely to emerge in treatment, recommend forms of intervention, and offer guidance about likely outcomes
4. To aid in the differential diagnosis of emotional, behavioral, and cognitive disorders
5. To monitor treatment over time, to evaluate the success of interventions, or to identify new issues that may require attention as original concerns are resolved

6. To manage risk, including minimization of potential legal liabilities and identification of untoward treatment reactions
7. To provide skilled, empathic assessment feedback as a therapeutic intervention in itself. (p. 129)

Within the scope of personality assessment items 1 to 4 are of obvious importance to the psychodiagnostician.

Meyer et al. (2001) clarified the critical distinction between "psychological testing" and "psychological assessment":

> Psychological testing is a relatively straightforward process wherein a par-
> ticular scale is administered to obtain a specific score (e.g., a scaled subtest
> score on a Wechsler scale). Subsequently, a descriptive meaning can be ap-
> plied to the score on the basis of normative, nomothetic findings. In contrast,
> psychological assessment is concerned with the clinician who takes a variety
> of test scores, generally obtained from multiple test methods, and considers
> the data in the context of history, referral information, and observed behav-
> ior to understand the person being evaluated, to answer the referral ques-
> tions, and then to communicate findings to the patient, his or her significant
> others, and referral sources. (p. 143)

Psychological assessment is a task that uses test-derived information in
combination with the patient's historical data, presenting complaints, and
interview results, along with information derived from behavioral observations and third parties to disentangle competing diagnostic possibilities.
The process is "far from simple and requires a high degree of skill and sophistication to be implemented properly" (p. 144).

Psychological assessment includes a wide range of information sources
that provide distinctive types of information (McClelland, 1980). A summary of these methods and their limitations is presented in Table 16.1. Notably, performance-based personality tests, such as the Rorschach, elicit
data about behavior in unstructured settings or implicit dynamics related
to an understanding of perception and motivation. These types of tests,
however, are limited by the individual's engagement in the task and the
specific stimulus materials used in the task.

Thus, the assessment clinician establishes an evaluation framework that
systematically develops information concerning the client's personality
functioning using multiple information sources and methods. None of the
ordinarily used sources or methods is without its drawbacks. As discussed
later, concordance levels between sources and methods are low because
various sources and methods of assessment provide independent and distinctive information about the individual being assessed. The challenge is
to understand how information may be integrated into meaningful
personality description, assessment, and diagnosis.

TABLE 16.1

Meyer et al.'s (2001) Range of Assessment Methods and Their Constraints

Method	Constraints
Unstructured interviews	Range of topics considered and ambiguities in the interpretation of this information
Structured interviews and self-reports	Patient's motivation to communicate frankly and his or her ability to make accurate judgments
Performance-based personality tests (e.g., Rorschach, TAT)	Patient's engagement in the task and the nature of the stimulus materials
Performance-based cognitive tests	Patient's motivation, task engagement, and setting
Observer rating scales	Parameters of the particular type of relationship (e.g., spouse, coworker, therapist) and the setting in which observations are made

Note. Taken from Meyer et al. (2001). Psychological testing and psychological assessment: A review of evidence and issues. *American Psychologist, 56,* 128–165.

PSYCHOLOGICAL ASSESSMENT AS APPLIED CLINICAL SCIENCE

The scientist–practitioner approach (i.e., Boulder model) to psychological assessment is established on foundations of scientific procedure and informed by empirical research findings. Shakow (1976) described the scientist–practitioner psychologist as

> A person who, on the basis of systematic knowledge about persons obtained primarily in real-life situations, has integrated this knowledge with psychological theory, and has consistently regarded it with the questioning attitude of the scientist. In this image, clinical psychologists see themselves combining the idiographic and nomothetic approaches, both of which appear to them significant. (p. 554)

In this context, practice is "strictly an applied scientific activity, with praxis dictated by a sound body of scientific knowledge" (Stricker & Trierweiler, 1995, p. 996). "The clinical setting can be regarded as a laboratory for the clinician and must be approached with the same discipline, critical thinking, imagination, openness to falsification, and rigor that characterizes the scientist in the traditional laboratory" (p. 998). Through the context of discovery (Reichenbach, 1938), initial hypotheses are derived from referral questions, assessment methods are selected and administered (Acklin, 2002), and hypotheses are initially tested, accepted, and rejected.

Through the more rigorous logic of justification (Reichenbach, 1938), careful integration of source material using a nomothetically based and idiographically applied configurational approach (Stricker & Gold, 1999) permits the refinement of inferences and development of conclusions. The integration of scientific values and modes of thought "leads to the generation of internally consistent formulations that are consistent with all extant data, both local and more general" (Stricker & Trierweiler, 1995, p. 998).

Scientifically based assessment includes at least three elements. First, it involves the application of a *heteromethod* procedural methodology that integrates sources and methods of clinically relevant information into a unified description of the individual being assessed (Stricker & Gold, 1999). Second, scientifically based assessment considers nomothetic and idiographic aspects of analysis:

> The *nomothetic* approach to assessment is part of the science of psychology's search for lawful relationships in human behavior.… An *idiographic* approach to assessment is aimed at understanding the singular ways in which many characteristics fit together within the context of the life of one person. (p. 240)

Scientifically based assessment psychology has come to recognize a relatively low degree of association between differing data sources in personality assessment and diagnosis. Meyer (2002) wrote that, "sophisticated clinicians and researchers should expect associations of about .20 to .30 between alternative data sources, and this should fuel the motivation to systematically gather data from multiple independent sources whenever an accurate understanding of the patient is required" (p. 89). He noted further:

> Cook and Campbell (1979) illuminated how the construct validity of nomothetic research can be seriously compromised by monomethod or mono-operation bias. As such, optimal nomothetic research maximizes construct validity by obtaining data from multiple methods of assessment, multiple sources of information, and multiple operational definitions of the target construct. (p. 90)

Third, critical thinking is essential to scientifically disciplined psychological assessment. Focus on the falsifiability of hypotheses and consideration of alternative hypotheses are an aspect of critical thinking and an antidote to common biases and heuristics that weaken clinical judgment (Garb, 1994a, 1994b; Garb 1996; Garb, 1998). To promote sound clinical thinking, Meyer (2002) concluded that clinicians should seek to minimize monomethod and mono-operational bias in their clinical work by synthesizing information gathered from multiple sources consistent with the recommendations of Stricker & Gold (1999). By creating multiple sources of information in an assessment paradigm designed to elicit unique response configurations, clinicians operate within a classical view of test battery administration (Acklin, 2002; Rapaport, Gill, & Schafer, 1968). That is, varying methods of source information replicate the convergent and discriminant validation (Campbell & Fiske, 1959) process in the formation, refinement, and acceptance of inferences emerging from the data sources (Wiggins, 1973).

PERSONALITY ASSESSMENT AND THE INNER WORLD

Personality functioning is not limited to publicly observable aspects of behavior. Millon (1969) defined personality as "those intrinsic and pervasive modes of functioning which emerge from the entire matrix of the individual's developmental history, and which now characterize his or her perceptions and ways of dealing with the environment" (p. 221). In another context, Millon (1981) defined personality "as a complex pattern of deeply embedded psychological characteristics that are largely unconscious, cannot be eradicated easily, and express themselves automatically in almost every facet of functioning ... individual and pervasive these traits comprise the individual's distinctive pattern of perceiving, feeling, thinking, and coping" (p. 8).

Thus, personality encompasses the subjective experience of the individual. Subjective experience encompasses the primary fact that humans inhabit bodies (derived from Freud's [1961] notion that "the ego is first and foremost a bodily ego," p. 26; Lakoff & Johnson, 1999); the feeling life and motives (i.e., wishes, fears, anticipations); and the welter of inner subjectivity (i.e., what psychoanalysts call unconscious fantasy or psychic reality, Arlow, 1985; Solorow & Atwood, 1989). Inner experience is revealed in the stream of consciousness, fantasy, memories, dreams, beliefs and attitudes, and creative products in the arts and humanities. As such, an experiential or phenomenologic approach to the self is necessary for an understanding and full appreciation of persons.

The self is the locus of affective experience, sense of agency, and basis of self-awareness and reflectivity (Blatt & Bers, 1993). "The experiences of affect, agency, and reflective self-awareness define the self in ways that are consistent with the experiential aspects of traditional psychoanalytic thought, such as the topographical model with its specifications of consciousness and awareness" (p. 172). The raw material and aboriginal language of human subjectivity is fantasy. Fantasy life has been described from a variety of theoretical concepts (Pine, 1988): imagoes (Josephs, 1989), complexes (Jacobi, 1999), object representations (Kernberg, 1976), internalized working models (Carlson & Sroufe, 1995), and more lately, from a cognitive perspective, schemas (Blatt, 1995). Blatt asserted that "various forms of psychopathology in adults are determined, in large part, by differential impairments of the schemas of the representational world that occur as a consequence of serious disruptions of the relationships between child and caregivers" (p. 1).

The role of the unconscious, a concept rejected as a factor in mental life during the short-lived hegemony of behaviorism and scientism of the 1960s, has been resurrected (Epstein, 1994; Greenwald, 1992). The inner, intrapsychic life of the individual forms the substrate for observable behavior and thoroughly pervades it. As such, the inner life and methods for assessing its dynamics are critical to the psychodiagnostic task. The pervasiveness of the inner life and the way in which "the interpersonal and the intrapsychic realms create, interpenetrate, and transform each other in a subtle and complex manner" (Mitchell, 1988, p. 9) are the basis for the "projective hypothesis" (Frank, 1939). All aspects of a person's perceptions, feelings, attitudes, beliefs, and behavior are intertwined to form a unity (Rapaport et al., 1968). Consequently, knowledge concerning the inner life of the individual is crucially relevant for understanding an individual's experience and behavior and in the psychodiagnostic assessment and diagnosis of personality and personality disorders.

OBJECT RELATIONS THEORY
AND THE REPRESENTATIONAL WORLD

With the advent of psychoanalysis, Freud and his followers laid down theoretical postulates concerning psychological development (McWilliams, 1994; Tyson & Tyson, 1990) represented in the psychosexual stages of libidinal development and intrapsychic structuralization. Developments in psychoanalytical ego psychology further refined the structural–developmental approach to understanding inner experience (Blanck & Blanck, 1975) and laid the foundation for the object relations theories of Klein, Guntrip, Fairbairn, Sandler, and others (Urist, 1980). More recently, with a shift toward cognitive psychology, developmental factors are less emphasized, and greater emphasis is given to internalized images or representations of self and others, represented in cognitive psychology as schemas and in attachment theories as internalized working models.

In a classic contribution, Sandler and Rosenblatt (1962) described the concept of the representational world. In reference to Freud's ideas about the superego, Sandler and Rosenblatt quote Freud (1940/1964) who wrote that at about the age of 5 years,

a portion of the external world has, at least partially, been given up as an object and instead, by means of identification, taken into the ego—that is, has become an integral part of the internal world. This new mental agency continues to carry on the functions which have hitherto been performed by the corresponding people in the external world. (p. 131)

Sandler and Rosenblatt (1962) noted that the developing child "creates, within its own perceptual or representational world, images and organizations of his internal as well as external environment" (p. 132). They write that "a representation can be considered to have a more or less enduring existence as an organization or schema which is constructed out of a multitude of impressions" (p. 133). The internalization of object relations refers "to the internalization of units of affective state, object representation, and self-representation" (Kernberg, 1976, p. 75). The organization and developmental maturity of the representational world—based on the internalization of early life relational scenarios—establishes the individual's character (Kernberg, 1976; Shapiro, 1965).

Personal life is characterized by consistency and repetitiveness of states of mind that give a quality of consistency to the personality. In a global sense, these engrained predispositions to perceive, feel, and behave constitute a person's character and identity. Moore and Fine (1968) defined character as

that aspect of personality ... which reflects the individual's habitual modes of bringing into harmony his own inner needs and the demands of the external world. It is a constellation of relatively stable and constant ways of reconciling conflicts between the various parts of the psychic apparatus to achieve adjustment in relation to the environment. Character therefore has a permanent quality that affects the degree and manner of drive discharge, defenses, affects, specific object relationships, and adaptive functioning in general. (p. 25)

Atwood and Stolorow (1980) linked character to the representational world:

We propose that a strictly psychoanalytical description of a person's character is always a description of his representational world (i.e., of those distinctive, archaically determined, affectively colored configurations of self and object representations which recurrently and unconsciously structure the person's subjective experiences and conduct). (p. 280)

Subsequently, Atwood and Stolorow (1984) stated that "personality structure is the structure of a person's experience" (p. 33), and that "character is coextensive with the structure of a subjective world" (p. 34). They added that character structure is not merely a passive template for perceiving, but a proactive program from acting in the world. On this point, Shapiro (1968) wrote:

The neurotic person does not simply suffer neurosis, as, essentially, one suffers tuberculosis or a cold, but actively participates in it, functions, so to speak, according to it, and, in ways that sustain its characteristic experiences; he sees, at any point, no serious alternative to whatever particular act or interest has just this effect. (p. 20)

The object or representational world operates as a guidance system for perceiving, thinking, feeling, and acting. Building on Fairbairn's notions that internalized objects are crystallized experiences deriving from negative early relationships, Rubens (1994) wrote about the active and dynamic nature of object relations:

Such a subsystem seeks at all times to express itself and have experience in accordance with the template based on the formative *intolerable* experiences which define its existence. Thus the existence of such an endopsychic structure leads to the seeking of relationships that will be consonant with the specific neurotic paradigms of early experience, to the distortion of current relationships so they can be experienced in accordance with such paradigms, and to the patterning of activity in the world so as to be expressive of such a relationship. (p. 163)

Consistent with Fairbairn's notion of crystallization of negative early experience and the link between character and behavior, Kernberg (1976) wrote:

The final outcome of pathological identification processes is character pathology. The more rigid and neurotic the character traits are, the more they reveal that a past pathogenic internalized object relation (representing a particular conflict) has become "frozen" into a character trait. (p. 79)

Although these theoretical constructs focus on the development and substance of mental and emotional life, they are relevant to the lived experience of the person because they reflect phenomenologic dimensions of fantasy, feeling, perception, and enactment.

EGO STATE AND OBJECT RELATIONS THEORIES

Ego state theory emerged from the work of Federn (1952) and others, reflecting the singular importance of subjective experience as a clinical construct of psychodiagnostic importance. Ego states are experiential states of feeling, perception, and thought, which form the basis of a person's enactments in interpersonal situations. Of particular relevance to Rorschach psychology, Horowitz (1983) discussed modes of representation of thought: enactive, image, and lexical. Imagistic modes of representation are represented in "introjects, fantasies, body images, and relationships between objects" (p. 86). Object representations consist of "important transactions [that] will be repeated and, with repetition, will gain in structural clarity and development so that they come to act as organizers of new information" (p. 87). Horowitz (1998) extended the concept of ego states to states of mind, which reflect a "combination of conscious and unconscious experience with patterns of behavior that can last for a short or long period of time. Each person has a repertoire of recurrent states of mind]" (p. 13).

States of mind are characterized by feeling, perception, level of regulation (undermodulated, overmodulated, well-modulated, and shimmering), type of motivation (wished for or dreaded states), and person schemas (Horowitz, 1998, p. 15). States of mind differ from "one another not only in terms of prevailing emotion or expressed feelings, but in the apparent style or the degree of control" (Horowitz, 1988, p. 13). Person schemas, synonymous with object representations, "remain as relatively unchanged in the mind even after the external aspects of the relationship are over" (Horowitz, 1991, p. 14). Person schemas have particular relevance for normal personality functioning and disorder. They demonstrate stable properties (Horowitz, 1988) and summarize past experience into "holistic composite forms, thus allowing incoming information to be measured against the existing composite for goodness of fit" (p. 13). Schemas that accord well with real stimuli "permit rapid organization of information;... schemas enhance stimuli that fit the schematic view and impede recognition of stimuli that do not" (p. 14). Whereas reification of schemas enables "rapid perception,... it may also lead to patterned and recurrent errors in interpreting and responding to stimuli that are actually different from schematic forms" (p. 14). This is of central significance for personality functioning, particularly in the case of personality disorders:

> Schemas of self and others enhance a sense of temporal continuity and coherence of identity. Conversely, aschematic conditions seem to lead to a loss of coherence of identity, experienced subjectively and symbolically as fragmentation of self and a loss of location of self in time. (Horowitz, 1988, p. 14)

Clinicians have proposed a variety of taxonomies for classifying personality organization and functioning. Horowitz (1998) proposed a five-level system, focusing on structural features that characterize intrapsychic functioning and interpersonal behavior reflecting states, controls, and person schemas: (a) well-developed, (b) neurotic, (c) narcissistically vulnerable, (d) borderline, and (e) fragmented. Of interest is Horowitz's insistence that these are not merely dispositional categories for third-party observation and classification, but features of the person's subjective experience of self and others.

Psychoanalytic developmental diagnosis is derived from theoretical foundations of classic drive theory, ego psychology, and object relations theory (Blanck & Blanck, 1975; Pine, 1990; Tyson & Tyson, 1990). Object relations theory focuses on internalized representations of self in relation to others and views character style as an attitudinal expression of these internalized object relations (Josephs, 1992). Kernberg (1976) integrated these notions in a psychoanalytic classification of character pathology with his tripartite classification of personality organization: neurotic, borderline, and psychotic. In Kernberg's framework, the organization of character pathology is based on the solidity of identity formation, quality and structural integrity of object representations, level of defensive operations, and proneness to regression and infiltration of primary process modes of thought.

Kernberg (1984) wrote:

Neurotic, borderline, and psychotic types of organization are reflected in the patient's overriding characteristics, particularly with regard to (1) his degree of identity integration, (2) the types of defenses he habitually employs, and (3) his capacity for reality testing. I propose that neurotic personality structure, in contrast to borderline and psychotic personality structures, implies an integrated identity. Neurotic personality structure presents a defensive organization centering on repression and other advanced or high-level defensive operations. In contrast, borderline and psychotic structures are found in patients showing a predominance of primitive defensive operations on the mechanism of splitting. Reality testing is maintained in neurotic and borderline organization but is severely impaired in psychotic organization. These structural criteria can supplement the ordinary behavioral or phenomenological descriptions of patients and sharpen the accuracy of the differential diagnosis of mental illness, especially in cases that are difficulty to classify (pp. 5–6).

In Kernberg's (1976) framework, severity of personality disorder is not limited to symptom presentation or outwardly observable behavior (as in the DSM), but includes underlying intrapsychic organization. Most hysterical, obsessive–compulsive, and depressive–masochistic characters are organized at the higher (neurotic) level of personality organization. Borderline, narcissistic, paranoid, schizoid, and psychopathic personalities may overlap both borderline and psychotic personality structures. These levels of personality organization, which are assessed through external means (behavior and modes of feeling, perceiving, and relating), also reflect modes of subjective experience.

THE RORSCHACH TEST'S CONTRIBUTION TO PERSONALITY ASSESSMENT AND DIAGNOSIS

Rorschach test interpretation is most effective when it is *integrative* (Acklin, 1994; Meloy, Acklin, Gacono, Murray, & Peterson, 1997), that is, when interpretation combines structural data with a nomothetic basis (e.g., empirically derived ratios, percentages, and indices) and theoretically derived content analyses with idiographic referents (Weiner, 2003). Despite recent controversies, the Comprehensive System (CS; Exner, 2003) for the Rorschach (Garb, Wood, Lilienfeld, Scott, & Nezworski, 2002; Lilienfeld, Wood, & Garb, 2000; see Acklin, 1999; Meyer, 2000; Viglione & Hilsenroth, 2001 for responses to these criticisms) remains the primary source of empirically derived and validated structural data for personality description. There is a voluminous empirical literature focusing on various personality constructs and Rorschach indices, percentages, and ratios.

Using "sign" approaches to Rorschach assessment, several recent studies have found that certain Rorschach variables are related to DSM-IV Axis II personality disorder criteria. For example, Hilsenroth, Hibbard, Nash, and Handler (1993) found that Rorschach measures of defenses and aggression effectively discriminated narcissistic personality patients from a nonclinical sample and from DSM-IV cluster A, cluster C, and other cluster B personality disorders. Blais, Hilsenroth, and Fowler (1998) reported that color balance (FC+CF+C) and texture (T) codes were strongly correlated with histrionic personality disorder (HPD). In addition, these two Rorschach variables were significantly correlated with seven of the eight HPD criteria. The total number of Rorschach color responses (FC+CF+C) was positively correlated with DSM HPD criteria (2, 3, 4, and 5), whereas texture responses were positively correlated with criteria 1, 5, 6, 7, and 9 (Blais & Hilsenroth, 1998).

In a follow-up study, Blais, Hilsenroth, Castlebury, Fowler, and Baity (2001) explored the incremental validity of Rorschach variables relative to Minnesota Multiphasic Personality Inventory-2 (MMPI-2) personality disorder scales (Colligan, Morey, & Offord, 1994; Morey, Waugh, & Blashfield, 1985) in predicting DSM-IV cluster B criteria. In this study of 57 psychiatric outpatients, two Rorschach variables (FC+CF+C and T) performed incrementally above and beyond the MMPI-2 HPD scales in identifying DSM-IV HPD criteria. In fact, when both MMPI-2 scales and the Rorschach variables were entered simultaneously into the regression equation, only the Rorschach variables were independent predictors of the DSM-IV HPD criteria.

Theoretically derived approaches to the Rorschach test broaden the test's application to personality assessment and diagnosis (Frank, 1995a; Lerner, 1991; Pine, 1988; Rosenen, 1990; Schafer, 1954). Bridging the gap between experience, percept, and score, Schafer's (1954) ego psychological approach focused on thematic analysis of individual responses as highly revealing of styles of thought and feeling. Reflecting on the nature of projection in approaching Rorschach inkblots, Schafer regarded the subject's "perceptual styles as enduring, integrated response tendencies which have remained in the service of and reflect enduring configurations of drives, defenses, and adaptive efforts, and the imagery with which these are associated" (p. 115). Combining both drive and ego psychological perspectives, the work of Robert Holt (1970) has particular relevance for the Rorschach test in terms of studying and understanding the subjective experience of persons, with specific reference to Rorschach assessment, classification and psychodiagnosis of personality disorders. Holt and colleagues (Holt, 1970; Holt & Havel, 1960) devised a comprehensive scoring system for Rorschach percepts that illuminates the content, structural, and defensive features of responses to the cards. Holt focused on the role of primary process thinking and associated defensive functioning revealed in Rorschach percepts, phenomena directly related to the differential diagnosis of level of personality structure and organization (Acklin, 1992, 1993, 1994; Kernberg, 1976).

Object relations approaches to Rorschach test interpretation have come to predominate in both clinical practice and research (Frank, 1995b; Stricker & Healey, 1990) with a large, developing empirical literature. Sidney Blatt and colleagues (Blatt, Brenneis, Schimick, & Glick, 1976a, 1976b; Blatt & Lerner, 1983; Blatt, Wild, & Ritzler, 1975) developed a Rorschach Concept of the Object Scale that uses structural–developmental theory as a means to assess the features of Rorschach responses. Their investigations have demonstrated solid empirical associations between features of internalized object representations and differing types of psychopathology, including borderline personality organization. The Mutuality of Autonomy Scale (MOAS; Urist, 1977, 1980; Urist & Schill, 1982) characterizes the structural and interactional features of object representations. Harder, Greenwald, Wechsler, and Ritzler (1984) found the MOAS to be useful as an indicator of psychopathology. Rorschach data on object representations also has been found very useful in the diagnosis of antisocial personality disorder and underlying personality organization (Gacono, 1990; Gacono & Meloy, 1992; Gacono, Meloy, & Berg, 1992).

Self psychological approaches to the Rorschach assessment situation and interpretation emerged in 1988 (Arnow & Cooper, 1988). Following the work of Kohut, Rorschach responses are viewed as a reflection of the state of the self (a self-representation), as a perception of an archaic self-object, and as an indication of how new objects will be experienced (p. 56). More recently, self psychological approaches to the Rorschach have been described by Silverstein (1999), who assessed mirroring, idealization, and twinship in Rorschach content.

Asserting that the Rorschach test is unparalleled in graphically assessing and displaying underlying structural, affective, and representational features of the test-taker's inner world, Acklin (1992, 1993, 1994) advocated integrating structural, theoretically derived, and thematic approaches, focusing on Kernberg's psychostructural diagnosis of personality organization. Acklin wrote that psychoanalytic research on boundary disturbance, structural integrity of object representations, assessment of drive-laden content, and use of structure in the assessment situation, in combination with Comprehensive System variables such as Special Scores, Weighted Sum 6, and the Schizophrenia Index (and the more recent Perceptual-Thinking Index) assist in the differential diagnosis of psychotic level of personality organization (Exner, 2002; Kleiger, 1999; Weiner, 2003).

Concerning the differential diagnosis of psychotic personality organization, Acklin (1992) wrote:

> The psychodiagnostician examining an individual with suspected psychotic personality organization might expect to find the following Rorschach characteristics: loading up of Special Scores, especially Level 2 special scores; a heavily Weighted Sum 6; Schizophrenia Index at a 4 or 5; disturbances and oddities of syntax and representation indicative of thought disorder; deterioration of Form Level; disturbances in the structural features of percepts, especially human percepts, failure of defensive operations and utilization of primitive defenses, expression of raw, drive-laden, primary process material, and themes of barrenness, emptiness, and malevolent interaction. (p. 460)

Concerning the differential diagnosis of borderline personality organization, Acklin (1993) wrote:

> Adequate functioning on high structure tests and deteriorated performance on projectives, especially the Rorschach, evidence of loosened thinking, boundary disturbance and thought disorder, malevolent object relations, dysphoria, poor stress tolerance, and labile emotionality. (p. 335)

Finally, concerning neurotic level of personality organizations, Acklin (1994) wrote:

> In terms of nomothetic data derived from the Comprehensive System, guided by a conceptual approach, one might expect the neurotic record to be characterized by banality (high Populars, high Intellectualization Index), without elevation of validity indicators (Lambda), affective overcontrol (reflected in predominance of FC responses in the Color Balance), generally adequate reality testing (X+% and F+%) and immaturity (predominance of FM over M, Human movement associated with animal content and Color Projection). (p. 7)

The Rorschach test is particularly useful in the differential diagnosis of borderline level of personality organization, integrating structural and theoretically derived indices assessing boundary disturbance, malevolence and maturity of object relations, defensive operations, affect management, and narcissism (Acklin, 1995). Borderline personality disorder and organization received considerable attention from Rorschach psychologists in the 1980s and 1990s, using both "sign" approaches (Exner, 1986; Gartner, Hurt, & Gartner, 1989) and theoretically derived scales (Acklin, 1995; Berg, 1990; Blais, Hilsenroth, Fowler, & Conboy, 1999; Cooper, Perry, & Arnow, 1988; Cooper, Perry, & O'Connell, 1991; Gacono et al., 1992; Hilsenroth et al., 1993; Johnston & Holzman, 1979; Lerner, 1990; O'Connell, Cooper, Perry, & Hoke, 1989; Perry & Cooper, 1989; Stuart et al., 1990). In general, there has been considerable empirical support for the borderline personality diagnosis within the context of the DSM framework and the theories of Gunderson (1984) and Kernberg (1976), who described borderline personality organization.

In combination with other sources of information, Rorschach test data have particular value in accessing experience-near images that reflect the subject's characteristic modes of experiencing and repertoire of ego states during the assessment process. The test-taking situation is a "real time" experience of immersion in the blots, eliciting and illuminating the individual's characteristic manner of dealing with a novel situation. In other words, the test subject's personality (i.e., characteristic manner of responding to and coping with experience) becomes manifest in the test situation.

Schachtel's (1966) Rorschach classic, *Experiential Foundations of Rorschach's Test*, focused on the experiential dimension of the assessment task. He wrote:

> I call the main approach I use ... "experiential" because it consists mostly in the attempt to reconstruct, to understand, and to make more explicit the experiences that the testee underwent in taking the test and his reaction to these experiences, specifically his way of approaching or avoiding and of handling the experience of the inkblots in the context of the test task. (p. 183)

Schachtel (1966), perhaps better than any other Rorschach commentator, described the profundity of Rorschach test data:

> The primary data elicited by Rorschach's test are not concepts but percepts...The data we study in Rorschach's test are what the testee saw in the blots and how he saw it, in the full concreteness of the percepts and with all the emotional overtones and undercurrents that color what he saw, and all the intellectual and emotional effort, its quality, its process, its smoothness, or conflicts which entered into the work of perceiving, associating, and judging the fitness of the percept. From his words, we try to reconstruct his experience. The score is merely an abstraction of this experience. (p. 261)

Schachtel added that "the visual impressions of the inkblots, openly received, will touch upon memories and sensibilities which resonate in the associations to the inkblot" (p. 45). Furthermore, one's "encounter" with the inkblots in the test situation

> ranges all the way from a full encounter with the inkblots in which the whole personality with all its layers is engaged on a wide range of levels of functioning, resulting in considerable variety and flexibility of experiences and responses, to an almost complete avoidance of the encounter by rejection of the test task or, more frequently, by the mobilization of massive defenses against all but the most superficial, stereotyped, and rigidly controlled responses. (p. 44)

Consistent with the view that Rorschach percepts reflect internal and idiographic imagery, Schafer (1954) viewed the test as accessing ego strivings in their imaginal language. Comparing Rorschach responses with dream and daydream images, he noted that the test "often briefly unlocks the book of our private imagery" (p. 75).

In contrast to other psychological test data—typically quantitative and nomothetic in nature—Rorschach percepts are the raw material of mentation and the end products of personality at work, yielding a sample of visual representations that reflect the individual's inner experience (Lerner, 1992, 1998; Schachtel, 1966). Although caution is advised in the use of individual responses for interpretation, the content of individual responses may be especially revealing, demonstrating a sample of private imagery: the repertoire of ego states that characterize the individual's inner life.

In nomothetic–idiographic methodology of personality assessment and diagnosis, Rorschach content contributes to an understanding of individual psychodynamics (Aronow & Reznikoff, 1976) including self-concept, attitudes toward significant others, perceptions of the environment, major concerns, and internal conflicts. In combination with empirically derived structural data (including observations of the work producing the response) individual responses, in their raw form, provide graphic representation of subjective experience and how people perceive themselves, others, and their world.

Assessment and diagnosis of personality disorder occurs in the context and methodology of comprehensive psychological assessment. The psychodiagnostician relies on multiple sources and methods, recognizing their independence, incompleteness, and inherent limitations. In contrast to other sources of psychological data, the Rorschach test makes a unique contribution in the systematic psychological assessment and diagnosis of personality functioning, taking its place as a heteromethod assessment approach in which independent source data—interviews, self-report personality inventories and checklists, and observer–informant assessment—are integrated via a disciplined and idiographic methodology. No individual source of information appears to be capable of standing alone in the assessment task. Integrating multiple data sources strengthens the network of interpretive hypotheses. Unlike other measures, the Rorschach test provides both nomothetic and idiographic information. The test's unique and critical position in the psychological assessment task, however, and its staying power as a frequently used clinical assessment tool reside in its ability to tap and express the primordial images and language of the individual's inner life.

REFERENCES

Acklin, M. W. (1992). Psychodiagnosis of personality structure: Psychotic personality organization. *Journal of Personality Assessment, 58,* 454–463.

Acklin, M. W. (1993). Psychodiagnosis of personality structure II: Borderline personality organization. *Journal of Personality Assessment, 61,* 329–341.

Acklin, M. W. (1994). Psychodiagnosis of personality structure: Neurotic personality organization. *Journal of Personality Assessment, 63,* 1–9.

Acklin, M. W. (1995). Integrative Rorschach interpretation. *Journal of Personality Assessment, 64,* 235–238.

Acklin, M. W. (1999). Behavioral science foundations of the Rorschach Test. *Assessment, 6,* 319–326.

Acklin, M. W. (2002). How to select personality tests for a test battery. In J. N. Butcher (Ed.), *Clinical personality assessment: Practical approaches* (2nd ed.). London: Oxford University Press.

Acklin, M., & Oliveira-Berry, J. (1996). Return to the source: Rorschach's Psychodiagnostics. *Journal of Personality Assessment, 67*(2), 427–433.

American Psychiatric Association. (2000). *Diagnostic and statistical manual of mental disorders* (4th ed., text revision). Washington, DC: APA Press.

Arlow, J. (1985). The concept of psychic reality and related problems. *Journal of the American Psychoanalytic Association, 33,* 521–535.

Arnow, D., & Cooper, S. (1988). Rorschach psychology of the self. In H. D. Lerner & P. M. Lerner (Eds.), *Primitive mental states and the Rorschach* (pp. 53–68). New York: International Universities Press.

Aronow, E., & Reznikoff, M. (1976). *Rorschach content interpretation.* New York: Grune & Stratton.

Atwood, G. E., & Stolorow, R. D. (1980). Psychoanalytic concepts and the representational world. *Psychoanalysis and Contemporary Thought, 3,* 267–290.

Atwood, G. E., & Stolorow, R. D. (1984). *Structures of subjectivity: Explorations of psychoanalytic phenomenology.* Hillsdale, NJ: Analytic Press.

Berg, J. (1990). Differentiating ego functions of borderline and narcissistic personality. *Journal of Personality Assessment, 55,* 537–548.

Blais, M. A., & Hilsenroth, M. J. (1998). Rorschach correlates of the DSM-IV histrionic personality disorder. *Journal of Personality Assessment, 70,* 355–364.

Blais, M. A., Hilsenroth, M. J., Castlebury, F., Fowler, J. C., & Baity, M. R. (2001). Predicting DSM-IV cluster B personality disorder criteria from MMPI-2 and Rorschach data: A test of incremental validity. *Journal of Personality Assessment, 76,* 150–168.

Blais, M. A., Hilsenroth, M. J., & Fowler, J. C. (1998). Rorschach correlates of the DSM-IV histrionic personality disorder. *Journal of Personality Assessment, 70*(2), 355–364.

Blais, M., A., Hilsenroth, M. J., Fowler, J. C., & Conboy, C. A. (1999). A Rorschach exploration of the DSM-IV borderline personality disorder. *Journal of Clinical Psychology, 55,* 563–572.

Blanck, G., & Blanck, R. (1975). *Ego psychology: Theory and practice.* New York: Columbia University Press.

Blatt, S. (1995). Representational structures in psychopathology. In D. Cicchetti & S. L. Toth, (Eds.), *Rochester Symposium on Developmental Psychopathology: Volume I. Emotion, cognition, and representation* (pp. 1–33). Rochester, NY: University of Rochester Press.

Blatt, S., Bers, S. A. (1993). The sense of self in depression: A psychodynamic perspective. In Z. Segal & S. Blatt (Eds.), *The self in emotional distress: Cognitive and psychodynamic perspectives* (pp. 171–217.). New York: Guilford.

Blatt, S. J., Brenneis, C. B., Shimick, J., & Glick, M. (1976a). *A developmental analysis of the concept of the object on the Rorschach.* Unpublished research manual, Yale University, New Haven, CT.

Blatt, S. J., Brenneis, C. B., Schimick, J., & Glick, M. (1976b). Normal development and psychopathological impairment of the concept of the object on the Rorschach. *Journal of Abnormal Psychology, 85,* 264–373.

Blatt, S J., & Lerner, H. (1983). The psychological assessment of object representation. *Journal of Personality Assessment, 47,* 7–28.

Blatt, S. J., Wild, C. M., & Ritzler, B. A. (1975). Disturbances of object representations in schizophrenia. *Psychoanalysis and Contemporary Science, 4,* 235–288.

Campbell, D. T., & Fiske, D. W. (1959). Convergent and discriminant validation by the multitrait multimethod matrix. *Psychological Bulletin, 56,* 81–105.

Carlson, E. A., & Sroufe, L. A. (1995). Contribution of attachment theory to developmental psychopathology. In D. Cicchetti & D. J. Cohen (Eds.), *Developmental psychopathology: Volume I. Theory and Methods* (pp. 581–617). New York: John Wiley.

Colligan, R. C., Morey, L. C., & Offord, K. P. (1994). The MMPI/MMPI-2 Personality Disorder Scales: Contemporary norms for adults and adolescents. *Journal of Clinical Psychology, 2,* 168–200.

Cook, T. D., & Campbell, D. T. (1979). *Quasi-experimental design: Design and analysis issues for field settings.* Boston: Houghton-Mifflin.

Cooper, S. Perry, J., & Arnow, D. (1988). An empirical approach to the study of defense mechanisms: I. Reliability and preliminary validity of the Rorschach Defense scales. *Journal of Personality Assessment, 52,* 187–203.

Cooper, S., Perry, J., & O'Connell, M. (1991). The Rorschach Defense Scales: II. Longitudinal perspectives. *Journal of Personality Assessment, 56,* 191–201.

Epstein, S. (1994). Integration of the cognitive and psychodynamic unconscious. *American Psychologist, 49,* 709–724.

Exner, J. (1986). Some Rorschach data comparing schizophrenics with borderline and schizotypal disorders. *Journal of Personality Assessment, 50,* 455–471.

Exner, J. E. (2002). *The Rorschach: Basis foundations and principles of interpretation* (4th ed.). New York: John Wiley.

Exner, J. E. (2003). *The Rorschach: A comprehensive system* (4th ed.). New York: John Wiley.

Federn, P. (1952). *Ego psychology and the psychoses.* New York: Basic Books.

Frank, G. (1994). On the assessment of thought disorder from the Rorschach. *Psychological Reports, 75,* 375–383.

Frank, G. (1995a). An ego-psychological approach to the Rorschach. *Psychological Reports, 77,* 911–930.

Frank, G. (1995b). On the assessment of self- and object representations for the Rorschach: A review of the research and commentary. *Psychological Reports, 76,* 659–671.

Frank, L. (1939). Projective methods for the study of personality. *Journal of Psychology, 8,* 399–413.

Freud, S. (1961). The ego and the id. In J. Strachey (Ed.), *The standard edition of the complete psychological works of Sigmund Freud* (Vol. 19). London: Hogarth.

Freud, S. (1940/1961). An outline of psychoanalysis. In J. Strachey (Ed.), *The standard edition of the complete psychological works of Sigmund Freud* (pp. 2–78). London: Hogarth.

Gacono, C. B. (1990). An empirical study of object relations and defensive operations in antisocial personality disorder. *Journal of Personality Assessment, 54,* 589–600.

Gacono, C. B., & Meloy, J. R. (1992). The Rorschach and the DSM-III-R antisocial personality. *Journal of Clinical Psychology, 48,* 393–406.

Gacono, C. B., Meloy, J. R., & Berg, J. L. (1992). Object relations, defensive operations, and affective states in narcissistic, borderline, and antisocial personality disorder. *Journal of Personality Assessment, 59,* 32–49.

Garb, H. N. (1994a). Judgment research: Implications for clinical practice and testimony in court. *Applied and Preventive Psychology, 3,* 173–183.

Garb, H. N. (1994b). Cognitive heuristics and biases in personality assessment. In L. Heath, R. S. Tindale, J. Edwards, E. Posavac, F. Bryant, E. Henderson-King, et al. (Eds.), *Applications of heuristics and biases to social issues: Social psychological applications to social issues* (Vol. 3). New York: Plenum Press.

Garb, H. N. (1996). The representativeness and past-behavior heuristics in clinical judgment. *Professional Psychology: Research and Practice, 27,* 272–277.

Garb, H. N. (1998). *Studying the clinician: Judgment research and psychological assessment.* Washington, DC: American Psychological Association.

Garb, H., Wood, J., Lilienfeld, S., Scott, O., & Nezworski, T. (2002). Effective use of projective techniques in clinical practice: Let the data help with selection and interpretation. *Professional Psychology: Research and Practice, 33,* 454–463.

Gartner, J., Hurt, S., & Gartner, A. (1989). Psychological test signs of borderline personality disorder: A review of the empirical literature. *Journal of Personality Assessment, 53,* 423–441.

Greenwald, A. (1992). New Look 3: Unconscious cognition reclaimed. *American Psychologist, 47,* 766–779.

Gunderson, J. (1984). *Borderline personality disorder.* Washington, DC: American Psychiatric Press.

Harder, D., Greenwald, D., Wechsler, S., & Ritzler, B. (1984). The Urist Mutuality of Autonomy Scale as an indicator of psychopathology. *Journal of Clinical Psychology, 40,* 1078–1083.

Hilsenroth, M., Hibbard, S., Nash, M., & Handler, L. (1993). A Rorschach study of narcissism, defense, and aggression in borderline, narcissistic, and cluster C personality disorders. *Journal of Personality Assessment, 60,* 346–361.

Holt, R. R. (1970). *Manual for the scoring of primary process manifestations in Rorschach responses* (10th draft). Research Center for Mental Health: New York University, New York.

Holt, R. R., & Havel, J. (1960). A method for assessing primary and secondary process in the Rorschach. In M. Rickers-Ovsiankina (Ed.), *Rorschach Psychology* (pp. 263–315). New York: John Wiley.

Horowitz, M. J. (1983). *Image formation and psychotherapy.* New York: Jason Aronson.

Horowitz, M. J. (1988). *Introduction to psychodynamics: A new synthesis.* New York: Basic Books.

Horowitz, M. J. (1998). Cognitive psychodynamics: From conflict to character. New York: John Wiley.

Horowitz, M. J. (1991). *Person schemas and maladaptive interpersonal patterns.* Chicago: The University of Chicago Press.

Jacobi, J. (1999). *Complex, archetype, and symbol in the psychology of C. G. Jung.* London: Routledge.

Johnston, M. H., & Holzman, P. S. (1979). *Assessing schizophrenic thinking.* San Francisco, CA: Jossey-Bass.

Josephs, L. (1989). The cleaning lady: The fate of an archaic maternal imago. *Psychoanalysis and Psychotherapy, 7,* 116–128.

Joseph, S. L. (1992). *Character structure and the organization of the self.* New York: Columbia University Press.

Kernberg, O. (1976). *Object relations theory and clinical psychoanalysis.* New York: Jason Aronson.

Kernberg, O. F. (1984). *Severe personality disorders: Psychotherapeutic strategies.* New Haven: Yale University Press.

Kleiger, J. (1999). *Disordered thinking and the Rorschach: Theory, research, and differential diagnosis.* Hillsdale, NJ: The Analytic Press.

Lakoff, G., & Johnson, M. (1999). *Philosophy in the flesh: The embodied mind and its challenge to Western thought.* New York: Basic Books.

Lerner, P. (1990). Rorschach assessment of primitive defenses: A review. *Journal of Personality Assessment, 54,* 30–46.

Lerner, P. (1991). *Psychoanalytic theory and the Rorschach.* Hillsdale, NJ: The Analytic Press.

Lerner, P. (1992). Toward an experiential psychoanalytic approach to the Rorschach. *Bulletin of the Menninger Clinic, 56,* 451–464.

Lerner, P. (1998). Schachtel and experiential Rorschach assessment. *Journal of Personality Assessment, 71,* 182–188.

Lilienfeld, S., Wood, J., & Garb, H. (2000). The scientific status of projective techniques. *Psychological Science in the Public Interest, 1,* 27–66.

McClelland, D. (1980). Motive dispositions: The merits of operant and respondent measures. In L. Wheeler (Eds.), *Review of Personality and Social Psychology* (Vol. 1, pp. 10–41). Beverly Hills, CA: Sage.

McWilliams, N. (1994). *Psychoanalytic diagnosis: Understanding personality structure in the clinical process.* New York: Guilford.

Meloy, R., Acklin, M. W., Gacono, C., Murray, J., & Peterson, C.A. (1997). *Contemporary Rorschach interpretation*. Mahwah, NJ: Lawrence Erlbaum Associates.

Meyer, G. (2000). On the science of Rorschach assessment. *Journal of Personality Assessment, 75*, 46–81.

Meyer, G., Finn, S., Eyde, L. D., Kay, G., Moreland, K., Dies, R. R., et al. (2001). Psychological testing and psychological assessment: A review of evidence and issues. *American Psychologist, 56*, 128–165.

Meyer, G. J. (2002). Implications of information gathering methods for a refined taxonomy of psychopathology. In L. E. Beutler & M. Malik (Eds.), *Rethinking DSM: A psychological perspective* (pp. 69–105). Washington, DC: APA Press.

Millon, T. (1969). *Modern psychopathology: A biosocial approach to maladaptive learning and functioning*. Prospect Heights, IL: Waveland Press.

Millon, T. (1981). *Disorders of personality DSM-III: Axis II*. New York: John Wiley.

Mitchell, S. A. (1988). *Relational concepts in psychoanalysis: An integration*. Cambridge, MA: Harvard University Press.

Moore, B. E., & Fine, B. D. (1968). *A glossary of psychoanalytic terms and concepts* (2nd ed.). New York: American Psychoanalytic Association.

Morey, L. C., Waugh, M. H., & Blashfield, R. K. (1985). MMPI scales for DSM-III personality disorders: Their derivation and correlates. *Journal of Personality Assessment, 49*(3), 245–251.

O'Connell, M., Cooper, S., Perry, J., & Hoke, L. (1989). The relationship between thought disorder and psychotic symptoms in borderline personality disorder. *Journal of Nervous and Mental Disease, 177*, 273–278.

Perry, J., & Cooper, S. (1989). An empirical study of defense mechanisms: I. Clinical interview and life vignette ratings. *Archives of General Psychiatry, 46*, 444–452.

Pine, F. (1988). The four psychologies of psychoanalysis and their place in clinical work. *Journal of the American Psychoanalytic Association, 36*, 571–596.

Pine, F. (1990). *Drive, ego, object, and self: A synthesis for clinical work*. New York: Basic Books.

Rapaport, D., Gill, M., & Schafer, R. (1968). *Diagnostic psychological testing*. New York: International Universities Press.

Reichenbach, H. (1938). *Experience and prediction*. Chicago: University of Chicago Press.

Rosner, S. (1990). Pine's four psychologies of psychoanalysis and the Rorschach. *Psychoanalysis and Psychotherapy, 8*, 103–111.

Rubens, R. L. (1994). Fairbairn's structural theory. In J. S. Grotstein & D. B. Rinsley (Eds.), *Fairbairn and the origins of object relations* (pp. 151–173). Oxford, England: Free Association Books.

Sandler, J. S., & Rosenblatt, B. R. (1962). The concept of the representational world. *Psychoanalytic Study of the Child, 17*, 128–145.

Schachtel, E. (1966). *Experiential foundations of Rorschach's test*. Hillsdale, NJ: The Analytic Press.

Schafer, R. (1954). *Psychoanalytic interpretation in Rorschach testing: Theory and application*. New York: Grune & Stratton.

Shakow, D. (1976). What is clinical psychology? *American Psychologist, 31*, 553–560.

Shapiro, D. (1965). *Neurotic styles*. New York: Basic Books.

Silverstein, M. (1999). *Self psychology and diagnostic assessment: Identifying selfobject functions through psychological testing*. Mahwah, NJ: Lawrence Erlbaum Associates.

Stolorow, R., & Atwood, G. (1989). The unconscious and unconscious fantasy: An intersubjective–developmental perspective. *Psychoanalytic Inquiry, 9,* 364–374.

Stricker, G., & Gold, J. R. (1999). The Rorschach: Toward a nomothetically based, idiographically applicable configurational model. *Psychological Assessment, 11,* 240–250.

Stricker, G., & Healey, B. J. (1990). Projective assessment of object relations: A review of the empirical literature. *Psychological Assessment: A Journal of Consulting and Clinical Psychology, 2,* 219–230.

Stricker, G., & Trierweiler, S. (1995). The local clinical scientist: A bridge between science and practice. *American Psychologist, 50,* 995–1002.

Stuart, J., Western, D., Lohr, N., Benjamin, J., Becker, S., Vorus, N., et al. (1990). Object relations in borderlines, depressives, and normals: An examination of human responses on the Rorschach. *Journal of Personality Assessment, 55,* 296–318.

Trull, T. J., Widiger, T. A., Useda, J. D., Holcomb, J., Doan, B., Axlerod, S. R., et al. (1998). A structural interview for the assessment of the Five-Factor Model of personality. *Psychological Assessment, 10,* 229–240.

Tyson, P., & Tyson, R. (1990). *Psychoanalytic theories of development: An integration.* New Haven: Yale University Press.

Urist, J. (1977). The Rorschach test and the assessment of object relations. *Journal of Personality Assessment, 41,* 309.

Urist, J. (1980). Object relations. In R. H. Woody (Ed.), *Encyclopedia of clinical assessment* (Vol. 1, pp. 821–833). San Francisco: Jossey-Bass.

Urist, J., & Schill, M. (1982). Validity of the Rorschach mutuality of autonomy scale: A replication using excerpted responses. *Journal of Personality Assessment, 46,* 450–454.

Viglione, D., & Hilsenroth, M. (2001). The Rorschach: Facts, fictions, and future. *Psychological Assessment, 13,* 452–471.

Weiner, I. B. (2003). *Principles of Rorschach interpretation* (2nd ed.). Mahwah, NJ: Lawrence Erlbaum Associates.

Wiggins, J. S. (1973). *Personality and prediction.* Reading, MA: Addison-Wesley.

Author Index

L

Subject Index

A

Abnormality, self-reports of, 30–31
ABPP, *see* American Board of Professional Psychology
Abuse
    borderline personality disorder and sexual, 173, 181
    paranoid character and child, 61
    paranoid symptoms and history of, 60
Academic success, obsessive-compulsive personality disorder and, 315
Achievement, narcissistic personality disorder and, 226
Achromatic color responses, depressive personality disorder and, 376, 377
Active dependency, 314
Adolescence
    antisocial personality disorder and, 149
    onset of personality disorders in, 4–5
    onset of schizotypal personality in, 111
Adulthood
    onset of personality disorders in early, 4–5
    onset of schizotypal personality disorder in early, 111
Affect
    antisocial personality disorder and, 156
    borderline personality disorder and, 182
    borderline personality disorder case example and, 196
    Rorschach and assessment of, 44
Affect cluster
    depressive personality disorder and, 376–377

schizoid personality disorder case example, 96, 102–103
schizotypal personality disorder case example, 129
Affective experience, self as locus of, 428
Affective functioning, histrionic personality disorder and, 208
Affective instability
    borderline personality disorder and, 173, 174, 181–182
    borderline personality disorder case example and, 194
Affective ratio, avoidant personality disorder and, 276
Agency
    interpersonal relatedness and, 16, 17
    self and, 428
Aggression
    antisocial personality disorder and, 14–151, 160
    egodystonic, 149
    histrionic persolity disorder and, 206
    narcissistic personality disorder and, 227–229, 229
    schizoid personality disorder case example and, 104–105
Aggressive content responses
    antisocial personality disorder and, 150–151, 155
    depressive personality disorder and, 378
    paranoid personality disorder and, 68, 69
Aggressive impulsivity, borderline personality disorder and, 173, 174–175

459